Luxemburger Juristische Studien –
Luxembourg Legal Studies

edited by

Faculty of Law, Economics and Finance
University of Luxembourg

Volume 17

Catherine Warin

Individual Rights under European Union Law

A study on the relation between rights, obligations and interests in the case law of the Court of Justice

Nomos

The Deutsche Nationalbibliothek lists this publication in the Deutsche Nationalbibliografie; detailed bibliographic data are available on the Internet at http://dnb.d-nb.de

ISBN 978-3-8487-5469-4 (Print)
978-3-8452-9623-4 (ePDF)

British Library Cataloguing-in-Publication Data
A catalogue record for this book is available from the British Library.

ISBN 978-3-8487-5469-4 (Print)
978-3-8452-9623-4 (ePDF)

Library of Congress Cataloging-in-Publication Data
Warin, Catherine
Individual Rights under European Union Law
A study on the relation between rights, obligations and interests in the case law of the Court of Justice
Catherine Warin
584 p.
Includes bibliographic references and index.

ISBN 978-3-8487-5469-4 (Print)
978-3-8452-9623-4 (ePDF)

1st Edition 2019

to Thomas

'Qu'est-ce en effet que d'être libres ? c'est raisonner juste, c'est connaître les droits de l'homme ; & quand on les connaît bien, on les défend de même.'[1]

Voltaire

1 Voltaire, 'Onzième lettre écrite par le proposant à M. Covelle,' *Œuvres complètes de Voltaire, Tome 46* (1784 La Société littéraire-typographique) 453.

Acknowledgements

This book is a revised version of the PhD thesis which I wrote between 2013 and 2017 at the Faculty of Law of the University of Luxembourg.

I am immensely thankful to Professor Herwig Hofmann, who supervised my work with enthusiasm and kindness. I would like to sincerely thank him for having trusted me with this project, and for having always been available for challenging and enlightening discussions. His advice and feedback have been essential for orienting and refining my reflection and for sustaining my motivation. I am also grateful for the inspiring example he has provided as a lawyer and an academic. It has been an honour and a pleasure to work under his guidance.

I would like to thank the members of my evaluation committee, Professor Jörg Gerkrath and Professor Luc Heuschling, for their kind availability and the valuable advice they provided me with. I also thank Judge Allan Rosas and Professor Loïc Azoulai for showing interest in my research and for having accepted to be part of the PhD defence jury. I deeply appreciate that they took time out of their busy schedules to read my thesis and to come to the Faculty of Law for the defence and I am grateful for their insightful suggestions for preparing this book for publication.

The University of Luxembourg has been a wonderful place to do a PhD, and I express my gratitude to the academic and administrative staff of the Faculty of Law. The many fruitful discussions in seminars and workshops organised at the Doctoral School of Law have broadened my perspectives and helped me improve the quality of my work. I want to warmly thank the colleagues and friends who proofread my manuscript and provided me with encouragements and emotional support along the way: Fatima Chaouche, Clelia Lacchi, Janine Silga, Edoardo Stoppioni, Allison Östlund, Zheni Zhekova, Bucura Mihaescu and Marie Marty.

While I worked on my thesis I had the pleasure of participating in different workshops and conferences where I could present my research, which greatly benefitted from the ensuing discussions. I would like to acknowledge in particular the organisers and participants of the 2017 French-German Doctoral Seminar in comparative public law in Heidelberg and the 2017 W.G. Hart Legal Workshop in London, for their valuable feedback and suggestions. Working on blogdroiteuropéen has also been an instructive experience and I would like to thank Olivia Tambou for her trust and her support.

I want to thank Audrey Ducoup for being such a truthful and supportive friend, and Catherine Schneiders and Barbara-Andréa Cid-Leyton-Prieux for their friendship and encouragements. In addition, I would like to acknowledge the friends I made at Passerell, especially my dear Cassie Adélaïde, for her endless energy, her patience and her support, and to our volunteer lawyers for their inspiring commitment.

My gratitude then goes to Patrick Moffett, who was my Professor of English in the Lycée Condorcet's 'classes préparatoires,' who believed in me when I did not, and without whom I would not have made it into the Ecole Normale supérieure de Cachan. The ENS was my gateway into higher learning I and express my appreciation to Anthony Saber, head of the Department of English at the ENS, for his flexibility in accommodating my complex curriculum. In Cachan I also met Catalina Onofrei, whom I deeply thank for her since then unwavering and attentive friendship. I am also grateful to Flora Lucet, Juliette Mariani and Raphaëlle Lalo for their unconditional and benevolent friendship over many years.

I am deeply grateful to my family for their love, their unwavering support and their trust. I am particularly thankful to my parents who raised me with a thirst for knowledge and a love of learning; to my sister Laurence for being always so attentive and considerate; to my godmother Anne and to Marion, for their kindness and constancy.

This book is dedicated to my husband Thomas, the light in my world, who has always sincerely and steadily supported my projects – especially the PhD – and whom I can never thank enough for his invaluable patience, trust, and love.

Abbreviations

AC	Aarhus Convention
AG	Advocate General
AR	Aarhus Regulation
BVerfG	(German) *Bundesverfassungsgericht*
BVerwG	(German) *Bundesverwaltungsgericht*
CE	(French) *Conseil d'Etat*
CFI	Court of First Instance
CFR	Charter of Fundamental Rights
CFSP	Common Foreign and Security Policy
CJEU	Court of Justice of the European Union
Cons. const	(French) *Conseil constitutionnel*
CST	Civil Service Tribunal
ECI	European Citizens' Initiative
ECJ	European Court of Justice
ECS	European Social Charter
ECSC	European Coal and Steel Community
ECHR	European Convention for the Protection of Human Rights and Fundamental Freedoms
EEAS	European External Action Service
EU	European Union
HRA	Human Rights Act (United Kingdom)
ICJ	International Court of Justice
NGO	non-governmental organisation
TEC	Treaty on the European Community
TECE	Treaty establishing a Constitution for Europe
TEU	Treaty on the European Union
TFEU	Treaty on the Functioning of the European Union

Table of contents

Introduction

'If individual rights make your heart beat faster, then the EU is your Nirvana.'[2]

The *'longing to live in a fair world'* reflected in an amplifying rights language has been a *'global phenomenon'* of the second half of the twentieth century.[3] By placing individual rights at the heart of its language and logic in the landmark ruling *Van Gend en Loos*[4], the Court of Justice of what was then the European Economic Community gave a European response to this longing. The term *'right'* in European Union (EU) law is a very *'fluid'* one.[5] It covers rights that are born from obligations laid down in the Treaties[6] and in secondary legislation, to all individuals who have an interest in the enforcement of these obligations. In addition, filling the gaps of the original Treaty, the Court of Justice brought fundamental rights under its wing through the medium of the non-written general principles of law.[7] Many of these are now codified in the Charter of Fundamental Rights of the European Union.[8] Individual rights thus irrigate the whole constitutional system that has been building up on the basis of the *'new legal order'* established by the EEC Treaty.[9]

But perhaps the concept of rights is a victim of its own success. The word *'right'* has been used and abused so much that it is no longer clear

---

2 Judge O. Zetterquist, 'Fundamental Rights and the Fundamentals of the European Constitution' (Seminar at the University of Luxembourg, 26 June 2014).

3 M. Ignatieff, *The Rights Revolution* (Anansi 2000) 9.

4 Judgment of 5 February 1963, *Van Gend en Loos*, C-26/62, EU:C:1963:1.

5 G. De Burca, 'The Language of Rights and European Integration' in J. Shaw and G. More (eds), *New Legal Dynamics of European Union* (Clarendon Press 1995) 30.

6 Starting with the Treaty instituting the European Economic Community ('EEC Treaty'/'Treaty of Rome'), 1957 294 UNTS 17.

7 Judgment of 17 December 1970, *Internationale Handelsgesellschaft*, C-11/70, EU:C:1970:114.

8 Charter of Fundamental Rights of the European Union (OJ 2007 C 303/1) ('Charter'/ 'CFR')).

9 *Van Gend en Loos*, C-26/62, p. 12. On the notion of the EU legal order as a 'constitutional' system see A. Rosas and L. Armati, *EU Constitutional Law: An Introduction* (Hart 2012) 1-18.

what the term entails.[10] As pointed out by Prechal and Hancher, in Union law '*considerable uncertainty surrounds the concept of rights [...]. [A]s long as this concept is not clarified, it is not suitable as a tool for legal analysis. It may even be perilous, as it may result in fictive rights, as opposed to real rights.*'[11] Legal philosopher Raz expresses a similar concern when he writes that we seem to try to prove the importance of rights '*by calling anything of value a right*'.[12] This explains the growing '*dissatisfaction*' with the concept of rights and the '*strong skepticism*' with which some authors approach the concept.[13]

An additional element, perhaps more specific to the European Union context, causes rights to be considered with scepticism and distrust. Rights reflect a certain conception of their holders. Because of the specific nature of the Union's multilevel constitutional architecture, in which national courts are '*the ordinary courts*',[14] in pursuing their particular interests individuals play an essential part in ensuring the enforcement of Union law within the Member States and thus, the realisation of the Union's purposes. The notion of this virtuous circle, described as '*functional subjectivation*',[15] is certainly appealing. Yet it has been criticised on two main grounds. Firstly, this approach to rights is said to be instrumentalising individuals. Individual interests are seen as a mere pretext for enforcing obligations laid down in EU law, and thus advancing EU interests. Even fundamental rights are not immune to the suspicion of instrumentalisation, since the Court of Justice itself acknowledges that their integration was meant to preserve the integrity of the EU legal order.[16] Secondly, and consequently, the instrumentalisation of rights and their holders allegedly leaves behind those individuals whose interests do not converge with those of the Union. The intensity of the debate attests that the confusion lies not

10 P. Roubier, *Droits subjectifs et situations juridiques* (first published 1963, 2nd edn, Dalloz 2005) 47.

11 S. Prechal and L. Hancher, 'Individual Environmental Rights: Conceptual Pollution in EU Environmental Law?' (2001) 2 Yearbook of European Environmental Law 89 105.

12 J. Raz, 'On the Nature of Rights' (1984) 93 Mind 194.

13 De Burca, 'The Language of Rights and European Integration' 29 and 52.

14 Order of 22 December 1995, *Danielsson and Others v Commission*, T-219/95, EU:T:1995:219, para 77.

15 M. Ruffert, 'Rights and Remedies in European Community Law: a Comparative View' (1997) 34 Common Market Law Review 319 327. See also Masing, *Die Mobilisierung des Bürgers für die Durchsetzung des Rechts: europäische Impulse für eine Revision der Lehre vom subjektiv-öffentlichen Recht* 22.

16 Judgment of 6 March 2014, *Siragusa*, C-206/13, EU:C:2014:126, para 32.

only with the meaning of the concept of individual rights, but also with its underlying rationale, and the conception which it reflects of individuals and their relation to the EU legal system.

The entry into force of the Charter of Fundamental Rights along with the Treaty of Lisbon[17] was a turning point in the evolution of this system. The Charter embodies and amplifies the increasing reliance on rights in legal and political discourses. As a result, the intensified focus on fundamental rights is tangible in the case law: the Charter is now very often the starting point for reasoning on fundamental rights issues in the case law of the Court of Justice of the European Union (CJEU), with the Court relying less systematically on general principles of EU law as sources of such rights.[18] In addition, a distinction between '*rights*' and '*principles*' has been introduced in the Charter, implying that some 'fundamental rights' provisions do not contain 'rights'.[19] It is not clear which provisions correspond to each category, and how this new parameter connects with the other sources of rights which historically functioned without such a distinction. The paradoxical result is that, in the increasingly rights-centred legal system of the Union, the concept of individual rights is the source of growing confusion, and is more than ever in great need of clarification.

Against this backdrop, this study addresses the following questions. *Firstly, how does the relation between rights, obligations and interests define the nature and function of individual rights in the Union's legal order? Secondly, to what extent is the evolution of the Union's constitutional framework challenging the original concept of individual rights?*

These questions are addressed essentially by tracing the development of the CJEU's method for identifying individual rights and by mapping the relation between rights, obligations and interests that emerges from the case law. The basic characteristics of the concept of individual rights will be inferred from this relation. It should be stressed that although fundamental rights adjudication is becoming ever more important, it is not the central focus of this study. The case law on fundamental rights, as well as other

---

17 Treaty of Lisbon Amending the Treaty on European Union and the Treaty Establishing the European Community (OJ 2007 C 306/1) ('the Treaty of Lisbon').

18 J. Gerkrath, 'Les principes généraux du droit ont-ils encore un avenir en tant qu'instrument de protection des droits fondamentaux dans l'Union européenne ?' (2006) *Revue des Affaires Européennes - Law & European Affairs* 31; S. Peers, 'The Rebirth of the EU's Charter of Fundamental Rights' in C. Barnard and O. Odudu (eds), *The Cambridge Yearbook of European Legal Studies, Volume 13* (Hart 2011) 289.

19 Article 51(1) and Article 52(5) of the Charter.

types of rights with a specific label (for instance, fundamental freedoms), is examined through the lens of the basic concept of individual rights, i.e. in the light of the relation between rights, obligations and interests. The study scrutinises cases in which this relation took shape and is still developing. Perhaps the most obvious setting for exploring this relation is the situation of 'crisis' when an individual takes legal action (whether in national or EU courts) to protect a right that they consider has been violated. Other conducive situations arise when an individual's right becomes relevant due to other actors advancing their interests (not necessarily in the form of rights), requiring a balance of interests to be performed by the courts: this is the case law on the principle of proportionality and the prohibition of abuse of rights.[20] When looking at these various situations, it is important to keep in mind that in the case law and in the literature, the focus is often on the violation or the limitation of a right, while the step of pinpointing the right itself remains more or less implicit. We will need to beware of this implicit step. In addition, another type of cases rich in implicit indications should be considered. These are the cases where individual rights are minimised or even completely omitted from the judgment, whereas the reasoning gives weight to their traditional counterparts – obligations and interests.[21] The varying shift in emphasis on the three elements can shed light on the concept of individual rights.

The review of the case law is performed with one crucial pitfall in mind: that is, the dangers of linguistic and cultural biases. Words can be a source of tremendous conceptual blur, especially in legal studies,[22] where they convey (often unconscious) ideological preconceptions.[23] The issue is amplified in a multilingual and multinational environment such as the one in

20 Cornu, *Droit civil. Introduction. Les personnes. Les biens*, 56.

21 A notable example is Judgment of 23 April 1986, *Les Verts*, C-294/83, EU:C:1986:166.

22 W.N. Hohfeld, 'Fundamental Legal Conceptions as Applied in Judicial Reasoning' 1917 Yale Law Journal, Faculty Scholarship Series Paper 4378, 716 <http://digitalcommons.law.yale.edu/fss_papers/4378> accessed 13 August 2017; L. Heuschling, *Etat de droit, Rechtsstaat, Rule of law* (Nouvelle bibliothèque de thèses, Dalloz 2002) 5 ; E. Pic, 'Faire de la terminologie en droit?' (2007) Cahiers du CIEL 57; J.-P. Derosier, 'Enquête sur la limite constitutionnelle : du concept à la notion' (2008) 76 Revue française de droit constitutionnel 785 ; L. Wittgenstein, *Recherches philosophiques* (Gallimard 2014).

23 R. Van Gestel and H.-W. Micklitz, 'Why Methods Matter in European Legal Scholarship' (2014) 20 European Law Journal 292.

which EU law developed and still evolves.[24] Indeed, not all legal systems '*create rights in the same way under the same conditions*', nor do these various legal systems define rights, or the relation of rights with obligations and interests, in the same way.[25] It is likely that these different prisms have influenced the shaping of the EU concept of individual rights, and that they would also influence the way it is implemented. After all, the judges of the Court of Justice are all seasoned lawyers, most with extensive experience of practising or teaching the law of their respective Member States: they do not leave their conceptual baggage at the door of the Palais.[26] The conditions at the Court are thus ideal for confronting and blending various conceptions of rights. The variety of national influences is a source of richness but it also entails two risks. The first is to end up with a '*tower of Babel*' of irreconcilable conceptions of rights.[27] The second is '*the temptation to 'read' European law through the spectacles of national legal systems*'.[28] This is precisely why we need a clear and autonomous definition of a right at the EU level.[29] Yet, in order to avoid an approach biased by a '*missionary zeal*' at the

24 G.-R. De Groot, 'Law, Legal Language and the Legal system: Reflections on the Problems of Translating Legal Texts', in V. Gessner, A. Hoeland and C. Varga C, *European Legal Cultures* (Dartmouth 1996) 157-158.

25 N. Półtorak, *European Union Rights in National Courts* (Wolters Kluwer 2015) 7-8.

26 It is no secret that the legal cultures of the various Member States have greatly influenced the Court. See e.g. G.F. Mancini and D.T. Keeling, 'Language, Culture and Politics in the Life of the European Court of Justice' (1995) 1 Columbia Journal of European Law 397.

27 S. Prechal, 'Direct Effect Reconsidered, Redefined and Rejected' in J.M. Prinssen and A. Schrauwen (eds), *Direct Effect Rethinking a Classic of EC Legal Doctrine* (Europa Law Publishing 2002) 20.

28 S. Prechal and B. Van Roermund, 'Binding Unity in EU Legal Order: An Introduction' in S. Prechal and B. Van Roermund (eds), *The Coherence of EU Law: The Search for Unity in Divergent Concepts* (Oxford University Press 2008) 12; see also W. Van Gerven, 'Of Rights, Remedies and Procedures' (2000) 37 Common Market Law Review 501. Zumbansen has the same idea that '*we must first clarify our perspective, or, the historically and culturally based bias from which the analysis of this body of law is to take place. To decipher the language of European law we will need a better understanding of our own*'. P. Zumbansen, 'Semantics of European Law' (1999) 5 European Law Journal 114.

29 Beljin, 'Rights in EU Law'; J.W. Van Rossem, 'The Autonomy of EU Law: More is Less?' in R.A. Wessel and S. Blockmans (eds), *Between Autonomy and Dependence* (Between Autonomy and Dependence, T.M.C. Asser Press 2013); S. Turgis, 'Notions autonomes et concurrence des juges' (La concurrence des juges en Europe. Le dialogue en question(s), Faculté de Droit de Tours, 25-26-27 November 2015); D. Dero-Bugny, *Les rapports entre la Cour de justice de l'Union européenne et la Cour européenne des droits de l'homme* (Bruylant 2015) para 127.

service of an abstract European ideal or ideology,[30] we need to look at this common European legal culture without dismissing the influence and characteristics of national legal systems, especially those which have most influenced EU law at the various stages of its development.

For these reasons, this study relies on several strands of legal literature to inform the analysis of the case law. Firstly, legal philosophy and theories of rights provide analytical and conceptual tools, allowing rights to be comprehended from various angles, such as their form, their function, or their justification.[31] Moreover, theoretical and philosophical discussions of rights in different national contexts reflect concerns that are specific to each legal system. Identifying these specific features also allows pinpointing potential conceptual biases that might influence approaches to rights in EU legal studies, which often do not consciously rely on the analytical and explanatory schemes of legal theory.[32] Secondly, the book draws on the conceptions of rights, obligations and interests that shape national legal systems, especially of public and administrative law, which was the original field of development of EU law and thus also of the concept of individual rights. The main examples are the French, English and German legal systems, not only because they are the most linguistically accessible to the author of this study, but also more importantly, because these three legal systems have been the most influential in Europe.[33] We will therefore keep in mind that '*the rather rigid doctrinal definition of ('subjective') rights in German law, […] the rather loose concept of rights in common law […and…] the somewhat indolent view of rights in French law*'[34] may all have contributed to shaping the concept of individual rights under Union law. The task of sorting out the various doctrinal strands is guided and delineated by the objective of understanding the relation between rights, obligations and interests in Union law.

---

30 Walker, 'Legal Theory and the European Union' EUI Working Paper Law 2005/16 5.

31 L. Wenar, 'Rights' The Stanford Encyclopedia of Philosophy (Fall 2011 Edition), ed. E. Zalta <http://plato.stanford.edu/archives/fall2011/entries/rights/> accessed 10 November 2014.

32 Walker, 'Legal Theory and the European Union' 1.

33 M. Fromont, *Droit administratif des Etats européens* (Presses universitaires de France 2006) 351. Also important are works that provide a broader perspective on rights in the European legal culture, especially L. Medina Alcoz, *Libertad y autoridad en el derecho administrativo. Derecho subjetivo e interés legítimo: una revisión* (Marcial Pons 2016).

34 Prechal and Van Roermund, 'Binding Unity in EU Legal Order: An Introduction' 11.

Additionally, the book draws on the substantive existing body of doctrinal works in EU law. Many of these works approach individual rights by looking at how they relate to the EU legal order, while the studies that dissect the concept itself are as precious as they are scarce.[35] There is a substantial literature on the doctrine of direct effect, in which individual rights naturally feature as an essential component.[36] The literature also includes discussion of other characteristics of EU law which involve rights, such as the importance of the mechanism of proportionality review, the relation between EU and national law (especially in relationship to the debate on rights and remedies) and the evolution of the system of protection of fundamental rights, including debates over the Charter, notably its usefulness, relevance, and impact.[37] In particular, the implications of the distinction between rights and principles introduced at Article 51(1) and 52(2) of the Charter are intensely debated.[38] Not surprisingly, the writings on rights in EU law tend to reflect – both qualitatively and quantitatively – the national sensitivities to the issue. The orientations of the different writings on rights tend to confirm that there are '*as many versions of EU law as there are member states*', for both linguistic reasons (EU law is made, studied and applied in 24 different national languages) and systemic reasons (i.e. the interlocking of EU law with the national legal orders).[39] For instance, works on 'subjective rights' in EU law by German scholars are often focused on how the EU concept should be connected with the German concept of subjective right.[40] By contrast, the French-language literature on EU law often leaves rights in the background, but still provides important contributions

---

35 B. Thorson, *Individual Rights in EU Law* (Springer 2016).

36 E.g. S. Prechal, 'Direct Effect, Indirect Effect, Supremacy and the Evolving Constitution of the European Union' in C. Barnard (ed), *The Fundamentals of EU Law Revisited - Assessing the Impact of the Constitutional Debate* (Oxford University Press 2007).

37 E.g. T.-I. Harbo, 'The Function of the Proportionality Principle in EU Law' (2010) 16 European Law Journal 158; Van Gerven, 'Of Rights, Remedies and Procedures'; Ruffert, 'Rights and Remedies in European Community Law: a Comparative View'; K. Lenaerts, 'Exploring the Limits of the EU Charter of Fundamental Rights' (2012) 8 European Constitutional Law Review 375.

38 E.g. C. Hilson, 'Rights and Principles in EU Law: A Distinction Without Foundation?' (2008) 15 Maastricht Journal of European and Comparative Law 93.

39 Walker, 'Legal Theory and the European Union' 1-2.

40 E.g. N. Reich, "System der subjectiven öffentlichen Rechte' in the Union: A European Constitution for Citizens of Bits and Pieces' in Academy of European Law (ed), *Collected Courses of the Academy of European Law*, vol VI - 1 (Martinus Nijhoff Publishers 1998).

on the EU legal system of remedies, i.e. the means of enforcing rights.[41] It is hoped that by pulling these various doctrinal threads together it will be possible to shed light both on the inherent nature and structure of individual rights, and on their significance within the EU legal order.

The scope of the study is limited by the European Union's legal framework, meaning that the legal traditions of the Member States of the EU and the law of the European Convention for the Protection of Human Rights (ECHR)[42] are accounted for only in so far as they influence or interact with EU law in a manner that is relevant to understanding rights in the EU legal system. Within this system, individual rights arise in a variety of relations: relations between individuals and Member State authorities like in *Van Gend en Loos*, but also between individuals and the EU institutions, as well as 'horizontal' relations among individuals. Unlike in national legal systems, which often have distinct approaches to rights in public and private law, such a distinction indeed is '*not part of the grammar of EU law*'.[43] Therefore, the concept of individual rights is analysed as it developed and applies in both 'vertical' and 'horizontal' relations. The present research however limits itself to individual rights, that is, the rights of private individuals, excluding the rights of Member States or EU institutions that are also recognised under EU law. Moreover, it must be emphasised that the study explores the concepts of obligations and interests only in so far as they enlighten the concept of rights. Finally, a terminological clarification is necessary. The rights which the Court called '*individual*' in *Van Gend en Loos* have often been subsequently labelled '*subjective rights*'. The preferred term here is the original term of '*individual rights*', but with awareness that other terms may cover (fully or partially) the same concept.[44]

---

41 F. Berrod, *La systématique des voies de droit communautaires* (Dalloz, coll. Nouvelle bibliothèque de thèses 2003).

42 Council of Europe, *European Convention for the Protection of Human Rights and Fundamental Freedoms, as amended by Protocols Nos. 11 and 14*, 4 November 1950, ETS 5, available at: http://www.refworld.org/docid/3ae6b3b04.html [accessed 8 August 2017].

43 M. Claes, 'The European Union, its Member States and their Citizens' in D. Leczykiewicz and S. Weatherhill (eds), *The Involvement of EU Law in Private Law Relationships* (Hart Publishing 2013) 33.

44 Prechal explains that she uses the term 'individual rights' as an alternative to the continental law concept of 'subjective rights' because this expression '*does not make much sense in English*'. Prechal, 'Direct Effect, Indirect Effect, Supremacy and the Evolving Constitution of the European Union'45. In French law Virally reaches the same conclusion as Prechal, steering clear of the controversial term '*droit subjectif*' and choosing '*en désespoir de cause*' to use '*droit individuel*' instead to dis-

The study is organised as follows. *Part 1* traces the emergence and development of the EU concept of individual rights, highlighting two main characteristics: the correlation between rights and obligations, and the role of individual interests in bringing this correlation to life. It is argued that the relation between the three key elements that are rights, obligations and interests in EU law is the result of a double synthesis: between the influences of the legal systems of the Member States; and between the objectives of effectiveness of EU law and protection of individuals. Against this backdrop, the study moves on to assessing how the constitutional changes introduced by the Lisbon Treaty (especially the Charter of Fundamental Rights and its controversial distinction between 'rights' and 'principles') may impact the way in which individual rights are defined and identified. The study then turns to the evolving relation between rights and remedies and how it impacts (or may impact) our understanding of the concept of rights. The discussion brings to light two main difficulties for the application of the original model of rights, obligations and interests. The first one is a recurring pressure to identify rights based on the existence of an intention to protect specific interests, generating a resistance to the notion that any interest may trigger the translation of an obligation into a correlative right. The second one is a discrepancy between the methods for identifying rights, depending on whether they are claimed against Member States or individuals on the one hand, and against EU institutions on the other hand. This generates an asymmetry in the levels of protection of individuals.

Part 2 tests the concept of individual rights outlined in Part 1 by reviewing the case law on three categories of rights, corresponding loosely to three 'generations' of interests which have successively gained importance in the EU legal order, reflecting an increasingly broad and complex conception of the status of individuals. The three types of interests that are successively reviewed are economic individual interests, socio-economic and political individual interests, and collective interests. For each of these generations, Part 2 assesses the applicability and resilience of the original con-

---

tinguish the notion from that of objective law (*'droit'*). M. Virally, *La pensée juridique* (first published 1960, 3rd edn, Editions Panthéon-Assas, LGDJ 2010) 51. On comparative English and German terminology see P.G. Sack, 'Law and Custom: Reflections on the Relation between English Law and the English Language' in V. Gessner, A. Hoeland and C. Varga C, *European Legal Cultures* (Dartmouth 1996) 63-67. See also R. David, *International Encyclopedia of Comparative Law. Volume II - The Legal Systems of the World, Their Comparison and Unification. Chapter 3 - Sources of Law* (Mohr Siebeck 1984) 6.

cept of individual rights in the face of the previously identified factors of tension and evolution.

1. Modelling The Concept Of Individual Rights

'Van Gend en Loos *is Europe, with all its complexities.*'[45]

This first part presents the main characteristics of the original concept of individual rights under Union law and the main controversies around this concept, highlighting elements of stability as well as factors of evolution.

Section 1.1. opens on the account of the founding stories of *Algera, Van Gend en Loos* and *Defrenne II*, outlining an original concept of individual rights closely connected with the notions of obligations and interests. These basic characteristics may be traced in variable proportions to conceptual tools that pre-existed in the domestic systems of Member States of the EU, especially France, Germany, and the United Kingdom. This foray in national legal systems also allows to pinpoint preconceptions that influence both the development of legal concepts in EU law, and their analysis. Equipped with these conceptual tools and aware of the possible biases that they generate, we can turn back to Union law as such and analyse the justifications of individual rights, including fundamental rights, in the case law of the Court of Justice, and the heated debates to which they gave rise over the value and function of rights and their holders. Based on these elements the study highlights the double rationale of individual rights under Union law, at the basis of the defining relation of individual rights with obligations and interests.

Section 1.2 then focuses on a potentially disruptive element: the Charter of Fundamental Rights, integrated in primary law by the Treaty of Lisbon, promptly became the centre of gravity of the judicial and doctrinal discourse on rights. It is the result of a laboured compromise between contrasting views of rights (especially social rights) in the Member States. An important aspect of this compromise is the distinction between 'rights' and 'principles'[46] that, if understood strictly, potentially undermines the classically fluid conception of rights, allowing any provision (especially of primary law) phrased as an obligation or even an objective, to translate into a right if it is sufficiently clear and precise to be applicable in a given set

45 J.H.H. Weiler, 'Van Gend en Loos: The individual as subject and object and the dilemma of European legitimacy' (2014) 12 International Journal of Constitutional Law 94 103.

46 Article 51(1) and Article 52(5) of the Charter.

of concrete circumstances. The section therefore points out the main problems of interpretation that this distinction causes for the interpretation of the Charter, and it also highlights the potential consequences in terms of the nature and functions of individual rights within the Union's legal framework as a whole. In the light of these problems, the study argues in favour of upholding the original concept of individual rights, allowing for a consistent and a pluralistic approach to sources of rights.

Building on the discussion on the identification of rights, Section 1.3 moves on to the issue of their enforcement and focuses on the intensively debated relation between rights and remedies. This relation has been fuelled (much like the development of the concept of individual rights) by the meta-principle of effectiveness of EU law, leading to the modelling of the right to effective judicial protection. The evolution of this right is examined, especially in the light of the innovations of the Treaty of Lisbon: Article 47 of the Charter and Article 19(1) TEU. When it comes to the concrete implementation of these fundamental guarantees, however, we stumble across two main difficulties: first, the reluctance in the domestic legal systems of some Member States to acknowledge a broad conception of interest as a defining component of rights conferred by Union law and applied by national courts; secondly, the reluctance of the Court of Justice itself to apply this conception when individuals are claiming rights as correlatives of obligations of the EU institutions and administration.

In this first part, a definition of individual rights thus materialises in the shape of a tripartite relation between individual rights, correlative obligations, and individual interests in the fulfilment of these obligations. It allows to take stock of both the protective power of this concept, and the difficulties that arise in its implementation.

1.1. *The original concept of individual rights under Union law: foundations and justifications*

> *'I must say that I sometimes wonder whether I am on the same planet as some of the commentators. Taking part in the Court's deliberations, I see only a group of judges from different countries seeking to find acceptable legal solutions to practical legal problems.'*[47]

This section examines the first occurrences of the concept of individual rights in the early case law of the CJEU and highlights the original and defining relation of this concept with those of obligations and interests. These basic elements are then traced to potential influences from the legal systems of the Member States (1.1.1). Against this historical and comparative backdrop, the Court's method for approaching, identifying and applying rights is discussed in relation with the much-debated rationale of individual rights under Union law (1.1.2). Individual rights under Union law emerge as a blend of domestic conceptions of rights, obligations and interests, underpinned by the double concern of ensuring the effectiveness of EU law and protecting individual interests (1.1.3).

1.1.1. Historical and comparative elements

Three seminal cases set the stage for this study: *Algera, Van Gen den Loos,* and *Defrenne II.*[48] These judgments are founding in the sense that they introduced the three different types of relations in which individual rights come to life, and in the sense that they had powerful resonance in the subsequent case law (1.1.1.1). Having pinpointed the main features of rights that arise from these cases, the study moves on to the domestic legal systems of the Member States, analysing how the legal conceptions in these systems may have influenced the shaping of the EU concept of individual rights, and potentially bias our understanding of it (1.1.1.2).

---

47 Former CJEU Judge Edward, on the debate over direct effect: D.O.A. Edward, 'Direct Effect: Myth, Mess or Mystery?' in J.M. Prinssen and A. Schrauwen (eds), *Direct Effect Rethinking a Classic of EC Legal Doctrine* (Europa Law Publishing 2002) 3.

48 Judgment of 12 July 1957, *Algera and Others v Assemblée Commune*, Joined cases C-7/56 and C-3 to C-7/57, C:1957:7; *Van Gend en Loos,* C-26/62; *Defrenne v SABENA*, C-43/75.

1.1.1.1. The founding trilogy: Algera, Van Gend en Loos and Defrenne II

In the EU legal system, the rights of individuals first emerged successively as counterparts to obligations of EU institutions, Member States, and other individuals.

1.1.1.1.1. A first glint: Algera

The concept of individual rights first came up in *Algera*,[49] which also happens to be one of the first cases the Court of Justice ever ruled on. In this case, the plaintiffs were challenging the legality of several letters and communications of the Common Assembly of the European Coal and Steel Community (ECSC). The Court needed to address the shortcomings in the Treaty, as no existing legal provisions could help solve the issue. Following a comparative analysis of the administrative law of the six Member States,[50] the Court established that legally adopted administrative decisions brought rights to life, and that such rights could not be withdrawn. The court identified the nature, extent and limits of the 'individual right' of the plaintiffs by comparing the common approaches in the Member States. On this basis, it identified the obligations of the institution to act according to commonly accepted principles of law, and to accordingly protect and respect the rights and interests of individuals accordingly.

This early case is significant because it was the starting point for the CJEU's approach to using general principles of law to build a 'common law' of EU administrative procedure and a system of rights and obligations that was the basis for the later development of a system of fundamental

49 *Algera and Others v Assemblée Commune*, Joined cases C-7/56 and C-3 to C-7/57.

50 *Algera and Others v Assemblée Commune*, Joined cases C-7/56 and C-3 to C-7/57, p. 54: unless '*the Court is to deny justice it is therefore obliged to solve the problem by reference to the rules acknowledged by the legislation, the learned writing and the case-law of the member countries*.' See also N. De Vos, 'Europeanisering van het vertrouwensbeginsel. Betekenis van het Europese vertrouwensbeginsel voor de equivalente beginselen in Nederland, Frankrijk en België in het kader van een groeiend ius commune', Universiteit Utrecht 2011) 153. A. Grimmel, "This is not Life as it is Lived Here': The Court of Justice of the EU and the Myth of Judicial Activism in the Foundational Period of Integration through Law' (2014) 7 European Journal of Legal Studies 61 81 M. Barin, 'Depuis l'arrêt Algera, retour sur une utilisation "discrète" du droit comparé par la Cour de justice de l'Union européenne' in T. Di Manno (ed), *Le recours au droit comparé par le juge* (Bruylant 2014).

rights.[51] This approach has been enshrined in Article 6(3) TEU which identifies general principles of law as sources of fundamental rights. *Algera* also informs us about the genesis of rights in two ways. Firstly, rights in EU law emerged in the context of relations between individuals and the EU administration. It is in this context, and by extension in the context of vertical relations between individuals and public authorities in general, that they initially developed. Secondly, the original concept of right as it came up in Algera did not come out of the blue but instead is clearly derived from a comparison of the legal systems of the founding Member States and their conceptions of rights. The impossibility to rely on a literal reading of the multilingual and incomplete law legitimates the comparative method as a source of EU law[52] as well as a tool for understanding EU law in general and rights in particular. And so, with *Algera* the stage was set for the Big Bang.[53]

1.1.1.1.2. The Big Bang: Van Gend en Loos

The concept of rights gained further significance in EU law with the seminal, '*iconic*'[54] judgment in *Van Gend en Loos.*[55] This ruling is mostly famous for having laid down the principle of direct effect, i.e. the possibility for individuals to directly invoke acts of European legislation before national and European courts emerged as a distinctive feature of EU law. However, it has been pointed out that this was not particularly new, as direct effect was a well-known notion in public international law.[56] So, why has *Van*

51 In cases such as: Judgment of 12 November 1969, *Stauder*, C-26/69, EU:C:1969:57, *Internationale Handelsgesellschaft*, C-11/70; Judgment of 14 May 1974, *Nold v Commission*, C-4/73, EU:C:1974:51.

52 H.C.H. Hofmann, G.C. Rowe and A.H. Türk, *Administrative Law and Policy of the European Union* (Oxford University Press 2011) 112.

53 The expression 'Big Bang' is used by Zetterquist, 'Fundamental Rights and the Fundamentals of the European Constitution' to characterize *Van Gend en Loos.*

54 Weiler, 'Van Gend en Loos: The individual as subject and object and the dilemma of European legitimacy'.

55 *Van Gend en Loos,* C-26/62.

56 See e.g. F. Hagner, *Les particuliers et l'ordre juridique communautaire : l'égalité de traitement entre les hommes et les femmes* (euryopa - Institut européen de l'Université de Genève 2003) 58 ; M. Claes, *National Courts' Mandate in the European Constitution* (Hart Publishing 2006) 71 ; M. Rasmussen, 'Revolutionizing European Law: A history of the Van Gend en Loos judgment' (2014) 12 International Journal of Constitutional Law 136 139; Weiler, 'Van Gend en Loos: The individual as

Gend en Loos become such an essential '*part of the DNA of the European Union system*'?[57] The answer lies with the central role that it gave to individuals and the corresponding essential importance of their rights in the EU legal order.

The facts and the problem raised may be briefly recounted as follows. Van Gend en Loos, a transport company, was obliged to pay an increased tax on the import of chemicals from Germany into the Netherlands. It challenged this decision which it considered to be contrary to Article 12 of the EEC Treaty. This provision prohibited Member States from creating new taxes on imports, and from increasing the taxes above the level at which they were when the Treaty entered into force.[58] The Dutch administration argued that the increase in the tax was due to a change of classification of the chemicals, and therefore did not amount to an increase prohibited by Article 12. The Dutch court before which the dispute had been brought referred the matter to the Court of Justice, using the preliminary ruling procedure.[59] On the substance, two main issues were raised: could Van Gend en Loos rely on Article 12 before its national court? And if the answer was yes, did the contested duty constitute a violation of Article 12? It is in answering the first of these questions that the Court of Justice laid down essential elements both for the functioning of the EU legal system as a whole and for the definition and role of the concept of right in that system.

As a first step, the Court analyses the '*spirit*' and '*general scheme*' of the EEC Treaty and finds that this Treaty is intended to give rise to more than mere obligations between the contracting states, but rather, especially in light of its preamble and of the mechanisms that it institutes, '*a new legal order*'. Considering this teleological premise, rights are born to individuals

---

subject and object and the dilemma of European legitimacy'. Nollkaemper points out, however, that direct effect in public international law conceptually differs from direct effect in EC/EU law in that it is not focused on the invocability of that law by private parties and it classically has a broader range: A. Nollkaemper, 'The Direct Effect of Public International Law' in J.M. Prinssen and A. Schrauwen (eds), *Direct Effect Rethinking a Classic of EC Legal Doctrine* (Europa Law Publishing 2002) 179.

57 Weiler, 'Van Gend en Loos: The individual as subject and object and the dilemma of European legitimacy', 103.

58 Article 12 EEC: '*Member States shall refrain from introducing, as between themselves, any new customs duties on importation or exportation or charges with equivalent effect and from increasing such duties or charges as they apply in their commercial relations with each other*.'

59 Provided for at Article 177 EEC back then and Article 267 TFEU nowadays.

not only where they are expressly granted by EC law, '*but also by reason of obligations which the Treaty imposes in a clearly defined way upon individuals as well as upon the Member States and upon the institutions of the Community*'.[60] The Court then checks whether the provision at issue, Article 12 of the EEC Treaty, may give rise to rights of individuals vis-à-vis Member States. While the *telos*, as induced from the '*spirit and general scheme*' matters, the Court does not take into account what Augsberg calls the '*subjective*' intentions of the legislators – here, the drafters of the Treaty – i.e. whether they intended for Article 12 to grant individual rights or not.[61]

The next step of the analysis focuses on the '*wording*' of the Treaty;[62] yet, this should not be confused with a literal analysis in the strict sense. Indeed, it is not by chance that the wording comes third, after the spirit and general scheme; in presenting the criteria in this order the Court distances itself from classical treaty interpretation rules such as those from the Vienna Convention on the Law of Treaties.[63] The analysis of the wording is thus to be made in light of the spirit and general scheme that have been examined beforehand.[64] A strictly literal reading of Article 12 would reveal no

60 *Van Gend en Loos*, C-26/62, p. 12.

61 D. Chalmers and L. Barroso, 'What Van Gend en Loos stands for' (2014) 12 International Journal of Constitutional Law 105 114: '*EU law provisions are interpreted in light of their perceived objective. This objective is not, however, the original intent of the law-makers but rather some general point in the horizon to which the provision is believed to be moving*.' See also I. Augsberg, 'Methoden des europäischen Verwaltungsrechts' in J.P. Terhechte (ed), *Verwaltungsrecht der Europäischen Union* (1st edn, Nomos) 153.

62 *Van Gend en Loos*, C-26/62, p. 12.

63 T. Eijsbouts, 'Direct Effect, the Test and the Terms. In Praise of a Capital Doctrine of EU Law' in J.M. Prinssen and A. Schrauwen (eds), *Direct Effect. Rethinking a Classic of EC Legal Doctrine* (Europa Law Publishing 2002) 242. In The Vienna Convention, paragraph 1 of Article 31 entitled 'General rule of interpretation' provides that: '*A treaty shall be interpreted in good faith in accordance with the ordinary meaning to be given to the terms of the treaty in their context and in the light of its object and purpose*.' United Nations, *Vienna Convention on the Law of Treaties*, 23 May 1969, United Nations, Treaty Series, vol. 1155, p. 331, available at: http://www.refworld.org/docid/3ae6b3a10.html [accessed 15 December 2016] (Vienna Convention).

64 Eijsbouts further points out that a faulty English translation of the judgment (reproduced in many English language textbooks) originally required analysis of the wording of the provision, whereas it was the wording of the Treaty as a whole that mattered. Eijsbouts, 'Direct Effect, the Test and the Terms. In Praise of a Capital Doctrine of EU Law' 242. This in itself is a powerful call for caution against performing literal interpretation of isolated phrases in the multilingual EU legal system.

more than a prohibition on Member States to introduce new custom duties on imports or exports, and nothing about the consequences of this prohibition for individuals. In fact, this negative obligation is '*clear and unconditional*', and its nature '*makes it ideally adapted to produce direct effects in the legal relationship between Member States and their subjects*.' The obligation is phrased in such a way that its implementation requires no legislative intervention by the Member States. While the intervening Member States had argued that the prohibition being directed at them could not have effects for other parties, the Court dismisses these objections by stating that the fact that '*it is the Member States who are made the subject of the negative obligation does not imply that their nationals cannot benefit from this obligation*.'[65] Nothing prevents the obligation from translating into a right and thereby having the fullest possible effect. As Conway puts it, '*it was not necessary that the text contained an explicit statement, rather it was enough that the text did not explicitly exclude it.*'[66] Similarly, the fact that the Commission and the Member States have the possibility under the Treaty to bring before the Court a Member State not fulfilling its obligations, does not mean that individuals '*cannot plead these obligations ... before a national court*'.[67] The Court concludes that Article 12 '*must be interpreted as producing direct effects and creating individual rights which national courts must protect*.'[68] Such rights are thus to be found even in provisions which are not explicitly intended to confer rights on individuals.[69]

A few years later, the *Simmenthal* ruling, building on this original finding, made clear that these rights consist in legal relations between subjects of law, the prerogatives of whom must be protected by the judge via a full control of the dispute. Direct applicability of EC law provisions means that

---

65 *Van Gend en Loos*, C-26/62, p. 13. For further details about the case and especially the objections of Member States to the Commission's proposal see Rasmussen, 'Revolutionizing European Law: A history of the Van Gend en Loos judgment.'

66 G. Conway, *The Limits of Legal Reasoning and the European Court of Justice* (Cambridge University Press 2012) 27.

67 *Van Gend en Loos*, C-26/62, p. 13. See also A.H. Türk, *The Concept of Legislation in European Community Law - A Comparative Perspective* (Kluwer 2006) 87 and B. De Witte, 'Direct Effect, Primacy and the Nature of the Legal Order' in G. De Burca and P. Craig (eds), *The Evolution of EU Law* (2nd edn, Oxford University Press 2011), 326.

68 *Van Gend en Loos*, C-26/62, p.13.

69 W. Van Gerven, 'Articles 30, 48, 52 and 59 after *Keck & Mithouard*, and Protection of Rights Arising from Directives after *Faccini Dori*' (1996) Columbia Journal of European Law 217 233; C. Joerges, 'The Law in the Process of Constitutionalizing Europe' EUI Working Papers, Law 2002/4, 7.

'these provisions are ... a direct source of rights and duties for all those affected thereby, whether Member States or individuals, who are parties to legal relationships under Community law'. This consequence stretches to *'any national court whose task it is as an organ of a Member State to protect, in a case within its jurisdiction, the rights conferred upon individuals by Community law'.*[70] Essentially, the Treaty constitutes an immediate source of rights – and obligations – for all those concerned, whether Member States or individuals; and these rights are identifiable by reference to the criteria of clarity and unconditionality. The significance of *Van Gend en Loos* thus lies with how the Court used the mechanism of direct effect in order to equate the obligations which the Treaty imposed on Member States with rights for individuals.[71]

1.1.1.1.3. Defrenne II or the far-reaching effects of direct effect

In addition to rights claimed against EU Institutions and against the administrations of the Member States, already in *Van Gend en Loos* a third context had been acknowledged. The CJEU therein explicitly stated that clear and precise obligations under EU law should also be enforceable *'in actions between individuals before a national court'* where individuals could plead *'infringements of those obligations'.*[72] The Court refined this position *Defrenne II.*[73] This case helps understand how the Court identifies individual rights and it shows how this concept irrigates the whole EU legal system and contributes to its dynamism.

Just as Article 12 EEC, the direct effect of which was established in *Van Gend en Loos*, Article 119 is phrased as an obligation addressed to Member States and not as a right. This time it is a positive obligation: Article 119 EEC (now Article 157 TFEU[74]) requires Member States to eliminate dis-

70 Judgment of 9 March 1978, *Simmenthal*, C-106/77, EU:C:1978:49, para 15-16. N. Foulquier, *Les droits publics subjectifs des administrés. Emergence d'un concept en droit administratif français du XIXè au XXè siècle* (Dalloz 2003) 202.

71 T. Eilmansberger, 'The Relationship between Rights and Remedies in EC Law: in Search of the Missing Link' (2004) 41 Common Market Law Review 1199 1203.

72 *Van Gend en Loos*, C-26/62, p. 13.

73 *Defrenne v SABENA*, C-43/75 (This case is often referred to as *Defrenne II* because it must be distinguished from a previous case on a related issue: Judgment of 25 Mai 1971, *Defrenne v. Belgian State*, C-80/70, EU:C:1971:55). See Rosas and Armati, *EU Constitutional Law: An Introduction* 79.

74 Consolidated Version of the Treaty on the Functioning of the European Union (TFEU), OJ 2008 C 115/47.

crimination between men and women in professional settings. The Court starts by admitting that the complete implementation of the aim pursued by that article '*may in certain cases involve the elaboration of criteria whose implementation necessitates the taking of appropriate measures at Community and national level*.'[75] But the provision itself is sufficient to identify *some* forms of the direct discrimination which it prohibits. In this case, Ms. Defrenne, a stewardess, is forced to retire at the age of 40 like all her female colleagues, while her male colleagues may continue doing the exact same job until they reach the age of 55. This implies that they reach higher levels of salaries and retirement pensions. There is therefore no need to apply any further criteria to see that she is being discriminated against based on her gender. This corresponds to a case '*where men and women receive unequal pay for equal work carried out in the same establishment or service*'[76]. In this situation, '*the court is in a position to establish all the facts which enable it to decide whether a woman worker is receiving lower pay than a male worker performing the same tasks*.'[77] '*In such situation, at least, Article 119 is directly applicable and may thus give rise to individual rights which the courts must protect.*'[78]. Therefore Article 119 grants Ms. Defrenne a right that she can claim against her employer (in other words, it has direct horizontal effect).[79] This judgment clarifies and consolidates the *van Gend en Loos* method in three fundamental ways.

Firstly, like in *van Gend en Loos*, the Court states that in order to determine whether Article 119 has direct effect one should consider '*the nature of the principle of equal pay, the aim of this provision and its place in the scheme*

75 *Defrenne v. SABENA*, C-43/75, para. 19.

76 *Defrenne v. SABENA*, C-43/75, para. 22.

77 *Defrenne v. SABENA*, C-43/75, para. 23.

78 *Defrenne v. SABENA*, C-43/75, para. 24.

79 D. Simon, 'SABENA is dead, Gabrielle Defrenne's case is still alive: the old lady's testament...' in M. Poiares Maduro and L. Azoulai (eds), *The Past and Future of EU law: the Classics of EU Law Revisited on the 50th Anniversary of the Rome Treaty* (Hart 2010); N. Reich, 'The Impact of the Non-Discrimination Principle on Private Autonomy' in D. Leczykiewicz and S. Weatherhill (eds), *The Involvement of EU Law in Private Law Relationships* (Hart Publishing 2013); Millénaire 3, 'L'antidiscrimination, une volonté de l'Union européenne' Discriminations "raciales" et politiques antidiscriminatoires - Fiche n°1 <http://www.millenaire3.com/uploads/tx_ressm3/syntheses_discrim_fiche1.pdf> accessed 14 April 2015. *Defrenne II* is remembered as a horizontal direct effect case, however the issue would probably be framed differently today because *SABENA* was a public-owned company. Indeed, in direct effect cases the Court has since then developed a very broad conception of public authorities: see especially Judgment of 12 July 1990, *Foster and others v British Gas*, C-188/89, EU:C:1990:313, para 20).

of the Treaty.'[80] As Pollicino remarks, this amounts to engaging in teleological interpretation, '*furthering the aims of the Treaty by recourse to dynamic criteria and purposive considerations*'.[81] Systemic considerations also play a role (with '*scheme*' corresponding to '*système*' in the French version).[82] The Court notices that Article 119 '*forms part of the social objectives of the Community, which is not merely an economic union, but is at the same time intended, by common action, to ensure social progress and seek constant improvement of living and working conditions, as is emphasised by the preamble to the Treaty.*'[83] The teleological and systemic methods of interpretation are employed to give priority to the proclaimed objectives of the Treaty(ies), especially the objective of European integration;[84] this leads the Court to acknowledge, within the system established by the Treaty, the particular importance of the principle of equal treatment.

However, this is as far as the search for the intentions of the authors goes. In fact, while the greater aims (those constituting the *telos*) of the Treaty play a role in the Court's analysis, Article 119 itself is not subjected to an intentionalist analysis. The only relevant question for determining whether it gives rise to rights is whether the obligation contained therein passes the test of direct effect. The Court does not look for what may have been the subjective intention of the lawmaker in drafting this specific provision. The nature of the provision, or its designation in the Treaty, is irrelevant to determine whether it has direct effect: in the case at hand, the Member States had argued that the provision at issue, being the expression of a 'principle' of non-discrimination, could as such under no circumstances have direct effect.[85] The Court's reply was the clear-cut statement that '*it is impossible to put forward an argument against its direct effect based on the use in this article of the word "principle", since, in the language of the Treaty, this term is specifically used in order to indicate the fundamental nature of certain provisions, as is shown, for example, by the heading of the first part of the*

80 *Defrenne v. SABENA*, C-43/75, para. 7.

81 O. Pollicino, 'Legal Reasoning of the Court of Justice in the Context of the Principle of Equality Between Judicial Activism and Self-restraint' (2004) 5 German Law Journal 283 294.

82 Dero-Bugny, *Les rapports entre la Cour de justice de l'Union européenne et la Cour européenne des droits de l'homme* para 128.

83 *Defrenne v. SABENA*, C-43/75, para. 7.

84 N. Fennelly, 'Legal Interpretation at the European Court of Justice' (1996) 20 Fordham International Law Journal 656; Conway, *The Limits of Legal Reasoning and the European Court of Justice*, 210.

85 *Defrenne v. SABENA*, C-43/75, para. 28.

Treaty which is devoted to "Principles"'.[86] Likewise, the subject-matter of the provision is just as irrelevant to determine whether there is direct effect: Article 119 EEC contained an obligation to achieve an objective of social policy - a field which, '*by nature, involves a certain degree of freedom of action on the part of the national authorities*'; but this did not matter as long as the provision passed the *van Gend en Loos* test.[87] The link between direct effect and enforceable individual rights is also made clear in the judgment, when the Court recalls *Van Gend en Loos* by stating that a provision phrased as an obligation addressed to the Member States does not exclude the granting of rights to individuals: '*as the Court has already found in other contexts, the fact that certain provisions of the Treaty are formally addressed to Member States does not prevent rights from being conferred at the same time on any individual who has an interest in the performance of the duties thus laid down*'.[88] The Court grants direct horizontal effect to an obligation clearly addressed to Member States, thus acknowledging that such an obligation may also be binding on individuals and '*allowing individuals to vindicate their rights arising from these provisions against other individuals*'.[89]

Secondly, *Defrenne II* exemplifies the importance of concrete circumstances for identifying an individual right in a Treaty provision. The Court checks whether, in a given situation, the provision alone suffices to detect a right (and the violation of a right) even though it might not be sufficient in another situation. This is why the Court admits that Article 119 may require implementing measures but still finds that some aspects of this provision directly and immediately grant a right to Ms. Defrenne. This reading of *Defrenne II* is supported in the literature: '*in the context of direct effect,*

---

86 *Defrenne v. SABENA*, C-43/75, para. 28. This has also been highlighted by Prechal: S. Prechal, 'Rights v principles, or how to remove fundamental rights from the jurisdiction of the courts' in J. De Zwaan, J.H. Hans and F.A. Nelissen (eds), *The European Union: An Ongoing Process of Integration - Liber Amicorum Alfred E Kellermann* (T.M.C. Asser Press (The Hague) 2004) and S. Prechal, 'EU Gender Equality Law: a source of inspiration for other EU legal fields?' (2008) European Gender Equality Law Review 10.

87 Pollicino, 'Legal Reasoning of the Court of Justice in the Context of the Principle of Equality Between Judicial Activism and Self-restraint' 294.

88 *Defrenne v. SABENA*, C-43/75, EU:C:1976:56, para. 31. W. Van Gerven, 'Remedies for Infringements of Fundamental Rights' (2004) 10 European Public Law 261 268.

89 See also concerning horizontal direct effect (of Article 48 EEC) the Judgment of 15 December 1995, *Union royale belge des sociétés de football association and Others v Bosman and Others*, C-415/93, EU:C:1995:463 and Türk, *The Concept of Legislation in European Community Law - A Comparative Perspective* 88.

we need to know not only whether a provision confers rights on individuals in the abstract, but also whether it confers rights on individuals in the current proceedings.'[90] Thus, rather than abstract criteria, the Court has developed a set of tools which help determine how any provision may be applied to any concrete situation. In this sense, *Defrenne II* confirms that whenever a rule is phrased in a way that allows it to be technically, practically applicable by a national court, then it has direct effect,[91] which means that it is enforceable by individuals before this court, even if it is phrased as an obligation and not as a right. The Court demonstrates great flexibility in the assessment of these criteria: unconditionality means that the operation of a given provision is not dependent on further action being taken by Union or national authorities.[92] This requirement may even be waived in many cases, precisely like in *Defrenne II* when the Court held that the requirement of further action did not prevent a provision from having direct effect after the deadline for that further action.[93]

Thirdly, *Defrenne* highlights the significance of interests and their combination with duties in order to identify corresponding rights. One particularly significant paragraph in *Defrenne II* deserves to be quoted again here: '*the fact that certain provisions of the Treaty are formally addressed to Member States does not prevent rights from being conferred at the same time on any indi-*

90 C. Hilson and T. Downes, 'Making sense of rights: Community rights in E.C. law' (1999) European Law Review 121 138 quoting P. Eleftheriadis, 'The Direct Effect of Community Law: Conceptual Issues' (1996) 16 Yearbook of European Law 205 211. Their position is that direct effect cannot be the attribute of rules themselves, as legal effects instead depend on the application of those rules in concrete cases.

91 Simon, 'SABENA is dead, Gabrielle Defrenne's case is still alive: the old lady's testament...' 270; S. Robin-Olivier, 'The evolution of direct effect in the EU: Stocktaking, problems, projections' (2014) 12 International Journal of Constitutional Law 165 169. In the same vein, the Court sometimes uses the expression of a 'legally perfect' norm, in the sense that it does not lack any element for it to be directly applicable: Judgment of 27 June 1989, Kühne, C-50/88, EU:C:1989:262, para 26, and Judgment of 22 May 1980, *Regina v Secretary of State for Home Affairs, ex parte Santillo*, C-131/79, EU:C:1980:131, para 13 – as pointed out by AG Trstenjak: Opinion of AG Trstenjak in *Dominguez*, C-282/10, EU:C:2011:559, para 135.

92 A Community provision is unconditional where it is not subject, in its implementation or effects, to the taking of any measure either by the institutions of the Community or by the Member States – as clarified in Judgment of 3 April 1968, *Molkerei Zentrale Westfalen-Lippe v Hauptzollamt Paderborn*, C-28/67, EU:C:1968:17, p. 153.

93 Hartley, *The Foundations of European Union Law* 214.

vidual who has an interest *in the performance of the duties thus laid down*'.[94] This echoes an argument which the Commission had submitted in *Van Gend en Loos* but which had not been explicitly addressed by the Court in the grounds of judgment back then, i.e. that '*the fact that a Community rule is, as regards its form, directed to the states does not of itself take away from individuals* who have an interest in it *the right to require it to be applied in the national courts*'.[95] The notion of interest is thus closely linked to that of a right, which can be claimed by anyone who has an interest in the fulfilment of the corresponding obligation.[96]

Defrenne II is a very enlightening case: building on *Van Gend en Loos*, it derives a right from a positive obligation and, in so doing, it also makes the predominance of the teleological and systemic methods of interpretation very clear, while limiting the relevance of the literal and intentionalist methods. Moreover, the ruling emphasizes the importance of concrete circumstances and of individual interest for identifying and applying a right. With this combination of rights, obligations, and interests, the Court in the *Algera-Van Gen den Loos-Defrenne II* trilogy laid down the essential parameters for developing the concept of individual rights under EU law.

1.1.1.2. Rights, obligations and interests in domestic legal systems

This section provides a comparative overview of the legal systems from which the Court may have drawn inspiration for designing the basic concept of individual rights. The use of comparative law to answer legal questions arising in the EU legal order was legitimised already in *Algera*.[97] Awareness of the legal conceptions from which the Court drew inspiration can thus help understand the development of individual rights in the EU legal order.[98] The main examples are the French, English and German legal

94 *Defrenne v. SABENA*, C-43/75, para. 31 (emphasis added).

95 *Van Gend en Loos*, C-26/62, p. 7 (emphasis added).

96 The Court reasserted this in *Angonese*, relying on *Defrenne* to hold that Article 48 had direct horizontal effect: Judgment in *Angonese*, C-281/98, EU:C:2000:296, paras 34-35. See also Judgment of 11 December 2007, *The International Transport Workers' Federation and The Finnish Seamen's Union*, C-438/05, EU:C:2007:772, para 58.

97 As pointed out above p. 32. See *Algera and Others v Assemblée Commune*, Joined cases C-7/56 and C-3 to C-7/57, p. 54.

98 See the justification of this approach in the introduction to this study, p. 19.

systems, which have been the most influential in Europe.[99] Special attention is paid to notions and discussions that overlap with the characteristics identified in the *Algera-Van Gend en Loos-Defrenne* trilogy, namely the relation between rights, obligations and interests.

1.1.1.2.1. The limited relevance of rights and the emphasis on obligations and interests in the French legal culture

First-year law students in French law faculties are taught that the law is organised around the *summa divisio* between objective law (sources of law) and subjective rights (the angle from which persons and acts are studied).[100] Against this backdrop, the elementary relation that structures all legal norms is the one between the holder of a right and the debtor of the corresponding obligation.[101] Subjective rights are further divided into patrimonial and extra patrimonial rights, which spread into further subdivisions in the style of a '*jardin à la française*'.[102] The notion of '*droit subjectif*' is an essential notion in private law.[103] This is reflected in the intensity of the debates over the definition of subjective rights. These have been subjected

99 M. Fromont, *Droit administratif des Etats européens* (Presses universitaires de France 2006) 351.

100 Cornu defines a 'droit subjectif' as follows : '*une prérogative reconnue à une personne par le droit objectif, pour la satisfaction d'un intérêt personnel*'. G. Cornu, *Droit civil. Introduction. Les personnes. Les biens* (8th edn, Montchrestien 1997) 13 and 25. See also J. Carbonnier, *Droit civil : Introduction, Les personnes* (Presses universitaires de France 1984); J.-L. Aubert, E. Savaux, *Introduction au droit et thèmes fondamentaux du droit civil* (Sirey 2016).

101 Virally, *La pensée juridique* 43-44.

102 Kaczmarek, *La Responsabilité pour fait normal : Etude critique sur son originalité en matière civile extracontractuelle* 260. See also Cornu, *Droit civil. Introduction. Les personnes. Les biens* 26; N. Deleuze and A. Bertrand-Mikovic, *Introduction générale au droit : le droit objectif, les droits subjectifs, l'action en justice* (Studyrama 2005); J.-C. Ricci, *Droit civil - Les biens* (Hachette Education 2013).

103 Kaczmarek, *La Responsabilité pour fait normal : Etude critique sur son originalité en matière civile extracontractuelle* 263, citing e.g.: O. Ionescu, *La notion de droit subjectif dans le droit privé* (Sirey 1931) 182; G. Michaleides-Nouaros, 'L'évolution récente de la notion de droit subjectif' (1966) Revue trimestrielle de droit civil 216, where the notion of a subjective right is described as the '*notion première ou centrale, sur laquelle est construit tout le système du droit privé moderne*'.

to various categorisations[104] and discussions over whether a broad conception such as that of '*appartenance-maîtrise*' defended by the Belgian civil law theorist Dabin,[105] should be preferred over a more restrictive theory of rights such as Roubier's.[106] It is also still debated whether the purpose of subjective rights is primarily to protect interests or to protects goods,[107] and whether subjective rights are defined more by the power they rely on or by the interest that they protect.[108] Cornu's classic and synthetic definition proposes that a '*droit subjectif*' is an interest that is legally protected under (objective) law.[109] In a slightly expanded version, a subjective right may be defined as an individual prerogative that is provided for by objective law, and that gives 'power' to act and/or allows for the satisfaction of a personal interest.[110] The importance of subjective rights in the French legal discourse, especially in the context of the growing significance of fundamental rights,[111] has even been described as the '*pulvérisation du droit en droits subjectifs*'.[112]

Why is it, then, that the French view of rights has been characterised by outside observers as '*somewhat indolent*'?[113] The branch of French law from which the Court of Justice originally drew inspiration was public and administrative law.[114] In this discipline, the focus is traditionally not on

104 For instance, Virally distinguishes between '*droits-pouvoirs*' on the one hand, and '*droits-libertés*' and '*droits-intérêts*' on the other hand. Virally, *La pensée juridique* 52.

105 F. Ost, *Droit et intérêt, vol. 2 : Entre droit et non-droit, l'intérêt : essai sur les fonctions qu'exerce la notion d'intérêt en droit privé* (M. Van de Kerchove ed, Publications des Facultés universitaires Saint-Louis 1990.).

106 In addition, Roubier proposed another type categorisation, distinguishing '*droits subjectifs*' from '*libertés*'. See Roubier, *Droits subjectifs et situations juridiques.*

107 Kaczmarek, *La Responsabilité pour fait normal : Etude critique sur son originalité en matière civile extracontractuelle* 350.

108 Cornu, *Droit civil. Introduction. Les personnes. Les biens* 25. E. Gaillard, *Le pouvoir en droit privé* (BEBYAI 1985).

109 Cornu, *Droit civil. Introduction. Les personnes. Les biens* 26.

110 E. Gaillard, *Le pouvoir en droit privé* (BEBYAI 1985).

111 F. Hourquebie, 'Les droits publics subjectifs: échec de l'importation d'une théorie allemande en droit administratif français?' in F. Melleray (ed), *L'argument de droit comparé en droit administratif français* (Bruylant 2007).

112 J. Carbonnier, *Droit et passion du droit* (Flammarion 1996) 121 ; A.-C. Aune, *Le phénomène de multiplication des droits subjectifs en droit des personnes et de la famille* (Presses Universitaires d'Aix-Marseille 2007).

113 Prechal and Van Roermund, 'Binding Unity in EU Legal Order: An Introduction' 11.

114 See *Algera and Others v Assemblée Commune*, Joined cases C-7/56 and C-3 to C-7/57.

rights. The indifference to – or even skepticism towards – individual rights is due at least in part to the influence of Léon Duguit, who developed an objectivist conception of public law based on social solidarity and in so doing minimised the relevance of individual rights.[115]

In his theory individual rights are rather viewed as residual, i.e. what remains in between the various individual duties based on the common good – this, by the way, also justifies why individuals are defined only as subordinate to the administration. In his *Traité de droit constitutionnel*, Duguit developed a critique of legal subjectivism, i.e. a system in which the law (the whole set of legal rules, referred to as '*droit objectif*' in order to distinguish it from '*les droits*') is derived from subjective rights which are posited as the first legal reality.[116] As Waline later analysed, in an objectivist system, the starting point is objective law, i.e. all legal rules, while in a subjectivist system objective law is logically and chronologically secondary, its mission being to ensure the rights of individuals. Duguit fought the idea according to which the single purpose of all norms was to ensure the protection of subjective rights of individuals, such rights being considered as powers to require a certain behaviour (action or non-action) from other persons. In Duguit's view, the individual will plays no role in the generation of legal effects: while the human will acts on the human body, the consequences of such actions are then construed by the law; this, in his view, legitimates an objectivist legal system.[117] For both Hauriou and Duguit, this does not prevent the legal system from protecting '*la personne hu-*

115 R. Bonnard, 'Léon Duguit. Ses oeuvres. Sa doctrine' (1929) Extrait de la Revue du Droit public et de la Science politique en France et à l'Etranger 5; L. Duguit, 'Souveraineté et liberté - Neuvième leçon, La souveraineté nationale à l'intérieur. La liberté de l'individu.' Revue générale du droit online, 2014, numéro 18567 <www.revuegeneraledudroit.eu/?p=18567> accessed 31 July 2016; L. Duguit, 'Les doctrines juridiques objectivistes' Extraits de la Revue du Droit public et de la Science politique en France et à l'Etranger (Octobre-Novembre-Décembre 1927), Revue générale du droit online, 2014, numéro 17072 <www.revuegeneraledudroit.eu/?p=17072> accessed 31 July 2016.

116 L. Duguit, *Manuel de droit constitutionnel* (4th edn, E. De Boccard 1923) (see in particular the Introduction pp.1-12); L. Duguit, *Traité de droit constitutionnel* (2nd edn, Fontemoing 1921); Y. Eminescu, 'Les juristes roumains et l'essor du droit comparé à l'Ecole de droit de Paris' (1989) 41 Revue internationale de droit comparé 737 752; J. Agudo Gonzalez, 'Evolucion y negacion del derecho subjetivo' (2011) Revista Digital de Derecho Administrativo 9; Foulquier, *Les droits publics subjectifs des administrés. Emergence d'un concept en droit administratif français du XIXè au XXè siècle*; J. Dabin, *Le droit subjectif* (Dalloz 2008) 5.

117 M. Waline, *L'individualisme et le droit* (Dalloz 2007) 204.

maine'.[118] Simply, on the whole, Duguit views subjective rights as no more than the possible reflex application of objective law to particular, individual situations.[119]

Even Roubier, who was challenging Duguit's radically objectivist point of view, considered that many positions which may be thought to be subjective rights in themselves are in fact reflex effects of objective law, rendering the notion of subjective rights irrelevant.[120] Hourquebie has suggested that this objectivist conception of administrative law is essentially due to the 'sanctification' ('*sacralisation*') of the State, which prohibits its limitation by law and therefore leads to the sanctification of the public power itself. In this context, little importance is granted to the subjective elements such as the personal situation of the applicant. The task of the administrative court is to control the legality of an act in the light of the law; only secondarily does the action for annulment help individuals defend their personal situation.[121]

In this setting, rights have only limited significance for the understanding of legal relations in the framework of public law. Instead, the main remedy in French administrative law remains the '*recours pour excès de pouvoir*', which is often characterised as a remedy of a deeply objective nature.[122] This remedy is open to any person whose (material or moral) interests are affected by an administrative act – the consequence being that the category of persons whose challenge is admissible is very broad.[123] Although some restrictions have been introduced over time, the principle re-

118 Bioy, *Droits fondamentaux et libertés publiques* 29.

119 Roubier, *Droits subjectifs et situations juridiques* 80; Kaczmarek, *La Responsabilité pour fait normal : Etude critique sur son originalité en matière civile extracontractuelle* 268.

120 Roubier, *Droits subjectifs et situations juridiques* 135.

121 M. Fromont, 'L'influence du droit français et du droit allemand sur les conditions de recevabilité du recours en annulation devant la Cour de Justice des Communautés européennes' [1966] Revue trimestrielle de droit européen 47 48; E. Ballot, *Les insuffisances de la notion de droits fondamentaux* (mare & martin 2014) 207.

122 Hourquebie, 'Les droits publics subjectifs: échec de l'importation d'une théorie allemande en droit administratif français?'; J. Masing, *Die Mobilisierung des Bürgers für die Durchsetzung des Rechts: europäische Impulse für eine Revision der Lehre vom subjektiv-öffentlichen Recht* (Duncker & Humblot 1997) 83.

123 Fromont, *Droit administratif des Etats européens* 166. See also M. Rousset and O. Rousset, *Droit administratif - Tome 2. Le contentieux administratif* (2nd edn, Presses universitaires de Grenoble 2004) 119-124.

mains nowadays.[124] The criterion of '*intérêt pour agir*' opens the way to court to any person, including associations defending collective interests.[125] It may be decomposed into two elements: the potential adverse effect, and the individual's proximity to the decision.[126] More generally, this means that individuals play a role in the legal system not by exercising rights but by proving interests.[127] This 'subjective' filter exists mainly in order to avoid the risk of *actio popularis*[128] in an otherwise essentially objective procedure.[129]

In this system, the plaintiff serves primarily as instrument to the observance of objective law, and only secondarily (if at all) he is perceived in terms defending his own rights.[130] The focus on the respect of objective obligations of the authorities is to be traced back to the traditional idea according to which the existence of a discretionary power excluded *ipso facto* any possibility for individuals to have subjective rights (which materialised during the nineteenth century in the distinction between '*actes de contentieux*' and '*actes discrétionnaires*'). Of course, in its contemporary form, the margin of action which is left to the administration in order to ensure the protection of the '*intérêt général*' does not amount to the absence of individual rights – it rather leads to a limitation of their scope of application.[131] In addition, rights are relevant in French public law in the shape of '*droits fondamentaux*' or '*libertés fondamentales*', or somehow superior principles, which are then analyzed and categorized according to various meth-

124 N. Poulet-Gibot Leclerc, *Droit administratif: sources, moyens, contrôles* (Bréal 2007) 230, Masing, *Die Mobilisierung des Bürgers für die Durchsetzung des Rechts: europäische Impulse für eine Revision der Lehre vom subjektiv-öffentlichen Recht* 200.

125 Fromont, *Droit administratif des Etats européens* 166. See also the judgment of the French Conseil d'Etat: Syndicat des propriétaires et contribuables du quartier Croix-de-Seguey-Tivoli, CE, 21 décembre 1906, Rec. p. 962.

126 J.M. Auby, Les recours juridictionnels contre les actes administratifs spécialement économiques dans le droit des Etats membres de la CEE (Commission européenne, Etudes, Série concurrence - rapprochement des législations, 1971) 46.

127 V. Bolgar, 'L'intérêt général dans la théorie et dans la pratique' (1965) 17 Revue internationale de droit comparé 329; K. Sibril, 'Définition de la notion d'intérêt en droit administratif français', Université de Bretagne occidentale - Brest 2012).

128 Pinault, *Rapport de la délégation française* 47.

129 Sibril, 'Définition de la notion d'intérêt en droit administratif français' 263.

130 A. Von Arnaud, 'Theorie und Methode des Grundrechtsschutzes in Europa - am Beispiel des Grundsatzes der Verhältnismässigkeit' (2008) Europarecht 41 60.

131 Hourquebie, 'Les droits publics subjectifs: échec de l'importation d'une théorie allemande en droit administratif français?' 205.

ods.[132] The existence of an infringed right is also relevant in another type of remedy, which while of modest relative importance in the traditional French system of remedies,[133] has gained importance in the past years: the '*recours de pleine juridiction*' or '*de plein contentieux*'.[134]

It remains true, however, that the legitimacy of citizens for requesting the observance of rules of public law lies primarily with their function as '*surveillants de l'Administration*'; in the words of Hauriou, in a '*recours pour excès de pouvoir*', individuals have '*un intérêt personnel sans doute, mais en même temps ils agissent dans l'intérêt de la Puissance publique; dans l'instance engagée, ils ne sont pas des parties en cause défendant leur droit, leur situation se rapproche de celle d'un ministère public poursuivant la répression d'une contravention*'.[135] Or as rephrased by Masing, '*the citizen does not only defend its private sphere against the State, [...] he exercises a public function above all*'.[136] In this respect the French system significantly differs from the German system.

1.1.1.2.2. The German emphasis on subjective rights and protective intention

Unlike the French system of control of public action, which was built mainly on objective elements, the German legal system relies on a theoreti-

132 E.g. M. Levinet, *Théorie générale des droits et libertés* (4th edn, L.G.D.J. , Anthemis/Nemesis 2012); X. Bioy, *Droits fondamentaux et libertés publiques* (Monchrestien, Lextenso éditions 2011).

133 M. Pinault, *Rapport de la délégation française* (8ème colloque de l'Association des Conseils d'Etat et des Juridictions administratives suprêmes de l'Union européenne, du 12 au 15 mai 1982, Copenhague - 'La notion de l'intérêt en contentieux administratif (intérêt personnel, intérêt collectif, l'action populaire) notamment en matière d'environnement', 1982).

134 Even this classic distinction between recours pour excès de pouvoir and recours de plein contentieux is now being challenged by the development of a third way: the 'recours de plein contentieux objectif': H. Lepetit-Collin, *Recherches sur le plein contentieux objectif* (L.G.D.J., collection Thèses 2011).

135 M. Hauriou, 'Recours pour excès de pouvoir et tierce opposition, Note sous Conseil d'Etat, 8 décembre 1899 (Ville d'Avignon), 15 décembre 1899 (Adda) S. 1900.3.73' Revue générale du droit on line, 2015, numéro 15407 <www.revuegeneraledudroit.eu/?p=15407> accessed 22 January 2016.

136 Masing, *Die Mobilisierung des Bürgers für die Durchsetzung des Rechts: europäische Impulse für eine Revision der Lehre vom subjektiv-öffentlichen Recht* 198: '*der Bürger verteidigt nicht nur und auch nicht in erster Linie seine Privatsphäre gegenüber dem Staat, sondern übt eine öffentliche Funktion aus.*'.

cal and philosophical tradition that conceives of individual or 'subjective' rights as an end in themselves, to be protected against the public powers. The doctrinal works in German public and administrative law are thus based on the premise that the guarantee of subjective rights is an essential condition for a liberal, democratic and social political system oriented towards the rule of law.[137]

The conception of the relation between individuals and the State under German public law emerged in the context of the German constitutional monarchy and the development of the *Rechtsstaat*.[138] The status and role of the individual are closely linked to the conception of the (mainly antagonistic) relation between individual and public interests, respectively of the citizen and the state.[139] For instance, Thoma defined the public community as an entity to which other legal subjects may oppose subjective rights, or towards which they may have legal obligations.[140] Kelsen connected rights with corresponding obligations by explaining that '*the right in the specific sense of the word is the legal power to enforce an existing duty*'.[141] Within the State, subjective rights are the medium for acknowledging the citizen as a *Rechtssubjekt* with a personality and a fundamental place in the German legal order.[142] Perhaps precisely because of its importance, the notion of subjective public rights has been the object of intense debate. Two opposing views were famously embodied by Windscheid, who defined a subjective right as a power granted by the legal system, and Jhering, who

137 Maurer, *Allgemeines Verwaltungsrecht* 164.

138 A. Gaillet, 'Chronique de droit administratif allemand (2012) ; 1. Le droit au recours des associations : l'orientation subjective du procès administratif allemand à l'épreuve du droit européen et conventionnel de l'environnement' (2013) Droit administratif. See also Heuschling, *Etat de droit, Rechtsstaat, Rule of law*; A. Gaillet, *L'individu contre l'Etat. Essai sur l'évolution des recours de droit public dans l'Allemagne du XIXè siècle* (Dalloz 2012).

139 Masing, *Die Mobilisierung des Bürgers für die Durchsetzung des Rechts: europäische Impulse für eine Revision der Lehre vom subjektiv-öffentlichen Recht* 14. This, although the dominant vision, is of course debated. For instance, Jhering conceived of each individual's struggle for their rights as a civic duty that the State had to support, because this phenomenon was at the heart of the realisation of the law. R. von Jehring, *La lutte pour le droit* (Dalloz 2006, first published 1890), O. Jouanjan ed., O. De Meulenaere trans; Melot, 'La conception wébérienne des droits subjectifs : un parcours de l'histoire économique au débat sur la légitimité politique' 143.

140 Thoma, 'Das System der subjektiven öffentlichen Rechte und Pflichten' 369.

141 H. Kelsen, *General Theory of Norms* (Oxford University Press 1991) 324, cited in Alexy, *A Theory of Constitutional Rights* (Oxford University Press 2002) 117.

142 German Constitution: Article 1 I, 2 I GG.

described subjective rights as legally protected interests.[143] Jellinek famously argued that it was possible to reconcile the 'interest' and the 'will' or 'power' as defining elements of the right, since an interest is defined as such by the subjective will. In his very influential general theory of subjective public rights, he therefore defined subjective public rights by combining a formal element – the will-power, i.e. the possibility to act in court, with a material element – the legally protected interest.[144] Subjective public rights are thus conditioned on the existence of an interest defined by the law and of a means of defending it in court.

The relation between rights and obligations is defined against the backdrop of the distinction between '*objektives Recht*' (the sum of all rules of law and the basis for legal duties) and '*subjektives Recht*'. No subjective right exists without a corresponding objective duty; the subjective public right is derived from objective norms.[145] But the connection between rights and obligations exists only in a certain limited context, i.e. where a public duty entails a corresponding subjective right: in that case, the obligation and the right will indeed be closely linked, as two sides of a medal.[146] On the other hand, however, it is possible to have an objective public duty without a corresponding subjective right. Such is the case for most public law norms, which lay down obligations for the administration, solely in the public interest, without giving individuals the possibility

143 B. Windscheid, *Lehrbuch des Pandektenrechts* (T. Kipp ed, 9th edn, Buddeus 1906) 156; R. von Jhering, *Der Geist des römischen Rechts auf den verschiedenen Stufen seiner Entwicklung*, (Benno Schwabe 1954 8th ed) 339. Both are cited in Alexy, *A Theory of Constitutional Rights*, 115. See also M. Smith, 'Four German Jurists. II' (1896) 11 Political Science Quarterly 278 289; Voßkuhle and Kaiser, 'Grundwissen – Öffentliches Recht: Das subjektiv-öffentliche Recht' 17; S. Schlacke, *Überindividueller Rechtsschutz: Phänomenologie und Systematik überindividueller Klagebefugnisse im Verwaltungs- und Gemeinschaftsrecht, insbesondere am Beispiel des Umweltrechts* (Mohr Siebeck 2008) 37.

144 G. Jellinek, *System der subjektiven öffentlichen Rechte* (1905) 44: '*Der Wille ist das notwendige Mittel, durch welches das 'Etwas' zum Gute oder Interesse wird*'. See also Capitant, *Les effets juridiques des droits fondamentaux en Allemagne* 38; Alexy, *A Theory of Constitutional Rights* 117 ; Masing, *Die Mobilisierung des Bürgers für die Durchsetzung des Rechts: europäische Impulse für eine Revision der Lehre vom subjektiv-öffentlichen Recht* 89; Sibril, 'Définition de la notion d'intérêt en droit administratif français"13; Voßkuhle and Kaiser, 'Grundwissen – Öffentliches Recht: Das subjektiv-öffentliche Recht' 17.

145 D. Capitant, *Les effets juridiques des droits fondamentaux en Allemagne* (L.G.D.J. 2001) 36; Maurer, *Allgemeines Verwaltungsrecht* 144.

146 A. Voßkuhle and A.-B. Kaiser, 'Grundwissen – Öffentliches Recht: Das subjektiv-öffentliche Recht' (2009) Juristische Schulung 16.

to require the execution of these obligations in court.[147] This is consistent with the emphasis in the literature on the idea that the protection of an individual's rights is not a mere side-effect or 'reflex' of objective norms, but rather the essential characteristic of the system.[148]

This essential characteristic is also enshrined in the German Constitution, Article 19 IV of which provides that any person whose subjective rights are violated by the public powers may challenge this behaviour in court.[149] The practical significance of these rights is that they grant the possibility to require in court the execution of the laws which concern him or her (*'gerichtlichen Durchsetzbarkeit'*).[150] The technical definition of a subjec-

---

147 R. Alexy, 'Rights and Liberties as Concepts' in M. Rosenfeld and A. Sajo (eds), *Oxford Handbook of Comparative Constitutional Law* (Oxford Handbook of Comparative Constitutional Law, Oxford University Press 2012) 286. Alexy emphasises a sort of hierarchy between rights and duties, insisting that duties can exist without rights while the opposite is impossible. He explains, 'A has a right that B do X' is logically equivalent to 'it is obligatory that B do X vis-à-vis A.' So, for instance, saying that A has a right against B that B grant A asylum means the same as 'B is vis-à-vis A obligated to grant A asylum.' But Alexy insists that not every obligation or duty implies a right. An obligation which is not relationally phrased, e.g. 'it is obligatory that B do X,' does *not* imply that A would have a right that B do X. See also Masing, *Die Mobilisierung des Bürgers für die Durchsetzung des Rechts: europäische Impulse für eine Revision der Lehre vom subjektiv-öffentlichen Recht* 63; Voßkuhle and Kaiser, 'Grundwissen – Öffentliches Recht: Das subjektiv-öffentliche Recht.'

148 G. Jellinek, *System der subjektiven öffentlichen Rechte* (1905) 44; R. Melot, 'La conception wébérienne des droits subjectifs : un parcours de l'histoire économique au débat sur la légitimité politique' in M. Coutu and G. Rocher (eds), *La légitimité de l'Etat et du droit autour de Max Weber* (La légitimité de l'Etat et du droit autour de Max Weber, Presses Université Laval 2005) 148; Fromont, 'L'influence du droit français et du droit allemand sur les conditions de recevabilité du recours en annulation devant la Cour de Justice des Communautés européennes' 48 and 56.

149 Maurer, *Allgemeines Verwaltungsrecht* 164; Masing, *Die Mobilisierung des Bürgers für die Durchsetzung des Rechts: europäische Impulse für eine Revision der Lehre vom subjektiv-öffentlichen Recht* 128; Voßkuhle and Kaiser, 'Grundwissen – Öffentliches Recht: Das subjektiv-öffentliche Recht' 17.

150 Some important rulings of the German Constitutional Court manifest this strict distinction between 'objective' and 'subjective' considerations. In the *Schleyer* case (BVerfGE 46, 160) the Constitutional Court reasoned in terms of State duties to protect citizens as a whole (against terrorist activities), not of subjective rights (of the individual who had been kidnapped by terrorists). In the *Kalkar* case (BVerfGE 49, 89) where a farmer was challenging an authorization to build an atomic plant near his property, the Constitutional Court carefully distin-

tive right is based on the reference to a legal capacity of enforcement,[151] the legal power for a citizen to require a certain behaviour or action from the State.[152] The provision of Article 19 IV GG finds further expression in the German law on administrative procedure and in the *Schutznorm* doctrine, which guides the application of this law.[153] The (so far) dominant *Schutznorm* doctrine (rooted in Jhering's work) identifies a '*subjektives Recht*' (i.e. a right which an individual may claim against the administration) in a norm that does not only aim to protect public interests, but instead, or at least also, the interests of individual citizens.[154] Only those individuals targeted by such an explicitly protective norm (*Schutznorm*) can bring an action before an administrative court. Therefore, what matters is the normative intention to protect specific interests, identifiable in that norm. The simple fact that a legal requirement brings advantages to an individual does not constitute ground for a subjective right; the subjective right exists only if these advantages were intended by the legislator.[155]

The main two questions for identifying a subjective public right can be summarised as follows: 1) is there a rule of law that compels the administration to act in a certain way? and 2) does this rule aim – if not exclusively, at least primarily – at protecting individual citizens?[156] The succession of

---

guished between constitutional rights and '*objective legal protective duties derivable from the constitutional rights system*'. It followed the same approach in *Müllheim-Kärlich* (BVerfGE 53, 30). Alexy, *A Theory of Constitutional Rights* 301.

151 Alexy, *A Theory of Constitutional Rights* 117; Maurer, *Allgemeines Verwaltungsrecht* 164.

152 Maurer, *Allgemeines Verwaltungsrecht* 164.

153 § 42.II A Verwaltungsgerichtsordnung, 21.1.1960, BGBI. I 1960 p. 17. J. Bok, 'Judicial Review of Administrative Decisions by the Dutch Administrative Courts: recours objectif or recours subjectif? A Survey including French and German law' in F.A.M. Stroink (ed), *Judicial Lawmaking and Administrative Law* (Intersentia nv 2005) 162. M. Künnecke, *Tradition and Change in Administrative Law: an Anglo-German comparison* (Springer 2007) 42.

154 BVerfGE 27, 297/307. Bok, 'Judicial Review of Administrative Decisions by the Dutch Administrative Courts: recours objectif or recours subjectif? A Survey including French and German law' 163.

155 R. Thoma, 'Das System der subjektiven öffentlichen Rechte und Pflichten' in H. Dreier (ed), *Rechtsstaat - Demokratie - Grundrechte* (Mohr Siebeck 1932) 383; Fromont, 'L'influence du droit français et du droit allemand sur les conditions de recevabilité du recours en annulation devant la Cour de Justice des Communautés européennes' 58; H. Maurer, *Allgemeines Verwaltungsrecht* (17 edn, Beck 2009) 164 ; Ruffert, 'Rights and Remedies in European Community Law: a Comparative View' 311.

156 Maurer, *Allgemeines Verwaltungsrecht* 167; Voßkuhle and Kaiser, 'Grundwissen – Öffentliches Recht: Das subjektiv-öffentliche Recht' 17.

these two questions is consistent with the idea that an obligation can exist autonomously from a right (question 1 may well have a positive answer even though question 2 does not). The answer to the second question will depend on the intentional inclusion, by the legislator, of a protective aspect in the obligation; if no such intention can be detected, the obligation will not translate into a subjective right.[157]

While this approach applies in the specific scope of the law on administrative procedure, it has far-reaching conceptual and practical implications in terms of the relation between rights and the means of enforcing them. The notion of a subjective public right may have been originally the consequence of an action in court, but it has now become the condition for such an action. The consequence is that interests that are not individually and intentionally protected by law, are excluded from the protection offered by German administrative procedural law.[158]

1.1.1.2.3. The focus on duties and remedies in the English legal tradition

Just like in continental legal systems, in the English legal tradition there is an assumption that '*duties precede rights logically and chronologically*'. This assumption can be traced back to Holmes, who emphasised that, '*while there are in some cases legal duties without corresponding rights, we never see a legal right without either a corresponding duty or a compulsion stronger than the duty*'.[159] As Williams puts it, '*[n]o one ever has a right to do something: he only has a right that someone else shall do (or refrain from doing) something. In other*

157 Capitant, *Les effets juridiques des droits fondamentaux en Allemagne* 33.

158 For instance, groups can defend only their interests as legal persons, not the interests of their individual members. See the ruling by the German federal administrative tribunal on an association of engineers: BVerwG, 3.12.1959, MDR 1960 338. Auby, Les recours juridictionnels contre les actes administratifs spécialement économiques dans le droit des Etats membres de la CEE, 49; Fromont, 'L'influence du droit français et du droit allemand sur les conditions de recevabilité du recours en annulation devant la Cour de Justice des Communautés européennes' 58.

159 O.W. Holmes, 'Codes, and the Arrangement of the Law' (1870) 5 American Law Review, quoted in M. Graziadei, 'Rights in the European Landscape: A Historical and Comparative Profile' in S. Prechal and B. Van Roermund (eds), *The Coherence of EU Law The Search for Unity in Divergent Concepts* (Oxford University Press 2008) 72.

words, every right in the strict sense relates to the conduct of another.'[160] Where the English legal tradition stands apart from its continental counterparts, is in how it ignores the notion of an opposition between subjective rights and objective law[161] and tones down the issues that may arise from the relationship between individual and public interests.[162] Indeed, traditionally '*English public law has been more concerned with wrongs than rights, being primarily focused on whether public authorities have breached the obligations imposed on them by legislation.*'[163] In addition, Sales observes that traditionally there was little space for rights discourse because the English way to reason about law was focused on the sovereignty of Parliament and the early theory of common law.[164] Thus in the English legal culture, duties and remedies make the language of rights redundant.[165] This applies also on the constitutional level: '*the common law does not generally speak in the language of constitutional rights.*'[166]

As a consequence, in the English legal tradition the law of remedies matters at least as much as substantive law; in public law, remedies were the way to enforce the duties of public bodies, following the principle '*ubi remedium, ibi obligatio*' (which also meant that if no writ was available, then there was no duty to be enforced).[167] English administrative law has

160 G. Williams, 'The Concept of Legal Liberty' (1956) 56 Columbia Law Review 1129 1145, quoted in M.H. Kramer, 'Rights Without Trimmings' in M.H. Kramer, N.E. Simmonds and H. Steiner (eds), *A Debate Over Rights* (A Debate Over Rights, Oxford University Press 1998) 14.

161 K. Campbell, 'Legal Rights' The Stanford Encyclopedia of Philosophy (Fall 2013 Edition), ed E. Zalta <http://plato.stanford.edu/archives/fall2013/entries/legal-rights/≥ accessed 10 November 2014.

162 N.E. Simmonds, 'Rights at the Cutting Edge' in M.H. Kramer, N.E. Simmonds and H. Steiner (eds), *A Debate Over Rights* (A Debate Over Rights, Oxford University Press 1998) 126.

163 Sales, 'Rights and Fundamental Rights in English Law' 89.

164 P. Sales, 'Rights and Fundamental Rights in English Law' (2016) 75 The Cambridge Law Journal 86.

165 Graziadei, 'Rights in the European Landscape: A Historical and Comparative Profile' 71; on the English system of remedies in public law, and how its development is intimately linked with that of substantive public law, see M. Sunkin, 'Remedies Available in Judicial Review Proceedings' in D. Feldman (ed), *English Public Law* (English Public Law, 2nd edn, Oxford University Press 2009).

166 *R. v Lord Chancellor, ex p. Witham* [1998] Q.B. 575, 581, per Laws J., cited in Sales, 'Rights and Fundamental Rights in English Law' 87.

167 P. O'Callaghan, 'Reversing Ubi Remedium Ibi Jus in the Common Law: The Right of Privacy' (2007) 15 European Review of Private Law 659. The 'cousin' principle in private law is '*ubi remedium ibi jus*', signalling that the notion of rights was more relevant for private law than for public law.

been through a tremendous evolution in the second half of the twentieth century, especially with the introduction in the 1980s of a 'sufficiency of interest test' for admissibility to judicial review in public law.[168] Nevertheless, the fundamental principle remains that there should be a remedy available for any wrong.[169] One only has to open a book on English public law and check the table of contents in order to observe that in English judicial review, the emphasis is on remedies rather than on rights,[170] reflecting the prominent place of principles of procedural justice in the English legal system.[171]

Nevertheless, and even though the '*obligation-dominated days of public law*' and the emphasis on procedural principles have left their mark,[172] a shift has undeniably taken place and rights (including now from domestic sources) are becoming more important in the English legal system.[173] Substantive rights have drawn more attention in the recent years since the 1998 Human Rights Act,[174] which incorporates the ECHR in national law.[175] The consecration through the HRA of ECHR rights against public bodies has led to the creation of new remedies linked with those rights and to the integration of an 'ubi ius, ibi remedium' principle alongside the traditional 'ubi remedium, ibi obligatio' and 'ubi remedium, ibi jus'.[176] This causes some conceptual confusion especially since in many instances

---

168 P. Craig, 'Access to Mechanisms of Administrative Law' in D. Feldman (ed), *English Public Law* (English Public Law, 2nd edn, Oxford University Press 2009) 767.

169 D. Feldman, 'Remedies for Violations of Convention Rights' in D. Feldman (ed), *English Public Law* (English Public Law, 2nd edn, Oxford University Press 2009) 827; Fromont, *Droit administratif des Etats européens* 64; Heuschling, *Etat de droit, Rechtsstaat, Rule of law* 296.

170 E.g.: *English Public Law* (2nd edn, Oxford University Press 2009); A. Le Sueur, M. Sunkin and J.E.K. Murkens, *Public Law. Text, Cases, and Materials* (2nd edn, Oxford University Press 2010).

171 Bignami, 'Creating European Rights: National Values and Supranational Interests' (2005) 11 Columbia Journal of European Law 241 272.

172 Feldman, 'Remedies for Violations of Convention Rights'; see also E. Palmer, *Judicial Review, Socio-Economic Rights and the Human Rights Act* (Hart Publishing 2007) 105.

173 Sales, 'Rights and Fundamental Rights in English Law' 86.

174 Human Rights Act 1998 [United Kingdom of Great Britain and Northern Ireland], 9 November 1998; hereafter 'HRA'.

175 Le Sueur, Sunkin and Murkens, *Public Law. Text, Cases, and Materials* 681. See also Prechal, 'Does Direct Effect Still Matter?' 1053.

176 Feldman, 'Remedies for Violations of Convention Rights'; Sunkin, 'Remedies Available in Judicial Review Proceedings'; O'Callaghan, 'Reversing Ubi Remedium Ibi Jus in the Common Law: The Right of Privacy'.

where the focus is on 'remedy', this remedy happens to also constitute a 'right'.[177] Still, the array of grounds for judicial review has been broadened and now includes not only various types of illegality, but also infringement of due process requirements and violation of an HRA right.[178]

Moreover, rights have been theorised and intensely discussed by English legal scholars. One important example is the resonance in English legal theory of Hohfeld's analytical prism for what he called '*fundamental legal conceptions*'.[179] Hohfeld thought and wrote in the American context but, as Graziadei stresses, his contribution to the analysis of rights was '*the work of a straightforward-looking common lawyer*'[180] and it has become unavoidable in the English debate over the theory of rights. Hohfeld's aim was to provide tools for practical purposes, i.e. methods that could be used in concrete problems of litigation – or at least to make lawyers aware of how these methods were already being used.[181] In order to understand complex legal notions, he relied on the idea that the claimant's legal position (or entitlement) is necessarily related to the defendant's position[182] and proposed to work with a network of interrelated notions, rather than complex, isolated concepts.[183] Hohfeld thus distinguished four types of jural correlatives, i.e. four pairs of concepts, one being an entitlement and the other the corresponding disablement:[184] *right (claim)/duty*, *privilege (liberty)/no-right*, *power/liability*, *immunity/disability*. The basic idea being: '*we should always*

177 P. Birks, 'Rights, Wrongs, and Remedies' (2000) 20 Oxford Journal of Legal Studies 1; J.N.E. Varuhas, 'Judicial Review: Standing and Remedies' (2013) 72 The Cambridge Law Journal 243.

178 Sunkin, 'Grounds for Judicial Review: Illegality in the Strict Sense'; S.H. Bailey, 'Grounds for Judicial Review: Due Process, Natural Justice, and Fairness' in D. Feldman (ed), *English Public Law* (2nd edn, Oxford University Press 2009); Fromont, *Droit administratif des Etats européens* 192.

179 W.N. Hohfeld, 'Some Fundamental Legal Conceptions as Applied in Judicial Reasoning'; W.N. Hohfeld, 'Fundamental Legal Conceptions as Applied in Judicial Reasoning'.

180 Graziadei, 'Rights in the European Landscape: A Historical and Comparative Profile' 84.

181 Hohfeld, 'Fundamental Legal Conceptions as Applied in Judicial Reasoning' 712.

182 Graziadei, 'Rights in the European Landscape: A Historical and Comparative Profile' 84.

183 Bennet, 'Le droit et l'analyse philosophique des droits selon W.N. Hohfeld' (2011) 21 Klesis Revue philosophique 133 143.

184 Hohfeld, 'Fundamental Legal Conceptions as Applied in Judicial Reasoning' 712; Campbell, 'Legal Rights'. For a detailed analysis of Hohfeldian concepts see e.g. A. Rotolo and G. Sartor, 'Deontic Logic. Introductory materials', Summer

look at both sides of any legal advantage.[185] The subtleties of the Hohfeldian conceptual scheme have been subjected to innumerable interpretations and counter-interpretations, criticism and counter-criticism.[186] But the fundamental characteristic of Hohfeld's approach remains in the idea that each legal conception gains meaning from its relation with another (or with other) conception(s).[187] In this perspective, it is not so much that duties 'give rise' to rights or that rights 'imply' duties, but rather that '*one's rights* are *duties in someone else just as one's duties* are *rights in someone else*.' In other words, right or duty are two different ways of talking about the same legal relation.[188] This is what Kramer calls the '*Correlativity Axiom*'.[189]

A recurring criticism of Hohfeld's work regrets that this approach establishes a conceptual hierarchy between duties and rights, the former being more 'fundamental' than the latter. MacCormick has severely questioned the utility and relevance of Hohfeld's work by stating that to '*rest an account of claim rights* solely *on the notion that they exist whenever a legal duty is imposed by a law intended to benefit assignable individuals... is to treat rights as being simply the "reflex" of logically prior duties. Accordingly, for any statement about rights there could always be substituted a statement about duties*

School on Law and Logic, European University Institute and Harvard Law School 2015 <http://lawandlogic.org/coursebasic/session-5-2-2/> accessed 25 August 2015. Hohfeld also identified four types of jural opposites but these are not directly relevant to the present study, which focuses on the correlation between obligations and rights observed in the founding cases *Van Gend en Loos* and *Defrenne II*.

185 J. Waldron, 'A Rights-Based Critique of Constitutional Rights' (1993) 13 Oxford Journal of Legal Studies 18 27.

186 Works in which awareness of this ongoing controversy is particularly acute, and in which an explicit intention to solve it is announced, include: P. Schlag, 'How to Do Things With Hohfeld' (2014) 78 Law and Contemporary Problems ; Kramer, Simmonds and Steiner, *A Debate Over Rights*; J.M. Finnis, 'Some Professorial Fallacies About Rights' (1972) Scholarly Works ; A. Halpin, 'Rights, Duties, Liabilities, and Hohfeld' (2007) 13 Legal Theory 23; E. Engle, 'Taking the Right Seriously: Hohfeldian Semiotics and Rights Discourse' (2010) 3 The Crit 84. Furthermore, all references about Hohfeld cited in the present work propose interpretations of his work with more or less significant (and more or less conscious) variations.

187 W.N. Hohfeld, 'Some Fundamental Legal Conceptions as Applied in Judicial Reasoning' (1913) 23 Yale Law Journal ; Schlag, 'How to Do Things With Hohfeld' 4. See also Hohfeld, 'Fundamental Legal Conceptions as Applied in Judicial Reasoning.'

188 Schlag, 'How to Do Things With Hohfeld' 17.

189 Kramer, 'Rights Without Trimmings' 24.

which would be at a more fundamental level analytically.'[190] Similarly, Waldron has analysed Hohfeld's understanding of rights as being always subordinate to '*the more primitive notion of a duty*'.[191] Gewirth has called this the '*correlativity objection*', which states that if right and duty designate one and the same legal relation, then one of these concepts is useless and redundant, and it has to be the right, since the notion of duty is necessary for the law to impose normative requirements. In this sense, the correlativity of rights and duties is even used to negate the relevance of the notion of rights for legal theory.[192] In addition, the influential legal philosopher Raz proposed to define rights by considering that '*x has a right*' if '*an aspect of x's well-being (his interest) is a sufficient reason for holding some other person(s) to be under a duty*', thus dismissing the idea of a correlativity between rights and duties.[193] One of his objections to most formulations of the correlativity thesis is that they do not sufficiently take into account '*the dynamic aspect of rights*' and the ability of rights to create new duties depending on concrete circumstances, so that '*there is no closed list of duties which correspond to the right*'.[194]

Rights can also be apprehended from the perspective of their function. This debate takes the shape of a competition between two strands of theoretical legal thinking: the will theory and the interest theory.[195] The discussion resembles and even overlaps with the German debate on similar issues.[196] Indeed, the will and interest theories have been competing '*literally for ages*'.[197] Schematically, will theorists (including Hart, Kelsen, Steiner) ar-

190 N. MacCormick, 'Rights in Legislation' in P.M.S. Hacker and J. Raz (eds), *Law, Morality and Society: Essays in Honour of HLA Hart* (Law, Morality and Society: Essays in Honour of HLA Hart, Clarendon Press 1977) 199 quoted in Kramer, 'Rights Without Trimmings' 24.

191 J. Waldron, *The Right to Private Property* (Clarendon Press 1988) 68, quoted in Kramer, 'Rights Without Trimmings' 26.

192 A. Gewirth, 'Why Rights are Indispensable' (1986) 95 Mind 329 330. The correlativity objection was developed by Hart: see e.g. in H.L.A. Hart, 'Bentham on Legal Rights' in H.L.A. Hart (ed), *Essays on Bentham: Jurisprudence and Political Theory* (Essays on Bentham: Jurisprudence and Political Theory, Clarendon Press 1982) 181.

193 Raz, 'On the Nature of Rights' 195 and 199-200.

194 Raz, 'On the Nature of Rights' 208.

195 The debate between interest theorists and will theorists overlaps with the Hohfeldian analysis of rights; on both sides (will and interest) there are Hohfeldians and non-Hohfeldians. Kramer, Simmonds and Steiner, *A Debate Over Rights* 4.

196 Alexy, *A Theory of Constitutional Rights* 115.

197 Wenar, 'Rights'.

gue that a right is characterised by the power which it grants its owner over others' duties to act in a particular way; while interest theorists (including Bentham, Lyons, MacCormick, Raz, Kramer) stress that the defining feature of a right is its function to protect an interest of the right-holder.[198] According to the latter conception, then, having a right means having a shield against interference or non-assistance to an aspect of one's well-being.[199] This is why the interest theory is sometimes referred to as the benefit theory. The will theory often contends that rights and claims are not equivalent, meaning that, the label of 'rights' can be applied only to claims that are coupled with genuine powers of enforcement. On the contrary, in the interest theory, right and claim can be used interchangeably.[200]

A connected debate takes place concerning the relation between individual interests and community interests. Dworkin famously defined rights '*as trumps over some background justification for political decisions that states a goal for the community as a whole*'.[201] Raz, on the contrary, rejects the view that the primacy of individual rights represents the individual's standpoint against the public good. He argues instead that the range and nature of common goods determine the options available to individuals and define

---

198 MacCormick, 'Rights in Legislation'; Roubier, *Droits subjectifs et situations juridiques* 67; Wenar, 'Rights'; S. Van Duffel, 'From Objective Right to Subjective Rights: The Franciscans and the Interest and Will Conceptions of Rights' National University of Singapore, 2 <http://ssrn.com/abstract=1467455>; R. Cespedes, 'Hohfeld's Taxonomy Revisited: an Update from the Theory of Rights and Modern Public Law, Family Law and Human Rights Law' 'Tis Forty Years Since: Britain & Ireland in Europe, Europe in Britain & Ireland' The changing landscape of theory and practice, The University of Edinburgh, Edinburgh Law School, 2-3 September 2013 3. The two strands of will and interest may in turn be subdivided into several sub-theories: see e.g. Eleutheriadēs' work where three versions of the interest theory and three versions of the will theory are discussed: P.Z. Eleutheriades, *Legal Rights* (Oxford University Press 2008) 6; see also Simmonds about the many '*insipid contemporary descendants*' of the original will and interest theories: Simmonds, 'Rights at the Cutting Edge' 118.

199 J. Waldron, 'Critical Notice' (1985) 94 Mind 281 291; Kramer, Simmonds and Steiner, *A Debate Over Rights* 2; Bengoetxea and Jääskinen, 'Rights and Diverse Effects in EU Law: A Hohfeldian Approach to the Doctrine of Direct Effect of Directives' in R. Banakar (ed) *Rights in Context - Law and Justice in Late Modern Society* (Ashgate 2010) 286.

200 Yet, Hohfeld's account of jural relations may still fit in the vision of both interest theorists and will theorists, since '*a Hohfeldian claim* can *be combined in a single person with a Hohfeldian power of enforcement/waiver but does not* have *to be so combined.*' Kramer, 'Rights Without Trimmings' 65.

201 R. Dworkin, 'Rights as Trumps' in J. Waldron (ed), *Theories of Rights* (Oxford University Press 1984) 153.

their well-being.[202] All in all, given the limited practical relevance of the concept of rights in the English legal system, it is very interesting to see the intensity and depth of the debate over rights and their relation with duties and interests in English legal theory.

1.1.1.2.4. The EU concept of individual rights as an original blend of influences

In the second half of the twentieth century, the main characteristics of the legal systems sketched out above have converged in many respects.[203] The traditionally objectivist French system increasingly takes into account individual rights.[204] German lawyers no longer think exclusively in terms of subjective public rights (for instance, special provisions provide for the inclusion of third parties in some procedures).[205] English lawyers do think in terms of rights much more than they did a century ago. However, the differences were more clear-cut half a century ago when the EU legal system started developing (and became a powerful factor of convergence). Therefore, without dismissing the nuances, it is possible to identify some of the distinctive features in the legal systems of the Member States and to assess in what proportions they may have influenced the shaping of the EU concept of individual rights.

There is a common continental opposition between objective and subjective elements of legal norms.[206] The difference between the French and

---

202 J. Raz, 'Rights and Individual Well-Being' (1992) 5 Ratio Juris 127.

203 Masing, *Die Mobilisierung des Bürgers für die Durchsetzung des Rechts: europäische Impulse für eine Revision der Lehre vom subjektiv-öffentlichen Recht* 103 and 118.

204 Regarding the evolution of French administrative law see J. Sirinelli, 'La subjectivisation du recours pour excès de pouvoir' (2016) Revue française de droit administratif 529.

205 Gaillet notes that '[à] *l'heure de l'observation d'une tendance à la "subjectivisation" du droit administratif français, il est significatif de relever que, en Allemagne, ce sont bien les limites d'un procès construit autour de la notion de droits publics subjectifs qui sont mises en avant.*' Gaillet, 'Chronique de droit administratif allemand (2012), 1. Le droit au recours des associations : l'orientation subjective du procès administratif allemand à l'épreuve du droit européen et conventionnel de l'environnement'.

206 As opposed to a lesser concern for this distinction in English law, as summarized by Simmonds, 'Rights at the Cutting Edge' 126: '*the general issue underlying a concern for the integrity of private rights, and the problematic relationship between "rights" and "law", tends to be nearer to the surface of debate in those countries that distinguish "law" from "rights" by the distinction between "objective" and "subjec-*

German systems lies with the main point of focus as an operational concept: in French public law, priority is given to duties imposed on the administration, not to the rights of individuals. In German public law, on the contrary, rights have acquired an essential operational value.[207] In between these two models of public law, there is a spectrum of other domestic legal systems with various definitions and roles for rights, duties and interests. Closest to the objective French-style system (with the broadest conception of interest as a filter for challenging administrative decisions) are probably Belgium[208] and Luxembourg.[209] Across the objective/subjective spectrum

---

tive" rights: for this way of expressing the distinction makes it abundantly clear that we have here a question of the relationship between the projects or preferences of the individual and the impersonal demands of the collectivity.'.

207 The transsystemic dialogue also takes place between the English and the continental lawyers, with Alexy relying for instance on Hohfeld's legal conceptions to organise his own reflection on constitutional rights in the German legal system. Alexy, *A Theory of Constitutional Rights* 301; R. Alexy, 'Rights and Liberties as Concepts' in M. Rosenfeld and A. Sajo (eds), *Oxford Handbook of Comparative Constitutional Law* (Oxford Handbook of Comparative Constitutional Law, Oxford University Press 2012) 286. By contrast, the Hohfeldian approach has not much permeated into the French legal discourses, with Bennet providing one of the very rare French language discussions on Hohfeld's contribution to legal thinking: see Bennet, 'Le droit et l'analyse philosophique des droits selon W.N. Hohfeld.'

208 M. Paques and L. Donnay, 'Juridiction ordinaire et juridiction administrative en droit belge' <https://orbi.ulg.ac.be/bitstream/2268/9929/1/Juridiction%20ordinaire%20et%20juridiction%20administrative%20n%20droit%20belge.pdf> accessed 24 January 2016; C. de Roy, 'Visie op de verhoudingen tussen burger en bestuur enerzijds, en tussen bestuur en rechter anderzijds, en de gevolgen hiervan op de organisatie van het administratief contentieux' jura falconis, jg 39, 2002-2003, nr 3, 429 <https://www.law.kuleuven.be/jura/art/39n3/deroy.htm> accessed 24 January 2016; F. Ost, *Droit et intérêt, vol. 2 : Entre droit et non-droit, l'intérêt : essai sur les fonctions qu'exerce la notion d'intérêt en droit privé* (Publications des Facultés universitaires Saint-Louis 1990).

209 The latter drew inspiration from French law, the influence of which is strongly perceptible in administrative procedure where 'intérêt pour agir' is decisive, so that a right becomes effective in court when it corresponds to an interest. Luxembourg is a good illustration of hybridisation, since in addition to its current Belgian-style catalogue of liberties and rights at the constitutional level, there are ongoing discussions on the inclusion of the notion of human dignity, following the German model of protection of fundamental rights. M. Feyereisen, J. Guillot and S. Salvador, *Procédure administrative contentieuse* (Promoculture Larcier 2013) 190. F. Delaporte, 'Droit luxembourgeois et droits européens', Interview by C. Warin, (*blogdroiteuropéen*, 2016) <https://blogdroiteuropeen.com/2016/11/10/droit-luxembourgeois-et-droits-europeens-interview-de-francis-delaporte-partie-2/> accessed 20 March 2017.

the Dutch, Italian and Spanish cases are in an intermediary position.[210] It was probably not a coincidence that the question in *Van Gend en Loos* came from the Netherlands, a legal system which also acknowledges subjective rights. The question was phrased in terms of 'rights', providing the Court of Justice with a good opportunity to pick up the notion.[211] The Italian legal system relies both on 'legitimate interests' (*interessi legitimi*) and on 'subjective rights' (*diritti soggettivi*). A legitimate interest is an individual interest that is connex to the public interest and is indirectly protected through the protection of the public interest, whereas a subjective right corresponds to an interest that is directly attributed to a characterised individual and protected.[212] Not unlike in French law, the condition for a legitimate interest to be admitted before an administrative court is that it coex-

210 Fromont, *Droit administratif des Etats européens* 164.

211 *Van Gend en Loos*, C-26/62. R. Widdershoven and A.W.H. Meij, *Europees recht en het Nederlands bestuursrecht: preadviezen* (Samson H.D. Tjeenk Willink 1996); J.H. Jans and K.J. de Graaf, 'Bevoegdheid = verplichting? Enkele opmerkingen over de uitspraak van het Hof van Justitie in de zaak Kühne & Heinz (2004) Nederlands tijdschrift voor Europees recht 98; W.W. Geursen, 'Handhaving van het objectieve gemeenschapsrecht via het effectiviteitsbeginsel vs. subjectieve rechtsbescherming via het nationaalrechtelijke verbod op reformatio in peius' (2009) Nederlands tijdschrift voor Europees recht 131; Hagner, *Les particuliers et l'ordre juridique communautaire : l'égalité de traitement entre les hommes et les femmes* 60.

212 The distinction between is enshrined in Article 113 of the 1948 Constitution. Constitution of Italy, 22 December 1947 (English version available at: http://www.refworld.org/docid/3ae6b59cc.html, accessed 20 March 2017); Italian Council of State, Opinion of 26 February 1965; Auby, Les recours juridictionnels contre les actes administratifs spécialement économiques dans le droit des Etats membres de la CEE 15. A. di Majo, *La tutela civile dei diritti*, vol 3 (4th edn, Giuffrè editore 2003) 19; Claes, *National Courts' Mandate in the European Constitution*, note 28; Auby, 'Les recours juridictionnels contre les actes administratifs spécialement économiques dans le droit des Etats membres de la CEE' 8; R. Caranta, 'Governmental Liability after Francovich' (1993) 52 Cambridge Law Journal 272 287. The distinction matters because of the consequences on the form of protection that will be granted to the individual. More specifically, the civil courts will control the administration's action when subjective rights are at stake, and administrative tribunals will deal with issues of legitimate interests. Di Majo, *La tutela civile dei diritti* 21. Auby, 'Les recours juridictionnels contre les actes administratifs spécialement économiques dans le droit des Etats membres de la CEE' 15. See also the CJEU's *Salgoil* case, in which an Italian court had enquired as to whether direct effect gave rise to a subjective right or a legitimate interest according to the Italian categorisation. Judgment of 19 December 1968, *Salgoil v Ministerio del commercio con l'estero*, C-13/68, EU:C:1968:54. The Court held that the national courts must grant immediate protection, but that

ists with a public interest established by law.[213] The concept of interest is also essential for identifying 'subjective rights' and determining access to Spanish administrative courts.[214] Because they refer to 'subjective rights', the Italian and Spanish systems have sometimes been said to have an equivalent to the *Schutznorm* doctrine[215]: in fact, their notion of a legitimate interest is closer to a French actual interest than to a German protected interest in the meaning of the *Schutznorm* doctrine.

Nevertheless, the German model of subjective legality review is not isolated: with the latest enlargements of the Union to Eastern European countries, an increasing number of Member States function with a similar system.[216] Continuing hybridation thus takes place in the EU, between different conceptions of the relation between rights, obligations and interests.

---

the classification of these rights and the corresponding jurisdictions are left to national law.

213 Di Majo, *La tutela civile dei diritti* 22.

214 Medina Alcoz, *Libertad y autoridad en el derecho administrativo. Derecho subjetivo e interés legítimo: una revisión* 206.

215 A. Türk, *Judicial Review in EU law* (Edward Elgar Publishing 2010) 258 and see Opinion of AG Darmon in *Vreugdenhil*, C-282/90, EU:C:1992:12 para 54 where he notes that not only in German law, but also in Belgian, Italian and Danish law must a subjective right be breached in order for State liability to be acknowledged.

216 For example, Croatian administrative law is centered around the relation between subjective rights and remedies and the literature relies on German administrative law doctrine. B. Babac, 'La nouvelle procédure administrative et le nouveau contentieux administratif en Croatie - Sur quelques implications des différences dans le traitement de l'objet du litige administratif au regard du contrôle de la légalité de l'action administrative' (2012) 49 Zbornik radova Pravnog fakulteta u Splitu 325. In Poland, the right to court is conditioned by the existence of a legal interest arising from provisions of law, although not necessarily from provisions intended to protect a specific group of individuals; however, it is still narrower than the CJEU's broad understanding of interest and closer to the German conception of a protected interest allowing to identify a subjective right. N. Półtorak, 'Changes in the Level of the National Judicial Protection Under the EU Influence on the Example of the Polish Legal System' in M. Bobek (ed), *Central European Judges Under the European Influence* (Hart Publishing 2015) 234. The recent enlargements have not, however, caused a radical shift in the balance, since the Bulgarian code of administrative procedure only requires a 'legitimate interest' in challenging an administrative measure (Article 27(2)(5) of the Bulgarian Administrative Procedure Code, in force from 12.7.2006, amend. sg. 27/25 March 2014 (English translation available at http://www.cadastre.bg/node/7941, accessed 19 March 2017). The Romanian system classically functioned with 'subjective rights' corresponding to legally identified and protected individual interests; a reform in 2004 opened the courts to individuals

Political scientists who developed the realist theory tell us that the most powerful Member States are the one who are able to '*upload*' their system of rights onto the EU institutions.[217] Given the strong influence of French administrative law on EU law, it is no surprise that the French objective conception of the relationship between the citizen and the state, focused on the objective '*principe de légalité*' and materialising in the *recours pour excès de pouvoir*, was the starting point for the development of the European system of legality review.[218] Like in French public law, the citizens are conceived as participants in a process of good administration.[219] However, something happened in *Van Gend en Loos* that does not happen (or much more moderately) in the French system: by using a language of rights (thereby accepting the suggestion of the referring Dutch court), the CJEU (deliberately?) put individuals under the spotlight, granting them a status and value similar to that which individuals have in German public law.[220] Yet, there is also an essential difference between individual rights under EU

---

who could demonstrate either a traditional 'subjective right' or a 'legitimate interest'. A. Cernat, 'The Term of Subjective Right in the Romanian Public Law Doctrine' [2005] Manager - Juridical; 'Le Tiers et le droit public - Le rapport roumain' Association Henri Capitant, Journées panaméennes, 18 au 22 mai 2015, Les tiers <http://www.henricapitant.org/storage/app/media/pdfs/evenements/tiers_droits_public_2015/Roumanie_7.pdf>..

217 Bignami, 'Creating European Rights: National Values and Supranational Interests' 255; Hagner, *Les particuliers et l'ordre juridique communautaire : l'égalité de traitement entre les hommes et les femmes* 91-94. According to the realist theory, the institutions, might anticipate the preferences of the Member States: this includes the Court of Justice self-constraining in accordance with the reactions it foresees: G. Garrett, 'The Politics of Legal Integration in the European Union' (1995) 49 International Organization 171. Limits of the analysis are highlighted by supporters of the neo-functionalist theory: W. Mattli and A.-M. Slaughter, 'Law and Politics in the European Union: A Reply to Garrett' (1995) 49 International Organization 183.

218 Masing, *Die Mobilisierung des Bürgers für die Durchsetzung des Rechts: europäische Impulse für eine Revision der Lehre vom subjektiv-öffentlichen Recht* 196.

219 Masing, *Die Mobilisierung des Bürgers für die Durchsetzung des Rechts: europäische Impulse für eine Revision der Lehre vom subjektiv-öffentlichen Recht* 83 and Hourquebie, 'Les droits publics subjectifs: échec de l'importation d'une théorie allemande en droit administratif français?'.

220 The EU legal order could therefore be compared to the German legal order as it was at the time where the notion of subjective public right gained significance under the influence of Jellinek, allowing '*shadow rights*' (*Rechtsreflexe*) derived from objective principles, to turn into enforceable entitlements. In this respect, indeed, the mechanism of direct effect shows a similar concern. Reich, "System der subjectiven öffentlichen Rechte' in the Union: A European Constitution for Citizens of Bits and Pieces' 169. See also Melot, 'La conception wébérienne des

law, and the German subjective public rights. In German law, the simple fact that the individual is concerned (*eine nur tatsächliche Betroffenheit*) and would gain a factual and coincidental advantage from an objective norm is not sufficient to ground a subjective right.[221] In EU law, on the contrary, and as the Court made clear in *Defrenne II*, it is more than sufficient.[222] The originality of the EU concept of individual rights is thus that, as a result of a hybridation process between the objective and subjective legality control,[223] it turns individuals into agents of EU law (like in French public law) by asserting their value as individuals (like in German public law) instead of camouflaging this value behind that enforcement function. The English influence is perhaps not so easily pinpointed – unsurprisingly, given that it was not represented at the Court in the early times of the Community. However, the flexibility with which English lawyers approach rights (echoing the Hohfeldian idea that fundamental legal conceptions are better thought of as sets of jural correlatives) does resemble the simplicity and fluidity of the original EU concept of rights.[224] The next step in this study will be to assess the underlying rationale for the introduction and application of this concept in the EU legal order.

---

droits subjectifs : un parcours de l'histoire économique au débat sur la légitimité politique' 148.

221 Masing, *Die Mobilisierung des Bürgers für die Durchsetzung des Rechts: europäische Impulse für eine Revision der Lehre vom subjektiv-öffentlichen Recht* 105.

222 *Defrenne v SABENA*, C-43/75, para 31: '*the fact that certain provisions of the Treaty are formally addressed to the Member States does not prevent rights from being conferred at the same time on any individual who has an interest in the performance of the duties thus laid down*'. Maurer, *Allgemeines Verwaltungsrecht* 170; Voßkuhle and Kaiser, 'Grundwissen – Öffentliches Recht: Das subjektiv-öffentliche Recht' 17; Masing, *Die Mobilisierung des Bürgers für die Durchsetzung des Rechts: europäische Impulse für eine Revision der Lehre vom subjektiv-öffentlichen Recht* 189; Reich, "System der subjectiven öffentlichen Rechte' in the Union: A European Constitution for Citizens of Bits and Pieces' 164.

223 Barents, 'EU Procedural Law and Effective Legal Protection'.

224 In addition, it can already be pointed out that the English influence is clearly perceptible in the development of a specific type of rights, that is, procedural rights, which developed in the case law of the Court of Justice following the accession of the United Kingdom to the EC. This will be developed further in Section 2.1.3.2. (see p. 308).

1.1.2. The concept of rights as a convergence point for EU and individual interests

In the previous section, we explored domestic legal systems in search of the origins of the basic constitutive elements of individual rights in Union law. The present section addresses the question of why the Court of Justice designed such a concept. For this purpose, it reviews the classic recurring debates over the justifications and functions of individual rights under EU law. The first angle from which to approach the question is the CJEU's overarching method of interpretation, entailing a strong concern for the effectiveness of EU law and a focus on teleological considerations with which the EU concept of rights is imprinted (1.1.2.1). Beyond this instrumentalist understanding of rights, the development of EU fundamental rights however revealed a second dimension to this concept (1.1.2.2). A third possibility is to approach rights from a 'negative' perspective, looking at how they may be limited by applying the principle of proportionality and the prohibition of abuse of rights: this analysis confirms and refines the complex and essential functional relation between rights and interests (1.1.2.3).

1.1.2.1. The effectiveness rationale of individual rights under EU law

'The vigilance of individuals concerned to protect their rights amounts to an effective supervision in addition to the supervision entrusted [...] to the diligence of the Commission and of the Member States.'[225] In light of this argument advanced by the Court in *Van Gend en Loos*, the concern for the effectiveness of EU law has consistently been characterised in the literature as the rationale underlying the doctrine of direct effect, and thus also as the principle at origin of the creation of rights under EU law – the existence of rights being justified by their function of ensuring the effectiveness of EU law.

1.1.2.1.1. Effectiveness as a meta-rule of interpretation

The above citation from *Van Gend en Loos* shows that already in the early times of the Community the Court was concerned with 'effective' supervision of the application of EU law by the Member States. The concern was

---

225 *Van Gend en Loos*, C-26/62, p. 13.

later famously developed and theorised under a variety of (sometimes converging, sometimes conflicting) doctrines and labels – most notably the principle of effectiveness that arose from the *Rewe* line of case law, and the requirement of effective judicial protection.[226] In its more primitive form, however, the overarching principle of effectiveness mainly expresses '*the core value*', i.e. '*the proper functioning of the EU*', functioning as a pragmatic guide for the interpretation of EU law, a '*judicial meta-rule of interpretation*'.[227] Understood as such, the effectiveness of EU law is closely associated with teleological considerations – also noticeable in *Van Gend en Loos*, with the 'spirit' of the Treaty as starting point for the reasoning.[228] Indeed, as Everling explains, the ECJ '*interprets the competence norms and the Treaty as a whole not restrictively to preserve the rights of the Member States but objectively and teleologically according to the goals of the Treaty. The Court orients itself at the meaning and systematic location of the dispositions in the Treaty and at the effet utile, the "practical effectiveness", of the provisions affected, this means an interpretation in which the provision can fulfil the function for which it is insert in the Treaty*'.[229] In this sense, effectiveness plays the role of a compass, en-

---

226 On the interchangeability of these expressions see U. Šadl, 'The Role of Effet Utile in Preserving the Continuity and Authority of European Union Law: Evidence from the Citation Web of the Pre-accession Case Law of the Court of Justice of the EU' European Journal of Legal Studies, Summer 2015 - Volume 8 - Issue 1 <http://www.ejls.eu/18/209UK.htm> accessed 8 January 2017. This is yet another example of a key concept of EU law for which the Court does not use fixed terminology. The principle of full effect is often described as wider than that of *Rewe* effectiveness, and has been held by e.g. Krommendijk to '*comprise both the PEJP and Rewe effectiveness.*' J. Krommendijk (2016), 1404. See also S. Prechal and R. Widdershoven, 'Redefining the Relationship between "Rewe-effectivenesss" and Effective Judicial Protection' (2011) 4 Review of European Administrative Law 31; A. Östlund, 'Effectiveness of European Union Law versus Procedural Protection. Tracing the tension throughout the case-law of the Court of Justice on *ex officio* review by the national judge' (PhD thesis, University of Luxembourg 2017) 254.

227 M. Ortino, 'A Reading of the EU Constitutional Legal System Through the Principle of Effectiveness' (Cahiers de droit européen - Les principes généraux du droit de l'Union européenne, Brussels, 10 September 2015).

228 *Van Gend en Loos*, C-26/62, p. 22.

229 U. Everling, 'The European Union Between Community and National Policies and Legal Orders' in A. Von Bogdandy A and J. Bast (eds), *Principles of European Constitutional Law* (Hart Publishing 2006) 700. In the same vein Ortino suggests that '*the constitutional legitimacy of a European or national measure is not only assessed against EU legal rules, but also against EU objectives. This point of view provides an additional explanation for the principle of effectiveness: in a context where a*

suring that the interpretation process stays on course towards the *telos* of an '*ever closer Union*'.[230]

This is consistent with the methods of interpretation which the Court relies on, including when defining and identifying rights. The literature on legal interpretation reveals that four main methods of interpretation may be distinguished, and are generally combined, in various proportions, by the judges of the CJEU.[231] A first method is the *intentionalist* or *originalist* (also called subjective, psychological, and linked with a historical-genetical method) approach: this method refers to the intent of the authors of the text: what the legislator meant, intended to say. This allegedly leaves little

---

clear and hierarchical set of objectives and interests is not provided for by the Treaties, and where the EU legal system must be permanently adapted to political, social, cultural and economic changes, the principle of effectiveness represents a reliable assessment criterion, and thus an essential element of stability [...].' Ortino, 'A Reading of the EU Constitutional Legal System Through the Principle of Effectiveness'. See also H. Rasmussen, 'Towards a Normative Theory of Interpretation of Community Law' [1992] The University of Chicago Legal Forum 135.

230 Rasmussen, 'Towards a Normative Theory of Interpretation of Community Law' 137. Also, the exact relation between effectiveness and *telos* is not clear-cut. Grimmel argues that over time the emphasis in the Court's reasoning has shifted from teleological considerations to arguments concerning the useful effect of EU law. A. Grimmel, "This is not Life as it is Lived Here": The Court of Justice of the EU and the Myth of Judicial Activism in the Foundational Period of Integration through Law' (2014) 7 European Journal of Legal Studies 61 77. For a critical discussion of the Court's reliance on effectiveness as an interpretation guide, see Rasmussen, who points out that '*it is no secret that the judges themselves constitute the source of the absolute effectiveness* contention': Rasmussen, 'Towards a Normative Theory of Interpretation of Community Law' 148.

231 The review that is proposed here relies in particular on the following works: Y. Galmot, 'Réflexions sur le recours au droit comparé par la Cour de justice des Communautés européennes' (1990) Revue française de droit administratif 255; J. Rideau, 'Ordre juridique de l'Union européenne - Sources non écrites' JurisClasseur Europe Traité, Cote 04 para 24; M. Dederichs and R. Christensen, 'Inhaltsanalyse als methodisches Instrument zur Untersuchung von Gerichtsentscheidungen, vorgeführt am Beispiel der Rechtssprechung des EuGH' in F. Müller and I. Burr (eds), *Rechtssprache Europas. Reflexion der Praxis von Sprache und Mehrsprachigkeit im supranationalen Recht* (Duncker & Humblot 2004) 307; R. Guastini, 'L'interprétation de la constitution' in M. Troper and D. Chagnollaud (eds), *Traité international de droit constitutionnel* (Dalloz 2012); K. Lenaerts and J.A. Gutierrez-Fons, 'To Say What the Law of the EU Is: Methods of Interpretation and the ECJ' (2014) 20 Columbia Journal of European Law 3; Augsberg, 'Methoden des europäischen Verwaltungsrechts' 147; Conway, *The Limits of Legal Reasoning and the European Court of Justice* 20; A. Basset, *Pour en finir avec l'interprétation. Usage des techniques d'interprétation dans les jurisprudences constitutionnelles française et allemande* (Institut universitaire Varenne 2015).

space for jurisprudential creation, as the court bases its interpretation on the intention expressed by the author, e.g. by referring to preparatory works. A second method is the *literal* (also called textual, objective or grammatical) method: the judge starts from the text itself to solve difficulties. Various techniques may be used, relying on context, grammatical interpretation, or the confrontation of different linguistic versions. This method leaves more space for the judge's creativity (depending on the choice of interpretation techniques). A third method is the *teleological* (also called functional and sometimes purposive) method: the judge refers to the purpose of the texts, what the authors wanted to do or obtain; he may interpret more or less freely, as he may also adapt these objectives to have them coincide with political, economic and social evolutions. It is generally acknowledged as the method which is the most likely to foster jurisprudential creativity. A fourth method is the *systemic* (or contextual) method: often combined with method n°3, it is a type of reasoning by which the judge draws the consequences from a system which he has deduced from a group of norms.[232] The lines between these various approaches are rarely clear-cut. In particular, the distinction between the intentionalist and teleological methods is not always easy to make. Sometimes these two methods are even completely merged by some authors,[233] while others find that they overlap only in some cases.[234] In the intentionalist method, the reference to the intention of the authors of a law is a form of 'originalist' interpretation; the subjective intention may be identified, more or less empirically, by using the preparatory work. In the teleological method, on the contrary, the subjective intention of the legislator is only secondary; the drafters are attributed an objective intention on the basis of an assumption as to what should be a 'rational' or 'reasonable' intention.[235] As we have seen in the founding cases, this subtle distinction is very relevant for EU rights, since in order to identify these rights the Court does rely on the

---

232 A fifth method is less often referred to: Dederichs and Christensen consider that the reference to earlier case law (precedent) is a distinct method of interpretation: M. Dederichs and R. Christensen, 'Inhaltsanalyse als methodisches Instrument zur Untersuchung von Gerichtsentscheidungen, vorgeführt am Beispiel der Rechtsprechung des EuGH' 317.

233 E.g. G. Beck, *The Legal Reasoning of the CJEU* (Hart 2012) 187.

234 Conway, *The Limits of Legal Reasoning and the European Court of Justice* 20.

235 Guastini, 'L'interprétation de la constitution' 487; Augsberg, 'Methoden des europäischen Verwaltungsrechts' 153.

telos identified in the Treaty – and the '*general scheme*' of the text[236] – but does not search for the intention underlying a specific provision.[237]

This observation is not specific to the Court's method for identifying rights. It is congruent with the Court's method of interpretation in general. As Hartley points out, while the Court naturally looks at the wording of the provision at issue and tries to make sense of it in the context of the instrument as a whole, it is '*much more willing than an English court to depart from the literal meaning of the words to achieve this*' and it '*makes little attempt to establish the actual subjective intention of the authors of the text.*'[238] Several reasons account for the limited use of these two methods of interpretation. Regarding the literal method, of course, the issue of linguistic discrepancies comes to mind – adding to other obscurities of the text, they make the literal meaning of the words particularly difficult to identify, which might explain why the Court '*does not put a great deal of weight*' on that literal meaning.[239] The systemic and purpose-oriented interpretation solves the issue of not having a single unequivocal text to apply but rather several language versions (all with equal legal value) of a text.[240] Regarding the intentionalist approach, one reason for not resorting to it is that '*in the case of an agreement reached after hard bargaining, there may be no common intention – only an agreement on a form of words.*' Hartley also suggests another reason: '*the Court prefers to interpret texts on the basis of what it thinks they should be trying to achieve; it moulds the law according to what it regards as the needs of the Union*', i.e. according to the *telos* of the Union.[241] This corresponds to Kramer's recommendation that '*instead of striving to unearth the intentions of the people who have forged a norm, an interpreter can approach as a constructive endeavour the task of positing an objective or a purpose which the norm ad-*

236 *Van Gend en Loos*, C-26/62, p. 12.

237 As observed p. 37 concerning *Defrenne v SABENA*, C-43/75.

238 T.C. Hartley, *The Foundations of European Union Law* (Oxford University Press 2010) 71.

239 Hartley, *The Foundations of European Union Law* 64.

240 E. Paunio and S. Lindroos-Hovinheimo, 'Taking Language Seriously: An Analysis of Linguistic Reasoning and Its Implications in EU Law' (2010) 16 European Law Journal 395. See also T. Schilling, 'Beyond Multilingualism: On Different Approaches to the Handling of Diverging Language Versions of a Community Law' (2010) 16 European Law Journal 47.

241 Hartley, *The Foundations of European Union Law* 72. See also Fennelly, 'Legal Interpretation at the European Court of Justice'; Conway, *The Limits of Legal Reasoning and the European Court of Justice* 210.

vances.'[242] Poiares Maduro has even suggested that there is a '*meta-teleological*' dimension in the Court's interpretative process and that teleological and systemic elements of interpretation are closely connected: '*it is not simply the* telos *of the rules to be interpreted that matters but also the telos of the legal context in which those rules exist*.'[243] The Court's method for identifying rights is thus consistent with its approach to the interpretation of EU law as a whole: guided by the meta-principle of effectiveness, and predominantly systemic and teleological, rather than intentionalist and literal.

1.1.2.1.2. An instrumentalist conception of rights and individuals?

In light of the omnipresent effectiveness rationale, it has been argued that individual rights were born merely as a '*by-product*'[244] of the direct applicability of a provision. Scholarship has repeatedly stressed that the empowerment of individuals was justified by the necessity to effectively implement EC law, while the protection of individuals in itself was not of primary significance.[245] In other words, at the time of *Van Gend en Loos*, '*the protection of individual rights was probably not at the top of the Court's agenda at that time anyway. "Objective" Community law occupied that place.*'[246] The diagno-

242 Kramer, 'Rights Without Trimmings' 86. Advantage of the teleological method: it allows to be clear and transparent about the telos, the big picture, so that the debate can be fuelled over what this telos is/should be. Augsberg, 'Methoden des europäischen Verwaltungsrechts' 164.

243 M. Poiares Maduro, 'Interpreting European Law: Judicial Adjudication in a Context of Constitutional Pluralism' (2007) 1 European Journal of Legal Studies 1 5 and M. Lasser, *Judicial Deliberations. A Comparative Analysis of Judicial Transparency and Legitimacy* (Oxford University Press 2004) 359; Conway, *The Limits of Legal Reasoning and the European Court of Justice* 22.

244 Eilmansberger, 'The Relationship between Rights and Remedies in EC Law: in Search of the Missing Link' 1203. E.F. Hinton, 'Strengthening the Effectiveness of Community Law: Direct Effect, Article 5 EC, and the European Court of Justice' (1998) 31 NYU Journal of International Law and Politics 307.

245 Masing, *Die Mobilisierung des Bürgers für die Durchsetzung des Rechts: europäische Impulse für eine Revision der Lehre vom subjektiv-öffentlichen Recht* 46; Eilmansberger, 'The Relationship between Rights and Remedies in EC Law: in Search of the Missing Link' 1203; E.F. Hinton, 'Strengthening the Effectiveness of Community Law: Direct Effect, Article 5 EC, and the European Court of Justice' (1998) 31 NYU Journal of International Law and Politics 307.

246 Eilmansberger, 'The Relationship between Rights and Remedies in EC Law: in Search of the Missing Link' 1204.

sis was shared by Coppen and O'Neill in an aptly titled article.[247] In a similar manner, former Advocate General Jacobs has expressed his understanding that the recognition of individual rights in *Van Gend en Loos* was instrumental to the notion of effectiveness.[248] Thus, as Ortino points out, the principle of direct effect has been introduced in *Van Gend en Loos* '*with a view to overcoming political and technical obstacles to the effectiveness of EU law. [...] it is a supplementary enforcement device conceived within the EU legal system to greatly increase the pressure on Member States to comply with their EU obligations [...]*'. Under the lens of effectiveness, direct effect is indeed primarily '*a supplementary enforcement device*';[249] the Court's reaction against '*the first manifestations of systematic opposition of the governments regarding the loyal execution of their obligations*'.[250] This mechanism (and the rights it generated) provided a way to '*persuade national judges to adopt and develop their roles as 'Community' judges, and supply the necessary sanctions to enforce rules*' of EC law.[251] Regarding the enforcement of directives, it has been remarked that it is more difficult for Member States to disregard decisions from their own courts, than decisions from a more or less remote court in Luxembourg.[252] The advantage for the Community is boosted by the fact that having individuals rely on direct effect is also more simple and politically less dangerous than for the Commission to initiate treaty violation procedures.[253] Individual rights thus appear as particularly efficient tools

247 J. Coppel and A. O'Neill, 'The European Court of Justice: Taking Rights Seriously?' (1992) 29 Common Market Law Review 669. This article has been criticised and deconstructed by Weiler and Lockhart in a two-part article: J.H.H. Weiler and N.J.S Lockhart, "Taking Rights Seriously' Seriously: The European Court and its Fundamental Rights Jurisprudence - Part I' (1995) 32 Common Market Law Review 51 and J.H.H. Weiler and N.J.S. Lockhart, "Taking Rights Seriously' Seriously: the European Court and its Fundamental Rights Jurisprudence - Part II' (1995) 32 Common Market Law Review 579.

248 F.G. Jacobs, 'The Evolution of the European Legal Order' (2004) 41 Common Market Law Review 303 309.

249 Ortino, 'A Reading of the EU Constitutional Legal System Through the Principle of Effectiveness'.

250 P. Pescatore, 'Van Gend en Loos, 3 February 1963: A view from within' in M. Poiares Maduro and L. Azoulai (eds), *The Past and Future of EU Law: The Classics of EU Law Revisited on the 50th Anniversary of the Rome Treaty* (Hart 2010) 5.

251 Ward, 'More than an 'Infant Disease'. Individual Rights, EC Directives, and the Case for Uniform Remedies' 50.

252 D. Curtin, 'Directives: the Effectiveness of Judicial Protection of Individual Rights' (1990) 27 *Common Market Law Review* 709.

253 F. Becker and A. Campbell, 'The Direct Effect of European Directives: Towards the Final Act?' (2007) 13 Columbia Journal of European Law 401 405.

for ensuring the implementation of obligations imposed by EU law, particularly on Member States, remarkably allowing for '*[a] high level of compliance, [an] automatic acceptance of Community supremacy and Community obligations in almost all cases*'.[254]

Symmetrically, in their doctrinal work on rights, EU lawyers have been focusing, according to Walker, on '*how rights discourse contributes to an understanding of the relationship in terms of formal competence, practical efficacy and relative legitimacy between the new supranational order on the one hand and other overlapping legal orders on the other*'.[255] Thus, the teleological premises on which the Court relied in its founding cases in order to affirm the uniqueness of the EU legal system and its relationship to national legal orders[256] find an extension in the doctrinal conception of EU law in general, and EU rights in particular, as instrumental to EU integration.[257] In the neo-functionalist terms of political scientists, the idea is that the Court gave individual litigants a personal stake in community law, i.e. '*the Court created a pro-community constituency of private individuals by giving them a direct stake in promulgation and implementation of community law.*'[258] In other words, neo-functionalist integration theory relies on the 'spillover' effect of rights (or rules that defend interests of persons) to foster integration.[259] In addition, however, '*the Court was careful to create a one-way ratchet by permitting individual participation in the system only in a way that would advance*

---

254 W. Wallace, 'Europe as a Confederation: the Community and the Nation-State' (1982) 21 Journal of Common Market Studies 57 61; see also J.H.H. Weiler, 'Community, Member States and European Integration: Is the Law Relevant?' (1982) 21 Journal of Common Market Studies 39.

255 Walker, 'Legal Theory and the European Union' 3.

256 Especially the doctrine of direct effect (*Van Gend en Loos*, C-26/62, p. 12) and the complementary doctrine of primacy (Judgment of 15 July 1964, *Costa v E.N.E.L.*, C-6/64, EU:C:1964:66, p. 593). On the relation between both doctrines see e.g. Hagner, *Les particuliers et l'ordre juridique communautaire : l'égalité de traitement entre les hommes et les femmes* 67.

257 D. Mitrany, 'The Prospect of Integration: Federal or Functional' (1965) 4 Journal of Common Market Studies 119, Walker, 'Legal Theory and the European Union' 8.

258 A. Burley and W. Mattli, 'Europe Before the Court: A Political Theory of Legal Integration' (1993) 47 International Organization 41 60.

259 J. Shaw, 'Citizenship of the Union: Towards Post-National Membership?' in Academy of European Law (ed), *Collected Courses of the Academy of European Law*, vol VI - 1 (Martinus Nijhoff Publishers 1998) 279.

community goals'[260] – and this further supports the idea that individuals and their rights were primarily instrumental to European integration.

Those who emphasise the instrumentalist justification of rights under EU law usually consider that the main interest pursued is of an economic nature, i.e. economic integration and the establishment of a common market.[261] Admittedly, neo-functionalist theories and the doctrine of 'integration through law' strongly influenced EU construction in the 1960s and again in the 1980s, i.e. at times where the European integration project remained centred around the four fundamental freedoms and competition law.[262] In this perspective, the individual is perceived mainly as an economic agent whose rights constitute tools for achieving a higher objective of economic integration. Contemporary works looking back critically at the early developments of EU law, since *Van Gend en Loos* and the development of European supranational law, emphasise that individuals were considered primarily as '*factors of production*'[263] or as '*agents of market integration*'[264] fulfilling the function of ensuring the application of the doctrine of effectiveness,[265] an approach which Dani considers is an explanation for the '*current*

260 According to Burley and Mattli, the typical illustration of this 'one-way ratchet' is the very restrictive approach to action for annulment as '*citizens who are net losers from integrative decisions by the council or the commission cannot sue to have those actions declared ultra vires*.' Burley and Mattli, 'Europe Before the Court: A Political Theory of Legal Integration' 60-62. On the neo-functionalist theory see further: S. Saurugger, *Théories et concepts de l'intégration européenne* (Presses de la Fondation nationale des sciences politiques 2009).

261 N. Bernard, 'A 'New Governance' Approach to Economic, Social and Cultural Rights in the EU' in T. Hervey and J. Kenner (eds), *Economic and Social Rights under the EU Charter of Fundamental Rights A Legal Perspective* (Hart 2003) 248; G.S. Katrougalos, 'The Implementation of Social Rights in Europe' (1996) 2 Columbia Journal of European Law 277 304.

262 K. Lenaerts, 'Les défis actuels de la Cour de justice,' Interview by O. Tambou (*blogdroiteuropéen*, 2016), <https://blogdroiteuropeen.com/2016/04/01/interview-du-president-koen-lenaerts-partie-2-les-defis-actuels-de-la-cjue/> accessed 6 July 2016. L. Azoulai, '"Integration through law" and us' (2016) 14 International Journal of Constitutional Law 449; J.-P. Jacqué, 'The Role of Law in European Integration,' in V. Gessner, A. Hoeland and C. Varga, *European Legal Cultures* (Darthmouth 1996).

263 T. Blanchet, 'Evolution of EU citizenship and the rights attached to it' (Conference - EU Citizenship and Justice, Luxembourg, 14th and 15th September 2015).

264 M. Dani, 'The subjectification of the citizen in European public law' EUI Working Paper, Law 2015/02, 7.

265 Coppel and O'Neill, 'The European Court of Justice: Taking Rights Seriously?.'

commodification of workers'.[266] Dani uses the term '*subjectification*' to insist on the fact that the individual becomes 'subjected' to a purpose which is beyond his/her own interests. Similarly, Borowski argues that '*the interests of the individual as such play no decisive role*' in the implementation of fundamental freedoms.[267] This reading is further supported by the fact that historically the ECJ seemed less preoccupied by granting individual protection against Community institutions than against Member States.[268]

The instrumentalisation of rights – and of their holders – by EU law has been the object of criticism, casting doubts even on the pertinence of rights discourses. For instance, Prechal and Hancher have suggested that '*by invoking the language of individual rights, the ECJ tries to benefit from the mystique of the term in order to ensure that the requirements which it formulates are more readily accepted in the national legal orders. After all, in the supranational context the protection of individual citizens' rights seems a much more laudable project than merely stipulating that Member States must be controlled*'.[269] Likewise, De Burca, while admitting that relying on rights '*offers a means to develop a moral and ethical foundation for the Community, and to contribute to the development of a sense of European identity and a commitment to a European society, in a way which may further the process of political integration*', warns that '*it is possible for the language of rights in Community law*

266 Dani, 'The subjectification of the citizen in European public law'.

267 M. Borowski, 'The Charter of Fundamental Rights in the Treaty on European Union' in M. Trybus and L. Rubini (eds), *The Treaty of Lisbon and the Future of European Law and Policy* (Edward Elgar 2012) 203.

268 Eilmansberger, 'The Relationship between Rights and Remedies in EC Law: in Search of the Missing Link' 1207, citing as examples, prominent cases where actions for annulment were dismissed: Judgment of 13 May 1971, *International Fruit Company and Others v Commission*, C-41 to C-44/70, EU:C:1971:53; Judgment of 11 July 1985, *Salerno and Others v Commission and Council*, C-87/77, C-130/77, C-22/83, C-9 and C-10/84, EU:C:1985:318; Judgment of 8 October 1986, *Leussink-Brummelhuis v Commission*, C-169/83 and C-136/84, EU:C:1986:371; Judgment of 7 July 1987, *Etoile commerciale and CNTA v Commission*, C-89/86 and C-91/86, EU:C:1987:337; Judgment of 21 November 1989, *UCDV v Commision*, C-244/88, EU:C:1989:588; Judgment of 27 March 1990, *Cargill v Commission*, C-229/88, EU:C:1990:138; Judgment of 19 May 1992, *Mulder and Others v Council and Commission*, Joined cases C-104/89 and C-37/90, EU:C:1992:217. See also A. Arnull, 'The action for annulment: A case of double standards?' in D. O'Keefe D and A. Bavasso (eds), *Judicial Review in European Union Law* (Kluwer Law International 2000) 177; Półtorak, *European Union Rights in National Courts* 252.

269 Prechal and Hancher, 'Individual Environmental Rights: Conceptual Pollution in EU Environmental Law?' 105.

to paper over deep national divisions and cultural differences, to suggest a moral content to Community policies which in reality further essentially market goals, and to hold out the promise of protection for human rights whilst actually delivering little of practical benefit to individuals as opposed to corporations and legal persons'; which is why she recommends that EU lawyers exercise '*strong skepticism*' with regard to the rhetoric of rights.[270] Without dismissing this warning, it is still possible to look beyond the instrumentalist justification of rights and to acknowledge that the development of fundamental rights adds another dimension to the value of rights and their holders in the EU legal order.

1.1.2.2. Asserting the intrinsic value of individuals: the development of EU fundamental rights

The analysis of individuals as mere means to a greater end, with rights as tools to achieve that end, has limits that have also been emphasised in the literature. For instance, it has been pointed out that the term 'Community' already indicated an idea that went beyond a purely economic concern.[271] Milutinović suggests that *van Gend en Loos* could also be understood as the affirmation of individual rights with the best arguments possible at that time, i.e. the instrumental-type arguments – but with these arguments serving in fact as a pretext to make subjective rights inherent in the system of the Treaty.[272] The same goes for the primacy of economic considerations, which the founders of Europe assumed would lead to political integration,[273] ultimately more efficiently than what the failed political union

270 De Burca, 'The Language of Rights and European Integration' 52.

271 Blanchet, 'Evolution of EU citizenship and the rights attached to it'. The Court of Justice also builds on this notion of a 'Community' in landmark cases such as *Les Verts*, C-294/83: the Court famously held at para 23 that the EEC was '*a Community based on the rule of law, inasmuch as neither its Member States nor its institutions can avoid a review of the question whether the measures adopted by them are in conformity with the basic constitutional charter, the Treaty*'.

272 V. Milutinovic, *The 'Right to Damages' under EU Competition Law: from Courage v Crehan to the White Paper and Beyond* (Kluwer Law International 2010) 89.

273 W. Abelshauser, ''Integration à la Carte' The Primacy of Politics and the Economic Integration of Western Europe in the 1950s' in S. Martin (ed), *The Construction of Europe Essays in Honour of Emile Noël* (Kluwer Academic Publishers 1994) especially 3-4.

around the European Defence Community had managed.[274] Moreover, even admitting that individual rights have been mainly (or exclusively, depending on the interpretation) instrumental to other ends in the early stages of the Community, the later developments of Community law took a different direction. Borowski concedes a distinction between what he calls instrumental rights, granted to individuals so that they ensure the proper functioning of the internal market, and fundamental rights, the purpose of which is to protect the interests of individuals in themselves, '*as a value in itself*'.[275] The inclusion of fundamental rights in the Court's ambit thus relativises the purely instrumentalist explanation for the existence of rights in the EU legal order.

The Treaty of Rome contained no bill of rights and no provision on judicial review for potential violations of fundamental human rights. This did not prevent the Court from identifying 'rights' in the Treaty, deriving them from the obligations therein laid down, but it left open the issue of whether other rights arising from other sources could be relevant. Concerning the ECSC Treaty, the Court had ruled out the possibility for an individual to rely on fundamental rights protected by national law against a decision of the ECSC High Authority.[276] The Court of Justice was however pressured into integrating fundamental rights in the EU legal system, most prominently in 1967 when the German Constitutional Court declared itself competent for assessing the validity of German acts that implement EC legislation, especially with regard to fundamental rights protected by the German Constitution. This was valid, so the *Bundesverfassungsgericht* ruled, '*so long*' as the Community's integration process has not reached the stage

274 See e.g. R.T. Griffiths, 'Europe's First Constitution: The European Political Community, 1952-1954' in S. Martin (ed), *The Construction of Europe Essays in Honour of Emile Noël* (Kluwer Academic Publishers 1994) 19-37.

275 Borowski, 'The Charter of Fundamental Rights in the Treaty on European Union' 203.

276 Judgment of 4 February 1959, *Stork & Co. v High Authority of the European Coal and Steel Community*, C-1/58, EU:C:1959:4, para 4: '*under Article 8 of the treaty the High Authority is only required to apply Community law. It is not competent to apply the national law of the Member States. Similarly, '[...] the Court is only required to ensure that in the interpretation and application of the Treaty, and of rules laid down for implementation thereof, the law is observed. It is not normally required to rule on provisions of national law. Consequently, the High Authority is not empowered to examine a ground of complaint which maintains that, when it adopted its decision, it infringed principles of German constitutional law '[...]*'.

of having a catalogue of fundamental rights. The Italian Constitutional Court held a similar position.[277]

The subsequent rulings of the Court of Justice can be read as a reaction to that pressure. The Court made clear in the benchmark ruling *Stauder* that '*fundamental human rights*' form an integral part of the '*general principles of Community law*' and are as such '*protected by the Court*',[278] demonstrating that '*while in the early stages of the development of Community law, the Court's main aim seemed to be to guarantee the* objective *lawfulness of the administrative action, later on the idea of protecting the* subjective *rights of the individual has in addition to the objective standards played a more and more important role*'.[279] In *Internationale Handelsgesellschaft* the Court then recognised the influence of the constitutional traditions of Member States in shaping these general principles. Fundamental rights are thus protected by the Community and not as rights guaranteed by a variety of national constitutions. The Court held that the protection of these fundamental rights was to be ensured within the structure and in light of the objectives of the Community.[280] The *Nold* ruling in 1974 added another source of inspiration: international treaties on the protection of human rights, especially

277 BVerfGE 37, 271 (the so-called '*Solange*' judgment) and Judgment of the Italian Constitutional Court of 27 December 1973, Case 183/73, *Frontini and associates*, Giurisprudenza Costituzionale, 1973, 2406. Hagner, *Les particuliers et l'ordre juridique communautaire : l'égalité de traitement entre les hommes et les femmes* 76; Coppel and O'Neill, 'The European Court of Justice: Taking Rights Seriously?' 682; Commission Memorandum on Accession of the Communities to the European Convention on Human Rights (COM (79) final, Bulletin of the European Communities, Supplement 2/79) 6-7. See also M. Cartabia, 'The Italian Constitutional Court and the Relationship Between the Italian legal system and the European Union' in A.-M. Slaughter, A. Stone Sweet and J.H.H. Weiler (eds), *The European Court and National Courts – Doctrine and Jurisprudence. Legal Change in Its Social Context* (Hart 1998) 133-146.

278 *Stauder*, C-26/69, para 7 and subsequent case law, e.g. *Nold v Commission*, C-4/73, para 13 and Judgment of 13 December 1979, *Hauer*, C-44/79, EU:C:1979:290, para 15.

279 J. Schwarze, 'Sources of European Administrative Law' in S. Martin (ed), *The Construction of Europe Essays in Honour of Emile Noël* (Kluwer Academic Publishers 1994) 189.

280 *Internationale Handelsgesellschaft*, C-11/70, para 3. Hagner, *Les particuliers et l'ordre juridique communautaire : l'égalité de traitement entre les hommes et les femmes* 77. The ECJ restated in *Hoechst* that EC law may not be interpreted in a manner which would be inconsistent with the fundamental rights protected by EC law (Judgment of 21 September 1989, *Hoechst AG v Commission*, C-46/87, EU:C:1989:337).

the ECHR.[281] Rights may thus be found not only in written EU law, but also in non-written general principles, which channel the influences of national and international legal traditions of protecting fundamental human rights.[282]

While this highlights the intrinsic value that is recognised to individuals under EU law, the instrumentalist explanation for rights does not lose its relevance. The development of fundamental rights in the EU legal order at the very least coincides with the Court's recurring concern for the legitimacy, effectiveness and supremacy of EU law and the realisation of its integrative purpose. As the Court itself stated in *Internationale Handelsgesellschaft*, '*recourse to the legal rules or concepts of national law in order to judge the validity of measures adopted by the institutions of the Community would have an adverse effect on the uniformity and efficacy of Community law.*'[283] Looking back, Weiler has argued that '*[c]learly, at first, the Court was motivated less by a genuine concern for fundamental rights, than by its wish to consolidate the supremacy of Community law and its own authority*'.[284] Likewise, Harbo suggests to read *Internationale Handelsgesellschaft* in the light of the search for democratic legitimacy: '*The need to bind the reasoning to some objectifiable structure of formal and substantial character increases in proportion with the competences of the courts. Binding itself to some acknowledged principles according to which (a court) will conduct its reasoning in hard cases could be a way of compensating for the lack of democratic legitimacy.*'[285]

We can take the reasoning further by looking at the landmark *Hauer* case, in which the Court recognised the fundamental right to property as a general principle. This was justified by the following argument: citing *In-*

---

281 *Nold v Commission*, C-4/73, para 12. Then in *Rutili* the ECHR becomes an even more solid source of general principles, as the Court elaborates its own definition of trade union freedom based on the definitions of the ECtHR: Judgment of 28 October 1975, *Rutili*, C-36/75, EU:C:1975:137. See further: Judgment of 15 May 1986, *Johnston v Chief Constable of the Royal Ulster Constabulary*, C-222/84, EU:C:1986:206; *Hoechst AG v Commission*, C-46/87; Judgment of 18 June 1991, *ERT v DEP*, C-260/89, EU:C:1991:254. G. Arestis, 'Fundamental rights in the EU: three years after Lisbon, the Luxembourg perspective' College of Europe Research Papers in Law 2/2013.

282 D. Simon, 'Y a-t-il des principes généraux du droit communautaire?' (1991) 14 Droits 73; H. Ruiz Fabri, 'Principes généraux du droit communautaire et droit comparé' (2007) 45 Droits 127.

283 *Internationale Handelsgesellschaft*, C-11/70, para 3.

284 Weiler, 'Community, Member States and European Integration: Is the Law Relevant?' 52.

285 Harbo, 'The Function of the Proportionality Principle in EU Law' 164.

ternationale Handelsgesellschaft, the Court states that '*the question of a possible infringement of fundamental rights by a measure of the Community institutions can only be judged in the light of Community law itself. The introduction of special criteria for assessment stemming from the legislation or constitutional law of a particular Member State would, by damaging the substantive unity and efficacy of Community law, lead inevitably to the destruction of the unity of the Common Market and the jeopardizing of the cohesion of the Community*'.[286] The need to recognise an autonomous fundamental right to property for individuals is thus derived from the need to ensure the 'unity', 'efficacy' and 'cohesion' of the Community and its legal order. In *Hauer* this translates practically into looking for a 'precise' answer, which is not provided by the Treaty, by browsing through the solutions that exist in the Member States – not just the State in which the question originates.[287] The Court maintained the *Internationale Handelsgesellschaft* rationale in *Siragusa*, holding that the reason for the objective of protecting fundamental rights in EU law '*is the need to avoid a situation in which the level of protection of fundamental rights varies according to the national law involved in such a way as to undermine the unity, primacy and effectiveness of EU law*'.[288]

The motives of European integration and EU law effectiveness as reasons for fundamental rights protection are also perceptible in the Court's differentiated approach to fundamental rights protection depending on whether an act of a Member State or an act of the EU itself is under scrutiny. *Wachauf*[289] was the first case where the Court openly assessed the validity of an act of a Member State by reference to EC fundamental rights. A German tenant farmer had requested compensation for the discontinuance of his production of milk, in accordance with EC legislation. However, under German law application by tenants for compensation was subject to consent of the landlord. Wachauf's landlord had denied consent and therefore Wachauf could not obtain compensation. He challenged the German legislation, arguing that it violated his right to property. While the Court did not directly rule on whether there was a violation of EU fundamental

286 *Hauer*, C-44/79, para 14.

287 *Hauer*, C-44/79, EU:C:1979:290, paras 20-22.

288 *Siragusa*, C-206/13, para 32.

289 Judgment of 13 July 1989, *Wachauf v Bundesamt für Ernährung und Forstwirtschaft*, C-5/88, EU:C:1989:321.

rights, it made clear that even where Member States have discretion in how to implement EU law, they must still respect EU fundamental rights.[290]

Then in *ERT* the Court built on *Wachauf*, assessing public policy derogations on grounds of fundamental rights.[291] There is a difference between *Wachauf* and *ERT*, in that in *Wachauf* the Court subordinated the fundamental rights of the individual to the objectives of the Community;[292] by contrast, in *ERT* the Court held that derogations from economic freedoms, even allowed by the Treaty, must respect EU fundamental rights.[293] Coppel and O'Neill's explanation for this difference is that in *Wachauf* the validity and implementation of a Community provision was at issue, whereas *ERT* was focused on a provision of national legislation. Therefore, they argue that there are 'two standards': one for Community acts, where fundamental rights must be interpreted in the light of Community objectives, and one for national acts derogating from Community law, where fundamental rights constrain Member State action. In their view, the Court thus '*clearly subordinates human rights to the end of closer economic integration in the Com-*

290 *Wachauf v Bundesamt für Ernährung und Forstwirtschaft*, C-5/88, paras 18-19. See also D. Chalmers, G. Davies and G. Monti, *European Union Law: Cases and Materials* (2nd edn, Cambridge University Press 2010) 252-253.

291 *ERT v DEP*, C-260/89 (with reference to *Wachauf* at para 41).

292 *Wachauf v Bundesamt für Ernährung und Forstwirtschaft*, C-5/88, para 18. See also Judgment of 17 January 1989, *Vainker v Parliament*, C-293/87, EU:C:1989:8, para 54; Judgment of 11 July 1989, *Schräder v Hauptzollamt Gronau*, C-265/87, EU:C:1989:303, para 15; *Von Deetzen*, C-44/89, para 28; Judgment of 10 January 1992, *Kühn v Landwirtschaftskammer Weser-Ems*, C-177/90, EU:C:1992:2, para 16; Judgment of 5 October 1994, *Germany v Council*, C-280/93, EU:C:1994:367, para 78; Judgment of 13 December 1994, *SMW Winzersekt v Land Rheinland-Pfalz*, C-306/93, EU:C:1994:407, para 22; Judgment of 17 October 1995, *The Queen v Minister of Agriculture, Fisheries and Food, ex parte Fishermen's Organisations and Others*, C-44/94, EU:C:1995:325, para 55; Judgment of 13 July 1995, *O'Dwyer and Others v Council*, Joined cases T-466/93, T-469/93, T-473/93, T-474/93 and T-477/93, EU:T:1995:136; Judgment of 15 April 1997, *Irish Farmers Association and Others v Minister for Agriculture, Food and Forestry, Ireland and Attorney General*, C-22/94, EU:C:1997:187, para 27; Judgment of 28 April 1998, *Metronome Musik v Music Point Hokamp*, C-200/96, EU:C:1998:172, para 21. In Schmidberger the Court refers instead to a 'social purpose' of the right: Judgment of 12 June 2003, *Schmidberger*, C-112/00, EU:C:2003:333, para 80. In *Kadi I* the term is 'function in society': Judgment of 3 September 2008, *Kadi and Al Barakaat International Foundation v Council and Commission ('Kadi I')*, Joined cases C-402/05 P and C-415/05 P, EU:C:2008:461, para 355.

293 Coppel and O'Neill, 'The European Court of Justice: Taking Rights Seriously?' 674-678 and 683-685.

munity.'[294] The development of fundamental rights case law thus suggests that the instrumental conception of rights retains its relevance, but it is insufficient for explaining the full role that rights play in this system. The analysis above instead points to the convergence of values of protection of individuals and ensuring the legitimacy of the Community and the effectiveness of its law.

1.1.2.3. Rights in the balance of interests: is it all relative?

Another possible way to consider the concept of a right is to take a 'negative' approach and look at where rights stop. Since rights materialise interests in the EU legal order, they are the typical subjects of proportionality tests. In post-World War II constitutional systems the principle of proportionality has become a central mechanism for balancing competing interests.[295] This principle reflects the idea that seemingly conflicting or contrary norms may be reconciled to a balancing point. An individual right may be balanced with another individual right, but also with a norm that reflects collective or general interests. Below are successively examined the development of the principle of proportionality, and then its specific manifestation in the prohibition of abuse of rights. Both notions inform us about how the relation between rights and interests plays out in concrete circumstances.

1.1.2.3.1. Rights, interests and the proportionality principle

The EU notion of proportionality first appeared in *Fédéchar* in 1956, at the time connected with the notion of a '*balance of interests*'.[296] It became close-

294 Coppel and O'Neill, 'The European Court of Justice: Taking Rights Seriously?'692. For a less antagonistic reading of the *Wachauf*-style 'implementation cases' and the *ERT*-style 'derogation cases' see J. Snell, 'Fundamental Rights Review of National Measures: Nothing New under the Charter?' (2015) 21 European Public Law 285 287-290.

295 See Alexy's 'Weight Formula' in R. Alexy, 'On Balancing and Subsumption' (2003) Ratio Juris 433-449. See also S. Gardbaum, 'The structure and scope of constitutional rights' in T. Ginsburg, R. Dixon (eds.) *Comparative Constitutional Law* (Elgar Publishing 2011) 388.

296 Judgment of 29 November 1956, *Fédération charbonnière de Belgique v High Authority*, C-8/55, EU:C:1956:11; Judgment of 22 March 1961, *S.N.U.P.A.T. v High*

ly associated with rights, especially fundamental rights, in 1970 in *Internationale Handelsgesellschaft.*[297] In assessing the legality of a system of deposits for export licenses, checking whether the burden was not '*excessive*' and finding that the required amount was not '*disproportionate*', the Court drew inspiration from the German legal system and used for the first time a test of necessity and appropriateness as an express ground for review.[298] The proportionality principle then took a more precise shape in *Nold* where the Court looked at how rights of ownership were protected by national constitutional law: '*far from constituting unfettered prerogatives*', these rights '*must be viewed in the light of the* social function *of the property and activities protected thereunder. For this reason, rights of this nature are protected by law subject always to limitations laid down in accordance with the public interest. Within the Community legal order it likewise seems legitimate that these rights should, if necessary, be subject to certain limits justified by the overall objectives pursued by the Community*'.[299] This 'social function' of the right is highlighted in many prominent rulings on fundamental rights and proportionality. In *Hauer* the Court conducted a review of the justifications for limiting the right to property in all nine Member States and found that in all of them, '*numerous legislative measures have given concrete expression to that social function of the right to property*'[300]; the freedom to conduct a business must thus also be limited '*in the light of its social function*'.[301] The Court systematised this approach in *Wachauf*: '*The fundamental rights recognized by the Court are not absolute [...], but must be considered in relation to their social function. Consequently, restrictions may be imposed on the exercise of those rights, [...] provided that those restrictions in fact correspond to objectives of general interest pursued by the Community and do not constitute, with regard to the aim pur-*

Authority, Joined cases C-42/59 and C-42/59, EU:C:1961:5, p. 148 and (confronting public and private interests) p.159.

297 *Internationale Handelsgesellschaft*, C-11/70.

298 *Internationale Handelsgesellschaft*, C-11/70, paras 14 and 16. S. Carrera, *In Search of the Perfect Citizen? The Intersection Between Integration, Immigration, and Nationality in the EU* (BRILL 2009) 366; W. Sauter, 'Proportionality in EU Law: A Balancing Act?' in C. Barnard, A. Albors-Llorens, M.W. Gehring (eds), *Cambridge Yearbook of European Legal Studies, Vol 15* 439, 446; F. Bignami, 'Regulation and the courts: judicial review in comparative perspective' in F. Bignami and D. Zaring (eds), *Comparative Law and Regulation. Understanding the Global Regulatory Process* (Elgar 2016) 288-289.

299 *Nold v Commission*, C-4/73, para 14 (emphasis added).

300 Judgment of 13 December 1979, *Hauer*, C-44/79, EU:C:1979:290, para 20.

301 *Hauer*, C-44/79, para 32. See also *Schräder v Hauptzollamt Gronau*, C-265/87, para 15.

sued, a disproportionate and intolerable interference, impairing the very substance of those rights.'[302] In *Alliance for Natural Health*, the Court further acknowledged that the right to property and the freedom to pursue an economic activity '*form part of the general principles of Community law*' but, the Court adds, '*those principles are not absolute but must be viewed in relation to their social function*'.[303] This is important because it shows that the Court did not introduce the proportionality test in opposition to fundamental rights: instead, the possible limitation is inherent in their own 'social function' – showing no opposition, but instead a 'relation' between individual interests on the one hand, and the broader interests of the European society on the other hand.

The case law on the proportionality principle gives indications not only as to the rationale of rights but also as to how they are practically applied. In *Alliance for Natural Health*, the Court states the conditions for limiting the right to property and the freedom to pursue an economic activity: possible restrictions must '*correspond to objectives of general interest pursued by the Community and [must] not constitute in relation to the aim pursued a disproportionate and intolerable interference, impairing the very substance of the rights guaranteed*'.[304] Accordingly, the CJEU developed the review of compliance with the principle of proportionality as a three-step test. A textbook illustration of this test is *Afton Chemical*.[305] Afton was a UK-based manufacturer of MMT, a metallic fuel additive. It challenged the validity of a directive which imposed limits for MMT content in fuel.[306] Under the first level '*the principle of proportionality requires that measures adopted by European*

302 Judgment of 13 July 1989, *Wachauf v Bundesamt für Ernährung und Forstwirtschaft*, C-5/88, EU:C:1989:321, para 18. See also *Vainker v Parliament*, C-293/87, para 54; *Von Deetzen*, C-44/89, para 28; Judgment of 10 January 1992, *Kühn v Landwirtschaftskammer Weser-Ems*, C-177/90, EU:C:1992:2, para 16; *Germany v Council*, C-280/93, para 78; *SMW Winzersekt v Land Rheinland-Pfalz*, C-306/93, para 22; *Irish Farmers Association and Others v Minister for Agriculture, Food and Forestry, Ireland and Attorney General*, C-22/94, para 27; *The Queen v Minister of Agriculture, Fisheries and Food, ex parte Fishermen's Organisations and Others*, C-44/94, para 55; *Schräder v Hauptzollamt Gronau*, C-265/87, para 15; *Metronome Musik v Music Point Hokamp*, C-200/96, para 21. See also *Schmidberger*, C-112/00, para 80 and *Kadi I*, Joined cases C-402/05 P and C-415/05 P, para 355.

303 Judgment of 12 July 2005, *Alliance for Natural Health*, C-154/04, EU:C:2005:449, para 126.

304 *Alliance for Natural Health*, C-154/04, para 126 and case law cited.

305 Judgment of 8 July 2010, *Afton Chemical*, C-343/09, EU:C:2010:419.

306 Parliament and Council Directive No 2009/30/EC as regards the specification of petrol, diesel and gas-oil and introducing a mechanism to monitor and reduce

Union institutions do not exceed the limits of what is appropriate and necessary in order to attain the objectives legitimately pursued by the legislation in question'. Second, '*when there is a choice between several appropriate measures recourse must be had to the least onerous*' – a test of strict necessity. Third, '*the disadvantages caused must not be disproportionate to the aims pursued*', which corresponds to a stricto sensu proportionality requirement between means and outcome.[307]

The Court's continued reliance on the proportionality test for applying fundamental rights reflects a vision of the proportionality principle which in turn indicates a certain conception of rights. Harbo has pointed out the resemblance with Alexy's theory (developed with the German Constitutional Court as reference) according to which 'principles' are not absolute (as opposed to 'rules', which are norms either fulfilled or not) and may be weighed against other 'principles'. In Alexy's relativist understanding of rights, '*the proportionality principle is perceived as an instrument for the balancing of conflicting interests in a way that does not give priority to any of the interests.*'[308] According to Alexy, this means that the balancing can only be done on a case by case basis, depending on the legal and factual possibilities. Principles may therefore be described as '*optimisation requirements*'.[309] Overall, as Harbo explains, '*There is a clear link between Alexy's theory of rights as principles and the proportionality principle: since rights are principles and principles are optimisation requirements this means that their application requires proportionality analysis.*'[310] By contrast, the importance of proportionality analysis in the Court's case law on fundamental rights is hard to reconcile with Dworkin's theory according to which rights are 'trumps' that cannot be outweighed by policy or collective rights expressed through legislative acts.[311] Habermas sides with Dworkin, arguing that Alexy's vision endangers rights because it leaves no rational standards for balanc-

greenhouse gas emissions and amending Council Directive 1999/32/EC as regards the specification of fuel used by inland waterway vessels and repealing Directive 93/12/EEC (OJ L 140 p. 88).

307 *Afton Chemical*, C-343/09, para 45.

308 Harbo, 'The Function of the Proportionality Principle in EU Law' 166.

309 Alexy, 'Rights and Liberties as Concepts' 291; H. Avila, *Theory of Legal Principles* (Springer 2007) 9; A. Von Bogdandy, 'Founding Principles of EU Law: A Theoretical and Doctrinal Sketch' (2010) 16 European Law Journal 95 104; Borowski, 'The Charter of Fundamental Rights in the Treaty on European Union' 211; Hilson, 'Rights and Principles in EU Law: A Distinction Without Foundation?' 211.

310 Harbo, 'The Function of the Proportionality Principle in EU Law' 167.

311 Harbo observes that Dworkin's theory of law corresponds to the American legal tradition and is consistent with the absence of proportionality analysis from the

ing.[312] An additional argument against Alexy's approach is that it '*opens up for an inflationary use of, not only the terminology of rights, but also the concept of rights*', with '*dethronement of the legislator to the advantage of the judiciary*'.[313] Nevertheless, the Court's reliance on the 'social function' of fundamental rights may indicate why the arguments against the use of the proportionality test have not outbalanced those in favour of it. Again, the interests of the Community/Union play an essential part in the adjudication process. As Harbo argues, Alexy's '*relative understanding of rights can be defended from a democratic perspective because the way in which political processes are constructed gives reasons to believe that politics is (still) about the realisation of some kind of common good reaching beyond that of a calculus of consent.*'[314] In the EU context this notion of common good is assimilated with the purpose of European integration, with a resulting '*structural bias towards European relative supremacy over national interests*'.[315]

Despite the importance of the proportionality principle in EU fundamental rights adjudication, its relativist implications should not be exaggerated. The application of the proportionality test indeed also provides the opportunity to look at what, in a right, is *not* relative. Coming back to *Nold:* the Court back then already held that fundamental rights may '*be subject to certain limits justified by the overall objectives pursued by the Community*, on the condition that the substance of these rights is left untouched'.[316] In subsequent case law the Court often refers to the 'very substance' of the right.[317] The keywords listed at the beginning of the *Nold* judgment include the expression 'intangible substance of rights' – this has remained the only occurrence of this expression in CJEU case law, but it is

Supreme Court's 'tool box'. Harbo, 'The Function of the Proportionality Principle in EU Law' 168 and Dworkin, *Taking Rights Seriously*.

312 J. Habermas, *Between Facts and Norms: Contributions to a Discourse Theory of Law and Democracy* (W. Rehg trans, The MIT Press 1993); A. Sajó, *Abuse: The Dark Side of Fundamental Rights* (Eleven International Publishing 2006) 68; Harbo, 'The Function of the Proportionality Principle in EU Law' 166-169.

313 Harbo, 'The Function of the Proportionality Principle in EU Law' 168.

314 Harbo, 'The Function of the Proportionality Principle in EU Law' 170.

315 M. Goldoni, 'Constitutional Pluralism and the Question of the European Common Good' (2012) 18 European Law Journal 385 392. See also Harbo, 'The Function of the Proportionality Principle in EU Law' 172.

316 *Nold v Commission*, C-4/73, para 14 (emphasis added).

317 *Hauer*, C-44/79, para 23; *Schräder v Hauptzollamt Gronau*, C-265/87, para 15; *Wachauf*, C-5/88, para 15; Judgment of 8 April 1992, *Commission v Germany*, C-62/90, EU:C:1992:169, para 23; Judgment of 5 October 1994, *X v Commission*, C-404/92 P, EU:C:1994:361, para 18; *Metronome Musik v Music Point Hokamp*, C-200/96, para 21, *Schmidberger*, C-112/00, para 80.

interesting because 'intangible' etymologically refers both to something that *cannot be touched* and to something that *must not be touched*.[318] This suggests that the substance of a fundamental right is both difficult to grasp, and inviolable.

The substance of the right, its absolute part, is precisely also the most elusive part of it. In *Hauer*, the Court emphasises the need to check whether the 'very substance' of the right to property is infringed,[319] and finds that it is not, but without being very specific on the reasons.[320] The Court is a bit more precise in *Schräder*: again it stresses the importance of leaving the 'very substance' of the right untouched[321] and finds that the requirement for processors to pay a levy and pass it on to their suppliers has '*only a marginal effect upon the taxable person's freedom to pursue an occupation and consequently cannot impinge upon the very substance of that right*';[322] only then does it move on to proportionality.[323] The reasoning is similar in *Winzesekt* regarding the impairment of the freedom to pursue a trade or profession: the challenged regulation does not '*impair the very substance of the right freely to exercise a trade or profession relied on by Winzersekt since those provisions affect only the arrangements governing the exercise of that right and do not jeopardize its very existence.*' Only after this is clear, does the Court move on to assessing the proportionality of the limitation to the right.[324] And in *Kühn* the Court holds that the challenged provisions taken in the framework of the Common Agricultural Policy, '*which form part of a body of legislation intended to remedy the situation of surpluses on the milk and milk products market, correspond to the aims pursued by the Community in the general interest. They do not affect the very substance of the right to property and of the freedom to pursue an occupation because they do not affect the possibility for the operators in question to engage in the production of products other than milk on the holding concerned.*'[325] Only in concrete circumstances is it possible to assess whether the substance of a right is touched or not.

318 Centre National de Ressources Textuelles et Lexicales, http://www.cnrtl.fr/etymologie/intangible (Accessed 17 April 2017).

319 *Hauer*, C-44/79, para 23.

320 *Hauer*, C-44/79, para 30.

321 *Schräder v Hauptzollamt Gronau*, C-265/87, para 15.

322 *Schräder v Hauptzollamt Gronau*, C-265/87, para 18.

323 Judgment of 21 February 1991, *Zuckerfabrik Süderdithmarschen and Zuckerfabrik Soest v Hauptzollamt Itzehoe and Hauptzollamt Paderborn*, Joined cases C-143/88 and C-92/89, EU:C:1991:65, para 73.

324 *SMW Winzersekt v Land Rheinland-Pfalz*, C-306/93, para 24.

325 *Kühn v Landwirtschaftskammer Weser-Ems*, C-177/90, para 17.

1.1.2.3.2. Rights, interests and the prohibition of abuse of rights

An additional way to delineate a right is to consider the prohibition of abuse of rights. Many legal systems include some safeguards against 'abusive' exercise of rights.[326] These safeguards reflect two main concerns. As Foulquier explains, they find one justification in the preservation of the general good.[327] An additional justification is the balance between the exercise of different rights, in the spirit of Article 17 ECHR[328] and now also Article 54 of the Charter.[329] On the European level, the ECtHR dealt with

326 A non-exhaustive review of the literature on abuse of rights shows that it is a concern common to many legal systems; P.-E. Moyse, 'L'abus de droit : l'anténorme - partie II' (2012) 58 McGill Law Journal 1. Josserand in 1939 had already conducted a thorough study of abuse of rights both in the French (public and private law) context and in comparative law: L. Josserand, *De l'esprit des droits et de leur relativité. Théorie dite de l'abus des droits* (Dalloz 1939). Eck has traced the history of the notion specifically in French constitutional law: L. Eck, *L'abus de droit en droit constitutionnel* (L'Harmattan 2010). It is also a notion that has relevance in a variety of sectoral areas, such as intellectual property law: A.M. Ramadan, 'L'abus du droit de brevet : étude comparée de droit français et égyptien' (Thèse de doctorat en droit privé et sciences criminelles, Université de Montpellier et Université d'Alexandrie 2012); contract law: M.-C. Seyssel, 'L'abus de droit dans les contrats' (Thèse de doctorat en droit privé, Université Savoie Mont Blanc 2004); labour law: L. Bigiaoui-Duhamel, 'L'abus de droit en droit du travail' (Thèse de doctorat en droit privé, Université Paris 1 2002). On the prohibition of abuse of rights in international public law see R. Kolb, *La bonne foi en droit international public. Contribution à l'étude des principes généraux de droit* (The Graduate Institute 2000).

327 N. Nivert, 'Intérêt général et droits fondamentaux' (Thèse pour l'obtention du grade de Docteur en droit public, Université de la Réunion 2012) 315; Foulquier *Les droits publics subjectifs des administrés. Emergence d'un concept en droit administratif français du XIXè au XXè siècle* 345.

328 *'Prohibition of abuse of rights'*: *'Nothing in this Convention may be interpreted as implying for any State, group or person any right to engage in any activity or perform any act aimed at the destruction of any of the rights and freedoms set forth herein or at their limitation to a greater extent than is provided for in the Convention.'* Nivert, 'Intérêt général et droits fondamentaux' 273; Foulquier, *Les droits publics subjectifs des administrés. Emergence d'un concept en droit administratif français du XIXè au XXè siècle* 346.

329 *'Prohibition of abuse of rights'*: *'Nothing in this Charter shall be interpreted as implying any right to engage in any activity or to perform any act aimed at the destruction of any of the rights and freedoms recognised in this Charter or at their limitation to a greater extent than is provided for herein.'* The CJEU has not yet had the opportunity to interpret or apply this provision. The Explanations to the Charter explain that it is the equivalent of Article 17 ECHR.

this issue already in the early years of its existence.[330] By contrast, the CJEU rather slowly came to acknowledge the notion but over time the developing case law has been the object of doctrinal works as well,[331] such that there is now an EU theory of abuse of rights, and even a general principle of EU law prohibiting abuse of rights.[332] This general principle relies on the tension between the 'strict application' of a rule and its 'true spirit':[333] where the application of a rule of EU law leads to a result that does not meet the objectives pursued by that rule, abuse of rights may be identified.[334] This principle may be inconsistent with the original concept of rights in two ways.

Firstly, does it even make sense to talk of 'abuse of rights'[335]? As Gutteridge already pointed out almost a century ago, the term itself is '*of*

330 S. Van Drooghenbroeck, 'L'article 17 de la CEDH est-il indispensable ?' [2001] Revue trimestrielle des droits de l'homme (no spécial : Le droit face à la montée du racisme et de la xénophobie) 543; Y. Lecuyer, *Mémento de la jurisprudence de la CEDH* (Hachette Education 2012) 5. *Lawless v Ireland* (1 July 1961), *Parti communiste* 20 January 1957, *Glimmerveen and Hagenbeek* 11 October 1979.

331 Such as: L. Neville Brown, 'Is there a general principle of abuse of rights in European Community law?' in D. Curtin and T. Heukels (eds), *Institutional Dynamics of European Integration Essays in Honour of Henry G Schermers*, vol II (Martinus Nijhoff 1994); R.N. Ionescu, 'L'abus de droit en droit communautaire' (Thèse pour le doctorat en droit, Universitat Autònoma de Barcelona and Université Toulouse I - Sciences sociales 2009); A. Bobic, 'Prohibition of Abuse of Rights in EU Law' (Master's thesis, University of Zagreb, Faculty of Law, Jean Monnet Chair of European Public Law 2011).

332 Judgment of 5 July 2007, *Kofoed*, C-321/05, EU:C:2007:408, para 38; Judgment of 18 December 2014, *Schoenimport 'Italmoda' Mariano Previti and Others*, Joined cases C-131/13, C-163/13 and C-164/13, EU:C:2014:2455, para 46; Judgment of 18 May 2017, *Litdana*, C-624/15, EU:C:2017:389, para 31. A. Lenaerts, 'The General Principle of the Prohibition of Abuse of Rights: A Critical Position on Its Role in a Codified European Contract Law' (2010) 6 European Review of Private Law 1121 1138. See also Berrod, *La systématique des voies de droit communautaires* 906-907.

333 A. Lenaerts, 'The General Principle of the Prohibition of Abuse of Rights: A Critical Position on Its Role in a Codified European Contract Law' 1121.

334 Ionescu, 'L'abus de droit en droit communautaire' 381.

335 'Abuse of rights' has been the only expression used by the CJEU since Judgment of 14 December 2000, *Emsland-Stärke*, C-110/99, EU:C:2000:695. Prior to *Emsland* a variety of terms had been used, such as 'evasion', 'circumvent', 'avoidance', 'abuse', 'fraud'. Respectively in: Judgment of 7 February 1979, *Knoors v Staatssecretaris van Economische Zaken*, C-115/78, EU:C:1979:31, para 50; Judgment of 10 January 1985, *Leclerc and Others v Au Blé Vert and Others*, C-229/83, EU:C:1985:1, para 27; Judgment of 5 October 1994, *TV10 v Commissariaat voor de Media*, C-23/93, EU:C:1994:362, para 21; Judgment of 12 March 1996, *Pafitis and Others*,

doubtful elegance.[336] Along the same lines, Finnis argues that abuse of rights is a '*juridically improper concept*' since it refers to a prohibition and therefore signals in fact the absence of a right.[337] This objection is particularly relevant in the EU context given the correlativity observed so far between obligations and rights. Beyond this apparent contradiction, the abuse of rights may be analysed as a type of limitation by objective law on individual prerogatives.[338] In this sense the notion of abuse of rights may be the product of a tension between objective law and subjective rights.[339] It is therefore worth asking whether the notion of abuse of rights is compatible with the CJEU's classic approach which insists on correlativity rather than tension between 'law' and 'rights'.

Secondly, the classically decentralised enforcement of EU law within the domestic legal systems raises another issue. As explained in the previous section, the effectiveness of EU law has been a powerful rationale for rights in the development of the EU constitutional order. And in relation to this rationale, the rule is that any individual who has an interest in doing so can request the execution of a provision of EU law. The nature of the interest does not seem essential to the definition of the right. By contrast, the prohibition on abuse of rights suggests that some interests – or at least some motives, the distinction not being easily made – are not acceptable as triggers for rights. Is this prohibition compatible with the characteristics of rights that we have identified so far?

C-441/93, EU:C:1996:92, para 68; Judgment of 12 May 1998, *Kefalas and others v Elliniko Dimosio and Organismos Oikonomikis Anasygkrotisis Epicheiriseon*, C-367/96, EU:C:1998:222, para 20. Bobic, 'Prohibition of Abuse of Rights in EU Law' 3.

336 H.C. Gutteridge, 'Abuse of Rights' (1933) 5 Cambridge Law Journal 22.

337 Finnis, 'Some Professorial Fallacies About Rights' 387. See also Sajó pointing out the oxymoric nature of the term: Sajó, *Abuse: The Dark Side of Fundamental Rights* 32.

338 P. Ancel, 'Abus de droit (Interdiction de l' –)' in J. Andriantsimbazovina et al (eds) *Dictionnaire des Droits de l'Homme* (Presses universitaires de France 2008) 1-3. See also Nivert, 'Intérêt général et droits fondamentaux' 273.

339 Which, as Gutteridge points out, makes the notion especially difficult to grasp for English lawyers, for whom this tension has little relevance. Gutteridge, 'Abuse of Rights' 24, referring to Josserand, *De l'esprit des droits et de leur relativité. Théorie dite de l'abus des droits.* See also Sajó, *Abuse: The Dark Side of Fundamental Rights* 303.

The so-called 'Greek challenge' case series illustrate these questions. In the first of these cases, *Pafitis*,[340] shareholders had brought proceedings to seek the annulment of a decision to increase a company's capital taken without a prior general meeting and thus in breach of the Second Directive.[341] Advocate General Tesauro points out the risk in restricting the suspected abusive exercise of a right, i.e. the risk of hindering '*any exercise of it*'.[342] The Greek Civil Code however prohibits the exercise of a right '*where it manifestly exceeds the bounds of good faith or morality or the economic or social purpose of that right*'.[343] According to the Advocate General, the core problem with regard to EU law was not the existence of the rule in itself, but that '*the application of such a rule must not detract from the full effect and uniform application of Community law in the Member States*'.[344] Picking up on this, the Court ruled that '*uniform application and full effect of Community law would be undermined*' if minority shareholders were prevented from exercising their voting rights under the Second Directive solely because they were suspected, because they were in minority, or claiming the exercise of these rights abusively.[345] Thus, the Court does not express any general opposition towards safeguards against abuse of rights, but the full effect of EU law comes first.[346] While this does not help much to draw an autonomous definition of abuse of rights on the EU level, it is interesting for our purposes because it confirms the power of the effectiveness rationale of EU rights. This acceptance of domestic legislation on abuse of rights as long as it does not impair the effectiveness of EU law has been confirmed in rulings in a variety of policy areas: the freedom to supply services, the

340 *Pafitis and Others*, C-441/93. Other cases in the series include: *Kefalas*, C-367/96, EU:C:1998:222; Judgment of 23 March 2000, *Diamantis*, C-373/97, EU:C:2000:150. Bobic, 'Prohibition of Abuse of Rights in EU Law' 8.

341 Second Council Directive 77/91/EEC of 13 December 1976 on coordination of safeguards which, for the protection of the interests of members and others, are required by Member States of companies within the meaning of the second paragraph of Article 58 of the Treaty, in respect of the formation of public limited liability companies and the maintenance and alteration of their capital, with a view to making such safeguards equivalent (OJ L 26 p. 1).

342 Opinion of AG Tesauro in *Pafitis and Others*, C-441/93, EU:C:1995:368, paras 30-31.

343 Opinion of AG Tesauro in *Pafitis*, C-441/93, para 67.

344 Opinion of AG Tesauro in *Pafitis*, C-441/93, para 68.

345 *Pafitis and Others*, C-441/93, para 70.

346 A. Lenaerts, 'The General Principle of the Prohibition of Abuse of Rights: A Critical Position on Its Role in a Codified European Contract Law'.

freedom of establishment, the free movement of goods, social security, the common agricultural policy, and company law.[347]

The *Centros* case was a further significant step towards the definition of abuse of rights.[348] The Danish Department of Trade had refused to register a branch of a company established in the UK but in fact intending to do business exclusively in Denmark (which had more stringent national rules on principal establishments). Centros claimed that this was an infringement of its freedom of establishment and more specifically of Articles 52 and 58 of the EC Treaty, which specifically provided for the right to freely set up a secondary establishment. The Court admitted that '*a Member State is entitled to take measures designed to prevent certain of its nationals from attempting, undercover of the rights created by the Treaty, improperly to circumvent their national legislation or to prevent individuals from improperly or fraudulently taking advantage of provisions of Community law*',[349] according to settled case law. The Court then held that '*the fact that a national of a Member State who wishes to set up a company chooses to form it in the Member State whose rules of company law seem to him the least restrictive and to set up branches in other Member States cannot, in itself, constitute an abuse of the right of establishment. The right to form a company in accordance with the law of a Member State and to set up branches in other Member States is inherent in the exercise, in a single market, of the freedom of establishment guaranteed by the Treaty*.'[350] So the Court goes for a very broad interpretation of the material scope of the right – and accordingly, a narrow notion of abuse of right.[351]

---

347 See e.g. regarding freedom to supply services: Judgment of 3 December 1974, *Van Binsbergen* v *Bedrijfsvereniging Metaalnijverheid*, C-33/74, EU:C:1974:131, para 13; *TV 10* v *Commissariaat voor de Media*, C-23/93, para 20; regarding freedom of establishment: *Knoors*, C-115/78, para 25; Judgment of 3 October 1990, *Bouchoucha*, C-61/89, EU:C:1990:343, para 14; regarding the free movement of goods: *Leclerc and Others* v *Au Blé Vert and Others*, C-229/83, para 27; regarding social security: Judgment of 2 May 1996, *Brennet* v *Paletta*, C-206/94, EU:C:1996:182, para 24; regarding the common agricultural policy: Judgment of 3 March 1993, *General Milk Products* v *Hauptzollamt Hamburg-Jonas*, C-C-8/92, EU:C:1993:82, para 21; regarding company law, *Kefalas and Others v Elliniko Dimosio and Organismos Oikonomikis Anasygkrotisis Epicheiriseon*, C-367/96, para 20. For a detailed analysis of these cases see Bobic, 'Prohibition of Abuse of Rights in EU Law'.

348 Judgment of 9 March 1999, *Centros*, C-212/97, EU:C:1999:126.

349 *Centros*, C-212/97, para 24.

350 *Centros*, C-212/97, para 27.

351 Bobic, 'Prohibition of Abuse of Rights in EU Law' 8. The *Centros* solution was confirmed and consolidated in Judgment of 5 November 2002, *Überseering*, C-208/00, EU:C:2002:632 and Judgment of 30 September 2003, *Inspire Art*,

Interestingly, in the early cases on abuse of rights the acceptance is justified by reference to 'rights' or 'interests' of the Member States. The Court admits that a Member State *'cannot be denied the right'* to take measures preventing abusive reliance on EU law by individuals.[352] In other cases, the Court finds that *'it is not possible to disregard the legitimate interest which a Member State may have in preventing certain of its nationals, by means of facilities created under the Treaty, from attempting wrongly to evade the application of their national legislation'*.[353] In *Centros* the term used was *'entitled'*[354] – echoing yet another notion close to that of right. The apparent interchangeability between 'right' and 'interest' in this context again highlights the strong connection between these two terms. In addition, this justification of the prohibition of abuse of rights confirms that it is a form of balancing between some individuals interests and some more general interests: the Court, when assessing the applicability of national legislation on abuse of rights, engages in a proportionality test.[355] In this sense, according to Van Gerven, the theory of abuse of rights is precisely no more and no less than an application of the proportionality principle.[356]

The analysis is complicated by the fluctuating definition of abuse of law in the case law. In *Diamantis*, *TV 10* and *Centros*, the focus was on whether the purpose of the rules relied on had objectively not been achieved.[357] In *Emsland* in the context of the common agricultural policy, a subjective

---

C-167/01, EU:C:2003:512. See Ionescu, 'L'abus de droit en droit communautaire' 97-107 concerning in particular the abuse of the freedom of establishment.

352 *Van Binsbergen* v *Bedrijfsvereniging Metaalnijverheid*, C-33/74, para 13; *TV 10* v *Commissariaat voor de Media*, C-23/93, para 20;.

353 *Knoors*, C-115/78, para 25; Judgment of 3 October 1990, *Bouchoucha*, C-61/89, EU:C:1990:343, para 14.

354 *Centros*, C-212/97, para 24.

355 *Centros*, C-212/97, para 34: *'national measures liable to hinder or make less attractive the exercise of fundamental freedoms guaranteed by the Treaty must fulfil four conditions: they must be applied in a non-discriminatory manner; they must be justified by imperative requirements in the general interest; they must be suitable for securing the attainment of the objective which they pursue; and they must notgo beyond what is necessary in order to attain it'* and case law cited. See also A. Zalasiński, 'Proportionality of Anti-Avoidance and Anti-Abuse Measures in the ECJ's Direct Tax Case Law' (2007) 35 Intertax 310-321; Ionescu, 'L'abus de droit en droit communautaire' 183.

356 Van Gerven, 'Principe de proportionnalité, abus de droit et droits fondamentaux' 307; Van Gerven, 'Remedies for Infringements of Fundamental Rights' 279-281.

357 *Diamantis*, C-373/97, *TV 10* v *Commissariaat voor de Media*, C-23/93, and *Centros*, C-212/97.

component was also required. The AG had greatly insisted on the abusive *intention* as a criterion for identifying abuse of rights.[358] The Court agreed to include this criterion but was careful to maintain the priority of the objective element, stating first that '*[a] finding of an abuse requires, first, a combination of objective circumstances in which, despite formal observance of the conditions laid down by the Community rules, the purpose of those rules has not been achieved*' and '*second, a subjective element consisting in the intention to obtain an advantage from the Community rules by creating artificially the conditions laid down for obtaining it.*'[359] The Court then added a last condition, this time not for identifying abuse of rights but rather to limit its application so that it would not harm the effectiveness of EU law: '*It is for the national court to establish the existence of those two elements, evidence of which must be adduced in accordance with the rules of national law, provided that the effectiveness of Community law is not thereby undermined*'.[360] Probably this was all the more important since in this case the Community's financial interests were at stake: the abuse of rights conferred by EU law was harming the Community's interests[361], not just the Member State's.

The relative weight of the objective and subjective criteria for assessing the existence of an abuse of rights has been clarified in subsequent case law and the priority goes to the objective component.[362] To take a recent example, in *WebMindLicenses* a Hungarian referring court was seeking interpretation of the VAT directive in order to assess whether the undertaking had committed an abuse of rights in order to circumvent Hungarian tax law and should therefore be sanctioned. The Court stated that '*preventing possible tax evasion, avoidance and abuse is an objective recognised and encouraged by the VAT Directive*'[363] (meaning that in this situation the interests of the Member States and those of the Union were converging). The Court then recalled that '*in the sphere of VAT, an abusive practice can be found to exist only*

---

358 Opinion of AG Alber in *Emsland-Stärke*, C-110/99, EU:C:2000:252, paras 80-82, building on the '*presumption*' that '*the abuse of rights as such does not merit protection*' to find that '*the pre-condition for a right of recovery based on general legal principles is therefore the intentional bringing about of circumstances which are contrary to the objectives of Community rules, with the aim of creating the formal conditions for obtaining an advantage*'.

359 *Emsland-Stärke*, C-110/99, paras 52-53.

360 *Emsland-Stärke*, C-110/99, para 54 and case law cited. Ionescu, 'L'abus de droit en droit communautaire' 366.

361 As emphasised by the Commission: *Emsland-Stärke*, C-110/99, para 37.

362 Ionescu, 'L'abus de droit en droit communautaire' 381.

363 Judgment of 17 December 2015, *WebMindLicenses*, C-419/14, EU:C:2015:832, para 35.

if, first, the transactions concerned, notwithstanding formal application of the conditions laid down by the relevant provisions of the VAT Directive and the national legislation transposing it, result in the accrual of a tax advantage the grant of which would be contrary to the purpose of those provisions and, secondly, it is apparent from a number of objective factors that the essential aim of the transactions concerned is solely to obtain that tax advantage'.[364] Thus, even the subjective intention to abusively obtain an advantage is assessed by reference to 'objective factors'.

The predominance of the objective aspect allows for the overall consistency of the CJEU's case law on rights. As already pointed out, the insistence on an individual's subjective intention when relying on a provision of EU law would challenge the broad conception of 'interest' as a component of the 'right', that the Court adopted in *Defrenne II*.[365] Instead, the Court was very clear in *Barbier* that the intention underlying an individual's claim could not in itself be considered as abusive and thus prevent him from relying on a rule of EU law: '*the fact that a Community national, whether a natural or a legal person, sought to profit from tax advantages in force in a Member State other than his State of residence cannot in itself deprive him of the right to rely on the provisions of the Treaty*'.[366] Although the notion of abuse of rights and the criteria for identifying it have been developed mainly in cases relative to economic freedoms and tax law, the same predominance of the objective component is to be found in other areas of EU law. A telling example is *Zhu and Chen*. A Chinese national was claiming the right to stay in the UK based on the right to free movement of her infant daughter, an Irish national. While the British authorities submitted that the baby was too young to exercise her rights under the treaties, the ECJ reached another conclusion: from the right of the child to stay in the UK, it derived the same right for the mother, without whom the child could not have effectively exercised her rights as an EU citizen.[367] Interestingly, the British government had suggested that Mrs Chen should not be

---

364 *WebMindLicenses*, C-419/14, para 36, citing Judgment of 21 February 2006, *Halifax and Others*, C-255/02, EU:C:2006:121, paras 74-75.

365 *Defrenne v SABENA*, C-43/75.

366 Judgment of 11 December 2003, *Barbier*, C-364/01, EU:C:2003:665, para 71. See also Judgment of 12 September 2006, *Cadbury Schweppes and Cadbury Schweppes Overseas*, C-196/04, EU:C:2006:544, para 36.

367 Judgment of 19 October 2004, *Zhu and Chen*, C-200/02, EU:C:2004:639. Advocate General Wathelet relies on the same reasoning in the *NA* case: Opinion of AG Wathelet in *NA*, C-115/15, EU:C:2016:259, paras 39-42. See also Judgment of 10 October 2013, *Alokpa and Moudoulou*, C-86/12, EU:C:2013:645, para 28.

allowed to stay in the UK because she had intentionally given birth in Northern Ireland so that the baby would benefit from the Irish *jus soli,* and gone back to the UK to assert her Irish (i.e. European) daughter's right to stay. The abusive conduct, the argument went, should not be rewarded by acknowledging such a right.[368] The Court however refused to frame the issue in terms of abuse of rights, holding that such an approach would amount to allowing a Member State (the UK) to restrict the effects of the grant of nationality by another Member State (Ireland), and that this was prohibited by EU law.[369] The possibly abusive intention of the individual matters only when it is established that the objective purpose of the rule on which he or she is relying is not being met. It thus has limited relevance for identifying rights, just like the intention underlying the EU norm itself.

To conclude on the principle of proportionality and the prohibition of abuse of rights, both constitute similar responses to situations where the relevant interests diverge rather than converge, so that the prohibition of abuse of rights may be considered as a specific application of the principle of proportionality outside 'fundamental rights' adjudication. The implication is that all rights, whether 'fundamental' or not, function in the same basic way, in two respects. First, rights are 'optimisation requirements';[370] 'principles' that can be limited and adapted in various ways depending on the situation. Second, they have an inherent 'substance' that cannot be subject to limitation. In addition, when applying either the proportionality principle or the prohibition of abuse of rights the Court relies on the double function of individual rights (serving both individual and EU interests) to bridge the gap and reach a solution.

1.1.3. Conclusions: the double rationale of individual rights under EU law

Milutinović has pointed out that it is still not clear '*whether it is the existence of individual rights that necessitated effective enforcement of Union law, or whether, on the contrary, it is the need for effective enforcement of Union law that necessitated the creation of individual rights.*'[371] While this debate could go on endlessly, it is at least possible to agree that rights have a double rationale, serving both the interests of their holders and those of the EU. Af-

---

368 *Zhu and Chen*, C-200/02, para 34.

369 *Zhu and Chen*, C-200/02, paras 39-40.

370 Alexy, *A Theory of Constitutional Rights* 65.

371 Milutinovic, *The 'Right to Damages' under EU Competition Law: from Courage v Crehan to the White Paper and Beyond* 16.

ter all, in the words of Weiler and Lockhart: '*[a]s is so common in life, altruism and opportunism are often intertwined*'.[372] Indeed, it cannot be expected that individuals will fight for the implementation of EU law unless they are also defending at the same time their own interests – especially since proceedings involving EU law are often highly technical, lengthy and costly.[373] In fact, from an effectiveness perspective, allowing '*any individual who has an interest in the performance of the duties*' laid down in the Treaty to claim the execution of these duties[374] is a brilliant trick: it makes the personal scope of the correlative rights extremely broad, which in turn ensures that a potentially infinite number of individuals can contribute to the enforcement of EU law.[375] There is of course a '*logic of mutuality*'[376] at work, since the individual citizen is put in an advantageous position, being supported by Community Law to obtain a benefit withheld by a Member State.[377]. Thus, '*[w]hilst being an agent moved by selfish ends, the individual remains committed to an institutional project*'.[378]

The convergence of EU and individual interests materialises into a mechanism that has been given different labels, notably that of '*functional subjectivation*', a term coined by Ruffert to describe how the whole system functions so as to ensure the effectiveness of EU law and the protection of indi-

372 Weiler and Lockhart, "Taking Rights Seriously' Seriously: The European Court and its Fundamental Rights Jurisprudence - Part I' 70.

373 Masing, *Die Mobilisierung des Bürgers für die Durchsetzung des Rechts: europäische Impulse für eine Revision der Lehre vom subjektiv-öffentlichen Recht* 185.

374 *Defrenne v. SABENA*, C-43/75, para. 31.

375 Eilmansberger, 'The Relationship between Rights and Remedies in EC Law: in Search of the Missing Link' 1205; see also Ruffert, 'Rights and Remedies in European Community Law: a Comparative View'.

376 Burley and Mattli, 'Europe Before the Court: A Political Theory of Legal Integration' 61.

377 De Witte, 'Direct Effect, Primacy and the Nature of the Legal Order'; see also Grzeszick who argues that the development of subjective rights in EU law had shown how the individual, by claiming his subjective rights, can become a motor for the implementation of objective law and therefore contribute to the protection of the interests of the Union: Grzeszick, 'Das Grundrecht auf eine gute Verwaltung - Strukturen und Perspektiven des Charta-Grundrechts auf eine gute Verwaltung' 179.

378 L. Azoulai, S. Barbou des Places and E. Pataut, 'Being a Person in the European Union' in L. Azoulai, S. Barbou des Places and E. Pataut (eds), *Constructing the Person in EU Law: Rights, Roles, Identities* (Bloomsbury Publishing 2016) 5. The authors also cite R. Lecourt, *L'Europe des juges* (Bruylant 1976) 260: '*When an individual appears before the judge to defend the rights he derives from the Treaties, that individual does not only act in his own interest, he immediately becomes an auxiliary agent of the Community*'.

vidual interests at once: as the obligation of the Member State amounts to a right for the individual, the latter in turn has an incentive to make sure that the obligation is respected. An action based on rights has effects beyond the individual sphere, since the individual, by claiming his or her rights, contributes to realizing the objectives of the Community (or now the Union).[379] Masing uses the term '*Versubjektivierung*' in a similar sense.[380] To use Poiares Maduro's expression, the '*subjectivation of the Treaties*'[381] thus forms a virtuous circle, which De Witte calls '*the useful effect of direct effect*'.[382] A classic example is EU competition law, where functional subjectivation takes the form of private enforcement. It is commonly admitted that allowing individuals to litigate against anticompetitive behaviours serves both the public interest and private individual interests.[383] The advantage of the notion of functional subjectivation is that it accounts for both these purposes, without necessarily assigning priority to one over the other. The rights claimed by individuals serve the double purpose of protecting individual interests *and* ensuring the enforcement of public obligations.[384]

379 Lecourt, *L'Europe des juges* 260; T. Von Danwitz, *Verwaltungsrechtliches System und europäische Integration* (Mohr Siebeck 1996) 230; Ruffert, 'Rights and Remedies in European Community Law: a Comparative View' 327; C. Callies, 'Kohärenz und Konvergenz beim europäischen Individualrechtsschutz - Der Zugang zum Gericht im Lichte des Grundrechts auf effektiven Rechtsschutz' (2002) 49 Neue Juristische Wochenschrift 3577 3579; Azoulai, 'L'autonomie de l'individu européen et la question du statut' EUI Department of Law Research paper 2013/14 4.

380 Masing, *Die Mobilisierung des Bürgers für die Durchsetzung des Rechts: europäische Impulse für eine Revision der Lehre vom subjektiv-öffentlichen Recht* 22.

381 M. Poiares Maduro, *We the Court* (Hart 1998) 9.

382 De Witte, 'Direct Effect, Primacy and the Nature of the Legal Order' 340.

383 Milutinovic, *The 'Right to Damages' under EU Competition Law: from Courage v Crehan to the White Paper and Beyond* 15; Masing, *Die Mobilisierung des Bürgers für die Durchsetzung des Rechts: europäische Impulse für eine Revision der Lehre vom subjektiv-öffentlichen Recht* 38.

384 This is also consistent with Habermas's co-originality thesis, which posits the co-originary emergence of democracy and rights, and of objective law and subjective rights. M. Loughlin, *Foundations of Public Law* (Oxford University Press 2010) 371; J. Habermas, *Faktizität und Geltung: Beiträge zur Diskurstheorie des Rechts und des demokratischen Rechtsstaats* (Suhrkamp 1992); U. Lapointe, 'Boyle, Martin. 2001. 'Chapitre I: Legal legitimacy and the Principles of Private and Public Autonomy', *Towards Justice and Validity: An Investigation into Habermas' Theory of Legitimacy*, Mémoire de maîtrise, Carleton University, pp. 6-45', in G. Fleury, U. Lapointe, L. Roch, V. Demers, 'Légitimité et gouvernance dans les oeuvres de Jürgen Habermas (Raison et légitimité et Droit et démocratie)'

Individual rights also embody another type of balance, between various domestic conceptions of the role of individuals. Like in French public law, in EU law each individual effectively becomes a *'legal vigilante'* of the public rule of law,[385] an *'attorney general',*[386] being assigned a controlling function (*Kontrollfunktion*).[387] However, something happens in EU law that does not happen (or much more moderately) in the French system: by using a language of rights in *Van Gend en Loos* (thereby accepting the suggestion of the referring Dutch court) and in subsequent case law, the CJEU (deliberately?) put individuals under the spotlight, granting them a status and value similar to that which individuals have in German public law. In EU law, the interests of the individuals and those of the Union do not just coincide, they converge into individual rights. Thus the mechanism of functional subjectivation also reflects the Court's refusal to choose between the French-style objective system and the German-style subjective system; it is instead the result of a compromise between the two ways.[388] It is also in harmony with the English system in so far as English lawyers avoid thinking in terms of antagonism between individual and collective

Chaire de responsabilité sociale et de développement durable ESG-UQAM, Recueil de textes CEH/RT-34-2005, Deuxième séminaire de la série annuelle 2004-2005 sur la gouvernance, 6 octobre 2005, 14-15; J. Habermas, *Droit et démocratie. Entre faits et normes* (Gallimard 1997), ch. 3 'Chapitre III : Reconstruction du droit' 97-149. The double rationale for rights in the EU legal system is also more in accordance with Raz's insistence on the harmony between individual rights and the interest of the community, than with Dworkin and Waldron's conception of rights as 'trumps' against the collectivity. On Dworkin's conception of rights as trumps: R. Dworkin, *Taking Rights Seriously* (Harvard University Press 1977), R. Dworkin, 'Rights as Trumps' in Waldron J (ed), *Theories of Rights* (Oxford University Press 1984). On Raz's vision of rights: J. Raz, 'Rights and Individual Well-Being' (1992) 5 Ratio Juris 127. Another line of argument against seeing rights as trumps is advanced by Gewirth, 'Why Rights are Indispensable'.

385 Weiler, 'Van Gend en Loos: The individual as subject and object and the dilemma of European legitimacy' 96 quoting Hartley, *The Foundations of European Union Law* (Chapter 7, 'Direct effect and national remedies').

386 Eilmansberger, 'The Relationship between Rights and Remedies in EC Law: in Search of the Missing Link' 1205.

387 Masing, *Die Mobilisierung des Bürgers für die Durchsetzung des Rechts: europäische Impulse für eine Revision der Lehre vom subjektiv-öffentlichen Recht* 22.

388 Widdershoven, 'Naar een bestuurs(proces)rechtelijk Ius Commune in Europa' 191.

interests.[389] The original concept of individual rights under EU law is therefore the result of a double synthesis: of EU and individual interests, and of various conceptions of the relation between rights, obligations and interests in the domestic legal systems of the Union's Member States.

1.2. Structural and conceptual challenges after Lisbon

> *'Protecting rights effectively is not the same thing as talking or thinking about rights'*.[390]

Section 1.1 has highlighted that the EU concept of individual rights is the result of a balancing exercise between a variety of influences and requirements, both in terms of its nature (closely related with obligations) and its double function (of protecting individual interests while simultaneously advancing Union interests). The present section assesses whether these basic features might be altered due to the introduction of the Charter of Fundamental Rights in the EU legal order. The Treaty of Lisbon has made the Charter a part of EU primary law and an essential, if not the major, point of focus when discussing rights (especially fundamental rights) and the relation between the different sources of rights (1.2.1). However, somewhat paradoxically, the distinction between rights and principles enshrined in Article 52(5) of the Charter suggests that not all provisions in this document on 'fundamental rights' contain 'rights'. This distinction deserves close attention because of its potential impact on our understanding of rights (1.2.2). These factors of evolution give rise to conceptual problems for identifying and applying rights, with potential implications for the functioning of the modified constitutional framework of the Union as a whole (1.2.3).

---

389 Ruffert, 'Rights and Remedies in European Community Law: a Comparative View' 327; see also Callies, 'Kohärenz und Konvergenz beim europäischen Individualrechtsschutz - Der Zugang zum Gericht im Lichte des Grundrechts auf effektiven Rechtsschutz' 3579; Azoulai, 'L'autonomie de l'individu européen et la question du statut' 4; Lecourt, *L'Europe des juges* 260. Regarding direct effect, Eijsbouts describes it as a compact of several distinct component legal traditions: one centred on right (Germany), one on result (France), one on remedies (England). Eijsbouts, 'Direct Effect, the Test and the Terms. In Praise of a Capital Doctrine of EU Law' 241.

390 Simmonds, 'Rights at the Cutting Edge' 115.

1.2.1. The reconfiguration of the EU fundamental rights landscape

By giving the Charter the value of primary law, the Treaty of Lisbon has reorganised the EU's system of protection of fundamental rights. The debate about the relation between the sources of fundamental rights matters not only because of its implications for how the EU system of protection of rights works, but also because of what it says about, and how it can affect, our underlying understanding of rights. This section first presents the Charter and the Explanations relating to the Charter, providing an overview of the history and content of these documents (1.2.1.1 and 1.2.1.2). Then this section assesses the place and role of the Charter in the complex EU network of sources of rights and highlights the shift of focus that has undeniably been taking place, both in the case law and in the literature, as the Charter seems to be becoming the centre of gravity in the judicial and doctrinal discourse on rights, as well as potential problems arising from this approach (1.2.1.3). Finally, this section argues that acknowledging the complementarity of the different sources of rights is key for avoiding these problems (1.2.1.4).

1.2.1.1. Genesis and content of the Charter

The Preamble to the Charter states that '*it is necessary to strengthen the protection of fundamental rights in the light of changes in society, social progress and scientific and technological developments by making those rights more visible in a Charter*'.[391] Indeed, the EU originally had no written bill of rights, and none of the original treaties contained provisions aimed at protecting fundamental human rights.[392] As we saw previously, the first rights were identified in Treaty provisions on fundamental freedoms.[393] Although the

391 Preamble to the Charter.

392 Borowski, 'The Charter of Fundamental Rights in the Treaty on European Union' 201.

393 Take for example the free movement of goods, which imposes limits and obligations on Member States with regard to collecting custom duties and gives rise to correlative rights. *Van Gend en Loos* is of course the archetypal illustration, other prominent cases on the free movement of goods include: Judgment of 16 June 1966, *Lütticke v Hauptzollamt Saarlouis*, C-57/65, EU:C:1966:34, Judgment in *Politi v. Ministero delle finanze*, C-43/71, EU:C:1971:122, Judgment of 6 October 1970, *Grad v Finanzamt Traunstein*, 9/70, EU:C:1970:78.

Court, starting with *Stauder*,[394] developed abundant case law on the protection of fundamental rights and thus mitigated the original lacuna,[395] the focus on fundamental freedoms to the detriment of other types of rights such as fundamental rights, social and political rights is a recurring element in the attempts to explain the problem of the Union's 'legitimacy gap'.[396]

1.2.1.1.1. The historical difficulties for consecrating the indivisibility of rights

In the twentieth century it became common ground in the socio-political and philosophical thought '*that individual interests in such basic social and economic necessities as food, shelter and the wherewithal to pay for them, carry sufficient moral force to justify the imposition of corresponding obligations on states for their protection, and that they should be accorded the status of human rights.*'[397] This, in spite of the diverging views on the role of the State in so-

394 *Stauder*, C-26/69.

395 A. Rosas and H. Kaila, 'L'application de la Charte des droits fondamentaux de l'Union européenne par la Cour de justice : un premier bilan' [2011] Il Diritto dell'Unione Europea 1.

396 The issue was pointed out by the Commission itself in Commission Memorandum on Accession of the Communities to the European Convention on Human Rights (COM (79) final, Bulletin of the European Communities, Supplement 2/79). The abundant literature on the topic includes T.J. Friedbacher, 'Motive Unmasked: The European Court of Justice, the Free Movement of Goods and the Search for Legitimacy' (1996) 2 European Law Journal 226; M.A. Wilkinson, 'Civil Society and the Re-imagination of European Constitutionalism' (2003) 9 European Law Journal 451; S. Smismans, 'European Civil Society: Shaped by Discourses and Institutional Interests' (2003) 9 European Law Journal 473; V. Breda, 'A European Constitution in a Multinational Europe or a Multinational Constitution for Europe?' (2006) 12 European Law Journal 330; S. Wernicke, 'Au nom de qui? The European Court of Justice between Member States, Civil Society and Union Citizens' (2007) 13 European Law Journal 380; A.J. Menendez, 'The European Democratic Challenge: The Forging of a Supranational Volonté Générale' (2009) 15 European Law Journal 277; La Torre, 'The Law beneath Right's Feet. Preliminary Investigation for a Study of the Charter of Fundamental Rights of the European Union'; Borowski, 'The Charter of Fundamental Rights in the Treaty on European Union' 202.

397 Palmer, *Judicial Review, Socio-Economic Rights and the Human Rights Act* 13. E. Millard, 'La justiciabilité des droits sociaux : une question théorique et politique' La Revue des droits de l'homme (en ligne), 452 <http://revdh.revues.org/159> accessed 10 January 2017.

cial issues, has translated into the affirmation of social values at the supranational level since the 1960s. The International Covenant on Economic, Social and Cultural Rights dates back to 1966.[398] It is, however, not insignificant that the United Nations were careful to enshrine these economic and social provisions in a document distinct from the International Covenant on Civil and Political Rights – a precaution reflecting the ideological conflict in the Cold War context.[399] Moreover, Article 2, Paragraph 1 of the ICESCR makes the realisations of economic, social and cultural rights conditional on the economic development of the signatory States, thus acknowledging that these rights have financial implications which may limit their implementation.[400] The question of the justiciability of social rights is indeed often treated as an issue in itself (distinct from the issue of how to apply rights in general).[401] Within the Council of Europe, the European Social Charter has been adopted and with more tangible impact, the ECHR has given rise to an increasing amount of cases where positive (social) obligations are imposed on the States.[402]

398 UN General Assembly, *International Covenant on Economic, Social and Cultural Rights*, 16 December 1966, United Nations, Treaty Series, vol. 993, p. 3, available at: http://www.refworld.org/docid/3ae6b36c0.html [accessed 11 December 2015] (ICESCR).

399 Fredman, *Human Rights Transformed. Positive Rights and Positive Duties* 66; Palmer, *Judicial Review, Socio-Economic Rights and the Human Rights Act* 14. Supiot, *Homo juridicus. Essai sur la fonction anthropologique du Droit* (Seuil 2005) 293.

400 '*Each State Party to the present Covenant undertakes to take steps, individually and through international assistance and co-operation, especially economic and technical, to the maximum of its available resources, with a view to achieving progressively the full realization of the rights recognized in the present Covenant by all appropriate means, including particularly the adoption of legislative measures.*' See Ballot, *Les insuffisances de la notion de droits fondamentaux* 177.

401 Millard explains very well how the justiciability of social rights is a political issue at least as much as a legal one: Millard, 'La justiciabilité des droits sociaux : une question théorique et politique'. See also R. Keat, 'Individual Rights as Social Rights' (2015) 24 Social & Legal Studies 618; J. Holmwood, 'Social Rights and Complex Freedom: A Comment on Fernando Atria' (2015) Social & Legal Studies 614; D. Garland, 'On the Concept of 'Social Rights' (2015) 24 Social & Legal Studies 622; F. Atria, 'Social Rights: A Reply' (2015) 24 Social & Legal Studies 628.

402 For detailed developments on this see Palmer, *Judicial Review, Socio-Economic Rights and the Human Rights Act* 59.

The EEC Treaty contained a few provisions on social policy but those were mostly aspirational rather than legally enforceable (e.g. Article 117).[403] In particular, the development of social rights in the CJEU's case law are often said to have been mainly ways to prevent distortions of competition, instead of primarily pursuing social objectives. In line with the more general diagnosis that rights are instrumental to an economic integration purpose, Advocate General Poiares Maduro has argued that '*EU social rights are not conceived as rights corresponding to social entitlements that EU citizens can claim with regard to the European polity. They are conceived, instead, either as an instrument of undistorted competition or as a guarantee that such competition will not affect the level of social protection afforded by the Member States.*'[404] Barnard has also suggested that, because of the priority given to the protection of competition, there might be an intrinsic limitation to the development of social rights in the EU legal system.[405]

Nevertheless, socio-economic rights have undeniably seeped into the EC legal system. Indeed, one of the leading cases on direct effect, decisive in establishing the ECJ's method for identifying rights, was also a leading case on a social right: i.e. *Defrenne II*, '*in which the Court tried to (…) assert the legal validity of the social provisions of the Treaties*'.[406] To a certain extent, it certainly succeeded, considering the abundance of antidiscrimination case law that followed.[407] However the 1980s saw the rise of concerns about the negative impact of economic integration in the absence of a social dimen-

403 S. Fredman and M. Wesson, 'Social, Economic, and Cultural Rights' in D. Feldman (ed), *English Public Law* (2nd edn, Oxford University Press 2009) 473; De Burca, 'The Language of Rights and European Integration' 29; Palmer, *Judicial Review, Socio-Economic Rights and the Human Rights Act* 86.

404 Poiares Maduro, 'The Double Constitutional Life of the Charter of Fundamental Rights of the European Union' 285.

405 C. Barnard, 'The 'Opt-Out' for the UK and Poland from the Charter of Fundamental Rights: Triumph or Rhetoric over Reality?' *The Lisbon Treaty*, vol 11 (Springer 2008). Barnard looks especially at the famous *Laval* and so-called *Viking* cases (Judgment of 18 December 2007, *Laval un Partneri*, C-341/05, EU:C:2007:809 and *The International Transport Workers' Federation and The Finnish Seamen's Union*, C-438/05) and argues in view of the CJEU's use of the proportionality test on the right to strike in relation with fundamental freedoms, that the limits imposed by EU law might turn out to be more restrictive than those of some national legal systems.

406 Katrougalos, 'The Implementation of Social Rights in Europe' 306.

407 Examples in the area of gender discrimination include: Judgment of 10 April 1984, *Von Colson and Kamann v Land Nordrhein-Westfalen*, C-14/83, EU:C:1984:153; Judgment of 26 February 1986, *Marshall v. Southampton and South-West Hampshire Area Health Authority*, C-152/84, EU:C:1986:84; *Foster and*

sion. This led to the 1989 Community Charter of the Fundamental Social Rights of Workers, in fact a political declaration with limited practical impact.[408] Then came the Maastricht Treaty with provisions on education, public health, economic and social cohesion, as well as a reference to the European Social Charter[409] in the Preamble.[410] The alarm bells rang even louder following the defeat of the first referendum on this Treaty in Denmark and the narrow success in France. The importance of reinforcing rights of [411]workers and citizens and strengthening economic and social inclusion was made even clearer: it was necessary to show that the Community was also '*concerned with individuals and their rights rather than simply with markets and monetary union*'.[412] In this context the 1993 Vienna World Conference which asserted the interrelationship between different types of rights (social, political, economic) may also have impacted the debate.[413]

With the Treaty of Amsterdam[414] and then the Treaty of Nice,[415] social policy acquired new value: the aims of the Community were officially no longer limited to common market, competitiveness, and economic development: now there were also other priorities such as a high level of employment and social protection, equality between men and women, environmental protection, and raising of the standard of living. Articles 136 to 143 EC gave competence to the Community on social issues. Article 136 EC (now Article 151 TFEU) laid down ambitious social objectives by refer-

---

others v British Gas, C-188/89; Judgment of 5 October 2004, *Pfeiffer and Others*, Joined cases C-397/01 to C-403/01, EU:C:2004:584.

408 Benlolo-Carabot, 'Chapitre 2. Les droits sociaux dans l'ordre juridique de l'Union Européenne' 92.

409 Council of Europe, *European Social Charter (Revised)*, 3 May 1996, ETS 163, available at: http://www.refworld.org/docid/3ae6b3678.html [accessed 19 April 2017.

410 Katrougalos, 'The Implementation of Social Rights in Europe' 306.

411 Treaty on the European Union (OJ 1992 191/1) ('Maastricht Treaty').

412 S. Holland, 'Economic and Social Cohesion in the 1990's' in S. Martin (ed), *The Construction of Europe Essays in Honour of Emile Noël* (Kluwer Academic Publishers 1994), see especially 84-85. Of course, this was not a universally accepted view. For instance, the UK goverment was mostly satisfied with exclusively economic integration: see H. W. Micklitz and S. Weatherhill, *European Economic Law* (Asghate Dartmouth 1997) 1-3.

413 Fredman and Wesson, 'Social, Economic, and Cultural Rights' 457.

414 Treaty amending the Treaty on the European Union, the Treaties establishing the European Communities and certain related acts (OJ 1997 C 340/1) ('Treaty of Amsterdam').

415 Treaty of Nice amending the Treaty on European Union, the Treaties establishing the European Communities and certain related acts (OJ 2001 C 80) ('Treaty of Nice').

ring to '*fundamental social rights*'.[416] This is corroborated by the fact that although Article 136 EC (now Article 151 TFEU) already laid down ambitious social objectives by referring to '*fundamental social rights*', the development of these rights was expected, according to paragraph 3, to '*ensue not only from the functioning of the internal market, which will favour the harmonisation of social systems, but also from the procedures provided for in the Treaties and from the approximation of provisions laid down by law, regulation or administrative action*'. Nevertheless, the realisation of social rights was still envisaged mostly as a result of the accomplishment of the common market, the good functioning of which remains the central objective in the Treaties.[417] The progress was double-edged since the Treaty seemed to distinguish and isolate social rights from the fundamental rights now referred to in Article 6(2) TEU.[418] The distinction sustains the notion of a '*second class*' status of social rights, '*generally depicted as being positive (requiring state expenditure for their realisation), programmatic (merely specifying goals or objectives to be achieved) and non-justiciable (not amenable to being involved by individuals as the basis of claims before courts), in contrast with the essentially negative and justiciable first generation rights.*'[419]

1.2.1.1.2. A step forward: the Treaty of Lisbon and the Charter

As summarised by Habermas, one of the causes of the existing democratic deficit is that '*the direct actionability of basic economic freedoms as subjective rights has removed decisions over alternative economic policies for the most part from the democratic process*'.[420] So, rights as they were originally conceived

---

416 Benlolo-Carabot, 'Chapitre 2. Les droits sociaux dans l'ordre juridique de l'Union Européenne' 87.

417 Benlolo-Carabot, 'Chapitre 2. Les droits sociaux dans l'ordre juridique de l'Union Européenne' 87.

418 Poiares Maduro, 'The Double Constitutional Life of the Charter of Fundamental Rights of the European Union' 285; Fredman and Wesson, 'Social, Economic, and Cultural Rights' 475.

419 J. Hunt, 'Fair and Just Working Conditions' in T. Hervey and J. Kenner (eds), *Economic and Social Rights under the EU Charter of Fundamental Rights A Legal Perspective* (Hart 2003) 47. See also, on the depiction of civil-political rights as subjective and social rights as objective obligations: X. Contiades and A. Fotiadou, 'Social rights in the age of proportionality: Global economic crisis and constitutional litigation' (2012) 10 International Journal of Constitutional Law 660 664.

420 J. Habermas, 'Democracy in Europe: Why the Development of the EU into a Transnational Democracy Is Necessary and How It Is Possible' (2015) 21 Euro-

might be part of the problem.[421] The Charter embodies the belief that they could also be part of the solution by reflecting *'values with which, intrinsically, most people can readily identify'*.[422] The Charter also constitutes an attempt to correct the EU's *'social deficit'*,[423] and has been welcome as a negation of the divide between civil-political rights and social rights, all included in a single document and organised thematically.[424] As Kenner argues, *'the Charter's proclamation of indivisible values and its express reference to solidarity alongside dignity, equality and freedom, sends a clear message that the EU*

---

pean Law Journal 546 547. See also Weiler, 'Van Gend en Loos: The individual as subject and object and the dilemma of European legitimacy'.

421 The original lack of a clear statement on individual rights is far from being the only reason suggested for the 'legitimacy gap'. Other often suggested reasons include the weakness of the European Parliament, the lack of transparency in policy-making, accountability issues. See Saurugger, *Théories et concepts de l'intégration européenne* 333-335 for a detailed review of the theories advancing explanations for the legitimacy gap and the democratic deficit, and an overview of the various theorisations of the notion of 'legitimacy'.

422 Kenner, 'Economic and Social Rights in the EU Legal Order: The Mirage of Indivisibility' 4. See also K. Lenaerts, 'Fundamental Rights to be included in a Community Catalogue' (1991) 16 European Law Review 367; D. Neacsu, 'The Draft of the EU Charter of Fundamental Rights: A Step in the Process of Legitimizing EU as a Political Entity and Economic-Social Rights as Fundamental Human Rights' (2001) 7 Columbia Journal of European Law 141; J.H.H. Weiler, 'A Constitution for Europe? Some Hard Choices' (2002) 40 Journal of Common Market Studies 563; Rosas and Kaila, 'L'application de la Charte des droits fondamentaux de l'Union européenne par la Cour de justice : un premier bilan' 9; Saurugger, *Théories et concepts de l'intégration européenne* 326; H. Raulus, 'The Charter of Fundamental Rights as a set of constitutional principles' in M. Trybus and L. Rubini (eds), *The Treaty of Lisbon and the Future of European Law and Policy* (The Treaty of Lisbon and the Future of European Law and Policy, Edward Elgar 2012) 181; E. Muir, 'The Court of Justice: a fundamental rights institution among others' in M. Dawson, B. De Witte and E. Muir (eds), *Judicial Activism at the European Court of Justice* (Edward Elgar 2013) 79. Back in 1979 the Commission listed as the main advantages of having the Community adhere to a catalogue of human rights (whether through accession to the ECHR, or through the drafting of its own fundamental rights document): *'Improving the image of Europe as an area of freedom and democracy'*, *'Strengthening the protection of fundamental rights in the Community'* and *'Strengthening of institutions'*. Commission Memorandum on Accession of the Communities to the European Convention on Human Rights (COM (79) final, Bulletin of the European Communities, Supplement 2/79) 11-12.

423 Katrougalos, 'The Implementation of Social Rights in Europe'.

424 Fredman and Wesson, 'Social, Economic, and Cultural Rights' 455.

institutions, when carrying out their obligations, will be bound to take note of the more elevated position that economic and social rights now occupy.'[425]

To a certain extent, this means that the often-criticised instrumental rationale of rights, oriented towards the integrative *telos* of the EU, does not disappear with the Charter: the insistence on rights remains a way of legitimising the European legal order and integration process,[426] meaning that rights remain means to an end. Nevertheless, the shift in emphasis from fundamental freedoms to fundamental rights denotes an evolution in the perception of the holders of these various rights: individuals are no longer perceived primarily as economic agents with market-related rights,[427] but also as citizens,[428] and even simply as persons, since many, if not most of the fundamental rights enshrined in the Charter are not reserved to EU citizens but instead apply to 'everyone'.[429] The accumulation of these levels

---

425 Kenner, 'Economic and Social Rights in the EU Legal Order: The Mirage of Indivisibility' 15. On the indivisibility of rights see also La Torre, 'The Law beneath Right's Feet. Preliminary Investigation for a Study of the Charter of Fundamental Rights of the European Union' 534 and the Communication from the Commission on the legal nature of the Charter of Fundamental Rights of the European Union, 28.10.2000 (COM (2000) 664 final). This has not solved all issues, however: implementation deficit of socio-economic rights: European Parliament resolution of 19 January 2017 on a European Pillar of Social Rights (2016/2095(INI).

426 De Burca, 'The Language of Rights and European Integration' 40.

427 A broad definition of 'worker' was developed starting with Judgment of 19 March 1964, *Unger v Bedrijfsvereniging voor Detailhandel en Ambachten*, C-75/63, EU:C:1964:19.

428 ;E. Meehan, 'Citizenship and the European Community' (1993) 64 The Political Quarterly 172; N. Reich, 'Union Citizenship - Metaphor or Source of Rights?' (2001) 7 European Law Journal 4; S. Kadelbach, 'Union Citizenship' in A. Von Bogdandy and J. Bast (eds), *Principles of European Constitutional Law* (Hart Publishing 2006); L. Azoulai, 'The (Mis)Construction of the European Individual. Two Essays on Union Citizenship Law' EUI Working Paper, Law 2014/14.

429 'Everyone' has the right to life (Article 2(1)), to the integrity of the person (Article 3(1), to liberty and security (Article 6), to respect for private and family life (Article 7), to protection of personal data (Article 8), to freedom of thought, conscience and religion (Article 10), to freedom of expression and information (Article 11), to freedom of assembly and of association (Article 12), to education (Article 14), to engage in work (Article 15(1)), to property (Article 17), to health care (Article 35), to an effective remedy and a fair trial (Article 47), to presumption of innocence (Article 48); 'everyone' is also equal before the law (Article 20); 'no one' shall be subjected to torture or inhuman or degrading treatment (Article 4), held in slavery or forced labour (Article 5), held guilty of any criminal offence on account of any act or omission which did not constitute a crimi-

emphasises the diversity of functions of EC law[430] and goes against a purely instrumentalist explanation for the codification of fundamental rights, especially socio-economic and social fundamental rights.

However, the negotiations over the drafting of the Charter by the First Convention, in 1999-2000, highlighted a conflict between two diametrically opposed visions (which, not surprisingly roughly corresponds to the schematic opposition between the English and continental visions of social rights described in the previous section). On the one hand, the United Kingdom, Denmark and the Netherlands were against making social rights legally enforceable.[431] In the context of the negotiations over the Charter, the United Kingdom was especially concerned over the right to strike.[432] On the other hand, governments such as the French and the Spanish rejected the idea of a systematic distinction between social and civil rights. In order to overcome the division, Guy Braibant introduced the notion of '*justiciabilité normative*',[433] allowing for two different degrees of justiciability: a

---

nal offence under national law or international law at the time when it was committed (Article 49), tried or punished twice for the same criminal offence (Article 50); and 'every person' has rights to good administration (Article 41),.

430 J. Shaw, 'Citizens' Rights and Access to Law' in H.-W. Micklitz and N. Reich (eds), *Public Interest Litigation before European Courts* (Nomos 1997) 243.

431 L. Burgorgue-Larsen, 'L'article II-112' in L. Burorgue-Larsen, A. Levade and F. Picod (eds), *Traité établissant une Constitution pour l'Europe : commentaire article par article Tome 2, Partie II La Charte des droits fondamentaux de l'Union* (Bruylant 2005) 683; Krommendijk, 'Principled Silence or Mere Silence on Principles? The Role of the EU Charter's Principles in the Case Law of the Court of Justice' 324; P. Craig, 'Rights, Legality, and Legitimacy' in P. Craig (ed) *The Lisbon Treaty: Law, Politics, and Treaty Reform* (Oxford University Press 2010) 216; Supiot, *Homo juridicus. Essai sur la fonction anthropologique du Droit* 310. On the Dutch view point see also R. Barents, 'Een grondwet voor Europa (VI): de grondrechten' (2005) Nederlands tijdschrift voor Europees recht 39 40.

432 Krommendijk, 'Principled Silence or Mere Silence on Principles? The Role of the EU Charter's Principles in the Case Law of the Court of Justice' 324.

433 EU Network of Independent Experts on Fundamental Rights, 'Commentary of the Charter" <http://ec.europa.eu/justice/fundamental-rights/files/networkcommentaryfinal_en.pdf> accessed 9 October 2015; G. Braibant, *La Charte des droits fondamentaux de l'Union européenne* (Seuil 2001) 45-46; Ballot, *Les insuffisances de la notion de droits fondamentaux* 202; Krommendijk, 'Principled Silence or Mere Silence on Principles? The Role of the EU Charter's Principles in the Case Law of the Court of Justice' 326; L. Burgorgue-Larsen, 'Ombres et Lumières de la constitutionnalisation de la Charte des droits fondamentaux de l'Union européenne' (2004) Cahiers de droit européen 683 683; Roman, 'La justiciabilité des droits sociaux ou les enjeux de l'édification d'un Etat de droit social'9.

compromise thus was found in a distinction between 'rights' and 'principles', enshrined at Article 51(1) and 52(5) of the Charter.[434]

The Charter did not become a full-fledged bill of rights overnight. On October 2, 2000, the EU Convention, specially constituted by the European Council to compose an EU draft Charter of Fundamental Rights, officially issued the said draft.[435] The Charter was then adopted in Nice as a non-binding instrument, which led some observers to regret the '*thinness*' of its original normative status.[436] Nevertheless, its high symbolic and political value was soon acknowledged by the EU Institutions[437] and both the Court of Justice and the ECtHR made use of it in their judgments.[438] The Treaty establishing a Constitution for Europe[439] would have made the Charter an integral part of the said Constitution. The rejection of that Treaty and the subsequent adoption of the Treaty of Lisbon have placed the

434 European Commissioner for Justice and Home Affairs Vitorino stated that this distinction was '*an important element of the overall consensus*'. Vitorino, Speaking points European Convention, 29 October 2002, Brussels, SPEECH/02/531.

435 More detailed accounts of the process: e.g. Neacsu, 'The Draft of the EU Charter of Fundamental Rights: A Step in the Process of Legitimizing EU as a Political Entity and Economic-Social Rights as Fundamental Human Rights'.

436 M. La Torre, 'The Law beneath Right's Feet. Preliminary Investigation for a Study of the Charter of Fundamental Rights of the European Union' (2002) 8 European Law Journal 515 533.

437 Rosas and Kaila, 'L'application de la Charte des droits fondamentaux de l'Union européenne par la Cour de justice : un premier bilan' 4-5. Commission Communication on the Charter of Fundamental Rights of the European Union, 13.9.2000 (COM(2000) 559 final). See also European Parliament resolution of 15 March 2007 on compliance with the Charter of Fundamental Rights in the Commission's legislative proposals: methodology for systematic and rigorous monitoring, 15.3.2007 (2005/2169(INI)).

438 Rosas and Kaila, 'L'application de la Charte des droits fondamentaux de l'Union européenne par la Cour de justice : un premier bilan' 6-8. Judgment of 30 January 2002, *max.mobil v Commission*, T-54/99, EU:T:2002:20, para 48 on Article 41 CFR; Judgment of 27 June 2006, *Parliament v Council*, C-540/03, EU:C:2006:429, paras 38 and 58 concerning the right to respect for private and family life and the rights of the child; Judgment of 13 March 2007, *Unibet*, C-432/05, EU:C:2007:163, para 37, citing Article 47 on principle of effective judicial protection. As for ECtHR judgments, see e.g. *Goodwin v United Kingdom*, n °28957/95 (ECHR 2002) paras 58 and 100, and *Bosphorus Hava Yollari Turizm ve Ticaret Anonim Şirketi v Ireland*, n°45036/98 (ECHR 2005), paras 80-81. See B. Dickson 'The EU Charter of Fundamental Rights in the case law of the European Court of Human Rights' European Human Rights Law Review 2015(1) 27.

439 Treaty establishing a Constitution for Europe, OJ 2004 C 310/1.

Charter in a different position, distinct from the Treaties yet of equal legal value, as laid down in Article 6(1) TEU.[440]

Resulting from a complex and laborious negotiation process, the Charter contains a broad range of types and generations of rights. It opens with an introductory Preamble which grounds the Charter in the Union's common 'values' while also insisting on protecting the diversity through which these values manifest. The rights are consecrated into the following categories: Dignity, Freedoms, Equality, Solidarity, Citizens' Rights, and Justice. The Charter is allegedly not meant to create new rights,[441] and instead consists in codification of pre-existing rights, many of them were recognised as fundamental rights through the medium of general principles of EU law – such as the right to an effective remedy (Article 47) and the various components of good administration. Others are more innovative and surprising, and build on pre-existing secondary legislation, such as the workers' right to participation in the undertaking (Article 27) or the right to the protection of personal data (Article 8). The catalogue thus includes civil and political rights as well as economic and social rights.[442] The final section entitled 'General Provisions' governs the interpretation and application of the other provisions, dealing with the 'Field of application' (Article 51), the 'Scope and interpretation of rights and principles' (Article 52, thus organised around a distinction between 'rights' and 'principles', to be further investigated below), the 'Level of protection' (Article 53) and the 'Prohibition of abuse of rights'. All this makes for a substantial and complex bill of rights, which is accompanied by an additional explanatory document.

---

440 Consolidated Version of the Treaty on European Union, OJ 2010 C 83/01 ('TEU').

441 Preamble to the Protocol on the application of the Charter of Fundamental Rights of the European Union to Poland and to the United Kingdom (2007 OJ C 306/156): '*Whereas the Charter reaffirms the rights, freedoms and principles recognised in the Union and makes those rights more visible, but does not create new rights or principles*'. L. Goldsmith, 'The Charter of Rights-A Brake Not an Accelerator' (2004) European Human Rights Law Review 473; Borowski, 'The Charter of Fundamental Rights in the Treaty on European Union' 213; C. Barnard, 'The "Opt-Out" for the UK and Poland from the Charter of Fundamental Rights: Triumph or Rhetoric over Reality?', *The Lisbon Treaty*, vol 11 (Springer 2008).

442 The juxtaposition was very difficult for some Member States, especially the UK, to conceptualise and accept. Goldsmith, 'The Charter of Rights-A Brake Not an Accelerator'; Barnard, 'The "Opt-Out" for the UK and Poland from the Charter of Fundamental Rights: Triumph or Rhetoric over Reality?' 4.

1.2.1.2. The Explanations to the Charter: an atypical 'tool of interpretation'

The Charter is complemented by a document called the 'Explanations to the Charter',[443] the existence of which is rather peculiar since no other instance of a constitutional document or of a 'bill of rights' type document being accompanied by such a document comes to mind. The Preamble of the Charter states that:

> *'This Charter reaffirms, with due regard for the powers and tasks of the Union and for the principle of subsidiarity, the rights as they result, in particular, from the constitutional traditions and international obligations common to the Member States, the European Convention for the Protection of Human Rights and Fundamental Freedoms, the Social Charters adopted by the Union and by the Council of Europe and the case-law of the Court of Justice of the European Union and of the European Court of Human Rights. In this context* the Charter will be interpreted by the courts of the Union and the Member States with due regard to the explanations *prepared under the authority of the Praesidium of the Convention which drafted the Charter and updated under the responsibility of the Praesidium of the European Convention.'*[444]

The Explanations themselves are introduced by the following paragraph:

> *'These explanations were originally prepared under the authority of the Praesidium of the Convention which drafted the Charter of Fundamental Rights of the European Union. They have been updated under the responsibility of the Praesidium of the European Convention, in the light of the drafting adjustments made to the text of the Charter by that Convention (notably to Articles 51 and 52) and of further developments of Union law. Although they do not as such have the status of law, they are a* valuable tool of interpretation intended to clarify the provisions of the Charter.'

The Explanations are thus presented as a 'tool of interpretation' to which courts interpreting and applying the Charter must pay 'due regard'. Looking then at the body of the Explanations, we find that they provide, for each Article of the Charter, the original source (or sources) in which the corresponding content was first developed. This is consistent with the

443 Explanations relating to the Charter of Fundamental Rights, 2007 OJ C 303/17 ('Explanations').

444 Preamble of the CFR, fifth paragraph. (emphasis added).

Preamble of the Charter stating that the Charter 'reaffirms' rights which 'result' from various instruments. The variety in terms of sources and intensity of inspiration from these sources is striking and reflects the diversity of the subject-matter of the Charter.

The sources cited, along with relevant case law, provide an exhaustive overview of legal instruments in which rights (not only fundamental rights) have been found in the history of the EU. The recurring sources, not surprisingly, include provisions of the Treaties (TEU, TFEU but also pre-Lisbon primary law), of the ECHR (sometimes in combination with relevant ECtHR case law),[445] of national constitutional traditions, as well as general principles of EU law. The latter are mentioned along with relevant CJEU case law. The case law of the Court of Justice is sometimes also mentioned as a source even if the provision does not clearly reflect a general principle of EU law.[446] In addition, a variety of international conventions feature in the Explanations.[447] There are also several references to EU secondary law in explanations on provisions on human trafficking,[448] data

445 One of the motives for giving a special place to the Explanations was that there had to be a way to include ECHR protection while simultaneously preserving the autonomy of the EU legal order. Burgorgue-Larsen, 'Ombres et Lumières de la constitutionnalisation de la Charte des droits fondamentaux de l'Union européenne' 671-673.

446 See for instance the explanatory paragraph on Article 41 on the right to good administration.

447 UN General Assembly, *Universal Declaration of Human Rights*, 10 December 1948, 217 A (III), available at: http://www.refworld.org/docid/3ae6b3712c.html [accessed 19 April 2017]; Council of Europe, *Convention for the Protection of Individuals with Regard to the Automatic Processing of Individual Data*, 28 January 1981, ETS 108, available at: http://www.refworld.org/docid/3dde1005a.html [accessed 19 April 2017]; European Social Charter; UN General Assembly, *Convention Relating to the Status of Refugees*, 28 July 1951, United Nations, Treaty Series, vol. 189, p. 137, available at: http://www.refworld.org/docid/3be01b964.html [accessed 19 April 2017]; Council of Europe, *Convention on Human Rights and Biomedicine*, 4 April 1997, ETS 164; UN General Assembly, *Convention on the Rights of the Child*, 20 November 1989, United Nations, Treaty Series, vol. 1577, p. 3, available at: http://www.refworld.org/docid/3ae6b38f0.html [accessed 19 April 2017]; UN General Assembly, *International Covenant on Civil and Political Rights*, 16 December 1966, United Nations, Treaty Series, vol. 999, p. 171, available at: http://www.refworld.org/docid/3ae6b3aa0.html [accessed 11 December 2015].

448 Council Framework Decision of 19 July 2002 on combating trafficking in human beings, OJ L 203, 01/08/2002 p.1-4.

protection[449] and labour law;[450] conventions concluded between EU Member States,[451] EU 'soft' law[452] and protocols or annexes to the Treaties. Customary law is also credited, with Article 49 being said to: '*[follow] the traditional rule*' of non-retroactivity. The Explanations even rely on fact, not law, as a basis for the prohibition of trafficking in human beings, referring to '*recent developments*' in organised crime and presenting Article 5, paragraph 3 as a response to these developments.

---

449 Parliament and Council Directive 95/46/EC of 24 October 1995 on the protection of individuals with regard to the processing of personal data and on the free movement of such data (OJ L 281 p. 31), Parliament and Council Regulation (EC) No 45/2001 of 18 December 2000 on the protection of individuals with regard to the processing of personal data by the Community institutions and bodies and on the free movement of such data (OJ L 8 p. 1) (the 'Data Protection Directive' and the 'Data Protection Regulation').

450 Parliament and Council Directive 2002/14/EC of 11 March 2002 establishing a general framework for informing and consulting employees in the European Community (OJ L 80 p. 29-34) Council Directive 98/59/EC of 20 July 1998 on the approximation of the laws of the Member States relating to collective redundancies (OJ L 225 p. 16-21), Council Directive 2001/23/EC of 12 March 2001 on the approximation of the laws of the Member States relating to the safeguarding of employees' rights in the event of transfers of undertakings, businesses or parts of undertakings or businesses (OJ L 82 p. 16), Council Directive 94/45/EC of 22 September 1994 on the establishment of a European Works Council or a procedure in Community-scale undertakings and Community-scale groups of undertakings for the purposes of informing and consulting employees (OJ L 254 p. 64), Council Directive 92/85/EEC of 19 October 1992 on the introduction of measures to encourage improvements in the safety and health at work of pregnant workers and workers who have recently given birth or are breastfeeding (tenth individual Directive within the meaning of Article 16 (1) of Directive 89/391/EEC) (OJ L 348 p. 1), Council Directive 96/34/EC of 3 June 1996 on the framework agreement on parental leave concluded by UNICE, CEEP and the ETUC (OJ L 145 p. 4).

451 Convention implementing the Schengen Agreement of 14 June 1985 between the Governments of the States of the Benelux Economic Union, the Federal Republic of Germany and the French Republic on the gradual abolition of checks at their common borders (OJ L 239, 22/09/2000, p. 19), Convention drawn up on the basis of Article K.3 of the Treaty on European Union, on the protection of the European Communities' financial interests (OJ C 316, 27/11/1995, p. 49), Convention drawn up on the basis of Article K.3 (2) (c) of the Treaty on European Union on the fight against corruption involving officials of the European Communities or officials of Member States of the European Union (OJ C 195, 25/06/1997, p. 2).

452 Community Charter of the Fundamental Social Rights of Workers, adopted at the meeting of the European Council held in Strasbourg on 9 December 1989.

The inspiration from these various sources is more or less loose depending on the provision. This is marked by a terminological gradation. Those provisions that are truly copied from other sources are explained with terms such as 'corresponds to', 'reproduces', 'is the same as', 'is the right guaranteed by', 'has the same wording' and 'therefore has the same meaning and the same scope'; and the explanatory paragraph on Article 36 even states that this provision 'is fully in line with' Article 14 TFEU. Where inspiration is looser one will see terms such as 'is/has been based on', 'draws on' (implying then a possibly different scope), 'is included in', 'has been taken over', 'is deduced primarily from', 'incorporates'. These terms reinforce the idea from the preamble that the Charter 'reaffirms' an array of rights originating in different sources, but does not as such create new rights.

Lastly, there is variety also in the way the different sources and types of inspiration are combined. Some fundamental rights already recognised as such by the Court, for instance the right to an effective remedy, are unsurprisingly explained by reference to general principles of EU law and ECHR (with the Explanations to Article 47 pointing out that the general principle shaped by CJEU's case law provides 'more extensive protection' than the relevant ECHR provisions). Other mixes of influences are more daring, such as the one at the basis of Article 8 on the protection of personal data: Treaty provisions (286 TEC, now 16 TFEU and 39 TEU), Council of Europe instruments (Article 8 ECHR and Council of Europe Convention for the Protection of Individuals with regard to Automatic Processing of Data), and the Data Protection Directive and Regulation. The right to the protection of personal data therefore is 'upgraded' to the status of fundamental right.[453] However, the explanations indicate that the directive and the regulation '*contain conditions and limitations*' for the exercise of this right, making clear that pre-existing instruments of secondary law may condition and limit the exercise of a right enshrined in the Charter.

Following the order of the provisions in the Charter, the Explanations end with substantial developments on the Charter's 'General provisions'.[454] Each of these provisions is explained with an introductory sentence focused on the aim underlying it: '*the aim of Article 51 is to…*', '*the purpose of Article 52 is to…*', Article 53 '*is intended to*'. By contrast with the diversity of

453 K. Lenaerts, "In the Union we trust': Trust-enhancing principles of Community law' (2004) 41 Common Market Law Review 317 322.

454 See an analysis of the Charter's General provisions: S. Peers, 'Taking Rights Away? Limitations and Derogations', in S. Peers, A. Ward (eds), *The European Union Charter of Fundamental Rights* (Hart Publishing 2004) 141 154-160.

sources mentioned in other sections, in this section the Explanations rely mostly on CJEU case law and on the Treaties. The correspondence between Charter and ECHR provisions is listed in a systematic manner in the Explanations on Article 52. The Explanations on Article 52 especially, attempt to sort out the relationship between the Charter and the numerous sources that have given rise to the rights that it contains – and it is simultaneously an acknowledgement that Article 52 alone does not solve all the issues.

Although the Explanations are '*intended to clarify the provisions of the Charter*', they have also created the need for further clarification – concerning their own status and how they are to be used. The uncertainty was reflected in the questions asked by the UK Members of Parliament to Professor David Edward, former judge at the CJEU, when he was interviewed by the British Parliament's European Scrutiny Committee.[455] He pointed out that interpretation with 'due regard' in the French version of the Preamble is '*en prenant dûment en considération*', which he argues might even be '*slightly weaker than in English*'. In his view, the phrase means that '*you shall look at them, and you shall look at them seriously but you are not bound by them if your interpretation of the principal text in a given situation leads you to a different conclusion*'. Judging from the minutes of the interview, this did not enlighten the MPs, who were rather unsatisfied with his answers. Ironically, even the Court of Justice at first did not seem to know what to make of the Explanations: the first ruling mentioning the Explanations simply points out their uselessness for the issue at hand; this was case *DEB* admitting that the Explanations did not '*provide any clarification*' as to whether Article 47 applied also to legal persons.[456]

The insistence on the source or combination of sources for each right makes the Explanations look a bit like a summary of the preparatory works that led to the adoption of the Charter. Encouraging recourse to such documents for purposes of interpretation is an innovation in the EU legal order. As explained in Part I, the Court has traditionally used teleological and systemic arguments when interpreting provisions of EU law, especially when assessing the existence of rights in such provisions. Literal and intentionalist arguments, by contrast, were of little relevance in the Court's rea-

455 D.O.A. Edward, Oral Evidence Taken before the European Scrutiny Committee on Wednesday 17 November 2004, uncorrected transcript available at https://www.publications.parliament.uk/pa/cm200304/cmselect/cmeuleg/uc1064-ii/uc106402.htm (accessed 18 April 2017). V. Miller, The Treaty Establishing a Constitution for Europe: Part II (The Charter of Fundamental Rights) (House of Commons Library, Research Paper 04/85, 2004) 41-42.

456 Judgment of 22 December 2010, *DEB*, C-279/09, EU:C:2010:811, para 39.

soning. Accordingly, the Court classically paid no attention to the preparatory works that had led to the adoption of a provision under its scrutiny.[457] In so doing, it distanced itself from the classic methods of interpretation of international law.[458] However, Lenaerts has argued that the interpretative value of the Explanations should be higher than that of *travaux préparatoires* since the Charter itself (as well as Article 6(1), third sentence TEU) stresses the importance of the Explanations.[459] In the same vein, Burgorgue-Larsen has suggested that the Explanations should be understood as 'context' in the meaning of the Vienna Convention on the interpretation of Treaties, to be used as an element of interpretation of a treaty.[460]

It seems that these suggestions have been heard: the Court acknowledged expressly in *Åkerberg Fransson* that the Explanations '*have to be taken into consideration for the purpose of interpreting*' the Charter.[461] So far Advocates General have referred to the Explanations in a little less than a hundred cases, and the CJEU in slightly more than fifty cases.[462] These are not huge numbers relatively to the more than 1200 rulings and opinions involving the Charter itself, but they still denote that 'due regard' or at least 'regard' is being granted to the Explanations much more than to classic

457 S. Miettinen and M. Kettunen, 'Travaux to the Treaties: Treasures or trivia?' (European Studies Association conference, Boston 5 March 2015) suggest also that the explanation could work the other way around: as preparatory works were not systematically available, the Court was not incentivised to develop a reflex of checking them for guidance.

458 Vienna Convention, Articles 31 and 32; see especially Article 31, paragraph 1, which provides that "*A treaty shall be interpreted in good faith in accordance with the ordinary meaning to be given to the terms of the treaty in their context and in the light of its object and purpose*.' A. Kostova-Bourgeix, 'Cour de justice, 1er mars 2005, *A. Owusu c/ N.B. Jackson*, aff. C-281/02' Revue des affaires européennes 307, 314, points out that even though there is no explicit reference to preparatory works in most CJEU case law, it cannot be categorically excluded that this category of documents would still have an influence on how the judges reach the final solution to a case. In addition, EU international private law is a particular area where preparatory works are published in the form of communications in the official journal and probably have more direct influence on the interpretation of the relevant EU legal instruments.

459 Lenaerts, 'Exploring the Limits of the EU Charter of Fundamental Rights.'

460 Burgorgue-Larsen, 'Ombres et Lumières de la constitutionnalisation de la Charte des droits fondamentaux de l'Union européenne' 674.

461 Judgment of 26 February 2013, *Åkerberg Fransson*, C-617/10, EU:C:2013:105, para 20. See also Judgment of 5 April 2017, *Orsi*, Joined cases C-217/15 and C-350/15, EU:C:2017:264, para 19).

462 A search on the CJEU's website (www.curia.europa.eu) on 1 June 2017 showed 85 opinions and 57 judgments mentioning the Explanations.

preparatory works, which the Court has explicitly relied on in only three cases so far for interpreting the Treaties.[463] In two judgments on discrimination on the basis of religion, concerning the wearing of the Islamic headscarf in the workplace, the Court referred to the Explanations in order to emphasise the connection between the general principles of EU law, the ECHR and the Charter as sources of the right to freedom of conscience and religion.[464] The Explanations thus anchor the Charter in an intricate network of sources of rights. Yet they do not answer all questions on the relation between these different sources of rights.

1.2.1.3. The Charter at the heart of the rights discourse

The Treaty of Lisbon has included the Charter in the complex '*architectonic*' that constitutes the EU system of protection of fundamental rights.[465] To a certain extent, the Charter is even becoming the centre of gravity of this system. However, an excessive focus on the Charter, to the detriment of other sources of rights, could paradoxically weaken the system of protection of individuals in the EU legal order.

While there had been fears that the Charter would be relegated to '*a sort of purgatory*' because of its position outside of the Treaties,[466] the opposite is happening. It is often advocated that the new layer of protection that the Charter constitutes should be granted priority as a source of fundamental

---

463 These three cases were the so-called 'Euratom' case (Judgment of 12 April 2005, *Commission v United Kingdom*, C-61/03, EU:C:2005:210), the *Pringle* case (Judgment of 27 November 2012, *Pringle*, C-370/12, EU:C:2012:756, para 137), and *Inuit* where it even explicitly admits that preparatory works may also provide information relevant to the interpretation of a provision (Judgment of 3 October 2013, *Inuit Tapiriit Kanatami and Others v Parliament and Council*, C-583/11 P, EU:C:2013:625, para 50). S. Miettinen and M. Kettunen, 'Travaux to the Treaties: Treasures or trivia?' (European Studies Association conference, Boston 5 March 2015) 6-8.

464 Judgment of 14 March 2017, *G4S Secure Solutions*, C-157/15, EU:C:2017:203, para 27 and Judgment of 14 March 2017, *Bougnaoui and ADDH*, C-188/15, EU:C:2017:204, para 29.

465 Borowski, 'The Charter of Fundamental Rights in the Treaty on European Union' 205.

466 J. Baquero Cruz, 'What's Left of the Charter? Reflections on Law and Political Mythology' (2008) 15 Maastricht Journal of European and Comparative Law 65 68.

rights;[467] more concretely, that '*the Charter should be regarded as a starting point or primary source in identifying the existence of a particular right or principle*'.[468] This would imply that other classic sources of fundamental rights, such as the Treaties and general principles of EU law, would have a relatively lesser weight in the process of identifying such rights. The place left to general principles in this context varies from one author to the other. On the one hand, it has been suggested that they should retain an essential role in rights adjudication because of the crucial 'gap-filling' function that they fulfil.[469] On the other hand, it has been argued that the Charter could become the authoritative source of fundamental rights, with the general principles performing a more modest role, being '*dormant*' in most situations;[470] they would no longer constitute the '*core norms of human rights protection*' since the Charter has become '*the key fundamental standard*' of the EU legal order, while the general principles are '*only ancillary*' to it.[471] Proponents of the latter approach argue that an exclusive (or at least primary) focus on the Charter for matters of protection of fundamental rights would allow for more clarity and transparency and a more consistent definition of the limitations to these rights. Moreover, the option of seeing the Charter as an additional source of fundamental rights alongside the traditional sources is dismissed by many authors who insist that this would only '*add another layer of complexity to the present situation, instead of clarifying things*' and therefore lead to the creation of a legal '*junkspace*'.[472] Putting the Charter at the summit of the hierarchy of sources of rights is thus advocated as the solution which will guarantee the visibility of rights and legal certainty as to their applicability.

A connected argument is that the Charter signals a shift in the CJEU's role, from '*pro-integration court*' to a '*protecting court*' and '*human rights adju-*

467 Borowski, 'The Charter of Fundamental Rights in the Treaty on European Union' 216.

468 Raulus, 'The Charter of Fundamental Rights as a set of constitutional principles' 190.

469 B. Mihaescu Evans, 'The 'gaps' in protection stemming from the (problematic) coexistence of fundamental rights' sources in the EU legal order' (2016) Cahiers de droit européen.

470 M. Dougan, 'The Treaty of Lisbon 2007: Winning Minds, Not Hearts' (2008) 45 Common Market Law Review 617 664.

471 Lorenz, Groussot and Petursson, *The European Human Rights Culture - A Paradox of Human Rights Protection in Europe?* 172.

472 Baquero Cruz, 'What's Left of the Charter? Reflections on Law and Political Mythology' 67.

dicator'[473] – although it is not clear why these two roles (integration and protection) should be incompatible. The Charter could have an impact not only on the role of the Court but on how the latter performs it, as suggested by Muir: '*While for many years the EU, and therefore also the Court of Justice, was primarily focused on identifying fundamental rights, the new challenge is now to flesh out these rights: interpret them, identify their limits and balance them with each other.*'[474] The assumption is that the Charter unburdens the Court from the task of identifying rights and shifts its responsibility towards applying them.

Applying the Charter has for sure become daily business for the Court,[475] and it appears that indeed the Charter constitutes a welcome starting point for identifying rights. Advocate General Trstenjak has proposed that the Charter be used '*as the starting point of interpretation for all other rules of EU law, including general legal principles*'.[476] Similarly, Advocate General Cruz Villalón considers that the Charter is now the primary source of the prohibition on discrimination[477] and of the right to the respect for private and family life and the right to the protection of personal data[478], and that general principles become merely secondary as sources for the same rights. In the rulings of the Court of Justice there is now also a tendency to refer to the Charter as the primary source of fundamental rights, with more limited references to the Treaties and to the general principles of EU law than in the pre-Lisbon case law.[479] The Charter is very often the '*default starting point*'[480] for reasoning on fundamental rights issues in the CJEU's case law, with the Court relying less systematically on gener-

---

473 G. De Burca, 'After the EU Charter of Fundamental Rights: The Court of Justice as a Human Rights Adjudicator?' (2013) 20 Maastricht Journal of European and Comparative Law 168.

474 Muir, 'The Court of Justice: a fundamental rights institution among others' 85.

475 Rosas and Kaila, 'L'application de la Charte des droits fondamentaux de l'Union européenne par la Cour de justice : un premier bilan'; Arestis, 'Fundamental rights in the EU: three years after Lisbon, the Luxembourg perspective' 4. As of July 2017 the Charter had been cited in almost 1500 judgments and orders (precisely, 1429 on 12 July 2017).

476 Opinion of AG Trstenjak in *Dominguez*, C-282/10, EU:C:2011:559, para 74.

477 Opinion of AG Cruz Villalón in *Prigge e.a.*, C-447/09, EU:C:2011:321, para 26.

478 Opinion of AG Cruz Villalón in *Scarlet Extended*, C-70/10, EU:C:2011:255, para 26 to 34.

479 Peers, 'The Rebirth of the EU's Charter of Fundamental Rights' 289.

480 L. Pech, 'Between judicial minimalism and avoidance: the Court of Justice's sidestepping of fundamental constitutional issues in Römer and Dominguez' (2012) 49 Common Market Law Review 1841 1844.

al principles of EU law as sources of such rights.[481] This applies in cases concerning rights that have been 'upgraded' in the Charter, i.e. that did not pre-exist as general principles or fundamental rights, such as the right to protection of personal data, as exemplified in the *Volker* ruling.[482] In this case, two recipients of EU agricultural aid were challenging the validity of two regulations framing the publication of information on the beneficiaries of EU agricultural funds.[483] The Court started by referring to the Charter's legal value: '*In accordance with Article 6(1) TEU, the European Union recognises the rights, freedoms and principles set out in the Charter of Fundamental Rights of the European Union ('the Charter'), 'which shall have the same legal value as the Treaties*'; then it held that the validity of the provisions at issue had to be assessed '*in the light of the provisions of the Charter*', and finally zoomed in on article 8 of the Charter.[484] We see the same methodology of the Charter as starting point, in cases concerning fundamental rights that pre-existed the Charter, such as the right to effective judicial protection.[485]

---

481 Gerkrath, 'Les principes généraux du droit ont-ils encore un avenir en tant qu'instrument de protection des droits fondamentaux dans l'Union européenne?' 31; Peers, 'The Rebirth of the EU's Charter of Fundamental Rights' 289.

482 Judgment of 9 November 2010, *Volker und Markus Schecke and Eifert*, Joined cases C-92/09 and C-93/09, EU:C:2010:662.

483 Council Regulation (EC) No 1290/2005 of 21 June 2005 on the financing of the common agricultural policy (OJ L 209 p. 1), as amended by Council Regulation (EC) No 1437/2007 of 26 November 2007 (OJ L 322 p. 1) and Commission Regulation (EC) No 259/2008 of 18 March 2008 laying down detailed rules for the application of Regulation No 1290/2005 as regards the publication of information on the beneficiaries of funds deriving from the European Agricultural Guarantee Fund (EAGF) and the European Agricultural Fund for Rural Development (EAFRD) (OJ L 76 p. 28).

484 *Volker und Markus Schecke and Eifert*, Joined cases C-92/09 and C-93/09, paras 45-52. Rosas and Kaila, 'L'application de la Charte des droits fondamentaux de l'Union européenne par la Cour de justice : un premier bilan' 12.

485 In *DEB*, for instance, the question of the German referring court was focused on the meaning of the principle of effectiveness, which the Court connected with the general principle of effective judicial protection; yet in the light of Article 6(1) TEU and Article 51(1) CFR, the Court found it '*necessary to recast the question*' in terms of '*the principle of effective judicial protection as enshrined in Article 47 of the Charter*'. *DEB*, C-279/09, para 29 and 33 and Hofmann, 'Effective Judicial Remedies Before the National Courts'.

1.2.1.4. The dangers of a closed-circuit, Charter-centred approach and the necessary combination of sources for identifying and applying rights

Although it is hoped that the existence of and reliance on a Charter of rights would enhance the protection of individuals, this should not be taken for granted.[486] Among potential problems connected with the inclusion a Charter of rights in the Union's constitutional order, is the paradoxical risk of regression in the protection of rights, which Weiler emphasised in 2002. His point was that, given the use of the phrase '*guaranteed in accordance with the national laws governing the exercise of these rights*' in several provisions of the Charter,[487] there was a risk of '*deconstitutionalisation*' of some of the rights involved; on the basis of the Charter alone it could become very difficult to challenge an EU or national measure which simply replicated an existing law in one or more Member States.[488] In the same vein, in his Opinion in *Scattolon* Advocate General Bot outlined the problem with dissociating the protective system of the Charter and that which has been built in the case law: this would risk acknowledging a protective scope more limited than that of general principles.[489] A second issue lies with the risk of 'freezing' the case law on the protection of fundamental rights.[490] Indeed, the dynamic role of the EU Courts in identifying and defining new rights, and expanding the scope of existing rights, is also being challenged. This in turn undermines '*one of the truly original features of*

486 The potential drawbacks of equipping a legal system with a bill of rights are discussed also in non-EU settings. For instance, Waldron pointed out that '[a] *legal right that finds protection in a Bill of Rights finds it under the auspices of some canonical form of words in which the provisions of the charter are enunciated. One lesson of American constitutional experience is that the words of each provision in the Bill of Rights tend to take on a life of their own, becoming the obsessive catch-phrase for expressing everything one might want to say about the right in question.*' Waldron, *Law and Disagreement* 220; see also L.W. Sumner, *The Moral Foundation of Rights* (Clarendon Press 1987) 1.

487 Articles 9, 10, 14 and a similar phrase: '*in accordance with national laws and practices*' in Articles 16, 27, 28, 30, 34.

488 J.H.H. Weiler, 'A Constitution for Europe? Some Hard Choices' (2002) 40 Journal of Common Market Studies 563 576.

489 Opinion of AG Bot in *Scattolon*, C-108/10, EU:C:2011:211, para 120.

490 Burgorgue-Larsen, 'Ombres et Lumières de la constitutionnalisation de la Charte des droits fondamentaux de l'Union européenne' 681 - see especially her analysis of the Explanations, which could have '*la fâcheuse conséquence de congeler la jurisprudence en matière de protection des droits fondamentaux à l'échelle européenne*'.

the pre-Charter constitutional architecture in the field of human rights - the ability to use the legal system of each of the Member States as an organic and living laboratory of human rights protection which then, case by case, can be adapted and adopted for the needs of the Union by the European Court in dialogue with its national counterparts.' Ultimately the risk would be to induce *'a more inward-looking jurisprudence'*.[491]

A concrete illustration of these problems is provided by the early case law on Article 41 of the Charter, enshrining a 'right to good administration'. This provision codifies the body of various rights and principles that the Court had started developing from the early beginnings of the EEC[492] into a general principle of good administration.[493] The Charter has been described as *'really innovative'* for enshrining the guarantees of good administration *'not (...) in terms of objective legality in the public interest, but in the language of subjective public rights'*.[494] The following rights are listed in the Charter: the right to a fair and impartial treatment (Article 41(1) CFR), right to a decision within a reasonable time (Article 41(1) CFR), right to a fair hearing (Article 41(2) (a) and (b) CFR), right of access to the file (Article 41(2) CFR), right to a reasoned decision (Article 41(1), which overlaps with Article 296(2) TFEU), right to damage payments (Article 41(3) CFR), language rights (Article 41(4) CFR, also protected by Article 24(4) TFEU).[495] Although Article 41 has been welcomed as a significant step for-

491 Weiler, 'A Constitution for Europe? Some Hard Choices' 576.

492 E.g. *Algera and Others v Assemblée commune*, Joined cases C-7/56 and C-3 to C-7/57; Judgment of 4 July 1963, *Alvis v Council of the EEC*, 32/62, EU:C:1963:15. For an in-depth analysis of the principle of good administration and its components, see B. Mihaescu Evans, 'The right to good administration at the crossroads of the various sources of fundamental rights in the EU integrated administrative system' (PhD thesis, University of Luxembourg 2014). See also B. Grzesick, 'Das Grundrecht auf eine gute Verwaltung - Strukturen und Perspektiven des Charta-Grundrechts auf eine gute Verwaltung' (2006) Europarecht 161 and R. Bousta, 'Who Said There is a 'Right to Good Administration'? A Critical Analysis of Article 41 of the Charter of Fundamental Rights of the European Union' (2013) 19 European Public Law 481.

493 See e.g. *max.mobil v Commission*, T-54/99, para 48.

494 Dutheil de la Rochère, 'The EU Charter of Fundamental Rights, Not Binding but Influential: the Example of Good Administration', in Arnull, Eeckhout and Tridimas (eds), Continuity and Change in EU Law: Essays in Honour of Sir Francis Jacobs (Oxford University Press 2008), 157-171, 168.

495 The list is introduced by the phrase *'this right includes'* which tends to suggest that there could be other elements, i.e. elements which were developed as general principles of EU law and not explicitly codified in the Charter, like the duty of care, i.e. the obligation to examine carefully and impartially all relevant facts

ward for the protection of administrative procedural rights, it has rightly been pointed out that a literal reading of this provision does not correspond with the scope – personal, institutional, substantial – of the various guarantees of good administration which the Court had developed prior to the drafting of the Charter.[496] In particular, the restriction as to the institutional scope of application of Article 41 (EU institutions only) compared to the general principle of good administration is not consistent with the approach of the codification work, which was meant to increase the visibility and ultimately to strengthen the protection of fundamental rights under EU law.[497] A practical consequence lies with the elevated probability of finding gaps in protection of individuals between EU law applied by Member States and EU law applied by EU institutions: a strict conception of good administration based exclusively on the wording of the written provision instead of including also the case law on the general principle, would mean that individuals would not be protected in cases of indirect or composite administration where a national administration takes the final decision based on EU law.

This is exemplified by the early post-Lisbon rulings *Cicala, M.* and *Y.S. and others*,[498] which sent unclear and fluctuating signals. In *Cicala*, the Court declined to answer questions on the interpretation of Article 41 because the dispute did not fall within the scope of EU law, yet it pointed out that the provision is addressed '*solely to the Institutions, bodies, offices and agencies of the EU*',[499] which appeared like an implicit exclusion of Member States' activities from its scope. In the *M.* case the Court avoided addressing the limited scope of Article 41 and accepted that this provision was '*of gen-*

---

and aspects of a particular case. Judgment of 21 November 1991, *Technische Universität München v Hauptzollamt München-Mitte*, C-269/90, EU:C:1991:438.

496 H.C.H. Hofmann and B. Mihaescu, 'The Relation between the Charter's Fundamental Rights and the Unwritten General Principles of EU Law: Good Administration as the Test Case' 9 European Constitutional Law Review 73.

497 Heringa and Verhey, 'The EU Charter: Text and Structure' 30.

498 Judgment of 21 December 2011, *Cicala*, C-482/10, EU:C:2011:868, Judgment of 22 November 2012, *M.*, C-277/11, EU:C:2012:744, Judgment of 17 July 2014, *Y.S. and Others*, C-141/12 and C-372/12, EU:C:2014:2081. On the confrontation between *Cicala* and *Kamino*, the ambiguity arising from it, and the possibility that the rights under Article 41 CFR are applicable as general principles of EU law: A.W.G.J. Buijze, 'Het Hof van Justitie in Kamino-Datema: horen in bezwaar onder voorwaarden gesanctioneerd' (2014) Nederlands tijdschrift voor Europees recht 299 304.

499 *Cicala*, C-482/10, para 28.

eral application.[500] It gets more confusing with *Y.S. and others* concerning the scope of the right of access to file.[501] Applicants for residence in the Netherlands had been denied access to the legal analysis which provided internal advice on whether or not to grant them residence. To obtain access, they relied, among other provisions of EU law, on Article 41(2)(b) of the Charter. The Court stressed that Article 41 is addressed '*solely to the Institutions, bodies, offices and agencies of the EU*'[502] and on this basis declined to answer further questions of the Raad van State on the interpretation of Article 41, even though it acknowledged that this provision '*reflects a general principle of EU law*',[503] suggesting that the door might be open for similar claims against the Member States to be based on the general principle of good administration. This approach to good administration functioning through parallel but hermetically separate channels shows how a 'closed-circuit' approach, relying exclusively on Charter-defined rights, instead of making use the continuity between the Charter and the general principles to construe those rights, can become disadvantageous to individuals and thus counterproductive – insofar, of course, as the aim of introducing the Charter was indeed to provide better protection to individuals.[504]

This approach would also have consequences at the stage of applying the identified rights. An example is the position of Advocate General Cruz Villalón with regard to the principle of proportionality. As explained in the previous section, this principle has been applied by the Court as a general parameter of action ever since *Internationale Handelsgesellschaft.*[505] It was inserted in the EC Treaty in 1992 as the rule according to which the action of

500 Judgment of 22 November 2012, *M.*, C-277/11, EU:C:2012:744, paras 84. On the ambiguities in *M.* see S. Platon, 'Chronique de jurisprudence de droit administratif européen (année 2014)' (2015) Droit administratif.

501 *Y.S and Others*, Joined cases C-141/12 and C-372/12.

502 *Y.S and Others*, Joined cases C-141/12 and C-372/12, para 67, referring to *Cicala*, C-482/10, para 28.

503 *Y.S and Others*, Joined cases C-141/12 and C-372/12, para. 68.

504 More recent case law such as *WebMindLicenses* indicates a shift towards a reading of the Charter provision in more harmonious connection with the general principles of law on the basis of which it was drafted. The Court therein held that while Article 41 as such did not apply to Member States, the general principle of good administration which it reflected did impose obligations on the Member States and as a consequence, also granted rights to individuals (in that case, the right to a fair hearing). *WebMindLicenses*, C-419/14, paras 84-85. Advocate General Wathelet had pointed out the inconsistency in the Court's previous case law: Opinion of AG Wathelet in *WebMindLicenses*, C-419/14, EU:C:2015:606, para 136-138.

505 *Internationale Handelsgesellschaft*, C-11/70.

the Community must not exceed what is necessary to reach the objectives of the Union. This rule is now enshrined in the Treaty of Lisbon (Article 5(4) TEU), and Article 52 of the Charter of Fundamental Rights provides for another application of the general principle of proportionality, in the specific context of the Charter.[506] An exclusive focus on the Charter for matters of rights leads to an approach in which Article 52 would be the only basis for review of Charter rights, and reciprocally Charter rights would be controlled only through that filter. In his opinion on *Digital Rights Ireland*, the Advocate General argues that there are now 2 different types of proportionality review: Article 5(4) TEU would correspond to the proportionality principle framing the action of the EU, while Article 52(1) CFR would be used specifically for the review of infringement of fundamental rights.[507] This second type of review would be identical to that conducted by the European Court of Human Rights.[508] This suggestion, however, implicitly challenges the relevance of the abundant case law on the application of the principle of proportionality to fundamental rights issues and therefore potentially weakens this pre-existing system of protection of fundamental rights.

Fortunately, the system contains inherent safeguards against these pitfalls. As made clear in Articles 6(2) and 6(3) TEU, the Charter does not replace the former system of protection but is added to it, along with the possibility for the EU to accede to the ECHR. In addition, the Explanations state in the context of Article 52, concerning the rights in the Charter that also exist in the Treaties, that '*The Charter does not alter the system of rights conferred by the EC Treaty and taken over by the Treaties*'. The Explanations also highlight the approach underlying Article 52(4), according to which in so far as the Charter '*recognises fundamental rights as they result from the constitutional traditions common to the Member States, those rights shall be interpreted in harmony with those traditions*'. The Explanations make clear that this rule of interpretation '*has been based on the wording*' of Article 6(3) and '*takes due account of the approach to common constitutional traditions followed by the Court of Justice ...). Under that rule, rather than following*

506 H. Kombila-Ibouanga, 'La proportionnalité en tant que principe du droit de l'Union' (VIIIe Congrès mondial de droit constitutionnel, Mexico, 6-10 December 2010).

507 Opinion of AG Cruz Villalón in *Digital Rights Ireland*, C-293/12, EU:C:2014:845, para 133.

508 See Von Arnaud, 'Theorie und Methode des Grundrechtsschutzes in Europa - am Beispiel des Grundsatzes der Verhältnismässigkeit' on the parallel between the methods of the two courts.

a rigid approach of 'a lowest common denominator', the Charter rights concerned should be interpreted in a way offering a high standard of protection which is adequate for the law of the Union and in harmony with the common constitutional traditions.' In addition, Article 53 of the Charter itself is supposed to prevent a regressive process by stating: '*Nothing in this Charter shall be interpreted as restricting or adversely affecting human rights and fundamental freedoms as recognised, in their respective fields of application, by Union law and international law and by international agreements to which the Union or all the Member States are party (…), and by the Member States' constitutions*'. So, on the one hand, the Charter is not intended to alter the 'system of rights' established by the EC Treaty; on the other hand, its very existence as a source of rights is a new parameter. The challenge is to integrate this new parameter in the existing system.

The Lisbon architecture is designed so that sources of rights and obligations function together. Several provisions ensure the consistency of Charter requirements with those enshrined in other written sources of rights, starting with the Treaties (TEU and TFEU).[509] As the Court itself has emphasised in the *ONEm* case, Article 52(2) of the Charter requires that: '*[r]ights recognised by this Charter for which provision is made in the Treaties shall be exercised under the conditions and within the limits defined by those Treaties*'.[510] Regarding the general principles of EU law, Article 52(4) provides that '*(i)n so far as this Charter recognises fundamental rights as they result from the constitutional traditions common to the Member States, those rights shall be interpreted in harmony with those traditions*'. The Charter itself therefore enshrines a solid network of sources of rights.

It should be emphasised that there is a significant amount of contact points between the Charter and the Treaties, recognised in the Charter and the Explanations.[511] Examples of such duplicates include, as acknowledged in the Explanations, the right to the protection of personal data, enshrined at Article 8 of the Charter but based on Article 286 TEC, now replaced by Article 16 TFEU and Article 39 TEU; the freedom of assembly and association, at Article 12 CFR, of which Paragraph 2 corresponds to Article 10(4) TEU; the freedom to choose an occupation and the right to engage in work, at Article 15 CFR, which overlaps with Articles 26, 45, 49, 56 and

509 Craig, 'Rights, Legality, and Legitimacy' 226.

510 Judgment of 7 April 2016, *ONEm and M.*, C-284/15, EU:C:2016:220, para 33. In this case, the Court recognised the correspondence between Article 15(2) of the Charter and the free movement of workers guaranteed by Article 45 TFEU.

511 Barents uses the French term 'dédoublement': Barents, 'Een grondwet voor Europa (VI): de grondrechten' 42.

153 TFEU; the freedom to conduct a business (Article 16 CFR and Article 119 TFEU); the right not to be discriminated against (Article 21 CFR and Articles 18 and 19 TFEU); the protection of cultural, religious and linguistic diversity (Article 22 CFR and Article 3(3) TEU and Articles 17 and 167 TFEU); equality between men and women (Article 23 CFR and Article 157 TFEU); the rights of the child (Article 24 CFR and Article 81 TFEU); workers' right to information and consultation within the undertaking (Article 27 CFR and Articles 154 and 155 TFEU); the right to health care (Article 35 CFR and Article 168 TFEU); the right of access to services of general economic interest, laid down Article 36 CFR, which, according to the Explanations, sets out a principle in line with Article 14 TFEU; the right to environmental protection (Article 37 CFR and Article 3(3) TEU and Articles 11 and 191 TFEU; consumer protection (Article 38 CFR and Article 169 TFEU); the right to vote and stand as a candidate at European and municipal elections, which features at Articles 39 and 40 of the Charter and at Article 20(2) TFEU[512]; the right to good administration (Article 41 CFR and Articles 20, 25, 296 and 340 TFEU); the right of access to the European Ombudsman and the right to petition (Articles 43 and 44 CFR and Articles 20 and 228 TFEU); the freedom of movement and residence (Article 45 CFR and Articles 20(2)(a), 77, 78 and 79 TFEU); the right to diplomatic and consular protection (Article 46 CFR and Article 20 TFEU). As we can see, most of the Charter's provisions (and almost all of those which do not reproduce ECHR provisions) in fact correspond to Treaty provisions. Of course, most of these duplicates are not exact duplicates; rather, the provisions of the Charter and those of the Treaties overlap to a variable extent – which makes a coherent interpretation of primary EU law even more difficult. Further connections exist even though they are not cited in the Explanations, such as the relation between Article 47 CFR on the right to effective judicial protection and Article 19(1) TEU on the obligation for Member States to provides remedies. The list of connections is virtually endless.

Moreover, just as there is a long list of contact points between the Charter and the Treaties, many fundamental rights exist in the form of both general principles of EU law and Charter provisions, and even very often, simultaneously as Treaty provisions, which adds an extra layer of complexity to the network of sources of fundamental rights. Article 6(3) TEU now states that fundamental rights '*shall constitute general principles of the*

512 See Opinion of AG Cruz Villalón in *Delvigne*, C-650/13, EU:C:2015:363, paras 40 and 43 Judgment of 6 October 2015, *Delvigne*, C-650/13, EU:C:2015:648, para 41.

Union's law', thereby requiring general principles to keep playing a role in fundamental rights adjudication.[513] The Charter itself alludes to general principles, with Article 53(4) requiring that: '*In so far as this Charter recognises fundamental rights as they result from the constitutional traditions common to the Member States, those rights shall be interpreted in harmony with those traditions*'. More generally, all of EU judge-made law retains relevance in the new system integrating the Charter. As pointed out by Lenaerts, the Explanations themselves, referring to a variety of CJEU judgments, are evidence that the case law pre-dating the Charter is applicable in interpreting the meaning of its provisions.[514] The general principles of EU law therefore must be taken into account, along with relevant Treaty provisions, in the interpretation of Charter provisions. There is of course a long list of fundamental rights for which these three types of sources are relevant. An example of a substantial right is the principle of equal remuneration for men and women, which is enshrined both in Article 23 of the Charter and in Article 157 TFEU, while also having been developed and detailed in a long line of case law which started with the *Defrenne* ruling.[515] An example of a procedural right is the requirement of effective judicial protection: although it is now laid down in Article 47 of the Charter, it is a product of the case law on general principles, justified by the obligation of Member States under the principle of sincere cooperation to ensure the effectiveness of the rights of individuals.[516] It is therefore difficult to ignore the complementarity between the Charter provision and the general principle, not to

513 C. Semmelmann, 'General Principles in EU Law between a Compensatory Role and an Intrinsic Value' (2013) 19 European Law Journal 457 468.

514 K. Lenaerts, 'Exploring the Limits of the EU Charter of Fundamental Rights' (2012) 8 European Constitutional Law Review 375.

515 *Defrenne v SABENA*, C-43/75.

516 *Rewe v Landwirtschaftskammer für das Saarland*, 33/76, para 5; Judgment of 16 December 1976, *Comet BV v Produktschap voor Siergewassen*, C-45/76, EU:C:1976:191, para 12; *Simmenthal*, C-106/77, paras 21 and 22; Judgment of 9 November 1983, *Ammistrazione delle finanze dello Stato v San Giorgio*, C-199/82, EU:C:1983:318, para 12. Judgment of 19 June 1990, *The Queen v Secretary of State for Transport, ex parte Factortame*, C-213/89, EU:C:1990:257, para 19; Judgment of 14 December 1995, *Peterbroeck, Van Campenhout & Cie v Belgian State*, C-312/93, EU:C:1995:437, para 12; *Unibet*, C-432/05, para 38. The Court of Justice has repeatedly referred to the common constitutional traditions of the Member States and Articles 6 and 13 of the ECHR, as sources of the EU right to effective judicial protection. See e.g.: *Johnston v Chief Constable of the Royal Ulster Constabulary*, C-222/84, paras 18 and 19; Judgment of 15 October 1987, *Unectef v Heylens*, C-222/86, EU:C:1987:442, para 14; Judgment of 25 July 2002, *Unión de Pequeños Agricultores*, C-50/00 P, EU:C:2002:462, para 39; *Kadi I*, Joined cases

mention the additional requirement to ensure effective legal protection as enshrined in Article 19 TEU.[517] These numerous replicates attest that '*the substantive meaning and scope of EU fundamental rights cannot be divorced*' from the general principles of EU law.[518] The dissociation is not only undesirable, it is also practically unfeasible.

The Court does not favour a compartmentalised approach in the interpretation and application of Charter rights. This is clear from the post-Lisbon case law on the principle of proportionality. Admittedly, in some cases, it has conducted a proportionality review based only on Article 52(1) CFR, with no mention of Article 5(4) TEU.[519] Yet there is also an amount of case law that applies the principle of proportionality as enshrined in Article 5(4) TEU, and/or as a general principle of EU law, and as interpreted by the Court in the pre-Lisbon era, to more recent fundamental rights cases.[520] In the abovementioned *Volker* case the Court referred to *Schmidberger* to ground the proportionality review, insisting that the right to the protec-

C-402/05 P and C-415/05 P, para 335; Judgment of 16 July 2009, *Mono Car Styling*, C-12/08, EU:C:2009:466, para 47; Judgment of 18 March 2010, *Alassini and Others*, C-317 to C-320/08, EU:C:2010:146, para 61. L.Y.M. Parret, 'Effectieve rechtsbescherming: eindeloos potentieel, ongeleid projectiel?' (2012) Nederlands tijdschrift voor Europees recht 157 158; H.C.H. Hofmann, 'Effective Judicial Remedies Before the National Courts' in A. Ward and others (eds), *The EU Charter of Fundamental Rights* (The EU Charter of Fundamental Rights, Hart 2014).

517 Judgment of 16 May 2017, *Berlioz Investment Fund*, C-682/15, EU:C:2017:373, para 44: '*According to Article 47 of the Charter, entitled 'Right to an effective remedy and to a fair trial', everyone whose rights and freedoms guaranteed by the law of the Union are violated has the right to an effective remedy before a tribunal. The obligation imposed on the Member States in the second subparagraph of Article 19(1) TEU, to provide remedies sufficient to ensure effective legal protection in the fields covered by Union law, corresponds to that right*'. See also Judgment of 26 July 2017, *Sacko*, C-348/16, EU:C:2017:591, paras 29-30.

518 D. Augenstein, 'Engaging the Fundamentals: On the Autonomous Substance of EU Fundamental Rights Law' (2013) 14 German Law Journal 1917 1927.

519 Judgment of 17 October 2013, *Schwarz*, C-291/12, EU:C:2013:670, para 34; Judgment of 28 November 2013, *Council v. Manufacturing Support & Procurement Kala Naft*, C-348/12 P, EU:C:2013:776; Judgment of 17 October 2013, *Schaible*, C-101/12, EU:C:2013:661, para 27; Judgment of 27 May 2014, *Spasic*, C-129/14 PPU, EU:C:2014:586.

520 In para 37 of Judgment of 19 June 2012, *Jaramillo v EIB*, T-234/11 P, EU:T:2012:311, there is no reference to Article 52: the principle of proportionality as enshrined in Article 5(4) TEU is applied in relation with the alleged violation of Article 47 (right to effective remedy). In its Judgment of 27 February 2014, *Ezz e.a. v Council*, T-256/11, EU:T:2014:93, the General Court refers to 52(1) but also explains that the principle of proportionality is a general principle

tion of personal data '*is not (...) an absolute right, but must be considered in relation to its function in society*'.[521] Another telling example is *Sky Österreich*. In this case, the Court had to review the legality of a provision of a directive requiring broadcasting companies which had acquired exclusive broadcasting licenses for sports events, to allow their competitors to partially broadcast these events. The balancing exercise between the freedom to conduct a business protected by Article 16 CFR, and the freedom to receive information (Article 11(2) CFR) is based on Article 52(1) CFR, but this provision is applied in the light of earlier case law on proportionality, which does not specifically involve fundamental rights.[522] In this situation the Court found that the obligations on the holders of the exclusive licenses were '*not disproportionate in the light of the aims*' which the directive pursued and were '*such as to ensure a fair balance between the various rights and fundamental freedoms at issue*'.[523] In *Digital Rights Ireland*, instead of elaborating on AG Cruz Villalón's abovementioned suggestion, the Court has relied precisely on cases such as *Volker* and *Sky Österreich* in order to apply the principle of proportionality enshrined in Article 52(1) of the Charter.[524] The Court's application of the principle of proportionality does not reflect a 'closed-circuit' conception of the Charter's structure, nor a will to break from the pre-Lisbon approach to applying rights.

Another element of continuity in the case law on the principle of proportionality is in the notion that a right has an intangible core. This is despite the lexical switch that seems to have taken place, from the obligation to respect in any event the '*very substance*' of the right that was laid down in the case law,[525] to the obligation laid down at Article 52(1) CFR to '*re-*

---

of EU law (para 205, and see also *Volker und Markus Schecke and Eifert*, Joined cases C-92/09 and C-93/09, para 74).

521 *Volker und Markus Schecke and Eifert*, Joined cases C-92/09 and C-93/09, para 48, citing *Schmidberger*, C-112/00, para 80.

522 Judgment of 22 January 2013, *Sky Österreich*, C-283/11, EU:C:2013:28, para 50, citing *Afton Chemical*, C-343/09. See also Opinion of AG Bot in *Sky Österreich*, C-283/11, EU:C:2012:341, para 47, equating the principle of proportionality with a general principle of EU law.

523 *Sky Österreich*, C-283/11, para 67.

524 Judgment of 8 April 2014, *Digital Rights Ireland and Seitlinger and Others*, C-293/12, EU:C:2014:238, paras 38 and 46.

525 *Nold v Commission*, C-4/73, *Hauer*, C-44/79, para 23; *Schräder v Hauptzollamt Gronau*, C-265/87, para 15; *Wachauf*, C-5/88, para 15; *X v Commission*, C-404/92 P, para 18, *Commission v Germany*, C-62/90, para 23; *Metronome Musik v Music Point Hokamp*, C-200/96, para 21, *Schmidberger*, C-112/00, para 80. See also p. 82 of this work.

spect the essence' of the rights guaranteed by the Charter. Are these terms – 'substance' and 'essence' – interchangeable? In his Opinion in *Berlioz*, Advocate General Wathelet appears to assume as much, when in order to assess the legality of the limitation of the right to an effective remedy, he refers to settled case law on the prohibition to affect the 'very substance' of the right and then uses the term 'essence' as prescribed by Article 52(1) CFR.[526] The Court has acknowledged the terminological shift in a more gradual way. In some post-Lisbon cases it controls whether fundamental rights granted by the Charter are not infringed upon in their 'very substance', as required by 'settled case law' (i.e. also pre-Lisbon case law).[527] In *Digital Rights Ireland*, it used the term 'essence', finding that the retention of data required by Directive 2006/24[528] was not '*such as to adversely affect the essence*' of the right to privacy and the other rights laid down in Article 7 CFR, nor that of the right to the protection of personal data enshrined in Article 8 CFR, because the directive included appropriate safeguards in the form of obligations on Member States to ensure that appropriate technical and organisational measures were taken.[529]

Also assessing the possible infringement of the 'essence' of a right, in *Schrems* the Court held that '*legislation permitting the public authorities to have access on a generalised basis to the content of electronic communications must be regarded as compromising the essence of the fundamental right to respect for private life, as guaranteed by Article 7 of the Charter*'. In addition, '*legisla-*

526 Opinion of AG Wathelet in *Berlioz Investment Fund*, C-682/15, EU:C:2017:2, paras 82 and 84-85.

527 E.g., *Boudjlida*, C-249/13, para 43, concerning the right to be heard, enshrined at Articles 41(2), 47 and 48 of the Charter as pointed out at para 31. Para 43 refers to: *Alassini and Others*, C-317/08 to C-320/08, para 63; Judgment of 10 September 2013, *G. and R.*, C-383/13 PPU, EU:C:2013:533, para 33; and Judgment of 26 September 2013, *Texdata Software GmbH*, C-418/11, EU:C:2013:588, para 84, all referring to the (pre-Lisbon) Judgment of 15 June 2006, *Dokter and Others*, C-28/05, EU:C:2006:408, para 75. Another example is Judgment of 20 September 2016, *Ledra Advertising v Commission and ECB*, C-8/15 P, EU:C:2016:701, paras 70-75.

528 Parliament and Council Directive 2006/24/EC of 15 March 2006 on the retention of data generated or processed in connection with the provision of publicly available electronic communications services or of public communications networks and amending Directive 2002/58/EC (OJ L 105 p. 54).

529 *Digital Rights Ireland and Seitlinger and Others*, C-293/12, para 39-40. Another case where there is a detailed assessment of whether the 'essence' of rights (the freedom to conduct a business and the freedom of establishment) has been violated is Judgment of 21 December 2016, *AGET Iraklis*, C-201/15, EU:C:2016:972, paras 82-88.

tion not providing for any possibility for an individual to pursue legal remedies in order to have access to personal data relating to him, or to obtain the rectification or erasure of such data, does not respect the essence of the fundamental right to effective judicial protection, as enshrined in Article 47 of the Charter'.[530] While this case is historical because it was the first judgment striking down an EU act because of a violation of the essence of a fundamental right, it does not reflect a conceptual break from earlier case law. The fundamentals observed in the founding cases on proportionality review[531] remain. *Schrems* confirms that there are limits to the relativist implications of the proportionality principle, in the sense that although rights are relative, they have an absolute core or 'essence', the infringement of which is prohibited in any case, without the need to engage in a balancing exercise. The essence of the right, albeit elusive and mostly escaping the possibility of an abstract definition,[532] becomes identifiable in concrete circumstances such as those which led to the *Schrems* case.

The above developments suggest that the Union's constitutional design, as renewed by the Treaty of Lisbon and especially the integration of the Charter in the network of sources of fundamental rights, does not favour a radical break in our approach to fundamental rights. In spite of the undeniable power of attraction of the Charter as a source of rights, the Lisbon architecture remains a pluralistic system of sources of rights. As a consequence, the Court's original approach to identifying and applying rights is not intrinsically challenged by the post-Lisbon constitutional architecture. The potential impact of an additional, more specific new parameter now needs to be considered: the distinction between rights and principles.

1.2.2. The distinction between rights and principles in the Charter: a new parameter?

While the inclusion of a Charter of rights in our legal system is an innovation of the Treaty of Lisbon, the Charter itself contains another innovation: the distinction between 'rights' and 'principles' (1.2.2.1). The reason for introducing the distinction between rights and principles lies with the diverging national conceptions of social guarantees and the disagreement of

530 Judgment of 6 October 2015, *Schrems*, C-362/14, EU:C:2015:650, paras 94-95.

531 See p. 82 of this work.

532 E.g., concerning the difficulty to identify the 'essence' or 'core' of the *ne bis in idem* principle, see View of AG Jääskinen in *Spasic*, C-129/14 PPU, EU:C:2014:739, paras 83-90.

the negotiating Member States as to whether the Charter should have included social elements (1.2.2.2). Perhaps precisely because it is the result of a laboured compromise, the rights/principles dichotomy enshrined in the Charter is far from clear in its meaning and consequences, and has thus given rise to a variety of suggestions with regard to how it should be used in interpreting the Charter (1.2.2.3). The dichotomous nature of this interpretative tool certainly has important potential implications for interpretation and application of the Charter (1.2.2.4) as well as for the concept of rights and its place and function in the EU legal system (1.2.2.5).

1.2.2.1. Basis for the distinction

The basis for the distinction between rights and principles is to be found in the final title of the Charter, which includes transversal provisions on the interpretation and application of the other titles. More specifically, the distinction between rights and principles is laid down in Articles 51(1) and 52(5) of the Charter.

The first paragraph of Article 51 entitled '*Field of application*' reads:

> '*The provisions of this Charter are addressed to the institutions, bodies, offices and agencies of the Union with due regard for the principle of subsidiarity and to the Member States only when they are implementing Union law. They shall therefore* respect the rights, observe the principles and promote the application thereof *in accordance with their respective powers and respecting the limits of the powers of the Union as conferred on it in the Treaties.*' (emphasis added)

The fifth paragraph of Article 52 entitled '*Scope and interpretation of rights and principles*' provides the following specification:

> '*The provisions of this Charter which contain* principles may be implemented by legislative and executive acts *taken by institutions, bodies, offices and agencies of the Union, and by acts of Member States when they are implementing Union law, in the exercise of their respective powers. They shall be* judicially cognisable only in the interpretation of such acts and in the ruling on their legality.' (emphasis added)

As we can see, Articles 51(1) and 52(5) CFR introduce a dichotomy between 'rights' and 'principles.' However, the background elements to this distinction are contradictory. As a result of a compromise in the negotiations which led to drafting the Charter, Article 51(1) provides that rights are to be 'respected' while principles are to be 'observed.'

The Explanations to Article 52(5) read:

> *'Paragraph 5 clarifies the distinction between 'rights' and 'principles' set out in the Charter. According to that distinction, subjective rights shall be respected, whereas principles shall be observed (Article 51(1)). Principles may be implemented through legislative or executive acts (adopted by the Union in accordance with its powers, and by the Member States only when they implement Union law); accordingly, they become significant for the Courts only when such acts are interpreted or reviewed. They do not however give rise to direct claims for positive action by the Union's institutions or Member States authorities. This is consistent both with case-law of the Court of Justice (cf. notably case-law on the 'precautionary principle' in Article 191(2) of the Treaty on the Functioning of the European Union: judgment of the CFI of 11 September 2002, Case T-13/99 Pfizer v Council, with numerous references to earlier case-law; and a series of judgments on Article 33 (ex-39) on the principles of agricultural law, e.g. judgment of the Court of Justice in Case 265/85 Van den Berg [1987] ECR 1155: scrutiny of the principle of market stabilisation and of reasonable expectations) and with the approach of the Member States' constitutional systems to 'principles', particularly in the field of social law. For illustration, examples for principles, recognised in the Charter include e.g. Articles 25, 26 and 37. In some cases, an Article of the Charter may contain both elements of a right and of a principle, e.g. Articles 23, 33 and 34.'*

Although Article 52(5) supposedly (according to the Explanations) 'clarifies' the distinction between rights and principles, in fact while the consequences of this distinction are laid down in the Explanations, neither the Charter nor the Explanations actually provide systematic criteria for distinguishing 'rights' from 'principles'. A few provisions are cited as examples of principles, and others as examples of provisions which contain both 'rights' and 'principles', but there is no indication as to how one should distinguish between the rights and the principles in such provisions. Article 52(5) seemingly associates the notion of principles with a form of limited justiciability, which was reportedly introduced in order to limit the enforceability by individuals of certain Charter provision, especially those containing social rights, at the request of some Member States.[533] This request, however, was somewhat conflicting with the ambition to make fun-

533 Goldsmith, 'The Charter of Rights-A Brake Not an Accelerator', J. Krommendijk, 'Principled Silence or Mere Silence on Principles? The Role of the EU Charter's Principles in the Case Law of the Court of Justice' (2015) 11 European Con-

damental rights more visible and accessible to EU citizens, and even more with the aspiration to proclaim the indivisibility of the various types of rights (civil, political, and social rights).[534] Therefore, the new distinction is the result of a compromise between two opposite visions. Yet, the compromise is not clear-cut: it has been pointed out repeatedly in the literature that not all provisions of Title IV, i.e. the 'social' chapter, correspond to what one could understand (more or less intuitively) as principles, while provisions elsewhere in the Charter may also be 'principles' and not 'rights'.[535] The exact meaning and implications of the distinction between rights and principles are left to interpretation. The conceptual underpinnings to EU rights have been explored in the previous section, but since the Charter opposes rights to principles, the latter concept also needs to be analysed, as well as its relationship with the concept of rights.

The term 'principle', as several authors have rightly pointed out, does not have one fixed meaning in EU law. For an EU lawyer the term 'principle' is perhaps most evocative of the category of general principles, on which the Court extensively relied to fill various gaps in EU law. More generally, the notion of general principles is familiar to continental lawyers.[536] Yet the overlap between the historical category of general principles of EU law and the newly introduced notion of principles is incomplete at best.[537] What is

---

stitutional Law Review 321 656, Barnard, 'The 'Opt-Out' for the UK and Poland from the Charter of Fundamental Rights: Triumph or Rhetoric over Reality?', Baquero Cruz, 'What's Left of the Charter? Reflections on Law and Political Mythology' 65, K. Lenaerts, 'Exploring the Limits of the EU Charter of Fundamental Rights' (2012) 8 European Constitutional Law Review 375 399; Craig, 'Rights, Legality, and Legitimacy' 216.

534 Guðmundsdóttir, 'A Renewed Emphasis on the Charter's Distinction Between Rights and Principles: Is a Doctrine of Judicial Restraint More Appropriate?' 686; M. Benlolo-Carabot, 'Chapitre 2. Les droits sociaux dans l'ordre juridique de l'Union Européenne' 95.

535 Lorenz, Groussot and Petursson, *The European Human Rights Culture - A Paradox of Human Rights Protection in Europe?* 196.

536 J. R. Toubes Muniz, 'Legal Principles and Legal Theory' (1997) 10 Ratio Juris 267 267.

537 S. Prechal, 'The relation between the rights arising from the Charter and general principles of law (responding to H.C.H. Hofmann)' (The protection of fundamental rights in the EU: future challenges - Conference on EU Litigation, Centre for European Law of the University of Luxembourg and Institut Universitaire International Luxembourg, 22 October 2012); C. Semmelmann, 'General Principles in EU Law between a Compensatory Role and an Intrinsic Value' (2013) 19 *European Law Journal* 457; Hofmann and Mihaescu, 'The Relation between the Charter's Fundamental Rights and the Unwritten General Principles of EU Law: Good Administration as the Test Case' 73.

more, on the whole EU law is '*not very principled when it comes to the use of the term principle*',[538] so that the term can refer to objectives, values, standards, rules, key notions or concepts, or general prescriptions.[539] It features in a variety of Treaty provisions.[540] For instance, the principles in Title I of the TEU, such as the principle of sincere cooperation, have been described as founding principles.[541] Another important example is of course the principle of non-discrimination. As observed in *Defrenne II*, the UK had argued that the ban on discrimination was '*a general statement of principle*' and that therefore its application should have been left, according to the UK, to the legislative action of Member States.[542] The argument had not convinced the Court back then and this principle was found to give rights to individuals even in horizontal situations.[543] Since then, admittedly, the '*anarchie sémantique*' has reached a point where Van Meerbeeck doubts that the Court would still characterise, as it did in *Defrenne*, the term 'principle' as one used to 'indicate the fundamental nature of certain provisions'.[544] In any case, even though the Charter is supposedly intended to be consolidating the Court's case law, its use of the term 'principle' does nothing to clarify that case law.

In an attempt to better understand this distinction, which is far from self-explanatory from the perspective of an EU lawyer, one may turn to le-

538 S. Prechal, 'The relation between the rights arising from the Charter and general principles of law' (The protection of fundamental rights in the EU: future challenges, Luxembourg, 22 October 2012).

539 J. Van Meerbeeck, 'Les principes généraux du droit de l'Union européenne' in I. Hachez and others (eds), *Les sources du droit revisitées Volume 1 - Normes internationales et constitutionnelles* (Anthemis 2012) 165; see also D. Simon, 'Y a-t-il des principes généraux de droit communautaire?' (1991) 14 Droits 73.

540 Von Bogdandy, 'Founding Principles of EU Law: A Theoretical and Doctrinal Sketch' 104.

541 Krommendijk, 'Principled Silence or Mere Silence on Principles? The Role of the EU Charter's Principles in the Case Law of the Court of Justice' 328; Von Bogdandy, 'Founding Principles of EU Law: A Theoretical and Doctrinal Sketch' 106.

542 Krommendijk, 'Principled Silence or Mere Silence on Principles? The Role of the EU Charter's Principles in the Case Law of the Court of Justice' 325.

543 *V. SABENA*, C-43/75, para. 28: '*it is impossible to put forward an argument against its direct effect based on the use in this article of the word "principle", since, in the language of the Treaty, this term is specifically used in order to indicate the fundamental nature of certain provisions, as is shown, for example, by the heading of the first part of the Treaty which is devoted to "Principles"*'.

544 *Defrenne v. SABENA*, C-43/75, para. 28. Van Meerbeeck, 'Les principes généraux du droit de l'Union européenne' 165.

gal theory and see how the rights/principles distinction fits in, or overlaps with, the general theoretical debate on the notion of principles. The term 'principle' evokes the rule/principle distinction which was developed by legal theorists such as Dworkin and Alexy. In Dworkin's words, a rule is an '*all or nothing*' standard, i.e. a rigid standard, while a principle is not.[545] Based on this negative definition of principles, all provisions of the EU treaties which relate to fundamental rights may be closer to Dworkin's conception of principles than to his conception of rules. As Borowski points out, the appropriateness of the distinction between rights and principles distinction for limiting judicial implementation of some Charter provisions is therefore questionable: according to the Dworkinian terminology, indeed, judicially enforceable rights of the individual amount to 'principles'.[546] Likewise, the Court usually works as though all rights conferred by EU law are Dworkinian principles, i.e. the limits of rights can be adapted so that they can be balanced with other rights or even other requirements.[547] Indeed, the essential role of proportionality analysis in the Court's case law shows that EU fundamental rights fit Robert Alexy's characterisation of principles (for which he relied on Dworkin's work) as optimisation requirements.[548] The opposition between rights and principles thus does not seem to correspond to the classic concepts of rights and principles in legal theoretical thought. In fact, rather than an opposition, there seems to be an overlap between these concepts.

The above overview tends to confirm Borowski's analysis that '*[t]he artificial 'rights'/'principles' dichotomy cannot (…) be reconciled with jurisprudential terminology, with traditional terminology in European law, or with tradi-*

545 R. Dworkin, *Taking Rights Seriously* (Harvard University Press 1977) 90; S.J. Shapiro, 'The "Hart-Dworkin" Debate: A Short Guide for the Perplexed' *University of Michigan Law School, Public Law and Legal Theory Working Paper Series, Working Paper No* 77 (March 2007) <http://ssrn.com/abstract=968657> accessed 27 June 2015; S. Law, 'The Rationales, Reasoning and Methodology Underpinning the Judicial Recognition of Principles of Union Law' (Cahiers de Droit européen - Les principes généraux du droit de l'Union européenne, Bruxelles, 10 September 2015); Toubes Muniz, 'Legal Principles and Legal Theory' 269.

546 Dworkin, *Taking Rights Seriously* 90; Borowski, 'The Charter of Fundamental Rights in the Treaty on European Union' 211.

547 Borowski, 'The Charter of Fundamental Rights in the Treaty on European Union' 211.

548 Alexy, 'Rights and Liberties as Concepts' 291; H. Avila, *Theory of Legal Principles* 9; C. Hilson, 'Rights and Principles in EU Law: A Distinction Without Foundation?' 211.

tional categories in the analysis of judicial review.'[549] The roots of this original distinction therefore deserve more specific attention: these are to be traced in the domestic legal systems of EU Member States.

1.2.2.2. A consequence of the diverging conceptions of social rights and principles in domestic legal systems

The growing importance of social rights gave a new dimension to the debate on the functions and justification of rights.[550] Not in all EU constitutional or legal traditions are social entitlements considered as 'rights' (in the sense that is emerging from this research, i.e. closely correlated with obligations, and fuelled by individual interests). The use of rights as tools to advance social objectives at the EU level has been a source of intense controversy between the Member States. Instead, it is acknowledged that the inclusion of social 'principles' in the Charter followed the examples of some national constitutions (or constitutional documents): the Explanations state that the distinction is consistent '*with the approach of the Member States' constitutional systems to 'principles', particularly in the field of social law*'.[551] It is of course not new that EU law would develop its own concepts based on a benchmarking of what exists in the legal systems of its Member States: think for instance of the Court's method in *Algera*.[552] What is not clear is to what extent and in what proportions the various national uses of the notion of principles served as a source of inspiration for the new rights/principles distinction in the Charter.

The use of principles, instead of rights, to constitutionalise the social protection of citizens occurs in several Member States. But it is important to keep in mind that the notion of principle does not necessarily mean the same thing in the various legal systems where it is used to characterise social constitutional provisions. Conversely, not all social constitutional provisions are labelled as principles. A brief inventory of the different national

549 Borowski, 'The Charter of Fundamental Rights in the Treaty on European Union' 212.

550 Benlolo-Carabot, 'Chapitre 2. Les droits sociaux dans l'ordre juridique de l'Union Européenne' 85; On social and economic rights in the Charter see T. Hervey and J. Kenner (eds), *Economic and Social Rights under the EU Charter of Fundamental Rights. A Legal Perspective* (Hart 2003).

551 Explanations on Article 52.

552 *Algera and Others v Assemblée Commune*, Joined cases C-7/56 and C-3 to C-7/57. See p. 32 of this work.

approaches to social provisions at the constitutional level indicates that there are two main models of protection of social rights in Europe:[553] the liberal model, which is essentially the United Kingdom and which corresponds to the absence of constitutional social rights; and the continental model, which may be subdivided into several branches.

In the United Kingdom, there is of course no written constitutional document that would acknowledge social requirements. The notion of constitutional principles does come up (in the context of Bill of Rights case law)[554] but it is not applied to social issues. Even after the Second World War and the birth of the British Welfare State, justiciable social rights were not recognized as being grounded in the common law; instead, social guarantees '*were considered moral principles directive of the legislature's choices, and primarily encouraged the development of the social statutory legislation.*'[555] Later on, the UK imported the ECHR via the Human Rights Act, but never considered transposing socio-economic rights such as those from the European Social Charter, of which the UK is also a signatory.[556] An example of a social 'right' which does not exist as such in the UK is the 'right to strike': trade unions enjoy immunity in some conditions only and strike is illegal unless those conditions are fulfilled – this has been maintained by both Labour and Conservative government, based on the argument that it helps preserve a flexible labour market.[557] In the same vein, lately there has been a movement to transfer social services towards the private sector, which limits their acknowledgement as responsibilities of the state.[558]

There are at least three reasons for the United Kingdom's reluctance to regard socio-economic rights as justiciable. The first reason is the fear of heavy financial implications and increasing the financial burden on the State.[559] The second reason lies with the indeterminacy of socio-economic rights and the idea that the means to achieve such rights are themselves

553 Katrougalos, 'The Implementation of Social Rights in Europe'.

554 M. Elliott, 'Constitutional Legislation, European Union Law and the Nature of the United Kingdom's Contemporary Constitution' (2014) 10 Columbia Journal of European Law 379.

555 Katrougalos, 'The Implementation of Social Rights in Europe' 280.

556 S. Fredman and M. Wesson, 'Social, Economic, and Cultural Rights' in D. Feldman (ed), *English Public Law* (2nd edn, Oxford University Press 2009) 453.

557 Barnard, 'The 'Opt-Out' for the UK and Poland from the Charter of Fundamental Rights: Triumph or Rhetoric over Reality?' 10.

558 Katrougalos, 'The Implementation of Social Rights in Europe' 280.

559 Krommendijk, 'Principled Silence or Mere Silence on Principles? The Role of the EU Charter's Principles in the Case Law of the Court of Justice' 325; Fredman and Wesson, 'Social, Economic, and Cultural Rights' 462.

subject to contestation and should be left to the political process.[560] As Krommendijk has analysed, there is '*a reluctance to have the judiciary decide on such broad issues because of the lack of expertise among judges, but also, and above all, because of the idea that such decisions should be made by democratically elected governments and parliament*'.[561] The third reason is that in the Common Law vision, there is a 'positive'/'negative' dichotomy between social rights (or rather social principles?) which require positive action on the part of the state, and civil and political rights which are meant to protect the individual against the state.[562] Indeed, the opposition between socio-economic rights and others is based on two different visions of the relationship between the individual and the state: traditional human rights theory conceives human rights as protection of individuals against the state, which constitutes a potential threat to liberty; on the other hand, socio-economic rights correspond to a positive vision of the state, which is considered essential to the protection of liberty.[563] Against this backdrop, the debate is intense as to the possible justiciability of social rights: as explained by Palmer, political theorists argue over whether '*social rights can be legitimately constitutionalised in* democratic societies' and constitutional lawyers discuss just as intensely the question whether '*social rights can be effectively enforced through sustainable and meaningful remedies*'.[564] For all these reasons, the social provisions of the Charter belong to what Lord Goldsmith has described as '*sensitive areas*' in the English context.[565]

The dichotomy between social rights and other rights is much less significant in the continental approach to socio-economic rights. The types of

560 Fredman and Wesson, 'Social, Economic, and Cultural Rights' 462.

561 Krommendijk, 'Principled Silence or Mere Silence on Principles? The Role of the EU Charter's Principles in the Case Law of the Court of Justice' 325.

562 Fredman and Wesson, 'Social, Economic, and Cultural Rights' 462; K.G. Young, 'Rights and Queues: On Distributive Contests in the Modern State' (2016) 55 Columbia Journal of Transnational Law 65 74; M. Khosla, 'Making social rights conditional: Lessons from India' (2010) 8 International Journal of Constitutional Law 739 740.

563 Fredman and Wesson, 'Social, Economic, and Cultural Rights' 456. Porat also distinguishes between 'negative' and 'socio-economic' rights: Porat, 'Rights-Based Law v. Duty-Based Law: Old Dilemma, New Perspective' Hebrew University of Jerusalem Legal Research Paper No 16-04 <http://papers.ssrn.com/sol3/papers.cfm?abstract_id=2696463> accessed 12 January 2016 48.

564 Palmer, *Judicial Review, Socio-Economic Rights and the Human Rights Act* 19. For an in-depth contestation of the dichotomy between social and other rights see S. Fredman, *Human Rights Transformed. Positive Rights and Positive Duties* (Oxford University Press 2008).

565 Goldsmith, 'The Charter of Rights-A Brake Not an Accelerator' 476.

rights which correspond to the innovative 'Solidarity' section of the Charter have been imbedded in a notion of social state or at least of social policy (either an overarching principle or a collection of social 'rights'/provisions) that is a typical feature of continental Western European constitutionalism (it is called 'continental' because the United Kingdom does not have that feature, although Ireland does to some extent). Indeed, the continental model includes a formal recognition of the Social State as a constitutional principle; Katrougalos traces this back to the Bismarckian model, to the French revolutionary model and to the influence of Catholic corporatism.[566] Of course, the European landscape of social rights is more complex than a binary opposition between the British and the continental models. Indeed, there is a variety of approaches within the broad category of continental conceptions of social rights.

In several Member States, social constitutional provisions are associated with no or limited justiciability: they lay down obligations for the State without opening a claim to individuals. Spain and Ireland are examples of such an approach. The Spanish constitution clearly distinguishes between basic rights, rights and duties of citizens, and a section titled 'Governing Principles of Economic and Social Policy' in which most provisions start with the phrase '*the authorities shall*'; the authorities have broad discretion as to how to implement these provisions.[567] In Ireland, Article 45 of the Constitution falls under the title '*Guiding principles of social policy*' and these principles are explicitly excluded from justiciability in an introductory paragraph which is strangely reminiscent of Article 52(5) of the EU Charter: '*The principles of social policy set forth in this Article are intended for the general guidance of the Oireachtas. The application of those principles in the making of laws shall be the care of the Oireachtas exclusively, and shall not be cognisable by any Court under any of the provisions of this Constitution.*'[568] Other constitutions do not explicitly use the term 'principle' or an equiva-

566 Katrougalos, 'The Implementation of Social Rights in Europe' 283; Neacsu, 'The Draft of the EU Charter of Fundamental Rights: A Step in the Process of Legitimizing EU as a Political Entity and Economic-Social Rights as Fundamental Human Rights' 145.

567 M. Poiares Maduro, 'The Double Constitutional Life of the Charter of Fundamental Rights of the European Union' in T. Hervey and J. Kenner (eds), *Economic and Social Rights under the EU Charter of Fundamental Rights A Legal Perspective* (Hart 2003) 286; Spanish Constitution, 1978 (Agencia Estatal Boletín Oficial del Estado).

568 Article 45 of the Irish Constitution (Constitution of Ireland, 1937, last amended on 29 August 2015). The Oireachtas is the legislature of Ireland. See also D. Bilchitz, 'Article Review: David Bilchitz on Matthias Klatt's 'Positive Rights: Who

lent, but also frame social requirements as obligations of the State, not directly justiciable by individuals. The Dutch constitution, for instance, contains several social provisions but they are clearly phrased as obligations of the State, as opposed to rights which individuals could claim. The Finnish constitution also contains many social provisions phrased as missions of the State. The Scandinavian model is characterised by a strict observance of the principle of equality in the implementation of social rights, even though the Scandinavian constitutions themselves contain little about such rights.[569] The Swedish constitution presents the state as a welfare State, the aim of which is to ensure social welfare of citizens, but again no enforceable rights can be directly derived from this general requirement. The Greek constitution contains a long catalogue of social rights, which are not directly justiciable and therefore function in a way similar to the 'principles' of the Irish or Spanish constitutions.[570]

At the other end of the spectrum, a number of Member States function with justiciable social rights at the constitutional level. In Portugal a very exhaustive and detailed catalogue of social rights is included in the constitution, and these very detailed provisions are clearly fundamental subjective rights, for which there is a specific mechanism of judicial review (Art 279).[571] The Belgian constitution includes a short list of social provisions in which are phrased as rights, in Article 23.[572] The Italian constitution also contains social rights, some of which are acknowledged as subjective rights by the constitutional court.[573]

France and Germany are somewhere in between.[574] The French example shows that social 'principles' are not systematically associated with limited

---

Decides? Judicial Review in Balance" International Journal of Constitutional Law Blog, August 26, 2015, 359 <http://www.iconnectblog.com/2015/08/article-review-david-bilchitz-on-matthias-klatts-positive-rights-who-decides-judicial-review-in-balance> accessed 27 August 2015.

569 Katrougalos, 'The Implementation of Social Rights in Europe.'

570 M.E. Butt, J. Kübert and C.A. Schultz, *Droits sociaux fondamentaux en Europe* (Document de travail, Parlement Européen, Direction générale des études, Séries affaires sociales, SOCI 104 FR, 2000).

571 M. Brito Vieira and F. Carreira da Silva, 'Getting rights right: Explaining social rights constitutionalization in revolutionary Portugal' (2013) 11 International Journal of Constitutional Law 898 902.

572 Belgian Constitution, 1831, as coordinated in 1994, last modified in 2014, Art. 23.

573 Butt, Kübert and Schultz, *Droits sociaux fondamentaux en Europe*.

574 Another intermediary group, about which information is less available to the author, appears to be post-communist European countries, strongly influenced by the continental model (especially in its German form) but still in transition.

justiciability. The preamble to the Constitution of 1958 establishes the continued constitutional value of the preamble to the Constitution of 1946. In this document, a series of political, economic and social '*principes*' that were deemed '*particulièrement nécessaires à notre temps*' were laid down. Such principles reflect the post-war context and provide for the right to strike, the freedom to constitute trade unions, the right to participate to the collective determination of working conditions, equal rights for men and women, children's rights, etc.[575] Within the 1946 catalogue a distinction is commonly made in the literature between '*droits-libertés*' and '*droits-créances*'.[576] Interestingly, rights are also here defined by reference to the corresponding obligations: *droits-libertés* are correlatives of negative obligations on the State, whereas *droits-créances* are correlatives of positive obligations. The latter category is more controversial precisely because such rights require positive action (and often expenses) from the State, yet they may be relied on directly by individuals – a recent example of such a *droit-créance* is the right to housing.[577] Significantly for the present research, in the French context, rights and principles are not mutually exclusive

---

W. Sadurski, 'Constitutional Courts in the Process of Articulating Constitutional Rights in the Post-Communist States of Central and Eastern Europe, Part I: Social and Economic Rights' EUI Working Paper Law 2002/14.

575 French Constitution of 4 October 1958, last modified on 23 July 2008 and Preamble to the French Constitution of 27 October 1946.

576 F. Rangeon, 'Droits-libertés et droits-créances : les contradictions du préambule de la Constitution de 1946' in G. Koubi (ed), *Le Préambule de la constitution de 1946 : antinomies juridiques et contradictions politiques* (Le Préambule de la constitution de 1946 : antinomies juridiques et contradictions politiques, Presses universitaires de France 1996) et C. Rapoport, 'L'opposabilité des "droits-créances" constitutionnels en droit public français' (Communication présentée aux journées de l'association française de droit constitutionnel, www.droitconstitutionnel.org/congresParis/comC8/RapoportTXTpdf, accessed 20 March 2017).

577 The exact nature of this right is still subject to debate - it seems to be developing mostly into procedural right, rather than an obligation as to the result. V. Kapsali, 'L'opposabilité du droit au logement précisée par le Conseil d'Etat' (2013) Droit administratif. See also in relation to ECHR *Tchokontio Happi v France*, n °65829/12 (ECHR 2015) and R. Rivais, 'Strasbourg garantit le droit au logement opposable' SOS Conso, Le Monde <http://sosconso.blog.lemonde.fr/2015/04/17/strasbourg-garantit-le-droit-au-logement-opposable/> accessed 17 April 2015. More generally, a very rich special issue of *La Revue des droits de l'homme* reflects the intensity of the debate on the justiciability of social rights in the French context, containing the following contributions: D. Roman, 'La justiciabilité des droits sociaux ou les enjeux de l'édification d'un Etat de droit social' La Revue des droits de l'homme (en ligne), 2 <http://revdh.revues.org/635> accessed 1 September 2016; T. Gründler, 'La doctrine des libertés fondamentales à la

concepts: for instance, the right to strike was consecrated as a '*principe*' in the 1946 Constitution ('*Le droit de grève s'exerce dans le cadre des lois qui le réglementent*'[578]) but it is acknowledged as a justiciable constitutional right.[579] Therefore, it seems that the CJEU's answer in *Defrenne II* to the British argument that the prohibition on discrimination could not give rise to a right because it was labelled 'principle',[580] applies both in EU and in French law: 'principle' or '*principe*' signals the fundamental importance of a particular requirement, it does not prevent it from being relied on by individuals (i.e. in the EU context, from giving rise to a right). It should also be emphasised that France was one of the Member States that pushed the most for the inclusion of social rights in the Charter,[581] which shows the importance of this category of rights in the French legal system. Germany was perhaps less insistent on this, probably because while the German Constitution posits a general principle of social state (*Sozialstaatsprinzip*), it only lays down one specific right, the mothers' right to assistance, which the term '*Anspruch*' clearly identifies as a claim, i.e. a justicia-

recherche des droits sociaux' La Revue des droits de l'homme (en ligne), 103 <http://revdh.revues.org/122> accessed 5 September 2016; I. Boucobza and D. Robitaille, 'Standards jurisprudentiels et contrôle de l'obligation étatique. Des contrôles à géométrie variable' La Revue des droits de l'homme (en ligne), 298 <http://revdh.revues.org/142> accessed 5 September 2016; D. Roman, 'Les droits civils au renfort des droits sociaux. L'interchangeabilité des droits fondamentaux dans le discours judiciaire.' La Revue des droits de l'homme (en ligne), 320 <http://revdh.revues.org/144> accessed 1 September 2016; V. Donier and others, 'Les débiteurs des droits sociaux' La Revue des droits de l'homme (en ligne), 388 <http://revdh.revues.org/161> accessed 1 September 2016.

578 Preamble to the French Constitution of 27 October 1946, recital 7.

579 Cons. const., 25 juillet 1979, n° 79-105 DC, *Droit de grève à la radio et à la télévision.* For a overview and discussion of the case law on this principle see L. Gay, 'Droit de grève et liberté syndicale dans la jurisprudence constitutionnelle : des libertés "particulières"?' Nouveaux Cahiers du Conseil constitutionnel n°45 (Le Conseil constitutionnel et le droit social) - October 2014.

580 *Defrenne v. SABENA*, C-43/75, para. 28.

581 Rapoport points out that that some 'droits-créances' from the French system have been transposed into the Charter as 'principles' in Articles 34 CFR ('Social security and assistance) and 35 CFR ('Health care'): 'L'opposabilité des "droits-créances" constitutionnels en droit public français' 3.

ble right:[582] other social 'goals' were excluded from the text of the Constitution because they were not deemed precise enough.[583]

The use of principles as vectors of social guarantees at the EU level is a result of the blending of this very broad array of national conceptions of the role of the State in social matters. In fact, the dichotomy reflects at best a short majority of national constitutional systems – which, anyway, are probably too heterogeneous in their approaches to social provisions for these approaches to be melted into a single balanced one at the EU level. While this is not necessarily a problem in itself, the Explanations turn it into a problem by suggesting that national constitutional approaches should be relied on in order to understand the rights/principles distinction, without specifying which approaches are actually relevant. It remains up to the reader to try to make sense of a requirement of limited justiciability – introduced at the request of UK, Netherlands, Denmark who did not want to be bound by social rights[584] – conveyed by the category of 'principles' – from French and Spanish inspiration, more specifically Article 53(3) of the Spanish Constitution,[585] which provides for guiding principles in social and economic policy, and the French 'principes à valeur constitutionnelle'.[586] The inconsistency is almost insurmountable.[587] Given the status of the distinction within the Charter (i.e. one of the horizontal provisions

582 Article 6(4) of the German Constitution: '*Every mother shall be entitled to the protection and care of the community*' ('*Jede Mutter hat Anspruch auf den Schutz und die Fürsorge der Gemeinschaft*'). Basic Law for the Federal Republic of Germany, 23 May 1949 (English version available at: http://www.refworld.org/docid/4e64d9a02.html, accessed 21 March 2017).

583 K.-P. Sommermann, *Staatsziele und Staatszielbestimmungen* (Mohr Siebeck 1997) 355; V. Brohm Winfried, 'Soziale Grundrechte und Staatszielbestimmungen in der Verfassung', JuristenZeitung, 1994, 213 ; C. Fercot, 'Précision et droits de l'Homme dans les ordres juridiques allemand et suisse' La Revue des droits de l'homme (en ligne) 7 - 2015 <http://revdh.revues.org/1330> accessed 7 June 2016 5-6.

584 Burgorgue-Larsen, 'L'article II-112' 683; Krommendijk, 'Principled Silence or Mere Silence on Principles? The Role of the EU Charter's Principles in the Case Law of the Court of Justice' 324; Barents, 'Een grondwet voor Europa (VI): de grondrechten' 40; Craig, 'Rights, Legality, and Legitimacy' 216.

585 Spanish Constitution, 1978.

586 T. Von Danwitz and K. Paraschas, 'A Fresh Start for the Charter: Fundamental Questions on the Application of the European Charter of Fundamental Rights' (2012) 35 Fordham International Law Journal 1396; Lorenz, Groussot and Petursson, *The European Human Rights Culture - A Paradox of Human Rights Protection in Europe?* 195.

587 H.J.Th.M. Van Roosmalen and A. Pahladsingh, 'Het Handvest van de grondrechten van de Europese Unie: beweging in de rechtspraak' (2013) Nederlands

that should guide the interpretation of the substantive provisions) it is not surprising that there have been many (contradictory) suggestions regarding its meaning and consequences. Most of the discussion in the literature is focused on two main issues: the criteria for practically applying the rights/ principles distinction, and the consequences that this distinction entails.

1.2.2.3. Possible criteria for the distinction

The different theories as to the interpretation of the distinction between rights and principles cannot be used if it is not clear, in the first place, how the distinction is to be made – in other words, according to which criteria should we distinguish a 'right' from a 'principle'? Two main approaches to that problem may be identified.[588] One consists in an intentionalist approach, the other in a series of variants of the direct effect test.

The first possibility for applying the distinction and identifying rights and principles is what may be called the intentionalist approach. It consists in trying to discern whether the drafters intended each particular provision to function as a right or a principle – with the idea that several Charter provisions are labelled 'right' or 'principle'.[589] Yet the terminology in the Charter itself is not very helpful, as there are only three provisions which are labelled as 'principles': Article 23 on the principle of equality, Article 37 on sustainable development, and Article 49 on the legality and proportionality of criminal offences and penalties. Moreover, the latter provision in fact corresponds to a 'right' in the meaning of the Charter; and it seems there are more than just two or three 'principles' in the whole Charter.[590] Among the proponents of a purely intentionalist approach, Lord Goldsmith thus recommends to focus on the phrasing of each provision to determine whether the intention of the authors was to establish a justiciable right or a principle. When the word 'principle' does not appear in the

---

tijdschrift voor Europees recht 83 87; Krommendijk, 'Principled Silence or Mere Silence on Principles? The Role of the EU Charter's Principles in the Case Law of the Court of Justice'.

588 Other criteria have occasionnally been suggested, e.g. the equation between rights and prohibition, and principles and positive action, but easily dismissed in light of the positive phrasing of some provisions labelled rights. Craig, 'Rights, Legality, and Legitimacy' 218.

589 A.W. Heringa and L. Verhey, 'The EU Charter: Text and Structure' (2001) 8 Maastricht Journal of European and Comparative Law 11 14.

590 Krommendijk, 'Principled Silence or Mere Silence on Principles? The Role of the EU Charter's Principles in the Case Law of the Court of Justice' 330.

wording of a provision, the '*drafting method*' would still indicate whether it should be construed as a right or a principle: '*the Union recognises and respects*' or the reference to '*national law and practices*' (meaning that a margin of discretion would be left to national authorities) would indicate a principle (i.e. not a justiciable right).[591]

The various provisions of the Charter have not been explicitly or systematically categorised, neither in the Charter nor in the Explanations.[592] The latter document may however be of help for categorising certain provisions; the phrase '*the principle(s) set out in this Article*' is indeed a recurrent one, describing Articles 26, 34, 35, 37, 38. Moreover, the Explanations on Article 36 even make explicit use of the right/principle divide by stating that Article 36 '*does not create any new right*' and instead '*merely sets out*' a '*principle*'. However, with regard to other provisions the Explanations are more confusing than they are helpful, since the Explanations on Article 52(5) point out that some provisions '*may contain both elements of a right and a principle*', citing Articles 23, 33, 34 as examples in a list that does not seem to be exhaustive. In order to overcome that kind of difficulty, some refined criteria have been proposed. According to Krommendijk's thorough review of the literature the most commonly suggested criterion (also closest to Goldsmith's vision) is whether the provision aims to protect the rights of individuals.[593] According to the new distinction, the counterpart to Charter principles consists in Charter 'rights' – or, as the Explanations emphasise, 'subjective rights'. While this term 'subjective' is seldom used in English[594] it is strongly evocative of the German doctrine of subjective public rights based on the *Schutznorm* theory, and according to which an

---

591 Goldsmith, 'The Charter of Rights-A Brake Not an Accelerator' 476. Gordon and Moffatt also take the view that the reference to 'national law and practices' will significantly limit the impact of the Solidarity section of the Charter: Gordon and Moffatt, *EU Law in Judicial Review* (2nd edn, Oxford University Press 2014) 383. See also Sever who argues that Article 27, because of the restriction it contains, is insufficient to in itself confer rights on individuals. S. Sever, 'General Principles of Law and the Charter of Fundamental Rights' (Cahiers de droit européen - Les principes généraux du droit de l'Union européenne, Brussels, 10 September 2015).

592 In fact, as Borowski points out, the substantive provisions were for the most part drafted in 2000, i.e. before the distinction was introduced in 2004; the distinction therefore played little role in the original text. Borowski, 'The Charter of Fundamental Rights in the Treaty on European Union' 211.

593 Krommendijk, 'Principled Silence or Mere Silence on Principles? The Role of the EU Charter's Principles in the Case Law of the Court of Justice' 332.

594 Prechal explains that she uses the term 'individual rights' as an alternative to the continental law notion of 'subjective rights'. The use of this expression originates

individual will have access to court if the provision allegedly violated by the public authorities is clearly intended to protect individual interests.[595] Following this logic, then, a provision where no such intention is detectable could be categorised as a 'principle', i.e. a public obligation not directly enforceable by individuals, as opposed to an expressly intended 'right', i.e. a rule directly justiciable in court. Considering the genesis of the Charter, an additional filter could be the socio-economic character of the provisions which, according to Lord Goldsmith, it itself would indicate that these '*are not justiciable as such until implemented by detailed legislation.*'[596] This limited justiciability of the provisions of the Solidarity title, although it may have been intended by at least part of the drafters, is however not supported (nor, admittedly, excluded) by the text of the Charter itself.

A different group of suggested approaches may be identified, reminiscent of the direct effect test that we know from *Van Gen den Loos*.[597] Heringa and Verey rely on '*generally accepted practice*' to suggest that 'rights' correspond to '*clear and well-defined obligations on the states to which enforceable subjective rights correspond*', while '*principles indicate less precise "objectives" and basic, fundamental premises that may give rise to rights but that need further clarification before they can be enforced*'. This general approach can be subdivided into several versions. Some authors have attempted to use the

---

in the need to distinguish between 'law' and 'rights', since these two notions have merged into one single word – 'droit' in French, 'Recht' in German. This has resulted in the distinction between 'droit objectif'/'objektives Recht' (norms) and 'droit subjectif'/'subjektives Recht'. See Prechal, 'Direct Effect, Indirect Effect, Supremacy and the Evolving Constitution of the European Union' 45 (footnote 40); Prechal and Van Roermund, 'Binding Unity in EU Legal Order: An Introduction'. See also on the distinction between 'law' and 'rights': S. Beljin, 'Rights in EU Law' in S. Prechal and B. Van Roermund (eds), *The Coherence of EU Law The Search for Unity in Divergent Concepts* (Oxford University Press 2008) 95; J. Rivers, '*A Theory of Constitutional Rights* and the British Constitution', in R. Alexy, *A Theory of Constitutional Rights* (J. Rivers tr, Oxford University Press 2002) xxiii. A search in the Court's database on 1 April 2017 reveals that, at least in English, the Court does prefer the adjective '*individual*' to the adjective '*subjective*': the search for 'individual rights' (in the plural) gives 390 judgments and 281 opinions of AGs. The search for 'individual right' (in the singular) gives 201 judgments and 131 opinions of AG. By contrast, only 81 judgments and 83 opinions of AG contain the term 'subjective rights' and 77 judgments and 85 opinions of AGs include 'subjective right'.

595 See p. 52 of this work.

596 Goldsmith, 'The Charter of Rights – A Brake Not an Accelerator' 476.

597 *Van Gend en Loos*, C-26/62.

direct effect test to categorise the provisions of the Charter as either 'rights' or 'principles'. For instance, it has been suggested that some of these provisions '*appear to be fully judicial rights since they are sufficiently clear and precise*', such as Articles 27, 28, 32, 33(2) and 34(2).[598] In the same vein, Craig insists that '*there is no reason why an individual should not be able to bring a legal rights-based claim against a State that sought to charge*' for placement services, since Article 29 provides that everyone has the right to a free placement service. A similar argument may be brought forward with regard to Articles 30 and 31, as '*there is no reason why*' they should not be cognisable in court.[599] This 'no reason why' motto is perfectly consistent with the Court's finding in *Van Gend en Loos* that nothing prevents Article 12 EEC from being relied on by individuals.[600] There are also some suggestions to focus on whether a provision depends on further implementation, or on the margin of discretion left to the authorities.[601] All these tests contain elements of a same familiar method for identifying rights, i.e. the direct effect test. However, the fact that different authors assign the 'right' tag to different provisions shows the difficulty in an abstract, a priori classification of the Charter's provisions. Prechal thus sensibly insists that the assessment should be carried out in each concrete and particular case: '*Whether or not a provision containing a fundamental right can be relied upon in concrete cases involves an assessment that is best performed by the courts. In fact, it boils down to a question of direct effect. That is, the courts have to determine whether or not the provisions at issue are "unconditional and sufficiently precise" to be applied* for the purposes relied upon *by the individual concerned.*'[602] This suggestion finds further support if we look at the implications of applying an *a priori* filter to the provisions of the Charter.

---

598 Lorenz, Groussot and Petursson, *The European Human Rights Culture - A Paradox of Human Rights Protection in Europe?* 196.

599 Craig, 'Rights, Legality, and Legitimacy' 218.

600 *Van Gend en Loos*, C-26/62, p. 13: the fact that '*it is the Member States who are made the subject of the negative obligation does not imply that their nationals cannot benefit from this obligation*'.

601 Krommendijk, 'Principled Silence or Mere Silence on Principles? The Role of the EU Charter's Principles in the Case Law of the Court of Justice' 333. See also M. De Mol et al., 'Inroepbaarheid in rechte van het Handvest van de Grondrechten van de Europese Unie: Toepassingsgebied en het onderscheid tussen 'rechten' en 'beginselen'', 60 SEW (2012) 222.

602 Prechal, 'Rights v principles, or how to remove fundamental rights from the jurisdiction of the courts' 183.

1.2.2.4. Consequences of applying the distinction to Charter provisions

Assuming that 'rights' and 'principles' may be distinguished, what is the consequence for a Charter provision of falling into one or the other category? Article 51(1) of the Charter tells us that rights must be '*respected*' and principles '*observed*'. In addition, the EU and the Member States implementing EU law must also '*promote the application*' of the principles. It has occasionally been argued that the distinction should simply be dismissed as irrelevant. On the contrary, others argue that it should become the main tool for distinguishing between justiciable rights and non-justiciable obligations. Somewhere in between, the theory of exclusionary effects has been suggested as a middle ground.

Perhaps the easiest way out (which does not necessarily make it a bad way out) is the position defended by Hilson. His argument is that the distinction is irrelevant to the functioning of EU law and the application of Charter provisions,[603] and that a strictly literal construction of the right/principle distinction laid down in the Charter simply does not work. This is congruent with Van Leuven's work showing how it is impossible to assume that principles would fall into the category of soft law while rights would constitute hard law.[604] Similarly, Borowski dismisses the relevance of the distinction by stating: '*one would expect that the distinction between 'subjective rights' and mere 'objective principles' plays no decisive role in cases heard before the ECJ, for the scheme of judicial review in the Union is based on the French system, in which 'illegality' is key, not the violation of rights.*'[605] This is in line with the characteristics of the correlativity model in the sense that the phrasing of a provision either as a right or as an obligation, has little relevance for the justiciability of the said provision. A problem with such an option is that it leads to ignoring the status of Articles 51(1) and 52(5) as horizontal provisions which should guide the interpretation of the substantive provisions of the Charter. It is therefore difficult and questionable to just try to bypass the questions raised by the distinction.

Another problem is that the distinction is in fact being put to use in a number of cases which, although limited so far, cannot simply be ignored. Some Advocates General have attempted to make sense and use of the distinction, especially by presenting rights and principles as mutually exclu-

---

603 Hilson, 'Rights and Principles in EU Law: A Distinction Without Foundation?'.

604 N. Van Leuven, 'Droits et principes de la Charte des droits fondamentaux de l'Union européenne : pas d'opposition simple entre hard law et soft law'.

605 Borowski, 'The Charter of Fundamental Rights in the Treaty on European Union' 212.

sive concepts. Advocate General Cruz Villalón's Opinion in *Association de Médiation Sociale* provides an elaborate reflection on the issue. The Advocate General construes the distinction between rights and principles as meaning that provisions of the Charter which are phrased as obligations for Member States and EU Institutions cannot translate into rights for individuals. Since "*principles' are characterised by the concept of obligation*', the obligatory nature of some provisions would allow them to identify them as principles and it would simultaneously exclude the possibility for individuals to directly claim the corresponding rights.[606] Advocate General Jääskinen argues along the same lines in *Schönberger*, that Article 52(5) CFR implies that some Charter provisions '*are not considered to be individual rights*'.[607] In the same vein, in *Wojciechowski*, the Belgian state argued that Article 34 on social security and social assistance only laid down a principle and therefore could not be claimed by an individual. Advocate General Mengozzi supported this view and maintained this position in the *Melchior* case concerning the same provision.[608] In none of these cases has the Court endorsed the proposed solution, or even expressly addressed the meaning of the rights/principles distinction.[609] The closest that the Court got to directly addressing the distinction was in *Glatzel:* Article 26 of the Charter requiring the integration of disabled persons, was labelled as a principle

606 Opinion of AG Cruz Villalón in *Association de médiation sociale*, C-176/12, EU:C:2013:491, paras 50-51.

607 Opinion of AG Jääskinen in *Schönberger*, C-261/13 P, EU:C:2014:2107, paras 57-58.

608 Opinion of AG Mengozzi in *Wojciechowski*, C-408/14, EU:C:2015:393, para 24 and para 67. Ultimately, however, the Court solved the issue without deeming it necessary to use Article 34 of the Charter, focusing instead on the principle of sincere cooperation enshrined at Article 4(3) TEU and the deriving obligation to apply the EU legislation protecting pension rights. Opinion of AG Mengozzi in *Melchior*, C-647/13, EU:C:2014:2301, paras 60-62. Again the Court did not deem it necessary to use Article 34 of the Charter and held that in light of the principle of cooperation the domestic legislation at issue was contrary to EU law. Judgment of 4 February 2015, *Melchior*, C-647/13, EU:C:2015:54.

609 In *AMS* the Court reached a solution without expressly relying on the rights/principles distinction (see below p. 351 for an analysis of the Court's solution). Some Advocates General also steer clear from the rights/principles distinction even when national courts ask for an interpretation of it. For instance, in *Daouidi*, Barcelona's social tribunal seemed to have integrated the distinction between 'rights' having (even horizontal) direct effect and 'principles' requiring consistent interpretation, and AG Bot did not address the corresponding question: Opinion of AG Bot in *Daouidi*, C-395/15, EU:C:2016:371, para 30 (see the 4th question).

(based especially on the Explanations[610]) and the Court explained that '*it must be given more specific expression in European Union or national law. Accordingly, that article cannot by itself confer on individuals a subjective right which they may invoke as such*'.[611]

These scarce explicit applications of the distinction echo the doctrinal position according to which rights are justiciable provisions whereas principles are not. According to the Explanations, principles do not '*give rise to direct claims for positive action by the Union's institutions or Member States authorities*'. In other languages the restriction is phrased as follows: '*begründen ... keine direkten Ansprüche auf den Erlass positiver Massnahmen durch die Organe der Union oder die Behörden den Mitgliedstaaten*'/'*ne donnent ... pas lieu à des droits immédiats à une action positive de la part des institutions de l'Union ou des autorités des Etats membres*'/'*geven ... geen aanleiding tot directe eisen tot het nemen van positieve maatregelen door de instellingen van de Unie of de overheden van de lidstaten*'. The common denominator is clearly the absence of 'direct' (or 'immédiat' in French) effect of those provisions of the Charter which qualify as principles. From this perspective, Charter principles may be construed as never directly usable in court; instead, they would be justiciable only through EU or national measures implementing EU law and giving expression to these principles. For example, according to Lord Goldsmith, a principle is by essence opposed to a justiciable right; Goldsmith does not even understand principles as obligations for the Member States or the EU institutions to act, since they '*become significant for the courts only when acts implementing the principles are interpreted or reviewed.*'[612] Likewise, Commissioner Vitorino argued that there should be '*a right where the holder is clearly designated*' and a principle '*where the Union is referred to as having to respect or recognize a specific value such as a healthy environment or protection of consumers*'.[613] Those provisions which can be identified as rights would apply to individual situations, while principles would only define general matters and outcomes for guiding the action of public bodies.[614]

---

610 Judgment of 22 May 2014, *Glatzel*, C-356/12, EU:C:2014:350, para 74.

611 *Glatzel*, C-356/12, paras 77-78.

612 Goldsmith, 'The Charter of Rights-A Brake Not an Accelerator' 476. This view is also supported by Ladenburger: C. Ladenburger, 'European Institutional Report' in J. Laffranque (ed), *The Protection of Fundamental Rights Post-Lisbon: The Interaction between the Charter of Fundamental Rights of the European Union, the European Convention on Human Rights and National Constitutions* (Reports of the XXC FIDE Congress, Tallinn, 2012).

613 Commissioner Vitorino cited by Craig, 'Rights, Legality, and Legitimacy' 216.

614 Robin-Olivier, 'The evolution of direct effect in the EU: Stocktaking, problems, projections' 169.

Depending on what kind of binding force we want for the Charter, viewing Charter principles as non-binding, guiding provisions may be seen as the ideal solution (for instance from Lord Goldsmith's perspective), but one may, on the contrary, find regrettable that this interpretation restricts the potential impact of the Charter. Moreover, the genesis of the Charter limits the relevance of this interpretation: according to the Commission, certain rights envisaged at the beginning have not been included '*because they were seen as simply setting policy objectives (…) this is the case as regards the right to work or right to an equitable wage*'.[615] By contrast this would suggest that the elements that have eventually been included, even the Charter's 'principles', are meant to do more than just set out objectives.

As a middle ground, Guy Braibant's notion of '*normative justiciability*' was introduced in an attempt to bridge the gap between those Member States who insisted on including social provisions in the Charter and those who were very reluctant to see such provisions be granted the label of fundamental rights.[616] This notion provides for the invalidation of rules which violate principles occupying a higher place in the hierarchy of norms, as opposed to subjective justiciability corresponding to the possibility for a norm to be relied on before a judge in order to obtain individual satisfaction.[617] In this vein, 'principles' would have normative justiciability while 'rights' would be subjectively justiciable. This solution is conceptually very close to the distinction that Lenaerts makes between 'exclusionary effects' or 'invocabilité d'exclusion' as opposed to 'invocabilité de substitution': '*whilst principles may not impose positive obligations on the EU, or, as the case may be, on national authorities, they may however be relied upon with a view to setting aside conflicting legislation.*' The EU and national legislators would thus be prevented from adopting regressive measures contrary to the prin-

615 Commission Communication on the Charter of Fundamental Rights of the European Union, 13.9.2000 (COM(2000) 559 final).

616 EU Network of Independent Experts on Fundamental Rights, 'Commentary of the Charter" <http://ec.europa.eu/justice/fundamental-rights/files/networkcommentaryfinal_en.pdf> accessed 9 October 2015; G. Braibant, *La Charte des droits fondamentaux de l'Union européenne* (Seuil 2001) 45-46; Ballot, *Les insuffisances de la notion de droits fondamentaux* 202; Krommendijk, 'Principled Silence or Mere Silence on Principles? The Role of the EU Charter's Principles in the Case Law of the Court of Justice' 326; L. Burgorgue-Larsen, 'Ombres et Lumières de la constitutionnalisation de la Charte des droits fondamentaux de l'Union européenne' 683; Roman, 'La justiciabilité des droits sociaux ou les enjeux de l'édification d'un Etat de droit social'9.

617 Ballot, *Les insuffisances de la notion de droits fondamentaux* 192.

ciples enshrined in the Charter.[618] In other words, the idea is to grant partial direct effect to Charter principles. In this vision, the justiciability of principles is not rejected; instead, rights and principles correspond to different degrees of justiciability. Burgorgue-Larsen sums up this interpretation of the rights/principles distinction by proposing that rights work as swords while principles function as shields.[619]

This balanced solution could, however, be criticised for again limiting the impact of provisions labelled as 'principles', which coincide at least partially with those provisions that are described as the most innovative, those that have the potential to offer new types of protection to individuals – that is, the 'Solidarity' provisions. In addition, it can also be viewed as redundant given that the direct effect test already provides an exhaustive solution for assessing the ability of a rule to give rise to rights, covering both exclusionary and substitutive effects.[620] Or, on the contrary, if considered as a filter to be applied preliminarily to performing a direct effect test, it still requires 'principles' to be identified *a priori*, and barred from having full direct effect.[621] This is not inconsistent with the likely rationale behind the rights/principles distinction, i.e. '*restraint in the interpretation and application of the Charter's provisions*'.[622] As Krommendijk pointed out, too broad an interpretation of Charter provisions as 'rights' would translate into too many opportunities for individuals to challenge democratically established

618 Lenaerts, 'Exploring the Limits of the EU Charter of Fundamental Rights' 400; see also O. De Schutter, 'Les droits et principes sociaux dans la Charte des droits fondamentaux de l'Union européenne' in J.Y. Carlier and O. De Schutter (eds), *La Charte des droits fondamentaux de l'Union européenne* (Bruylant 2002), and Guðmundsdóttir, 'A Renewed Emphasis on the Charter's Distinction Between Rights and Principles: Is a Doctrine of Judicial Restraint More Appropriate?' 693.

619 Burgorgue-Larsen, 'Ombres et Lumières de la constitutionnalisation de la Charte des droits fondamentaux de l'Union européenne'.

620 In the pre-Lisbon setting the distinction between exclusion and substitution had already been proposed e.g. by AG Léger and ignored by the Court, who instead relied on a classic direct effect test. See Opinion of AG Léger, *Linster*, C-287/98, EU:C:2000:3 and Judgment of 19 September 2000, *Linster*, C-287/98, EU:C:2000:468. S. Prechal and L. Hancher, 'Individual Environmental Rights: Conceptual Pollution in EU Environmental Law?' (2001) 2 Yearbook of European Environmental Law 89 95.

621 Lorenz, Groussot and Petursson, *The European Human Rights Culture - A Paradox of Human Rights Protection in Europe?* 196.

622 Prechal, 'Rights v principles, or how to remove fundamental rights from the jurisdiction of the courts' 184.

EU and national acts and measures,[623] bringing grist to the mill of those who argue that direct effect sustains the legitimacy deficit in the EU.[624] Nevertheless, this approach has the potential to foster more than 'restraint'. An inversion takes place: while direct effect constituted the test for detecting rights, now we need to know first whether a provision qualifies as a right or principle, only then do we determine whether it has direct effect. This is not only inconsistent with the original direct effect test, which is essentially circumstancial, as *Defrenne II* already showed.[625] Identifying too many Charter provisions as 'principles' would indeed leave individuals empty handed.[626] Moreover, the fear that the Charter would give rise to an excessive number of rights is unfounded at least insofar as, since the Charter applies to Member States only when they are implementing EU law, '*there is no direct effect or supremacy for the Charter provisions alone, and there is no power for the ECJ or national courts to apply the Charter rights or principles independently.*'[627]

This overview emphasises the difficulty to reach a consensus either on the criteria or on the consequences of the distinction between rights and principles – and the difficulties inherent in the abstract categorisation of provisions which are meant to be applied to concrete cases.

1.2.2.5. Potential problems for rights within the Union's constitutional structure

The rights/principles polarisation raises a number of issues that stretch beyond the Charter itself, since it potentially affects the relation between primary and secondary EU law as sources of rights. As discussed above, the abundance of these contact points renders impossible a 'closed-circuit' approach to the Charter that would include a method of interpretation distinct from that which applies to other sources of rights. Instead, what we need is a harmonised method for identifying rights in all sources of EU

623 Krommendijk, 'Principled Silence or Mere Silence on Principles? The Role of the EU Charter's Principles in the Case Law of the Court of Justice' 322.

624 Weiler, 'Van Gend en Loos: The individual as subject and object and the dilemma of European legitimacy'.

625 *Defrenne v SABENA*, C-43/75. See p. 40 of this work.

626 Krommendijk, 'Principled Silence or Mere Silence on Principles? The Role of the EU Charter's Principles in the Case Law of the Court of Justice' 322.

627 Raulus, 'The Charter of Fundamental Rights as a set of constitutional principles' 187.

fundamental rights. In this respect, we know that according to the Explanations, several Charter provisions are based at least in part on pre-existing EU secondary legislation. In addition, Article 52(2) makes clear that Charter rights corresponding to Treaty provisions must be exercised '*under the conditions and limits*' defined by the Treaties. This also has implications beyond primary law, because as Craig points out, often a Treaty provision will be '*set in general terms*' while '*the more specific conditions for its exercise*' will be laid down in secondary legislation. Craig thus asks whether '*Article 52(2) is applicable in these instances, such that conditions and limits contained in a regulation or directive would then impose constraints on the interpretation of an analogous Charter right*'.[628] To this already complex relation between the Charter and Union secondary law, Article 52(5) adds that Charter principles '*shall be judicially cognisable only in the interpretation*' and '*in the ruling on [the] legality*' of acts taken by the Union or Member States to implement these provisions. If Article 52(5) is to be understood as laying down a method of interpretation centred on the rights/principles divide, the question arises what are we to make of all the contact points between the Charter and other sources of fundamental rights.[629]

Article 52(5) has been interpreted by Lord Goldsmith as meaning that principles should be used to review only the legislation adopted to implement them.[630] In line with this interpretation, in *AMS* Advocate General Cruz Villalón suggested that secondary law could be controlled with regard to Charter principles only by confronting them to a first layer of secondary legislation which would be explicitly intended to apply these principles.[631] It has been pointed out, however, that such an interpretation would prevent applicants from challenging measures which clearly violate

628 Craig, 'Rights, Legality, and Legitimacy' 228.

629 This issue has been pointed out by Lenaerts and Gutiérrez-Fons, who support an interpretation of the rights/principles distinction based on the concept of exclusionary effects precisely because too restrictive an interpretation of the term 'principle' would cause serious problems for the interpretation of Charter provisions which contain both a Charter principle and a general principle of EU law, such as the precautionary principle (Art. 37 CFR) and ultimately this would cause the scope of protection of the Charter to retract. Lenaerts, 'Exploring the Limits of the EU Charter of Fundamental Rights' 403; Lenaerts and Gutierrez-Fons, 'The Place of the Charter in the EU Constitutional Edifice' 1576.

630 Goldsmith, 'The Charter of Rights-A Brake Not an Accelerator' 476.

631 Opinion of AG Cruz Villalón in *Association de médiation sociale*, C-176/12, ECLI:EU:C:2013:491.

Charter 'principles', as long as they do not give expression to them.[632] This is an intuitively disturbing result and also a break from the *Van Gend en Loos/Defrenne* approach which established that the provision at issue only needs to be sufficiently clear, precise and unconditional to identify a violation in a given case, for it to be enforceable. The provisions of the Charter which correspond to pre-existing Treaty provisions or general principles are to a certain extent protected from the restrictive effects of the rights/principles distinction because of the existing case law which is to be taken into account when interpreting Charter provisions.[633] The problem, as already pointed out, is more acute when it comes to guarantees which did not have a clear status of fundamental rights prior to their inclusion in the Charter, i.e., most articles from the Solidarity Title. It is also exacerbated in the case of provisions containing restrictions such as '*under the conditions provided for by Union law and national law and practices*' or equivalent propositions.[634] Should these provisions (of which many Solidarity provisions) never give rise to rights in the classic *Van Gen den Loos* sense because they depend on further implementing measures?

The notion of implementing legislation as a barrier blocking the legality review of other secondary legislation with regard to primary EU law could already be detected in the arguments over the *Defrenne II* case back in 1975.

---

632 Burgorgue-Larsen, 'L'article II-112' 687; Lenaerts, 'Exploring the Limits of the EU Charter of Fundamental Rights' 400 ; K. Lenaerts and J.A. Gutierrez-Fons, 'The Place of the Charter in the EU Constitutional Edifice' in S. Peers and others (eds), *The EU Charter of Fundamental Rights A Commentary* (Hart Publishing 2014) 1577.

633 However, since Article 52(5) is meant to apply transversally to the whole Charter, the rights/principle distinction would need to be applied consistently to provisions laying down both 'old' and 'new' fundamental rights.

634 These restrictions are phrased in slightly different ways across the Charter: '*in accordance with the national laws*' in Article 9 (Right to marry and right to found a family), Article 10 (Freedom of thought, conscience and religion), Article 14 (Right to education), Article 16 (Freedom to conduct a business); '*in the cases and under the conditions provided for by Union law and national laws and practices*' in Article 27 (Workers' right to information and consultation); '*in accordance with Union law and national laws and practices*' in Article 28 (Right of collective bargaining and action) and Article 30 (Protection in the event of unjustified dismissal); '*in accordance with the rules laid down by Union law and national laws and practices*' in Article 34 (Social security and social assistance); '*under the conditions established by national laws and practices*' in Article 35 (Health care); '*as provided for in national laws and practices, in accordance with the Treaties*' in Article 36 (Access to services of general economic interest). This is reinforced by Article 52(6) CFR stating that '*Full account shall be taken of national laws and practices as specified in this Charter*'.

Article 119 EEC was a programmatic provision; it was not phrased as a right and it required further implementing measures by the Member States in order to eliminate discrimination in the workplace (all characteristics which make it resemble a Charter 'principle' in the light of the criteria that have been discussed above). One argument of the British and Irish governments against the direct applicability of Article 119 was that the transposition period for the directive which aimed to specify the requirements of that provision (especially by ensuring judicial protection to workers wronged by failure to apply the principle of equal pay) had not yet expired. In other words, they argued that the directive should be preventing the direct application of the primary law provision from which it was derived as long as it was not itself applicable.[635] To a French lawyer, this linear and hermetic conception of the hierarchy of norms could be reminiscent of the French *loi-écran* theory. According to this theory, which dates back to the French Revolution and is connected with a strong emphasis on a strict separation of powers, an act implementing a law will be deemed valid even if the conformity of the law with the constitution (or with international obligations) has not been established, and that law will block the possibility for an administrative court to control the constitutionality of the act.[636] Thus the concept of 'legislative screen' makes sense in the light of French judicial history, especially given the division of competences between the *Conseil d'Etat* and the *Conseil Constitutionnel* (and even in this context it is controversial).[637]

However, in the constitutional framework of the Union, where there is no such division of competences, it is more difficult to justify preventing

---

635 See the summary of the written observations submitted to the Court, *Defrenne v. SABENA*, C-43/75, p. 459-461.

636 Judgments of the French Conseil d'Etat: Arrighi, CE, section, 6 nov 1936, Rec. p 966 (loi-écran in the context of 'contrôle de constitutionnalité') and Nicolo, CE, ass., 20 oct 1989, n°108243 (loi-écran in the context of 'contrôle de conventionnalité'); M. Lasser, *Judicial Transformations: The Rights Revolution in the Courts of Europe* (Oxford University Press 2009) 1 and 27-33; V. Schnebel, 'Le juge administratif, un nouveau juge de la constitutionnalité des lois? 14 November 2011 <http://chevalierdesgrandsarrets.com/2011/11/14/le-juge-administratif-un-nouveau-juge-de-la-constitutionnalité-des-lois/> accessed 20 April 2015 ; Poulet-Gibot Leclerc, *Droit administratif: sources, moyens, contrôles* 50; F. Hagner, *Les particuliers et l'ordre juridique communautaire : l'égalité de traitement entre les hommes et les femmes* 72.

637 J. Gicquel and J.-E. Gicquel, *Droit constitutionnel et institutions politiques* (Montchrestien, Lextenso éditions 2008) 105. See also F. Batailler, *Le Conseil d'Etat, Juge constitutionnel* (L.G.D.J. 1966).

the Court from controlling the compatibility of secondary law with fundamental rights protected by primary law.[638] Concerning the relation between Charter provisions and national legislation of Member States, the Court held, concerning Article 28 CFR on the right to collective bargaining, the Court has interpreted the restriction '*in accordance with Union law and national laws and practices*' by recognising that these national laws and practices must be taken into account in the protection of the fundamental right, but that conversely '*that right must be exercised in accordance with European Union law.*'[639]

In *Defrenne*, the Court rejected the argument of the Member States, stating that '*no implementing provision, whether adopted by the Institutions of the Community or by the national authorities, could adversely affect the direct effect of Article 119*'.[640] A contemporary reaffirmation of this solution is to be found in the controversial *Kücükdeveci* case, where it was asked whether the prohibition on age discrimination in the workplace, as detailed in Directive 2000/78,[641] could be relied on by Mrs Kücükdeveci against her employer. The Court explained that Directive 2000/78 '*gives specific expression*' to the principle of non-discrimination on grounds of age. The consequence was that the requirement of non-discrimination became sufficiently precise to have direct (horizontal) effect and thus provided the tools to identify both the rights of Ms. Kücükdeveci and the violation of those rights. The national court was thus under a duty to disapply the contrary provisions of national law.[642] Importantly, the Court expressly drew an analogy with *Defrenne II* when stating that the directive gives specific expression to the general principle of non-discrimination.[643] The cited paragraph from *Defrenne II* indicated that the directive on the principle of equal pay for men and women provided '*further details regarding certain aspects of the material scope of Article 119*' and adopted '*various provisions whose essential purpose [was] to improve the legal protection of workers who may be wronged by failure to apply the principle of equal pay laid down by Article 119.*' It is almost

638 Borowski, 'The Charter of Fundamental Rights in the Treaty on European Union' 212.

639 Judgment of 15 July 2010, *Commission v Germany*, C-271/08, EU:C:2010:426, paras 38-43. Rosas and Kaila, 'L'application de la Charte des droits fondamentaux de l'Union européenne par la Cour de justice : un premier bilan' 25.

640 *Defrenne v. SABENA*, C-43/75, para 64.

641 Council Directive 2000/78/EC of 27 November 2000 establishing a general framework for equal treatment in employment and occupation (OJ 2000 L 303, p.16).

642 Judgment of 19 January 2010, *Kücükdeveci*, C-555/07, EU:C:2010:21, para 51.

643 *Defrenne v SABENA*, C-43/75, para 54.

as if the Court was minimising the substantive input of the directive. In *Kücükdeveci*, we have a general principle and Charter provision instead of a Treaty provision, but the idea is also that the main source of the right is in primary law and not in the directive, meaning also that the latter does not function as a 'legislative screen'.[644] Consistently with this solution, in another case on non-discrimination on grounds of age Advocate General Bobek has argued that '*as long as the provisions at issue fall within the scope of EU law through the operation of Directive 2000/78, the scope of protection of the Charter is triggered*' and that the relationship between the Charter and the Directive is '*one of concretisation and complementarity*', so that '*the provisions of the Charter constitute the ultimate yardstick of validity of EU secondary law*'.[645]

In the context of applying Treaty provisions, a further argument against the 'legislative screen' has been made by Advocate General Szpunar in his Opinion on the *AKT* case on social policy, more specifically on temporary agency work. Pointing out that Article 56 TFEU on the freedom to provide services had already been found to have direct effect (including horizontal direct effect), he explained that '*prior to the adoption of Directive 2008/104, national measures which restricted the use of temporary agency work, and therefore also raised an obstacle to the provision of services in that area, potentially fell within the scope of the prohibition laid down in Article 56 TFEU*'; therefore, '*it would be somewhat illogical to permit such measures to escape that prohibition merely because it is now given specific expression in Directive 2008/104 and because directives do not, in principle, apply directly to relationships between individuals*'.[646] Although in *AKT* the Court did not address that issue, the Advocate General's argument may be generalised so that it applies also to the Charter: a provision of primary law which fulfils the criteria for di-

644 An additional clarification is provided in *Dansk Industri*, a more recent age discrimination case, in which the Court explained that Directive 2000/78 was adopted in order to '*facilitate the practical implementation of the principle of equal treatment and, in particular, to specify various possible exceptions to that principle, circumscribing those exceptions by the use of a clearer definition of their scope*'. Judgment of 19 April 2016, *DI*, C-441/14, EU:C:2016:278, para 23.

645 Opinion of AG Bobek in *Abercrombie & Fitch Italia*, C-143/16, EU:C:2017:235, paras 26-28. The Court did not expressly validate or invalidate this approach but controlled the compatibility of the national provision at issue with '*Directive 2000/78, which gives specific expression, in the domain of employment and occupation, to the principle of non-discrimination on grounds of age, now enshrined in Article 21 of the Charter*'. Judgment of 19 July 2017, *Abercrombie & Fitch Italia*, C-143/16, EU:C:2017:566, para 17.

646 Opinion of AG Szpunar in *AKT*, C-533/13, EU:2014:2392, para 138-144.

rect effect should not be denied such effect only because it is being implemented through an instrument of secondary law – or, for that matter, because it has not been implemented.[647] Yet this is exactly what would happen if some Charter provisions abstractly labelled as 'principles' could as a consequence be used only in review of legislation through which they would be implemented.

1.2.3. Conclusions: structural continuity and conceptual instability

This section has examined the potential implications, for the original concept of rights, of introducing the Charter in the EU legal order. From a structural perspective, the main finding is that the Union's renovated constitutional architecture does not call for a revolution in the approach to sources of fundamental rights; it rather reinforces the need to take these sources in connection with one another, applying a unified method of interpretation. This is arguably the only way to make sense of the abundance of contact points between provisions of the Charter and rights enshrined in other instruments of primary and secondary, written and non-written EU law.

From a conceptual perspective, the introduction of a distinction between 'rights' and 'principles' is more challenging. Read literally and understood as laying down mutually exclusive concepts, this distinction has the potential to alter (and restrict) the classic definition of a right in EU law, by undermining the notion that any obligation (of primary or secondary law) has the potential to turn into a right. This is not only a hypothetical problem: we have seen examples in a limited number of judgments and opinions and in the literature, of the distinction between rights and principles being construed as a binary opposition. As a consequence the possibility that a given provision may amount to a right is dismissed on the

647 In another case, AG Szpunar has further argued that, conversely (and consistently with *Defrenne II*) the absence of implementing national measures cannot hinder the application of the right that stems from Article 56, because otherwise '*the exercise of that directly applicable provision, which confers a subjective economic right on [the applicant in the main proceedings], would be frustrated*'. Opinion of AG Szpunar in *Unibet International*, C-49/16, EU:C:2017:270, para 62.

sole ground that it is labelled a principle and thus 'merely' lays down an obligation.[648]

An underlying methodological problem is that the a priori categorisation of Charter provisions into 'rights' and 'principles' would lead to readjusting the relative relevance of conditionality and concrete circumstances in the process of identifying rights. One of the main characteristics of the correlation between obligations and rights, as established in the founding cases, is that its expression is dependent on concrete circumstances. *Defrenne II* illustrated this pragmatic conception of the rights-obligations correlation which allowed a partly conditional Treaty obligation to give rise to a directly applicable right.[649] A more restrictive, all-or-nothing understanding of conditionality – of the type that the UK was pushing for – would have led to a very different result, where an obligation conditioned to further measures would have automatically been prevented from giving rise to rights. In the same way, taking the rights/principles filter as a starting point for identifying rights in a provision minimises the importance of concrete circumstances, and thus restricts the array of situations where it would be possible to identify rights.

The risk of blocking the translation of an obligation into a right is greater for rules which have not yet been applied for a long time (i.e. social provisions of the Charter) and for the interpretation of which we cannot rely on a long line of case law based on general principles. Of course, the introduction of the rights/principles distinction was precisely to limit the impact of these provisions. Nevertheless, the implications of a rigid understanding of the distinction that is advocated in part of the literature and applied in a (for now marginal) number of cases, are more fare reaching, potentially affecting the historically dynamic role of the Court in identifying and applying rights. Ultimately, the conception of rights and principles as mutually exclusive concepts could generate a paradox: in our increasingly rights-focused system, the concept of rights itself would be restricted, *'to the detriment of individuals who are said to be located at the heart of the activities of the Union.'*[650] The more strictly the distinction will be interpreted, the more spectacular the break from the original concept of rights.

---

648 *Glatzel*, C-356/12; Opinion of AG Cruz Villalón in *Association de médiation sociale*, C-176/12 ; Opinion of AG Jääskinen in *Schönberger*, C-261/13 P; Opinion of AG Mengozzi in *Wojciechowski*, C-408/14. See p. 124 of this work.

649 *Defrenne v SABENA*, C-43/75. See p. 40 and p. 96.

650 Prechal, 'Rights v principles, or how to remove fundamental rights from the jurisdiction of the courts' 184.

1.3. *Protecting rights in the EU legal order: the relation between rights and remedies*

'That rights would be practically useless without remedies does not make remedies constitutive of rights'.[651]

We have looked in Sections 1.1 and 1.2 at the basic definition and functions of individual rights, and taken of stock the conceptual challenges that have arisen as a result of the constitutional reconfiguration performed by the Treaty of Lisbon. One important finding is that individual rights fulfil a double function of protecting individual interests and simultaneously advancing the interests of the EU as a whole. This means that the effectiveness of individual rights is crucial in the EU legal system. The importance of this requirement is reflected in the pivotal role of the right to an effective remedy, which comes in support of other rights conferred by EU law and ensures their effective enforcement. Our understanding of the relation between rights and remedies is thus closely related to our conception of rights. Although the concept of a remedy is crucial in the case law and in doctrinal discussions, it has only recently been introduced in written primary law, through the Treaty of Lisbon: according to Article 47 of the Charter, '*everyone whose rights and freedoms guaranteed by the law of the Union are violated has the right to an effective remedy before a tribunal (...)*'.[652]

This section highlights the various parameters at work in the implementation of individual rights under EU law, and assesses the conceptual and practical impacts for the relation between rights and remedies. For this purpose, it is important to keep in mind that rights do not have to be expressly phrased as such, since they can be correlatives of obligations, and can be activated by a variety of interests that are not necessarily pre-defined.[653] The notion of remedies is thus understood here as encompassing

651 MacCormick, *Institutions of Law* (Oxford University Press 2007) 286.

652 In addition, also an innovation of the Treaty of Lisbon, Article 19(1), second subparagraph requires Member States to '*provide remedies sufficient to ensure effective legal protection in the fields covered by Union law*'.

653 Therefore, definitions of remedies that are too focused on the protective intention of the legislator should be avoided. For instance, a definition of remedies as '*legal instruments whose aim is to protect rights from being violated*' (Półtorak, *European Union Rights in National Courts* 9) would be too restrictive for a starting point: it is not to be excluded that actions not expressly designed to protect rights may function as remedies.

the means of enforcing rights and/or make good their infringement,[654] which are governed and made operational by procedures.[655] The right-remedy relation in EU law has been shaped by the dynamism of the right-obligation correlativity, which, combined with the meta-principle of effectiveness of EU law, fostered the development of the right to an effective legal remedy and of correlative obligations of Member States (1.3.1). However, in the EU's complex *'de-central and multi-jurisdictional enforcement system'*,[656] some difficulties make the virtuous circle less virtuous: there is indeed a recurring tendency to restrict remedies, manifesting also a more restrictive conception of individual rights (1.3.2). The Court's response to this tendency is not homogeneous: the analysis will shed light on a discrepancy between the approach to rights which individuals claim in the enforcement system of their Member States, and the protection of rights afforded to individuals in direct actions before the EU Courts (1.3.3).

1.3.1. The right to an effective remedy, an illustration of the correlativity between obligations and rights

The historical and conceptual foundation of the right to an effective judicial remedy is the meta-principle of effectiveness of EU law (1.3.1.1.). With rights increasingly perceived as an end in themselves, the right to effective judicial protection, set out in Article 47 CFR, evolved into a more autonomous imperative, the link with the effectiveness of EU law being less systematically acknowledged (1.3.1.2). Yet the correlativity dynamic is still at work and detectable in how the evolution of the *right* to effective judicial protection of individual rights is mirrored in the extension of the corresponding *obligation* to provide the remedies for effectively enforcing these rights (1.3.1.3)

---

654 The definition of remedies as means of enforcing rights is from F.G. Wilman, 'The end of the absence? The growing body of EU legislation on private enforcement and the main remedies it provides for' (2016) 53 Common Market Law Review 887 891, citing A.P. Kominos, *EC Private Antitrust Enforcement: Decentralised Application of EC Competition Law by National Courts* (Hart 2008). The definition focused on making good infringements is from Van Gerven, 'Of Rights, Remedies and Procedures.'

655 Van Gerven, 'Of Rights, Remedies and Procedures.'

656 Hofmann, 'The Right to an 'Effective Judicial Remedy' and the Changing Conditions of Implementing EU Law' 19.

1.3.1.1. The relation between effectiveness and the right to an effective remedy

We have already seen that the effectiveness of EU law constitutes a powerful justification for the existence of individual rights. Once the connection is made between the empowerment of individuals and the purpose of ensuring the effectiveness of EU law, the tendency of EU law to open individual remedies before national courts as widely as possible[657] makes perfect sense. While effectiveness first appeared in the case law distinctly from the concept of rights,[658] the underlying effectiveness rationale that was at work in the seminal cases on individual rights was then legitimised and systematised by finding its justification in the principle of sincere cooperation enshrined in Article 5 EC. In *Rewe*,[659] the Court held that since the prohibition on charges having an effect equivalent to custom duties had direct effect and conferred rights on individuals, the principle of sincere cooperation required that those rights be protected by national courts, which in so doing also had to respect the principles of equivalence and effectiveness.[660] These principles set the limits of the national procedural autonomy of Member States.[661] Famously, the principle of equivalence requires Member States to provide remedies in case of infringement of EU law which are

657 Masing, *Die Mobilisierung des Bürgers für die Durchsetzung des Rechts: europäische Impulse für eine Revision der Lehre vom subjektiv-öffentlichen Recht* 38.

658 The Court held in a 1961 case that Article 67 of the ECSC Treaty (framing the prohibition of anticompetitive practices in the coal and steel industry) was '*designed to enable the juristiction of the Community to impinge on national sovereignty in cases where, because of the power retained by the Member States, this is necessary to prevent the effectiveness of the Treaty from being considerably weakened and its purpose from being seriously compromised.*' Judgment of 23 February 1961, *De gezamenlijke Steenkolenmijnen in Limburg v High Authority*, C-30/59, EU:C:1961:2, p. 24. Concerning EEC competition law, the Court held in 1969 that '*The EEC Treaty has established its own system of law, integrated into the legal system of the Member States, and which must be applied by their courts. It would be contrary to the nature of such a system to allow Member States to introduce or retain measures capable of prejudicing the effectiveness of the Treaty*'. Judgment of 13 February 1969, *Walt Wilhelm and Others v Bundeskartellamt*, C-14/68, EU:C:1969:4, para 6. Półtorak, *European Union Rights in National Courts* 40.

659 *Rewe v Landwirtschaftskammer für das Saarland*, C-33/76.

660 *Rewe v Landwirtschaftskammer für das Saarland*, 33/76, para 5. See e.g. L.M. Ravo, 'The role of the Principle of Effective Judicial Protection and its Impact on National Jurisdictions', *Sources of Law and Legal Protection (Triestine Lecture 1)* (EUT Edizioni Università di Trieste 2012) 109.

661 Półtorak, *European Union Rights in National Courts* 33: '*Procedural autonomy (…) may not be considered a normative but merely a descriptive principle. The concept de-*

equivalent to those which exist in case of infringement of national law, and the principle of effectiveness requires that the conditions set out in national law to use these remedies must not be framed so as to render virtually impossible or excessively difficult the exercise of the rights conferred by EU law. Subsequent case law confirmed that the obligation for Member States to provide effective judicial protection for the rights conferred by EU law is based on the principle of sincere cooperation and the notions of equivalence and effectiveness.[662] The latter notion, in particular, has flourished and become key in structuring the relation between rights and remedies in EU law.

With the *Johnston* ruling the Court drew the consequences from its findings in *Rewe*.[663] Ten years after *Defrenne II*, the fight against gender discrimination again provided momentum for further definition and protection of

---

scribes a certain reality, which is admission, in the absence of Union legislation and frequently also of competence in this respect, of independent actions by Member States in developing procedures and institutional structures for the fulfilment of obligations resulting from the Union system'. M. Bobek, 'Why There is no Principle of 'Procedural Autonomy' of the Member States', in B. de Witte and H. Micklitz (eds), *The European Court of Justice and the Autonomy of the Member States* (Intersentia 2012). Neframi, 'Quelques réflexions sur l'article 19, paragraphe 1, alinéa 2, TUE et l'obligation de l'Etat membre d'assurer la protection juridictionnelle effective dans les domaines couverts par le droit de l'Union'. On the legal foundations and definitions of national procedural autonomy see A. Östlund, 'Effectiveness of European Union Law versus Procedural Protection. Tracing the tension throughout the case-law of the Court of Justice on *ex officio* review by the national judge' (PhD thesis, University of Luxembourg 2017) 19-25.

662 *Comet BV v Produktschap voor Siergewassen*, 45/76, para 12; *Simmenthal*, C-106/77, paras 21 and 22; *Ammistrazione delle finanze dello Stato v San Giorgio*, C-199/82, para 12; *The Queen v Secretary of State for Transport, ex parte Factortame*, C-213/89, para 19; *Peterbroeck, Van Campenhout & Cie v Belgian State*, C-312/93, para 12; Judgment of 14 December 1995, *Van Schijndel v Stichting Pensioenfonds voor Fysiotherapeuten*, C-430/93 and C-431/93, EU:C:1995:441, para 17; *Unibet*, C-432/05, para 38. L.Y.M. Parret, 'Effectieve rechtsbescherming: eindeloos potentieel, ongeleid projectiel?' 158; H.C.H. Hofmann, 'Effective Judicial Remedies Before the National Courts' in A. Ward and others (eds), *The EU Charter of Fundamental Rights* (The EU Charter of Fundamental Rights, Hart 2014); on the principle of equivalence: N.J.M. De Munnik, 'Geen ambsthalve toepassing van Europees recht. Vragen van het CBb inzake Van der Weerd e.a. beantwoord' (2007) Nederlands tijdschrift voor Europees recht 246. See also Judgment of 8 June 2017, *Freitag*, C-541/15, EU:C:2017:432, para 42.

663 *Johnston v Chief Constable of the Royal Ulster Constabulary*, C-222/84. Already the *Von Colson* ruling indicated a similar solution regarding the interpretation of Council Directive 76/207/EEC of 9 February 1976 on the Implementation of the Principle of Equal Treatment for Men and Women as Regards Access to Employ-

individual rights. Mrs Johnston had been working in the auxiliary police of Northern Ireland, on the basis of three-year contracts which were regularly renewed. As women did not bear firearms, they could not accomplish certain missions, and the Chief Constable decided that it was no longer necessary to renew the contracts of female employees. Mrs Johnston challenged this decision, based on the equal treatment directive, especially on Article 6 according to which any person who deems himself/herself discriminated against must be able to claim his/her rights before a court. The Industrial Tribunal of Belfast submitted a reference for a preliminary ruling on the interpretation of the directive. One of the questions referred was whether the Member States were required to ensure the effective control by national courts over compliance with EU law. The Court first noted that the directive required that the observance of the rights laid down in it be effectively ensured by national courts. In a second step, the Court identified this requirement as a general principle of law which existed both in common constitutional traditions and in international law (especially in the ECHR);[664] as a consequence, the requirement could be generalised and extended beyond the sole framework of the directive. Read together, the directive and the general principle meant that all persons have the right to an effective judicial remedy against measures which they consider contrary to the principle of equal treatment. More specifically, a rule of national law that would suppress any possibility to go to courts to claim rights protected by EU law would be contrary to the principle of effective judicial control.[665]

---

ment, Vocational Training and Promotion, and Working Conditions (OJ L 39 p. 40) (the 'Equal Treatment Directive'). The Court did not require a specific type of sanction against discrimination in hiring, but the sanction had to '*guarantee real and effective judicial protection*': *Von Colson and Kamann v Land Nordrhein-Westfalen*, C-14/83, para 23. Hagner, *Les particuliers et l'ordre juridique communautaire : l'égalité de traitement entre les hommes et les femmes* 146.

664 The Court of Justice has repeatedly referred to the common constitutional traditions of the Member States and Articles 6 and 13 of the ECHR, as sources of the EU right to effective judicial protection. See e.g.: *Johnston*, C-222/84, paras 18 and 19; *Unectef v Heylens*, 222/86, para 14; *Unión de Pequeños Agricultores*, C-50/00 P, para 39; *Unibet*, C-432/05, para 37; *Kadi I*, Joined cases C-402/05 P and C-415/05 P, para 335; *Mono Car Styling*, C-12/08, para 47; *Alassini and Others*, C-317 to C-320/08, para 61. Hofmann, 'The Right to an 'Effective Judicial Remedy' and the Changing Conditions of Implementing EU Law' 1; Callies, 'Kohärenz und Konvergenz beim europäischen Individualrechtsschutz - Der Zugang zum Gericht im Lichte des Grundrechts auf effektiven Rechtsschutz' 3577.

665 *Johnston*, C-222/84, paras 17 to 20. Półtorak, *European Union Rights in National Courts* 10.

This judgment sheds light on the concept of rights in two ways. Firstly, it reiterates the Court's finding in *Van Gend en Loos* that individual rights can be born from obligations of the Member States:[666] here, the (procedural) right to an effective remedy was deduced from the obligation of the Member States to ensure that the (substantive) rights conferred by EU law may be effectively relied upon before national courts by the persons concerned. In addition to the substantive focus on the issue of gender discrimination, *Johnston* has another common trait with *Defrenne.* Let us remember that the Court had held that although Article 119 EEC required implementing measures in order to be fully effective, some aspects of this provision did immediately grant a right to Ms. Defrenne.[667] A similar reasoning occurs in *Johnston.* The Court admits that Article 6 of the directive '*does not contain, as far as sanctions for any discrimination are concerned, any unconditional and sufficiently precise obligation which may be relied upon by an individual.*' Yet, the Court adds that '*in so far as it follows from that article, construed in the light of a general principle which it expresses, that all persons who consider themselves wronged by sex discrimination must have an effective judicial remedy, that provision is sufficiently precise and unconditional to be capable of being relied upon as against a Member State which has not ensured that it is fully implemented in its internal legal order*'.[668] In other words, the provision is not sufficiently clear and precise for implementation of all its aspects, but it is sufficiently clear and precise for the purposes of the concrete case. The difference with *Defrenne* is that here the provision is read in light of a general principle of law, which contributes to making it 'clear' and 'precise'.[669]

Secondly, *Johnston* establishes '*a link between rights and the existence of a remedy*': the obligation for Member States to ensure effective judicial protection means that the requirement of a remedy is the logical consequence of the existence of a right.[670] This logical connection was confirmed in *Pe-*

---

666 *Van Gend en Loos*, C-26/62.

667 *Defrenne v SABENA*, C-43/75, paras 23-24.

668 *Johnston*, C-222/84, para 58.

669 This use of a broad range of instruments, including general principles, in order to assess the possibility for a given provision to grant rights in a concrete situation, is not exceptional in the Court's case law. Also in the field of non-discrimination, this approach was crucial in cases such as *Mangold* and *Kucukdeveci.* Judgment of 22 November 2005, *Mangold*, C-144/04, EU:C:2005:709; *Kücükdeveci*, C-555/07.

670 W. Van Gerven, 'Bridging the Unbridgeable - Community and National Tort Laws After Francovich and Brasserie' in H.-W. Micklitz and N. Reich (eds), *Public Interest Litigation before European Courts*, vol 1997 (Nomos 1997) 63. The

terbroeck[671] where Court also relied on the derivation of the right to effective legal protection from the principle of sincere cooperation. The Brussels Court of Appeal had referred questions to the Court of Justice in the context of a dispute on the legality of a non-resident tax on the Dutch company Peterbroeck. Peterbroeck relied on EC law to argue that the application to a company having its seat in the Netherlands of a rate of tax higher than that applicable to a Belgian company constituted an obstacle to freedom of establishment prohibited by Article 52 EEC. The problem was that Peterbroeck raised this argument only when the dispute reached the stage of appeal, beyond the time limits imposed by Belgian procedural law. The plea was therefore inadmissible under Belgian law. The question referred to the Court of Justice was whether Community law precluded the application of a domestic procedural rule whose effect was to prevent the national court from considering of its own motion whether a measure of domestic law was compatible with a provision of Community law. In its answer the Court recalled the crucial obligation of Member States to protect the '*rights which individuals derive from the direct effect of Community law*', stressing that '*under the principle of cooperation laid down in Article 5 of the Treaty, it is for the Member States to ensure the legal protection which individuals derive from the direct effect of Community law*'. Consequently, in the absence of procedural rules governing the matter, it is for each domestic legal system to lay down the procedural rules to protect those rights, all this while respecting the principles of equivalence and effectiveness.[672]

This obligation is not just theoretical: in *Peterbroeck*, the Court examined the practical implications for the litigant of the Belgian procedural rule at issue, i.e., time limits for raising before the Court of Appeal a new plea based on Community law. The Court held that the existence of time limits was not in itself objectionable, but that the conditions attached to these limits were too restrictive in practice and therefore did not respect the requirement of effective judicial protection.[673] Ultimately, it is by examining

causal link from right to remedy is also made clear in *Unectef v Heylens*, C-222/86, para 14: '*since free access to employment is a fundamental right which the Treaty confers individually on each worker of the Community, the existence of a remedy of a judicial nature against any decision of a national authority refusing the benefit of that right is essential in order to secure for the individual effective protection for this right*'.

671 *Peterbroeck, Van Campenhout & Cie v Belgian State*, C-312/93.

672 *Peterbroeck, Van Campenhout & Cie v Belgian State*, C-312/93, para 12 and case law cited.

673 *Peterbroeck, Van Campenhout & Cie v Belgian State*, C-312/93, paras 16 to 20.

the concrete effects of a rule on the individual that the Court evaluates whether the obligations of Member States (here, the principle of sincere cooperation), and therefore also the rights of this individual, have been respected. *Peterbroeck* thus exemplifies the close link between the obligations of public authorities and the rights of individuals, and it confirms that in EU law the remedy is determined by the existence of the right, and not the other way around.[674]

The relation between effectiveness and effective legal protection remains subject to debate,[675] but *Rewe, Johnston* and *Peterbroeck* leave no doubt that there is a close connection between the two notions and that the latter developed on the basis of the former. The principle of effective judicial protection has been described as an application of the principle of effectiveness,[676] or even '*a more robust manifestation*' of it.[677] Ravo considers that '*the obligation placed upon national courts, intended as a means for ensuring effectiveness of EU law at national level, turned out to be an indirect instrument for granting judicial protection to individuals, whose concern for their rights constitutes an important additional form of enforcement of EU law*'.[678] In this light, the requirement of judicial protection appears as a logical consequence of the mechanism of functional subjectivation. The classic dual rationale of rights (which matter both in themselves *and* as instruments for ensuring the effectiveness of EU law) thus shapes not only the concept of individual rights but also the requirement of effective judicial protection.

674 Eilmansberger, 'The Relationship between Rights and Remedies in EC Law: in Search of the Missing Link' 1236; Van Gerven, 'Of Rights, Remedies and Procedures' 307.

675 Prechal points out that on this issue the case law itself is somewhat '*drifting*'. Prechal, 'Member State Liability and Direct Effect: What's the Difference After All?' 315. Neframi 2016, Lacchi CMLR, Safjan.

676 J.M. Fernandez Martin, 'El principio de tutela judicial efectiva de los derechos subjetivos derivados del Derecho comunitario: evolución y alcance' [1994] Revista de Instituciones europeas 845; Półtorak, *European Union Rights in National Courts* 46-47. On the distinction between effectiveness and effective judicial protection see also Parret, 'Effectieve rechtsbescherming: eindeloos potentieel, ongeleid projectiel?'.

677 S. Prechal and R. Widdershoven, 'Redefining the Relationship between 'Rewe-effectiveness' and Effective Judicial Protection' (2011) 4 Review of European Administrative Law 31 39.

678 Ravo, 'The role of the Principle of Effective Judicial Protection and its Impact on National Jurisdictions' 110.

1.3.1.2. The limited autonomisation of the right to an effective remedy from the instrumental effectiveness rationale

Article 47 of the Charter, entitled 'Right to an effective remedy and to a fair trial', provides that:

> *Everyone whose rights and freedoms guaranteed by the law of the Union are violated has the right to an effective remedy before a tribunal in compliance with the conditions laid down in this Article.*
> *Everyone is entitled to a fair and public hearing within a reasonable time by an independent and impartial tribunal previously established by law. Everyone shall have the possibility of being advised, defended and represented.*
> *Legal aid shall be made available to those who lack sufficient resources in so far as such aid is necessary to ensure effective access to justice.*

As observed more generally, the Charter is now at the heart of fundamental rights discourses. In this context Article 47 has become the centre of gravity of the discussion on the effective protection of individual rights. In this evolution three phases may be distinguished: in the first cases mentioning Article 47, the Court highlighted the roots of the right therein enshrined and its connection with the objective requirement of effectiveness; in a second phase, Article 47 became used increasingly in autonomy from its foundations, with a focus on its value for individuals rather than the system as a whole; in a third phase, the Court seems to have reached a balancing point, embracing the double rationale of the right to an effective remedy.

1.3.1.2.1. Article 47 before Lisbon

The first phase started even before the Charter became legally binding: in *Unibet*, the Court acknowledged the right to effective judicial protection as a general principle of EU law, based both on the ECHR and the Charter. This was read – rightly, in the light of later developments – as a first step towards the acknowledgement of the legal value of the Charter.[679] *Unibet* has also been characterised as the Court's first effort '*in articulating the rela-*

679 *Unibet*, C-432/05, para 37; Van Waeyenberge and Pecho, 'L'arrêt Unibet et le traité de Lisbonne - un pari sur l'avenir de la protection juridictionnelle effective'; A. Arnull, 'Case C-432/05, Unibet (London) Ltd and Unibet (International) Ltd v Justitiekanslern, judgment of the Grand Chamber of 13 March 2007' (2007) 44 Common Market Law Review 1763.

tionship between effectiveness and effective judicial protection'.[680] The *Impact* case works along the same lines: the principles of effectiveness and equivalence materialise the obligation of Member States to ensure the effective judicial protection of rights of individuals.[681]

The first *Kadi* ruling[682] is famous because the Court therein affirms the importance of fundamental rights in the Community, and its own legitimacy to check the legality of international instruments against those fundamental rights.[683] It is also significant because when the Court performs the review of the contested acts against EU fundamental rights, the concepts of rights and obligations are tightly interwoven. A series of resolutions of the UN Security Council, called the Member States of the UN to freeze the financial assets of persons and entities whom the Security Council's sanctions committee had designated as being associated with Al-Qaida or the Taliban. To implement these resolutions that Council of the EU adopted a regulation that provided for the freezing of financial assets of these persons and entities, listed in an annex to the regulation, to be regularly updated based on the UN resolutions.[684] Mr Kadi, a Saudi resident, and Al Barakaat International Foundation, based in Sweden were included in this list and challenged the Regulation before the Court of First Instance, arguing that the Council had no competence to adopt such legislation and that the Regulation breached several of their fundamental rights, especially the right to property and the rights of the defence. The CFI dismissed the claims, based on the primacy of international law on EU law.[685] By contrast, the Court of Justice then decided on appeal that, as a constitu-

680 Prechal and Widdershoven, 'Redefining the Relationship between "Rewe-effectiveness" and Effective Judicial Protection' 44.

681 Judgment of 15 April 2008, *Impact*, C-268/06, EU:C:2008:223, paras 47-48.

682 *Kadi I*, Joined cases C-402/05 P and C-415/05 P.

683 C.R.J.J. Rijken, 'Het Hof als hoeder van de fundamentale rechten in de zaak Kadi en Al Barakaat' (2009) Nederlands tijdschrift voor Europees recht 140.

684 Council Regulation (EC) No 881/2002 of 27 May 2002, imposing certain specific restrictive measures directed against certain persons and entities associated with Usama bin Laden, the Al-Qaida network and the Taliban, and repealing Council Regulation (EC) No 467/2001 prohibiting the export of certain goods and services to Afghanistan, strengthening the flight ban and extending the freeze of funds and other financial resources in respect of the Taliban of Afghanistan (OJ L 139 p. 9).

685 Judgment of 21 September 2005, *Kadi v Council and Commission*, T-315/01, EU:T:2005:332.

tional guarantee, the EU courts must control the validity in light of fundamental rights of all acts within its jurisdiction.[686]

With regard to the rights of the defence, '*in particular the right to be heard, and the right to effective judicial review of those rights*',[687] the Court recalled in *Kadi* that in order to allow for proper judicial control the EU authority had to communicate the grounds for the decision adversely affecting an individual, so that the latter could assess whether there were reasons to challenge the decision. The connection between objective, systemic requirements and subjective individual guarantees is emphasised by the Court's recollection that the observance of the obligation to communicate the grounds '*is necessary both to enable the persons to whom restrictive measures are addressed to defend their rights in the best possible conditions and to decide, with full knowledge of the relevant facts, whether there is any point in their applying to the Community judicature, and to put the latter fully in a position in which it may carry out the review of the lawfulness of the Community measure in question which is its duty under the EC Treaty*'.[688] An obligation not respected (the obligation to communicate the grounds for a decision) translates into a violated right (the rights of defence), '*which has had the further consequence that the principle of effective judicial protection has been infringed*' because the applicants have not been able to defend their rights properly before the CFI.[689] The Court finds that the pleas alleging breach of defence rights, especially the right to be heard, and of the principle of effective judicial protection, are well founded. Holding that the measures in addition constitute an excessive restriction of the right to property, the Court invalidates the measures.[690] In the end in *Kadi* the *principle* of effect-

686 *Kadi I*, Joined cases C-402/05 P and C-415/05 P, para 285: '*the obligations imposed by an international agreement cannot have the effect of prejudicing the constitutional principles of the EC Treaty, which include the principle that all Community acts must respect fundamental rights, that respect constituting a condition of their lawfulness which it is for the Court to review in the framework of the complete system of legal remedies established by the Treaty.*'.

687 *Kadi I*, Joined cases C-402/05 P and C-415/05 P, para 334. The Court mentions the Charter as a source of this right at para 335.

688 *Kadi I*, Joined cases C-402/05 P and C-415/05 P, para 337, citing *Unectef v Heylens*, C-222/86, para 15. See also Judgment of 22 April 2015, T-320/09, *Planet v Commission*, EU:T:2015:223, para 77 and case law cited.

689 *Kadi I*, Joined cases C-402/05 P and C-415/05 P, para 352.

690 More precisely, the Court allows the Council three months to solve the identified issues, acknowledging that the efficacy of the asset freezing measures does require a suprise effect and immediate application and that, while there was no

ive judicial protection is construed as a combination of a *right* (for individuals) and an *obligation* (for public bodies, here, the EU institutions).

In the same way, in *Alassini*[691] the Court combined the principle of effectiveness and the fundamental right to effective judicial protection.[692] Against the backdrop of a dispute between users and providers of telephone services, this case concerned the interpretation of the principle of effective judicial protection in relation to Italian legislation under which an attempt to achieve an out-of-court settlement was a mandatory condition for the admissibility before the courts of actions in certain disputes under the 'Universal Service Directive'.[693] To begin with, the Court conducted a systemic analysis by checking the Italian procedural rules at issue against the principles of equivalence and effectiveness. In other words, it controlled that the Member State respects its obligation under the principle of effective judicial protection, since '*those requirements of equivalence and effectiveness embody the general obligation on the Member States to ensure judicial protection of an individual's rights under EU law*';[694] The Court found that the Italian system fulfilled those requirements. The Court did not develop its position on the respect of the principle of equivalence since the issue has not been raised; as for effectiveness, it checked how the system in general might affect the possibility for individuals to exercise their rights. The requirement to go through an out-of-court procedure does not in itself impair that possibility.[695] Then the Court shifted the perspective and considered effective judicial protection as a right under Article 47 of the Charter; it found that there was a limitation to this right, but not a disproportionate one. To sum up, there was a double control: firstly, whether the Member

---

obligation to state reasons or hear the concerned persons before they were put on the list, the authorities should afterwards have done in a reasonable timeframe.

691 *Alassini and Others*, C-317 to C-320/08.

692 Parret, 'Effectieve rechtsbescherming: eindeloos potentieel, ongeleid projectiel?' 162; Ravo, 'The role of the Principle of Effective Judicial Protection and its Impact on National Jurisdictions.'

693 Parliament and Council Directive 2002/22/EC of 7 March 2002 on Universal Service and users' rights relating to electronic communications networks and services ('Universal Service Directive') (OJ L 108 p. 51).

694 *Alassini and Others*, C-317 to C-320/08, para 49. E. Neframi, 'Quelques réflexions sur l'article 19, paragraphe 1, alinéa 2, TUE et l'obligation de l'Etat membre d'assurer la protection juridictionnelle effective dans les domaines couverts par le droit de l'Union' in C. Boutayeb (ed), *La Constitution, l'Europe et le droit Mélanges en l'honneur de Jean-Claude Masclet* (Publications de la Sorbonne 2013) 808.

695 *Alassini and Others*, C-317 to C-320/08, para 60.

State respected its *obligations* with regard to effective judicial protection; secondly, whether the restriction to effective judicial protection as a *right* was proportionate.

This case has been described as uncoupling the procedural right from the procedural obligation because it reached '*opposite solutions with respect to the compatibility of the same national procedural rule*',[696] given that the Court did not identify a restriction when testing the respect of the principle of equivalence, whereas it did find a limitation to the right to effective judicial protection. Admittedly, each issue appears '*neatly separated*', with both reviews having '*a specific focus of their own*'.[697] Yet, both reviews lead to the same conclusion, i.e. that the national rule at issue complies with the EU procedural requirements. Moreover, in the first review (of effectiveness) while the Court does not explicitly find that there is a limitation of the principle of effectiveness, it does insist in paragraphs 58 and 59 that the national court must assess whether in some specific circumstances '*the exercise of rights conferred by the Universal Service Directive might be rendered in practice impossible or excessively difficult for certain individuals*' and whether the possibility for interim measures is ensured.[698] The wheel comes full circle at the end of the second layer of review (effective judicial protection) when the Court holds that '*the national procedure at issue in the main proceedings also complies with the principle of effective judicial protection, subject to the conditions referred to in paragraphs 58 and 59 of this judgment*'.[699] Therefore, this case illustrates, rather than undermines, the complementarity between the principle of effectiveness and the right to effective judicial protection.

1.3.1.2.2. After Lisbon, Article 47 in the spotlight

In a second phase of case-lawmaking on Article 47, corresponding to the Charter becoming legally binding, more emphasis is put on the right to benefit from this protection, than on the obligation to ensure it. The shift appears very clearly in *DEB*.[700] DEB was a company seeking reparation

696 Ravo, 'The role of the Principle of Effective Judicial Protection and its Impact on National Jurisdictions' 113.

697 Prechal and Widdershoven, 'Redefining the Relationship between 'Rewe-effectiveness' and Effective Judicial Protection' 45.

698 *Alassini and Others*, C-317 to C-320/08, paras 58-59.

699 *Alassini and Others*, C-317 to C-320/08, para 66.

700 *DEB*, C-279/09.

from Germany for the delay in the transposition of directives intended to ensure non-discriminatory access to the national gas networks.[701] It had applied for legal aid in order to bring this action, but the aid was denied on the basis of national legislation refusing such aid to legal persons in the absence of a 'public interest'. The question of the German referring court was focused on the meaning of the principle of effectiveness, which the Court connected with the general principle of effective judicial protection.[702] However, in the light of Article 6(1) TEU and Article 51(1) CFR, the Court found it '*necessary to recast the question*' in terms of whether '*the principle of effective judicial protection as enshrined in Article 47 of the Charter*'[703] applied to legal (as well as natural) persons. Article 47 was then the centre of gravity of the reasoning, leading to the conclusion that it '*must be interpreted as meaning that it is not impossible for legal persons to rely on that principle and that aid granted pursuant to that principle may cover, inter alia, dispensation from advance payment of the costs of proceedings and/or the assistance of a lawyer*'.[704] The Court did not rely on the general principle nor consider whether the right might be connected with obligations of the Member States, such as the principle of sincere cooperation. For this reason, *DEB* has been characterised as an example of how the right enshrined in Article 47 '*can also be decoupled from the effectiveness principle*'.[705]

There could be several complementary explanations for this approach. The first that comes to mind is that the Court took this case as an occasion to make a statement on the value of the Charter as a source of fundamental rights shortly after its entry into force, and on its relation with the ECHR as a source of fundamental rights. The Court made clear that its reliance on ECtHR case law to reach a conclusion in *DEB* was justified by Article 52(3) of the Charter, which requires this approach for Charter rights corresponding to those guaranteed in the ECHR, and by the Explanations on Article 47, which also refer to ECtHR case law.[706] Another possible reason

701 Parliament and Council Directive 98/30/EC of 22 June 1998 concerning common rules for the internal market in natural gas (OJ L 204 p. 1) and Parliament and Council Directive 2003/55/EC of 26 June 2003 concerning common rules for the internal market in natural gas and repealing Directive 98/30/EC (OJ L 176 p. 57).

702 *DEB*, C-279/09, para 29.

703 *DEB*, C-279/09, para 33. Hofmann, 'Effective Judicial Remedies Before the National Courts'.

704 *DEB*, C-279/09, para 59.

705 Safjan, 'A Union of Effective Judicial Protection. Addressing a multi-level challenge through the lens of Article 47 CFREU'.

706 *DEB*, C-279/09, paras 35-36.

is that the traditional case law on the principle of effectiveness might have been of little use in the reasoning. There did not seem to be much in EU law or case-law about the issue of legal aid to legal persons, and there was no consistent approach across the Member States on this issue,[707] whereas ECtHR case-law contained many relevant elements.[708] In addition, a classic solution relying on the general principle of effective judicial protection and the obligations which it entails for Member States, including the duty of sincere cooperation, would have risked bringing to light a conflict between the 'effectivess of EU law' rationale of individual rights, and the German notion of public interest that was restricting these rights. The Court performed a systemic analysis and held that '*the inclusion of the provision relating to the grant of legal aid in the article of the Charter relating to the right to an effective remedy indicates that the assessment of the need to grant that aid must be made on the basis of the right of the actual person whose rights and freedoms as guaranteed by EU law have been violated, rather than on the basis of the public interest of society, even if that interest may be one of the criteria for assessing the need for the aid*'.[709] This put the individual right under the spotlight, rather than the notion of public interest, and thus avoided a direct and unnecessary confrontation between the requirements of the EU and national (German) legal orders.

Whichever the underlying motives, *DEB* validates an application of the requirement of effective judicial protection independently from its conceptual roots.[710] Following the assimilation of the Charter into primary law as laid down by Article 6(1) TEU, Article 47 of the Charter has become the main basis for the right to an effective remedy.[711] The relevance of general principles of law (along with the 'obligational' underpinnings to the

707 *DEB*, C-279/09, para 44.

708 Reviewed in paras 45-50 of *DEB*, C-279/09.

709 AG Mengozzi had been more daring and more intrusive in his Opinion, suggesting that the German court should take into ccount that '*the preservation of the effectiveness of EU law – and, by extension, the safeguarding of the rights that individuals derive from it – may constitute 'public interests' that should be taken into consideration when adjudicating on an application for legal aid submitted by a legal person*'. Opinion of AG Mengozzi in *DEB*, C-279/09, EU:C:2010:489, para 103.

710 This happened in other cases always citing *DEB:* E.g. Judgment of 28 July 2011, *Samba Diouf*, C-69/10, EU:C:2011:524, para 49; Judgment of 6 November 2012, *Otis and Others*, C-199/11, EU:C:2012:684, paras 46 to 49; Judgment of 31 January 2013, *D. and A.*, C-175/11, EU:C:2013:45, para 80; Judgment of 16 July 2014, *Hassan v Council*, T-572/11, ECR, EU:T:2014:682. para 88.

711 D. Simon, 'Protection juridictionnelle effective' (2011) Europe comm. 38.

'right') for the reasoning is toned down, while the Charter is effectively the starting point of the analysis.

In the same vein, *Texdata*[712] suggests that by contrast with the founding case law where the right to an effective legal remedy was derived from an obligation on the Member States, there is an inversion of this original relation. An Austrian branch of a German software company had been imposed penalties by the Landesgericht Innsbruck for having failed to submit annual accounts. Texdata argued that the absence of prior notice before imposition of a penalty breached the principles of effective judicial protection and respect for the rights of the defence. The Oberlandesgericht Innsbruck has been careful to request interpretation both of the '*general legal principle (Article 6(3) TEU) of effective judicial protection (principle of effectiveness)*' and of '*the principle of the right to a fair hearing laid down in the second paragraph of Article 47 of the Charter (Article 6(1) TEU) and in Article 6(2) of the ECHR (Article 6(1) TEU)*'.[713] So the Austrian court, in the way it phrased its question, was showing awareness of the original connection between the obligational aspect of effective judicial protection, and the right to a fair hearing. Yet the Court, much like it had in *DEB*, refocused the question on '*the general principle of the right to effective judicial protection and the principle of respect for the rights of the defence, as entrenched in Article 47 of the Charter and in Article 6(2) of the ECHR*', thus limiting the general principle to its expression as a right in the Charter. It then reintroduced the notion of an obligation on the Member States: '*[i]n order to ensure the observance of that fundamental right within the European Union, the second subparagraph of Article 19(1) TEU lays down that Member States are to provide remedies sufficient to ensure effective legal protection in the fields covered by [EU] law*'.[714] The complementarity between the right (Article 47 CFR) and the obligation (article 19(1) TEU) is thus acknowledged, but there seems to be an inversion of the original relationship between the obligation of the Member States to ensure access to an effective remedy, and the rights of individuals to have access to such a remedy.[715]

This does not correspond to the vision of effective judicial protection that Advocate General Mengozzi had developed in his Opinion. Indeed, the latter was also referring both to Article 47 of the Charter and to Article

712 *Texdata Software GmbH*, C-418/11.

713 *Texdata Software GmbH*, C-418/11, para 25.

714 *Texdata Software GmbH*, C-418/11, paras 77-78.

715 The Court ultimately held that the immediate imposition of the penalty in the circumstances of the case was not in principle in breach of the '*principle of effective judicial protection*'.

19(1) TEU, but he was doing so in a more balanced way, without establishing a hierarchy between the right and the obligation.[716] In the judgment, the fundamental right appears to be, precisely, the fundamental requirement, while the obligation for the Member State to organise its judicial system adequately is the consequence of the right enshrined in the Charter.

The inversion is also clear in the prominent *Kadi II* ruling, which construes individual rights as the basis and justification for corresponding obligations. In this case, Mr Kadi was (again) challenging a regulation that implemented a decision by the UN Security Council to put him on its sanctions list and freeze his financial assets.[717] This case exemplifies how obligations can be derived from rights and imposed on public authorities: it seems as though the individual right preexisted the obligation rather than the other way around. A whole section of this long judgment deals with the scope and implications of the rights of the defence and of the right to effective judicial protection.[718] This right, with its corollary the right to a reasoned decision, is introduced in the reasoning by a statement that it is '*affirmed in Article 47 of the Charter*'.[719] Once these Charter provisions have been established as sources of the rights considered (with no mention of general principles of law) they translate into what the Court calls a '*dual procedural obligation*', i.e. the obligation to give reasons for the decision and the obligation to ensure that the individual may effectively make known his views on the grounds advanced against him.[720] The Court then mentions *TU München* and Article 296 TFEU as further bases for the duty of care and the duty to state reasons for the response to the comments made by the individual on the original summary of reasons.[721] These du-

---

716 Opinion of AG Mengozzi in *Texdata Software*, C-418/11, EU:C:2013:50, paras 81 et seq.

717 Judgment of 18 July 2013, *Commission and Others v Kadi ('Kadi II')*, Joined cases C-584/10 P, C-593/10 P and C-595/10 P, EU:C:2013:518. For an explanation of the main issues raised in this case see e.g. A.A. Franken and P.T.C. Van Kampen, 'Toetsing van plaatsing op een sanctielijst na Kadi II' (2014) Nederlands tijdschrift voor Europees recht 116.

718 *Kadi II*, Joined cases C-584/10 P, C-593/10 P and C-595/10 P, paras 97 to 134.

719 *Kadi II*, Joined cases C-584/10 P, C-593/10 P and C-595/10 P, paras 99-100. The same method applies to the rights of the defence (right to be heard and right of access to the file), which appear to be derived exclusively, in the Court's reasoning, from Article 41(2) CFR. See also Judgment of 21 December 2011, *France v People's Mojahedin Organisation of Iran*, C-27/09 P, EU:C:2011:853, para 66, and *Council v. Manufacturing Support & Procurement Kala Naft*, C-348/12 P, para 67.

720 *Kadi II*, Joined cases C-584/10 P, C-593/10 P and C-595/10 P, para 113.

721 *Kadi II*, Joined cases C-584/10 P, C-593/10 P and C-595/10 P, paras 114 to 116.

ties and the procedural obligations mentioned earlier are blended together into '*procedural safeguards*'.[722] '*The effectiveness of the judicial review guaranteed by Article 47 of the Charter*' requires a certain conduct from the Court performing the review; so, the right set out in the Charter justifies an obligation on a public body.

Similarly, in analysing the errors of law made by the General Court, again the Court focuses on how the respect of the rights of the defence and of the right to effective judicial protection requires a certain behaviour both from the authorities (disclosing the reasons, enabling the individual to make known his observations, examine carefully and impartially whether the reasons alleged are well-founded) and from the Court itself (to examine '*whether the reasons relied on in the summary provided by the Sanctions Committee are sufficiently detailed and specific and, where appropriate, whether the accuracy of the facts relating to the reason concerned has been established*').[723] Thus the procedural rights are not only posited as the starting point of the reasoning; they also serve as justification for obligations at each step of the reasoning.[724]

1.3.1.2.3. The continuing complementarity between effectiveness and the right to an effective remedy

However, in a third strand of case law the complementarity between effectiveness and effective judicial protection resurfaces. In *Morcillo and Gar-*

722 *Kadi II*, Joined cases C-584/10 P, C-593/10 P and C-595/10 P, para 118.

723 *Kadi II*, Joined cases C-584/10 P, C-593/10 P and C-595/10 P, para 135-136.

724 The General Court also relies abundantly on *Kadi II* e.g. in the *Ayadi* case (Judgment of 14 April 2015, *Ayadi v Commission*, T-527/09 RENV, EU:T:2015:205), in *Al-Faqih* (Judgment of 28 October 2015, *Al-Faqih and Others v Commission*, T-134/11, EU:T:2015:812, paras 59-65) and in *Makhlouf v Council* (Judgment of 21 January 2016, *Makhlouf v Council*, EU:T:2016:27, paras 37-50 and 85-86). Each time it follows the same methodology of using Charter rights, especially Article 41(2) and Article 47, as starting points for determining whether the corresponding obligations have been respected. In *Mikhalchanka* the Court even adopted a purely subjective focus, citing only the subjective rationale underlying the rights of the defense: Judgment of 10 May 2016, *Mikhalchanka v Council*, T-693/13, EU:T:2016:283, para 46 (citing *Kadi II*): '*afin que cette personne puisse défendre ses droits dans les meilleures conditions possibles et décider en pleine connaissance de cause s'il est utile de saisir le juge de l'Union*'.

cia,[725] in order to determine whether the Spanish system of mortgage enforcement proceedings is compatible with EU fundamental rights, the Court starts by recalling the concept of national procedural autonomy, from which flow the principles of equivalence and effectiveness; this '*implies a requirement of judicial protection, which is also guaranteed by Article 47 of the Charter*'.[726] Having connected the right in the Charter with the pre-existing principle of effective judicial protection, the Court then relies on the case law on that principle and finds that the system of enforcement at issue is incompatible with EU law. So, instead of only acknowledging the collision between national procedural autonomy and the right to effective judicial protection, the Court insists on the link between those two requirements, which materialises in the principle of effectiveness. The violation of this principle inherent in the principle of national procedural autonomy amounts to a violation of the right to an effective remedy and is therefore contrary to EU law.

The connection is also clear in *Agrokonsulting*,[727] in which the Court was asked whether Article 47(1) CFR and the principles of equivalence and effectiveness precluded a rule of Bulgarian procedural law which required individuals to challenge an act of an administrative body before the court of the district where this body was located – i.e., for the body responsible for agricultural aid schemes, in Sofia. The referring court pointed out that it infringed the right to effective judicial protection by requiring farmers to go all the way to the capital when they wanted to challenge a decision.[728] The Court first examined the contested rule against the requirements of equivalence and effectiveness principles, then checked whether Article 47 was respected when a farmer could bring a case relating to agricultural aid only at the seat of the competent administrative authority. The Court held that this rule was not in principle prohibited under EU law, provided that it did not cause individual procedural problems in terms, inter alia, of the duration of the procedure.[729] This, according to Judge Safjan, '*show[s] that*

725 Judgment of 17 July 2014, *Sánchez Morcillo and Abril García*, C-169/14, EU:C:2014:2099.

726 *Sánchez Morcillo and Abril García*, C-169/14, para 35. See also Judgment of 6 October 2015, *Orizzonte Salute*, C-61/14, EU:C:2015:655, para 48.

727 Judgment of 27 June 2013, *Agrokonsulting-04*, C-93/12, EU:C:2013:432.

728 For more details on the case, especially the Bulgarian background, see A. Kornezov, 'When David Teaches EU Law to Goliath: A Generational Upheaval in the Making' in M. Bobek (ed), *Central European Judges Under the European Influence* (Hart Publishing 2015) 258.

729 *Agrokonsulting-04*, C-93/12, para 61.

the right and the principles [of equivalence and effectiveness] can be treated harmoniously'[730] – exactly like in *Alassini.*

As noted by AG Kokott in her Opinion in *Puškár,* a case on data protection, '*in recent times, the principle of effectiveness has increasingly been associated with the right to effective legal protection under Article 47(1) of the Charter*.'[731] Kokott however cites a recent judgment that is '*no longer based on the principle of effectiveness, but solely on Article 47(1)*'[732], i.e., *Star Storage.*[733] In fact, this observation needs to be qualified. *Star Storage* was a case concerning the right to a remedy in public procurement law. The Court explained that the obligation on Member States, provided for in the relevant directives, to ensure the availability of review mechanisms in public contract award procedures,[734] was an expression of the right enshrined in Article 47 CFR.[735] However, in the reasoning leading to this statement, the Court had abundantly stressed the connection between the effectiveness of EU law and the right to a remedy, highlighting that the relevant provisions of the directives were '*designed to reinforce the existence, in all Member States, of effective remedies, so as to ensure the effective application of the EU rules on the award of public contracts (...)*'[736] and insisting that the effectiveness of the directives must not be hindered.[737] So the principle of effectiveness even here is strongly linked with the right to a remedy – which in fact reinforces

730 Safjan, 'A Union of Effective Judicial Protection. Addressing a multi-level challenge through the lens of Article 47 CFREU'.

731 Opinion of AG Kokoktt in *Puškár*, C-73/16, EU:C:2017:253, para 49, with note 19 citing as additional examples of the Court citing jointly Article 47 and the principle of effectiveness: Judgment of 11 April 2013, *Edwards and Pallikaropoulos,* C-260/11, EU:C:2013:221, para 33; Judgment of 6 October 2015, *East Sussex County Council,* C-71/14, EU:C:2015:656, para 52; Judgment of 13 October 2016 *Polkomtel,* C-231/15, EU:C:2016:769, paras 23-24.

732 Opinion of AG Kokoktt in *Puškár*, C-73/16, para 49, with note 20.

733 Judgment of 15 September 2016, *Star Storage and Others,* Joined cases C-439/14 and C-488/14, EU:C:2016:688.

734 Council Directive 89/665/EEC of 21 December 1989 on the coordination of the laws, regulations and administrative provisions relating to the application of review procedures to the award of public supply and public works contracts (OJ L 395 p. 33), Article 1(3); Council Directive 92/13/EEC of 25 February 1992 coordinating the laws, regulations and administrative provisions relating to the application of Community rules on the procurement procedures of entities operating in the water, energy, transport and telecommunications sectors (OJ L 76 p. 14), Article 1(3).

735 *Star Storage and Others,* Joined cases C-439/14 and C-488/14, paras 45-46.

736 *Star Storage and Others* ,Joined cases C-439/14 and C-488/14, para 41.

737 *Star Storage and Others,* Joined cases C-439/14 and C-488/14, paras 43-44.

AG Kokoktt's ultimate conclusion that '*Article 47(1) of the Charter and the principle of effectiveness ultimately embody the same legal principle and may be examined jointly using the rules in Articles 47(1) and 52(1) of the Charter*'.[738]

The case law on effective judicial protection since the Charter became part of the EU legal order suggests that effectiveness and effective judicial protection are not decoupled, but rather used in complementarity. This complementarity both confirms and embodies the dual rationale of individual rights in EU law, both objective (effectiveness of EU law) and subjective (protection of the individual). The nature of the relation between effectiveness and effective judicial protection is therefore not radically altered; rather, the evolution consists mostly in a fluctuation in the relative importance of these two requirements in the judicial discourse, manifesting in the increased visibility of the right to an effective remedy. As we shall now see, this has the virtuous effect of intensifying the correlative obligation to provide remedies.

1.3.1.3. Article 19(1) TEU and the extension of the positive obligation to ensure the effectiveness of rights

The first rights which the Court identified in the Treaty were derived from prohibitions, i.e. negative obligations: e.g., the prohibition on the creation of new taxes on imports in *Van Gend en Loos*, the ban on discrimination in *Defrenne*. Likewise, as a counterweight to national procedural autonomy, effective judicial protection is often framed as a negative obligation on the Member States: in *Safalero* the Court stated that '*while it is, in principle, for national law to determine an individual's standing and legal interest in bringing proceedings, Community law nevertheless requires that the national legislation* does not undermine *the right to effective judicial protection*'.[739] Yet we are now witnessing the development of effective judicial protection from a negative obligation into a positive obligation, and an evolution of the corresponding right.[740] In *Unibet* the Court held that the EC Treaty '*was not*

738 Opinion of AG Kokoktt in *Puškár*, C-73/16, EU:C:2017:253, para 51.

739 Judgment of 11 September 2003, *Safalero*, C-13/01, EU:C:2003:447, para 50 (emphasis added). Similar phrases feature in Judgment in *Verholen and Others v Sociale Verzekeringsbank Amsterdam*, C-87/90 to C-89/90, EU:C:1991:314, para 24; *Mono Car Styling*, C-12/08, para 49; *Unibet*, C-432/05, para 42.

740 On the distinction between negative and positive obligation applied to effectiveness and effective judicial protection, see Prechal and Widdershoven, 'Redefining the Relationship between 'Rewe-effectiveness' and Effective Judicial Protec-

intended to create new remedies in the national courts to ensure the observance of Community law other than those already laid down by national law [...]. It would be otherwise only if it were apparent from the overall scheme of the national system in question that no legal remedy existed which made it possible to ensure, even indirectly, respect for an individual's rights under Community law [...]'.[741] This was a first hint towards the possibility that there might be more than just a negative obligation. This possibility was reinforced by the introduction of Article 19(1) TEU by the Treaty of Lisbon. This provision requires in its second sentence that '*Member States shall provide remedies sufficient to ensure effective legal protection in the fields covered by Union law*'. The question thus arises whether Article 19 TEU imposes a positive obligation that may in turn give rise to an enhanced right to effective judicial protection.[742]

The first rulings where the Court relied on Article 19(1) TEU were cases where the consistency of the EU legal system as a whole was being challenged: for instance, in Opinion 1/09 on the project to create a unified patent court, Article 19(1) TEU was among the provisions analysed by the Court in order to draw conclusions on the system of judicial review framed by the Treaties.[743] Later on, in *Inuit* the applicants argued that the classically restrictive interpretation of Article 263, paragraph 4, TFEU on the possibility for individuals to bring actions for annulment of EU legislative acts was too restrictive and thus breached Article 47 CFR. In response, the Court stated that, as it had already emphasised in Opinion 1/09, '*judicial review of compliance with the European legal order is ensured, as can be seen from Article 19(1) TEU, by the Court of Justice and the courts and tribunals of the Member States*'.[744] The Court then studied the architecture of the Treaties, especially the system of judicial review laid down therein, and reaffirmed that it was for the Member States to establish a system of legal remedies which ensure the respect of the right to effective judicial protec-

---

tion' and A.F.M. Brenninkmeijer, 'The Influence of Court of Justice Case Law on the Procedural Law of the Member States' in J.A.E. Vervaele (ed), *Administrative Law Application and Enforcement of Community Law in the Netherlands* (Kluwer 1994). See also Van Gerven, 'Of Rights, Remedies and Procedures'.

741 *Unibet*, C-432/05, paras 40-41.

742 For a discussion on the potential implications of Article 19(1) see Neframi, 'Quelques réflexions sur l'article 19, paragraphe 1, alinéa 2, TUE et l'obligation de l'Etat membre d'assurer la protection juridictionnelle effective dans les domaines couverts par le droit de l'Union'.

743 Opinion of 8 March 2011, 1/09, EU:C:2011:123, paras 66 and 71.

744 *Inuit Tapiriit Kanatami and Others v Parliament and Council*, C-583/11 P, para 90.

tion.[745] Indeed, '*that obligation on the Member States was reaffirmed by the second subparagraph of Article 19(1) TEU [...]*'[746] but '*neither the [TFEU] nor Article 19 TEU intended to create new remedies before the national courts to ensure the observance of [EU] law other than those already laid down by national law*',[747] with a reference to *Unibet*, where the Court had held that the EC Treaty likewise expressed no such intention.[748] This is peculiar given that Article 19(1) TEU, a brand-new provision, did not exist in the EC Treaty at the time of *Unibet*. Also surprising is the reliance on the 'intention' underlying the provision, or rather on the absence of intention to create new remedies. Finally, the Court concluded that neither Article 47 of the Charter nor Article 19(1) TEU '*require that an individual should be entitled to bring actions (against EU legislative acts) before the national courts*'.[749] The first important case on Article 19(1) therefore was not very promising as to its potential concrete effects.

Even in *Telefónica*, where the applicant in the main proceedings was alleging a violation of its rights under Article 47, Article 19(1) was used not to decide upon the practical consequences of the obligations of the Member States, but merely to emphasize the consistency of the system: '*Judicial review of compliance with the European Union legal order is ensured, as can be seen from Article 19(1) TEU, by the Court of Justice and the courts and tribunals of the Member States. To that end, the FEU Treaty has established, by Articles 263 TFEU and 277 TFEU, on the one hand, and Article 267 TFEU, on the other, a complete system of legal remedies and procedures designed to ensure judicial review of the legality of European Union acts, and has entrusted such review to the European Union judicature.*'[750] Therefore the Court used Article 19(1) rather defensively, as proof that the Treaties did indeed constitute a 'complete system of remedies'. It did not check whether the provision might be granting rights as such.

In a still pending case, Portuguese judges have challenged the reduction of their salaries, arguing that this measure is infringing the principle of judicial independence, relying both on Article 47 CFR and Article 19(1), sec-

745 *Inuit Tapiriit Kanatami and Others v Parliament and Council*, C-583/11 P, para 100 and *Unión de Pequeños Agricultores*, C-50/00 P, para 41.

746 *Inuit Tapiriit Kanatami and Others v Parliament and Council*, C-583/11 P, para 101.

747 *Inuit Tapiriit Kanatami and Others v Parliament and Council*, C-583/11 P, para 103.

748 *Unibet*, C-432/05, para 40.

749 *Inuit Tapiriit Kanatami and Others v Parliament and Council*, C-583/11 P, para 106.

750 Judgment of 19 December 2013, *Telefónica v Commission*, C-274/12 P, EU:C:2013:852, para 57, with reference to *Inuit Tapiriit Kanatami and Others v Parliament and Council*, C-583/11 P, paras 90 and 92.

ond subparagraph TEU. Unlike the referring court, which assumes that these provisions embody the same principle, in his Opinion AG Saugmandsgaard Øe has taken the view that they differ in '*purpose*' and '*wording*',[751] and therefore assessed separately the applicability of each provision to the case at hand. According to the AG, the second subparagraph of Article 19(1) is '*primarily procedural in nature*',[752] and covers effective judicial protection in the strict sense, excluding the right to a fair hearing before an independent court. He then assesses separately whether Article 47 CFR, which does include this right, is respected by the salary reductions and finds no incompatibility.

This compartmentalised approach is to be contrasted with the reasoning in *Client Earth*.[753] This case suggests that Article 19(1) may impact the extent of the obligations of Member States obligations regarding effective judicial protection. A British NGO, ClientEarth, had initiated proceedings against the Secretary of State for the Environment and requested that the UK's air quality plans be revised, based on Directive 2008/50/EC on ambient air quality.[754] The British court asked: '*what (if any) remedies must a national court provide as a matter of European law in order to comply with Article 30 of ... Directive [2008/50] and/or Article 4 TEU or 19 TEU?*'[755] Admittedly, the British court had itself mentioned Article 19 TEU along with Article 4 TEU and the directive, but the Court may well have avoided mentioning that provision in its answer. Having recalled the *Unibet* case law and the principle of sincere cooperation, which requires that the Member States ensure judicial protection of an individual's rights under EU law, it added that '*Article 19(1) TEU requires Member States to provide sufficient remedies to ensure effective legal protection in the fields covered by EU law.*'[756] Combined with the consequences of the direct effect of directive provisions which are clear and sufficiently precise, it follows that persons concerned by the limit values set by the directive and exceeded after the transposition period '*must be in a position to require the competent authorities, if necessary by bringing an action before the courts having jurisdiction, to establish*

751 Opinion of AG Saugmandsgaard Øe in *Associação Sindical dos Juízes Portugueses*, C-64/16, EU:C:2017:395, para 62.

752 Opinion of AG Saugmandsgaard Øe in *Associação Sindical dos Juízes Portugueses*, C-64/16, para 63.

753 Judgment of 19 November 2014, *ClientEarth*, C-404/13, EU:C:2014:2382.

754 Parliament and Council Directive 2008/50/EC of 21 May 2008 on ambient air quality and cleaner air for Europe, (OJ L 152 p. 1).

755 *ClientEarth*, C-404/13, para 23.

756 *ClientEarth*, C-404/13, para 52.

an air quality plan' which complies with the directive.[757] Of course, Article 19(1) TEU is not used autonomously here, but rather in combination with another obligation laid down in the Treaty (the obligation of sincere cooperation)[758] and with obligations laid down in a directive. This set of obligations creates an enforceable legal position for the individuals concerned. It is not to be excluded that the positive obligation in Article 19(1) would be increasingly interpreted, in the future, as the requirement to actively take necessary measures.[759]

In addition, the obligation contained in Article 19(1), second subparagraph, has lately been characterised as the correlative of the right contained in Article 47 of the Charter. The connection appears in *Liivimaa Lihaveis,* a case in which the Court held that the impossibility to appeal the decisions of a transnational body which was allocating EU funds was incompatible with the requirement of effective judicial protection and therefore constituted a breach of Article 47 of the Charter.[760] It relied on the symmetrical considerations that '*[t]he first paragraph of Article 47 of the Charter provides that everyone whose rights and freedoms guaranteed by EU law are violated has the right to an effective remedy before a tribunal in compliance with the conditions laid down in that article*' and that '*[t]o ensure that the right to an effective remedy within the EU is upheld, the second subparagraph of Article 19(1) TEU requires the Member States to provide remedies sufficient to ensure effective legal protection in the fields covered by EU law*'.[761]

To date, *Berlioz* is probably the case where the connection is most clearly spelled out: assessing '*whether there is a right to a remedy under Article 47*', the Court states that '*According to Article 47 of the Charter, entitled 'Right to an effective remedy and to a fair trial', everyone whose rights and freedoms guaranteed by the law of the Union are violated has the right to an effective remedy before a tribunal. The* obligation *imposed on the Member States in the second sub-*

757 *ClientEarth*, C-404/13, para 56.

758 On the relation between Article 4 TEU and Article 19(1) TEU see Neframi, 'Quelques réflexions sur l'article 19, paragraphe 1, alinéa 2, TUE et l'obligation de l'Etat membre d'assurer la protection juridictionnelle effective dans les domaines couverts par le droit de l'Union'.

759 The Court relied again on Article 19(1) TEU, quoting *ClientEarth*, in another case on participation in environment-related procedures: Judgment of 8 November 2016, *Lesoochranárske zoskupenie VLK*, C-243/15, EU:C:2016:838, para 50. See also Judgment of 14 June 2017, *Online Games and Others,* C-685/15, EU:C:2017:452, para 54.

760 Judgment of 17 September 2014, *Liivimaa Lihaveis*, C-562/12, EU:C:2014:2229, paras 71 and 74.

761 *Liivimaa Lihaveis*, C-562/12, paras 67-68.

paragraph of Article 19(1) TEU, to provide remedies sufficient to ensure effective legal protection in the fields covered by Union law, corresponds to that right'.[762] The correlation between rights and obligations thus also applies to the right to an effective remedy, the correlate of which is the obligation to ensure effective legal protection.

The case law on effective judicial protection sheds light on the concept of individual rights in two ways. Firstly, the basic correlation between rights and obligations remains relevant: there is a clear correlation between the right to an effective remedy and the obligation of Member States to provide this remedy. In this context, the dynamism of the correlation is striking. From the general objective requirement of effectiveness of EU law applied to situations where individual rights were identified, the Court developed a more specific individual right to a remedy to ensure the enforcement of these rights. This in turn translated into a concrete obligation for public authorities to provide effective remedies. The case law however tends to focus on rights rather than on obligations, especially in the post-Lisbon era.[763] This phenomenon (which may not be due, or not only, to the Court of Justice: it could well be a consequence of the tendency of l litigants and/or national courts to focus on rights), does not necessarily challenge the classic correlation between rights and obligations, which after all does not prevent the focus on the 'right' or 'obligation' aspect of a given rule, nor does it prevent the right from being relied on as the justification for the obligation. Indeed, a *justificational* focus, establishing a hierarchy between the right and the obligation, is not incompatible with their *logical* mutual entailment,[764] and the case law confirms as much. In fact, the variation in focus allows for a virtous circle: by deriving concrete con-

762 *Berlioz Investment Fund,* C-682/15, para 44 (emphases added) in line with AG Wathelet's assessment that '*Article 47 of the Charter cannot be treated independently of the second paragraph of Article 19 TEU, since under that provision Member States are required to provide 'remedies sufficient to ensure effective legal protection in the fields covered by Union law*''. Opinion of AG Wathelet in *Berlioz Investment Fund,* C-682/15, EU:C:2017:2, para 38. See a more detailed commentary on *Berlioz* below p. 171.

763 This is not just an impression from the cases analysed above. There are about 20 times more rulings involving Article 47 of the Charter than rulings where Article 19(1) is referred to. A search on the curia website on 30 July 2017 shows: 34 cases mentioning Article 19(1) TEU, versus 516 cases mentioning Article 47 CFR.

764 Kramer, 'Rights Without Trimmings' 26. This argument is used by Kramer to refute one recurring criticism of the Hohfeld's Correlativity Axiom, discussed above p. 56.

sequences from the 'right' aspect, the Court also reshapes and redefines the obligational aspect as well. Just like for rights in general, awareness of the dual rationale of effective judicial protection helps look at problems from two different angles and therefore allows to minimise blind spots in the protection of individual interests and in the implementation of EU law.[765] Secondly, the case law sheds light on the relation between rights and remedies, making clear that the latter are consequences of the former; the existence of the remedy is conditioned on the existence of a right. It must now be analysed how this unfolds practically in the Union's complex multilevel legal system.

1.3.2. The interest trigger: the stumbling block in the Union's pluralistic system of remedies

The EU functions with a pluralistic system of enforcement of rights. The remedies for rights conferred by EU law are available in two parallel systems: on the one hand, a central system of remedies against the EU institutions before the EU courts; on the other hand, a decentralised system of enforcement of rights within domestic legal frameworks, before national courts (referring questions to the CJEU if necessary) further subdivided into as many systems as there are Member States in the Union.[766] This complex architecture has specific implications for the EU concept of individual rights. The decentralised system of remedies means that EU rights must find their way through a variety of channels designed to apply 'rights' that may not always correspond to the EU concept of rights, and domestic systems struggle especially with the broad notion of interest as a trigger for rights conferred by EU law. The Court's case law, especially through the mechanism of the preliminary ruling, of course constitutes a unifying force ensuring that the rights conferred by EU law are effectively applied and protected in all Member States (1.3.2.1). However, by contrast another problem becomes clear, specific to the enforcement of rights taking place directly before the CJEU, which does not in this context show the same eagerness to protect individual interests (1.3.2.2).

765 See Porat, 'Rights-Based Law v. Duty-Based Law: Old Dilemma, New Perspective' on the importance of neglecting neither the rights-based nor the duty-based perspective on legal norms.

766 Callies, 'Kohärenz und Konvergenz beim europäischen Individualrechtsschutz - Der Zugang zum Gericht im Lichte des Grundrechts auf effektiven Rechtsschutz' 3578.

1.3.2.1. The decentralised system of national remedies and the protective norm issue

The founding cases on rights and remedies that we reviewed the previous section arose in the context of the decentralised enforcement of rights. A distinctive feature of EU law is indeed that it grants rights to individuals and requires the Member States to make these rights effective by providing appropriate remedies.[767] As Ruffert observes, this situation creates a practical distinction between rights and remedies, unknown to many domestic systems of Member States such as Germany.[768] Likewise, Eilmansberger acknowledges that ever since *Rewe* and *Comet* the Court has instituted a '*division of labour for the enforcement of Community rights*', i.e. that creating rights is the mission of the EU while creating the remedies for enforcing these rights is a matter left to the national lawmakers.[769] This distinction should therefore be the starting point for understanding the relation between rights and remedies in EU law.[770] The Court repeatedly relied on the meta-principle of effectiveness to 'invent' remedies where rights were insufficiently protected by existing domestic remedies, creating in turn new difficulties in the implementation of rights on the domestic level

767 Azoulai, 'L'autonomie de l'individu européen et la question du statut' 3; Foulquier, *Les droits publics subjectifs des administrés. Emergence d'un concept en droit administratif français du XIXè au XXè siècle* 271.

768 Ruffert, 'Rights and Remedies in European Community Law: a Comparative View' 333.

769 *Rewe v Landwirtschaftskammer für das Saarland*, C-33/76; *Comet BV v Produktschap voor Siergewassen*, C-45/76; Eilmansberger, 'The Relationship between Rights and Remedies in EC Law: in Search of the Missing Link' 1200. Eilmansberger however argues that this division is inadequate and calls for a redistribution of labour between EU and national law, i.e. make sure that remedies are made a defining part of rights at the EU level instead of being left to national lawmakers. See also Ruffert, 'Rights and Remedies in European Community Law: a Comparative View' 333.

770 Türk, *The Concept of Legislation in European Community Law - A Comparative Perspective* 100. See also Ruffert, 'Rights and Remedies in European Community Law: a Comparativc Vicw'.

1.3.2.1.1. Remedies before national courts as consequences of rights under EU law

The first example is the principle of Member State liability for violations of EU law, which is one of the '*practically most important substantive remedies capable of effectively enforcing rights under EU law*'.[771] The right to compensation by the Member States of damages caused by violations of EU law was first laid down in *Francovich*, based on a reminder of the correlation between obligations of public authorities and rights of individuals (with a reference to *Van Gend en Loos* and *Costa v ENEL*): '*the Treaty has created its own legal system, which is integrated into the legal systems of the Member States and which their courts are bound to apply. The subjects of that legal system are not only the Member States but also their nationals. Just as it imposes burdens on individuals, [Union] law is also intended to give rise to rights which become part of their legal patrimony. Those rights arise not only where they are expressly granted by the Treaty but also by virtue of obligations which the Treaty imposes in a clearly defined manner both on individuals and on the Member States and the [Union] institutions*'.[772] The principle of the liability of national public authorities for violations of EU law is a logical consequence of that approach and has even been characterised in the literature as a general principle of EU law, especially given that it is '*inherent in the system of the Treaty*'. It is therefore a very good illustration of the close link between the obligations of the EU and the Member States on the one hand, and the rights of individuals on the other hand. However, the EU principle of public liability requires closer attention because of the other way in which it involves the concept of a right. Indeed, rights are part of the *criteria* for establishing EU or Member State liability.

In *Francovich*, the conditions for Member State liability were listed as follows: ', *[t]he first of those conditions is that the result prescribed by the directive should entail the grant of rights to individuals. The second condition is that it should be possible to identify the content of those rights on the basis of the provisions of the directive. Finally, the third condition is the existence of a causal link between the breach of the State' s obligation and the loss and damage suffered by the injured parties*.'[773] These conditions, the Court stated, were '*sufficient to give rise to a right on the part of individuals to obtain reparation, a right found-*

771 Hofmann, 'The Right to an 'Effective Judicial Remedy' and the Changing Conditions of Implementing EU Law' 11.

772 Judgment of 19 November 1991, *Francovich and Bonifaci v. Italy*, Joined cases C-6/90 and C-9/90, EU:C:1991:428, para 31.

773 *Francovich and Bonifaci v. Italy*, Joined cases C-6/90 and C-9/90, para 40.

ed directly on Community law'.[774] In the case in point, the provisions at issue were several articles from Directive 80/987/EEC on the protection of employees in the event of insolvency of the employer.[775] The Court held that they were sufficiently precise and unconditional as regards the content of the guarantee claimed and as regards the persons who are entitled to that guarantee. But the directive did not give sufficiently precise indications as to the public authority which should be liable to provide that guarantee, therefore it did not have direct effect.[776] It was clear, however, that the result required by the directive entailed '*the grant to employees of a right to a guarantee of payment of their unpaid wage claims*', and the content of this right could be identified, so that the first two conditions were fulfilled and that employees had a right '*to obtain reparation of loss and damage caused to them as a result of failure to transpose*'.[777]

This essential case is very enlightening as regards the role that rights play in the process of acknowledging a right to damages. Firstly, the connection between rights and obligations appears again in the list of conditions laid down by the Court: the first condition refers to 'rights' while the third condition refers to a corresponding 'obligation'. Secondly, this judgment shows that in order to identify a right, it is important to think also in terms of obligations: here, there could be no directly applicable right because it was not clear who was the addressee of the correlative obligation. The correlation supported by the effectiveness rationale, as the Court held that '*[t]he full effectiveness of Community rules would be impaired and the protection of the rights which they grant would be weakend if individuals were unable to obtain redress when their rights are infringed by a breach of Community law for which a Member State can be held responsible.*'[778] Thirdly, *Francovich* also shows that the infringed rule does not need to have direct effect for it

---

774 *Francovich and Bonifaci v. Italy*, Joined cases C-6/90 and C-9/90, para 41.

775 Council Directive 80/987/EEC of 20 October 1980 on the approximation of the laws of the Member States relating to the protection of employees in the event of the insolvency of the employer (OJ L 283 p. 23).

776 *Francovich and Bonifaci v. Italy*, Joined cases C-6/90 and C-9/90, para 22 and paras 25-26. As Claes points out, however, it does not mean that the provisions cannot have direct effect in other cases: Claes, *National Courts' Mandate in the European Constitution*, 80.

777 *Francovich and Bonifaci v. Italy*, Joined cases C-6/90 and C-9/90, para 44.

778 *Francovich and Bonifaci v. Italy*, Joined cases C-6/90 and C-9/90, para 33. The next important case on Member State liability was Judgment of 5 March 1996, *Brasserie du pêcheur v Bundesrepublik Deutschland and The Queen v Secretary of State for Transport, ex parte Factortame*, Joined cases C-46/93 and C-48/93, EU:C:1996:79, which is analysed in this work p. 256.

to be considered as 'intended' to confer rights on individuals: while the applicant could not rely on the provision of the unimplemented directive in the sense that it did not have direct effect, the Court did find that the relevant provision of the directive entailed the grant of rights on individuals. And so, in the words of Caranta, *Francovich 'marks the birth of a "jus commune", of a law common to all the Member States and to the Community itself, in the field of the judicial protection of individuals against public powers'.*[779]

In developing the principle of Member State liability, the Court held that enforceable rights are created by the provisions of EU law themselves, and not as a result of a Court judgment against a Member State. The *Waterkeyn* ruling made clear that the purpose of judgments resulting from actions for failure to fulfil obligations '*is primarily to lay down the duties of Member States when they fail to fulfil their obligations. Rights for the benefit of individuals flow from the actual provisions of Community law having direct effect in the Member States' internal order.*'[780] This proves not only that the enforceability of a right does not depend upon a prior judgment of the CJEU, but also that individual rights are indeed inherent in obligations of Member States.[781] Remedies are necessary consequences of the existence of these rights/obligations.

Further examples of remedies required to ensure the effectiveness of rights conferred by Union law include the obligation for a national court to provide interim relief,[782] the obligation to review the legality of a decision taken at the national level as a result of a composite administrative

---

779 R. Caranta, 'Governmental Liability after Francovich' (1993) 52 Cambridge Law Journal 272 297.

780 Judgment of 14 December 1982, *Procureur de la République v Waterkeyn*, C-314/81, EU:C:1982:430, para 15.

781 A. Barav, 'Enforcement of Community Rights in the National Courts: the Case for Jurisdiction to Grant an Interim Relief' (1989) 26 Common Market Law Review 369 382; D. Ruiz-Jarabo Colomer, 'Once Upon a Time--Francovich: From Fairy Tale to Cruel Reality?' in M. Poiares Maduro and L. Azoulai (eds), *The Past and Future of EU Law: the Classics of EU Law Revisited on the 50th Anniversary of the Rome Treaty* (Hart Publishing 2010) 407; V. Milutinovic, The 'Right to Damages' under EU Competition Law: from Courage v Crehan to the White Paper and Beyond (Kluwer Law International 2010) 70. See also Judgment of 20 September 2001, *Courage and Crehan*, C-453/99, EU:C:2001:465, paras 19-29.

782 In *Factortame*, the Court held that '*any provision of a national legal system and any legislative, administrative or judicial practice which might impair the effectiveness*' of EU law by withholding from the national courts the power to set aside national legislative provisions was incompatible with the very essence of Community law. This meant that there was an obligation on national court to grant interim relief where there was no equivalent form of protection of rights under national

procedure,[783] the obligation to provide for actions for prohibitive or mandatory injunctions,[784] the compensation for violation of rights.[785] It seems that only where the concern for effectiveness stops, does the principle of national procedural autonomy begin: in the *Salgoil* case, an Italian court enquired as to whether direct effect gave rise to a subjective right or a legitimate interest according to the Italian categorisation. The distinction was key in Italian law because it determined whether the case would be judged by a civil or an administrative court. The ECJ held that the courts must grant immediate protection to the rights conferred by EU law (i.e., provide sufficient remedies), but left the categorisation of these rights to national law,[786] implying that it would not meddle into domestic procedural systems as long as the effectiveness of rights conferred by EU law was ensured.

---

law – interim relief was understood as a means of guaranteeing '*real and effective judicial protection*'. *The Queen v Secretary of State for Transport, ex parte Factortame*, C-213/89, paras 29-30. The principle of effectiveness was also at stake on another level: there was concern as to the effectiveness the preliminary ruling mechanism if there was no possibility for the national court to grant interim relief until it got an answer from the CJEU. Rasmussen, 'Towards a Normative Theory of Interpretation of Community Law' 147. Hofmann, 'The Right to an 'Effective Judicial Remedy' and the Changing Conditions of Implementing EU Law' 9.

783 Judgment of 3 December 1992, *Oleificio Borelli v Commission*, C-97/91, EU:C:1992:491. Hofmann, 'The Right to an 'Effective Judicial Remedy' and the Changing Conditions of Implementing EU Law' 11; Mihaescu Evans, 'The right to good administration at the crossroads of the various sources of fundamental rights in the EU integrated administrative system' 98.

784 In environmental law: Judgment of 25 July 2008, *Janecek*, C-237/07, EU:C:2008:447; in anti-discrimination law: Judgment of 10 July 2008, *Feryn*, C-54/07, EU:C:2008:397. H.-W. Micklitz, 'The ECJ between the Individual Citizen and the Member States - A plea for a judge-made European law on remedies' EUI Working Paper Law 2011/15, 13. See also Wilman on how these injunctions have developed also in EU secondary law: Wilman, 'The end of the absence? The growing body of EU legislation on private enforcement and the main remedies it provides for' 909-918.

785 Compensation for anticompetitive behaviour: *Courage and Crehan*, C-453/99; Judgment of 13 July 2006, *Manfredi*, Joined cases C-295/04 to C-298/04, EU:C:2006:461. Compensation for antidiscriminatory practices: Judgment of 17 July 2008, *Raccanelli*, C-94/07, EU:C:2008:425. Micklitz, 'The ECJ between the Individual Citizen and the Member States - A plea for a judge-made European law on remedies' 13.

786 Judgment of 19 December 1968, *Salgoil v Ministerio del commercio con l'estero*, C-13/68, EU:C:1968:54.

1.3.2.1.2. Domestic courts and the Schutznorm pressure

The requirement to effectively protect EU rights thus led to the development of a *'judge-made Law on Remedies*',[787] constantly probing the limits of Member States' procedural autonomy, which is limited by the requirements of equivalence and effectiveness.[788] The mobilisation of EU individuals that the Court has organised since *Van Gend en Loos* in order to implement EU law translates into a requirement for all Member States to admit that any interest in enforcing a norm of EU law should allow access to court to the individual claiming it: for some Member States, this entails tremendous changes in their system of access to court.[789] The problem in fact goes both ways: not only does EU law puts pressure on Member States; conversely, the debates at the national level on how to integrate EU law requirements have an impact on how the rights conferred by EU law come to life when claimed by individuals. And indeed, the problem is more acute in some domestic legal systems than in others.

The French conception of remedies is not too problematic with regard to the protection of rights conferred by EU law, provided that these rights are acknowledged. In the French legal order, difficulties manifested mostly in the reception of principles such as direct effect and supremacy and admitting that EU law (including rights granted by it) could have precedence over national law.[790] In other words, the French legal system may contain some resistance to acknowledging EU sources of rights and obligations, but not so much to means of enforcing them.[791] In terms of remedies, the French definition of *intérêt à agir* seems to overlap with the ECJ's use of the

---

787 Micklitz, 'The ECJ between the Individual Citizen and the Member States - A plea for a judge-made European law on remedies'.

788 *Rewe v Landwirtschaftskammer für das Saarland*, C-33/76.

789 Callies, 'Kohärenz und Konvergenz beim europäischen Individualrechtsschutz - Der Zugang zum Gericht im Lichte des Grundrechts auf effektiven Rechtsschutz' 3578.

790 See e.g. the reluctance to review individual decisions based on EU law provisions with direct effect since the *Cohn-Bendit* ruling by the French Conseil d'Etat: Ministre de l'intérieur c/ Cohn-Bendit, CE, ass, 22 déc 1978, Rec. Lebon p. 524. J.H. Jans and J.M. Prinssen, 'Direct Effect: Convergence or Divergence? A Comparative Perspective' in J.M. Prinssen and A. Schrauwen (eds), *Direct Effect Rethinking a Classic of EC Legal Doctrine* (Europa Law Publishing 2002) 109. This page has been turned, however, with the Judgment of the French Conseil d'Etat: Mme Perreux, CE, ass., 30 oct 2009, n°298348.

791 The Danish Supreme Court seems to have a similar kind of problem for accepting the general principles of EU law can be sources of rights, especially in horizontal situations. Danish Supreme Court (Højesteret), 6 December 2016, Case

notion of interest in cases where it identifies rights. Yet this overlap is incomplete. As discussed in Section 1.2., the common feature is that interest opens the access to court in both the French and the EU system.[792] However, at the EU level it also determines the possibility for the Court to acknowledge the 'right' equivalent of a given obligation, whereas French administrative courts will check the *intérêt à agir* without translating the subsequent issue into a matter of rights. Still, this system does not prevent individuals from claiming their rights under EU law before French courts.

By contrast, complex problems arise in the implementation of rights, as conceptualised in EU law, in the German and German-inspired systems of remedies, designed to enforce 'subjective' public rights.[793] As Prechal has noted, the problem with the notion of a *Schutznorm* is that it causes confusion when it comes with the understanding that direct effect and creation of rights are one and the same thing.[794] This has led German courts and legal scholars to consider that the intention to create a substantive individual right (the *Schutznorm* requirement) was a pre-requisite for direct effect. As a consequence, it has been argued both before the Court and in the literature that only individuals whose interests are intended to be protected by the EU provisions at issue may rely on them.[795] A concrete example, advanced by Voßkuhle and Kaiser, is that of a directive which aims to protect

---

15/2014 (First Chamber), *DI v Estate of A.* For a commentary of this case see: G. Zaccaroni, 'Ultra vires review e applicazione orizzontale del principio di non discriminazione sulla base dell'età : una riflessione (a freddo) su Dansk Industri,' SIDIBlog, May 2017, <http://www.sidiblog.org/2017/05/04/ultra-vires-review-e-applicazione-orizzontale-del-principio-di-non-discriminazione-sulla-base-delleta-una-riflessione-a-freddo-su-dansk-industri/> accessed 13 August 2017.

792 See p. 60 of this work.

793 See p. 52 of this work. Drexl recommends to not think in terms of German 'subjective rights' in the context of EU law. J. Drexl, 'Competition Law as Part of the European Constitution' in A. Von Bogdandy and J. Bast (eds), *Principles of European Constitutional Law* (Hart Publishing 2006) 655.

794 Prechal, 'Member State Liability and Direct Effect: What's the Difference after All?'.

795 See the arguments of the Dutch government and AG Fennelly in the *Lemmens* case: Judgment of 16 June 1998, *Lemmens*, C-227/97, EU:C:1998:296, and Opinion of AG Fennelly in *Lemmens*, C-227/97, EU:C:1998:61; in the literature: Hilson and Downes, 'Making sense of rights: Community rights in E.C. law' 131 who are, in Prechal's words, "*smuggling' an interest requirement into the concept of direct effect*'. See S. Prechal, 'Member State Liability and Direct Effect: What's the Difference After All?' (2006) 17 European Business Law Review 299 313. E. Staebe, *Rechtsschutz bei gemeinschaftswidrigen Beihilfen vor europäischen und deutschen Gerichten* (Duncker & Humblot 2001) 193-195.

public health. Such a directive would be seen in German law as protecting individuals only by reflex, and therefore insufficient to ground subjective public rights. Indeed, the aim to protect individual interests is the essential criterion for granting a subjective public right. On the contrary, under EU law actual interest will be sufficient for an individual to require the execution of the obligations laid down in the directive.[796]

Germany is not the only Member State where such problems arise: a Polish example is the judgment of the Sąd Najwyższy (the Polish Supreme Court) showing how EU law impacts the understanding of *locus standi* in Polish law. This was a case about a complaint lodged by an undertaking against the decision of a regulatory authority, regarding effective competition on the domestic telecommunication market. As the undertaking was not a party to the administrative proceedings which had led to the decision, Polish law did not allow it to challenge it in court. This was held in first and second instance, but then the Supreme Court held that the Polish concept of party to proceedings could not hold against the EU obligation to grant the right of appeal against a decision to an entity affected by the decision. It relied on provisions of the Framework Directive on electronic communications networks and services (Article 4(1) of which provides that '*any user or undertaking providing electronic communications networks and/or services who is affected by a decision of a national regulatory authority has the right of appeal against the decision*')[797] and on the EU principle of effective legal protection.[798]

This interpretation has been indirectly confirmed by the CJEU in a preliminary ruling on an Austrian case *Tele2*. In the context of administrative market analysis proceedings conducted by the Austrian telecommunications control commission (TCK), a provider of electronic communications networks and services had requested the latter to grant it party status and access to the file. However, Austrian law (much like Polish law prior to the decision of the Polish Supreme Court) provided that only undertakings in

796 Voßkuhle and Kaiser, 'Grundwissen – Öffentliches Recht: Das subjektiv-öffentliche Recht' 18; Masing, *Die Mobilisierung des Bürgers für die Durchsetzung des Rechts: europäische Impulse für eine Revision der Lehre vom subjektiv-öffentlichen Recht* 14.

797 Parliament and Council Directive 2002/21/EC of 7 March 2002 on a common regulatory framework for electronic communications networks and services (OJ L 108 p. 33) ('Framework Directive').

798 Order of the Sąd Najwyższy of 20 February 2008, III SK 23/07. N. Półtorak, 'Changes in the Level of the National Judicial Protection Under the EU Influence on the Example of the Polish Legal System' in M. Bobek (ed), *Central European Judges Under the European Influence* (Hart Publishing 2015) 234.

respect of which specific obligations were imposed, amended or withdrawn, could be party to market analysis proceedings.[799] The Court confirmed that the term 'affected' in Article 4(1) was meant that not only the addressee of a decision, but also all '*users and undertakings in competition with such an undertaking which are not themselves addressees of that decision but the rights of which are adversely affected by it*', must be allowed to challenge the decision.[800] We find here again the broad conception of interest that triggers the application of rights granted by EU law, and requires the availability of remedies to ensure the effectiveness of these rights.

Another judgment on a case from Austria further illustrates the point. In *Zuchtverband*,[801] an association of breeders for ponies opposed the recognition of competing organisation of breeders for Shetland ponies. The applicable EU law provisions stemmed from Directive 90/427 on the conditions applicable to intra-Community trade in equidæ and the complementary Decision.[802] Article 2 of the Decision provided that '*[t]he authorities of the Member State concerned must grant official approval or recognition to any organisation or association which maintains or establishes a stud-book, provided it meets the conditions laid down in the Annex*' and that these authorities '*may refuse*' to recognise such an organisation if it endangers the preservation of the breed or if the breed is already part of another organisation's stud-book. The Court assesses two questions: whether Article 2 binds the Member State into refusing authorisation in certain situations so that it gives rise to rights for individuals who would want to oppose the authorisation being granted to others; then whether there must be a '*judicial means of obtaining redress*' against the decision taken in application of the same provision. Concerning the first question, the Court construes Article 2 of the Decision as conferring on the authorities of the Member States discretion allowing them, in specific circumstances, to refuse an application.[803] Acknowledging a right to require refusal from the authorities

799 Judgment of 21 February 2008, *Tele2 Telecommunication*, C-426/05, EU:C:2008:103.

800 *Tele2 Telecommunication*, C-426/05, para 48.

801 Judgment of 11 November 2004, C-216/02, *Zuchtverband für Ponys*, EU:C:2004:703.

802 Council Directive 90/427/EEC of 26 June 1990 on the zootechnical and genealogical conditions governing intra-Community trade in equidæ (OJ L 224 p. 55) and Commission Decision 92/353/EEC of 11 June 1992 laying down the criteria for the approval or recognition of organizations and associations which maintain or establish stud-books for registered equidae (OJ L 192 p. 63).

803 *Zuchtverband für Ponys*, C-216/02, para 34.

'*would amount to doing away*' with that discretion.[804] In a classic direct effect reasoning the Court therefore holds that the Zuchtverband is not entitled to demand that competent authorities refuse to recognise or approve the new association. Concerning the second question the Court finds that, as a consequence of the answer to the first question, there is no requirement stemming from EU law that Member States should provide a judicial means of obtaining redress against the decision to grant recognition to the competing organisation.[805] In accordance with the correlativity model, *Zuchtverband* thus perfectly illustrates that where there is no obligation there is no right,[806] and that where there is no right there is no remedy.[807]

There is a small inconsistency, however. In its brief answer the Court relies on Advocate General Ruiz-Jarabo Colomer's line of argument without specifying exactly which aspect it endorses. One of the arguments put forward by the Advocate General concerns the scope of protection allowed by Article 2. '*In the light of the purpose of*' this provision he insists that only the organisations seeking recognition which may rely on its content: '*existing associations and organisations do not appear in that provision as the holders of rights: they are only mentioned, indirectly, when the competent authorities are entrusted with assessing, in order to approve a new association or organisation, whether it may jeopardise the operation or improvement or selection programme of one which is already active*'.[808] This takes us back onto the 'protective intention' track, looking for an intended beneficiary for the provision. Dougan, because of the Advocate General's conclusions, interprets the Court's ruling as meaning that the claimant was not within the protective scope of the Decision.[809] In addition to being unnecessary for reaching a

804 *Zuchtverband für Ponys*, C-216/02, para 36.

805 *Zuchtverband für Ponys*, C-216/02, paras 38-40.

806 Prechal observes that, '*[a]s the corresponding right of an individual must be ascertainable with sufficient precision, it can only exist as a correlative of the obligation when the latter is sufficiently defined*'. Prechal, 'Member State Liability and Direct Effect: What's the Difference After All?' 308.

807 Reich has described this as the turning upside down of the *ubi ius - ibi remedium* principle. N. Reich, 'Horizontal Liability in EC Law: Hybridization of Remedies for Compensation in Case of Breaches of EC Rights' (2007) 44 Common Market Law Review 705 718.

808 Opinion of AG Ruiz-Jarabo Colomer in *Zuchtverband für Ponys*, C-216/02, ECLI:EU:C:2004:25, paras 38-39.

809 M. Dougan, 'Who Exactly Benefits from the Treaties? The Murky Interaction Between Union and National Competence over the Capacity to Enforce EU Law', *The Cambridge Yearbook of European Legal Studies, Volume 12* (Hart 2010) 99 and 111.

solution, this argument implicitly based on the notion of a protected interest is also inconsistent with the rest of the reasoning, which otherwise constitutes a straightforward application of the right-obligation correlation and the conception of remedies as consequences of rights and obligations.[810]

Perhaps in part due to the sometimes contradictory signals, some national courts keep looking for 'subjective rights' in order to filter access to court. The question how to identify the rights of third parties to an administrative procedure came up again in *Olainfarm*.[811] Olainfarm, a pharmaceutical company, held an authorisation to market a medicinal product in Latvia. When another pharmaceutical company applied for and received an authorisation to market a generic of the same product, Olainfarm brought an action before the district administrative court in order to seek annulment of that authorisation. It relied on Article 10 of Directive 2001/83/EC on medicinal products, which provided as a condition for granting the authorisation that the reference to the product registered by the manufacturer of the reference product should be founded on the verification of a series of conditions.[812] The Court's preliminary ruling is interesting not only because of the answer but also because of how the question itself was phrased. The Latvian court's question was whether there is a 'subjektīvas tiesības' – the term was translated into English as 'individual right' but retained the equivalent of 'subjective' in many other language versions of the ruling[813] – to bring an action '*or in other words [...] the right to a judicial remedy [...] to determine whether the manufacturer of the generic product made lawful, well-founded reference to the product registered by the manufacturer of the reference product, relying on Article 10 of the directive*'.[814] The referring court thus appears to be looking for a right of access to court (i.e. a remedy) without acknowledging that this is conditioned on the existence of another right. This question therefore illustrates the *Schutznorm*-type of bias that shapes questions of interpretation of EU law.

---

810 Reich, 'Horizontal Liability in EC Law: Hybridization of Remedies for Compensation in Case of Breaches of EC Rights' 718.

811 Judgment of 23 October 2014, *Olainfarm*, C-104/13, EU:C:2014:2316.

812 Directive 2001/83/EC of the European Parliament and of the Council of 6 November 2001 on the Community code relating to medicinal products for human use (OJ L 311 p. 67) as amended by Regulation (EC) No 1394/2007 of the European Parliament and of the Council of 13 November 2007 (OJ L 324 p. 121 and corrigendum OJ 2009 L 87 p. 174).

813 For example, respectively in the French, German, Dutch and Spanish versions: 'droit subjectif', 'subjektives Recht', 'subjectief recht', 'derecho subjetivo'.

814 *Olainfarm*, C-104/13, para 22.

The Court however steers clear from the dogmatically loaded term of '*subjective*' right and incorporates the requirement of Article 47 of the Charter into the question, thus reframed into whether the combination of Article 10 of the Directive and Article 47 confer a right to challenge the granting of an authorisation.[815] Then, while the Latvian court and the parties were focusing on assessing whether the directive intends to grant a right, the Court's answer shows that this has little relevance. Instead, what matters is that for granting authorisations the administration must respect the conditions laid down at Article 10, especially those concerning the reference medicinal product. '*It is apparent that that provision confers a concomitant right on the holder of the [marketing authorisation] for the former medicinal product to demand that the rights attaching to him by virtue of those conditions are observed*'.[816] Here again we witness the simultaneous emergence of obligations and corresponding rights. In light of Article 47 CFR requiring that a right must be protected by a remedy, the Court deduces from the existence of these rights, the requirement of a remedy for enforcing them.[817]

Contrast this result with *Zuchtverband*: in that case, the third party was challenging a decision that was taken within the administration's margin of discretion. The administration was under no obligation to act in the way requested by the applicant, who therefore had no correlative right, so that the question of a remedy became pointless. By contrast, in *Olainfarm*, the decision must based on conditions laid down in the Directive: the obligation is clear and gives rise to a correlative right. So in both cases, the question whether there must be a remedy is reframed into whether there is a right – and then is derived the answer (or, in the *Zuchtverband* case, the absence of need for an answer) regarding the remedy. The legislative intention to grant a right or a remedy is irrelevant.

The Court has indirectly addressed the protective intention issue in a more exhaustive way in the *Berlioz* case.[818] A joint stock company governed by Luxembourg law enjoyed an exemption from withholding tax for the

---

815 *Olainfarm*, C-104/13, para 36.

816 *Olainfarm*, C-104/13, para 37.

817 *Olainfarm*, C-104/13, para 39: '*It should therefore be recognised that the holder of a [marketing authorisation] for a medicinal product used as a reference product in an application for a MA under Article 10 of Directive 2001/83 is, by virtue of that provision, read in conjunction with Article 47 of the Charter, entitled to judicial protection in so far as concerns respect for his rights.*' See also Judgment of 14 March 2018, *Astellas Pharma*, C-557/16, EU:C:2018:181, paras 34-37.

818 *Berlioz Investment Fund*, C-682/15.

dividends received from its French subsidiary. The French tax administration asked the Luxembourgish tax administration for information in order to assess whether the exemption was justified. In turn the Luxembourgish administration requested information from Berlioz, which refused to give part of the requested information on the basis that it was not foreseeably relevant for the purpose of the investigation. As a result, Berlioz was imposed a pecuniary penalty for not complying with the information order. The Luxembourgish legislator facing criticism with respect to its tax information exchange policy had, in the meantime, suppressed the judicial review that used to be available to challenge the information order on which the penalty is based. The Luxembougish Administrative Court referred to the CJEU questions on on the interpretation of the applicable directive on administrative cooperation in the field of taxation[819] and Article 47 CFR in order to assess the compatibility of the Luxembourgish legislation with these instruments of EU law. According to its Article 1(1) the directive '*lays down the rules and procedures under which the Member States shall cooperate with each other with a view to exchanging information that is foreseeably relevant to the administration and enforcement of the domestic laws of the Member States*' concerning certain taxes. Article 5 further provides: '*[a]t the request of the requesting authority, the requested authority shall communicate to the requesting authority any information referred to in Article 1(1) that it has in its possession or that it obtains as a result of administrative enquiries*'. The interpretation of these provisions by the Court in the light of Article 47 CFR may, for our purposes, be divided into two main parts: firstly, the Court analyses whether there is a right to a remedy in the case at hand, and secondly, the Court assesses what this remedy consists in.

Firstly, having established, on the basis of Article 51(1) CFR, that the Charter is applicable to the case at hand,[820] the Court assesses whether the person requested is entitled under Article 47 CFR to challenge the legality of the information request. The Court answers in two steps. It first evaluates '*whether there is a right to a remedy under Article 47*' and in this context points out the correspondence between this provision and Article 19(1)TEU.[821] It then refers to the argument submitted by several governments that there is no right guaranteed by EU law to be protected by the

819 Council Directive 2011/16/EU of 15 February 2011 on administrative cooperation in the field of taxation and repealing Directive 77/799/EEC (OJ L 64 p. 1).

820 *Berlioz Investment Fund*, C-682/15, paras 32-42.

821 *Berlioz Investment Fund*, C-682/15, para 44: '*According to Article 47 of the Charter, entitled 'Right to an effective remedy and to a fair trial', everyone whose rights and freedoms guaranteed by the law of the Union are violated has the right to an effective*

remedy on the basis of Article 47 because the directive itself '*does not confer any rights on individuals*', since it '*covers only the exchange of information between tax administrations and confers rights only on them. Accordingly, a relevant person such as Berlioz could not claim on the basis of Article 47 of the Charter that it has a right to an effective remedy*'.[822] The Court admits that the '*directive does not impose any obligation for those authorities to give the taxpayer a hearing*'.[823] However, it points out the existence of a general principle of EU law guaranteeing '*protection against arbitrary or disproportionate intervention by public authorities in the sphere of the private activities of any natural or legal person*', which '*may be invoked by a relevant person, such as Berlioz, in respect of a measure adversely affecting him, such as the information order and the penalty at issue in the main proceedings, so that a relevant person can rely on a right guaranteed by EU law, within the meaning of Article 47 of the Charter, giving him the right to an effective remedy*'.[824] We can see here a concrete application of the interest component of a right in EU law: the right (here in the form of a general principle, which also lays down a negative obligation on public authorities) is activated in a situation where an individual is 'adversely affected' by a measure. This adverse effect on a person's interests is all it takes to activate a right and make it applicable in a concrete situation.

Then the Court assesses '*[t]he subject matter of the right to a remedy*' and finds that Article 47, paragraph 2 requires that '*the national court hearing an action against the pecuniary administrative penalty imposed on the relevant person for failure to comply with an information order must be able to examine the legality of that information order*'.[825] Therefore, '*a relevant person on whom a pecuniary penalty has been imposed for failure to comply with an administrative decision directing that person to provide information in the context of an exchange between national tax administrations pursuant to Directive 2011/16 is entitled to challenge the legality of that decision*'.[826] The double function of the right to an effective remedy is clearly acknowledged: it simultaneously protects individuals and ensures the legality review of national measures.

---

remedy before a tribunal. The obligation imposed on the Member States in the second subparagraph of Article 19(1) TEU, to provide remedies sufficient to ensure effective legal protection in the fields covered by Union law, corresponds to that right'. See also *Sacko*, C-348/16, paras 29-30.

822 *Berlioz Investment Fund*, C-682/15, para 45.

823 *Berlioz Investment Fund*, C-682/15, para 46.

824 *Berlioz Investment Fund*, C-682/15, paras 51-52.

825 *Berlioz Investment Fund*, C-682/15, para 56.

826 *Berlioz Investment Fund*, C-682/15, para 59.

Secondly, the Court performs this legality review, turning to the question whether the 'foreseeable relevance' of the information requested is a condition of the legality of the information order. The Court finds that Article 5 of the Directive *'imposes an obligation'* on the requested authority, to communicate to the requesting authority any information that it has or obtains; the 'wording' of the provision allows to conclude that *'the words 'foreseeably relevant' describe a necessary characteristic of the requested information'*, while the obligation on the requested authority to cooperate with the requesting authority *'does not extend to the communication of information that is considered not to have that characteristic.'*[827] This sets the limit to the 'discretion' of the requesting authority, which *'cannot request information that is of no relevance to the investigation concerned'*.[828] This limit is a condition of the legality of the information order addressed by the requested Member State to a relevant person and of the penalty imposed for failure to comply with that order.[829] The requested authority must assess the legality of the information order accordingly, i.e. not substitute *'its own assessment of the possible usefulness of the information sought for that of the requesting authority'*, but *'nevertheless verify whether the information sought is not devoid of any foreseeable relevance to the investigation being carried out by the requesting authority'*.[830] Correspondingly, while the judicial review *'may also concern the legality of (the) information order'*, in light of *'the requesting authority's discretion, (...) the limits that apply in respect of the requested authority's review are equally applicable to reviews carried out by the courts'*.[831]

This judgment illustrates the mechanism of functional subjectivation. It does not matter that the directive does not expressly confer rights on individuals: national measures taken within its scope are still subject to legality review requested by individuals. Also interesting is the connection between Article 47 CFR and Article 19(1), making clear that the coin metaphor ('right' and 'obligation' as two sides of the same coin) applies also to procedural rules.[832]

---

827 *Berlioz Investment Fund*, C-682/15, paras 62-63.

828 *Berlioz Investment Fund*, C-682/15, para 71.

829 *Berlioz Investment Fund*, C-682/15, para 74.

830 *Berlioz Investment Fund*, C-682/15, paras 76-78.

831 *Berlioz Investment Fund*, C-682/15, paras 83-85.

832 It also goes against the suggestion to read Article 19(1) as meaning that that *'the task of national courts is first and foremost to safeguard subjective rights granted by or derived from Union law'*, while the CJEU's mandate would rather indicate *'an orientation towards objective legality review'*. Barents, 'EU Procedural Law and Effective Legal Protection' 1437. In fact, *Berlioz* exemplifies the intrinsic link between these two functions.

The judgment is more puzzling in other respects. The right that justifies the existence of a remedy is the general principle of protection against arbitrary or disproportionate intervention by public authorities in the sphere of the private activities of individuals.[833] Yet once this is established the whole review is then focused on whether the obligations in the directive (identified especially by looking at exactly how much discretion they leave to the administrations) have been respected. It could be argued that these obligations are a specific application of the general principle. But the approach still differs from *Olainfarm*, where the right is deduced from the obligations contained in the directive, and then the remedy deduced from the right. The reasoning in *Berlioz* has the consequence of broadening the access to court: the identification of a right in the form of a general principle suffices to ground the right to a remedy; then the review assesses whether the general right is respected or not by looking at the specific obligation. This solution allows the Court to maintain the logical connection between the general right and the remedy: the right to an effective legal remedy is a consequence of another right (substantive or procedural), not a self-standing right.[834] The review then allows to identify further obligations, and to assess whether these have been respected in the concrete case. In the end, *Berlioz* is enlightening in how it equates the protection of individual rights and legality review (and in how the protection of individual interests triggers this legality review).

This section has showed that the persisting *Schutznorm* pressure and the emphasis on a German-inspired conception of a 'subjective right' does not only pose a problem at the stage of identifying the right. It also complicates the relation between the right and the remedy. Because it adds a filter in the process of identifying a right, it arguably provides in the end a less effective judicial protection of individual interests.[835] These individual interests, as we have seen, do not matter only in themselves but also because of how they converge with EU interests. So the protective intention ap-

833 This general principle had been recognised by the Court in *Hoechst AG v Commission*, C-46/87, para 19.

834 Unlike what is sometimes argued e.g. Półtorak, *European Union Rights in National Courts* 13 that the right to effective judicial protection is '*a self-contained subjective right derived from the EU system*' that does not necessarily serve the enforcement of substantial rights.

835 See the argument of O. Peiffert, 'Un possible malentendu en droit de l'Union européenne : le « droit subjectif » comme condition de l'effet direct' RTDeur (2017) 655. See also Medina Alcoz, *Libertad y autoridad en el derecho administrativo. Derecho subjetivo e interés legítimo: una revisión* 206.

proach generates a problem not only in terms of individual protection but also in terms of the effectiveness of EU law. Nevertheless, cases such as *Olainfarm* and *Berlioz* provide clear responses to the protective norm pressure and shape a system of rights and remedies that is ever more favourable to individuals, reinforcing the role of the latter as agents of EU interests in the domestic systems of remedies.

1.3.2.2. The system of remedies on the EU level and the 'rights deficit'[836]

Concerning remedies before the EU Courts for protecting rights against EU institutions, another type of issue arises in relation to effectiveness. The notion that individuals could claim rights before the EU institutions is not problematic in itself – *Algera*, the very first case on rights, arose precisely in that context.[837] The means of enforcement of the rights conferred on individuals by EU law before the EU institutions and administrations however raise several questions. So far, this study has depicted rights as – not exclusively, but at least in part – instrumental to the effectiveness of EU law and to the realisation of the integrative *telos*. What becomes of that powerful rationale, then, when rights are not claimed against Member States or individuals but against EU institutions, which one could legitimately expect to function as the agents *par excellence* of this *telos*? The Court's answer is to combine a systemic approach to remedies with a subjective filter used in a restrictive way, grounding a system of remedies that minimises the significance of individual rights and limits their protection.

1.3.2.2.1. The limited relevance of individual interests in the EU system of remedies

Let us first look at the emblematic ruling in *Les Verts*, in which the Court set out the logic of the EU's system of remedies.[838] In assessing the admissibility of the Green Party's action for annulment against a decision of the European Parliament concerning party expenses, the Court seems to be just as eager to ensure that there are appropriate remedies at the EU level as

---

836 The expression is borrowed from Walker, 'Legal Theory and the European Union' 3.

837 *Algera and Others v Assemblée Commune*, Joined cases C-7/56 and C-3 to C-7/57.

838 *Les Verts*, C-294/83.

in the domestic legal systems, positing famously: 'the *[EEC] is a Community based on the rule of law, inasmuch as neither its Member States nor its Institutions can avoid a review of the question whether the measures adopted by them are in conformity with the basic constitutional Charter, the Treaty. In particular, in Articles 173 and 184, on the one hand, and in Article 177, on the other, the Treaty established a complete system of legal remedies and procedures designed to permit the Court of Justice to review the legality of measures adopted by the Institutions*'.[839] On this premise the Court generously interpreted the existing law (or rather, the existing gap in the Treaty[840]) and held that an act of the European Parliament could be challenged by way of an action for annulment. However, unlike what happened in most of the cases on remedies that we have seen so far, here the Court's insistence on remedies is not coupled with insistence on individual rights – neither in the key passage cited above, nor in the whole *Les Verts* ruling. Instead, the remedies are associated with what seems to be a very objective form of legality review, in the sense that it is disconnected from the concern for the protection of individual rights or interests. In this respect, *Les Verts* differs significantly in spirit from *Van Gend en Loos* – even though both rulings relied on the spirit and scheme of the Treaty.[841]

Following the same approach in *Foto-Frost*, the Court set the limits to the assessment of validity of Community measures by national courts. In this case, an importer and exporter of goods was challenging a German decision based on a Commission decision regarding the post-clearance recovery of custom duties – the decision being itself based on a regulation.[842] The Court held that while national courts are entitled to reject arguments brought forward by the parties challenging the validity of such measures, where they consider those arguments to be valid they cannot of themselves declare the measures invalid and must instead refer to the Court of Justice for a preliminary ruling.[843] This conclusion was '*dictated by consideration of*

839 *Les Verts*, C-294/83, para 23.

840 Article 173 EEC then only provided for action for annulment against acts of the Council and the Commission.

841 *Van Gend en Loos*, C-26/62, p.13 and *Les Verts*, C-294/83, para 24. This common reference to the 'spirit' of the Treaty is pointed out by Von Bogdandy, 'Founding Principles of EU Law: A Theoretical and Doctrinal Sketch' 98.

842 Council Regulation (EEC) No 1697/79 of 24 July 1979 on the post-clearance recovery of import duties or export duties which have not been required of the person liable for payment on goods entered for a customs procedure involving the obligation to pay such duties (OJ L 197 p. 1).

843 Judgment of 22 October 1987, *Foto-Frost v Hauptzollamt Lübeck-Ost*, C-314/85, EU:C:1987:452, paras 14-15.

the necessary coherence of the system of judicial protection established by the Treaty'; the Court further observed that '*requests for preliminary rulings, like actions for annulment, constitute means for reviewing the legality of acts of the Community institutions*'.[844] So the preliminary ruling on validity is framed not in terms of protection of individuals but in terms of objective legality review. Then the Court cited *Les Verts*[845] and concluded: '*Since Article 173 gives the Court exclusive jurisdiction to declare void an act of a Community Institution, the coherence of the system requires that where the validity of a Community act is challenged before a national court the power to declare the act invalid must also be reserved to the Court of Justice.*'[846]

This solution has been criticised for having '*removed the power to rule on the validity of Community legal enactments from the national level*' against the spirit of the Treaty.[847] In fact, the decision is not particularly surprising in view of the Court's steady preference for systemic reasoning and insistence on coherence.[848] What is more surprising, especially after *Johnston*,[849] is the absence of reflection on, or even just acknowledgement of, the connection between the review system and the individual rights that are at stake. Not once does the term 'right' come up in the judgment. Yet the heart of the concrete matter was precisely a question of what an individual could claim based on the regulation at issue. The Court observed that Article 5(2) of Regulation 1697/79 '*(laid) down three specific requirements which must be fulfilled before the competent authorities may waive the post-clearance recovery of duties. That provision must be interpreted as meaning that if all those requirements are fulfilled the person liable is entitled to the waiver of the recovery of the duty in question*'.[850] In other words: where conditions were fulfilled, the individual concerned had a right to see the administration waive the recovery of the duty – which was indeed the case, as the Court found after having assessed the three conditions. In the method and the result, this looks very

844 *Foto-Frost v Hauptzollamt Lübeck-Ost*, C-314/85, para 16.

845 *Foto-Frost v Hauptzollamt Lübeck-Ost*, C-314/85, para 16, citing *Les Verts*, C-294/83, para 23.

846 *Foto-Frost v Hauptzollamt Lübeck-Ost*, C-314/85.

847 Rasmussen, 'Towards a Normative Theory of Interpretation of Community Law' 153.

848 M. Dawson, 'How Does the European Court of Justice Reason? A Review Essay on the Legal Reasoning of the European Court of Justice' (2014) 20 European Law Journal 423 426.

849 *Johnston*, C-222/84.

850 *Foto-Frost v Hauptzollamt Lübeck-Ost*, C-314/85, para 22.

much like a direct effect test, except that rights are never mentioned.[851] The contrast with *Van Gend en Loos* is strong when considering that then, too, an individual was claiming a right not to pay a certain duty – and the Court had acknowledged that right based on systemic considerations, especially the role given to individuals within the system of the Treaty. It seems that where a measure of EU law is being challenged, this role matters a lot less than where a national measure is allegedly threatening the effectiveness of EU measures.

Foto-Frost also differs from *Van Gend en Loos* in the sense that it fails to connect the rights of individuals and the obligations of the authorities. The Court deduces from the 'entitlement' of the individual, that the Commission decision denying that entitlement is invalid.[852] Compare this expeditious reasoning with the one held in *Mecanarte,* where the exact same entitlement was being claimed (i.e. based on Article 5(2) of Regulation 1697/79) but against a decision of national authorities: having recalled the solution from *Foto-Frost* making clear the existence of an entitlement where the conditions are fulfilled, the Court adds the following: '*If the person liable is so entitled, the competent national authorities are required not to effect post-clearance recovery, otherwise that entitlement would be worthless*'.[853] The 'entitlement' of an individual is thus equated with a 'requirement' on the authorities, based on the effectiveness of the former. The correlativity axiom thus plays a part, but a less explicit one, in the assessment of EU acts than of national acts.[854]

---

851 See also Judgment of 23 May 1989, *Top Hit Holzvertrieb v Commission*, C-378/87, EU:C:1989:209, para 18; Judgment of 12 July 1989, *Binder v Hauptzollamt Bad Reichenhall*, C-161/88, EU:C:1989:312, para 16; Judgment of 27 June 1991, *Mecanarte-Metalurgica da Lagoa v Alfandega do Porto*, C-348/89, EU:C:1991:278, para 12; Judgment of 14 May 1996, *Faroe Seafood and Føroya Fiskasøla*, C-153/94, EU:C:1996:198, para 84, all maintaining that if the three conditions are satisfied, '*the person liable is entitled to the waiver of the recovery*'. The same phrase is found in Judgment of 12 December 1996, *Ministero delle Finanze v Foods Import*, C-38/95, EU:C:1996:488, para 25, even though the referring court had expressly asked whether *Foto-Frost* meant that there was an individual 'right' (see the third question at para 8), which the Court did not pick up on.

852 *Foto-Frost v Hauptzollamt Lübeck-Ost,* C-314/85, paras 27-28.

853 *Mecanarte-Metalurgica da Lagoa v Alfandega do Porto*, C-348/89, para 13.

854 Article 5(2) was also at stake in a a case where individual applicants were challenging acts of national authorities that the Court eventually used the term 'right', stating that the regime set out by this provision '*makes the right of the person liable to pay customs duties not to have post-clearance recovery effected by the competent authorities subject to three conditions*': Judgment of 12 December 1996,

The predominance of systemic considerations is also clear in *Zuckerfabrik.* In this case a sugar producer had initiated proceedings to suspend the enforcement of a German measure based on a Community regulation introducing a special levy on sugar and the national court referred to the Court of Justice for a preliminary ruling on the validity of this regulation.[855] The Court acknowledged that '*the legal protection guaranteed by Community law includes the* right *of individuals to challenge, as a preliminary issue, the legality of such regulations before national courts and to induce those courts to refer questions to the Court of Justice for a preliminary ruling.*'[856] Swaine has argued that in this assertion of a protective approach to individual rights *Zuckerfabrik* anticipated *Francovich.*[857] Nevertheless, the right in *Zuckerfabrik* is merely instrumental to legality review, as the Court then highlights (like in *Foto-Frost*) the parallelism of purpose between the action for annulment and the preliminary ruling on validity – both '*means for reviewing the legality of acts of the Community institutions*.'[858] The possibility for a national court to grant interim relief awaiting a CJEU ruling on validity is then ultimately justified by the '*coherence of the system of interim legal protection*':[859] as interim relief is available both in actions for annulment and in domestic proceedings involving a reference for preliminary ruling on interpretation, it should also be available in proceedings where a preliminary ruling on validity is awaited.[860] However, the national court must '*take account of the interest of the [Union]*' and not set aside the EU act without proper guarantees in this respect[861] - so that the individual's interest in

Olasagasti and Others v Amministrazione delle Finanze dello Stato, Joined cases 47 to 50/95, C-60/95, C-81/95, C-92/95 and C-148/95, EU:C:1996:489, para 32.

855 Council Regulation (EEC) No 1914/87 of 2 July 1987 introducing a special elimination levy in the sugar sector for the 1986/87 marketing year (OJ L 183 p. 5).

856 , *Zuckerfabrik Süderdithmarschen and Zuckerfabrik Soest v Hauptzollamt Itzehoe and Hauptzollamt Paderborn*, Joined cases C-143/88 and C-92/89, para 16 (emphasis added).

857 E.T. Swaine, 'Subsidiarity and Self-Interest: Federalism at the European Court of Justice' (2000) 41 Harvard International Law Journal 1 30.

858 *Zuckerfabrik Süderdithmarschen and Zuckerfabrik Soest v Hauptzollamt Itzehoe and Hauptzollamt Paderborn*, Joined cases C-143/88 and C-92/89, para 18, referring to *Foto-Frost v Hauptzollamt Lübeck-Ost*, C-314/85, para 16.

859 *Zuckerfabrik Süderdithmarschen and Zuckerfabrik Soest v Hauptzollamt Itzehoe and Hauptzollamt Paderborn*, Joined cases C-143/88 and C-92/89, para 18.

860 *Zuckerfabrik Süderdithmarschen and Zuckerfabrik Soest v Hauptzollamt Itzehoe and Hauptzollamt Paderborn*, Joined cases C-143/88 and C-92/89, paras 18-19.

861 *Zuckerfabrik Süderdithmarschen and Zuckerfabrik Soest v Hauptzollamt Itzehoe and Hauptzollamt Paderborn*, Joined cases C-143/88 and C-92/89, para 30.

seeing a potentially illegal EU act set aside apparently matters less than the Union's interest in the implementation of this act.

The insistence on 'coherence' rather than on individual rights in the Court's approach to the preliminary ruling on validity was confirmed when the *Foto-Frost* story repeated itself two decades later: in *Schul* the Court had to deal with a reference for preliminary ruling on the validity of a provision of a Commission regulation that implemented the basic regulation on the organisation of the sugar market.[862] Prior to assessment of validity, the referring court asked if it was under an obligation to request that assessment, given that a very similar provision from another regulation had already been declared invalid by the CJEU in another procedure. The Court essentially copied its reasoning from *Foto-Frost* and reached the conclusion that even in such a situation the national court still had to ask for a preliminary ruling on validity.[863] It then assessed the validity of the challenged provision by referring to the basic regulation which '*unambiguously*' laid down the course to follow for determining cif prices, making '*no provision for an exception*'. Again, the (incidentally positive) implications for the individual of the objectively identified obligation are not addressed.

1.3.2.2.2. The restrictive conception of individual interest in the action for annulment

In cases such as *Les Verts*, *Foto-Frost* and *Schul*, the outcome of applying this objective approach to legality review of EU measures was positive for the individuals concerned even though their interests were not part of the equation. The problem is that in the context of this objective approach, where interest does become a parameter, it functions as a restrictive filter, rather than as an empowering tool for individuals. This is apparent in the case law on the infamously strict criterion of direct and individual con-

862 Respectively, Commission Regulation (EC) No 1423/95 of 23 June 1995 laying down detailed implementing rules for the import of products in the sugar sector other than molasses (OJ L 141 p. 16) and Council Regulation (EEC) No 1785/81 of 30 June 1981 on the common organisation of the markets in the sugar sector (OJ L 177 p. 4), as amended by Council Regulation (EC) No 3290/94 of 22 December 1994 on the adjustments and transitional arrangements required in the agriculture sector in order to implement the agreements concluded during the Uruguay Round of multilateral trade negotiations (OJ L 349 p. 105) ('the basic regulation').

863 Judgment of 6 December 2005, *Gaston Schul* C-461/03, EU:C:2005:742, paras 17-24, especially para 22 citing *Les Verts*, C-294/83.

cern, '*le filtre le plus étanche pour les recours en annulation émanant de particuliers*';[864] originally laid down in Article 173 EC.

Ironically, in the historical ruling on this issue – just a few months after *Van Gend en Loos – Plaumann*, the Court started with a first step affirming the importance of individual interest. An importer of clementines was challenging a Commission decision refusing to authorise Germany to suspend customs duties on imports of clementines from third countries. The Commission argued that because the decision was addressed to a Member State, the action for annulment lodged against it by a private individual was not admissible. The Court replied that '*the second paragraph of Article 173 does allow an individual to bring an action against decisions addressed to 'another person' which are of direct and individual concern to the former, but this Article neither defines nor limits the scope of these words. The words and the natural meaning of this provision justify the broadest interpretation. Moreover provisions of the Treaty regarding the right of interested parties to bring an action must not be interpreted restrictively. Therefore, the Treaty being silent on the point, a limitation in this respect may not be presumed*.'[865] The Court thus relied on a broad understanding of 'interest' to reject the Commission's first argument. By contrast,[866] then, it laid down a very restrictive understanding of the criterion of individual concern: '*[p]ersons other than those to whom a decision is addressed may only claim to be individually concerned if that decision affects them by reason of certain attributes which are peculiar to them or by reason of circumstances in which they are differentiated from all other persons and by virtue of these factors distinguishes them individually just as in the case of the person addressed*.'[867] This interpretation of individual concern coupled with the requirement of direct concern has become the main and most criticised filter in the action for annulment.

---

864 Van Waeyenberge and Pecho, 'L'arrêt Unibet et le traité de Lisbonne - un pari sur l'avenir de la protection juridictionnelle effective' 131.

865 Judgment of 15 July 1963, *Plaumann v Commission of the EEC*, C-25/62, EU:C:1963:17, p. 106-107. See also Judgment of 17 September 1980, *Philip Morris v Commission*, C-730/79, EU:C:1980:209, para 5.

866 The inconsistency has also been noted by Berrod, *La systématique des voies de droit communautaires* 25.

867 Adding then: '*In the present case the applicant is affected by the disputed Decision as an importer of clementines, that is to say, by reason of a commercial activity which may at any time be practised by any person and is not therefore such as to distinguish the applicant in relation to the contested Decision as in the case of the addressee*.' *Plaumann v Commission of the EEC*, C-25/62, p. 107.

This filter is a peculiar hybrid, again a mix of German and French influences.[868] It was reportedly inspired by the German conception of the action for annulment as a way to settle an issue between the administration and an individual, not a mechanism to ensure legality review.[869] The idea was that the Member States would protect the collective interests of their nationals, if necessary by challenging regulatory acts.[870] The regulatory function of the institutions would be protected by restricting the range of individuals allowed to challenge these acts.[871] The Court's understanding of individual concern and interest however differs from the German *Schutznorm* filter, which is focused on the nature of the rule invoked by the individual, not on that of the rule that is being challenged.[872] The similarity with the German system lies with how the subjective filter serves as a restriction to the individual's access to court, by requiring a direct affectation of the applicant's individual legal situation.[873] This was reportedly an intentional departure from the French approach, based on individual interest in a broad sense, which was at the root of the previous action for annulment in the ECSC Treaty.[874] In fact, this French filter has not been completely dismissed, since Court actually *also* tests the interest in bringing

868 B. Grzeszick, *Rechte und Ansprüche. Eine Rekonstruktion des Staatshaftungsrechts aus den subjektiven öffentlichen Rechten* (Mohr Siebeck 2002) 494-495.

869 Ruffert, 'Rights and Remedies in European Community Law: a Comparative View' 325, Fromont, 'L'influence du droit français et du droit allemand sur les conditions de recevabilité du recours en annulation devant la Cour de Justice des Communautés européennes' 51-52.

870 Petersen, 'L'influence possible du droit anglais sur le recours en annulation auprès de la Cour de justice des communautés européennes' 259 and M. Lagrange, 'L'Ordre Juridique de la C.E.C.A. vu à travers la jurisprudence de sa Cour de Justice', Revue du droit public, 1958, 850.

871 E. Petersen, 'L'influence possible du droit anglais sur le recours en annulation auprès de la Cour de justice des communautés européennes' [1966] Revue trimestrielle de droit européen 256 257.

872 On the German *Schutznorm* doctrine see p. 52 of this work.

873 Fromont, 'L'influence du droit français et du droit allemand sur les conditions de recevabilité du recours en annulation devant la Cour de Justice des Communautés européennes' 63: '*la Cour a, en fait, adopté les solutions allemandes : elle exige une atteinte directe à la situation juridique individuelle du requérant. L'expression de droit public subjectif n'est pas utilisée, mais sa substance a été reprise par la Cour de justice*'.

874 Berrod, *La systématique des voies de droit communautaires* 578-579. Fromont, 'L'influence du droit français et du droit allemand sur les conditions de recevabilité du recours en annulation devant la Cour de Justice des Communautés européennes' 60-61. AG Lagrange pointed out in his Opinion in *Conf. des prod. de fruits v Conseil CEE*, C-16/62, EU:C:1962:40, p. 482, that the EEC Treaty was

proceedings, i.e. the interest of the applicant '*in seeing the contested measure annulled*'.[875]

As a consequence, an individual who has an interest (in the broad sense) in challenging an EU act that he suspects of being illegal, but who is not the addressee of that act nor is directly and individually concerned by it, cannot do so unless the act entails further implementing measures which the Member States must take, and which may then be challenged in national courts, with the possibility of a reference for validity concerning the EU act at issue. The standing conditions remained unchanged in Article 230, paragraph 4 of the EC Treaty and in spite of some slight adjustments,[876] the Court has maintained its restrictive interpretation of these

---

more liberal than the ECSC Treaty concerning the definition of persons having access to the Court, and concerning the nature of the grounds for application, but that it was stricter than the ECSC Treaty with regard to the conditions to be fulfilled before certain measures may be challenged.

875 On the notion of interest in bringing proceedings and the distinction with direct and individual concern, see Opinion of AG Bobek in *Bionorica SE and Diapharm GmbH & Co. KG v European Commission,* Joined cases C-596/15 P and C-597/15 P, EU:C:2017:297, paras 47-57 and para 146. The interest in bringing proceedings must be vested and present: Judgment of 14 September 1995, *Antillean Rice Mills e.a. v Commission,* T-480/93 and T-483/93, EU:T:1995:162, para 59; Judgment of 14 April 2005, *Sniace SA v Commission*, T-141/03, EU:T:2005:129, para 25; Judgment of 7 September 2009, *Liga para Protecção da Natureza v Commission*, T-186/08, EU:T:2009:309, para 58. The measure must have brought 'a distinct change' in the applicant's legal position, see e.g.: Judgment of 22 March 2000, *Coca-Cola v Commission*, T-125/97 and 127/97, EU:T:2000:84, para 77; Judgment of 26 October 2000, *Carlo Ripa di Meana and Others v Parliament*, T-83/99, EU:T:2000:244, para 30; Judgment of 13 October 2011, *Deutsche Post and Germany v Commission,* C-463/10 P, EU:C:2011:656, para 37; Judgment of 23 April 2018, *One of Us and Others v Commission,* T-561/14, EU:T:2018:210, para 70. See also Ward, 'More than an 'Infant Disease'. Individual Rights, EC Directives, and the Case for Uniform Remedies' 58.

876 Especially Judgment of 18 May 1994, *Codorniu v Council,* C-309/89, EU:C:1994:197 according to which a regulation may concern some individuals directly and individually even though it is general relatively to others. Hagner, *Les particuliers et l'ordre juridique communautaire : l'égalité de traitement entre les hommes et les femmes* 26. The Court has also slightly relaxed its stance on the admissibility of actions for annulment initiated by groups and associations. The criterion of individual concern was first applied in such a restrictive way that it was practically impossible for associations representing collective interests of producers or traders to pass the admissibility test. See Judgment of 14 December 1962, *Conf. des prod. de fruits v Conseil CEE,* Joined cases C-16 and C-17/62, EU:C:1962:47; and Judgment of 10 July 1986, *DEFI v Commission,* C-282/85, EU:C:1986:316, para 16. However in Judgment of 13 December 2005, *Commis-*

conditions, even in the face of the Opinion of AG Jacobs in *UPA*, who argued that the system was inconsistent with the right to effective judicial protection[877] and suggested that the '*only satisfactory solution*' would be to re-interpret the notion of individual concern and '*to recognise that an applicant is individually concerned by a Community measure where the measure has, or is liable to have, a substantial adverse effect on his interests.*'[878] In addition to the advantages that the AG listed in support of this solution,[879] this would have had the merit of granting the same level of protection to individuals whose interests where affected by an EU measure, than to those whose interests protected by EU law were affected by a national measure.[880] This Opinion was issued at a time where the CFI had to rule on *Jégo Quéré*, a fishing company had lodged an action for annulment against several provisions of Regulation 1162/2001. The CFI rejected all arguments regarding individual concern: it was not sufficient that the claimant was the only fishing company in a specific zone. Nevertheless, since the regulation did not require any implementing measures to be taken by Member

---

sion v Aktionsgemeinschaft Recht und Eigentum, C-78/03 P, EU:C:2005:761, para 70 the Court ruled that with regard to the admissibility of an action seeking the annulment of a general aid scheme, an association set up to promote the collective interests of a category of persons, could be regarded as being individually concerned to the extent to which '*the position of its members in the market substantially affected*' by the aid scheme which was the subject of the contested decision. See also Judgment of 22 December 2008, *British Aggregates v Commission*, C-487/06 P, EU:C:2008:757, para 33.

877 Opinion of AG Jacobs in *Unión de Pequeños Agricultores v Council*, C-50/00 P, EU:C:2002:197, paras 38-39.

878 Opinion of AG Jacobs in *Unión de Pequeños Agricultores v Council*, C-50/00 P, para 102.

879 Which he summarised at para 102, arguing that the proposed solution ensures that '*applicants are granted a true right of direct access to a court which can grant a remedy, cases of possible denial of justice are avoided, and judicial protection is improved in various ways*'; it '*removes the anomaly under the current case-law that the greater the number of persons affected the less likely it is that effective judicial review is available*'; '*the increasingly complex and unpredictable rules on standing are replaced by a much simpler test which would shift the emphasis in cases before the Community Courts from purely formal questions of admissibility to questions of substance*'; and '*such a re-interpretation is in line with the general tendency of the case-law to extend the scope of judicial protection in response to the growth of powers of the Community institutions*'.

880 *Defrenne v SABENA*, C-43/75, para 31 : '*the fact that certain provisions of the Treaty are formally addressed to the Member States does not prevent rights from being conferred at the same time on any individual who has an interest in the performance of the duties thus laid down*'.

States, the CFI found that the claimant would be deprived of all remedies, an unacceptable situation in a Community based on the rule of law – and that the action was therefore admissible.[881] In this the CFI was following AG Jacobs' call for evolution. Yet in *UPA* the Court of Justice did not follow the AG and instead stuck to its 'tunnel vision' on this issue, maintained its traditional interpretation of the criterion of direct and individual concern, and held that the action was inadmissible.[882] This was again justified by the systemic and coherence-based vision of remedies laid down in the famous passage from *Les Verts*.[883]

With the Treaty of Lisbon, the structure of the former Article 230, paragraph 4 EC was modified, so that Article 263, paragraph 4 TFEU now allows a natural or legal person to challenge not only as was previously the case an act '*addressed to that person*' or which is of '*direct and individual concern to them*', but also against '*a regulatory act which is of direct concern to them and does not entail implementing measures*'. In *Inuit*, the Court had to interpret this new possibility and especially to determine what was meant by a regulatory act. The Court performed a predominantly literal and historical analysis of Article 263, by contrast with much of its case law; the only systematic element of interpretation was in the reference to Article 19(1), 2nd sentence TEU, suggesting that it was still left to the Member States to fill in the gaps that remained in terms of direct access to the EU courts.[884] The Court held that the notion of regulatory act excludes legislative acts, and that the limited possibility for individuals to challenge legislative act is not problematic in the light of Article 19(1) TEU nor in the light of Article 47, especially since the protection conferred by the latter provision '*does not require that an individual should have an unconditional entitlement to bring an action for annulment of European Union legislative acts directly before the Courts of the European Union*'.[885] This is not particularly

---

881 Van Waeyenberge and Pecho, 'L'arrêt Unibet et le traité de Lisbonne - un pari sur l'avenir de la protection juridictionnelle effective' 136.

882 Callies, 'Kohärenz und Konvergenz beim europäischen Individualrechtsschutz - Der Zugang zum Gericht im Lichte des Grundrechts auf effektiven Rechtsschutz' 3580.

883 *Unión de Pequeños Agricultores*, C-50/00 P, para 40. See also Judgment of 1 April 2004, *Commission v Jégo-Quéré*, C-263/02 P, EU:C:2004:210, para 30; Judgment of 30 March 2004, *Rothley and Others v Parliament*, C-167/02 P, EU:C:2004:193, para 46.

884 Waelbroeck and Bombois, 'Des requérants 'privilégiés' et des autres... A propos de l'arrêt Inuit et de l'exigence de protection juridictionnelle effective des particuliers en droit européen' 32-37.

885 *Inuit Tapiriit Kanatami and Others v Parliament and Council*, C-583/11 P, para 105.

surprising in the sense that although Article 47 of the Charter is generally considered as sufficiently clear and precise to give rise to rights, in some situations its implementation is naturally subject to some conditions, such as those of Article 263, paragraph 4. However, even if legislative acts are to be excluded from the notion of 'regulatory acts', the Court could have seized *Inuit* as an opportunity to broaden the criterion of 'individual concern', and thus made the action for annulment more accessible to individuals, as was precisely the point of the new version of Article 263.[886] The persistence of this restrictive definition of individual concern, making other kinds of individual interests irrelevant for accessing the EU courts, is all the more problematic that the action for annulment serves as a reference point for approaching other remedies, so that the restrictive vision irrigates the whole system of EU remedies.[887]

1.3.2.2.3. Union liability: the Schutznorm temptation

The founding cases on the conditions for liability of the Union reveal the same restrictive vision. Unlike the regime of Member State liability, which

---

886 Waelbroeck and Bombois, 'Des requérants 'privilégiés' et des autres... A propos de l'arrêt Inuit et de l'exigence de protection juridictionnelle effective des particuliers en droit européen' 35-41.

887 D. Simon (ed), F. Mariatte and D. Ritleng, *Contentieux de l'Union européenne : 1/ Annulation, exception d'illégalité* (Lamy 2010) 311-312; M. Jaeger, 'Les voies de recours sont-elles des vases communicants?' in G. C. Rodríguez Iglesias (ed), *Mélanges en hommage à Fernand Schockweiler* (Nomos 1999). For instance, the plea of illegality under Article 277 TFEU is only possible if it does not amount to circumventing the time limits of the action for annulment (see Judgment of 14 December 1962, *Wöhrmann v Commission of the EEC*, C-31/62, EU:C:1962:49). The same restriction applies to the incidental review on validity under Article 267 TFEU (Judgment of 9 March 1994, *TWD v Bundesrepublik Deutschland*, C-188/92, EU:C:1994:90, para 20). Hofmann, Rowe and Türk, *Administrative Law and Policy of the European Union* 861 and 867; Hagner, *Les particuliers et l'ordre juridique communautaire : l'égalité de traitement entre les hommes et les femmes* 28. Yet this kind of incidental review is not an exhaustive palliative to the other restrictions that apply in an action for annulment, given that it can only be, precisely, 'incidental' to a principal action. In the same way, the action for failure to act remains in the shadow of the action for annulment. I. Daukšienė and A. Budnikas, 'Has the action for failure to act in the European Union lost its purpose?' (2014) 7 Baltic Journal of Law & Politics 209. For detailed developments on the action for failure to act and how it differs from and relates to the action for annulment see D. Simon, *Contentieux de l'Union européenne : 2/ Carence, Responsabilité* (Lamy 2011).

is purely judge-made, the principle of Union liability for violations of EU law has been enshrined in the Treaties since the origins of the Union: successively in Article 40 of the ECSC Treaty,[888] Articles 178 and 215 EEC, Article 288 EC, and now in Article 340 TFEU and Article 41(3) CFR.[889] The detailed conditions for awarding damages to individuals for violation of EU law by the institutions were however laid down in the case law and were much more restrictive than the conditions for claiming Member State liability. At least, unlike what *Plaumann* had originally implied, the award of damages arising out of Union action is not strictly conditioned to admission of an action for annulment.[890] The Court made that clear in *Schöppenstedt*, holding (against the Commission's submission) that the action for damages '*was introduced as an autonomous form of action*', so that the inadmissibility of an action for annulment against a given act does not entail the inadmissibility of an action for damages suffered as a result of the same act.[891] However, a different kind of restriction was laid down in *Schöppenstedt*: the Court conditioned the liability of the Union arising out

888 Treaty establishing the European Coal and Steel Community (ECSC Treaty/ Treaty of Paris), 18 April 1951, 261 UNTS 140, Expired by its terms 23 July 2002.

889 Article 340, second sentence, TFEU: '*In the case of non-contractual liability, the Union shall, in accordance with the general principles common to the laws of the Member States, make good any damage caused by its institutions or by its servants in the performance of their duties*'. Article 41(3) of the Charter: '*Every person has the* right *to have the Union make good any damage caused by its institutions or by its servants in the performance of their duties, in accordance with the general principles common to the laws of the Member States*'. In addition, Article 268 TFEU provides that the CJEU has exclusive jurisdiction in disputes regarding the non-contractual liability of the Union.

890 *Plaumann v Commission of the EEC*, C-25/62, p.108: the Court had stated that '*An administrative measure which has not been annulled cannot of itself constitute a wrongful act on the part of the administration inflicting damage upon those whom it affects.The latter cannot therefore claim damages by reason of that measure. The Court cannot by way of an action for compensation take steps which would nullify the legal effects of a decision which, as stated, has not been annulled*'.

891 Judgment of 2 December 1971, *Zuckerfabrik Schöppenstedt v Council*, C-5/71, EU:C:1971:116, paras 2-3. See also Judgment of 24 October 2000, *Fresh Marine v Commission*, T-178/98, EU:T:2000:240, para 38, and Order of 30 September 2009, *Ivanov v Commission*, T-166/08, EU:T:2009:375, para 51. Nevertheless, the requirement of coherence is still implemented by reference to the action for annulment, since the Court dismisses an action for damages which '*is actually aimed at securing withdrawal of an individual decision which has become definitive or where it amounts to a misuse of procedure.*' Judgment of 27 June 2000, *Meyer v Commission*, T-72/99, EU:T:2000:170, para 36 and see also Judgment of 24 September 1996, *Dreyfus v Commission*, T-485/93, EU:T:1996:126, para 68.

of legislative acts to a '*sufficiently serious breach of a superior rule of law for the protection of the individual.*'[892] So, in addition to a potential *Schutznorm*-type of restriction since the rule of law breached had to provide for the protection of individuals, there was also an additional filter, i.e. the requirement that the norm breached be a 'superior' rule of law. These requirements are thus much more stringent than those that apply for Member State liability and make it more difficult for individuals to defend their interests before the EU courts.

An approach slightly more favourable to individuals was developed for liability arising from administrative acts of the EU institutions. Administrative acts may be defined as individual and concrete, as opposed to legislative acts which are of general application.[893] The seminal case in this area was *Adams*, concerning a breach of the Commission's duty of confidentiality which the Court found gave rise to damages without examining the requirement of a 'superior rule of law for the protection of the individual.'[894] This category is however limited: a 'decision' can be considered 'legislative', in which case the applicants claiming damages on its basis will have to demonstrate that the restrictive conditions of liability arising of legislative acts are fulfilled.[895] In addition, even in the case of an administrative act there can be wide discretion, making it difficult to prove liability.[896] Overall, the more flexible conditions for liability arising out of administrative acts did not radically open the possibility for individuals to claim damages from the EU institutions, but perhaps this was paving the way for the more

892 *Zuckerfabrik Schöppenstedt v Council*, C-5/71, para 11. A. Biondi and M. Farley, *The Right to Damages in European Law* (Kluwer Law International 2009) 107. This condition was maintained in subsequent rulings: e.g.: Judgment of 4 October 1979, *Ireks-Arkady GmbH contre Conseil et Commission des Communautés européennes*, C-238/78, EU:C:1979:226, para 9; Judgment of 17 December 1981, *Ludwigshafener Walzmühle v Council and Commission*, Joined cases C-197 to C-200, C-243, C-245 and C-247/80, EU:C:1981:311, para 19; Judgment of 14 January 1987, *Zuckerfabrik Bedburg v Council and Commission*, C-281/84, EU:C:1987:3, para 18; Judgment of 6 June 1990, *AERPO and Others v Commission*, C-119/88, EU:C:1990:231 para 8.

893 Grabitz, 'Liability for Legislative Acts' 1.

894 Judgment of 7 November 1985, *Adams v Commission*, C-154/83, EU:C:1985:448.

895 Judgment of 10 December 1998, *Schröder and Thamann v Commission*, C-221/97 P, EU:C:1998:597.

896 Judgment of 16 January 1996, *Candiotte v Council*, T-108/94, EU:T:1996:5. P. Aalto, *Public liability in EU law: Brasserie, Bergaderm and beyond* (Bloomsbury Publishing 2011) 83-84.

significant change that came with *Bergaderm.*[897] In this judgment, the Court established '*an objective of convergence*' between the systems governing the liability of the Union and of the Member States.[898] Since then, the conditions for Union liability are aligned on the *Brasserie* criteria[899] and the assessment of the '*sufficient seriousness*' criterion is performed by reference to discretion and whether the institution gravely and manifestly disregarded that discretion.[900]

The overall picture remains that the Union liability regime has been historically more restrictive – that is, less favourable to individuals, than the Member State liability regime for violation of (potentially the same) rights.[901] As Caranta observed in the aftermath of *Francovich*, '*the court is more demanding of Member States than in respect of [Union] organs; this attitude is difficult to condone, because what is at stake in both cases is the remedy*

897 Judgment of 4 July 2000, *Bergaderm and Goupil v Commission*, C-352/98 P, EU:C:2000:361; M. Wathelet and J. Wildermeersch, *Contentieux européen* (2 edn, Larcier 2014) 353.

898 Aalto, *Public liability in EU law: Brasserie, Bergaderm and beyond* 4.

899 *Bergaderm and Goupil v Commission*, C-352/98 P, para 42: '*Community law confers a right to reparation where three conditions are met: the rule of law infringed must be intended to confer rights on individuals; the breach must be sufficiently serious; and there must be a direct causal link between the breach of the obligation resting on the State and the damage sustained by the injured parties (*Brasserie du Pêcheur and Factortame, *paragraph 51)*'. U. Saüberlich, *Die außervertragliche Haftung im Gemeinschaftsrecht. Eine Untersuchung der Mehrpersonenverhältnisse* (Springer 2005) 22.

900 E.g. Judgment of 10 December 2002, *Commission v Camar and Tico*, C-312/00 P, EU:C:2002:736, paras 54-55; Judgment of 12 July 2005, *Commission v CEVA and Pfizer*, C-198/03 P, EU:C:2005:445, para 64. E. Bagińska, *Damages for Violations of Human Rights* (Springer 2015) 433.

901 See prominent cases where actions for annulment were dismissed, cited by Eilmansberger, 'The Relationship between Rights and Remedies in EC Law: in Search of the Missing Link' 1207: Judgment of 13 May 1971, *International Fruit Company and Others v Commission*, C-41 to C-44/70, EU:C:1971:53; Judgment of 11 July 1985, *Salerno and Others v Commission and Council*, C-87/77, C-130/77, C-22/83, C-9 and C-10/84, EU:C:1985:318; Judgment of 8 October 1986, *Leussink-Brummelhuis v Commission*, C-169/83 and C-136/84, EU:C:1986:371; Judgment of 7 July 1987, *Etoile commerciale and CNTA v Commission*, C-89/86 and C-91/86, EU:C:1987:337; Judgment of 21 November 1989, *UCDV v Commision*, C-244/88, EU:C:1989:588; Judgment of 27 March 1990, *Cargill v Commission*, C-229/88, EU:C:1990:138; *Mulder and Others v Council and Commission*, Joined cases C-104/89 and C-37/90.

for the infringement of [Union] law;[902] and thus the protection of the rights conferred by Union law.

1.3.3. Conclusions on the right-remedy relation: looking at both sides of the story

The story of the relation between rights and remedies in Union law is that of a virtuous circle. Individual rights, as we have seen, are crucial for the effectiveness of EU law. In turn, the requirement of effectiveness applied to individual rights shaped the principle of effective judicial protection, requiring Member States to refrain from applying procedural requirements that would hinder the exercice by individuals of the rights conferred by EU law. The Treaty of Lisbon validated this principle by enshrining it in Article 47 of the Charter as the right to an effective remedy, reinforced by the positive obligation of Member States under Article 19(1) TEU to provide adequate remedies, demonstrating again that rights and obligations function together in a dynamic correlation. The more rights were derived from EU law, the more remedies were 'invented', with Member States required to accordingly adapt their procedures. This has not been easy, especially in some legal systems functioning with a '*Schutznorm*' approach to rights and remedies, exercising judicial and doctrinal pressure to condition the identification of a right to the existence of a clear intention to protect individuals and grant them a remedy.[903] Still, the Court has consistently reasserted that, since remedies are consequences of rights, any situation where there is an individual interest in activating an obligation of a public authority will require a remedy to be provided for the correlative right. This is exemplified in cases such as *Olainfarm* and *Zuchtverband*, in which the Court reframes questions of national courts in terms that make the protective intention underlying a norm irrelevant.[904] *Berlioz* is probably the most clear-cut contemporary restatement of the Court's classic approach to rights and remedies,[905] illustrating the potential of this approach for addressing the contemporary challenges of our time, such as the growing transnational integration of Member State administrations implementing Union law.

902 Caranta, 'Governmental Liability after Francovich' 285. See also A. Arnull, 'The action for annulment: A case of double standards?' 177.

903 See p. 165 of this work.

904 *Olainfarm*, C-104/13; *Zuchtverband für Ponys*, C-216/02, discussed in this work p. 199.

905 *Berlioz Investment Fund*, C-682/15, discussed in this work p. 202.

There is a darker side to the narrative. Most cases on the development of the right to effective judicial protection are cases on remedies in Member States, brought before the Court by way of preliminary ruling. Exceptions are of course *Kadi I* and *II*, reflecting a strong stance of the Court on the protection of fundamental rights.[906] But the instrumental rationale of rights was also very strong in these rulings, in the sense that the CJEU was affirming the protection of individual rights, perhaps not so much against the acts of EU institutions as against the reach of international law into the EU legal order. Viewed in this light, the *Kadi* rulings constitute a statement on the autonomy of EU law,[907] which as it so happens, also benefits individuals.[908] Of course, as long as the result is there, it does not matter what the motives are. The problem for individuals arises when the Court no longer sees the instrumental rationale for rights. In cases where individuals challenge acts of EU institutions, there is a much lesser concern for rights, as well as a much looser connection between rights and remedies.[909] The conditions for direct access to the EU courts, especially in the condition of direct and individual concern in the action for annulment, and the requirement of a superior rule of law for the protection of the individual in the action for liability, limit the relevance of individual interests as triggers for legality review. Indeed, they create a bias for the identification of rights, the existence of which is analysed only once a stringent interest filter has been applied. This bias, by contrast, is absent in references for preliminary rulings on interpretation, where the CJEU's case law tends to weaken or

906 *Kadi I*, Joined cases C-402/05 P and C-415/05 P; *Kadi II*, Joined cases C-584/10 P, C-593/10 P and C-595/10 P.

907 Muir depicts the CJEU as the '*guardian of the autonomy of the EU legal order*': Muir, 'The Court of Justice: a fundamental rights institution among others' 80.

908 The same observation has been made on *Schrems* case, the first case in which the Court invalidated an act of an EU institution on the basis of the violation of the essence of a fundamental right and also because it violated Article 47 of the Charter. The Court spelled out that '*the very existence of effective judicial review designed to ensure compliance with provisions of EU law is inherent in the existence of the rule of law*' (*Schrems*, C-362/14, para 95). The Commission decision that was struck down however concerned the level of protection of European Facebook users under the American system, so that the judgment was also, much like the *Kadi* cases, a response to 'external' threats to the fundamental rights of EU citizens. See Editorial comments, 'EU law as a way of life' (2017) 54 Common Market Law Review 357 364: '*it may prove much easier to find the proper institutional design for protecting European citizens from external threats, as was the case in Kadi and Schrems, than to protect an individual citizen from internal threats whilst circulating in Europe.*'

909 Notably in *Les Verts*, C-294/83, as observed p. 207 of this work.

even dismiss existing domestic procedural filters, so that a broad notion of interest typically triggers the application of rights conferred by EU law in national courts.

Thus, the *ubi ius ibi remedium* principle is not at its best in situations where individuals challenge acts of the EU authorities, rather than those of their Member States. A more restrictive approach to rights and interests take shape, that is reminiscent of the *Schutznorm* doctrine, with the result that where there is no remedy there is no right. That is exactly the problem that the mechanism of direct effect (supported by the effectiveness rationale) is meant to suppress when individuals rely on obligations of Member States to request the enforcement of correlative rights. In view of the '*changing conditions of implementation of EU law marked by an ever closer co-operation of the executive branches of power on the EU level and the levels of the Member States*',[910] this double standard in the identification and application of rights is more questionable than ever, since it does not only limit the protection of individual interests, but also weakens the role of individuals as agents of legality review. In this sense, this situation undermines the rationale of individual rights in the Union's legal system.

1.4. Conclusion of Part 1

The first part of this work has approached the concept of individual rights under EU law from three main angles. It has explored in Section 1.1 the historical foundations of this concept and the justification for its key role in the EU legal order. Challenges arising from the introduction of the Charter of Fundamental Rights in the Union's constitutional architecture have been discussed in Section 1.2. Finally, Section 1.3 focused on the often-problematic relation between rights and remedies, which reveals some diverging conceptions of individual rights. This in turn complicates their identification and enforcement. The findings inform the two defining features of the concept of individual rights: namely, the correlation between rights and obligations, and the functional relation between rights and interests.

Concerning the correlation between rights and obligations, it is the beating heart of the original method for identifying individual rights conferred by EU law. The Court first applied this method to provisions of pri-

910 Hofmann, 'The Right to an 'Effective Judicial Remedy' and the Changing Conditions of Implementing EU Law' 2.

mary law: all it took for granting an individual right was the identification of a clear and unconditional obligation. The correlation has become the guiding thread for deriving rights also from obligations enshrined in all types of secondary law instruments. Conversely, the 'obligational' aspect of a norm can be deduced from the right that it grants, especially in the case law on fundamental rights. The implications of the correlation between rights and obligations thus reach much further than its original area of application, i.e. that of the mechanism of direct effect.[911] It allows to approach all sources of potential rights in a simple way, as many legal theorists have suggested in the wake of Hohfeld's influential work:[912] when considering one obligation and the corresponding right, '*[t]he existence of each is a necessary and sufficient condition for the existence of the other*'.[913] The right and the obligation are thus two sides of the same medal, '*two different perspectives of exactly the same norm*'.[914] Whatever the starting point (obligation or right), it can be recharacterised as the corresponding jural correlative. In other words, as proposed by Bengoetxea and Jääskinen, the jural relations of EU law can also be decomposed into Hohfeldian 'molecules' (i.e. rights and duties), so that the '*obligations of Member States, which are Hohfeldian burdens, are transformed into Hohfeldian entitlements of individuals.*'[915] The same approach can apply for describing rights arising in relations

911 According to Prechal, the concept of direct effect '*has become so wide and diluted that it has lost its explanatory value. It says about Community law provisions nothing else than what holds true for any rule of national law and it should be treated accordingly.*' S. Prechal, 'Does Direct Effect Still Matter?' (2000) 37 Common Market Law Review 1047 1068. A similar argument is advanced in Prechal, 'Direct Effect Reconsidered, Redefined and Rejected'; and in Gordon and Moffatt, *EU Law in Judicial Review* 66. See Claes, *National Courts' Mandate in the European Constitution* for a comprehensive reply to this argument. However, direct effect precisely retains at the very least an '*explanatory value*' for the concept of individual rights in EU law, both with regard to the definition of a right by reference to an obligation and with regard to the method for how to assess the existence of a right.

912 Hohfeld, 'Fundamental Legal Conceptions as Applied in Judicial Reasoning' and see p. 40 of this work.

913 Kramer, 'Rights Without Trimmings' 26.

914 B. Porat, 'Rights-Based Law v. Duty-Based Law: Old Dilemma, New Perspective'. Porat also suggests another metaphor to described the right-duty correlativity: '*a one-way door on one side of which is written 'push' (duty) and on the other, 'pull' (right): no matter from which direction you approach, the door remains the same door*'.

915 Bengoetxea and Jääskinen, 'Rights and Diverse Effects in EU Law: A Hohfeldian Approach to the Doctrine of Direct Effect of Directives' 288. On the idea that rights and duties can be approached as 'molecules' of complex jural relations see also Wenar, 'Rights'.

among individuals, or between individuals and the EU institutions. In order to be workable and useful, this basic idea of a correlation between rights and obligations requires two important clarifications.

Firstly, this correlation does not mean that rights and obligations are interchangeable for all purposes. If it were so, it would be at odds with the increasingly rights-focused legal and political discourse of our times (especially since the introduction of the Charter in the EU legal order), which appears to grant much more value to rights than to corresponding obligations (for better or for worse).[916] That is why it is important to point out that logical *correlation* should not be confused with *causation* or moral *justification*.[917] In other words, if one so wishes (or if one legal system so posits), rights can be morally superior to duties without affecting the correlativity of the two notions. Likewise, the rights-obligations correlativity can work both with a justification that attaches primary importance to rights and secondary importance to duties, and *vice versa*. As Kramer points out, '*a justificational focus does not commit anyone to the notion of an existential or analytical hierarchy*'.[918] Viewed in this light, the idea of a correlation between rights and obligations has many advantages. A first advantage is its explanatory power. It highlights the logical consistency between cases where rights are derived from duties (like in the early cases) and those where the opposite operation is performed (such as *Kadi II*[919]). A second advantage is that it allows to approach the protection of rights in a consistent and constructive manner even in an evolving constitutional framework. For instance, the various guarantees encompassed under the umbrella-principle of good administration were traditionally phrased as obligations, yet their inclusion in the form of a list of rights under Article 41 of the Charter has not rendered the pre-Charter case law on good administra-

916 This is the concern of Loughlin, who argues that '*[s]ince rights and duties are twin aspects of a reciprocal relationship, this looks like a distinction without a difference. But in practice, this inversion has had an important effect on the way governmental authority is constituted. It is when rights are given positive institutional effect that this effect is disclosed. This positivisation of the basic rights of citizens has the potential to reconfigure the architecture of public law*'. M. Loughlin, *The Idea of Public Law* (Oxford University Press 2003) 114. See also Azoulai, 'L'individu européen et la question du statut' 1.

917 Kramer, 'Rights Without Trimmings' 27; Gewirth, 'Why Rights are Indispensable'; A. Gewirth, 'Rights and Duties' (1988) 97 Mind 441.

918 Kramer, 'Rights Without Trimmings' 38.

919 *Kadi II*, Joined cases C-584/10 P, C-593/10 P and C-595/10 P. See p. 151 of this work.

tion irrelevant.[920] That is to say, the correlation provides a conceptual reference point that is stable over time and over constitutional evolutions, and that is workable no matter which aspect (right or obligation) the legislator or the constituent emphasises.

Secondly, the correlation between rights and obligations is to be understood as a dynamic relation. Indeed, the correlation allows to identify rights *in concrete circumstances*. This means that for a given duty there is a potentially infinite number of right-holders.[921] Typically, all individuals active in cross-border trade may rely on a Member State's duty not to impose customs duties: this is the *Van Gend en Loos* scenario. It also means, as we know from *Defrenne II*, that depending on the concrete circumstances of a given case, a provision may or may not give rise to a right. The criteria of clarity, precision and unconditionality, used for circumscribing an obligation and its correlative right, allow an assessment of the *practical* applicability of a provision, not an abstract decision on whether a given obligation has a correlative right.[922] This is why even some ambiguous provisions, lacking clarity and/or precision, have been found to create rights for individuals.[923] Additionally, a norm may give rise to different rights and obligations depending on the concrete situation. For instance, as established in *Francovich*, a directive providing for an employee's right to a guarantee of payment of unpaid wage may give rise, when the correlative duty is breached, to a right to compensation for the damage suffered.[924] The correlation is dynamic also in the sense that it applies not to isolated norms, but to norms integrated in a rich legal architecture composed of many sources of obligations and rights. In the just mentioned *Francovich* example, the right to damages was deduced from the duty of Member States to implement directives, combined with a general principle of Member State liability. Likewise, the general principles of good administration and effective

---

920 See p. 98 of this work.

921 Hilson and Downes, 'Making sense of rights: Community rights in E.C. law' 3.

922 *Defrenne v SABENA*, C-43/75. See p. 40 of this work.

923 Gordon and Moffatt, *EU Law in Judicial Review* 18 and see e.g. *Regina v Secretary of State for Home Affairs, ex parte Santillo*, C-131/79. See also Hartley, *The Foundations of European Union Law* 210 and Dashwood, 'The Principle of Direct Effect in European Community Law' (1982) 16 Journal of Common Market Studies 229.

924 *Francovich and Bonifaci v. Italy*, Joined cases C-6/90 and C-9/90. See p. 162 of this work.

judicial protection remain relevant even now that Articles 41 and 47 of the Charter are available.[925]

The first part of this study also emphasises the function of interests as powerful triggers for ensuring the enforcement of obligations and rights laid down by provisions of EU law. The seminal cases *Van Gend en Loos* and *Defrenne II* made it clear that any individual who has an interest in doing so may request the execution of obligations imposed by the Treaties upon Member States or individuals. Correlative rights are deduced from these obligations.[926] And since the immediate consequence of identifying a right is that there must be a remedy to enforce it, the identified rights are immediately operational.[927] As illustrated in *Berlioz*, individuals, by protecting their own interests, also fulfil a crucial function of activating a process of legality review. This is the virtuous circle that has been described as functional subjectivation.[928] In addition, interests constitute an essential parameter in the adjudication process since rights must be balanced with other rules reflecting other interests, as exemplified by the case law on the proportionality principle and the prohibition of abuse of rights. However, the notion of interest is also the stumbling block in the debates over how to identify and apply the rights conferred by EU law. The unease manifests itself in two main problems.

The first problem is the recurring *Schutznorm* pressure. Under the *Schutznorm* doctrine, a typical feature of the German legal system but also present in the systems of other EU Member States, an individual right may be identified in a provision only if there is a clearly expressed intention to protect a precisely defined individual interest.[929] The attempts to transpose this approach to individual rights under EU law is problematic in two respects. Firstly, it generates confusion in the process of identifying the rights conferred by EU law: the application of the *Schutznorm* doctrine prevents obligations which are not expressly intended to protect individuals, from

925 In the same vein see Hofmann and Mihaescu, 'The Relation between the Charter's Fundamental Rights and the Unwritten General Principles of EU Law: Good Administration as the Test Case' 93.

926 '*[...] the fact that certain provisions of the Treaty are formally addressed to Member States does not prevent rights from being conferred at the same time on any individual who has an interest in the performance of the duties thus laid down.*' *Defrenne v. SABENA*, C-43/75, para. 31.

927 Azoulai, 'L'autonomie de l'individu européen et la question du statut' 3: '*[les droits] sortent tout armés des Traités*'.

928 Ruffert, 'Rights and Remedies in European Community Law: a Comparative View' 327. See also above p. 96.

929 See p. 37 of this work.

translating into correlative rights. Secondly, and consequently, it hinders the access to a remedy (which should be the immediate consequence of the identification of a right conferred by EU law). This in turn challenges the role of individuals in ensuring the effective enforcement of EU law. Since the introduction of the Charter, the debate over the distinction between 'rights' and 'principles' has added a new dimension to this pre-existing issue. The exclusive focus on whether a provision was intended as a justiciable 'right' as opposed to a non-justiciable 'principle' that is advocated in part of the literature amounts in fact to applying a *Schutznorm* filter to the provisions of the Charter and it thus unnecessarily restricts its protective potential.

The second and connected problem is the discrepancy between the level of protection of rights that is granted at the EU level and that granted to individuals against their Member States. The traditional conditions that must be fulfilled for an individual to be able to challenge an EU act, based on the violation of his rights, are very restrictive compared to the broad interest criterion that the Court itself has established as sufficient to claim rights conferred by EU law before a domestic court.[930] This is particularly clear in the standing conditions of the action for annulment. The traditional case law on Union liability also reflects a restrictive conception of individual interests as triggers for rights. These restrictions have the same effect as the application of a *Schutznorm* filter. By the latter, some obligations cannot translate into correlative rights even for individuals who would have some interests in it, meaning that the role of individuals for activating the process of judicial review, which is so crucial in the decentralised enforcement of EU law, is not recognised in the relations between individuals and the EU institutions.

The basic characteristics of individual rights under EU law and the recurring problems in their identification and application lead to the conclusion that the underlying rationale of this concept, the requirement of effectiveness, is both very powerful and highly contentious. On the one hand, the Court has relied on this principle to develop a very dynamic and flexible approach to individual rights. On the other hand, the effectiveness rationale has led to the suspicion that individual rights are merely the symptom of instrumentalisation of individuals for the realisation of the Union's *telos*. Of course, this is not necessarily a problem as long as the result is a

930 Callies, 'Kohärenz und Konvergenz beim europäischen Individualrechtsschutz - Der Zugang zum Gericht im Lichte des Grundrechts auf effektiven Rechtsschutz' 3579.

win-win situation, i.e. as long as there is indeed a convergence between the interests of individuals and those of the EU. The problem arises outside this win-win situation. The question thus arises as to how inclusive EU law can be of an increasing variety of interests, and how adaptable the original concept of individual rights can prove in the light of these evolving realities.

2. Individual Rights And Three Generations Of Interests

'The interpretation of the system to be favoured is that which provides the fullest protection or, perhaps more accurately, the least incomplete protection, for all the interests involved'.[931]

The first part of this study has highlighted the essential relation between rights, obligations and interests and accordingly suggested to approach individual rights as correlatives of obligations, triggered by the existence of interests arising in concrete circumstances. It has also identified the difficulty for national courts, sometimes even for the Court of Justice itself, to consistently rely on a broad conception of interest as a trigger for individual rights, and the tendency to restrict this conception, thus narrowing also the concept of rights.

The second part of this study assesses the resilience and relevance over time of the original relation between rights, obligations and interests, by testing it on a series of cases spanning from the early judgments of the Court of Justice, to its contemporary case law. For this purpose, the cases are sorted out according to successive phases in the evolution of the Union's legal order. Rights are often categorised in different 'generations' in the literature. A recurring criterion is the type of interest that the rights protect, such as economic, social, or political interests.[932] It is a pertinent criterion for assessing the stability (or instability) of the concept of individ-

931 Opinion of AG Mancini in *Luxembourg v Parliament,* C-230/81, EU:C:1982:417.

932 Eilmansberger, 'The Relationship between Rights and Remedies in EC Law: in Search of the Missing Link', F. Bignami, 'Three Generations of Participation Rights in European Administrative Proceedings' Jean Monnet Working Paper 11/03; Walker, 'Legal Theory and the European Union' 3, Micklitz, 'The ECJ between the Individual Citizen and the Member States - A plea for a judge-made European law on remedies' 9, Guðmundsdóttir, 'A Renewed Emphasis on the Charter's Distinction Between Rights and Principles: Is a Doctrine of Judicial Restraint More Appropriate?' 687; N. Marty, 'La Notion de Bonne Administration: À la Confluence des Droits Européens et du Droit Administratif Français' (PhD thesis, University of Montpellier 2007) 469. See also D. Curtin and K. Mortelmans, 'Application and Enforcement of Community Law by the Member States: Actors in Search of a Third Generation Script', in D. Curtin and T. Heukels (eds), *Institutional Dynamics of European Integration, Essays in Honour of H.G. Schermers*, vol. II, (Martinus Nijhoff Publishers 1994). Concerning 'generations' of remedies: E.T. Swaine, 'Subsidiarity and Self-Interest: Federalism at the

ual rights over time, given that the interest trigger is the most problematic aspect for the conceptualisation of individual rights. The variety of typologies proposed in the literature however attests to the implausibility of strict categorisation (for example, a woman's interest in not being discriminated against on the basis of her gender in the workplace can be considered both from an economic or from a social perspective). Nevertheless, the increasing variety of rights protecting an ever-broader array of interests parallels the deepening integration of the legal system of the Union, and the multiplication of roles that individuals are granted in this setting.[933]

Accordingly, this study successively scrutinises three main generations of rights corresponding to three main types of interests, which although sometimes overlapping, schematically correspond to phases in the evolution of the Union's legal order, with specific focus points and problems. The three types of rights are thus distinguished according to the types of interests by which they predominantly (but not exclusively) appear to be triggered. The first generation of rights encompasses those that are triggered by economic interests, reflected mainly in the case law on the fundamental freedoms and competition law (Section 2.1). The second generation covers socio-economic and political interests, paralleling the evolving conception of individuals as more than mere economic actors (Section 2.2.). The third generation corresponds to interests that cannot be strictly individualised and may therefore be called 'collective' interests (Section 2.3).

2.1. *Individual rights and economic interests*

The genesis of individual rights in EU law is tightly linked with the protection of economic interests. After all, the main aim of the original EEC Treaty was the development of an *Economic* Community, and *Van Gend en Loos* itself was about the direct effect of Treaty provisions relating to the free movement of goods. The present section scans the broad array of situations covered by the treaties and involving a variety of economic actors and

---

European Court of Justice' (2000) 41 Harvard International Law Journal 1 17. In other, non-EU contexts: M. Klatt, 'Positive rights: Who decides? Judicial review in balance' (2015) 13 International Journal of Constitutional Law 354 255; Engle, 'Taking the Right Seriously: Hohfeldian Semiotics and Rights Discourse' 99.

933 L. Azoulai, S. Barbou des Places and E. Pataut 'Being a Person in the European Union' in L. Azoulai and others (eds), *Constructing the Person in EU Law: Rights, Roles, Identities* (Bloomsbury Publishing 2016).

interests. Taking as a reference point the basic concept of individual rights as correlatives of obligations, triggered into existence by individual interests, it traces how the Court of Justice refined, adjusted and enriched its original method for identifying rights in order to address various challenges in the areas of fundamental freedoms (2.1.1) and competition law (2.1.2), and through mechanisms that generally protect individual interests in EU economic law (2.1.3). This section confirms the dynamism and flexibility of the original concept of individual rights.

2.1.1. Individual rights and the Fundamental Freedoms

The provisions relating to the four fundamental freedoms were the first in which the Court of Justice identified individual rights. This section examines how the EU concept of rights originally developed in the case law on free movement (predominantly the free movement of goods, which had the most weight in the original Treaty), and on the customs union (designed precisely to enable the exercise of the four freedoms). Two main categories of cases for this development may be distinguished: direct effect cases (2.1.1.1), and cases on the liability of Member States and the Union for violations of EU law (2.1.1.2). The analysis confirms the conceptual continuity between rights in direct effect cases and rights in liability cases. This continuity is however more reluctantly acknowledged by the Court in cases where Union liability (as opposed to Member State liability) is at stake (2.1.1.3).

2.1.1.1. The direct effect of fundamental freedoms in the wake of Van Gend en Loos

Historically, the development of the concept of rights under EU law is closely intertwined with the case law on the direct effect of provisions relating to fundamental freedoms. In this line of case law, the capacity of Treaty provisions to create rights for individuals was systematised first, followed by the recognition of directly applicable rights contained in secondary law provisions.

2.1.1.1.1. Fundamental freedoms in primary law

Van Gend en Loos made clear that a Treaty provision phrased as a prohibition on the Member States (the *telos* of which is the realisation of an internal market where goods would circulate freely) gave rise to a correlative individual right.[934] This principle was then applied to other provisions of the EEC Treaty, such as Article 30 EEC, which prohibited quantitative restrictions and measures having equivalent effect. In *Ianelli v Meroni* the Court held that this prohibition was '*mandatory and explicit*' and that its implementation did not require '*any subsequent intervention of the Member States or Community institutions*', therefore it had '*direct effect and create[d] individual rights which national courts must protect (...)*.'[935] The same approach was applied in *Capolongo*, concerning Article 13(2) EEC. This provision required the progressive abolition of charges having an effect equivalent to customs duties. The Court read this obligation to abolish as comprising '*a clear and precise prohibition*', which had '*no reservation allowing States to subject its implementation to a positive measure of domestic law or to an intervention by the institutions of the Community*'. This prohibition lent itself, '*by its very nature, to producing direct effects in the legal relations between Member States and their subjects*'.[936]

In retrospect, this was a step towards the more general idea that any obligation (whether negative or positive) may translate into a right. This became clear when in *Lütticke* the Court focused on the effects of a positive obligation imposed by EU law on the Member States.[937] Alfons Lütticke GmbH imported milk powder from Luxembourg into Germany and was imposed a duty labelled 'turnover equalisation tax'. The undertaking went to court challenging this duty and the German court thus raised the question of the direct effect of Article 95 EEC.[938] The first paragraph of Article 95 prohibited Member States from levying internal taxation at a rate higher for imported products than for domestic ones, and the third paragraph further required the Member States to repeal or amend any provisions that might conflict with the probibition. The Court held that the latter provision contained a prohibition in the form of a '*clear and unconditional obligation*', constituting a '*complete, legally perfect*' rule '*capable of pro-*

934 *Van Gend en Loos*, C-26/62.

935 Judgment of 22 March 1977, *Ianelli v Meroni*, C-74/76, EU:C:1977:51, para 13.

936 Judgment of 19 June 1973, *Capolongo v Azienda Agricola Maya*, C-77/72, EU:C:1973:65, para 11.

937 *Lütticke v Hauptzollamt Saarlouis*, C-57/65.

938 Now slightly modified into Article 110 TFEU.

ducing direct effects on the legal relationships between the Member States and persons within their jurisdiction'. Also in line with the seminal rulings on direct effect, the Court added that '*the fact that this article describes the Member States as being subject to the obligation of non-discrimination does not imply that individuals cannot benefit from it.*'[939] Regarding the third paragraph, it did include a 'period of grace' for Member States to take the necessary measures; however, after the expiration of this period, '*the general rule*' laid down at Article 95 '*emerge[d] fully with full force*' and the third paragraph left '*no discretion to the Member States with regard to the date*' by which the operations had to have been carried out.[940] The Court therefore concluded that Article 95, including the positive obligation enshrined in the third paragraph, did have direct effect and create individual rights.[941] As Dashwood observes, the discretion allowed by the provision was thus '*the crucial factor*' in assessing its ability to confer rights.[942] Whether the obligation is phrased in negative or positive terms does not matter for the assessment. This is confirmed by the Court referring in subsequent case law to the obligations of Articles 12, 13 and 95 EEC and recalling that these '*have direct effect and create individual rights which the national courts must protect*',[943] without distinguishing between negative and positive obligations.

The consequences of *Lütticke* were examined in *Molkerei*,[944] where a German court having asked whether the third paragraph of Article 95 had created a 'breach in legislative sovereignty' in the field of internal taxation. The Court's first step was to re-use the method and terms of *Van Gend en Loos*, looking at the 'wording' of Article 95, the 'character and spirit' of the Treaty. The 'objective' of the Treaty '*to establish a Common Market the functioning of which is of direct concern to interested parties in the Community*', implies that '*Community law [...] not only imposes obligations on individuals but is also intended to confer upon them rights which become part of their legal her-*

939 *Lütticke v Hauptzollamt Saarlouis*, C-57/65, p. 210.

940 *Lütticke v Hauptzollamt Saarlouis*, C-57/65, p. 210.

941 *Lütticke v Hauptzollamt Saarlouis*, C-57/65, p. 211. See also Judgment of 17 February 1976, *Rewe-Zentrale v Hauptzollamt Landau-Pfalz*, C-45/75, EU:C:1976:22, para 9, and Judgment of 22 February 2001, *Gomes Valente*, C-393/98, EU:C:2001:109, para 33.

942 *Lütticke v Hauptzollamt Saarlouis*, C-57/65; Dashwood, 'The Principle of Direct Effect in European Community Law' 231; Hartley, *The Foundations of European Union Law* 211.

943 Judgment of 16 December 1992, *Demoor and Others v Belgian State*, Joined cases C-144/91 and C-145/91, EU:C:1992:518, para 22. See also Judgment of 23 April 2002, *Nygård*, C-234/99, EU:C:2002:244, para 51.

944 *Molkerei Zentrale Westfalen-Lippe v Hauptzollamt Paderborn*, C-28/67.

itage. These rights arise not only where they are expressly granted by the Treaty but also by reason of obligations which the Treaty imposes in a clearly defined way upon individuals as well as upon the Member States and upon the institutions of the Community.' Against this backdrop the Court then reiterated that Article 95 fulfilled the criteria for conferring rights.[945] In arguing this case, Germany showed resistance to this approach, which would '*result in the recognition of wider rights for individuals than those available to the Community itself*.' However, the Court replied: '*It is not possible to base an argument […] on a comparison of the rights conferred by this provision on individuals, on the one hand, and the powers conferred on the Community institutions, on the other. Every time a rule of Community law confers rights on individuals, those rights […] may be safeguarded by proceedings brought before the competent national courts.*[946]

The same approach applies not only to provisions relating to the free movement of goods, but also to other fundamental freedoms enshrined in the Treaty, as a taxation case on the free movement of workers demonstrates: in *Schumacker* the Court held that Article 48 EC, the provision laying down this right,[947] was conversely '*capable of limiting the right of a Member State to lay down conditions concerning the liability to taxation of a national of another Member State and the manner in which tax is to be levied on the income received by him within its territory*' because it did not allow a Member State to treat a national of another Member State less favourably than its own nationals in the same situation.[948] There is a correlation between the right of the individual and the limitation of the Member State's 'right' to organise its tax system (i.e. an obligation not to take certain measures). The use of the term 'right' for a Member State as well as for an individual reinforces the idea that the identification of 'rights' should be understood above all as a *relational* issue and that someone's right can always be rephrased in terms of someone else's obligation.

A connected question, then, is how far the 'obligational' counterpart to the right stretches. This question arose in *San Giorgio*[949] with regard to the restitution of monies obtained through unlawful import duties. For a long

945 *Molkerei Zentrale Westfalen-Lippe v Hauptzollamt Paderborn*, C-28/67, p. 152.

946 *Molkerei Zentrale Westfalen-Lippe v Hauptzollamt Paderborn*, C-28/67, p. 153.

947 Now Article 45 TFEU.

948 Judgment of 14 February 1995, *Finanzamt Köln-Altstadt v Schumacker*, C-279/93, EU:C:1995:31, para 24. . See also an earlier case on taxation of workers in Luxembourg: Judgment of 8 May 1990, *Biehl v Administration des contributions*, C-175/88, EU:C:1990:186.

949 *Ammistrazione delle finanze dello Stato v San Giorgio*, C-199/82.

time, it had not been clear whether such restitution was required under Community law or whether it just happened to exist in all Member States.[950] The company San Giorgio had to pay health inspection charges which were levied contrary to the Community legislation on the importation of dairy products from other Member States. It then went to court to reclaim these amounts. The national court ordered the finance administration to repay San Giorgio, but the administration appealed the ruling, relying on a series of provisions from national law in order to argue that the charges had not constituted a burden on the company since the latter had simply passed them on to the buyers of its products. Previously, in similar situations, Advocates General had already issued opinions in favour of understanding directly effective provisions as entailing the right to recover charges that were unlawully levied.[951] The Court of Justice finally took *San Giorgio* as an occasion to demarcate the material extent of the right to the free movement of goods: on the one hand, '*entitlement to the repayment of charges levied by a Member State contrary to the rules of Community law is a consequence of, and an ajunct to, the rights conferred on individuals by the Community provisions prohibiting charges having an effect equivalent to custom duties or, as the case may be, the discriminatory application of internal taxes.*'[952] The right is thus classically derived from an obligation of the Member State (*in casu*, a prohibition on customs duties). Interestingly, in reaction to the breach of this obligation it also gives rise to the further obligation to

950 *Rewe* and *Comet* had left this question open (*Rewe v Landwirtschaftskammer für das Saarland*, C-33/76; *Comet BV v Produktschap voor Siergewassen*, C-45/76). The *Pigs and Bacon* ruling had previously already hinted towards the acknowledgement of a right to restitution of monies: Judgment of 26 June 1979, *Pigs and Bacon v Commission*, C-177/78, EU:C:1979:164. Swaine, 'Subsidiarity and Self-Interest: Federalism at the European Court of Justice' 25.

951 Opinion of AG Reischl in *Just*, C-68/79, EU:C:1979:272; Opinion of AG Reischl in Amministrazione delle finanze dello Stato v Denkavit italiana, C-61/79, EU:C:1980:2; Opinion of AG Reischl in *Cucchi v Avez*, C-77/76, EU:C:1977:68. Swaine, 'Subsidiarity and Self-Interest: Federalism at the European Court of Justice' 20.

952 *Ammistrazione delle finanze dello Stato v San Giorgio*, C-199/82, para 12. See also *Comateb and Others v Directeur général des douanes and droits indirects*, C-192/95 to C-218/95, para 20; Judgment of 8 March 2001, *Metallgesellschaft and Others*, C-397/98 and C-410/98, EU:C:2001:134, para 84; Judgment of 19 July 2012, *Littlewoods Retail and Others*, C-591/10, EU:C:2012:478, para 24 and Judgment of 14 June 2017, *Compass Contract Services*, C-38/16, EU:C:2017:454, para 29.

set 'right' the 'wrong'[953], by repaying duties that should not have been levied.

On the other hand, the Court demonstrates pragmatism in assessing the limits of the right. It does not oppose a national system that would disallow the repayment of unduly levied charges *'where to do so would entail unjust enrichment of the recipients. There is nothing in Community Law therefore to prevent courts from taking into account, under their national law, of the fact that the unduly levied charges have been incorporated in the price of the goods and thus passed on to the purchasers.'* Therefore national provisions which prevent the reimbursement of taxes, charges and duties levied in breach of EU law are not contrary to EU law *' where it is established that the person required to pay such charges has actually passed them on to other persons.'*[954] Therefore, although the Court insists on ensuring the full effectiveness of the rights protected by EU law,[955] it does not object to national mechanisms that would prevent abuse of such rights, as long as these mechanisms are reasonable, e.g. do not have excessively stringent requirements of proof.[956]

In the wake of *San Giorgio*, a long line of case law on 'passing-on' defences against restitution developed.[957] The more recent way in which the Court phrases the principle is an excellent illustration of the stability of the

953 Eilmansberger, 'The Relationship between Rights and Remedies in EC Law: in Search of the Missing Link' 1219.

954 *Ammistrazione delle finanze dello Stato v San Giorgio,* C-199/82, para 13.

955 *Ammistrazione delle finanze dello Stato v San Giorgio,* C-199/82, para 12: the Court recalled the principles of equivalence and effectiveness and refers *inter alia* to *Rewe v Landwirtschaftskammer für das Saarland,* C-33/76; *Comet BV v Produktschap voor Siergewassen,* C-45/76. Fernandez Martin, 'El principio de tutela judicial efectiva de los derechos subjetivos derivados del Derecho comunitario: evolución y alcance' 858; Swaine, 'Subsidiarity and Self-Interest: Federalism at the European Court of Justice' 20.

956 *Ammistrazione delle finanze dello Stato v San Giorgio,* C-199/82, paras 14 to 17. Ionescu, 'L'abus de droit en droit communautaire' 349. On the prohibition of abuse of rights see also above p. 88.

957 Judgment of 27 May 1981, *Amministrazione delle Finanze dello Stato* v. *Essevi SpA and Carlo Salengo*, C-142 and C-143/80, EU:C:1981:121, para 35; Judgment of 25 February 1988, *Bianco and Girard v Directeur général des douanes and droits indirects*, C-331/85, C-376/85 and C-378/85, EU:C:1988:97, para 13; Judgment of 14 January 1997, *Comateb and Others v Directeur général des douanes and droits indirects,* C-192/95 to C-218/95, EU:C:1997:12, para 29; Judgment of 9 February 1999, *Dilexport Srl* v. *Amministrazione delle Finanze dello Stato*, C-343/96, EU:C:1999:59, para 47; Judgment of 21 September 2000, *Michailidis,* C-441/98 and C-442/98, EU:C:2000:479, para 34; Judgment of 2 October 2003, *Weber's Wine World and Others*, C-147/01, EU:C:2003:533, paras. 86 et seq; Judgment of 9

classic correlation between the rights of individuals and the obligations of Member States: '*the right to a refund of charges levied in a Member State in breach of the rules of European Union law is the consequence and complement of the rights conferred on individuals by provisions of European Union law prohibiting such charges. The Member State is therefore required in principle to repay charges levied in breach of European Union law*'.[958] In Eilmansberger's view, the acceptance of this line of defence has led to a fundamental alteration of the content of the EC right to restitution, as the '*right not to be charged certain taxes*' becomes a '*mere right not to be economically injured by this tax*'.[959] However, considering that individual rights are triggered by interests,[960] this is not such a disturbing alteration, since the economic interest (here, the interest in not being economically harmed by the tax) indeed contributes to shaping the right and triggering its concrete application.[961]

Another issue is whether the basic right-obligation correlation applies when fundamental freedoms are invoked in horizontal relations.[962] The Court has addressed this issue with a straightforward application of *Defrenne II*, relying especially on its two key lessons, i.e. that '*the fact that cer-*

December 2003, Case C-129/00, *Commission* v. *Italy*, EU:C:2003:656, paras. 35 et seq. Eilmansberger, 'The Relationship between Rights and Remedies in EC Law: in Search of the Missing Link' 1220. In addition, the distinction between the right to refund of overpaid VAT and the right to deduct VAT is discussed in Opinion of AG Sánchez-Bordona in *Compass Contract Services*, C-38/16, EU:C:2017:163.

958 See e.g. Judgment of 20 December 2017, *Caterpillar Financial Services*, C-500/16, EU:C:2017:996, para 35; Judgment of 6 September 2011, *Lady & Kid and Others*, C-398/09, EU:C:2011:540, para 17.

959 Eilmansberger, 'The Relationship between Rights and Remedies in EC Law: in Search of the Missing Link' 1221-1223.

960 See the conclusions of Part 1, p. 193 of this work.

961 As the Court recently recalled in order to distinguish claims for repayment of overpaid VAT from claims for deduction of input tax: '*the claim for repayment of overpaid VAT (…) helps to offset the consequences of the tax's incompatibility with EU law by neutralising the economic burden which that tax has wrongly imposed on the trader who, in fact, has ultimately borne it*'; it is '*specifically the fact that the VAT is not due which underlies the right to recover*'. *Compass Contract Services*, C-38/16, paras 30-31, and Judgment of 20 October 2011, *Danfoss and Sauer-Danfoss*, C-94/10, EU:C:2011:674, para 23. By contrast, the right to deduct VAT '*is based on the existence of a tax that is due*', and from the burden of which the taxable person is to be freed: *Compass Contract Services*, C-38/16, para 36.

962 Robin-Olivier, 'The evolution of direct effect in the EU: Stocktaking, problems, projections' 176; D. Wyatt, 'Horizontal effect of fundamental freedoms and the right to equality after *Viking* and *Mangold*, and the implications for Community competence' (2008) 4 Croatian Yearbook of European Law and Policy 1.

tain provisions of the Treaty are formally addressed to the Member States does not prevent rights from being conferred at the same time on any individual who has an interest in compliance with the obligations thus laid down' and that '*the prohibition on prejudicing a fundamental freedom laid down in a provision of the Treaty that is mandatory in nature, applies in particular to all agreements intended to regulate paid labour collectively*'.[963] Based on this, the Court established the horizontal direct effect of the free movement of workers[964] in *Angonese*,[965] and the horizontal direct effect of the freedom of establishment[966] in *Viking*, so that this freedom may also '*be relied on by a private undertaking against a trade union or an association of trade unions*'.[967]

The acknowledgment of the horizontal direct effect of fundamental freedoms has opened the possibility of liability of private individuals for violations of these freedoms, especially in the case *Raccanelli*. This landmark case in the development of the EU law of horizontal liability,[968] concerned an Italian national who went to do research at a Max Planck Institute in Germany and could not work under an employment contract because of his nationality, and had to settle for a grant instead. The Court took this

963 *Defrenne v SABENA*, C-43/75, paras 31 and 39.

964 Back then Article 48 EC, now Article 45 TFEU.

965 *Angonese*, C-281/98, paras 34-36.

966 Back then Article 43 EC, now Article 49 TFEU.

967 *The International Transport Workers' Federation and The Finnish Seamen's Union*, C-438/05, paras 58-61. *Laval un Partneri*, C-341/05. It should be pointed out that in order to recognise the fundamental character of the right to collective action, the Court relied, among other sources, on the Charter (which was not yet binding back then): see paras 43-44 of the judgment. Having identified the fundamental right, in *Viking* and *Laval* the Court was then mostly concerned with how to balance it with the more classic economic fundamental freedoms. These cases have been abundantly commented in the literature: e.g., C. Barnard, 'The 'Opt-Out' for the UK and Poland from the Charter of Fundamental Rights: Triumph or Rhetoric over Reality?' 12-13; E. Paunio and S. Lindroos-Hovinheimo 'Taking Language Seriously: An Analysis of Linguistic Reasoning and Its Implications in EU Law' (2010) 16 European Law Journal 395 412; L. Uibo, 'Defending Estonia's interests in the Court of Justice of the European Union' Estonian Ministry of Foreign Affairs Yearbook 2010 <http://www.vm.ee/en/yearbook-201 0> accessed 14 February 2017 89; M . Goldoni, 'Constitutional Pluralism and the Question of the European Common Good' (2012) 18 European Law Journal 385 392.

968 Reich, 'Rights without Duties? Reflections on the State of Liability Law in the Multilevel Governance System of the Community: Is There a Need for a More Coherent Approach in European Private Law?'. H.-W. Micklitz, 'The ECJ between the Individual Citizen and the Member States - A plea for a judge-made European law on remedies' EUI Working Paper Law 2011/15, 13.

opportunity to confirm that the free movement of workers materialised in the right not to be discriminated against on the basis of one's nationality, which had horizontal direct effect.[969] This meant that the obligation not to discriminate between German citizens and citizens of other Member States (a correlative of the doctoral researcher's right not to be discriminated against, as a worker entitled to free movement) also applied to the Max Planck Society as a private employer.[970] An additional related issue was whether, where such an obligation (and the corresponding right) has been breached, national law should provide individuals with legal means of seeking compensation. The Court's answer was that, where EU law does not provide for any specific measure to be taken when that right has been violated, it is for the national court to decide on the '*nature of the compensation*'. While this leaves space to the national legislator and courts, at the same time it still presupposes that there must be a compensation.[971] This development highlights the potential of fundamental freedoms, depending on the concrete circumstances, to give rise to a variety of rights against different holders of correlative obligations.

2.1.1.1.2. Fundamental freedoms in secondary law

Concerning provisions of secondary law, the correlation between obligations and rights was also decisive in *Politi*, the first case on the direct effect of regulations.[972] What came in question was the relation of Italian legislation providing a duty for administrative services and a statistical levy on imports from other Member States and from third countries with a set of regulations on the common organisation of the European market in pig meat.[973] Having recalled previous case law which had established that the Italian duty constituted a charge having an effect equivalent to custom du-

---

969 *Raccanelli*, C-94/07, para 41, *Angonese*, C-281/98, para 29. D. Weber, 'Some Remarks on the Application of Community Law, Its Legal Effects and the Relationship between These Concepts' in P. Pistone (ed), *Legal Remedies in European Tax Law* (IBFD 2009) 51.

970 *Raccanelli*, C-94/07, para 48.

971 *Raccanelli*, C-94/07, para 52.

972 *Politi v. Ministero delle finanze*, C-43/71, EU:C:1971:122.

973 Council Regulation (EEC) No 20 of 4 April 1962 on the gradual establishment of the common organization of the market in pigmeat (OJ of 20.4.1962 p. 945) and Council Regulation (EEC) No 121/67/EEC of 13 June 1967 on the common organization of the market in pigmeat (OJ of 19.6.1967, p. 2283).

ties and as such was prohibited,[974] the Court went on to assess whether the relevant provisions of the regulations were '*immediately applicable within the national legal system*' and as such created '*individual rights*' for national courts to protect. It found that, as laid down at the second paragraph of Article 189 EEC,[975] regulations '*shall have general application*' and '*shall be... directly applicable in all Member States*'. Just like it had in *Van Gend en Loos* and *Defrenne II*, the Court easily equated the obligations of the Member States with the rights of individuals: '*by reason of their nature and their function in the system of the sources of Community law, regulations have direct effect and are as such, capable of creating individual rights which national courts must protect*'.[976]

In addition, in *Politi* the Court was also asked to rule on the exact moment when these rights came to existence. The automaticity of the creation of rights as a consequence of obligations laid down in regulations thus appeared even more clearly as the Court stated that '*the prohibition on the imposition of those charges by the Member States and, therefore, the right of individuals to require its observance, [...] came into existence on the date on which*

974 *Politi v. Ministero delle finanze*, C-43/71, para 7.

975 Now Article 288 TFEU.

976 *Politi v. Ministero delle finanze*, C-43/71, para. 9. Despite the apparent equation here of direct applicability with direct effect, it has been observed that both notions do not always overlap exactly. Dashwood, 'The Principle of Direct Effect in European Community Law' 230; Gordon and Moffatt, *EU Law in Judicial Review* 18; J. Gerkrath, 'Direct Effect in Germany and France' in J.M. Prinssen and A. Schrauwen (eds), *Direct Effect Rethinking a Classic of EC Legal Doctrine* (Europa Law Publishing 2002) 131; S. Gáspár-Szilágyi 'The Primacy and Direct Effect of EU International Agreements' (2015) 21 European Public Law 343 351. As Claes points out, however, the Court itself does not explicitly make a distinction: Claes, *National Courts' Mandate in the European Constitution* 75. Moreover, the distinction does not appear to be decisive with regard to the creation of rights. See also Judgment of 10 October 1973, *Fratelli Variola Spa v Amministrazione delle finanze dello Stato*, C-34/73, EU:C:1973:101: the Court therein held that the prohibition on 'charges having equivalent effect' to customs duties in Council Regulation 19/62/EEC of 4 April 1962 on the Progressive Establishment of a Common Organisation of the Market in Cereals' (OJ 1962 30/933) and Council Regulation 120/67/EEC of 13 June 1967 on the common organization of the market in cereals (OJ 1967 2269/67) had the same meaning as in the Treaty (paras 2-3) and added at para 8: '*owing to its very nature and its place in the system of sources of Community law, a regulation has immediate effect and, consequently, operates to confer rights on private parties which the national courts have a duty to protect*'. See also Judgment of 17 September 2002, *Muñoz and Superior Fruiticola*, C-253/00, EU:C:2002:497, para 27.

the [...] levy systems took effect.'[977] The Court confirmed this interpretation in *Fratelli Variola*, holding that the Member States could not introduce legislation adapting the requirements concerning the entry into force of a regulation: '*This is particularly true as regards the date from which the Community rule becomes operative and creates rights in favour of private parties. The freedom of each Member State to vary [...] the date on which a Community rule comes into force is excluded by reason of the need to ensure uniform and simultaneous application of Community law throughout the Community.*'[978] This means that when enshrined in regulations, the obligations for Member States and the corresponding rights for individuals emerge simultaneously and immediately, and that the Member States must refrain from hindering the exercise of these rights. This explanation in *Fratelli Variola* also highlights the double rationale underlying the development of the direct effect doctrine – the protection of individual rights being tightly linked with the application of EU law.

Also in relation to the free movement of goods, *Grad*[979] was the first ruling in which the Court applied the *van Gend en Loos* method to a decision in order to assess whether such an instrument could contain an individual right.[980] Just as for Treaty provisions, '*the fact that decisions are addressed to specific persons does not mean that they cannot affect the legal position of other persons*'.[981] Moreover, the fact that regulations have direct effect by their nature does not prevent other types of legal instruments from having direct effect.[982] On the contrary, such a position would compromise the effectiveness of the decision.[983] '*Therefore, in each particular case, it must be ascertained whether the nature, background and wording of the provision in question are capable of producing direct effects in the legal relationships between the ad-*

977 *Politi v. Ministero delle finanze*, C-43/71, para. 11.

978 *Fratelli Variola Spa v Amministrazione delle finanze dello Stato*, C-34/73, para 15.

979 *Grad v Finanzamt Traunstein*, 9/70.

980 The decision at issue was Council Decision of 13 May 1965 on the harmonization of certain provisions affecting competition in transport by rail, road and inland waterway (OJ special edition 1965 p. 67), read in light of First Council Directive of 11 April 1967 on the harmonisation of legislation of Member States concerning turnover taxes (OJ Special Edition 1967 p. 14).

981 Türk, *The Concept of Legislation in European Community Law - A Comparative Perspective* 90.

982 *Grad v Finanzamt Traunstein*, 9/70, para 5. Bast, 'Legal Instruments' 378.

983 *Grad v Finanzamt Traunstein*, 9/70, para 5, later highlighted again in Judgment of 22 September 1988, *Land de Sarre v Ministre de l'Industrie*, C-187/87, EU:C:1988:439, para 19.

dressee of the act and third parties.'[984] Following the same method as in past seminal cases, the Court found that the relevant provisions of the decision at hand were unconditional and sufficiently clear and precise and, as such, gave rise to rights for individuals.[985] Thus, the *Grad* ruling echoes *van Gend en Loos* and *Defrenne II* in the way it connected rights, obligations, interests and effectiveness: here, too, the Court stated that the obligation imposed on the addressee of a decision may be invoked by any person who has '*an interest in the fulfilment of this obligation*',[986] with effectiveness as the underlying justification.

With regard to the identification of rights in decisions, the *Hansa Fleisch* case added the precision that, just as a right is born no later than its corresponding obligation, it also does not exist *before* the obligation from which it is derived and deduced. In the context of harmonising the health safeguards across the common market for meat, Decision 88/408 set standard levels for health inspection fees to be implemented by December 31, 1990.[987] As of May 1989, the regional administration of Schleswig Holstein set fees that were higher that these standard levels. The Hansa Fleisch company challenged these fees by invoking the direct effect of decisions, which were established in *Grad*. The Court first noted, in an answer to an argument submitted by the German authorities, that although the clear and precise provision on which Hansa Fleisch was relying on contained a possibility for derogation, this did not make it conditional and devoid of direct effect, especially given that the possibility for derogation was strictly sub-

984 *Grad v Finanzamt Traunstein*, 9/70, para 6.

985 *Grad v Finanzamt Traunstein*, 9/70, para 9. Regarding decisions the same method was applied later in: Judgment of 12 December 1990, *Kaefer and Procacci v French State*, C-100/89, EU:C:1990:456, para 24; Judgment of 10 November 1992, *Hansa Fleisch v. Landrat des Kreises Schleswig-Flensburg*, C-156/91, EU:C:1992:423, paras 12-13; Judgment of 28 September 1999, *Fruchthandelsgesellschaft Chemnitz v Commission*, T-254/97, EU:T:1999:178, para 29 and case law cited. Also of interest is the *Sace* ruling, delivered shortly after *Grad*, on the possibility for a decision combined with provisions from the Treaty and from a directive to give rise to individual rights. The Court focused on the substance and function of the measure at issue, rather than the form (para 13), identified the nature of the obligation, and then established that it was '*capable of producing direct effects*' between '*the Member State and its subjects*': Judgment of 17 December 1970, *Spa Sace v Ministero delle finanze*, C-33/70, EU:C:1970:118, paras 13-14 and 18. Dashwood, 'The Principle of Direct Effect in European Community Law' 239.

986 *Grad v Finanzamt Traunstein*, 9/70, para. 5.

987 Council Decision 85/73/EEC of 15 June 1988 on the levels of the fees to be charged for health inspections and controls of fresh meat pursuant to Directive 85/73/EEC (OJ L 194/24).

ject to judicial review.[988] Then the Court came to the issue of how to determine the precise moment when the rights identified in the decision came into existence. The Court made clear that '*the possibility granted to individuals of relying on a decision as against the Member States to which it is addressed is based on the binding nature of the decision vis-à-vis its addressees. Consequently, where the decision grants the Member State a specified period in which to comply with the obligations resulting from it, the decision may not be relied on by individuals as against the Member States before the expiry of the period in question.*'[989] The temporal simultaneity of the obligation and the right thus add up with the material equivalence between the obligation and the right. This further supports the notion of right and obligation as a pair of jural correlatives – or as two sides of a single medal.

This applies to provisions of directives, although this was not such an obvious conclusion as illustrated by the *Van Duyn* case. Ms Van Duyn, a Dutch national, was recruited by the Church of Scientology to work in the UK. She was denied a work permit by the British authorities on grounds of public policy. She claimed that this was contrary to Article 48 EEC on the free movement of workers and to the requirements of Directive 64/221, which provided a framework for Member States imposing restrictions to entry on their territory based on grounds of public policy, public security or public health.[990] Mrs Van Duyn was relying on Article 3(1) of Directive 64/221, which required that '*measures taken on grounds of public policy or public security shall be based exclusively on the personal conduct of the individual concerned.*' The question arose: can non-transposed (or incorrectly transposed) directives give rise to rights? The British government submitted observations and had a suggestion for an answer: it proposed to clearly deny that directives could never have direct effects or, as a consequence, give rise to individual rights. This submission relied on the very nature of directives, which, unlike regulations, were intended to be binding on the Member States as to the ends that they defined, but not the means for reaching these ends. Just like it had in *Grad*, the Court flatly rejected this *a contrario* approach based on the nature of regulations and made clear instead that the requirement of useful effect implies that individuals must have the pos-

988 Judgment of 10 November 1992, *Hansa Fleisch v. Landrat des Kreises Schleswig-Flensburg*, C-156/91, EU:C:1992:423, paras 15-16.

989 *Hansa Fleisch v. Landrat des Kreises Schleswig-Flensburg*, C-156/91, paras 19-20.

990 Council Directive 64/221/EEC of 25 February 1964 on the co-ordination of special measures concerning the movement and residence of foreign nationals which are justified on grounds of public policy, public security or public health (OJ 056, 04/04/1964, p. 850).

sibility to rely on the act before their national courts.[991] Thereby the Court manifested that for detecting a right in a provision of a directive after the expiration of the transposition period, the method is the same as for identifying a right in any other provision of EU law: the Court examines the nature, general scheme and wording of the provision in order to check whether it is unconditional, precise and clear.[992] Regarding the requirement of clarity, where a provision might not be completely clear the Court may provide an interpretation by way of a preliminary ruling.[993] The Court therefore held that Article 3(1) of the Directive fulfilled all conditions for having direct effect. This point, however, was tempered by the Court's answer to the last question, which was about how the concept of public policy should be interpreted and used in the assessment of the personal conduct of the individual concerned. The Court acknowledged that the Member States were allowed '*an area of discretion*' when they apply this concept[994] and could take into account the fact that the individual was associated with an organisation conducting activities potentially harmful to society. Ultimately, the assessment of the degree of discretion left to the Member State proved decisive and allowed for a restriction of Mrs Van Duyn's right to free movement under Article 48 EEC.

991 Judgment of 4 December 1974, *Van Duyn v. Home Office,* C-41/74, EU:C:1974:133, para 12. J. Bast, 'Legal Instruments' in A. Von Bogdandy and J. Bast (eds), *Principles of European Constitutional Law* (Hart Publishing 2006) 378. Šadl, 'The Role of Effet Utile in Preserving the Continuity and Authority of European Union Law: Evidence from the Citation Web of the Pre-accession Case Law of the Court of Justice of the EU' 35. With regard to directives the Court reasserted this in later cases such as: Judgment of 1st February 1977, *Verbond nederlandse ondernemingen v Inspecteur der invoerrechten en accijnzen,* C-51/76, EU:C:1977:12, paras 22-23; Judgment of 5 April 1979, *Ratti,* C-148/78, EU:C:1979:110, para 19, Judgment of 19 January 1982, *Becker,* C-8/81, EU:C:1982:7, para 21.

992 *Van Duyn v. Home Office,* C-41/74, paras 11 to 14. See also Judgment of 12 May 1987, *Traen,* Joined cases C-372 to 374/85, EU:C:1987:222, para 25; Judgment of 20 September 1988, *Beentjes v State of the Netherlands,* C-31/87, EU:C:1988:422, para 43; Judgment of 23 February 1994, *Comitato di coordinamento per la difesa della Cava and Others v Regione Lombardia and Others,* C-236/92, EU:C:1994:60, paras 8-9.

993 *Van Duyn v. Home Office,* C-41/74, para 14.

994 *Van Duyn v. Home Office,* C-41/74, para 18. Šadl, 'The Role of Effet Utile in Preserving the Continuity and Authority of European Union Law: Evidence from the Citation Web of the Pre-accession Case Law of the Court of Justice of the EU' 35.

Van Duyn is nonetheless remembered as having sanctioned the possibility for directives to give rise to rights – a matter which was confirmed and refined in subsequent case law. In *Fratelli Costanzo,* the issue was whether a directive provision could be relied on by an individual challenging the result of a tendering procedure led by local authorities such as municipalities. The Court recalled that the unconditionality and sufficient precision of a provision means that an individual may rely on it if the State has failed to implement it by the end of the period prescribed or has implemented it incorrectly. '*It is important to note that the reason for which an individual may [...] rely on the provisions of a directive in proceedings before the national courts is that the obligations arising under those provisions are binding upon all the authorities of the Member States.*'[995] The Court further advanced the underlying logic by adding that as long as the conditions for relying on the provisions of a directive before a national court are met, it would be inconsistent not to require that all public authorities and bodies of the administration also apply these provisions.[996] Therefore, if an obligation imposed on a Member State fulfils the conditions for giving rise to an individual right, the obligation must be respected by all types of public authorities so that the effectiveness of this right is ensured.[997] Here again the basic correlation between obligations and rights is verified.

The application of this model, however, was not always so straightforward, as the *Becker* case on turnover tax exemplifies.[998] The German law transposing the Sixth VAT Directive[999] came into force on January 1st, 1980. The transposition period for the directive, however, had expired one year earlier. Ms Becker, a self-employed credit negotiator, applied for tax exemptions for that time window, i.e. the tax year 1979, relying on provisions of the directive. The German authorities, however, refused to acknowledge

995 Judgment of 22 June 1989, *Fratelli Costanzo v. Comune di Milano,* C-103/88, EU:C:1989:256, paras 29-30, with reference to *Becker,* C-8/81, and *Marshall v. Southampton and South-West Hampshire Area Health Authority,* C-152/84.

996 *Fratelli Costanzo v. Comune di Milano,* C-103/88, para 31. Fernandez Martin, 'El principio de tutela judicial efectiva de los derechos subjetivos derivados del Derecho comunitario: evolución y alcance' 883.

997 The Court later systematised this approach in *Foster e.a. v British Gas,* C-188/89 (see below p. 338). Wernicke, 'Au nom de qui? The European Court of Justice between Member States, Civil Society and Union Citizens' 401.

998 *Becker,* C-8/81.

999 Council Directive 77/388/EEC of 17 May 1977 on the harmonisation of the laws of the Member States relating to turnover taxes - Common system of value added tax: uniform basis of assessment (OJ L 145 p. 1) (the 'Sixth VAT Directive').

the direct effect of these provisions. Just like in *Van Duyn*, the Court again rejected the argument that consisted in opposing regulations having direct effect by their very nature, to directives;[1000] and it relied on considerations of effectiveness: the effectiveness of the directive '*would be diminished in persons were prevented from relying upon it in proceedings before a court and national courts were prevented from taking it into consideration as an element of Community law*.'[1001] Therefore, '*wherever the provisions of a directive appear [...] to be unconditional and sufficiently precise, those provisions may, in the absence of implementing measures adopted within the prescribed period, be relied upon as against any national provision which is incompatible with the directive or in so far as the provisions define rights which individuals are able to assert against the state.*'[1002] This is where confusion arises: the last limb of the passage, i.e. a sort of requirement that individual rights be defined in the directive if one wants to rely on this directive, has been read especially by German authors as an acknowledgement of the *Schutznorm* doctrine, in the sense that there would have to be a clear intention to protect a defined interest, in order to identify a right.[1003]

Yet, the Court does not actually use this requirement to test whether the relevant directive provisions have direct effect.[1004] The Court tested the precision and unconditionality of the provision, paying closer attention to unconditionality which was the aspect most disputed in this case.[1005] Unconditionality was again assessed by reference to the degree of discretion left in the provision: '*Whilst the Sixth Directive undoubtedly confers upon the Member States varying degrees of discretion as regards implementing certain of its provisions, individuals may not for that reason be denied the right to rely on any provisions which owing to their particular subject-matter are capable of being severed from the general body of provisions and applied separately.*' Indeed, the obligation to implement the directive '*would be rendered totally ineffectual if the Member States were permitted to annul, as the result of their inactivity, even those effects which certain provisions of a directive are capable of producing by*

1000 *Becker*, C-8/81, para 21.

1001 *Becker*, C-8/81, para 23.

1002 *Becker*, C-8/81, para 25.

1003 As pointed out by: E. Staebe, *Rechtsschutz bei gemeinschaftswidrigen Beihilfen vor europäischen und deutschen Gerichten* 194; Ruffert, 'Rights and Remedies in European Community Law: a Comparative View' 312. On the *Schutznorm* doctrine in German law see p. 52 and on the problem it causes in EU law see the conclusion of Part 1 p. 228.

1004 Ruffert, 'Rights and Remedies in European Community Law: a Comparative View' 313.

1005 *Becker*, C-8/81, para 27.

virtue of their subject-matter.[1006] As a consequence, the Court held that a mandatory exemption, even subject to certain conditions, may also be characterised as 'unconditional' and therefore may confer rights.[1007] Thus, in the process of identifying individual rights the opposite relation between discretion and unconditionality is sustained by the recurring concern for the effectiveness of EU law. This silver lining of the *Becker* case was confirmed in a later case in which the Court quoted *Becker* yet applied only the test of precision and unconditionality to identify individual rights in a directive.[1008] This test has been used in multiple cases since then.[1009]

It must be pointed out that the criteria for assessing the ability of an obligation to translate into a right (i.e. precision, clarity and unconditionality) are applied in a flexible and pragmatic way. In fact, these are all used as instruments for assessing the discretion left by the norm, and the cases emphasise the opposition relation between discretion and unconditionality. In the context of proceedings on value added tax, the Court has held that that Article 11 of the second VAT Directive[1010] allowed the Member States a margin of discretion, but that the national court would have to give effect to the provision, when individuals relied on it, if that margin was exceeded.[1011] The Court later added that '*[a] provision of EU law is unconditional where it sets forth an obligation which is not qualified by any condition, or subject, in its implementation or effects, to the taking of any measure ei-*

1006 *Becker*, C-8/81, para 29.

1007 Weber, 'Some Remarks on the Application of Community Law, Its Legal Effects and the Relationship between These Concepts' 48.

1008 *Comitato di coordinamento per la difesa della Cava and Others v Regione Lombardia and Others*, C-236/92, para 8. Ruffert, 'Rights and Remedies in European Community Law: a Comparative View' 314. See also Hilson and Downes, 'Making sense of rights: Community rights in E.C. law' 131.

1009 E.g. *Pfeiffer and Others*, Joined cases C-397/01 to C-403/01, para 103; Judgment of 15 January 2014, *Association de médiation sociale*, C-176/12, EU:C:2014:2, para 31; Judgment of 15 May 2014, *Almos Agrárkülkereskedelmi*, C-337/13, EU:C:2014:328, paras 31-35; Judgment of 9 October 2014, *Traum*, C-492/13, EU:C:2014:2267, paras 47-48; Judgment of 25 June 2015, *Indėlių ir investicijų draudimas et Nemaniūnas*, C-671/13, EU:C:2015:418, paras 58-60; Judgment of 6 October 2015, *T-Mobile Czech Republic et Vodafone Czech Republic*, C-508/14, EU:C:2015:657, para 52.

1010 Council Directive 67/228/EEC of 11 April 1967 on the harmonisation of legislation of Member States concerning turnover taxes (OJ 71/1303 p. 14).

1011 *Verbond nederlandse ondernemingen v Inspecteur der invoerrechten en accijnzen*, C-51/76. Dashwood, 'The Principle of Direct Effect in European Community Law' 240.

ther by the institutions of the European Union or by the Member States.'[1012] Moreover, the Court sometimes added a condition of completeness of the norm, precisely because completeness excludes discretion.[1013] One such instance was a case on the freedom to provide services and the freedom of establishment in the French overseas territories, concerning the applicability of a provision of a Council decision. There the Court also made it clear that '*an unconditional provision is one which leaves no discretion to the Member States*'.[1014] Discretion thus serves as the overarching criterion for assessing of the existence of rights. Of course, as pointed out by Prechal, discretion is always a matter of degree, which is indicated by clues such as precision, clarity, and unconditionality.[1015] This means on the one hand that discretion does not exclude direct effect: where a Member State has exercised its

---

1012 Judgment of 16 July 2015, *Larentia + Minerva*, C-108/14, EU:C:2015:496, para 49; See also Judgment of 3 September 2014, *GMAC UK*, C-589/12, EU:C:2014:2131, para 30; Judgment of 15 May 2014, *Almos Agrárkülkereskedelmi*, C-337/13, EU:C:2014:328, para 32 and case law cited. See also Opinion of AG Wathelet in *Ambisig*, C-46/15, EU:C:2016:137, para 24.

1013 E.g. Judgment of 22 September 1983, *Auer v Ministère Public*, C-271/82, EU:C:1983:243, para 16: directive provisions which '*impose on each Member State clear, complete, precise and unconditional obligations which exclude the possibility of discretionary assessments*' may be relied on by individuals before national courts. See also Judgment of 15 December 1983, *Rienks*, C-5/83, EU:C:1983:382, para 8 and Judgement of 15 January 1986, *Hurd v Jones*, C-44/84, EU:C:1986:2, para 47. Hofmann and Mihaescu, 'The Relation between the Charter's Fundamental Rights and the Unwritten General Principles of EU Law: Good Administration as the Test Case' 94. A Community provision is unconditional where it is not subject, in its implementation or effects, to the taking of any measure either by the institutions of the Community or by the Member States: *Molkerei Zentrale Westfalen-Lippe v Hauptzollamt Paderborn*, C-28/67, p. 152; *Comitato di coordinamento per la difesa della Cava and Others v Regione Lombardia and Others*, C-236/92, para 8.

1014 Judgment of 12 December 1990, *Kaefer and Procacci v French State*, C-100/89, EU:C:1990:456, para 26.

1015 Prechal, 'Does Direct Effect Still Matter?' 1062. On discretion and the inverse relationship with the existence of rights see also Foulquier, *Les droits publics subjectifs des administrés. Emergence d'un concept en droit administratif français du XIXè au XXè siècle*. On discretion more generally: Hofmann, Rowe and Türk, *Administrative Law and Policy of the European Union* 498. On the relation between precision and rights, see the special issue of *La Revue des droits de l'homme*, 'Précision et droits de l'Homme', including the following contributions, all relevant to the present discussion: C. Roulhac, 'Introduction' La Revue des droits de l'homme (en ligne) 7 - 2015 <http://revdh.revues.org/1312> accessed 7 June 2016; J.-J. Sueur 'Imprécision des droits de l'Homme : quelle imprécision?' La Revue des droits de l'homme (en ligne) 7 - 2015 <http://revdh.

discretion in adopting national measures which are in fact incompatible with the directive, it is still possible for individuals to rely on the relevant directive provision.[1016] On the other hand, when discretion is allowed concerning the determination of the scope of application, individuals falling outside that scope under national measures cannot rely on the directive.[1017]

2.1.1.1.3. The direct effect of international agreements

The category of international agreements has raised specific problems with regard to the identification of rights. This may be due to motives of a political nature related to the autonomy of the EU from the international legal order.[1018] Another explanation is more focused on the originality of the EU legal order. Martines suggests that we can infer from the distinction made by the Court in *van Gend en Loos* between the new EC legal order and classic international legal order, that classic international agreements are not

---

revues.org/1313> accessed 7 June 2016, T. Acar 'Appréhender l'imprécision des droits : approche linguistique' La Revue des droits de l'homme (en ligne) 7 - 2015 <http://revdh.revues.org/1191> accessed 7 June 2016; A. Gelblat 'Appréhender l'imprécision des droits : approche stratégique' La Revue des droits de l'homme (en ligne) 7 - 2015 <http://revdh.revues.org/1341> accessed 7 June 2016; E. Millard 'Précision et effectivité des droits de l'homme' La Revue des droits de l'homme (en ligne) 7 - 2015 <http://revdh.revues.org/1215> accessed 7 June 2016; C. Fercot 'Précision et droits de l'Homme dans les ordres juridiques allemand et suisse' La Revue des droits de l'homme (en ligne) 7 - 2015 <http://revdh.revues.org/1330> accessed 7 June 2016; I. Hachez 'Précision et droits de l'homme dans l'ordre juridique belge : focus sur la notion polysémique d'effet direct' La Revue des droits de l'homme (en ligne) 7 - 2015 <http://revdh.revues.org/1261> accessed 7 June 2016.

1016 Concerning the Sixth VAT Directive: Judgment of 17 February 2005, *Linneweber and Akritidis*, Joined cases C-453/02 and C-462/02, EU:C:2005:92, paras 34-37; Judgment of 28 June 2007, *JP Morgan Fleming Claverhouse Investment Trust and The Association of Investment Trust Companies*, C-363/05, EU:C:2007:391, para 61; Judgment of 15 February 2017, *British Film Institute*, C-592/15, EU:C:2017:117, paras 25-26.

1017 *British Film Institute*, C-592/15, paras 23-24: Article 13A(1)(n) of the Sixth VAT Directive provides that '*certain cultural services*' may be exempted from VAT, meaning that there is discretion in determining the exempted cultural services.

1018 C. Mayeur-Carpentier, L. Clément-Wilz and F. Martucci, 'Chronique de droit administratif et droit de l'Union européenne, 1er janvier 2012 - 1er juillet 2012' (2012) Revue française de droit administratif 961 969.

designed to confer rights upon individuals.[1019] As a consequence, '*before concluding that a private person can enforce the right conferred by a provision contained in an agreement binding the EU before a national tribunal, the ECJ has to verify whether the agreement is reproducing those conditions which can be assimilated to those of the EU legal order*'.[1020] And indeed, although there is still room for debate, the Court's position has stabilised into the following 'two-tier' approach[1021]: '*the provisions of an international agreement to which the European Union is a party can be relied on* … [in an action for annulment or exception based on illegality of secondary law] *where, first, the nature and the broad logic of that agreement do not preclude it and, secondly, those provisions appear, as regards their content, to be unconditional and sufficiently precise*'.[1022] This is not essentially different from the Court's method in *Van Gend en Loos*. The originality is that, while the answer to the first leg of the test is known to be positive in direct effect cases concerning 'internal' EU law, the question must be asked for each international agreement.

Therefore, firstly, the possibility for a provision of an international agreement to directly grant individual rights will be assessed by reference to the general scheme of that agreement, its nature and broad logic.[1023] The case law on rules of international trade provides an example of how this is done. While the Court of Justice, prior to the creation of the World Trade

1019 The notion of direct effect existed in public international law before it was introduced in EC/EU law, but it was not so closely associated with rights. Nollkaemper, 'The Direct Effect of Public International Law'.

1020 Martines, 'Direct Effects of International Agreements of the European Union' (2014) 25 The European Journal of International Law 129 137.

1021 J. Wouters and D. Van Eeckhoutte, 'Giving Effect to Customary International Law Through European Community Law' in J.M. Prinssen and A. Schrauwen (eds), *Direct Effect Rethinking a Classic of EC Legal Doctrine* (Europa Law Publishing 2002) 216. The first case in which the Court followed such an approach was *Kupferberg*: Judgment in *Hauptzollamt Mainz v Kupferberg & Cie*, C-104/81, EU:C:1982:362.

1022 *Council and Others v Vereniging Milieudefensie and Stichting Stop Luchtverontreiniging Utrecht*, Joined cases C-401/12 P to C-403/12 P, para 54 and case law quoted, especially: Judgment in *Intertanko and Others*, C-308/06, EU:C:2008:312, para 45; Judgment of 9 September 2008, *FIAMM and Others v Council and Commission*, C-120/06 P and C-121/06 P, EU:C:2008:476, paras 110 and 120; Judgment of 21 December 2011, *Air Transport Association of America and Others*, C-366/10, EU:C:2011:864, para 54.

1023 S. Van Raepenbusch, *Droit institutionnel de l'Union et des Communautés européennes* (De Boeck 2000) 379.

Organisation (WTO), had consistently denied direct effect to GATT rules,[1024] under WTO law it then identified provisions which could exceptionally be invoked to review EC measures. The specific conditions making this possible were laid down in the *Nakajima* case: the Court held that it was empowered to review the legality of the conduct of the EU Institutions in the light of WTO law, where the Community intends to implement a 'particular obligation' assumed in the context of the WTO.[1025] The rationale of the *Nakajima* exception was later explained by Advocate General Geelhoed: '*In a case where it is clear that a Community measure was specifically intended to implement a particular obligation of WTO law, the Community legislature has essentially chosen to limit its own scope of manoeuvre by itself 'incorporating' that obligation into Community law*'.[1026] However, it is not easy to apply such an exception, because '*the Court has not set out a clear, consistent and defensible principle distinguishing those cases in which the Nakajima exception applies, from those cases in which it does not*'.[1027] Yet, this exception may be considered as an extension of the 'nature and broad logic' condition: it is not only the international legal instrument itself which is examined, but also the intention of the EC/EU to implement it in its own legal system.

As we can see, in the context of international agreements the purpose underlying such instruments are much more significant to the Court than the intentions of the authors of a regulation or directive when it comes to identifying rights in such instruments. This can be explained by the nature of these agreements and their position at the interface between EU law and international law. While the *telos* of the EC/EU Treaty gives rise to a pre-

---

1024 Claes, *National Courts' Mandate in the European Constitution* 80. General Agreement on Tariffs and Trade, October 30, 1947, 61 Stat. A-11, 55 UNTS 194.

1025 Judgment in *Nakajima All Precision v Council*, C-69/89, EU:C:1991:186.

1026 Opinion of AG Geelhoed in *Franz Egenberger*, C-313/04, EU:C:2005:733, para 64.

1027 Opinion of AG Geelhoed in *Franz Egenberger*, C-313/04, para 68 and see A. Arcuri and S. Poli, 'What Price for the Community Enforcement of WTO Law?' EUI Working Paper 2010/01, 8. On the direct effect of WTO law see also H. Ruiz Fabri, 'Is There a Case - Legally and Politically - for Direct Effect of WTO Obligations?' (2014) 25 European Journal of International Law 151 and on the legacy of *Nakajima* S. Adam, P. Devisscher and P. Van Elsuwege, 'Chronique de jurisprudence communautaire : les relations extérieures (1er janvier 2006-31 décembre 2008)' (2009) Cahiers de droit européen 465 529.

sumption of direct effect,[1028] only if the international agreement is characterised by an intention to grant rights in the same way as the EU legal order can there be direct effect of (and reliance by individuals on) the obligations laid down.[1029]

The second step, then, is the test of precision and unconditionality, applied for example in the case law on association agreements containing commitments regarding the freedom of movement of workers. If the provision examined does not meet these conditions, then it does not directly confer rights on individuals. Such was the case in *Demirel*: the Court held that that a provision of an agreement concluded by the Community with non-member countries was directly applicable when, in lights of its wording and the purpose and of the nature of the agreement, the provision contains a clear and precise obligation which is not subject, to the adoption of any subsequent measure.[1030] The provisions of the EEC-Turkey association agreement[1031] on which Ms. Demirel was relying were '*phrased in very general terms*', requiring that the parties to the agreement must progressively secure the freedom of movement of workers between the EEC and Turkey. This did not amount to a sufficiently precise and unconditional obligation that could translate into an enforceable right.[1032]

By contrast, in the *Kziber* case the Court found that Article 41, paragraph 1 of the EEC-Morocco agreement,[1033] which established equality of treatment for Moroccan and EEC workers with regard to social security al-

1028 M. Wathelet, 'Du concept de l'effet direct à celui de l'invocabilité au regard de la jurisprudence récente de la Cour de justice' in M. Hoskins and W. Robinson (eds), *A True European. Essays for Judge David Edward* (Hart Publishing 2003) 369.

1029 Martines, 'Direct Effects of International Agreements of the European Union' 137.

1030 Judgment of 30 September 1987, *Demirel v. Stadt Schwäbisch Gmünd*, C-12/86, EU:C:1987:400, para 14 and Judgment of 10 September 1996, *Taflan-Met and Others*, C-277/94, EU:C:1996:315, para 24.

1031 Agreement creating an association between the European Economic Community and Turkey (OJ of 29.12.1964, L217, p. 3687), Articles 7 and 12.

1032 *Demirel v. Stadt Schwäbisch Gmünd*, C-12/86, paras 23-24. The absence of direct effect of the Ankara agreements has been confirmed more recently in the *Yedaş Tarim* case: Judgment of 30 March 2006, *Yedaş Tarim ve Otomotiv Sanayi ve Ticaret v Council and Commission*, T-367/03, EU:T:2006:96, paras 40-43. See also Gáspár-Szilágyi, 'The Primacy and Direct Effect of EU International Agreements' 369.

1033 Cooperation agreement between the European Economic Community and Morocco (OJ 1978 L274/2).

lowances, had direct effect.[1034] In a nutshell, the possibility for provisions of international agreements to give rise to individual rights depends on a two-step test similar to that which was performed in *Van Gend en Loos*: firstly, an analysis of the spirit, structure and nature of the agreement (teleological and systemic method), and secondly, the clear, precise and unconditional character of the obligation laid down in the provision at issue; in this second step, the search for the drafters' subjective intention to grant a right remains of limited importance.

The case law on the direct effect of fundamental freedoms shows that rights may be identified by reference to criteria such as precision, clarity and unconditionality of a norm, and more generally all criteria that may be relevant in assessing the discretion that this norm allows. This assessment in turn helps identifying the substance and limits of the obligation and of the corresponding right. The formula also works horizontally, as exemplified by the case law on the reliance on fundamental freedoms by individuals against other individuals. The correlation between rights and obligations and the role of interests in triggering the practical application of these jural correlatives applies also in the case law on the vertical direct effect of directives, confirming that the creation of rights is a consequence of, rather than a condition for, direct effect.[1035] This conclusion might be difficult to reconcile with the insistence on the 'protective intention' of the norm by supporters of the *Schutznorm* approach, an issue that shall now be further explored by looking at rights in the case law on public liability.

2.1.1.2. Rights in public liability

As one of the main areas of early development of EU law, fundamental freedoms litigation has been crucial in the development of the public liability regime under EU law – the notable exception being of course *Fran-*

1034 Judgment in *Office national de l'emploi v Kziber*, C-18/90, EU:C:1991:36; Van Gerven, 'Articles 30, 48, 52 and 59 after *Keck & Mithouard*, and Protection of Rights Arising from Directives after *Faccini Dori*' 234. See also Judgment of 20 April 1994, *Yousfi v Belgian State*, C-58/93, EU:C:1994:160, paras 16-19.

1035 Ruffert, 'Rights and Remedies in European Community Law: a Comparative View' 315; Prechal, 'Member State Liability and Direct Effect: What's the Difference After All?' 313; Staebe, *Rechtsschutz bei gemeinschaftswidrigen Beihilfen vor europäischen und deutschen Gerichten* 194; Reich, 'System der subjectiven öffentlichen Rechte' in the Union: A European Constitution for Citizens of Bits and Pieces' 180.

covich, which concerned not fundamental freedoms but labour law.[1036] As explained in Part 1, public liability encapsulates and illustrates important issues in the debate over the relation between rights and remedies. In particular, this debate is biased by the requirement of a 'rule intended to confer rights' and its unclear filiation with the *Schutznorm* doctrine.[1037] This doctrine originates in German law and focuses on whether a given provision specifically intends to protect individuals and thus to grant them rights; only if that intention can be pinpointed, may a right (to damages) be acknowledged.[1038] In the context of damages, this doctrine aims at limiting the cases where the State (or the Union) may be found liable.[1039] We have seen already how this approach can be problematic when it comes to identifying rights in directives. In liability cases, the tension is even stronger: does our basic model of rights, obligations and interests, sketched originally in the context of direct effect cases, hold water in light of the case law on public liability for violations of EU law? The Court's response to this *Schutznorm* pressure differs depending on whether it manifests in the context of Member State or Union liability, confirming the historical discrepancy pointed out in Part I.

2.1.1.2.1. Member State liability: discretion as the key criterion for identifying rights

After *Francovich*, the other typical illustration of the complementarity between direct effect and public liability is the historic ruling in *Brasserie du Pêcheur* and *Factortame*.[1040] Although the main question raised in that case was whether a Member State could be held liable for a breach of EU law performed specifically by its legislator, the judgment is also significant be-

1036 *Francovich and Bonifaci v. Italy*, Joined cases C-6/90 and C-9/90. See p. 192 of this work.

1037 Lenaerts, Maselis and Gutman, *EU Procedural Law* 516; Wathelet and Wildermeersch, *Contentieux européen* 341; Reich, 'Rights without Duties? Reflections on the State of Liability Law in the Multilevel Governance System of the Community: Is There a Need for a More Coherent Approach in European Private Law?' 13.

1038 See p.52 of this work, and for the problems raised by this doctrine for identifying rights in EU law, the conclusion of Part 1 p. 224 of this work.

1039 Türk, *Judicial Review in EU law* 258.

1040 Judgment of 5 March 1996, *Brasserie du pêcheur v Bundesrepublik Deutschland and The Queen v Secretary of State for Transport, ex parte Factortame*, Joined cases C-46/93 and C-48/93, EU:C:1996:79.

cause of the way it connects direct effect and State liability. The Court recalled its finding from *Francovich* that direct effect offers a '*minimum guarantee*' only and '*is not sufficient in itself to ensure the full and complete implementation of the Treaty*', so that '*the full effectiveness of Community law would be impaired if individuals were unable to obtain redress when their rights were infringed by a breach of Community law*'.[1041] In an answer to the German, Irish and Dutch governments who were arguing that Member State liability should exist only where the provisions breached did not have direct effect, the Court held exactly the opposite. It stressed the importance of the principle of liability and adds: '*It is all the more so in the event of infringement of a right directly conferred by a Community provision upon which individuals are entitled to rely before the national courts. In that event, the right to reparation is the necessary corollary of the direct effect of the Community provision whose breach caused the damage sustained.*'[1042] Member State liability thus appears as a complement to direct effect in order to simultaneously ensure the effectiveness of EU law and the protection of rights which individuals derive from it.[1043]

The Court then, unfaithful to the *Francovich* terminology, re-phrased the conditions for Member State liability as follows: '*Community law confers a right to reparation where three conditions are met: the rule of law infringed must be intended to confer rights on individuals; the breach must be sufficiently serious; and there must be a direct causal link between the breach of the obligation resting on the State and the damage sustained by the injured parties.*'[1044] It turns out that the first condition is '*manifestly*' satisfied because the relevant provisions – including the one which is phrased as a prohibition on the Member States - '*give rise to rights for individuals*', i.e. have direct ef-

1041 *Brasserie and Factortame*, Joined cases C-46/93 and C-48/93, paras 20-21. H.-M. Voigts, *Die Subjektivierung von Gemeinwohlinteressen als Demokratisierung der Verwaltung* (LIT Verlag 2016) 89.

1042 *Brasserie and Factortame*, Joined cases C-46/93 and C-48/93, para 20-22.

1043 U. Šadl, 'The Role of Effet Utile in Preserving the Continuity and Authority of European Union Law: Evidence from the Citation Web of the Pre-accession Case Law of the Court of Justice of the EU'. In the same vein Hinton argues that the rationale behind *Brasserie* and *Factortame* was that '*Member State actions undermined the effectiveness of Commmunity law because individuals did not possess adequate judicial protection for Member State breach of directly effective provisions*'. Hinton, 'Strengthening the Effectiveness of Community Law: Direct Effect, Article 5 EC, and the European Court of Justice' 335.

1044 *Brasserie and Factortame*, Joined cases C-46/93 and C-48/93, para 51.

fect.[1045] Direct effect and liability are thus not alternative mechanisms; they can exist simultaneously, being linked (rather than separated) by the concept of a right: a provision which confers directly effective rights on individuals necessarily fulfils the first liability condition. Eilmansberger convincingly argues that the capacity of the two provisions to create individual rights was based on their clear, precise and unconditional wording, '*and their resulting aptitude to be directly applied*'. The fact that this aptitude allows the provision to satisfy the condition of a rule intended to confer rights in his view prove that '*the rights protected under the State liability doctrine are not to be determined by the concrete legislative purpose or protective scope (*Schutzzweck*) of the Community rule in question.*'[1046] In other words, in this landmark ruling the Court shows no affinity with the upholders of the intentionalist approach. The unfortunate, but legitimate confusion arises from the phrasing of the first liability condition which requires a rule 'intended to confer rights.'

Then the Court examined the second liability condition: '*as regards both Community liability under Article 215 and Member State liability for breaches of Community law, the decisive test for finding that a breach of Community law is sufficiently serious is whether the Member State or the Community institution concerned manifestly and gravely disregarded the limits on its discretion*.' Regarding the criteria for examining this second condition, they include '*the clarity and precision of the rule breached, the measure of discretion left by that rule to the national or Community authorities, whether the infringement and the damage caused was intentional or involuntary, whether any error of law was excusable or inexcusable*,' and the breach will be sufficiently serious '*if it has persisted despite a judgment finding the infringement in question to be established, or a preliminary ruling or settled case-law of the Court on the matter from which it is clear that the conduct in question constituted an infringement*.'[1047] The Court held that in both cases at issue (except for some elements in the *Brasserie* case) earlier case law was sufficiently clear and unequivocal, so that the British legislator was in a position to understand and comply with the relevant EU law provisions; conversely, non-compliance thus amounted to a sufficiently serious breach of the rules at issue, meaning that the second liability condition was met. It is interesting to note that the German requirement of a '*Schutznorm*' being breached in order for damages to be

1045 *Brasserie and Factortame*, Joined cases C-46/93 and C-48/93, para 54 and case law cited.

1046 Eilmansberger, 'The Relationship between Rights and Remedies in EC Law: in Search of the Missing Link'1125.

1047 *Brasserie and Factortame*, Joined cases C-46/93 and C-48/93, paras 55-57.

awarded[1048] was clearly dismissed by the Court of Justice, which held that this rule possibly passed the test of equivalence, but definitely not the test of effectiveness.[1049] By contrast, the insistence on the clarity and precision of the rule breached and on the concrete circumstances in which the norm is to be construed is strongly reminiscent of the method which the Court had previously developed to assess the existence of a right, and of a violation of that right, in direct effect cases, such as *Defrenne II*. It is also in line with Advocate General Tesauro's observation that: '*the obligations of the Member States and of the Community institutions are directed above all, in the system which the Community has sought and sets out to be, to the creation of rights of individuals*'.[1050]

This being clear, the main issue then becomes how to identify the allegedly breached right and how to determine whether the breach gives rise to a further right to reparation. Therefore, like in direct effect cases, discretion is a key tool for reaching a solution. The array of tools that serve to assess the discretion left in a provision then comes in. A prominent case where the assessment of discretion is central in the Court's reasoning is *Norbrook*,[1051] a preliminary ruling on two directives relating to the approximation of national laws concerning veterinary medicinal products.[1052] The Norbrook Laboratories, which manufactured such products, challenged the British authorisation regime for the marketing of these products, which included conditions not provided for in the directives. One of the questions referred by the Court of Appeal of Northern Ireland was whether the United Kingdom could be held liable for damages caused by

---

1048 *Brasserie and Factortame*, Joined cases C-46/93 and C-48/93, para 7: '*in order for the State to be liable, the third party must be capable of being regarded as beneficiary of the obligation breached, which means that the State is liable for breach only of obligations conceived in favour of a third party*'.

1049 *Brasserie and Factortame*, Joined cases C-46/93 and C-48/93, paras 70-72. Berrod, *La systématique des voies de droit communautaires* 899.

1050 Opinion of AG Tesauro in *Brasserie du pêcheur v Bundesrepublik Deutschland and The Queen v Secretary of State for Transport, ex parte Factortame*, Joined cases C-46/93 and C-48/93, EU:C:1995:407, para 39. Ruffert, 'Rights and Remedies in European Community Law: a Comparative View' 307.

1051 Judgment of 2 April 1998, *Norbrook Laboratories v Ministry of Agriculture, Fisheries and Food*, C-127/95, EU:C:1998:151.

1052 Council Directive 81/851/EEC of 28 September 1981 on the approximation of the laws of the Member States relating to veterinary medicinal products (OJ L 317 p. 1) and Council Directive 81/852/EEC of 28 September 1981 on the approximation of the laws of the Member States relating to analytical, pharmaco-toxicological and clinical standards and protocols in respect of the testing of veterinary medicinal products (OJ L 317 p.16).

the refusal to grant an authorisation, based on these extra conditions. The Court of Justice held that the British authorisation regime was indeed in breach of EU law since the only conditions allowed were those listed in the directives. The Court then went on to assess Norbrook's right to damages. As regards the first liability condition, i.e. that the rule of law infringed must have been intended to confer rights on individuals, the Court found that an application for marketing authorisation may be refused only for the reasons '*laid down precisely and exhaustively*' in the directives, so that '*the scope of the right conferred on applicants for marketing authorisation may therefore be adequately identified on the basis of those directives.*' Again, the Court's fluctuating use of terminology may be confusing, but the reference to precision and exhaustiveness looks a lot like the application of a direct effect test. It is this test, rather than the search for an intention to grant a right, that allows the Court to find that the first condition is met.[1053]

Concerning the second liability condition, the Court recalled '*first, that a breach is sufficiently serious where a Member State, in the exercise of its legislative powers,has manifestly and gravely disregarded the limits on its powers [...] and, second, that where, at the time when it committed the infringement, the Member State in question was not called upon to make any legislative choices and had only considerably reduced, or even no, discretion, the mere infringement of Community law may be sufficient to establish the existence of a sufficiently serious breach [...]*'.[1054] The right clearly identified when testing the first condition amounts to absence of discretion for the Member State, meaning that any breach of that right constitutes a 'sufficiently serious breach.'

Similarly, in *Hedley Lomas*, the UK had imposed a ban on the export of animals for slaughter in Spain, based on the belief that animals would suffer unnecessarily in Spanish slaughterhouses. This was because Spain had transposed a directive against unnecessary cruelty against animals[1055] without providing for any penalty if compulsory stunning prior to slaughter was not actually performed. The company Hedley Lomas applied for a licence to export live sheep to Spain and was denied it by the British Government. The Court found that the ban was indeed contrary to EU law and then turned to the issue of damages.[1056] In order to check for the first lia-

1053 *Norbrook Laboratories v Ministry of Agriculture, Fisheries and Food*, C-127/95, para 108.

1054 *Norbrook Laboratories v Ministry of Agriculture, Fisheries and Food*, C-127/95, para 109.

1055 Council Directive 74/577/EEC of 18 November 1974 on stunning of animals before slaughter (OJ L 316 p.10).

1056 Hartley, *The Foundations of European Union Law* 252.

bility condition, the Court referred to an earlier case where the relevant provisions had been found to be '*directly applicable*' and to '*confer on individual rights which the courts of Member States must protect*', a result which '*flows on the one hand from the very nature of Articles 30 and 34 of the Treaty and on the other hand from Article 189 in the terms of which regulations are 'directly applicable in all Member States*''[1057] and thus found that the first liability condition is fulfilled.[1058] Regarding the second liability condition, the Court stated that where the Member State have '*considerably reduced, or even no, discretion, the mere infringement of Community law may be sufficient to establish the existence of a sufficiently serious breach*', as was the case here.

The similarities between the Court's method for identifying directly effective provisions and its method for finding a right for the purposes of State liability further appear in *Stockholm Lindöpark.*[1059] The company Stockholm Lindöpark is claiming damages from the Swedish state for incorrect transposition of the Sixth VAT. The Swedish court asks, first, whether the Swedish legislation is compatible with the relevant articles of this directive; second, whether these provisions conferred on individuals rights on which they could rely as against Member States before a national court; and third, whether there is a sufficiently serious breach of those provisions so as to make the Swedish state liable in damages. Having negatively answered the first question, the Court then rephrases the second question as follows: '*whether the provisions of Article 17(1) and (2) of the Sixth Directive, read together with those of Articles 2, 6 and 13, are sufficiently clear, precise and unconditional for an individual to rely on them as against a Member State before a national court.*'[1060] By relying on earlier case law on the Sixth Directive, the Court quickly establishes that these provisions have direct effect. Then, the Court points out that given this ability to confer rights on individuals, Lindöpark could rely on these provisions to pursue the debts owed by the Swedish State, even reatroactively, so that an action for damages may not be necessary.[1061] Thus, direct effect is construed as the main medium for applying rights, while liability comes in where direct effect has failed (or been failed).

1057 Judgment of 29 November 1978, *Redmond*, C-83/78, EU:C:1978:214, paras 66-67.

1058 Judgment of 23 May 1996, *The Queen v Ministry of Agriculture, Fisheries and Food, ex parte Hedley Lomas (Ireland)*, C-5/94, EU:C:1996:205, para 27.

1059 Judgment of 18 January 2001, *Stockholm Lindöpark*, C-150/99, EU:C:2001:34.

1060 *Stockholm Lindöpark*, C-150/99, para 29.

1061 *Stockholm Lindöpark*, C-150/99, para 35.

Yet the Court agrees to answer the third question, which focuses on the second liability condition. In so doing, it is implicitly accepting that the first condition is also met (since the final answer is that the breach of the provisions at issue can indeed render a Member State liable in damages).[1062] Then it assesses the second liability condition and finds that given the '*clear wording*' of the Sixth Directive, the Swedish State '*was not in a position to make any legislative choices and had only a considerably reduced, or even no, discretion. In those circumstances, the mere infringement of Community law may be sufficient to establish the existence of a sufficiently serious breach [...].*'[1063] Here again we have this parallel between the clarity of the norm, established when assessing the first condition, and the absence of discretion of the authority who must apply this norm, established when assessing the second condition. For identifying the right and the connected right to reparation, the Court here relies once more on the assessment of the discretion left in the provision, rather than the protective intention that might or might not be detected in this provision.

Discretion is also key in assessing whether the second condition is fulfilled, as seen in *British Telecommunications.*[1064] The first question which arose in this case was whether a Member State was goes as follows: is the Member State was free to determine which telecommunications services are to be excluded from the scope of implementation of Council Directive 90/531/EEC on procurement procedures of entities operating in the water, energy, transport and telecommunications sectors.[1065] The answer was no, because that power is vested in contracting entities themselves; therefore, the Member State is prohibited from exercising such a power. Indeed, the Court explained, that interpretation is consistent with the objective of the directive, which is '*to provide adequate legal protection for suppliers or contractors in the event of infringement of Community legislation on public procurement*'.[1066] The last question was whether, since the UK had in fact done what the directive prohibited, it may be liable in damages. The Court first recalled the conditions for the right to reparation as established in *Brasserie*

1062 *Stockholm Lindöpark*, C-150/99, para 42.

1063 *Stockholm Lindöpark*, C-150/99, paras 39-40.

1064 Judgment of 26 March 1996, *The Queen v H.M. Treasury, ex parte British Telecommunications*, C-392/93, EU:C:1996:131.

1065 Council Directive 90/531/EEC of 17 September 1990 on the procurement procedures of entities operating in the water, energy, transport and telecommunications sectors (OJ L 297 p. 1).

1066 *The Queen v H.M. Treasury, ex parte British Telecommunications*, C-392/93, para 26.

du Pêcheur, and stated that these conditions were applicable to the situation in which a Member State incorrectly transposes a directive.[1067] While the first liability condition was not explicitly examined, the Court's answer to the first question from the British court, based on a systemic and teleological interpretation of the provisions at issue and focusing on the objectives laid down in the preamble of the directive, did lead to the acknowledgement that the directive was intended to protect certain individuals (the suppliers and contractors). This was confirmed by the fact that the Court, when answering the question on liability, focuses directly on the second liability condition. Having listed the conditions from *Brasserie*, it then provided the elements which may help determine the existence of a sufficiently serious breach also based on past jurisprudence: '*a breach is sufficiently serious where, in the exercise of its legislative powers, an institution or a Member State has manifestly and gravely disregarded the limits on the exercise of its powers […]. Factors which the competent court may take into consideration include the clarity and precision of the rule breached […].*' The Court then assessed whether the facts amounted to a sufficiently serious breach of Community law in light of what it found to be a provision '*imprecisely worded and […] reasonably capable of bearing, as well as the construction applied to it by the Court in this judgment, the interpretation given to it by the United Kingdom in good faith […].*'[1068] The conclusion was that the UK's decision to determine the services to be excluded from the scope of application of the provisionin question was not a sufficiently serious breach of Community law. What we see here is a test of clarity and precision, not unlike the test applied in other contexts to check whether a provision grants directly effective rights; in this case it is applied to check whether the Member State went beyond the limits to its discretion. Ultimately, the intention to grant a right, even though it has been established in the first part of the Court's reasoning, does not matter as much as the lack of clarity and precision of the provision breached, which eliminates the possibility of acknowledging a right to reparation.

An additional illustration of this approach in cross-border taxation of dividends. The *Denkavit* case[1069] required interpretation of a provision of

1067 *The Queen v H.M. Treasury, ex parte British Telecommunications*, C-392/93, para 39-40.

1068 *The Queen v H.M. Treasury, ex parte British Telecommunications*, C-392/93, para 42-44.

1069 Judgment of 17 October 1996, *Denkavit Internationaal and Others v Bundesamt für Finanzen*, C-283/94, EU:C:1996:387.

the Parent-Subsidiary Directive,[1070] which provided for exemption in the State of the subsidiary from withholding tax upon distribution of profits, and of another provision of this directive, which gave Member States the option of making entitlement to that tax advantage subject to a minimum holding period which the Member States were free to set but which could not exceed two years. Having given an interpretation of the relevant provisions based on literal and purposive interpretation,[1071] the Court then assesses the possibility to grant damages and does not even check the first liability condition: the provision breached did not lay down a sufficiently clear obligation,[1072] which explains why there is no need to search for a correlative right.

In the same vein, the Court issued the famous *Köbler* judgment on the possibility for a Member State to be liable for a ruling of its supreme constitutional court, which had failed to refer to the CJEU for a preliminary ruling on the freedom of movement of workers enshrined at Article 48 EC and Article 7(1) of the Regulation on the free movement of workers.[1073] The Court held that this was indeed a rule intended to confer rights.[1074] This rule had been breached following the failure of the constitutional court to comply with its obligation under Article 234 EC (now Article 267 TFEU) to lodge a reference for preliminary ruling. However, the provision did not lay down a clear and precise obligation on the Member State on how to act in the specific circumstances of the case, nor could a solution be clearly delineated based on previous CJEU case law; in addition, it was this previous case law that led the constitutional court to the erroneous, but excusable conclusion that the case could be solved without referring to the Court of Justice for interpretation of Article 48.[1075] Therefore, no serious breach could be established, meaning in turn that no right to damages

1070 Council Directive 90/435/EEC of 23 July 1990 on the common system of taxation applicable in the case of parent companies and subsidiaries of different Member States (OJ L 225 p. 6).

1071 M. Tenore, 'The Scope for 'Consistent Interpretation' in the Area of Dividend Taxation' in P. Pistone (ed), *Legal Remedies in European Tax Law* (IBFD 2009) 37-41.

1072 *Denkavit Internationaal and Others v Bundesamt für Finanzen*, C-283/94, paras 50-53.

1073 Council Regulation (EEC) No 1612/68 of 15 October 1968 on freedom of movement for workers within the Community (OJ English Special Edition 1968 (II) p. 475).

1074 *Köbler*, C-224/01, paras 102-103.

1075 *Köbler*, C-224/01, para 122.

could be acknowledged.[1076] In light of this case, Dougan has argued that connecting right and obligation in the context of Member State liability is an artificial construction. In his view, even though the infringed 'right' is enshrined in Article 48 EC, the assessment of the 'sufficiently serious breach' is actually made by reference to the obligation of Article 234 EC.[1077] In fact, the correlativity between the right and the obligation retains its relevance in the context of State liability, if we consider that a given jural correlative is not to be taken in isolation, but rather arises out of a network of sources of obligations and rights. Indeed, it is not uncommon that an obligation (and correlative right) would arise not from one provision, but from a combination of provisions. In this case, the Court acknowledged the margin of appreciation of the constitutional court in applying Article 48 EC by reference to Article 234 EC. Conversely, one provision can contain the seed of several rights, to be materialised differently (or not at all) depending on the situation: it is not by chance that the Court generally assesses whether a provision gives rise to (or is intended to confer) 'rights' in the plural.

Sadly for European pigs, but interestingly for European human beings, the trade of pig meat has repeatedly been inspirational for clarifying the concept of rights in EU law. Almost four decades after *Politi* which made clear that individuals could derive rights from regulations,[1078] a contemporary reaffirmation that the correlation between obligations and rights is central to identifying rights is to be found in the *Danske Slagterier* case.[1079] This time it concerns the finding of rights in directives on the marketing of meat, including in liability cases. This case is a meaningful example essentially because of the contrast between the Advocate General's approach to the detection of individual rights, and the method eventually used by the Court. By an earlier judgment the ECJ had held that Germany had failed to fulfil its obligations under two directives on health problems and veterinary checks in intra-Community trade in fresh meat.[1080] A Danish association of slaughterhouse companies lodged an action for damages against

1076 *Köbler*, C-224/01, para 126.

1077 M. Dougan, 'Addressing Issues of Protective Scope within the Francovich Right to Reparation' (2017) 13 European Constitutional Law Review 124 128-130.

1078 *Politi v. Ministero delle finanze*, C-43/71. See p. 241 of this work.

1079 Judgment of 24 March 2009, *Danske Slagterier*, C-445/06, ECLI:EU:C:2009:178.

1080 Council Directive 64/433/EEC of 26 June 1964 on health conditions for the production and marketing of fresh meat (OJ English Special Edition 1963-64 p. 185), as amended by Council Directive 91/497/EEC of 29 July 1991 (OJ L

Germany, since it had suffered loss due to the incorrect transposition, which amounted to imposing a de facto import ban on meat from non-castrated male pigs from Denmark. Such a ban, precisely, was prohibited by the directives at issue. In order to determine whether the violation of this prohibition could give rise to damages, it was necessary to apply the *Francovich* test to the relevant provisions of the directives.

In order to perform this test, Advocate General Trstenjak first reviews the Court's case law on individual rights and quotes cases – including *Francovich, Norbrook,* and *StockholmLindöpark*[1081] - where the Court found that directives did grant individual rights. In her view, this was because these directives either explicitly granted either private law rights in the form of a right to compensation to employees or consumers, or public law rights vis-à-vis the authorities to a specific benefit. Only in these two scenarios, she argues, does a directive entail the grant of rights to individuals and thus fulfil the third branch of the *Francovich* test. Here, however, '*the purpose of those directives is not to protect the rights of producers and only Member States are obliged to take action*'.[1082] Advocate General Trstenjak thus upholds the view that obligations of Member States and rights of individuals should be dissociated. She argues that the Court's earlier case law '*cannot in any way mean ... that an individual right may be derived automatically from the imposition of an obligation of Member States*". She adds that '*the doctrine relating to 'subjective' public law rights supports the existence of a 'subjective' right if a provision of mandatory law is intended to serve not only the public interest but in addition at least the interest of particular individuals*.'[1083] Her conclusion is that since the obligations provided for by the directives do not translate into individual rights, the applicants cannot be granted damages because of the violation of these obligations. She leaves open the possibility that they might be awarded damages if the national court determines that the infringement of the directives amount to an infringement of the rights of citizens as established by Article 28 EC (primary law). In her view, the direct effect of EU law obligations and their justiciability as rights, including

268 p. 69) and Council Directive 89/662/EEC of 11 December 1989 concerning veterinary checks in intra-Community trade with a view to the completion of the internal market (OJ L 395 p. 13).

1081 *Francovich and Bonifaci v. Italy,* Joined cases C-6/90 and C-9/90; *Norbrook Laboratories v Ministry of Agriculture, Fisheries and Food*, C-127/95; *Stockholm Lindöpark,* C-150/99.

1082 Opinion of AG Trstenjak in *Danske Slagterier*, C-445/06, EU:C:2008:464, para 64-71.

1083 Opinion of AG Trstenjak in *Danske Slagterier*, C-445/06, para 72.

in liability suits, would thus be excluded from all directive provisions not expressly intended to grant individual rights. This view was also defended by five Member States who had submitted observations.[1084]

It is no coincidence that the Advocate General often refers to German law and legal literature in her Opinion – especially with regard to the doctrine of subjective public rights. She primarily relies on writings in the field of German public law; although she then extends her references to literature on EC/EU law, it is only German literature on the topic and she focuses on those writers who support the transposition of the German subjective rights doctrine into EU law for the purpose of identifying individual rights.[1085] However, the Court did not follow the Advocate General and instead clearly dismissed the intentionalist approach that she was pushing for. Instead, relying on *Brasserie* and *Factortame*,[1086] the Court first recalled that '*it is undisputed that Article 28 EC has direct effect in the sense that it confers on individuals rights upon which they are entitled to rely directly before the national courts and that breach of that provision may give rise to reparation*'. The directives at issue were further defining and giving concrete expression to these rights. The Court then maintained that it was perfectly conceivable that a provision laying down a negative obligation upon the Member States (and which in the case at issue clearly did not involve the slightest intention to grant rights to individuals) would translate into an individual right: '*the prohibition on Member States preventing importation gives individuals the right to market in another Member State fresh meat that complies with the Community requirements*'.[1087]

This correspondence between a prohibition for Member States and a right for individuals functions according to what Simon and Rigaux call '*la*

1084 D. Simon and A. Rigaux, 'La responsabilité des Etats membres en cas de violation du droit communautaire revisitée, ou comment le problème technique de l'odeur sexuelle des porcs non castrés conduit à trancher des questions fondamentales' (2009) 19 Europe, point 6.

1085 Opinion of AG Trstenjak in *Danske Slagterier*, C-445/06, paras 33-34. The cited literature on German public law includes: H. Maurer, *Allgemeines Verwaltungsrecht* (11 edn, Beck 1997); R. Alexy, *Theorie der Grundrechte* (Suhrkamp 1985); and references to Windscheid, Jhering and Jellinek. German-language literature on EU rights includes: M. Nettesheim, Die mitgliedstaatliche Durchführung von EG-Richtlinien (Duncker & Humblot 1999); S. Beljin, *Staatshaftung im Europarecht* (Beck 2000).

1086 *Brasserie du pêcheur v Bundesrepublik Deutschland and The Queen v Secretary of State for Transport, ex parte Factortame*, C-46/93 and C-48/93.

1087 *Danske Slagterier*, C-445/06, paras 22-24.

plus pure logique de l'‘effet réflexe’ du droit communautaire’.[1088] Just like in *van Gend en Loos*, the intentionalist interpretation, relying on a literal reading of the provision at stake, is irrelevant; a negative obligation (a prohibition) on the Member States simply translates into a (positive) right for individuals. Since this prohibition was itself a more precise version of the right to the free movement of goods enshrined in the Treaties, the Court concluded: ‘*individuals who have been harmed by the incorrect transposition and application of Directives 64/433 and 89/662 may rely on the right to the free movement of goods in order to be able to render the State liable for the breach of Community law*’.[1089] It also shows again how the first liability condition is fulfilled whenever the rule allegedly breached has direct effect. The second liability condition is not assessed explicitly by the Court – perhaps because the referring court did not focus on it, but the Court's final answer nevertheless constitutes an implicit acknowledgement that this condition is satisfied. Keeping in mind the liability cases we have seen above, it makes sense since a provision which is sufficiently clear and precise to give rise to directly effective rights conversely leaves the public authority no discretion in the fulfilment of the corresponding obligation.

The cases on Member State liability can be a significant source of confusion for one who seeks to define the nature and function of rights in this context. On the one hand, we have a requirement of a ‘rule intended to confer rights’ which could signal a break from the ‘classic’ conception of rights consecrated in *Van Gend en Loos*; on the other hand, such protective intention is often not researched by the Court, the focus being instead on the scope of the obligations and corresponding rights, the violation of which may give rise to damages. In fact, the protective intention may as an extra safeguard for individuals, giving them one more chance to pass the first leg of the liability test in cases where the rule on which they rely does not have direct effect. This is what had happened, for instance, in *Francovich*.[1090]

By contrast, if the direct effect of a provision has been established, the Court does not look for the intention to confer a right and considers the first liability condition to be fulfilled. In such a case it becomes rather sim-

1088 Simon and Rigaux, ‘La responsabilité des Etats membres en cas de violation du droit communautaire revisitée, ou comment le problème technique de l'odeur sexuelle des porcs non castrés conduit à trancher des questions fondamentales’ point 8.

1089 *Danske Slagterier*, C-445/06, para 26.

1090 *Francovich and Bonifaci v. Italy*, Joined cases C-6/90 and C-9/90. See p. 192 of this work.

ple to assess the second condition: since there is no discretion left to the Member State when a provision is sufficiently clear, precise, unconditional, exhaustive, etc. (depending, again, on the very flexible terminology) to give rise to directly effective rights, any breach of that provision would mean that the breach of EU law is 'sufficiently serious' and thus that the second condition is also fulfilled. In this respect, *Danske Slagterier* unequivocally confirms what *Brasserie* and *Factortame* already made clear. This judgment, and the way it radically differs from the assessment of the Advocate General, supports Ruffert's analysis of the earlier *Becker* case as meaning that a directive can grant rights even if no clear intention to grant rights is identifiable.[1091] Precisely, just like in direct effect cases, while the intention to confer a right *may* be inferred from the analysis, it does not condition the acknowledgement of a right, but merely facilitates it in some cases. This goes against the *Schutznorm* reading of the Court's approach to rights in liability cases (and possibly beyond). Advocate General Trstenjak pointed out that the interpretation alternative to her own would have '*every economic interest of market participants satisfied on the elimination of barriers to intra-Community trade*' translate into an individual right. In her view, *[t]he mere fact that an individual derives an advantage from a legal rule does not [...] establish in itself a 'subjective' right, but provides at most a favourable legal effect by rebound*.'[1092] Her argument precisely illustrates a recurring sticking point: this 'reflex' effect that is so limited in German law and other similar legal systems, is in fact inherent in EU individual rights and thus central to the functioning of EU law.[1093] The combination of an clearly defined obligation and an existing interest suffices, provided that infringement and damage are proven, to ground a right to reparation of the damage sustained.

2.1.1.2.2. Union liability: the fluctuating receptiveness to the Schutznorm approach

By comparison, the case law on Union liability indicates much less eagerness to acknowledge such a reflex effect, and to a certain extent it even in-

1091 Ruffert, 'Rights and Remedies in European Community Law: a Comparative View' 314.

1092 Opinion of AG Trstenjak in *Danske Slagterier*, C-445/06, para 72.

1093 Simon and Rigaux, 'La responsabilité des Etats membres en cas de violation du droit communautaire revisitée, ou comment le problème technique de l'odeur sexuelle des porcs non castrés conduit à trancher des questions fondamentales'

tegrates a *Schutznorm* approach. This was already so in an ECSC liability case, where the rule allegedly breached, i.e. the free movement of goods and the High Authority's obligation to take action to ensure respect of this freedom under the ECSC Treaty, was '*not intended to protect the interests of any third parties, but only the interests of the Community*' and therefore could not lead, if breached, to the award of damages.[1094]

However, one of the early cases on EEC liability suggested that, although a protective intention in the norm allegedly breached might be relevant, this protective intention should be understood in a generous way. In *Kampffmeyer*, German companies had been refused an import licence by the German authorities for a stock of French maize, and the ban had been confirmed by the Commission.[1095] The refusal had been based on determination by the Commission of the applicable intra-Community levies, on which the companies had relied for their strategy in requesting import licenses. These levies, as determined in a previous ruling, were in fact erroneous.[1096] The company decided to seek damages from the Commission for having wrongly applied EU legislation. Back then the conditions for liability were not yet set in their current shape and order. The Court started by examining the Commission's behaviour (which would nowadays amount to assessing the second liability condition). The Court found that the Commission had indeed incorrectly applied the relevant conditions and '*committed a wrongful act or omission capable of giving rise to liability on the part of the Community*'. At the time, the Court did not reason explicitly in terms of rights and focused instead on whether the rule '*intended to protect*' individual '*interests*'.[1097] The Commission argued that its duty to verify the legality of protective measures was '*not laid down in the interests of the applicants, but in the collective interest of the proper functioning of the common*

1094 Judgment of 14 July 1961, *Vloeberghs v High Authority*, C-9/60, EU:C:1961:18, p. 217. E. Grabitz, 'Liability for Legislative Acts' in H.G. Schermers, T. Heukels and P. Mead (eds), *Non-contractual liability of the European Communities* (Martinus Nijhoff Publishers 1988) 6.

1095 Judgment of 14 July 1967, *Kampffmeyer and Others v Commission of the EEC*, Joined cases C-5/66, C-13/66, C-16/66, C-21/66, EU/C/1967:31, p. 262.

1096 Judgment of 1 July 1965, *Toepfer v Commission of the EEC*, Joined cases C-106 and 107/63, EU:C:1965:65.

1097 There is no explicit reason why the lexical switch from 'interests' to 'rights' took place. It is possible that the Court adapted its language to be consistent with an increasing use of a rights language (both in the case law and the doctrine).

organisation of the markets in cereals.'[1098] However, by relying on the preamble of the relevant regulation, the Court found that the objectives of this regulation included not only the evolution in the agricultural markets, but also the development of the free movement of goods and, more specifically, '*the interests of the producers in the Member States and of free trade between these States*' were expressly mentioned. The Court found that even though the provisions at issue were '*of a general nature*', this did not prevent '*their including the interests of individual undertakings such as the applicants*'; and the Court went on: '[a]*lthough the application of the rules of law in question is not in general capable of being of direct and individual concern to the said undertakings, that does not prevent the possibility that the protection of their interests may be [...] intended by those rules of law.*'[1099] Unlike what would happen if the restrictive *Schutznorm* doctrine were applied, the intention to protect an individual interest does not need to be very specific or express – it seems like the slightest intention to protect an individual interest (even if it overlaps with a general one)[1100] is sufficient for the condition to be fulfilled, as was the case here in *Kampffmeyer*.[1101]

This impression was short-lived: not long afterwards the *Schöppenstedt* ruling led to the idea that the Court was acknowledging a much more restrictive *Schutznorm* test.[1102] Indeed, the Court established in *Schöppenstedt* that Community liability for the violation of legislative action involving

1098 *Kampffmeyer and Others v Commission of the EEC*, Joined cases C-5/66, C-13/66, C-16/66, C-21/66, p.252.

1099 *Kampffmeyer and Others v Commission of the EEC*, Joined cases C-5/66, C-13/66, C-16/66, C-21/66, p. 262; Mariatte and Munoz, *Contentieux de l'Union européenne / 2 - Carence. Responsabilité* 240; Lenaerts, Maselis and Gutman, *EU Procedural Law* 516.

1100 H.-M. Voigts, Die Subjektivierung von Gemeinwohlinteressen als Demokratisierung der Verwaltung (LIT Verlag 2016) 88; Saüberlich, *Die außervertragliche Haftung im Gemeinschaftsrecht. Eine Untersuchung der Mehrpersonenverhältnisse* 22.

1101 It should be noted however that the Court reserved calculation and award of damages until the German courts had determined the extent of the liability of the German State in this case, thus initiating an approach according to which EU liability can be invoked only once the legality of national measures implementing the EU act has been examined by national courts (if necessary also by recourse to preliminary ruling procedure). See a discussion of this requirement of a 'procedural detour' in Bebr, *Development of Judicial Control of the European Communities* 244-247. See also H. Schermers, *Judicial Protection in the European Communities* (Springer 2013) 316-318.

1102 S. Douglas-Scott, *Constitutional Law of the European Union* (Pearson Education 2002) 331; see also N. Reich, 'Rights without Duties? Reflections on the State

choices of economic policy required '*a sufficiently flagrant violation of a superior rule of law for the protection of the individual*',[1103] a condition that the Court maintained in subsequent rulings.[1104]

The same stringent requirement was for instance applied with regard to the EU system of allocation of powers which the Court, in the *Vreugdenhil* ruling, held was not a rule of law conferring rights on individuals for the purposes of damages. The European Commission had modified a regulation laying down the rules applicable to goods 'returned' to the customs territory of the Community.[1105] The system allowed goods which had been exported from the Community to then be re-imported free of import duties, and the provision added by the Commission introduced an exception for certain categories of goods. In an earlier judgment in a preliminary ruling procedure, the Court had found that this provision was invalid because it had not been adopted based on the correct procedure and thus did not respect the principle of institutional balance.[1106] As the Vreugdenhil company had originally been required to pay import duties on the goods it was re-importing, subsequently to the first procedure it introduced another one to seek damages from the Community. However, as regards the condition of '*a sufficiently serious breach of a superior rule of law for the protection of the individual*', the Court held that the aim of the institutional division of powers '*is to ensure that the balance between the institutions provided for in the Treaty is maintained, and not to protect individuals*' and that therefore a failure to observe this division could not on its own engage the Community's liability towards the traders concerned.'[1107] The Court focused on the addressees of the obligation (i.e., the Institutions), denying any relational im-

---

of Liability Law in the Multilevel Governance System of the Community: Is There a Need for a More Coherent Approach in European Private Law?' (2009) EUI Working Papers, Law 2009/10.

1103 *Zuckerfabrik Schöppenstedt v Council*, 5/71, para 11; A. Biondi and M. Farley, *The Right to Damages in European Law* 107. See also above p. 218.

1104 E.g.: *Ludwigshafener Walzmühle v Council and Commission*, Joined cases C-197 to C-200, C-243, C-245 and C-247/80, para 19; *Zuckerfabrik Bedburg v Council and Commission*, C-281/84, para 18; *AERPO and Others v Commission*, C-119/88, para 8.

1105 Commission Regulation No 1687/76 of 30 June 1976 laying down common detailed rules for verifying the use and/or destination of products from intervention, (OJ L 190 p. 1), amended by Commission Regulation (EEC) No 45/84 of 6 January 1984 (OJ L 7 p. 5).

1106 Judgment of 29 June 1989, *Vreugdenhil*, C-22/88, EU:C:1989:277.

1107 *Vreugdenhil v Commission*, C-282/90, paras 20-22; Simon (ed), Mariatte and Munoz, *Contentieux de l'Union européenne / 2 - Carence. Responsabilité* 242.

plications of the obligation and ignoring the other side of the medal: the potential correlative right of the concerned individuals.

Even more radical in this respect was *Lefebvre.* The CFI had to rule on the implementation of the common organisation of the market in bananas and held that certain provisions of the EC Treaty on the establishment of a common agricultural policy (now Articles 38(4) TFEU and 43(2) TFEU) could not be construed as conferring rights on individuals. This was because these provisions '*merely impose[d] obligations on the institutions; they [were] not intended to protect individuals.*' Therefore they were not superior rules of law the breach of which could cause the Community to incur liability.[1108] Here, the CFI differentiated between those provisions which establish general rules for the implementation of a policy, and those which are specifically *intended* to confer rights on individuals;[1109] in so doing, it explicitly opposed the obligations on the institutions and the protection of individuals.

The connection between obligations and rights is however not completely denied. It is indirectly validated by the importance, for determining whether the EU is liable in damages, of evaluating the discretion left to the EU institutions by the rule allegedly breached. In the case *Lütticke,* the applicant had lodged an action for damages against the Commission for failing to address to Germany a directive or a decision ordering it to abolish or at least reduce its turnover equalization tax on milk powder. The Commission had followed up on Germany's progress and required reduction, but not sufficiently according to the applicant. The ruling however highlights the discretion of the authorities on two levels. Firstly, EU law leaves discretion to the Member States in the process of reducing these taxes: in the exercise of the task of supervision '*account should be taken of the margin of discretion left to the Member States concerned*'.[1110] Secondly, the Court points out that, as the expert's report produced by the applicant shows, although the average rate for powdered milk should be lower, there are also a number of '*uncertain factors which may give rise to very different assessments, with the result that it is in general possible only to establish certain minimum and maximum limits between which several solutions appear equally justifiable*'.[1111] This can also be understood in terms of the discretion left to the Commission

1108 Judgment of 14 September 1995, *Lefebvre and Others v Commission,* T-571/93, ECR, EU:T:1995:163, para 41.

1109 Simon (ed), Mariatte and Munoz, *Contentieux de l'Union européenne / 2 - Carence. Responsabilité* 241.

1110 *Lütticke v Commission,* C-4/69, para 17.

1111 *Lütticke v Commission,* C-4/69, para 18.

in assessing the adequacy of the Member State's response. As a consequence, the Court dismissed the action for damages without applying any more specific criteria.

In other cases, a protective intention is found in the allegedly breached rule, and discretion is assessed in a second step in order to control the very stringently construed condition of a 'sufficiently serious breach'. In *Bayrische HNL*[1112] the Court clarified how this requirement was to be assessed. A Council Regulation on the compulsory purchase of skimmed-milk powder[1113] had been found null by a previous ruling on validity.[1114] The Court maintained the *Schöppenstedt* line of reasoning, according to which liability on account of a legislative measure involving choices of economic policy required '*a sufficiently serious breach of a superior rule of law for the protection of the individual*'.[1115] In this case, it admitted that the rule relied on (the prohibition on discrimination in the common organization of the agricultural markets, laid down in Article 40(3) EEC) was indeed designed for the protection of the individual. But it observed that in Member States generally, '*the public authorities can only exceptionnally and in special circumstances incur liability for legislative measures which are the result of choices of economic policy*'. This was justified by the consideration that the legislative process cannot always be hindered by the prospect of applications for damages.[1116] Therefore individuals active in sectors that come within the economic policy of the Union have to accept '*within reasonable limits certain harmful effects on their economic interests as a result of a legislative measure*', without being able to claim reparation even if the measure is found to be illegal. In a field where '*wide discretion*' is '*essential for the implementation of the Common Agricultural Policy*', '*the Community does not therefore incur liability unless the institution concerned has manifestly and gravely disregarded the limits on the exercise of its powers.*'[1117] This was not the case in the precise situation which required fixation of prices for feeding-stuff, considering

---

1112 Judgment of 25 May 1978, *HNL v Council and Commission*, Joined cases C-83 and C-94/76, 4, 15 and 40/77, EU:C:1978:113.

1113 Council Regulation (EEC) No 563/76 of 15 March 1976 on the compulsory purchase of skimmed-milk powder held by intervention agencies for use in feeding-stuffs (OJ L 67 p.18).

1114 Judgment of 5 July 1977, *Bela Mühle v Grows Farm*, C-114/76, EU:C:1977:116.

1115 *HNL v Council and Commission*, Joined cases C-83 and C-94/76, 4, 15 and 40/77, para 4.

1116 *HNL v Council and Commission*, Joined cases C-83 and C-94/76, 4, 15 and 40/77, para 5.

1117 *HNL v Council and Commission*, Joined cases C-83 and C-94/76, 4, 15 and 40/77, para 6. See also *Ireks-Arkady v Council and Commission*, C-238/78, para 10, *Etoile*

also that '*the effects of the regulation on the profit-earning capacity of the undertakings did not ultimately exceed the bounds of the economic risks inherent in the activities of the agricultural sectors concerned*.'[1118]

In the same vein, the *Quellmehl* ruling maintained that the damage alleged must go beyond the bounds of the normal economic risks inherent in the activities in the sector concerned[1119] but here, unlike in *HNL* the 'manifestly and gravely' condition was met, as the Court found after having laid down and the following criteria: the importance of the rule breached, the number of affected parties and the extent to which the group is well-defined, the degree of damage, and the absence of adequate justification.[1120] The second of these conditions indicates a concern that the action for damages might turn into an *actio popularis*. While such a solution makes sense if we worry exclusively about not hindering the EU legislator's action in the public interest, it is however questionable from the perspective of protection of individuals since it implies that the more diffuse the damageable consequences are, the less likely individuals are to obtain reparation.

The requirements became less stringent with the *Bergaderm* ruling, which is known for having aligned the conditions for EU liability with those for Member State liability, especially by dropping the requirement that the rule of law infringed be 'superior'.[1121] The CFI applied this solu-

commerciale and CNTA v Commission, Joined cases C-89/86 and C-91/86, para 16.

1118 *HNL v Council and Commission*, Joined cases C-83 and C-94/76, 4, 15 and 40/77, para 7.

1119 *Ireks-Arkady v Council and Commission*, C-238/78, para 11. See also Judgment of 4 October 1979, *DGV v Council and Commission*, Joined cases C-241, C-242 and C-246 to C-249/78, EU:C:1979:227, para 11; Judgment of 4 October 1979, *Dumortier v Council*, C-64/76, EU:C:1979:223, para 11; *Mulder and Others v Council and Commission*, Joined cases C-104/89 and C-37/90, para 13.

1120 *Ireks-Arkady v Council and Commission*, C-238/78, para 11. Grabitz, 'Liability for Legislative Acts' 9. See also Judgment of 27 June 1991, *Stahlwerke Peine-Selzgitter v Commission*, T-120/89, EU:T:1991:32, para 136. Other examples of cases where the stringent conditions were fulfilled and damages were awarded include: *Etoile commerciale and CNTA v Commission*, Joined cases C-89/86 and C-91/86 and Judgment of 26 June 1990, *Sofrimport SARL v Commission*, C-152/88, EU:C:1990:259. The liability in these cases was established for violation of the principle of protection of legitimate expectations, to be further analysed below p. 298.

1121 *Bergaderm and Goupil v Commission*, C-352/98 P, para 42 (citing *Brasserie du pêcheur v Bundesrepublik Deutschland and The Queen v Secretary of State for Trans-*

tion in *San Pedro*, noting that it did not matter whether or not the rule of law constituted a higher-ranking rule of law.[1122]

It seems however that there is more reluctance to truly align with the spirit of the first liability condition, which, as we have seen concerning Member State liability, does not involve a test of protective intention except where it might add some extra layer of protection for individuals.[1123] In some rulings the General Court indeed requires that '*the protection offered by the rule invoked must be effective vis-à-vis the person who invokes it and that person must […] be among those on whom the rule in question confers rights*'.[1124] In *Artegodan*, an undertaking had applied for damages incurred by a Commission decision withdrawing marketing authorisation for certain medicinal products. The company relied on the *Kampffmeyer* approach according to which damages may be awarded where the rule of law breached, while referring essentially to interests of a general nature, also ensures the protection of the individual interests of the undertakings concerned and the General Court ruled in favour of Artegodan, validating this broad conception of interest protection.[1125] Then the Court of Justice overturned the ruling by relying on *Vreugdenhil* and held that the system of division of powers between the institutions did not in itself intend to confer

---

port, ex parte Factortame, C-46/93 and C-48/93, para 51): '*Community law confers a right to reparation where three conditions are met: the rule of law infringed must be intended to confer rights on individuals; the breach must be sufficiently serious; and there must be a direct causal link between the breach of the obligation resting on the State and the damage sustained by the injured parties)*'. See also Judgment of 19 April 2007, *Holcim (Deutschland) v Commission*, C-282/05 P, EU:C:2007:226, para 47; *FIAMM and Others v Council and Commission*, Joined cases C-120/06 P and C-121/06 P, paras 172 and 173.

1122 Judgment of 19 October 2005, *Cofradía de pescadores 'San Pedro' de Bermeo and Others v Council*, T-415/03, EU:T:2005:365, para 85. The rule in question was the principle of relative stability of fishing activities of each Member States, which the applicants claimed the Council had infringed by transferring fishing quotas from Portugal to France. Aalto, *Public liability in EU law: Brasserie, Bergaderm and beyond* 41.

1123 See the conclusions of the previous section, p. 268.

1124 Judgment of 12 September 2007, *Nikolaou v Commission*, T-259/03, EU:T:2007:254, para 44; Judgment of 9 July 2009, *Ristic and others v Parliament*, T-238/07, EU:T:2009:263; Judgment of 3 December 2015, *CN v Parliament*, T-343/13, EU:T:2015:926, para 86.

1125 Judgment of 3 March 2010, *Artegodan v Commission*, T-429/05, EU:T:2010:60, para 89.

rights on individuals.[1126] The Court saw apparently no problem in citing *Bergaderm* in one paragraph and in the next to again require the infringement of '*a superior rule of law protecting individuals*'.[1127]

This did not prevent the General Court from further relying on *Kampffmeyer* in *Gap granen* regarding import duties on cereals,[1128] holding that although the relevant regulation[1129] aimed mainly towards the protection of the internal market and the Union's financial interests, its provisions on the determination of import prices were intended to ensure that import taxes were calculated in an objective, foreseeable and transparent way and that, therefore, they also ensured the protection of individual interests and had to be considered as rules intended to confer rights on individuals.[1130] Thus, the alignment of Union liability conditions on Member State liability conditions in *Bergaderm* certainly did not cause the influence of judgments such as *Schöppenstedt* and *Vreugdenhil* to disappear overnight. Still, little by little the EU Courts might draw the conclusions from *Bergaderm* and make clear that the *Schutznorm* doctrine in the context of Union liability is (at most) of very limited relevance.

2.1.1.3. Interim conclusions

The basic characteristics of rights identified in *Van Gend en Loos* and *Defrenne II* are abundantly and consistently illustrated in the case law on the direct effect of primary and secondary Union law relating to the funda-

---

1126 *Artegodan v Commission*, C-221/10 P, para 81: '*[…] whilst a failure to observe the system of the division of powers between the various institutions of the European Union, whose aim is to ensure that the balance between the institutions provided for in the Treaties is maintained, and not to protect individuals, cannot be sufficient on its own to render the European Union liable towards the traders concerned, the position would be different if a measure of the European Union were to be adopted which not only disregarded the division of powers between the institutions but also, in its substantive provisions, disregarded a superior rule of law protecting individuals*'.

1127 *Artegodan v Commission*, C-221/10 P, paras 80-81.

1128 Judgment of 16 May 2013, *Gap granen & producten v Commission*, T-437/10, EU:T:2013:248.

1129 Commission Regulation (EC) No 1249/96 of 28 June 1996 on rules of application (cereal sector import duties) for Council Regulation (EEC) No 1766/92 (OJ L 161 p. 125).

1130 *Gap granen & producten v Commission*, T-437/10, paras 22-24. See also in the area of the Common Foreign and Security Policy: Judgment of 23 November 2011, *Sison v Council*, T-341/07, EU:T:2011:687, para 47.

mental freedoms. Provisions that are sufficiently clear, precise and unconditional may be relied on by individuals who have an interest in doing so, no matter whether they are expressly phrased as rights or, more often, as negative or positive obligations. The question whether there is a protective intention underlying a given norm is of little relevance for assessing the ability of this norm to give rise to rights – neither directly effective rights, nor rights in liability cases. In both direct effect cases and Member State liability cases, the dual rationale of individual rights is very present and materialises in the mechanism of functional subjectivation: individuals by protecting their own interests, also contribute (with the assistance of national courts) to the enforcement of Union law.

The case law on the liability of the Union however outlines the limits of this conceptual harmony.[1131] There is some acceptance of the classic correlation between obligations and rights, from which concrete consequences are triggered where individual interests are identifiable, like in the early *Kampffmeyer* case. Still, overall, the Court is less faithful to the correlativity model and much more more sympathetic to the protective norm approach which requires that the interests or rights have been pre-defined so that they can be protected.[1132] Somewhat paradoxically (considering that the *Schutznorm* approach aims to identify 'subjective rights'), even the term 'right' rarely appears in EU liability cases, and individual rights do not have in this context the pivotal importance that they have in State liability cases. Since discretion is a key criterion in assessing public liability (of the Union as well as of Member States), we can reconstruct rights, even where they remain implicit, based on the idea that the probability to identify a right in a provision is inversely proportional to the degree of discretion allowed by this provision.[1133] However, the assessment of the violation by reference to the discretion left by the norm is not to the advantage of individuals, since the Court has been more prompt to acknowledge broad discretion to the EU legislator (than to Member States), making the requirement of a manifest and grave breach difficult to prove.

The case law on direct effect and damages in the area of fundamental freedoms therefore exemplifies two historical tensions in the development of individual rights under EU law. One is the *Schutznorm* pressure, which

1131 Aalto, *Public liability in EU law: Brasserie, Bergaderm and beyond* 42.

1132 Saüberlich has rightly observed that the *Schutznorm* doctrine appears to be less easily transposed to Member State liability than to Union liability: U. Saüberlich, *Die außervertragliche Haftung im Gemeinschaftsrecht. Eine Untersuchung der Mehrpersonenverhältnisse* (Springer 2005) 193.

1133 See especially p. 249 of this work.

the Court consistently resists in direct effect cases as well as in the case law on Member State liability. The other tension emerges when Union liability is added to the picture: it is the discrepancy between the system of identification and protection of rights on the Union level and the one on the level of the Member States.

2.1.2. Individual rights in EU competition law

Unlike fundamental freedoms, which have primarily a positive content for individuals and a negative content for Member States, EU competition law provisions have a negative content also for individuals. Antitrust provisions require individuals to abstain from certain behaviours, and public authorities to act in order to ensure that these prescriptions are respected. Provisions on State aid restrict the possibility for Member States to subsidise private undertakings if that would harm competition within the internal market. Nevertheless, there is no obstacle to the potential of duties in the area of competition law to translate into correlative rights for individuals interested in the performance thereof. This potential however does not materialise equally in all areas, as exemplified by the contrast between the relatively easy identification of rights in antitrust law (2.1.2.1), and the much more limited reliance on rights in the Court's reasoning on State aid issues (2.1.2.2).

2.1.2.1. Rules applying to enterprises: the development of horizontal liability

Antitrust provisions essentially regulate relations between competitors, and public authorities of course have an important role to play in these relations. The basic substantive framework of EU antitrust law is Section 1 (Rules applying to undertakings) of Chapter 1 (Rules on competition) of Title VII of the TFEU. This section comprises articles 101 to 106 TFEU.[1134] Article 101(1) lays down the general prohibition of '*agreements between undertakings, decisions by associations of undertakings and any concerted practices which may affect trade between the Member States and which have as their object or effect of prevention, restriction or distortion of competition within the Common Market*'. This provision was found by the Court already in 1962 in

1134 Formerly Articles 81 to 86 EC / Articles 85 to 89 EEC.

De Geus to be directly applicable, possibly also in proceedings between two private companies even though the issue was not directly addressed in that case.[1135] Later in *BRT v Sabam,* the ECJ was asked whether Article 9 of Regulation 17/62, which deprived national competition authorities of jurisdiction whenever the Commission opened proceedings to investigate a potential Article 101/102 infringement, also deprived national courts of their jurisdiction. The Court's answer was that the prohibitions of Articles 101(1) and 102 '*tend by their very nature to produce direct effects in relations between individuals*' and therefore '*create direct rights in respect of the individuals concerned which the national courts must safeguard*'.[1136] The Court confirmed this approach and drew practical consequences in *Delimitis,* holding that only were national courts not obliged to await a decision of the Commission if they were certain that there was no restriction of competition under Article 101(1) TFEU; they also could decide to deny exemption under Article 101(3) TFEU, if it seemed certain that the Commission would not grant an exemption.[1137] Competition law is thus a perfect area for looking not only at how (negative) obligations give rise to rights vertically (i.e. to individuals in their relations with public authorities), but also horizontally (i.e. to individuals in their relations with other individuals).

The Court has since then often stressed this idea that national courts play an essential role in safeguarding the rights that individuals derive from EU competition law.[1138] This requirement manifested in a number of judgments which have shaped a regime of civil liability for violations of EU competition law. Compared to public liability, horizontal liability for violations of EU law is a young field. Until the Damages Directive came into force, no EU legislation specifically provided for private rights of action

---

1135 Judgment of 6 April 1962, *De Geus en Uitdenbogerd v Bosch and others*, C-13/61, EU:C:1962:11.

1136 Judgment of 21 January 1974, *BRT v Sabam*, C-127/73, EU:C:1974:25, paras 16-17.

1137 Judgment of 28 February 1991, *Delimitis v Henninger Bräu*, C-234/89, EU:C:1991:91. V. Milutinović, 'The 'Right to Damages' in a 'System of Parallel Competences': A Fresh Look at *BRT v. SABAM* and its Subsequent Interpretation (July 1, 2013). ' Forthcoming in: P Lowe and M Marquis (eds), *European Competition Law Annual 2011: Integrating Public and Private Enforcement Implications for Courts and Agencies* (Hart Publishing, 2014) < https://ssrn.com/abstract=2293649> accessed 30 May 2017.

1138 Judgment of 5 June 2014, *Kone and Others*, C-557/12, EU:C:2014:1317, para 20; *Courage and Crehan*, C-453/99, para 23; *Manfredi*, Joined cases C-295/04 to C-298/04, para 39.

for damages.[1139] The first major developments were pretorian. Effectiveness proves here again to be at the heart of the EU system of rights and obligations.

In *Courage v Crehan*, a brewery sued one of its contractors, the operator of a pub, for unpaid beer deliveries. The contract included the obligation to buy a minimum quantity of beer at prices fixed by the brewery. The pub operator argued that this contract was in breach of EU anti-competitive rules and introduced a counter-claim for damages. While the referring court could pronounce the nullity of the contract, it could not, under English law, grant damages to the pub operator as the latter had voluntarily entered the illegal contract. The Court of Justice held that it was for the national courts to ensure that the rules of EU law '*take full effect*' and to '*protect the rights which they confer on individuals*'.[1140] And the existence of a right for '*any individual to claim damages for loss caused to him by a contract or by conduct liable to restrict or distort competition*' is strongly connected with the effectiveness of EU competition law, as the Court holds that it '*strengthens the working of the Community competition rules and discourages agreements or practices, which are frequently covert, which are liable to restrict or distort competition*', so that '*actions for damages before the national courts can make a significant contribution to the maintenance of effective competition in the Community*'.[1141] The consequence of the direct horizontal effect of Article 101 TFEU is that individuals must be allowed to seek reparation of damages caused by infringement of that provision by other private individuals.[1142] Civil liability is therefore strongly connected with the mechanism

---

1139 Directive 2014/104/EU of the European Parliament and of the Council of 26 November 2014 on certain rules governing actions for damages under national law for infringements of the competition law provisions of the Member States and of the European Union (OJ L 349 p. 1). A. Jones, 'Private Enforcement of EU Competition Law: A Comparison with, and Lessons from, the US (January 14, 2016)' in M. Bergström, M. Iacovides and M. Strand (eds), *Harmonising EU Competition Litigation: The New Directive and Beyond* (Hart Publishing 2016) - TLI Think! Paper 10/2016 Available at SSRN: https://ssrn.com/abstract=2715796 12.

1140 *Courage and Crehan*, C-453/99, para 15. Drexl, 'Competition Law as Part of the European Constitution' 652.

1141 *Courage and Crehan*, C-453/99, paras 26-27. See also Judgment of 14 June 2011, *Pfleiderer*, C-360/09, EU:C:2011:389, para 29; *Otis and Others*, C-199/11, para 42; Judgment of 16 May 2017, *Agria Polska and Others v Commission*, T-480/15, EU:T:2017:339, para 84.

1142 *Courage and Crehan*, C-453/99, paras 28-29. H.-W. Micklitz, 'The ECJ between the Individual Citizen and the Member States - A plea for a judge-made Euro-

of direct effect, just like Member State liability,[1143] and it obeys the same logic of relying on individuals (with the help of national courts) to ensure the effectiveness of EU law.

This logic continued unfolding in subsequent cases. The *Manfredi* ruling made clear that, in accordance with '*the principle of effectiveness and the right of any individual to seek compensation for loss caused by a contract or by conduct liable to restrict or distort competition*', full compensation must cover not only actual loss but also loss of profit and interest.[1144] In *Otis*, the Court added that the EU itself '*also enjoys that right*' to compensation.[1145] In order to reach that conclusion it had slightly extended the finding from *Manfredi* that 'any individual' could claim compensation for the harm suffered from an agreement of practice prohibited under Article 101(1) TFEU, and referred instead to 'any person'.[1146] The European Commission was therefore allowed to represent the EU for a civil claim before a domestic court.

The effectiveness rationale also supported a broader access to information by competitors for the purposes of claiming damages. The Court held in *Pfleiderer* that it was up to the national court to weigh up the respective interests in favour of disclosure of documents concerning a leniency programme and in favour of the protection of that information.[1147] The issue was dealt with again in *Donau Chemie*.[1148] In this case, competitors who were not parties to proceedings regarding leniency programmes had requested access to documents forming part of the file related to these proceedings, in order to subsequently submit an action for damages. Austrian law made access to this file subject to agreement of all parties in the proceedings. The referring court asked whether EU law, in particular the principle of effectiveness, precluded such a rule. In the form of preliminary observations, the Court listed a series of by then classic principles, relying on

---

pean law on remedies' EUI Working Paper Law 2011/15, 13; A. Jones, 'Private Enforcement of EU Competition Law: A Comparison with, and Lessons from, the US (January 14, 2016)' 13. Drexl, 'Competition Law as Part of the European Constitution' 646.

1143 Półtorak, *European Union Rights in National Courts*, 44.

1144 *Manfredi*, Joined cases C-295/04 to C-298/04, para 95. A. Jones, 'Private Enforcement of EU Competition Law: A Comparison with, and Lessons from, the US (January 14, 2016)' 13.

1145 *Otis and Others*, C-199/11, para 44.

1146 *Otis and Others*, C-199/11, para 43 and *Manfredi*, Joined cases C-295/04 to C-298/04, para 61.

1147 *Pfleiderer*, C-360/09, para 30.

1148 Judgment of 6 June 2013, *Bundeswettbewerbsbehörde v Donau Chemie AG and Others*, C-536/11, EU:C:2013:366.

iconic cases: the general ability of clearly defined obligations to give rise to rights for individuals (*Francovich*); the horizontal direct effect in particular of Article 101(1) TFEU (*Manfredi*) leading to the possibility to claim damages from competitors (*Courage and Crehan*); the duty of national courts to ensure effectiveness of EU law and protection of individual rights deriving thereof (*Simmenthal, Factortame, Courage and Crehan, Manfredi*); the instrumental rationale of the right to claim damages in such a situation, contributing to the effectiveness of EU law (*Courage and Crehan, Manfredi, Pfleiderer*); and the effectiveness of Article 101 TFEU as a limit to the procedural autonomy of Member States.[1149] In the light of these considerations, the Court then examined whether the rule of Austrian law at issue was compatible with the principle of effectiveness and the right to effective judicial protection. Recalling the principle laid down in *Pfleiderer* concerning the necessary weighing of interests by national courts prior to disclosing documents, the Court added: '*That weighing-up is necessary because, in competition law in particular, any rule that is rigid, either by providing for absolute refusal to grant access to the documents in question or for granting access to those documents as matter of course, is liable to undermine the effective application of, inter alia, Article 101 TFEU and the rights that provision confers on individuals.*'[1150] Indeed, on the one hand, systematic refusal would make it 'excessively difficult' to protect the right of third parties to claim compensation; on the other hand, generalised access is neither necessary (because not all documents are relevant to a liability claim) nor desirable, for it might affect the rights of private parties (protection of business secrecy and of personal data) as well as public interests, '*such as the effectiveness of anti-infringement policies in the area of competition law, because it could deter parties involved in infringements of Articles 101 TFEU and 102 TFEU from cooperating with the competition authorities*'.[1151] The national court must therefore assess the need for disclosure '*on a case-by-case basis*'.[1152] Consistently with the findings in *Pfleiderer*, the Court therefore concluded that that national rule at issue did not comply with the principle of effectiveness.

The logic of effectiveness of EU competition law, supporting a right to damages in horizontal situations, spreads to policy areas beyond competition law in the strict sense, as long as 'competitors' are involved. In *Muñoz*,

1149 *Bundeswettbewerbsbehörde v Donau Chemie AG and Others*, C-536/11, paras 20-28.

1150 *Bundeswettbewerbsbehörde v Donau Chemie AG and Others*, C-536/11, para 31.

1151 *Bundeswettbewerbsbehörde v Donau Chemie AG and Others*, C-536/11, paras 32-33, paras 41-48.

1152 *Bundeswettbewerbsbehörde v Donau Chemie AG and Others*, C-536/11, para 35.

a Spanish undertaking was seeking an order before an English court, to restrain a competitor from marketing table grapes in the UK under names that did not comply with Community legislation. The Court recalled that regulations '*confer rights on individuals which the national courts have a duty to protect*'.[1153] The Court then cited *Simmenthal, Factortame and Others* and *Courage and Crehan* to insist that '*the national courts, whose task it is to apply the provisions of Community law in areas within their jurisdiction, must ensure that they take full effect*'.[1154] Looking at the preambles of the applicable regulations on common quality standards,[1155] the Court found that these intended to ensure that '*products of unsatisfactory quality*' would be kept off the market and to encourage '*fair trading and market transparency*'; and concluded: '*accordingly, the full effectiveness of the rules on quality standards and, in particular, the practical effect of the obligations (laid down by the regulations) imply that it must be possible to enforce that obligation by means of civil proceedings instituted by a trader against a competitor.*' The Court then highlighted the powerful complementarity between public and private enforcement of EU law by insisting that the possibility of bringing civil proceedings '*strengthens the practical working of the Community rules on quality standards*'; it works as '*a supplement*' to the action of national authorities and thus contributes to ensuring '*fair trading and transparency of markets in the Community*'.[1156] Therefore traders must be able to enforce quality standards concerning fruit and vegetables through civil proceedings against their competitors.

The solution in *Muñoz* calls for three comments. Firstly, the Court does not search for an intention to grant a right in the regulations, which confer rights by their very nature. This approach contrasts which that of AG Geelhoed, who had suggested that conditions of action before national courts should be aligned on standing conditions to bring actions for annulment before the EU courts and thus be determined by the existence of '*an interest protected by*' the EU norm on which an individual is relying.[1157] The

---

1153 *Muñoz and Superior Fruiticola*, C-253/00, para 27, citing *Fratelli Variola*, C-34/73, para 8.

1154 *Muñoz and Superior Fruiticola*, C-253/00, para 28, citing *Simmenthal*, C-106/77, para 16, and *Courage and Crehan*, C-453/99, para 25.

1155 Council Regulation (EEC) No 1035/72 of 18 May 1972 on the common organization of the market in fruit and vegetables (OJ English Special Edition 1972 (II) p. 437) and Council Regulation (EC) No 2200/96 of 28 October 1996 on the common organization of the market in fruit and vegetables (OJ L 297 p. 1).

1156 *Muñoz and Superior Fruiticola*, C-253/00, paras 29-31.

1157 Opinion in *Muñoz and Superior Fruiticola*, C-253/00, EU:C:2001:697, para 73.

Court did not follow this advice and instead '*sent a clear signal that claimants do not need to be so entangled in the dispute as to be considered 'directly and individually concerned' before they acquire capacity to bring decentralised enforcement actions under Community law*'.[1158] Secondly, the teleological approach serves to objectively identify the purpose of these regulations in order to assess what is required in order to ensure their effective application. Thirdly, the Court heavily relies on effectiveness for reaching the conclusion that individual rights must be enforceable also through civil proceedings between individuals. This ruling is therefore completely in line with the seminal cases on direct effect and with the mechanism of functional subjectivation.

The potential breadth of the personal scope of the right to damages for violations of EU competition law appears even more clearly in *Kone*. Applicants challenged the compatibility with EU law of Austrian legislation, which posited that the causal link between a sustained loss and the existence of a cartel was considered, in the absence of a contractual link with a member of that cartel, to have been broken by the autonomous decision of the undertaking that is not a party to the cartel, and that such a situation excluded a right to compensation. The Court again held that the horizontal direct effect of Articles 101(1) and 102 TFEU implied the creation of '*rights for the individuals concerned*'.[1159] Damages for violation of these provisions must be a possibility in order to ensure '*full effectiveness*' of Article 101 TFEU.[1160] The instrumental rationale of the right to damages is again highlighted: this right '*strengthens the working of the European Union rules*' by discouraging anticompetitive behaviours, '*thereby making a significant contribution to the maintenance of effective competition in the European Union*'.[1161] The Court then recalled the existence of a procedural autonomy for Member States, limited by the principles of equivalence and effectiveness, and stressed the importance of ensuring the effectiveness of Articles 101 and 102 TFEU.[1162] The Member State's autonomy in defining the '*causal link*' must therefore be exercised '*taking into account the objective pursued by Article 101 TFEU*'.[1163] The full effectiveness of Article 101 TFEU

1158 *Muñoz and Superior Fruiticola*, C-253/00. Dougan, *National Remedies Before the Court of Justice. Issues of Harmonisation and Differentiation* (Hart Publishing 2004) 44.
1159 *Kone and Others*, C-557/12, para 20.
1160 *Kone and Others*, C-557/12, para 21.
1161 *Kone and Others*, C-557/12, para 23.
1162 *Kone and Others*, C-557/12, paras 24-26.
1163 *Kone and Others*, C-557/12, para 32.

would therefore be undermined '*if a person's right to claim compensation from another person for harm suffered depended, unconditionally, on the existence of a contractual link between those two persons*'. Having rejected this restrictive condition, the Court then left it to the national court to determine whether the cartel, in the circumstances of the case and in view of the specific aspects of the relevant market, could be liable in damages.[1164] The Damages Directive that came into force the same year is in line with this solution, since its Recital 13 makes clear that the right to compensation is not conditioned on the existence of a direct contractual relationship between the claimant and the infringing undertaking.

As pointed out by Eilmansberger, the red thread in these cases on the right to damages is the effectiveness of EU law, '*the central legal foundation for the finding of liability*'[1165] and more generally, consistently with what we had seen also in other contexts so far, the powerful rationale for individual rights in EU law. In *Courage* it was the effectiveness rationale that allowed the Court to deduce a new remedy from the existence of rights.[1166] Milutinović rightly suggests that 'BRT *represents, in a sense, a horizontalisation of the* Van Gend en Loos *principle, just as* Courage *represents a horizontalisation of the* Francovich/Brasserie du Pêcheur *principle.*'[1167] In both cases, the double function of private enforcement is very clear: on the one hand, there is a public interest function which is to '*boost the overall level of enforcement of the competition rules and the deterrent effect which these have on would-be infringers*'; on the other hand, there is a private interest function which is to '*safeguard the rights of individuals under Articles 101 and 102*'. Milutinović concludes that '*[t]he synthesis of these two antithetical functions is, of course, that a private plaintiff who acts out of his own private interest also protects the public interest.*'[1168] EU antitrust and antidumping law thus provides an excellent illustration of functional subjectivation, consolidating the conception of rights as correlatives of obligations, activated in the presence of (broadly understood) individual interests.

1164 *Kone and Others*, C-557/12, paras 33-34.

1165 Eilmansberger, 'The Relationship between Rights and Remedies in EC Law: in Search of the Missing Link' 1226.

1166 P. Rott, 'The Court of Justice's Principle of Effectiveness and its Unforeseeable Impact on Private Law Relationships' in D. Leczykiewicz and S. Weatherhill (eds), *The Involvement of EU Law in Private Law Relationships* (Hart Publishing 2013) 187.

1167 Milutinovic, *The 'Right to Damages' under EU Competition Law: from Courage v Crehan to the White Paper and Beyond* 5.

1168 Milutinovic, *The 'Right to Damages' under EU Competition Law: from Courage v Crehan to the White Paper and Beyond* 15.

This approach has however raised concerns as to whether the Court might be engaged on the slippery slope towards accepting the principle of an *actio popularis.*[1169] Yet, in *Courage* and *Manfredi* the claimants were affected by the anti-competitive practices[1170] – which means that individual interest remained relevant in triggering the right to reparation. In *Muñoz*, it could still be argued that there was a clear limit since the Court did not mention a right for individuals in general, but 'traders' and 'competitors'. The question is then whether the logic should extend beyond the (admittedly broad) context of interaction between competitors, and apply to other types of interests, such as those of consumers. *Kone* could well be paving the way to a positive answer, as the General Court suggested in a series of rulings on agreements and concerted practices by companies on the EU airfreight market.[1171] What these cases certainly demonstrate is that the *Schutznorm* doctrine does not apply in the context of civil liability any more than it does for Member State liability. In addition, the case law on

1169 Dougan, *National Remedies Before the Court of Justice. Issues of Harmonisation and Differentiation* 43. Eilmansberger, 'The Relationship between Rights and Remedies in EC Law: in Search of the Missing Link' 1128.

1170 Dougan, 'Who Exactly Benefits from the Treaties? The Murky Interaction Between Union and National Competence over the Capacity to Enforce EU Law' 90.

1171 The GC, relying on *Kone*, held that '*It cannot …[] be ruled out that a person held liable for an infringement of the competition rules found by the Commission may be required to pay compensation for the damage caused to customers of other persons held liable for the same infringement. In such a case, and where provided for by national law, indemnity proceedings between those parties may be brought before the national courts.*' Judgment of 16 December 2015, *Air Canada v Commission,* T-9/11, EU:T:2015:994, para 42; Judgment of 16 December 2015, *Koninklijke Luchtvaart Maatschappij v Commission*, T-28/11, EU:T:2015:995, para 47, Judgment of 16 December 2015, *Cathay Pacific Airways v Commission,* T-38/11, EU:T:2015:985, para 46; Judgment of 16 December 2015, *Cargolux Airlines v Commission,* T-39/11, EU:T:2015:991, para 41; Judgment of 16 December 2015, *Latam Airlines Group and Lan Cargo v Commission,* T-40/11, EU:T:2015:986, para 51; Judgment of 16 December 2015, *British Airways v Commission,* T-48/11, EU:T:2015:988, para 43; Judgment of 16 December 2015, *SAS Cargo Group and Others v Commission,* T-56/11, EU:T:2015:990, para 48; Judgment of 16 December 2015, *Air France-KLM v Commission,* T-62/11, EU:T:2015:996, para 49; Judgment of 16 December 2015, *Air France v Commission,* T-63/11, EU:T:2015:993, para 46; Judgment of 16 December 2015, *Martinair Holland v Commission,* T-67/11, EU:T:2015:984, para 38; Judgment of 16 December 2015, *Japan Airlines v Commission,* T-36/11, EU:T:2015:992, para 41; Judgment of 16 December 2015, *Singapore Airlines and Singapore Airlines Cargo v Commission,* T-43/11, EU:T:2015:989, para 47.

private liability for violations of EU competition law, just like the case law on public liability, attests to the dynamism of the correlation between rights and obligations, with rights containing the seeds for further obligations (to compensate violations) and corresponding rights (to compensation).

2.1.2.2. State aid: the limits of the instrumental rationale

The EU system of state aid control is rooted in the idea that a company which receives government support gains an advantage over its competitors.[1172] In order to ensure that competition on the EU market remains undistorted, State aid is therefore generally prohibited by the Treaties, although exceptions are allowed if advantages granted to some undertakings are justified by certain policy objectives.[1173] The main relevant provisions in the current treaty architecture are Articles 107, 108 and 109 TFEU (formerly Articles 87 to 89 EC / Articles 92 to 94 EEC). Save for some exceptions, Member States must notify all new aid measures to the Commission, which is in charge of controlling whether the prohibition and its exceptions are correctly applied: it approves aid measures, and has the power to recover incompatible State aid.

The first State aid case that we turn to is *Costa V ENEL.*[1174] This case is mainly remembered as having established the principle of supremacy of EU law, which in combination with the doctrine of direct effect laid down in *Van Gend en Loos*, allows maximal expansion of the useful effect of EU law. On one point, however, *Costa* stands in strong contrast with *Van Gend en Loos.* Mr Costa, as is well known, was challenging the nationalisation of the Italian electricity company. One of his lesser known arguments was that this nationalisation amounted to 'hidden' state aid, prohibited by Article 93 EEC (currently Article 108 TFEU). On this occasion the Court held that by including this provision in the Treaty, the Member States had agreed to bind themselves towards the Commission, but that this did not

1172 'State aid control' (*European Commission*, 12 September 2016) <http://ec.europa.eu/competition/state_aid/overview/index_en.html> accessed 20 June 2017.

1173 On the notion of State aid see M. Ebner and E. Gambaro, 'The Notion of State Aid' in A. Santa Maria (ed), *Competition and State Aid. An Analysis of the EC Practice* (Kluwer Law International 2007) 14-47.

1174 *Costa v E.N.E.L.*, C-6/64.

give rights to individuals.[1175] How is it that this iconic case, *Van Gend en Loos*'s constitutional twin, expresses such a different position on the ability of Treaty obligations on Member States to give rise to rights on individuals? The last part of Article 93(3) EEC being irrelevant for the main issue, the Court did not explain clearly why a different logic applied.

This specific logic was developed in other judgments. Article 93(3) EEC provides that '*[t]he Commission shall be informed [...] of any plans to grant or alter aid. If it considers that any such plan is not compatible with the common market having regard to article 107, it shall without delay initiate the procedure provided for in paragraph 2. The Member State concerned shall not put its proposed measures into effect until this procedure has resulted in a final decision*'. The Court confirmed the direct effect of this last sentence and its ability to give rise to rights, adding that '*the immediately applicable nature of this provision extends to the whole of the period to which it applies*'.[1176] Having also been asked whether this meant that the national court must of its own motion take account of the invalidity of a law granting aid in contravention of the prohibition laid down in Article 93(3), the Court replied that '*while the direct effect of the prohibition in question requires national courts to apply it without any possibility of its being excluded by rules of national law of any kind whatsoever, it is for the internal legal system of every Member State to determine the legal procedure leading to this result*'.[1177]

Since then the Court has repeatedly insisted on the role of national courts, '*whose involvement is the result of the direct effect*' of the prohibition laid down in the last sentence of Article 93(3) EEC,[1178] to ensure that the rights of individuals are safeguarded where the obligation to await a final

---

1175 *Costa v E.N.E.L.*, C-6/64, p. 596: '*[b]y so expressly undertaking to inform the Commission 'in sufficient time' of any plans for aid, and by accepting the procedures laid down in Article 93, the States have entered into an obligation with the Community, which binds them as States but creates no individual rights except in the case of the final provision of Article 93(3)*'.

1176 Judgment of 11 December 1973, *Lohrey v Bundesrepublik Deutschland and Others*, C-141/73, EU:C:1973:155, para 8. See also Judgment of 11 December 1973, *Lorenz GmbH v Bundesrepublik Deutschland and Others*, C-120/73, EU:C:1973:152, para 8.

1177 *Lohrey v Bundesrepublik Deutschland and Others*, C-141/73, para 9.

1178 *Fédération nationale du commerce extérieur des produits alimentaires and Others v France*, C-354/90, EU:C:1991:440, para 11; Judgment of 11 July 1996, *SFEI and Others*, C-39/94, EU:C:1996:285, para 39, Judgment of 21 November 1991.

decision of the Commission has been infringed.[1179] It has held that in case of breach of this provision, national courts must draw all necessary inferences for individuals '*as regards the validity of measures giving effect to the aid, the recovery of financial support granted in disregard of that provision and possible interim measures*'.[1180] The Court however insisted that tasks remains strictly separated: national courts even in such a situation, do not decide on the compatibility of the aid measures with EU law. This task remains '*the exclusive responsibility of the Commission, subject to review by the Court of Justice*'.[1181] Moreover, even if this final assessment validates the aid measure, it does not regularise *ex post facto* implementing measures taken in breach of the prohibition laid down by the last sentence of Article 93(3) EEC, '*since otherwise the* direct effect *of that prohibition would be impaired and the* interests of individuals, *which are to be protected by national courts, would be disregarded. Any other interpretation would have the effect of according a favourable outcome to the non-observance of that provision by the Member State concerned and would deprive it of its* effectiveness'.[1182]

The requirement to protect individual interests is however counterbalanced by the requirement to also take '*the Community interest fully into consideration*' in situations where applying the prohibition on putting aid into effect before the Commission has authorized it would in fact '*have the sole effect of extending the circle of recipients of the unlawful aid*'.[1183] So the Court insists on the duty of national courts to protect individual rights where the individual interests converge with those of the Community in making sure that the prohibition of Article 93(3) is observed (a typical *van Gend en Loos* approach); however, the rights of individuals derived from this provision stop where the interest of the Community begins.

1179 Judgment of 21 October 2003, *van Calster and Cleeren,* Joined cases C-261/01 and C-262/01, EU:C:2003:571, para 75; Judgment of 5 October 2005, *Transalpine Ölleitung in Österreich*, C-368/04, EU:C:2006:644, para 38; see also Judgment of 18 May 2017, *Fondul Proprietatea,* C-150/16, EU:C:2017:388, para 42.

1180 *Fédération nationale du commerce extérieur des produits alimentaires and Others v France*, C-354/90, para 12; See also *van Calster and Cleeren,* Joined cases C-261/01 and C-262/01, para 64; Judgment of 16 December 1992, *Lornoy and Others v Belgian State,* C-17/91, EU:C:1992:514, para 30.

1181 *Lornoy and Others v Belgian State,* C-17/91, para 30. See also Judgment of 27 November 2003, *Enirisorse,* Joined cases C-34/01 to C-38/01, EU:C:2003:640, para 42.

1182 *Van Calster and Cleeren,* Joined cases C-261/01 and C-262/01, para 64 (emphases added).

1183 *Transalpine Ölleitung in Österreich*, C-368/04, paras 57-58.

Another key State aid provision, Article 92 EEC (now Article 107 TFEU), does not of itself give rise to rights. The assessment of the compatibility of an aid with the common market is performed '*by means of an appropriate procedure which it is the Commission's responsibility to set in motion. [...] The parties cannot therefore simply, on the basis of Article 92 alone, challenge the compatibility of an aid with Community law before national courts or ask them to decide as to any compatibility which may be the main issue in actions before them or may arise as a subsidiary issue. There is this right however where the provisions of Article 92 have been applied by the general provisions provided for in Article 94 or by specific decisions under Article 93(2)*'.[1184] The Court added in *Lornoy* that '*the incompatibility of State aid with the common market is neither absolute nor unconditional*' and that *[i]ndividuals cannot therefore simply, on the basis of Article 92 alone, challenge the compatibility of an aid with Community law before the national courts or ask them to decide as the main or a subsidiary issue on any incompatibility.*'[1185] The argument that Article 92 EEC cannot of itself give rise to rights because it is dependent on further implementing measures constitutes a simple application of the *Van Gend en Loos* criteria. What is more at odds with the classic approach is the Court's insistence on the Commission's exclusive responsibility for enforcement of State aid law – rather than looking at the Commission and individuals as complementary agents of EU law enforcement.

This dissociation raises issues when EU State aid law intersects with EU antitrust law, which as we have seen in the previous section, is much more supportive of the active role of individuals in the enforcement of EU law. Such a problem arose in *Ianelli v Meroni*, concerning the validity of certain State aid measures by reference to Article 30 EEC (prohibiting restrictive measures). The Court maintained that private parties cannot challenge compatibility of an aid with EU law on the basis of Article 92 EEC (now 107 TFEU) alone, because it is the Commission's sole responsibility to set such a procedure in motion. However, the Court equally maintained that the prohibition of quantitative restrictions and measures having equivalent

1184 Judgment of 22 March 1977, *Steinike and Weinlig*, C-78/76, EU:C:1977:52, paras 9-10. The Court is however much more careful in the French version, where there is no mention of a 'droit', only of a 'possibilité': '*les particuliers ne sauraient... en invoquant le seul article 92, contester la compatibilité d'une aide...; ... par contre, cette possibilité est donnée dès lors que les dispositions visées de l'article 92 ont été concrétisées...*'. See also *Capolongo v Azienda Agricola Maya*, C-77/72, para 6.

1185 *Lornoy and Others v Belgian State*, C-17/91, para 29. See also *Demoor and Others v Belgian State*, Joined cases C-144/91 and C-145/91, para 25.

effect laid down in Article 30 EEC '*has direct effect and creates individual rights which national courts must protect*'.[1186] In situations where some aspects of an aid may be isolated and their compatibility with Treaty provisions other than those on State aid assessed without taking the aid as a whole, '*there are no reasons based on the division of powers under Articles 92 and 93*' that would lead to the conclusion that '*if other provisions of the Treaty which have direct effect are infringed, those provisions may not be invoked before national courts simply because the factor in question is an aspect of aid*' so that Article 30 EEC may be relied on against these aspects. On the contrary, the legality of an aid taken as a whole, where none of its elements could be isolated without impacting its object or functioning, is to be assessed exclusively through the Commission-initiated procedure in the framework laid down by Articles 107 to 109 TFEU.[1187] By insisting on the '*division of powers*' rather than on the complementarity between public and private enforcement of EU law this solution again highlights the limits of functional subjectivation.

The uncoupling of EU and individual interests also occurs in *Heineken*, a case concerning the scope of the notification requirement imposed on Member States.[1188] Heineken was a beneficiary of a tax allowance scheme, which the Dutch legislator altered during the course of an Article 93(2) EEC procedure opened by the Commission. Heineken challenged the reduction of the allowance and the Dutch court referred to the CJEU several questions, including the question whether Article 93(3) implied that the notification to the Commission by a Member State of a plan to grant aid must be immediately and clearly made known to all the interested parties. The Court held that Article 93(3) made no reference to such an obligation and that the objectives and context of that provision did not indicate such an obligation either: '*The sole purpose of the first sentence of Article 93(3) is to provide the Commission with the opportunity to review, in sufficient time and in the general interest of the Communities, any plan to grant or alter aid. At the same time, the interests of any individuals concerned are protected by Article 93(2), which requires the Commission, when it initiates the procedure provided for in that paragraph, to give notice to the interested parties to submit their comments.*'[1189] The notion of simultaneity implied by the expression 'at the

1186 *Ianelli v Meroni*, C-74/76, paras 12-13.

1187 *Ianelli v Meroni*, C-74/76, para 14. See also e.g. Judgment of 13 May 2015, *Niki Luftfahrt v Commission*, T-511/09, EU:T:284, para 216.

1188 Judgment of 9 October 1984, *Heineken*, Joined cases 91/83 and 127/83, EU:C:1984:307.

1189 *Heineken*, Joined cases 91/83 and 127/83, para 14.

same time' is in fact misleading, as the Court looks at which interests the provision *aims* to protect and finds that only EU interests are pursued by Article 93.

Some procedural rights are however granted to individuals in the EU legal framework on State aid. Article 93(2) (now 108(2) TFEU) requires that '*parties concerned*' must be notified before the Commission takes a decision in relation to aid. The *Intermills* case was an action for annulment of a decision which had not been individually notified to the applicant. The Court held that the 'parties concerned' '*are not only the (...) undertakings receiving aid but equally the persons, undertakings or associations whose interests might be affected by the grant of the aid, in particular competing undertakings and trade associations. In other words, there is an indeterminate group of persons to whom notice must be given.*'[1190] This is completely in line with the Court's classic approach to individual interests in relation with obligations of the administration: there is no predeterminate protected interest. But the story in *Intermills* does not conclude in a way very favourable to individuals: '*it follows that Article 93(2) does not require individual notice to be given to particular persons*' and that publication of a notice in the Official Journal is sufficient.[1191] So here, individual interest understood in a broad way actually lightens the obligation of the Commission. The bright side is that, as the Court held in subsequent rulings, the '*persons intended to benefit from the procedural guarantees provided by Article 93(2)*' can be considered to be directly and individually concerned for the purposes of an Article 263 TFEU action for annulment relying on the failure to respect these guarantees.[1192]

The broad notion of 'interested party' laid down in *Intermills* was codified at Article 1(h) of Regulation 659/1999, codifying and reinforcing the Commission practice on Article 88 EC (now 108 TFEU),[1193]: '*any Member State and any person, undertaking or association of undertakings whose interests might be affected by the granting of aid, in particular the beneficiary of the aid, competing undertakings and trade associations*'. The rights of interested parties were listed at Article 24 of the regulation: mainly, they consist in the right

1190 Judgment of 14 November 1984, *Intermills v Commission,* C-323/82, EU:C:1984:345, para 16.

1191 *Intermills v Commission,* C-323/82, para 17.

1192 Judgment of 2 April 1998, *Commission v Sytraval and Brink's France*, C-367/95 P, EU:C:1998:154, paras 40-41 and para 48; Judgment of 11 July 2007, *Asklepios Kliniken,* T-167/04, EU:T:2007:215, paras 49-52; *Commission v Aktionsgemeinschaft Recht und Eigentum*, C-78/03 P, paras 35-36.

1193 Council Regulation (EC) No 659/1999 of 22 March 1999 laying down detailed rules for the application of Article [108] TFEU (OJ L 83 p. 1).

to submit comments following a Commission decision to initiate a formal investigation procedure (Article 24(1) and the right to submit a complaint to inform the Commission of any alleged unlawful aid or misuse of aid (Article 24(2)).[1194]

Case *Kronoply and Kronotex* provide additional clarification on the notion of interested party. This case concerned the possibility for applicants to challenge a Commission decision not to raise objections to an aid granted by German authorities. Firstly, the Court held that the lawfulness of such a decision depended on whether there were doubts as to the compatibility of the aid with the common market, and that these doubts must trigger the initiation of a formal investigation procedure in which 'interested parties' can participate; therefore, the Court confirmed that the status of 'interested party' in the meaning of Article 1(h) was '*sufficient to distinguish individually, for the purposes of the fourth paragraph of Article 230 EC, the applicant contesting a decision not to raise objections*'.[1195] Secondly, the companies were not considered as direct competitors of the aid beneficiary (they just used the same raw material, i.e. industrial wood, for their production, making them rival purchasers of that material). The Commission raised the spectre of the *actio popularis*, arguing that by granting these companies the status of 'parties concerned' the General Court was '*opening the way for actions to be brought by members of the general public against Commission decisions in the field of State aid*'.[1196] The Court held that Article 1(h) did not rule out '*the possibility that an undertaking which is not a direct competitor of the beneficiary of the aid, but which requires the same raw material for its pro-*

1194 In Regulation 2015/1589 (which replaces Regulation 659/1999), Article 1(h) has remained identical and Article 24 has become Article 20, slightly altered so that paragraph (2) no longer refers to a right to submit a 'complaint' but simply a right to 'inform' the Commission. Council Regulation 2015/1589 of 13 July 2015 laying down detailed rules for the application of Article 108 of the TFEU (OJ L 248 p. 9).

1195 Judgment of 24 May 2011, *Commission v Kronoply and Kronotex*, C-83/09 P, EU:C:2011:341, paras 47-48. See also Judgment of 18 November 2010, *NDSHT v Commission*, C-322/09 P, EU:C:2010:701, paras 59-60; C-75/05 P and C-80/05 P, para 43; Judgment of 22 September 2011, *Belgium v Deutsche Post and DHL International*, C-148/09 P, EU:C:2011:603, para 54 and Judgment of 27 October 2011, *Austria v Scheucher-Fleisch and Others*, C-47/10 P, EU:C:2011:698, paras 43-44 and para 128; Judgment of 13 June 2013, *Ryanair v Commission*, C-287/12 P, EU:C:2013:395, para 55.

1196 *Commission v Kronoply and Kronotex*, C-83/09 P, para 61.

duction process, can be categorised as an interested party'.[1197] In order to be considered an interested party, the applicant therefore needed to demonstrate '*a legitimate interest in the implementation or non-implementation of the aid measures at issue*', which '*may consist, inter alia, in the protection of its competitive position, in so far as that position would be adversely affected by the aid measures*'.[1198] In this case, the increase in the prices of wood could reasonably be linked with the start of the aid beneficiary's activity, and the General Court had correctly held that the grant of the aid had '*potential adverse effects on [the applicants'] market position*'.[1199]

Although the notion of 'interested party' is defined generously, it gives rise only to the rights listed expressly in the regulation, instead of allowing individuals to rely on any obligation included therein. The Court has defined the scope of the rights that can be identified in connection with the status of interested party. This status allows individuals an action in order to safeguard their procedural rights, not an action calling into question the merits of a decision appraising the aid as such. For an action on these grounds, an individual will have to demonstrate that the standing conditions of Article 263 TFEU are fulfilled.[1200] The issue then intersects with that of the restrictive access to court in this context. This is exemplified by the famous *Telefonica* case where the Court confirmed that a Commission decision declaring an aid incompatible, since it entailed implementing measures by Spain, could not be challenged before the CJEU by an applicant not individually concerned by the decision.[1201]

The approach to the procedural rights of individuals is also restrictive. For instance, the *Scott* case concerned the interpretation of Article 15 of Regulation 659/1999, which provides that the powers of the Commission to recover aid shall be subject to a limitation period of 10 years. The second sentence of Article 15(2) provides that '*Any action taken by the Commission or by a Member State, acting at the request of the Commission, with regard*

1197 *Commission v Kronoply and Kronotex*, C-83/09 P, paras 64-65. See also Judgment of 27 October 2011, *Austria v Scheucher-Fleisch and Others*, C-47/10 P, EU:C:2011:698, para 132.

1198 *Commission v Kronoply and Kronotex*, C-83/09 P, para 66.

1199 *Commission v Kronoply and Kronotex*, C-83/09 P, para 69.

1200 *British Aggregates v Commission*, C-487/06 P, EU:C:2008:757, paras 28-30; Judgment of 9 July 2009, *3F v Commission*, C-319/07 P, EU:C:2009:435, para 31; Judgment of 5 November 2014, *Vtesse Network v Commission*, T-362/10, EU:T:2014:928, para 42.

1201 *Telefonica v Commission*, C-274/12 P. See also Judgment of 27 February 2014, *Stichting Woonpunt and Others v Commission*, C-132/12 P, EU:C:2014:100, para 44.

to the unlawful aid shall interrupt the limitation period.' The applicant argued that he should have been informed when such an action was taken and interrupted the limitation period. The Court acknowledged that private parties may have 'a practical interest' in being informed of action taken by the Commission which is capable of interrupting the limitation period, but that this '*cannot have the effect of making the application of the second sentence of Article 15(2) of Regulation No 659/1999 subject to the requirement that that action be notified to the beneficiary of the aid*',[1202] because the procedure '*takes place primarily between the Commission and the Member State concerned. It is initiated against that State and not against the beneficiaries*'.[1203] The Court concludes that the beneficiary of an aid is therefore not a 'party to the procedure' and cannot rely on a notification requirement.[1204] Ignoring the 'practical', factual interest of an individual in claiming the execution of an obligation, on the ground that this obligation arises in a procedure that does not expressly involve individuals: this strongly resembles a *Schutznorm* approach.

Still, the protection of individuals in State aid law is mainly procedural, in the sense that even those who are recognised as 'interested' parties do not have a right to any substantive result. Another, perhaps more fundamental issue is that the protection of individuals appears to be *peripheral* in this policy area. The assessment of EU interests is key, as it is the main criterion for evaluating whether an aid might be considered an acceptable exception to the general prohibition. Yet, unlike what happens in other policy areas (typically, antitrust law) these interests are not connected with those of individuals, but rather discussed in the case law as a completely distinct matter.[1205] The only context in which individual interests come back at the forefront is where a Member State has infringed its obligation

1202 Judgment of 6 October 2005, *Scott v Commission*, C-276/03 P, EU:C:2005:590, para 33.

1203 *Scott v Commission*, C-276/03 P, para 34.

1204 *Scott v Commission*, C-276/03 P, para 35.

1205 There are many State aid cases where the notion of public interest is addressed, but not in connection with individual interests. E.g. on the assessment of a 'common European interest': *Philip Morris v Commission*, C-730/79, Judgment of 8 March 1988, *Exécutif régional wallon v Commission*, Joined cases C-62/87 and C-72/87, EU:C:1988:132; on the notion of services of general economic interest: Judgment of 24 July 2003, *Altmark Trans and Regierungspräsidium Magdeburg*, C-280/00, EU:C:2003:415; Judgment of 8 March 2017, *Viasat Broadcasting UK v Commission*, C-660/15 P, EU:C:2017:178; on the relation between public interest in a Member State and Community interest: Judgment of 22 December 2008, *Regie Networks*, C-333/07, EU:C:2008:764.

to await a Commission decision: there, individual interest in the fulfilment of an obligation does give rise to rights which it is the duty of national courts to protect – although in so doing they must balance these rights with EU interests. In fact, we notice here the asymmetry already observed concerning public liability: individual rights are under the spotlight when they serve the purpose of ensuring the effectiveness of EU law in the relations between individuals and Member States; by contrast, in a context where it the legality of the actions of EU institutions is being challenged, interested individuals are not acknowledged as 'legal vigilantes' and are only granted 'residual' protection.

2.1.2.3. Interim conclusions

The study of the relation between rights, obligations and interests in competition law paints a very contrasted picture. The individual rights of competitors are key in ensuring the effectiveness of EU rules applying to undertakings. In this context, the Court has readily acknowledged the horizontal direct effect of relevant provisions, i.e. that the rights of competitors translate into obligations for others and vice-versa. This has paved the way towards a liability regime applicable in civil proceedings between competitors. By contrast to these many textbook examples of the mechanism of functional subjectivation, in State aid cases the 'vigilante' function of individuals is close to non-existent. The Commission has the exclusivity in controlling the implementation of EU law, which does not seem to be connected with the protection of individual interests. Some procedural rights are granted to individuals, but the effectiveness rationale is absent from the reasoning in these cases and the interest trigger is defined in a relatively narrow way. The discrepancy between the two policy areas precisely confirms that the ability of obligations under EU law to translate into correlative rights is strongly dependent on the effectiveness rationale.

2.1.3. The protection of economic interests across policy areas

The previous sections traced how the relation between rights, obligations and individual economic interests developed in specific sectoral areas of EU economic law. This section approaches this field transversally in order to test the consistency of this relation in the case law on the protection of legitimate expectations (2.1.3.1) and on administrative procedural rights (2.1.3.2).

2.1.3.1. How legitimate expectations give rise to rights

The principle of protection of legitimate expectations brings an additional twist to the correlativity model based on rights and obligations. In the CJEU's case law, the first occurrence of a requirement to protect legitimate expectations goes back to *Algera*, in which the Court pointed out that the unlawful withdrawal of the application to the applicants of the staff regulations meant that the latter were '*confronted with the prospect of a dismissal which meant the end of a career which they could legitimately rely on*', and that this had caused (non-material) damage for which they could claim compensation.[1206] It has become established case law that the withdrawal of an unlawful measures is permissible, provided that the withdrawal occurs within a reasonable time and provided that the Commission has had sufficient regard as to how far the applicant might have been led to rely on the lawfulness of the measure.'[1207] The first explicit enunciation of the concept was in *Lemmerz Werke* under the term '*Vertrauenschutz*'.[1208] It thus appears to have been inspired by German law, whereas it is not acknowledged by the French Conseil d'Etat (nor the Conseil constitutionnel) as a general principle of law.[1209] It was later formally acknowledged as the requirement

1206 *Algera and Others v Assemblée Commune*, Joined cases C-7/56 and C-3 to C-7/57, p. 66. See p. 32 of this work.

1207 Judgment of 3 March 1982, *Alpha Steel v Commission*, C-14/81, EU:C:1982:76, para 10; *Algera and Others v Assemblée Commune*, Joined cases C-7/56 and C-3 to C-7/57, p. 56, Judgment of 12 July 1962, *Koninklijke Nederlandsche Hoogovens en Staalfabrieken v High Authority*, C-14/61, EU:C:1962:28, p. 272; Judgment of 13 July 1965, *Lemmerz Werke v High Authority*, C-111/63, C:1965:76, p. 690.

1208 *Lemmerz Werke v High Authority*, C-111/63, p. 691: '*considering any position acquired by the applicant for which it could claim protection (Vertrauensschutz)*'. Hofmann, Rowe and Türk, *Administrative Law and Policy of the European Union* 178.

1209 However, the French courts make use of this principle when they apply EU law. The Conseil d'Etat has applied this principle when controlling the legality of French implementing measures of EU regulations. Conseil d'Etat, Fédération nationale des syndicats d'exploitants agricoles et autres du 11 juillet 2001, n°s 219494, 221021, 221274, 221275, 221421, Rec. F. Melleray, 'La revanche d'Emmanuel Lévy? L'introduction du principe de protection de la confiance légitime en droit public français' (2004) 56-57 Droit et société 143 147. See also: J.-M. Woehrling, 'La France peut-elle se passer du principe de confiance

to protect the individual's '*legitimate confidence*'[1210] and subsequently as the '*principle of protection of legitimate expectations*' forming '*part of the Community legal order*'.[1211] It was further consolidated as '*one of the fundamental principles of the Community*' in the *Dürbeck* case.[1212] The increasing number of references to this doctrine led Advocate General Lenz to state that it is '*undeniably part of [Union] law*'.[1213]

In EU law, the legal foundation of this principle is closely linked to the general principle of legal certainty,[1214] which reflects concerns of stability and foreseeability.[1215] Legal certainty essentially requires that subjects of the law know the law so that they can plan their actions accordingly. This requires that '*legal rules be clear and precise*' so that legal situations and relationships remain foreseeable.[1216] With regard to the transposition of directives the Court has stated that '*provisions of a directive must be implemented with unquestionable binding force and with the specificity, precision and clarity necessary to satisfy the requirements of legal certainty*'[1217] and that Member States have an obligation '*to establish a system of limitation periods that is sufficiently precise, clear and foreseeable to enable individuals to ascertain their*

légitime ?', *Gouverner, administrer, juger Liber amicorum Jean Waline, Mélanges en l'honneur de Jean Waline* (Dalloz 2002); 'Le juge administratif et le droit de l'Union européenne', Conseil d'Etat, 23 September 2015, <http://www.conseil-etat.fr/Decisions-Avis-Publications/Etudes-Publications/Dossiers-thematiques/Le-juge-administratif-et-le-droit-de-l-Union-europeenne> accessed 22 June 2017.

1210 Judgment of 5 June 1973, *Commission v Council*, C-81/72, EU:C:1973:60, para 13.

1211 Judgment of 3 May 1978, *Töpfer v Commission*, C-112/77, EU:C:1978:94, paras 18-19.

1212 Judgment of 5 May 1981, *Dürbeck v Hauptzollamt Frankfurt a. M.*, C-112/80, EU:C:1981:94, para 48.

1213 Opinion of AG Lenz in *Finsider v Commission*, Joined cases 63 and 147/84, EU:C:1985:253, p. 2865.

1214 Gordon and Moffatt, *EU Law in Judicial Review* 257 and Hofmann, Rowe and Türk, *Administrative Law and Policy of the European Union* 178 and see e.g. Judgment of 3 May 1978, *Töpfer v Commission*, C-112/77, EU:C:1978:94.

1215 C. Groulier, 'Norme permissive et droit public', Université de Limoges 2006) 509.

1216 Judgment of 15 September 2005, *Ireland v Commission*, C-199/03, EU:C:2005:548 para 69 and Judgment of 29 October 2009, *SKF*, C-29/08, EU:C:2009:665, para 77.

1217 Judgment of 15 October 2015, *Commission v Germany*, C-137/14, EU:C:2015:683, para 51 with reference to Judgment of 8 October 1996, *Dillenkofer and Others v Bundesrepublik Deutschland*, Joined cases C-178/94, C-179/94, C-188 to C-190/94, para 48.

rights and obligations.'[1218] Legal certainty, of which the principle of protection of legitimate expectations is the '*corollary*',[1219] therefore appears to be itself tightly connected with the Court's method for identifying rights by relying on the clarity and precisions of the norms.

Legitimate expectations can arise in a variety of cases:[1220] they can be based on legal acts conferring individual rights or benefits, although *S.N.U.P.A.T.* and *Hoogovens* made clear that changes of circumstances may justify revocation even of such acts;[1221] they can relate to the maintenance of existing legal positions; or they can be based on the conduct of the EU institutions. The cases analysed below exemplify how the principle of protection of legitimate expectations builds on the classic relation between rights, obligations and interests.

In *Sofrimport*, the company applied for annulment of Commission regulations and for damages for the harm which it had suffered by being prohibited to market apples from Chile in the Community.[1222] The Court em-

1218 Judgment of 28 January 2010, *Uniplex (UK)*, C-406/08, EU:C:2010:45, para 39 and case law cited. See also Judgment of 9 March 2017, *Poland v Commission*, C-105/16 P, EU:C:2017:191, para 54: '*le principe général de sécurité juridique, qui constitue un principe fondamental du droit de l'Union, exige, notamment, qu'une réglementation soit claire et précise, afin que les justiciables puissent connaître sans ambiguïté leurs droits et obligations et prendre leurs dispositions en conséquence*'. On legal certainty, see also Judgment of 16 December 2010, *Skoma-Lux*, C-339/09, EU:C:2010:781 and H. Van Eijken and M.J.M. Verhoeven, "Lost in translation'. Een bespreking van het arrest Skoma-Lux: de doorwerking van niet officieel gepubliceerde verordeningen' (2008) Nederlands tijdschrift voor Europees recht 165.

1219 Judgment of 15 February 1996, *Duff and Others*, C-63/93, EU:C:1996:51, para 20; Judgment of 19 March 1997, *Oliveira v Commission*, T-73/95, EU:T:1997:39, para 29.

1220 For a detailed overview of the case law on the protection of legitimate expectations see Hofmann, Rowe and Türk, *Administrative Law and Policy of the European Union* 178-190.

1221 *S.N.U.P.A.T. v High Authority*, Joined cases C-42/59 and C-42/59, p. 159 and *Koninklijke Nederlandsche Hoogovens en Staalfabrieken v High Authority*, C-14/61, p. 274.

1222 Commission Regulations (EEC) No 962/88 and No 984/88 of 12 and 14 April 1988 suspending the issue of import licences for dessert apples originating in Chile (OJ L 95 p. 10 and L 98, p. 37) and Commission Regulation (EEC) No 1040/88 of 20 April 1988 fixing quantities of imports of dessert apples originating in third countries and amending Regulation (EEC) No 962/88 suspending the issue of import licences for dessert apples originating in Chile (OJ L 102 p. 23).

phasised that Article 3(3) of Regulation 2707/72[1223] (on which the company was relying) provided that '*the measures provided for in paragraph 1 shall take account of the special position of products in transit to the Community*'. As the Court explained, the effect of that provision was '*to enable an importer whose goods are in transit to rely on a legitimate expectation that in the absence of an overriding public interest no suspensory measures will be applied against him.*'[1224] That provision thus qualifies as a superior rule of law intended to confer rights on individuals, since its purpose is '*to protect traders who import goods covered by that regulation into the Community from the unfavourable consequences of protective measures which might be adopted by the Community institutions*'.[1225] Having found that the first liability condition is fulfilled, the Court moves on to the second condition and holds that '*by failing completely to take account of the position of traders such as Sofrimport*', the Commission has committed a sufficiently serious breach of the principle of protection of legitimate expectations.[1226]

The Common Agricultural Policy and especially the Community's action on the milk market has given rise to several important cases concerning this principle. In *Mulder I*, the Court gave a preliminary ruling on the validity of Community regulations on additional levies on milk production.[1227] A milk producer had been encouraged by a Community measure to suspend production for a limited period in return for a premium, and then on this basis, was not allocated a milk production quota for the following year. The Court held that '*while a producer who had freely chosen to stop production for a certain period could not legitimately expect to be able to resume production under the same conditions as before, such a producer could legitimately expect not to be made subject to specific restrictions arising precisely from the fact that she or he had taken advantage of the option offered by the*

1223 Council Regulation (EEC) No 2707/72 of 19 December 1972 laying down the conditions for applying protective measures for fruit and vegetables (OJ English Special Edition 1972 (28 to 30 December), p. 3).

1224 *Sofrimport SARL v Commission*, C-152/88, para 16.

1225 *Sofrimport SARL v Commission*, C-152/88, para 26.

1226 *Sofrimport SARL v Commission*, C-152/88, para 27.

1227 Council Regulation (EEC) No 857/84 of 31 March 1984 adopting general rules for the application of the levy referred to in Article 5c of Regulation (EEC) No 804/68 in the milk and milk products sector (OJ L 90 p. 13), as supplemented by Commission Regulation No 1371/84 of 16 May 1984 laying down detailed rules for the application of the additional levy referred to in Article 5c of Regulation (EEC) No 804/68 (OJ L 132 p. 11).

Community legislation.'[1228] The regulation was partially invalidated because it breached the producers' legitimate expectations.

A later *Mulder* ruling on an action for annulment, still on regulation of the milk market, is interesting because of the way it distinguishes between two types of breaches of the principle of protection of legitimate expectations – one breach being sufficiently serious to pass the liability test, the other one being insufficiently serious.[1229] The first type of breach is where the Commission '*failed completely*' to take account of '*the specific situation of a clearly defined group of economic agents*' defined by the regulation at issue, i.e. the producers who were no longer allowed to market milk.[1230] The breach is sufficiently serious because, while the Commission had discretion as to how to take into account that situation, it did not have the discretion to decide not to take it into account at all. By contrast, in the second situation, the Community legislature made the choice to take into account the situation of those producers who wanted to get back in the milk market by setting a certain level of special references quantities; there, the Council was within the limits of its discretion.[1231] Only the first situation, thus, was found to be in breach of the principle of legitimate expectations, '*a general and superior principle of Community law for the protection of the individual*'[1232], and thus gave rise to liability of the Community. Consistently with what we have seen when looking at other liability cases, the key factor for assessing the existence of a right, and therefore a derived right to damages, is discretion.

The same method applied in *O'Dwyer*. Several Irish dairy farmers had applied for reparation of the damage which they claimed to have suffered as a result of the application of two Council Regulations amending milk production quotas[1233] in order to combat overproduction of milk. They argued that the legislative context prior to the adoption of the regulations at

---

1228 Judgment of 28 April 1988, *Mulder v Minister van Landbouw and Visserij*, C-120/86, EU:C:1988:213.

1229 E. Sharpston, 'European Community Law and the Doctrine of Legitimate Expectations: How Legitimate, and for Whom' (1990) 11 Northwestern Journal of International Law & Business 87 93.

1230 *Mulder and Others v Council and Commission*, Joined cases C-104/89 and C-37/90, paras 15-17.

1231 *Mulder and Others v Council and Commission*, Joined cases C-104/89 and C-37/90, paras 18-20.

1232 *Mulder and Others v Council and Commission*, Joined cases C-104/89 and C-37/90, para 15.

1233 Council Regulation 816/92 of 31 March 1992 amending Regulation 804/68 on the common organization of the market in milk and milk products (OJ L 86 p.

issue had given them a legitimate expectation that they would either see their quotas reinstated (depending on the case) or be paid compensation for the reduction of their quotas. They also asserted that the withdrawal, without any prior notice or transitional measures, of the compensation originally provided for constituted a violation of their legitimate expectations. In this respect the Court held that '*any economic operator to whom an institution has given rise to justified hopes may rely on the principle of protection of legitimate expectations*'.[1234] However, the Court added that, when the Community institutions have discretion to modify a situation, operators may not have a legitimate expectation that this situation will be maintained, particularly in the area of the common organization of the agricultural markets, '*whose purpose involves constant adjustments to meet changes in the economic situation.*'[1235] Determining milk quotas is thus typically a task where the Council has a broad power of appreciation to adjust to variations in the economic situations: therefore, '*no economic operator may entertain a legitimate expectation*' that the Council will not reduce the global milk production quantities, and therefore also the individual quotas.[1236] This corresponds to the idea that the broader the discretion that EU law grants to an institution, the less chances there are of identifying an individual right. The Court also looks at the problem from another, more subjective angle, recalling that '*where a prudent and discriminating economic operator could have foreseen the adoption of a Community measure likely to affect its interests, he cannot plead that his legitimate expectations have been infringed if the measure is adopted.*' In this case, the Court finds that a '*prudent and well-informed operator*'[1237] could indeed have foreseen the reduction of milk

---

83) and Council Regulation 748/93 of 17 March 1993 amending Regulation 3950/92 establishing an additional levy in the milk and milk products sector (OJ L 77 p. 16).

1234 *O'Dwyer and Others v Council*, Joined cases T-466/93, T-469/93, T-473/93, T-474/93 and T-477/93, para 48; *Opel Austria v Council*, T-115/94, para 93; Judgment of 14 July 1997, *Interhotel v Commission*, T-81/95, EU:T:1997:117, para 45; Judgment of 9 July 1999, *New Europe Consulting and Brown v Commission*, T-231/97, EU:T:1999:146, para 49; Judgment of 3 February 2005, *Chiquita Brands and Others v Commission*, T-19/01, EU:T:2005:31, para 255.

1235 *O'Dwyer and Others v Council*, Joined cases T-466/93, T-469/93, T-473/93, T-474/93 and T-477/93, para 48. The same applies to the area of protection against dumped imports, as the CFI held in Judgment of 18 September 1996, *Climax Paper Converters v Council*, T-155/94, EU:T:1996:118, para 110.

1236 *O'Dwyer and Others v Council*, Joined cases T-466/93, T-469/93, T-473/93, T-474/93 and T-477/93, para 49.

1237 *O'Dwyer and Others v Council*, Joined cases T-466/93, T-469/93, T-473/93, T-474/93 and T-477/93, paras 53-54.

quotas without compensation. This case illustrates how in order to apply the principle of protection of legitimate expectations, the Court follows a familiar method of looking at both sides of the medal: on the one hand, the objective assessment of the scope of the obligations of the institution (inversely correlated with the discretion allowed), and on the other hand the assessment of the subjective situation of the individual, taking into consideration his particular interests.

Since the milk quotas cases the principle of protection of legitimate expectations had been developed and consolidated in a variety of situations. In *Belgium and Forum 187 v Commission*, a State aid case, the Court has slightly rephrased the principle so that it covers not only 'economic operators' but '*any person*'.[1238] In addition, the principle is now clearly labelled by the General Court as a rule of law intended to confer rights on individuals.[1239] The interpretation of how it could give rise to a right to damages was further specified in *Citymo*. Relying on *Mulder*, the Court held that the rule allegedly breached, i.e. the principle of protection of legitimate expectations, was indeed a rule which conferred rights on individuals, so that the first liability condition was fulfilled.[1240] In order to assess the second liability condition, '*an assessment of the Commission's room for manoeuvre in the present case*' was necessary. In this case, the assurances given to the applicant seeking damages were '*precise, unconditional and consistent information from authorised and reliable sources*'. The Commission's behaviour then contradicted those assurances. Therefore, the 'sufficiently serious breach' condition was fulfilled.[1241] This implies that the intention of the authorities who issued the information does not matter. The assurances given can become binding and give rise to rights if they are precise, unconditional and consistent.[1242] The Court consistently states that the protection extends '*to any person in a situation in which an administrative authority has caused that*

1238 Judgment of 22 June 2006, *Belgium and Forum 187 v Commission*, Joined cases C-182/03 and C-217/03, EU:C:2006:416, para 147.

1239 Judgment of 28 April 2010, *BST v Commission*, T-452/05, EU:T:2010:167, para 156 and Judgment of 29 November 2016, *T & L Sugars and Sidul Açúcares v Commission*, T-279/11, EU:T:2016:683, para 58.

1240 Judgment of 8 May 2007, *Citymo v Commission*, T-271/04, ECR, EU:T:2007:128, paras 198-109.

1241 *Citymo v Commission*, T-271/04, ECR, para 138 and case law cited; Lewis and others, *Non-Contractual Liability of the EU for Damage Sustained by Women Who Received PIP Breast Implants* 9.

1242 Judgment of 17 March 2011, *AJD Tuna*, C-221/09, EU:C:2011:153 para 71-72; Judgment of 16 December 2010, *Kahla Thüringen Porzellan v Commission*, C-537/08 P, EU:C:2010:769 para 63 and case law cited; Judgment of 29 April

person to entertain expectations which are justified by precise assurances provided to him.'[1243] One more clear indication that the existence or absence of an *intention* to grant rights is not decisive in identifying actual rights.

The principle of protection of legitimate expectations can go so far as to generate individual rights even when legal provisions have not yet entered into force. In *Opel Austria*, the applicant was challenging the legality of a regulation withdrawing tariff concessions between Austria and the Community,[1244] by invoking the EEA Agreement, which had not yet entered into force.[1245] On this occasion, the Court of First Instance took into account the principle of good faith, a rule of international law which requires that States parties to an agreement refrain from acts which would defeat the object and purpose of a treaty even before the treaty enters into force.[1246] The CFI emphasised that '*the principle of good faith is the corollary in public international law of the principle of protection of legitimate expectations*'.[1247] It then held that '*traders may rely on the principle of protection of legitimate expectations in order to challenge the adoption by the institutions, during the period preceding the entry into force of that agreement, of any measure contrary to the provisions of that agreement which will have direct effect on them after it has entered into force*'. Consequently, '*the applicant is entitled to require a review of the legality of the contested regulation in the light of the provisions of the EEA Agreement which have direct effect after its entry into force.*'[1248] This could be a dissonance from the classic correlativity between rights and obligations: we

---

2004 in *Tokai Carbon e.a. v Commission* T-236/01, T-239/01, T-244/01 to T-246/01, T-251/01 and T-252/01, EU:T:2004:118, para. 15; Judgment of 1st December 2010, *Nolin v Commission*, F-82/09, EU:F:2010:154, paras 74-75. Mihaescu Evans, 'The right to good administration at the crossroads of the various sources of fundamental rights in the EU integrated administrative system' 117.

1243 Judgment of 21 February 2018, *Kreuzmayr*, C-628/16, EU:C:2018:84, para 46 and case law cited.

1244 Council Regulation (EC) No 3697/93 of 20 December 1993 withdrawing tariff concessions in accordance with Article 23(2) and Article 27(3)(a) of the Free Trade Agreement between the Community and Austria (General Motors Austria) (OJ L 343 p. 1).

1245 Agreement on the European Economic Area (EEA Agreement) (1994 OJ L1 572).

1246 Judgment of 22 January 1997, *Opel Austria v Council*, T-115/94, EU:T:1997:3, paras 90-91, citing ICJ Judgment of 25 May 1926, *German interests in Polish Upper Silesia*, CPJI, Series A, No7, pp. 30 and 39 and Vienna Convention, Article 18.

1247 *Opel Austria v Council*, T-115/94, para 93.

1248 *Opel Austria v Council*, T-115/94, paras 94-95. T. Lyons, *EC Customs Law* (Oxford University Press 2001) 189.

had seen in other cases such as *Hansa Fleisch*, that a right generally comes into existence simultaneously to its correlated obligation.[1249] In fact, and this is why it matters to look at both sides of the coin, the rationale for this solution is precisely on the side of the obligation. The principle of good faith has the effect of at least partly extending the temporal scope of the obligation to which the State (or here, the EU as a party to an international agreement) commits.[1250]

From this perspective, the rights arising from the principle of protection of legitimate expectations are the corollaries of the obligations to which the EU has committed and which are reinforced by the application of the principle of good faith. There is however, a strict limit to the principle of the protection of legitimate expectations, and this limit is dictated by the Court's usual concern for ensuring above all the respect and effectiveness of EU law: the principle '*cannot be relied upon against an unambiguous provision of EU law; nor can the conduct of a national authority responsible for applying EU law, which acts in breach of that law, give rise to a legitimate expectation on the part of a trader of beneficial treatment contrary to EU law*'.[1251]

C-628/16

Just like other rights, those rights arising from the principle of protection of legitimate expectations may be subjected to a sort of proportionality test. The Court indeed held in *CNTA* that, '*in the absence of an overriding public interest*', the Commission had infringed a superior rule of law by failing to couple the repeal of a set of rules with transitional measures for the protection of the expectations which a trader might legitimately have derived from the Community rules.[1252] By contrast, even if the Community

1249 *Hansa Fleisch v. Landrat des Kreises Schleswig-Flensburg*, C-156/91, discussed in this work p. 244.

1250 The principle of good faith in international public law can be likened to the EU Member States' duty of sincere cooperation under the EU treaties. G. De Baere and T. Roes, 'EU Loyalty as Good Faith' (2015) 64 International & Comparative Law Quarterly 829. The CJEU has connected good faith and sincere cooperation in *Intertanko* (D. Langlet and S. Mahmoudi, EU Environmental Law and Policy (Oxford University Press 2016)). The duty of sincere cooperation has comparable effects on obligations laid down in directives for which the transposition period has not yet expired: Judgment of 18 December 1997, *Inter-Environnement Wallonie*, C-129/96, EU:C:1997:628, para 45.

1251 See Judgment of 20 December 2017, *Erzeugerorganisation Tiefkühlgemüse*, C-516/16, EU:C:2017:1011, para 69 and case law cited.

1252 Judgment of 15 June 1976, *CNTA v Commission*, C-74/74, EU:C:1976:84, para 74 and *Belgium and Forum 187 v Commission*, Joined cases C-182/03 and C-217/03, para 149.

had first created a situation capable of giving rise to legitimate expectations, an overriding public interest may preclude transitional measures from being adopted in respect of situations which arose before the new rules came into force, but which are still subject to change.[1253] The Court has also insisted that in a case concerning the recovery of illegal aid that '*the interests of the Community must be taken fully into consideration in the application of a provision which requires the various interests involved to be weighed up before a defective administrative measure is withdrawn*'.[1254]

Although the principle of protection of legitimate expectations can be disconcerting at first, we see that rights arising from this principle fit within the classic model of rights, obligations, and interests. It has sometimes been suggested that legal certainty is based on objective criteria while the complementary principle of protection of legitimate expectations protects subjective rights.[1255] In fact, what comes out of the cases analysed above is that when applying the principle of protection of legitimate expectations, the Court relies both on objective considerations and on the subjective dimension of individual rights. On the one hand, the application of the principle serves a function of legality review, which is why the examination of the *obligations* binding the authorities and of the discretion which they allow is crucial. On the other hand, the Court assesses whether the particular individual was put in a situation such as to have legitimate expectations on which he could rely to pursue his *interests*. The combination of these two angles allows to determine the existence of a *right.* The EU principle of pro-

1253 Judgment of 17 July 1997, *Affish*, C-183/95 EU:C:1997:373, para 57; *Belgium and Forum 187 v Commission*, Joined cases C-182/03 and C-217/03, para 148; Judgment of 17 September 2009, *Commission v Koninklijke FrieslandCampina*, C-519/07 P, EU:C:2009:556, para 85 and Judgment of 19 July 2016, *Kotnik and others*, C-526/14, EU:C:2016:570, para 68. In the latter preliminary ruling, applicants were challenging the legality of national measures taken on the basis of the Communication from the Commission on the application, from 1 August 2013, of State aid rules to support measures in favour of banks in the context of the financial crisis (OJ C 216 p. 1) ('Banking Communication') and '*the objective of ensuring the stability of the financial system while avoiding excessive public spending and minimising distortions of competition*' was found to constitute such an overriding public interest (para 69).

1254 Judgment of 20 March 1997, *Land Rheinland-Pfalz v Alcan Deutschland*, C-24/95, EU:C:1997:163, para 24 and Judgment of 2 February 1989, *Commission v Germany*, C-94/87, EU:C:1989:46, para 12.

1255 J. Schwarze, *European Administrative Law* (Sweet & Maxwell 2006) 946 cited in De Vos, 'Europeanisering van het vertrouwensbeginsel. Betekenis van het Europese vertrouwensbeginsel voor de equivalente beginselen in Nederland, Frankrijk en België in het kader van een groeiend ius commune' 101.

tection of legitimate expectations reflects the hybridisation of two major legal systems – the French one focused on objective legality review, the German one based on a subjective conception of legality review.[1256] The result is again, the original double rationale of individual rights under EU law.

2.1.3.2. Administrative procedural rights

The development of procedural rights in EU administrative law also exemplifies this dual rationale, the Court having generally attempted to connect, rather than oppose, the general interests of good administration and the protection of individual interests. The limits to this approach however appear in the restrictive conception of these individual interests when it comes to granting access to the EU courts.

2.1.3.2.1. The dual rationale of administrative procedural rights

The founding case for the right to be heard in administrative proceedings was *Transocean Marine Paint.*[1257] Transocean was an association of marine paint manufacturers operating a world-wide sales network. It had already obtained an exemption under Article 85(3) EEC, but when it applied to get it renewed it had to go through proceedings again so that the Commission would check a list of conditions ensuring the absence of anti-competi-

1256 According to Woehrling this principle '*exprime le souci de placer à un très haut niveau la protection juridictionnelle des situations individuelles face à l'Etat dans un contexte de réaction au régime totalitaire antérieur*' J.-M. Woerhling, 'La France peut-elle se passer du principe de confiance légitime?', *Mélanges Jean Waline* (Mélanges Jean Waline, Dalloz 2002) 751. In the same vein, Melleray has analysed the principle as follows: '*il s'agit bien d'une valorisation affirmée des individus au détriment d'une puissance publique délégitimée par ses excès*'. Melleray, 'La revanche d'Emmanuel Lévy? L'introduction du principe de protection de la confiance légitime en droit public français' 148. De Vos has suggested that it is precisely because of this subjective dimension that the principle is not easily integrated into the French legal system. De Vos, 'Europeanisering van het vertrouwensbeginsel. Betekenis van het Europese vertrouwensbeginsel voor de equivalente beginselen in Nederland, Frankrijk en België in het kader van een groeiend ius commune' 11.

1257 Judgment of 23 October 1974, *Transocean Marine Paint Association v Commission*, C-17/74, EU:C:1974:106.

tive effects of the agreement. The negative final decision, however, relied on a decision which had not been notified to Transocean. The company challenged the decision, arguing that having not been notified of this condition it had not been in a position to make its views known on this point. The Court held that an individual '*whose interests are perceptibly affected by a decision taken by a public authority must be given the opportunity to make his point of view known*'.[1258] Relying on this principle, the Court annulled the decision and the Commission had to restart the proceedings for the exemption renewal.

It is probably no coincidence that this was one of the first competition cases before the Court after accession of the UK, and that the British Advocate General had in its Opinion conducted a comparative review of the legal systems of the Member States regarding the reception of the principle 'audi alteram partem' – an essential principle in English law – i.e. the requirement that '*an administrative authority, before wielding a statutory power to the detriment of a particular person, must in general hear what that person has to say about the matter, even if the statute does not expressly require it*', concluding that it deserved the rank of a general principle of EC law.[1259] This case is also significant in how it introduces the notion of interest in the system of procedural guarantees – whereas Advocate General Warner had not used this term in his Opinion. Perhaps the reference to affected 'interests' was a way for the Court, in this unprecedented incorporation of a common law principle into Community law, to slightly shift the balance back towards the more traditional influences of other Member States, especially that of France which gives great importance to this notion in administrative proceedings.[1260] It remained to be seen, however, how these 'interests' could be defined and in which circumstances they could be considered to have been 'perceptibly affected': the Court did not give precise indications in this respect – it seemed to simply accept that it was the case in

1258 *Transocean Marine Paint Association v Commission*, C-17/74, para 126.

1259 Bignami, 'Creating European Rights: National Values and Supranational Interests' 273-4; F. Bignami, 'Three Generations of Participation Rights in European Administrative Proceedings' Jean Monnet Working Paper 11/03 5. Advocate General Warner had observed that the principle was solidly rooted in the English, Danish, Irish and German legal systems and also in the process of being acknowledged in other Member States such as France, Belgium and Luxembourg. Opinion of AG Warner in *Transocean Marine Paint Association v Commission*, C-17/74, EU:C:1974:91, p. 1088-1089.

1260 See p. 30 of this work.

Transocean – and instead these answers have to be inferred from the case law.

The next step in the development of procedural guarantees was *Hoffmann-La Roche*.[1261] The Roche company had applied for annulment of a Commission decision which condemned it to pay a fine for abuse of dominant position. To examine the plea relating to irregularities in the administrative procedure, the Court started by emphasising the importance of the right to be heard, observance of which '*is in all proceedings in which sanctions, in particular fines or penalty payments, may be imposed a fundamental principle of Community law which must be respected even if the proceedings in question are administrative proceedings.*' The Court equates this right, which it labels a '*General Principle*',[1262] with the obligations imposed on the Commission by the relevant regulations, i.e. the duty to '*give the persons concerned the opportunity of putting forward their point of view with regard to the complaints made against them*' and '*in its decisions [to] deal only with those objections raised against undertakings and associations of undertakings in respect of which they have been afforded the opportunity of making known their views*'.[1263] By contrast with *Transocean*, here interests were not expressly mentioned, but could be inferred that the risk of a sanction or penalty – especially a fine or a penalty payment, i.e. a financial sanction – indeed corresponds to a situation where an individual's interests might be 'perceptibly affected'.[1264]

The case *Technische Universität München*[1265] has clarified the relation between the protection of individual interests in situations where they might be affected, and the procedural obligations of the administration. The TU München had brought into free circulation a microscope imported from Japan, on which the customs authorities of Munich demanded customs duties, relying on a Commission decision according to which the apparatus could not be imported free of customs into the Community given that

1261 Judgment of 13 February 1979, *Hoffmann-La Roche v Commission*, C-85/76, EU:C:1979:36.

1262 *Hoffmann-La Roche v Commission*, C-85/76, para 11. See also in e.g. Judgment of 29 June 1994, *Fiskano v Commission*, C-135/92, EU:C:1994:267, paras 38-39; Judgment of 6 December 1994, *Lisrestal*, T-450/93, ECR, EU:T:1994:290, para 42; Judgment in *Lisrestal*, C-32/95 P, EU:C:1996:402, para 21.

1263 *Hoffmann-La Roche v Commission*, C-85/76, para 9.

1264 Likewise in *Fiskano v Commission*, C-135/92, para 40: '*observance of the right to be heard requires that any person on whom a penalty may be imposed must be placed in a position in which he can effectively make known his view of the matters on the basis of which the Commission imposes the penalty*'.

1265 *Technische Universität München v Hauptzollamt München-Mitte*, C-269/90.

there were equivalent instruments available on the territory of the Community. In the proceedings between the university and the customs authorities, the German court lodged a reference for preliminary ruling to the Court of Justice on the validity of the Commission's decision. The university argued that the Commission had wrongly exercised its power of appraisal, especially by not respecting the right to be heard and not providing an adequate statement of reasons. Advocate General Jacobs expressed a vision of administrative procedural rights as tools to avoid a sanction but not as rights justiciable in themselves.[1266] He took the view that the Commission had failed to comply with the minimal requirement of both making a decision based on impartial expert advice and issuing a coherent statement of the scientific grounds for its decision. Consequently, based on an objective control of the administration's behaviour, he concluded that the Commission's decision is invalid.

The Court reached the same ultimate conclusion but based on a partly different reasoning, manifesting a different conception of the individual's function in the control of administrative action.[1267] The Court emphasised that the existence of the right to be heard is justified in any administrative procedure where the Commission holds a discretionary power, since discretion can be exercised properly, and its exercise controlled by the Court, only if the decision-making process is performed in strict respect of procedural requirements, which translate into individual rights.[1268] In order to effectively respect the right to be heard, the Commission should have allowed the University to '*put [its] own case and properly make [its] views known on the relevant circumstances and, where necessary, on the documents taken into account by the Community institution*'.[1269] The judgment also highlighted the insufficiency of the Commission's statement of reasons, which as a general rule '*must disclose in a clear and unequivocal fashion the reasoning followed by the Community authority which adopted the measure in question in such a way as to make the persons concerned aware of the reasons for the measure and thus enable them to defend their rights and to enable the Court*

1266 Opinion of AG Jacobs in *Technische Universität München v Hauptzollamt München-Mitte*, C-269/90, EU:C:1991:317, paras 41-43.

1267 As Tridimas puts it, this case '*brought to the fore a clash of conflicting philosophies of administrative law*'..

1268 *Technische Universität München v Hauptzollamt München-Mitte*, C-269/90, paras 13-14. J. Schwarze, 'Judicial Review of European Administrative Procedure' (2004) 68 Law and Contemporary Problems 85 95.

1269 *Technische Universität München v Hauptzollamt München-Mitte*, C-269/90, para 25.

to exercise its supervisory jurisdiction'.[1270] Thus, the protection of the procedural rights of the individuals and the feasibility of the judicial control of administrative action were put on the same level. The problem-solving potential of that balanced approach, embodying the dual rationale of procedural rights,[1271] materialises in the amount of cases in which *TU München* is referred to.[1272]

The 'affectation of interests' criterion is not fulfilled only in procedures susceptible of leading to sanctions, as exemplified in *TU München* and many other cases. In *Al-Jubail Fertilizer*, an anti-dumping case, the Court gave an extensive interpretation of this requirement: the right to be heard '*must be observed not only in the course of proceedings which may result in the imposition of penalties, but also in investigative proceedings prior to the adoption of anti-dumping regulations which, despite their general scope, may directly and individually affect the undertakings concerned and entail adverse consequences for them*'.[1273] This point was systematised in *Lisrestal*, in which several Portuguese organisations challenged a Commission decision to reduce

---

1270 *Technische Universität München v Hauptzollamt München-Mitte*, C-269/90, para. 26.

1271 Tridimas, *The General Principles of EU Law* 371. It is balanced also in the sense that it illustrates '*the role of the Court as the melting pot of national legal cultures*'. Tridimas, *The General Principles of EU law* 408.

1272 L. Azoulai, 'Le principe de bonne administration' in J.-B. Auby and J. Dutheil de la Rochère (eds), *Droit administratif européen* (Droit administratif européen, Bruylant 2007) 499; E. Vos, 'EU Risk Regulation reviewed by the European Courts' in M.B.A. Van Asselt, M. Everson and E. Vos (eds), *Trade, Health and the Environment - The European Union put to the test* (Routledge 2014). The *TU München* ruling is quoted e.g. in Judgment of 30 January 1992, *Schönherr v Economic and Social Committee*, T-25/90, ECR, EU:T:1992:8, para. 25; Judgment of 21 October 1992, *Maurissen v European Court of Auditors*, T-23/91, ECR, EU:T:1992:106, paras 41-47; Judgment of 18 mars 1993, *Parliament v Frederiksen*, C-35/92 EU:C:1993:104, para 13. See also, more recently, Judgment of 22 May 2012, *Aitic Penteo v OHIM - Atos Worldline*, T-585/10, ECR, EU:T:2012:251, para 37 ('*the duty to give reasons for individual decisions has two purposes: to allow interested parties to know the justifications for the measure so as to enable them to protect their rights and to enable the Union judicature to exercise its power to review the legality of the decision*').

1273 Judgment of 27 June 1991, *Al-Jubail Fertilizer Company and Others v Council*, C-49/88, EU:C:1991:276, para 15. See also: Judgment of 17 December 1997, *EFMA v Council*, T-121/95, EU:T:1997:198, para 84; Judgment of 18 December 1997, *Ajinomoto and The NutraSweet Company v Council*, T-159/94, EU:T:1997:209, para 83; Judgment of 19 November 1998, *Champion Stationery Mfg and others v Council*, T-147/97, EU:T:1998:266, para 55; Judgment of 21 November 2002, *Kundan and Tata v Council*, T-88/98, EU:T:2002:280, para 132.

financial assistance that originally been granted to them through the European Social Fund. The issue was typical of the multi-level, integrated EU administrative system:[1274] while the beneficiaries of the funding were expressly named in the decision, the addressee of the decision was the Member State through which the funds had been distributed. The undertakings challenged the decision, one of the grounds being that they had not had the chance to make their views known during the procedure. While the Commission had suggested that the right to be heard was not applicable because the procedure did not lead to a sanction,[1275] the Court rejected this approach and held that '*observance of the rights of the defence is a general principle of Community law which applies where the authorities are minded to adopt a measure which will adversely affect an individual*' and that accordingly '*the addressees of decisions which significantly affect their interests must be placed in a position in which they can effectively make known their views as regards the information on which the authorities intend to base their decision*'.[1276] It therefore became clear that interests are significantly affected not only where there is a risk of a sanction but also where a potential advantageous position is denied to an individual.[1277] In *Lisrestal*, the adverse effect consisted more specifically of '*the economic consequence of the decision to reduce the assistance*'.[1278]

In addition, the Court has held that '*in order to hold that the rights of the defence have been infringed, it is sufficient for it to be established that the non-disclosure of the documents in question might have influenced the course of the*

Bignami, 'Creating European Rights: National Values and Supranational Interests' 287; Mihaescu Evans, 'The right to good administration at the crossroads of the various sources of fundamental rights in the EU integrated administrative system' 171.

1274 H.C.H. Hofmann, 'Mapping the European administrative space' (2008) 31 West European Politics 662; H.C.H. Hofmann and A.H. Türk, 'The challenges of Europe's integrated administration' in E.O. Eriksen and C. Joerges (eds), *Law, Democracy and Solidarity in Europe's Post-National Constellation* (ARENA 2006).

1275 *Commission* v *Lisrestal and Others*, C-32/95 P, paras 31-34 J. Mendes, *Participation in EU Rule-Making. A Rights-Based Approach* (Oxford University Press 2011) 182.

1276 *Commission* v *Lisrestal and Others*, C-32/95 P, para 30. See also *Texdata Software*, C-418/11, para 83.

1277 J. Mendes, 'Participation and participation rights in EU law and governance' in H.C.H. Hofmann and A.H. Türk (eds), *Legal Challenges in EU Administrative Law Towards an Integrated Administration* (Edward Elgar 2009) 265.

1278 *Commission* v *Lisrestal and Others*, C-32/95 P, para 48. Mendes, *Participation in EU Rule-Making. A Rights-Based Approach* 182.

procedure and the content of the decision to the applicant's detriment'.[1279] Therefore, both the type of interests potentially affected, and the possibility that they might be affected, are construed generously by the Court. This has been often reasserted in the case law since then, and it applies both in procedures between individuals and the EU institutions[1280] and in procedures opposing individuals to national administrations,[1281] as well as in litigation between Member States and the EU institutions.[1282]

Consistently with this approach, the General Court has on several occasions found that the procedural obligations of the EU institutions entailed the protection of individuals and that their violations could give rise to Union liability. In *Fresh Marine* it was established that the breach of the duty of care could render the Community liable for damage.[1283] Likewise in *Airtours v Commission,* a Commission decision declared a concentration of two companies incompatible with the common market and was then an-

---

1279 Judgment of 25 October 2002, *Tetra Laval v Commission,* T-5/02, EU:T:2002:264, para 90 and case law cited.

1280 In *Windpark Groothusen,* for instance, the Court reaffirmed that there is a right to a hearing '*where the Commission contemplates the imposition of a penalty or the adoption of a measure likely to have an adverse effect on the person's legal position*': Judgment of 14 May 1998, *Windpark Groothusen v Commission*, C-48/96 P, EU:C:1998:223, para 47. See also: Judgment of 9 July 2003, *Vlaams Fonds voor Sociale Integratie van Personen met een Handicap v Commission*, T-102/00, EU:T:2003:192, para 59; Judgment of 14 June 2016, *Marchiani v Parliament,* C-566/14 P, EU:C:2016:437, para 51 and case law cited.

1281 In *Sopropé*, a Portuguese importer of footwear who refused to pay a duty and argued that it had not been granted sufficient time to submit its observations. The Court implicitly admitted that Sopropé's interests were significantly affected by the duty, which confirms that such affectation is not limited to sanctions, and instead covers also other cases where a financial burden is imposed on the individual: Judgment of 18 December 2008, *Sopropé,* C-349/07, EU:C:2008:746, para 36-37. See also Judgment of 22 October 2013, *Sabou*, C-276/12, EU:C:2013:678, para 38; Judgment of 3 July 2014, *Kamino International Logistics and Datema Hellmann Worldwide Logistics*, Joined cases C-129/13 and C-130/13, EU:C:2014:2041, paras 30 and 35.

1282 E.g. Judgment of 20 December 2017, *Spain v Council,* C-521/15, EU:C:2017:982, para 90: the requirement of impartiality must be complied with as a '*general principle of law in the context of administrative procedures that are initiated against Member States and are liable to result in decisions adversely affecting them*'. See also Judgment of 15 July 2004, *Spain* v *Commission*, C-501/00, EU:C:2004:438, para 52.

1283 *Fresh Marine v Commission,* T-178/98, para 61. J. Mendes, 'Discretion, Care and Public Interests in the EU Administration: Probing the Limits of Law' (2016) 53 Common Market Law Review 2 419.

nulled by the CFI.[1284] In the subsequent damages action based on a violation of the duty of diligence, the CFI insisted on the case law which recognised the protective nature of this duty and held that the criterion of a rule of law intended to confer rights on individuals was met.[1285] In *Idromacchine*, a State aid case, it held that the purpose of the obligation of professional secrecy laid down in Article 287 EC was to '*protect the rights conferred on individuals*' and that the Commission did not have broad discretion when applying that obligation; therefore, the breach alleged, a '*mere infringement*', amounted to a sufficiently serious infringement of a rule of law conferring rights on individuals, meaning that both the first and the second liability conditions were fulfilled.[1286]

2.1.3.2.2. The limits of this balanced vision

There are however limits to the protective power of administrative procedural rights. These limits correspond to two types of restriction of the possibility for an individual interest to trigger the activation a right. The first type concerns the definition of the individual interest, and the second concerns the type of measure that is challenged.

Concerning the limits to the acceptable individual interest, they were first set down in *Tradax*.[1287] A Dutch importer of maize challenged a duty through an action for failure to act, seeking a declaration that the Commission should have granted access to the information which had relied on for calculating the duty. The company had based its argument on the respect of its individual rights which it derived from principles such as the principle of good administration. More specifically, Tradax argued that the right to a hearing, which encompassed a right of access to documents, should apply to individuals affected by an implementing regulation. The Court

1284 Judgment of 6 June 2002, *Airtours v Commission*, T-342/99, EU:T:2002:146.

1285 Judgment of 9 September 2008, *MyTravel v Commission*, T-212/03, EU:T:2008:315, paras 49-50. Aalto *Public liability in EU law: Brasserie, Bergaderm and beyond* 117.

1286 Judgment of 8 November 2011, *Idromacchine and Others v Commission*, T-88/09, EU:T:2011:641, paras 24 and 56; confirmed by Judgment of 3 September 2013, *Idromacchine and Others v Commission*, C-34/12 P, EU:C:2013:552; M. Pittie and A. Jussiaux, 'Les recours en responsabilité non contractuelle devant le juge de l'Union européenne' in S. Mahieu (ed), *Contentieux de l'Union européenne Questions choisies* (Contentieux de l'Union européenne Questions choisies, Larcier 2014) 526.

1287 Judgment of 15 March 1984, *Tradax v Commission*, 64/82, EU:1984:106.

held that '*while it would be consistent with good administration for the Commission periodically to publish for the information of the traders concerned the main data taken into account in fixing cif prices*', this arrangement does not include a duty to reply to individual requests.[1288] The Court exclusively analysed the behaviour of the Commission, closely reviewing each step of the procedure, and concluded that the latter had no duty to provide information individually requested by the company. This is not inconsistent with the correlativity model, in the sense that in the absence of a duty, there would of course be no corresponding right. The problem with this judgment is that it is rather restrictive as to the role that individual interests may play in a procedure, making clear that there is no '*right for any person concerned (…) to be enabled to check whether the legislation in force (had) been correctly applied*'.[1289] The Court considered that being simply 'concerned' (or '*intéressé*' in the French version) was not equivalent to having one's interests 'perceptibly affected'. The Advocate General, whom the Court had followed, had also insisted that a measure having an impact on '*all traders*' did not lead to a duty towards '*individual traders*'.[1290]

In the same vein, in *Lisrestal* the Court had held that the applicants had a right to a hearing because they were '*directly and individually concerned*' by the decision, which '*named and expressly referred to the applicants as direct beneficiaries of the assistance granted.*'[1291] In *BEUC*, the Court held that an anti-dumping procedure involved no allegations against a consumer organisation and therefore could not result in a measure adversely affecting the latter, which therefore had no right to a hearing and no access to the file in such a procedure.[1292] This approach was reiterated in later case law, consolidating the analogy between the position of an addressee and the notion of significant affectation of an individual's interests,[1293] so that the activation of the right to be heard is conditioned on criteria similar to those of an ac-

1288 *Tradax v Commission*, 64/82, para 22.

1289 *Tradax v Commission*, 64/82, para 24.

1290 Opinion of AG Slynn, *Tradax v Commission*, C-64/82, EU:1983:300, p. 1386. Bignami, 'Creating European Rights: National Values and Supranational Interests' 338.

1291 *Commission v Lisrestal and Others*, C-32/95 P, para 45.

1292 Judgment of 28 November 1991, *BEUC v Commission*, C-170/89, EU:C:1991:450, para 19-21. Bignami, 'Creating European Rights: National Values and Supranational Interests' 338.

1293 In *Air Inter v Commission*, the Court accepted that applicants who were expressly named in a decision and therefore directly and individually concerned had a right to be heard in the procedure leading to the decision (Judgment of 19 June 1997, *Air Inter v Commission*, T-260/94, EU:T:1997:89). Conversely, the

tion for annulment – which, as already pointed out, are not very favourable to individuals.[1294] This results in preventing certain natural or legal persons from being heard in procedures where they might have an interest in intervening.

The Court's case law on procedural rights is also consistent with its restrictive approach to the function of individual interests in activating the legality review of measures taken in certain specific areas, such as State aid.[1295] In *max.mobil*,[1296] a telephone operator had lodged a complaint with the Commission, arguing that the Austrian authorities had granted to one of its competitors, advantages that were unlawful under EU State aid law. The Commission issued a decision refusing to act on this complaint and the company sought annulment of this decision. The CFI performed the rather classic operation of deriving a right from an obligation, by holding that the applicant's right to have his complaint examined could be deduced from the Commission's obligation to perform a diligent and impartial examination of complaints.[1297] Against this backdrop, the CFI held that the action was admissible, although it rejected it on substantial grounds. The case went on appeal and in his Opinion Advocate General Poiares Maduro argued that the obligation of diligent and impartial examination, which is derived from the principle of good administration, '*has an objective scope*' and '*is not carried out in relation to the person lodging the complaint, but first of all by reference to the general interest in sound administration and the proper application of the rules of the Treaty*'.[1298] The Court of Justice seemed to follow this approach when it held that '*no general principle of Community law*' gives standing to an undertaking for challenging a refusal by the Commission to initiate proceedings against a Member State for infringement of EU State law.[1299] This finding was however limited to the context of Article 90(3) EC (now Article 106(3) TFEU), which according to settled case law does not impose on the Commission an obligation to

General Court *Ristic and others v Parliament*, T-238/07 rejected the applicant's argument that his right to be heard had been violated, because the procedure could not be considered to have been initiatied 'against' this applicant. Mendes, *Participation in EU Rule-Making. A Rights-Based Approach* 182.

1294 As discussed at p. 212 of this work.

1295 See p. 250 of this work.

1296 Judgment of 22 February 2005, *Commission v max-mobil*, C-141/02 P, EU:C:2005:98.

1297 *Max.mobil v Commission*, T-54/99, paras 55-57.

1298 Opinion of AG Maduro in *Commission v max-mobil*, C-141/02 P, EU:C:2004:646, para. 56.

1299 *Commission v max-mobil*, C-141/02 P, para 72.

bring proceedings and based on which '*individuals cannot require the Commission to take a position in a specific sense*'.[1300] Therefore, '*the fact that max.mobil [had] a direct and individual interest in annulment of the Commission's decision to act on its complaint [was] not such as to confer on it a right to challenge that decision*'. Indeed, the letter itself did not produce legal effects and therefore was not challengeable by way of an action for annulment.[1301] For all these reasons, the Court held that the action was inadmissible.

The General Court generalised the implications of this judgment in *Arizona Chemical*. This case concerned companies that commercialised rosin, a chemical which a Commission Directive categorised as a skin sensitiser and which, as a result, was subjected to special conditions and restrictions for sale. The undertaking brought an action for annulment against the directives and an action for damages in compensation for the loss resulting from that classification. The applicants were arguing that the act they were contesting was administrative, individual and definitive, and that they therefore did not have to prove that they were individually and directly concerned in order for their action for annulment to be admissible.

The General Court, however, held that the contested act was an act of general application, and in that context, examined whether the applicants enjoyed specific procedural guarantees expressly laid down in the legislation in question and which would grant them a right of action. The applicants were arguing that they could rely on the Commission's duty of diligence in a procedure resulting in the adoption of measures of general application in the same way as they could rely on procedural guarantees in the context of a procedure resulting in the adoption of an administrative act of individual application. However, the GC characterised the duty of diligence as '*essentially an objective procedural guarantee arising from an absolute and unconditional obligation on the Community institution relating to the drafting of an act of general application and not the exercise of any individual right.*' Thus, even though the duty of diligence may be categorised as a '*procedural guarantee*', this in the GC's view does not mean that it confers rights directly on the operators taking part in a procedure leading to the adoption of measures of general application. The GC insisted that the duty of diligence was '*primarily an essential and objective procedural requirement, imposed in the public interest by legislation meeting the requirements of scientific objectivity*' and that its scope was to be distinguished from that in which it applied in procedures leading to the adoption of individual measures, '*in*

1300 *Commission v max-mobil*, C-141/02 P, para 69.
1301 *Commission v max-mobil*, C-141/02 P, para 70.

which the protective nature of the duty of diligence in relation to individuals has been recognised by the case-law.'[1302] The GC concluded that '*the existence of a duty of diligence cannot imply the grant of an individual procedural guarantee,*' especially in the process of drafting acts of general application.[1303] The contested directive therefore was not open to review under Article 230 EC.[1304] This result was thus reached essentially by denying the possibility for individuals to rely on an objective procedural requirement that exists for the public interest.

This solution has been maintained in Article 41 of the Charter, which proclaims the right for every person to be heard before an individual which would affect him or her adversely is taken: as the Court confirmed in *AJD Tuna*, '*that provision does not cover the process of enacting measures of general application*',[1305] so that an act of general application cannot be found invalid on the ground there was no consultation of operators likely to be affected by its measures.[1306]

2.1.3.3. Interim conclusions

This section has traced the transversal guarantees enshrined in the principle of protection of legitimate expectations and various administrative procedural rights as they apply in various areas of EU economic law. In this context, the basic concept of rights as correlatives of obligations activated by individual interests functions with some limitations. The correlativity between obligations and rights works in a very interesting and dynamic way in the application of the principle of protection of legitimate expectations. This principle allows for the identification of rights (and by reflex, correlative obligations) by combining an objective assessment of the discretion allowed on the administration, and the assessment of the subjective situation of the individual pursuing his or her interests. The case law also reflects a balanced vision of administrative procedural rights, simultaneously allowing individuals to protect their interests and the Court to control that the administration has complied with its obligations, as exemplified in *TU München*. This dual rationale is however altered when it comes

1302 Order of 14 December 2005, *Arizona Chemical and Others v Commission*, EU:T:2005:458, paras 86-88.
1303 *Arizona Chemical and Others v Commission*, EU:T:2005:458, para 89.
1304 *Arizona Chemical and Others v Commission*, EU:T:2005:458, para 92.
1305 *AJD Tuna*, C-221/09, para 49.
1306 *AJD Tuna*, C-221/09, para 53.

to challenging acts of the EU institutions: the conception of the adversely affected interest is narrower, and even in its restricted form, this kind of interest is not sufficient when it comes for challenging measures of general application on procedural grounds. In such a situation, the interests of the Union and those of individuals are no longer deemed to converge.

2.1.4. Conclusions

The cases analysed in this section on individual rights and economic interests illustrate how the relation between rights, obligations and interests has functioned as a structuring and structural force in the development of the legal system of the EU. It has supported the elaboration of many essential cogwheels of this system, starting with the emblematic doctrine of direct effect. Fundamental freedoms litigation provided many opportunities to refine this doctrine, and the basic concept of individual rights on which it relied. The examples consolidate the observation from Part 1 that obligations give rise to rights, no matter whether they are enshrined in provisions or primary or secondary law, as long as they are phrased in a way that makes them practically applicable.[1307] The protective intention underlying a norm plays a limited role in assessing whether it confers an individual right. What matters is the individual interest, allowing any individual to contribute to the enforcement of EU law by initiating a process of legality review. In addition, the case law on competition law confirms the implications of *Defrenne II* that the right-obligation correlation applies also in horizontal relations, i.e., in relations between private individuals such as competitors.[1308] Finally, the correlation is also illustrated by the development of administrative procedural rights, supported by a double rationale of ensuring the protection of individuals and enabling the legality review of the administrative process.

The added value of this section is that it also clarifies the relation between rights and discretion. The existence of discretion does not preclude the ability of a provision to confer rights on individuals, since assessing discretion is not an all-or-nothing issue but a matter of degree, assessed by reference to criteria such as are clarity, precision, and unconditionality· The probability of finding a right in a provision would thus be inversely pro-

1307 See the conclusions of Part 1 p. 224.

1308 *Defrenne v SABENA*, C-43/75. On the identification of individual rights in relations between competitors see p. 279.

portional to the degree of discretion allowed by the provision. This is illustrated not only in direct effect cases but also in the case law on Member State liability. A connected point is that the dynamism of the correlation appears clearly in liability cases where direct effect has failed or does not apply, giving rise to a further right (and correlative obligation) to reparation of the damage incurred. In the same way, the principle of protection of legitimate expectations, where circumstances allow it, generates new rights and correlative obligations.

By contrast, certain inconsistencies in the application of the concept of individual rights also come to light. Closer scrutiny of the case law on Union liability confirms the observation from Part 1 that in this context the Court is more sensible to the *Schutznorm* pressure. The review of State aid case law shows a similar result. This reinforces the idea already explored in Part 1[1309] that, where individuals are challenging decisions of the EU institutions, individual and EU interests are not perceived as converging. As a result, private interests are deprived of the ability to trigger individual rights and individuals are denied their function of agents of EU law.

2.2. *Individual rights beyond economic interests*

Mrs Defrenne and Mrs Johnston, two of the most prominent characters encountered in this study, were both victims of gender-based discrimination in the workplace. The significance of their cases for the development of rights (and remedies) in EU law has been repeatedly emphasised – in the case law, in the literature as well in this research. Their stories attest that the individual rights protecting interests that are not exclusively economic, are not new in the EU constitutional architecture. However, along with the evolution of the perception, roles and functions of individuals within this architecture, socio-economic, social and political rights have undeniably gained relative importance over the years. Some issues concerning these rights arise with new or renewed intensity following the Treaty of Lisbon. The purpose of this section is to look at this second 'generation' of rights and assess whether the classic obligation-right correlation and the functional relation between rights and interests apply in this context.

The first step will be to focus on the rights of workers, as they promptly developed additionally to the freedom of movement, in response to social realities in the workplace (2.2.1). Secondly, this section analyses the rights

1309 See p. 175 of this work.

that come with the status of Union citizen, clearly signalling that individuals are perceived no longer only as economic actors but also as social and political actors equipped with corresponding rights (2.2.2.). Thirdly, we will look at the rights of individuals seeking international protection in the EU and see that these rights work according to a model that is less protective of individuals than the classic concept of rights (2.2.3).

2.2.1. Socio-economic rights of workers

The protection of workers was originally developed instrumentally to the free movement of workers, yet it also reflects a social concern which was already part of the *telos* of the Community. As the Court pointed out in *Defrenne II*, social progress and the improvement of living and working conditions were already listed in the preamble of the EEC Treaty.[1310] *Defrenne II* also made clear that the conception of rights as correlates of obligations that had first been developed predominantly in the case law on fundamental freedoms and competition, also applied in the area of social policy. Social security law provides examples of identifying rights in classic vertical situations of individuals relying on EU law against Member States (2.2.1.1). Also in the context of 'vertical' relations between individuals and the EU as an employer, the case law on procedural rights in EU civil service law further illustrates the nature and function of rights under EU law (2.2.1.2). The case law on the prohibition of discrimination, the correlative right to equal treatment, and the interests relevant for activating these correlatives, adds important elements to the understanding of rights by tackling the issue of their identification and application in horizontal situations (2.2.1.3). Additionally, the 'younger' participation rights of workers exemplify the contemporary challenges to the original EU concept of rights (2.2.1.4).

2.2.1.1. Rights in EU social security law

Early in its history the Community imposed obligations on Member States concerning social security for migrant workers.[1311] From these obligations,

1310 *Defrenne v. SABENA*, C-43/75, para. 7.

1311 Council Regulation No 3 of 25 September 1958 on social security for migrant workers (OJ, English Special Edition 1952-1958(I), p. 63).

it should by now not come as a surprise that correlative rights could be identified in a variety of cases. The Court's very first preliminary ruling on social security was delivered in response to a reference originating in Luxembourg.[1312] Mr Simon, a Belgian national residing in the Grand Duchy and working for the Luxembourgish national rail company (SNCFL), died in a car accident during a leisure trip in Belgium. His widow brought proceedings against the (Belgian) insurer of the car driver who had caused the accident. She was joined in the proceedings by the SNCFL and by its sickness fund, claiming compensation respectively for expenses arising from the payment of benefit owed to the widow and for funeral expenses. They relied on the regulation on social security for migrant workers, Article 52(1) of which provided for a direct claim in favour of the person liable for payment of such benefits. The Luxembourgish court considered that the law applicable to the case was that of the place where the accident occurred, i.e. Belgian law, which provided no remedy for the sickness fund and the SNCFL, because their obligation to provide benefits arose from Mr Simon's Luxembourgish employment contract. Having found that the regulation applied to injuries sustained by migrant workers outside of their professional activity,[1313] the Court assessed the applicability of Article 52. This provision allowed Member States to conclude bilateral agreements in order to frame these types of claims, and the Belgian government was arguing that in the absence of such an agreement, Article 52 could not be relied on by individuals. In response, the Court noted '*the general nature*' of the terms of the first paragraph (aiming '*to secure the recognition by each Member State of any right of action pursued by the others in favour of the institution liable for payment of benefit against the third party liable [...]*'), and the '*peremptory*' wording of the provisions, which were therefore '*capable of direct application*'.[1314] In allowing for implementing provisions in the form of bilateral agreements, '*Article 52 in no way [made] the effect of the first paragraph dependent on the existence of such agreements*', the sole function of which was '*to provide detailed rules for its implementation, where necessary, without however rendering the direct effect of the provision in question subordi-*

1312 Judgment of 12 November 1969, *Caisse de maladie des CFL and Others v Compagnie d'assurance sur la vie et contre les accidents*, C-27/69, EU:C:1969:56.

1313 *Caisse de maladie des CFL and Others v Compagnie d'assurance sur la vie et contre les accidents*, C-27/69, para 7.

1314 *Caisse de maladie des CFL and Others v Compagnie d'assurance sur la vie et contre les accidents*, C-27/69, paras 15-18.

nate to them'.[1315] As a consequence, the Court held that there was indeed a direct right of action. This approach strongly resembles the Court's later finding in *Defrenne II* that the absence of implementing measures does not constitute an obstacle to the implementation (in the form of a right) of an obligation that is sufficiently clear and precise (or here, 'peremptory').

The correlation between obligations and rights is also verified in *Grimaldi*, which raised the question of the legal effects of two recommendations on how to deal with occupational diseases,[1316] and especially whether these could be relied on by individuals. Consistently with the *Becker* ruling, the Court first rejected again the *a contrario* argument based on the distinction between regulations having direct effect by their very nature, and other type of legal instruments.[1317] While admitting that recommendations were not intended to be binding, the Court still checked whether the substance of the act corresponded to its form, i.e. whether it in facts contained elements that would make it binding. Here indeed the recommendations contained nothing binding or presented as such; '*consequently, they [could not] create rights upon which individuals may rely before a national court*'.[1318] So again the classic *Van Gend en Loos* approach of assessing the existence of an obligation in order to identify the correlative right applies.

Following the same approach, the *BECTU* case added important precisions on the relation between a right contained in a directive, and the implementing measures taken by the national legislator. In *BECTU* the Court had to deal with a reference for preliminary ruling on the working time directive,[1319] coming again from the UK. The BECTU was a union of workers from the sectors of broadcasting, entertainment, cinema and theatre. These workers were mostly employed under short-term contracts and as a conse-

---

1315 *Caisse de maladie des CFL and Others v Compagnie d'assurance sur la vie et contre les accidents*, C-27/69, paras 19-20. This ruling illustrates the interchangeability, for practical purposes, of the terms '*direct applicability*', '*direct effect*', which the Court appears to use indifferently as properties of a norm that give rise to rights.

1316 Commission Recommendation to the Member States of 23 July 1962 concerning the adoption of a European schedule of occupational diseases (OJ 1962, 80, p. 2188) and Commission Recommendation 66/462 of 20 July 1966 on the conditions for granting compensation to persons suffering from occupational diseases (OJ 1966, 147, p. 2696).

1317 Judgment of 13 December 1989, *Grimaldi v Fonds des maladies professionnelles*, C-322/88, EU:C:1989:646, para 11 ; *Becker*, C-8/81.

1318 *Grimaldi v Fonds des maladies professionnelles*, C-322/88, paras 14-16.

1319 Council Directive 93/104/EC of 23 November 1993 concerning certain aspects of the organisation of working time, (OJ L 307 p. 18).

quence, they ended up being deprived of paid annual leave, by virtue of the British legislation transposing the working time directive. The BECTU challenged this legislation, arguing that Article 7 of the directive entitled '*every worker*' to paid annual leave. The Court characterised this provision as '*clear and precise*'[1320] and the corresponding entitlement as '*a particularly important principle of Community social law*'[1321] and found that the British legislation, by imposing '*a precondition for entitlement to paid annual leave which has the effect of preventing certain workers from any such entitlement*' amounted to negating '*an individual right expressly granted*' to '*all workers*' by the directive.[1322] Article 7 included the following precision: '*in accordance with the conditions for entitlement to, and granting of, such leave laid down by national legislation and/or practice*'. The Court held that this must be construed '*as referring only to the arrangements for paid annual leave adopted in the various Member States*', and not as a possibility to make the existence of the right, '*which derives directly from Directive 93/104 subject to any preconditions whatsoever.*'[1323] The directive '*does not allow Member States to exclude the very existence of a right*'.[1324] Even though the obligation and correlative right are subject to implementing measures, these measures cannot end up denying their very existence. This can also be read in terms of limits to the discretion of the Member States: while there may be discretion in determining some conditions to the application of the right, there is none with regard to the obligation of ensuring the existence of the right itself.

This approach also applies in liability cases. The *Larsy* case[1325] exemplifies how the clarity of the norm breached is key for identifying a right to reparation. This was a preliminary ruling on the interpretation of Regulation (EEC) No 1408/71 on the application of social security schemes to self-employed persons moving within the Community.[1326] The issue arose

1320 Judgment of 26 June 2001, *BECTU*, C-173/99, EU:C:2001:356, para 34.

1321 *BECTU*, C-173/99, para 43.

1322 *BECTU*, C-173/99, para 48 and para 55.

1323 *BECTU*, C-173/99, para 53.

1324 *BECTU*, C-173/99, para 55. See also Judgment of 20 January 2009, *Schultz-Hoff and Others*, Joined cases C-350/06 and C-520/06, EU:C:2009:18, para 46 and Judgment of 24 January 2012, *Dominguez*, C-282/10, EU:C:2012:33, para 19.

1325 Judgment of 28 June 2011, *Larsy*, C-118/00, EU:C:2001:368.

1326 Council Regulation (EEC) No 1408/71 of 14 June 1971 on the application of social security schemes to employed persons, to self-employed persons and to members of their families moving within the Community, as amended and updated by Council Regulation (EEC) No 2001/83 of 2 June 1983 (OJ L 230 p.6), as amended by Council Regulation (EEC) No 1248/92 of 30 April 1992 (OJ L 136 p. 7).

in proceedings between Mr Larsy and the Inasti (the Belgian social security organism for independent workers). Mr Larsy was a self-employed gardener living in Belgium near the French border and working both in France and Belgium. He applied for a retirement pension in both France and Belgium, and was awarded the pension first in Belgium, then also in France. Because the French authorities awarded him a pension, the Inasti adopted a decision to reduce his pension entitlement, based on Article 95a of Regulation 1408/71. However, a ruling by the ECJ on another case (concerning Mr Larsy's brother) made clear, that such a decision was an erroneous application of that provision; instead, based on Articles 12 and 46 of Regulation 1408/71, the applicant was entitled to the maximal calculation basis for a Belgian retirement pension even while he also received a pension from France.[1327] Based on this judgment, Mr Larsy challenged the Inasti's decision and the Inasti acknowledged that his pension rights were to be revised but stated that there were no damages to be paid. The Belgian court asked the CJEU whether the Inasti's behaviour fulfilled the condition of a sufficiently serious breach of Community law (implying that there was little doubt that the other two liability conditions[1328] were met).

The Court reasoned in two steps, distinguishing between the Inasti's application of Articles 12 and 46 of Regulation 1408/71, '*which entitled Mr Larsy to maintain a retirement pension calculated on a 45/45 basis, including for the period during which he enjoyed a retirement pension* [from the French authorities]' and Article 95a of the same regulation, '*which cannot limit that entitlement in time, contrary to Inasti's interpretation of the provision*'.[1329] Firstly, regarding Articles 12 and 46, the Court recalled, quoting *Brasserie*, that '*a breach of Community law will be sufficiently serious if it has persisted despite a preliminary ruling from the Court from which it is clear that the conduct in question constituted an infringement*'. Since there had been a preliminary ruling on the case of Mr Larsy's brother, '*comparable in every respect*' to the case at issue, and '*a clear answer*' as to how to apply the provisions, namely that Mr Larsy was entitled to have his retirement pension calculated on the maximum basis, the Court found that the Inasti had '*failed to draw all the consequences*' from the earlier judgment.[1330] Secondly, regarding Article 95a, the Court stated that '*regard must also be had to the clarity and precision of that provision*' and that '*the reply to be given [...], namely that Article 95a of*

1327 Judgment of 2 August 1993, *Larsy v INASTI*, C-31/92, EU:C:1993:166.

1328 I.e. the existence of a rule entailing rights and the existence of a causal link between the breach and the damage.

1329 *Larsy*, C-118/00, para 42.

1330 *Larsy*, C-118/00, paras 43-45.

Regulation No 1408/71 did not apply in the circumstances of the case, should not have been in any doubt, given the wording and purpose of that provision.' Therefore, the application of Article 95a, '*which resulted in limiting the effect of Articles 12 and 46 of that regulation in time, constitute[d] a serious breach of Community law.*'[1331] The Court added that the breach could not be justified by requirements of national law, since the principle of primacy required the Inasti to set aside the national provisions which may have prevented the application of Community law, especially those provisions having direct effect and from which Mr Larsy derived rights.[1332] The mention of the rights as a consequence of direct effect also indicates that the first liability condition was fulfilled. In the end, the solution to the *Larsy* case was based on a previous preliminary ruling having clarified the meaning of some of the provisions at issue (Articles 12 and 46), and on the clarity of the other provision (Article 95a). The clarity of the provisions breached (whether they are clear in themselves or following a preliminary ruling) made them easily applicable by the national authority and makes their erroneous application inexcusable, meaning that there has indeed been a serious breach of Community law.

In like manner, in the *Fuß* case the Court had to rule on the right to reparation for a fire officer whose employer had set a working time which exceeded the limit laid down by Directive 2003/88 on the organisation of working time.[1333] Here, the Court assesses the first liability condition by referring to earlier judgments which have established the direct effect of the relevant provision of the directive: '*in those circumstances, it appears obvious that Article 6(b) of Directive 2003/88 constitutes a rule of EU law intended to confer rights on individuals and that, therefore, the first condition for the existence of a right to reparation is met in the main proceedings.*'[1334] Concerning the second liability condition, the Court recalls the various judgments which have already shed light on the directive and left no doubt as to the meaning of the provision at issue. Therefore, the failure to comply with it '*occurred in obvious disregard of the Court's case law*' and thus constitutes a sufficiently serious breach of EU law.[1335] Again, the clarity of the norm breached (whether it was clear originally or was made clear through previ-

1331 *Larsy*, C-118/00, paras 46-47.

1332 *Larsy*, C-118/00, paras 50-52.

1333 Judgment of 25 November 2010, *Fuß*, C-429/09, EU:C:2010:717; Parliament and Council Directive 2003/88/EC of 4 November 2003 concerning certain aspects of the organisation of working time (OJ L 299 p. 9).

1334 *Fuß*, C-429/09, paras 33-35 and case law cited, and para 50.

1335 *Fuß*, C-429/09, paras 54-58.

ous rulings) and the corresponding denying of discretion to the authorities, is essential for identifying the violated right and the ensuing right to reparation.

Concerning the role of interests in triggering rights, the case law on the prohibition on gender discrimination has confirmed and refined this role and deserves a full section,[1336] but here we focus on one application of it in the field of social security: the *Verholen* case,[1337] on the interpretation of the directive on the progressive implementation of the principle of equal treatment for men and women in matters of social security.[1338] *Defrenne II* had already made clear that a woman could rely on that prohibition when she had an interest in doing so. *Verholen* exemplifies how interests can function as triggers for rights in a more complex way, and stretch their scope of application beyond their apparent protective scope. Among several joined cases, especially interesting is the case of Mr Heiderijk. Because of a distinction made by Dutch law between male and female workers regarding the conditions under which they could retire with a full pension, Mr Heiderijk's wife was regarded as uninsured during the time when Mr Heiderijk had been working in Germany. The consequence was that Mr Heiderijk's own pension was inferior to what it would have been had the situation been reverse (i.e. had the wife been working abroad, and the husband staying in the Netherlands with no employment). The question, as Advocate General Darmon pointed out, was '*rather delicate*' because until that point the discrimination had been relied on '*by the person who was its actual victim*'[1339] – precisely like in *Defrenne II*. Here, there was no doubt that Mrs Heiderijk's treatment was indeed contrary to the directive, but she was not a party to the proceedings – it was instead her husband, whose pension was being affected because of the discrimination she had suffered. Could he rely on the provisions of a directive which was not directly aimed at protecting him from discrimination? The Court held that '*the right to rely on the provisions of Directive 79/7 is not confined to individuals coming within the scope ratione personae of the directive, in so far as the possibility cannot be ruled out that other persons may have a direct interest in ensuring that the principle of*

1336 See below p. 336.

1337 *Verholen and Others v Sociale Verzekeringsbank Amsterdam*, C-87/90 to C-89/90.

1338 Council Directive 79/7/EEC of 19 December 1978 on the progressive implementation of the principle of equal treatment for men and women in matters of social security (OJ L 6 p. 24).

1339 Opinion of AG Darmon in *Verholen and Others v Sociale Verzekeringsbank Amsterdam*, C-87/90 to C-89/90, EU:C:1991:223, para 32.

non-discrimination is respected as regards persons who are protected'.[1340] Non-discrimination is thus not only a right with a pre-determined beneficiary: the directive determines the personal situations to which the prohibition on discrimination applies, but it does not limit the possibility for anyone who has a 'direct interest' to rely on this prohibition. Therefore, a husband who bears the effects of a national provision discriminating against his wife, should be allowed to rely on the directive before the national court.[1341]

Verholen reads like a sequel to *Defrenne II*: it confirms that any individual who has an interest to do so has a right to enforcement of the obligation of national authorities not to discriminate against another individual – meaning that the protective intention behind the obligation matters little in pinpointing the corresponding right and that the obligation does not need to be an obligation *towards* a determined person for it to qualify as a right. This is probably why *Verholen* has been described as an objective-focused ruling:[1342] the individual serves as an agent of enforcement of the objective prohibition on discrimination – that is, he contributes to the *effet utile* of EU law, according to the mechanism of functional subjectivation. Whether or not the provision identifies the individual who may be protected by a given duty is not relevant for determining whether that duty amounts to a right – and if the beneficiary is indeed identified, it also does not prevent other individuals from relying on the obligation. *Verholen* is thus hardly reconcilable with some doctrinal interpretations according to which the existence of rights depends on the identification of legislative intention to protect a specific interest.[1343]

1340 *Verholen and Others v Sociale Verzekeringsbank Amsterdam*, C-87/90 to C-89/90, para 23.

1341 This of course was possible '*only if his wife, who is the victim of the discrimination, herself comes within the scope of that directive*'; as this was not the case here, the situation did not fall within the scope of application of EU law. *Verholen and Others v Sociale Verzekeringsbank Amsterdam*, C-87/90 to C-89/90, para 25.

1342 R. Widdershoven, 'Naar een bestuurs(proces)rechtelijk Ius Commune in Europa' in E. Steyger, R. Widdershoven and A.W.H. Meij (eds), *Europees recht en het Nederlands bestuursrecht* (VAR-reeks 1996) 193.

1343 Hilson and Downes understand the interest theory as positing that '*a person can be said to have a right (...) if he or she is the intended beneficiary of a duty*' (although, as we have seen in Part 1, this is only one version of this theory). This version of the interest theory, they argue, applies in EU law where '*the idea of interpretation of legislative intention*' can be seen at work in the Court of Justice's case law, including *Verholen*. Hilson and Downes, 'Making sense of rights: Community rights in E.C. law' 123. See also Eilmansberger, 'The Relationship

2.2.1.2. Procedural rights in EU staff cases

EU staff cases have provided numerous opportunities for the development of administrative procedural rights. These cases are interesting not only because they confirm the basic rights-obligations correlation, but also because they indicate the type of interests that may trigger the application of rights. This section highlights that administrative procedural rights protect not only economic interests in the strict sense, but also career-related interests (which do not come down only to pecuniary interests) arising in procedures of recruitment, promotion, or dismissal.

Going back to the early times of the Community, the right to be heard first appeared in *Alvis.*[1344] Mr Alvis, a civil servant of the Council, was challenging his dismissal for disciplinary reasons. The Court emphasised the duty of the administration to allow its servants '*the opportunity of replying to allegations before any disciplinary decision is taken concerning them*'. The Court held that the rule of procedure considered here is a generally accepted principle of the national administrative law of the Member States, and deduced from this that the rule should also apply to the administration of the Community since it met '*the requirements of sound justice and good administration.*' The Court never referred to a 'right' to be heard, but only to the duty of the administration to hold such a hearing. The absence of a hearing left no choice to Mr Alvis but to apply to the Court for annulment of the decision, which signalled that the administrative (here, the disciplinary) procedure was flawed.[1345] The primary objective of judicial review is to correct this malfunctioning, rather than to expressly protect the individual interest of Mr Alvis. In this respect, the objective control of the administration's action seems to prevail over the concern of the respect for individual rights.

Nevertheless, the focus on the obligation of the administration is also linked with a subjective element, as the Court states that the observance of the requirement of good administration is even more important '*when, as in this case, the allegations are capable of resulting in the dismissal of the servant concerned*'.[1346] The Court's statement that the right to be heard is a rule

---

between Rights and Remedies in EC Law: in Search of the Missing Link' 1239 and 1241.

1344 *Alvis v Council of the EEC*, 32/62.

1345 *Alvis v Council of the EEC*, 32/62, p.57: '*In this case [...] the failure of the defendant to allow the applicant to submit his defence before his dismissal has undoubtedly encouraged the applicant to make an application to the Court*'.

1346 *Alvis v Council of the EEC*, 32/62, p. 55.

'*which meets the requirements of sound justice and good administration*'[1347] reflects, in the words of Tridimas, '*the dual rationale of the right to a hearing*' and of procedural rights in general: the instrumental rationale is the '*functional requirement promoting the quality of administration*' and the non-instrumental rationale is the '*requirement of formal justice akin to a human right and deriving from the rule of law.*'[1348] While the instrumental rationale is predominant in *Alvis*, at this early stage of the development of European administrative law, the non-instrumental aspect of the right to be heard is embryonic but nevertheless exists as a consequence of the obligation of the administration to hear the concerned person.

The risk of prejudice to an individual's interests as the trigger to the application of the general principle of the right to be heard was confirmed and consolidated in the 1970s. For instance, in *Mollett v Commission*, the Court relied on '*the general principle that when any administrative body adopts a measure which is liable gravely to prejudice the interests of an individual it is bound to put him in a position to express his point of view*'[1349] and annulled a decision that the applicant was physically unfit to be recruited. So, the right to be heard is triggered by a threat to individual interests also when these interests are not strictly quantifiable.

The recomposition of the network of sources of rights with the integration of the Charter in the EU legal order did not fundamentally alter this state of play. *Franchet and Byk,*[1350] which was decided after the proclamation of the Charter but before it became binding, illustrates a balanced approach to the different sources of procedural rights in administrative matters. Yves Franchet and Daniel Byk, respectively former Director-General and former Director of Eurostat, applied for compensation for damages due to the conduct of the Commission and OLAF in the investigations on irregularities in the financial management of Eurostat. Various components of the principle of good administration are mentioned in this case, based both on general principles and on Article 41 of the Charter. Firstly, the CFI relied on the '*principle of sound administration, the inter partes principle, the rights of the defence and the requirement of an investigation that consid-*

1347 *Alvis v Council of the EEC*, 32/62, p. 55.

1348 T. Tridimas, *The General Principles of EU Law* (2nd edn, Oxford University Press 2006) 371.

1349 Judgment of 13 April 1978, *Mollet v Commission*, C-75/77, EU:C:1978:84, para 21. See also Judgment of 9 November 2006, *Commission v De Bry*, C-344/05 P, EU:C:2006:710, para 37.

1350 Judgment of 8 July 2008, *Franchet and Byk v Commission*, T-48/05, ECR, EU:T:2008:257, paragraphs 151 to 156.

ers the evidence for and against the parties concerned, enshrined, inter alia, in the ECHR and the Charter'[1351] and held that these incontestably conferred rights on individuals for the purposes of assessing liability.[1352] Secondly, the plaintiffs had argued that OLAF was under an obligation to maintain the confidential nature of an investigation as long as no wrongdoing had been established. The Court held that, due to the '*right to good administration, provided for in Article 41 of the Charter, which states that that right includes the right of every person to have access to his or her file, while respecting the legitimate interests of confidentiality and of professional and business secrecy*',[1353] the administration was indeed under an obligation to '*avoid giving the press information concerning disciplinary proceedings which might damage the official concerned*'.[1354] Thirdly, the CFI recalled that '*the obligation to conduct administrative procedures within a reasonable time is a general principle of Community law which is enforced by the Community Courts and which, moreover, is set forth, as an element of the right to good administration, in Article 41(1) of the Charter*', the breach of which could entail the liability of the Community.

Franchet and Byk is important for this study in at least three ways. The first observation is that this case, by acknowledging the continued relevance of the general principle of good administration in combination with Article 41 CFR, provides '*an example of applied pluralism of sources of fundamental rights in the EU legal order*'.[1355] Secondly, the fluidity in the use of different sources also manifests in the interchangeability and complementarity of the terms and corresponding concepts of 'right', 'obligation' and 'principle'. The third interesting aspect is that this case illustrates how rights have the function of protecting a variety of interests, here the 'honour' and 'professional reputation' of the complainants, the harm to which lead the CFI to award them 56 000 euros for non-material damage.[1356] These three observations are all confirmed in the post-Lisbon case law on good administration in the context of EU civil service litigation.

Concerning the plurality of sources of rights, the CFI has acknowledged the contact points between different sources of administrative procedural

1351 *Franchet and Byk v Commission*, T-48/05, para 101, see also para 126.

1352 *Franchet and Byk v Commission*, T-48/05, paras 153-156.

1353 *Franchet and Byk v Commission*, T-48/05, para 257.

1354 *Franchet and Byk v Commission*, T-48/05, para. 214.

1355 Hofmann and Mihaescu, 'The Relation between the Charter's Fundamental Rights and the Unwritten General Principles of EU Law: Good Administration as the Test Case' 93.

1356 *Franchet and Byk v Commission*, T-48/05, para 411.

rights in a variety of other staff cases, pointing out that the Explanations themselves indicate that Article 41 of the Charter codifies the case law on the general principle of good administration.[1357] This includes not only the right to be heard but also the duty to state reasons, which is enshrined both in Article 296 TFEU and in Article 41(2)(c) CFR, reflecting the double rationale of this '*essential principle of EU law whose objective is, first, to provide the party concerned with the necessary information to enable him to ascertain whether or not the decision adversely affecting him is well founded and, secondly, to enable judicial review of the decision*'.[1358] This balanced approach has also been followed by the Civil Service Tribunal, for instance in *Guittet* where it first cites Article 41, paragraph 1 of the Charter and then refers to established case law on the principle of good administration and the duty of care, which of course date back to judgments delivered a long time before the entry into force of the Charter.[1359] Thus the CST reads the Charter provision and the general principle of law together, as a single continuous source of the right to good administration. The pluralism of sources anchors the right even more solidly in the EU legal order, so that the CST will control ex officio whether it has been respected, like *Bui Van*.[1360]

Concerning the correlativity between obligations and rights, it also remains relevant as exemplified in *GV v EEAS*.[1361] In this case, an employee claimed that there had been a manifest violation of his right to be heard before being dismissed by the European External Action Service (EEAS). The EEAS argued that as a new administrative structure it had not yet formalized all the decision-making processes required by EU case law. The CST answered that according to Article 51(1) CFR, the provisions of the Charter, especially Article 41, were addressed to the institutions and bodies of the EU, and that latter may not rely on internal difficulties to justify disrespecting norms of EU primary law. This applied all the more since the implementation of the requirements of Article 41(2)(a) presented no particular difficulty.[1362] This is quite similar to a direct effect test of identify-

1357 *BN v Parliament*, F-157/12, para 84; see also *Pipiliagkas v Commission*, F-96/13, EU:F:2015:29, para 54. See also *Z v Court of Justice*, F-88/09 and F-48/10, para 146 and case law cited.

1358 Judgment of 17 March 2015, *AX v ECB*, F-73/13, para 188.

1359 Judgment of 15 December 2015, *Guittet v Commission*, F-141/14, EU:F:2015:149, para 50-51 and case law cited.

1360 Judgment of 11 September 2008, *Bui Van v Commission*, F-51/07, EU:F:2008:112, paras 77-80.

1361 Judgment of 5 February 2016, *GV v EEAS*, F-137/14, EU:F:2016:14.

1362 *GV v EEAS*, F-137/14, para 77. See also Judgment of 24 April 2017, *HF v Parliament*, T-584/16, EU:T:2017:282, para 155.

ing a right based on its correlation with an obligation with a clearly determined content and addressee, not requiring further implementing measures.

The relevance of the correlation is also validated by the importance of discretion (as opposed to protective intention) as an indicator of the existence of a right, including for the purposes of awarding damages. The case of Ms *Staelen* provides an interesting example. Ms Staelen had applied for compensation for the damage she claimed to have suffered as a result of the Ombudsman's handling of her complaint concerning mismanagement by the European Parliament of the list of suitable candidates in a recruitment competition. Concerning the requirement of rule of law 'intended to confer rights' on individuals, the General Court provided an overview of the different possibilities that this rule covers according to the case law: '*the requirement is satisfied where that rule creates an advantage which could be defined as a vested right, is designed for the protection of the interests of individuals or entails the grant of rights to individuals, the content of those rights being sufficiently identifiable*' and where '*the rule of law breached, while referring essentially to interests of a general nature, also ensures the protection of the individual interests of the persons concerned.*'[1363] The protective intention underpinning a norm is thus only one of many possible indicators that this norm would qualify as a rule conferring rights.[1364] The principle of diligence, the right to good administration and the rules governing inquiries conducted by the Ombudsman are part of this broad array of rules 'intended to confer rights.'

The GC also insisted on the importance of discretion for assessing whether there was a 'sufficiently serious breach,' and applying it to the Ombudsman held that '*where the Ombudsman has discretion, only where he manifestly and gravely disregarded the limits on his discretion can there be a suffi-*

1363 Judgment of 29 April 2015 in *Staelen v Ombudsman*, T-217/11, EU:T:2015:238, para 73.

1364 The case of Bruno Gollnisch, a French Member of the European Parliament provides an additional illustration of this approach: in Judgment of 19 March 2010, *Gollnisch v Parliament*, T-42/06, EU:T:2010:102, the GC held at para 94 that the privileges and immunities '*expressly*' conferred by the Protocol on the Privileges and Immunities of the European Union and its officials, staff and Members of Parliament '*have a functional character, inasmuch as they are intended to avoid any interference with the functioning and independence of the Communities*,' and therefore have been '*provided in the public interest*.' This does not prevent the Protocol from also conferring '*an individual right on the persons concerned, compliance with which is ensured by the system of rights of recourse established by the Treaty*.' (Protocol (No 7) on the Privileges and Immunities of the European Union (OJ C 326, 26/10/2012 p. 266)).

ciently serious breach of Union law which can establish the liability of the European Union. By contrast, where, in the exercise of his functions, the Ombudsman has only considerably reduced, or even no, discretion, the mere infringement of Union law may be sufficient to establish the existence of such a sufficiently serious breach.'[1365] The GC found that the Ombudsman had discretion in his handling of complaints but held that he had manifestly and gravely disregarded the limits on his discretion in handling Ms Staelen's case, to whom it therefore awarded damages.

This judgment was in great part set aside by the Court of Justice in *Ombudsman v Staelen.*[1366] The Court of Justice admitted that there were indeed rules 'protecting individuals', not disavowing the GC's approach on that issue. In particular, the Court assessed whether there was '*a sufficiently serious breach of the Ombudsman's duty to act diligently*', which may be read as an implicit acknowledgement that this duty constitutes a 'rule intended to confer rights.' However, it found that these rules had not been '*manifestly and gravely disregarded*' in view of the specific circumstances of the case, in which the Ombudsman had shown no obvious lack of care.[1367] Again, the greater the discretion, the harder it is to prove that there was an obligation to behave in a certain way and the lower the probability of finding a right.

The third and last observation regarding the function of interests also stands if we look at recent staff cases: there is always an emphasis on interests as justifications for rights, as well as a broad understanding of these interests. For instance, according to the CST the right to be heard applies especially before adoption of an act that could have sensitive consequences for an employee's career evolution or career perspectives.[1368] And as exemplified by a recent case, the right to be heard protects interests of all parties to the proceedings, including the EU institutions themselves[1369] – showing again how the notion of interest matters more than any other characteristic attached to the person claiming the right to be heard (i.e., it is not, or not only, a matter of who is weaker or who is intended to benefit from the

1365 *Staelen v Ombudsman*, T-217/11, para 72.

1366 Judgment of 4 April 2017 in *European Ombudsman v Staelen*, C-337/15 P, EU:C:2017:256.

1367 *European Ombudsman v Staelen*, C-337/15 P, paras 37-41.

1368 Judgment of 19 June 2014, *BN v Parliament*, F-157/12, EU:F:2014:164, para 84; also quoted in Judgment of 15 April 2015, *Pipiliagkas v Commission*, F-96/13, EU:F:2015:29, para 54. See also Judgment of 5 December 2012, *Z v Court of Justice*, F-88/09 and F-48/10, EU:F:2012:171, para 146 and case law cited; Judgment of 14 May 2014, *Delacroix v EEAS*, F-11/13, EU:F:2014:91, paras 36-38.

1369 Judgment of 17 December 2009, *Réexamen M v EMEA*, C-197/09 RX-II, EU:C:2009:804, para 41.

rule). The emphasis on individual interest also means that '*not every infringement of the rights of the defence is to be penalised by annulment of the contested measure. That is the case where the unlawfulness of the contested measure did not influence its content*'.[1370] This is however strictly controlled: in a case where the applicant's employment contract with Frontex was not renewed, the Court considered that it could not be excluded that this decision '*could have been different if the applicant had been given a proper opportunity to make his point of view known regarding the level of his professional performance*' and that to hold '*that Frontex would have adopted the same decision, even after hearing the applicant, would render meaningless the fundamental right to be heard enshrined in Article 41(2)(a) of the Charter, since the very content of that right implies that the person concerned has the possibility of influencing the decision-making process at issue*'.[1371]

The case law on EU civil service litigation, thus confirms the flexibility and dynamism of the Court's approach for identifying rights, both at the level of sources of rights (a pluralist approach to a variety of sources) and in terms of the type of provisions that may give rise to rights (those that lay down obligations may translate into correlative rights, depending on the degree of discretion that they allow). It also shows that the Court is willing to accept a variety of career-related interests as triggers for activating these rights.

2.2.1.3. Rights in EU anti-discrimination law

When social rights are at stake, the issue of horizontal direct effect is as important as it is problematic. On the one hand, social guarantees have been the major stumbling block in the process of consolidating fundamental rights protection at the EU level because they are understood in very different ways from one Member State to the other;[1372] the broader the effects they are granted, the more problems arise in their implementation. On the other hand, excluding the application of social rights from private litigation may deprive them of any effect, given that these rights mostly apply in relations created by work contracts. It is therefore not surprising that most, if not all, of the essential case law of the Court of Justice on the horizontal

1370 *Bui Van v Commission*, F-51/07, para 81 and case law cited.

1371 Judgment of 17 September 2014, *Wahlström v Frontex*, F-117/13, EU:F:2014:215, paras 32-33. See also Judgment of 24 November 2015, *Marcuccio* v *Commission*, T-236/02, EU:T:2005:417, para 115.

1372 As discussed in this work p. 139.

application of rights, deals with social rights.[1373] *Defrenne II* has laid down the basis for equating rights and obligations in horizontal relationships (in this case, the right not to be discriminated against on the basis of one's age can be seen as one side of a medal, the other side being the duty of the employer not to discriminate[1374]). Some problems are however not fully solved, especially with regard to social rights enshrined in directives, since horizontal direct effect is in principle not possible for these instruments. Emblematic of this issue of horizontal effect is the prohibition of discrimination in the workplace on a variety of bases, including gender, age and religion.[1375]

2.2.1.3.1. The issue of horizontal direct effect in the light of the right-obligation correlation

As regards the limits to the potential of directives to create directly applicable rights, the Court drew the line in another case on gender-based difference in retirement age. In *Marshall*, an employee of the South-West Hampshire Area Health Authority challenged her employer's policy to send female employees into retirement at the age of sixty, while male employees could stay on the job until they were sixty-five. Mrs Marshall relied on the Equal Treatment Directive and there was no problem for determining the content of the unconditional and sufficiently precise obligation and the corresponding right, which indeed prohibited discrimination with regard to the retirement age.[1376] The problem was that the Britsh government argued here that the Health Authority was acting here not as a public body, but in its capacity of employer. The Court laid down the principle which still stands today: '*according to Article [288 TFEU] the binding nature of a directive, which constitutes the basis for the possibility of relying on the directive before a national court, exists only in relation to 'each Member State to which it is addressed'. It follows that a directive may not of itself impose obligations on an*

1373 Brunessen, 'Retour sur un classique. Quelques remarques sur la catégorie des principes généraux du droit de l'Union européenne' 1224.

1374 J. Vandamme, 'C'est arrivé près de chez vous! Het arrest Italmoda en het ontzeggen van rechten aan de particulier op grond van de EU-richtlijn' (2015) Nederlands tijdschrift voor Europees recht 154 157.

1375 See e.g. E. Ellis and P. Watson, *EU anti-discrimination law* (Oxford University Press 2012).

1376 *Marshall v. Southampton and South-West Hampshire Area Health Authority*, C-152/84, paras 52-55.

individual and that a provision of a directive may not be relied upon as such against such a person.'[1377] In defining the limits of the scope of rights potentially contained in a directive, the Court in fact looked at the scope of the corresponding obligations and found that the Treaty itself limited this scope by imposing them only on Member States. The *Marshall* solution is therefore perfectly consistent with the basic correlativity between obligations and rights, the scope of the latter mirroring the scope of the former.

The first way in which the Court managed to minimise the impact of the restriction for individuals claiming rights from directives was by adopting a broad understanding of *vertical* effect, so that *horizontal* effect would be an issue in a more limited number of cases. In *Marshall* the Court's reply to the UK's argument was that '*where a person involved in legal proceedings is able to rely on a directive as against the State he may do so regardless of the capacity in which the latter is acting, whether employer or public authority. In either case it is necessary to prevent the State from taking advantage of its own failure to comply with Community law*.'[1378] This reflects a broad conception of the State as a debtor of the obligations laid down in directives, the vertical direct effect of which functions as a deterrent against violations by Member States of these obligations. In *Foster v British Gas,* yet another case on gender discrimination in the workplace (more specifically at the British Gas Corporation) the Court systematised this position and held that any body which provides a public service under the control of the State '*and has for that purpose special powers beyond those which result from the normal rules applicable in relations between individuals*' is included among the bodies against which individuals may rely upon the provisions of a direc-

1377 *Marshall v. Southampton and South-West Hampshire Area Health Authority*, C-152/84, para 48. See also Judgment of 8 October 1987, *Kolpinghuis Nijmegen*, C-80/86, EU:C:1987:431, para 9; Judgment of 26 September 1996, *Arcaro*, C-168/95, EU:C:1996:363, para 36; Judgment of 17 December 1998, *IP*, C-2/97, EU:C:1998:613, para 25, Judgment of 22 September 1998, *Coote v Granada Hospitality*, C-185/97, EU:C:1998:424, para 17; Judgment of 13 July 2000, *Centrosteel*, C-456/98, EU:C:2000:402, para 15; *Pfeiffer and Others*, Joined cases C-397/01 to C-403/01, para 108; Judgment of 21 October 2010, *Accardo and Others*, C-227/09, EU:C:2010:624, para 45.

1378 *Marshall v. Southampton and South-West Hampshire Area Health Authority*, C-152/84, para 49.

tive.[1379] In a nutshell, individual rights contained in a directive may be claimed against any emanation of the State.[1380]

Besides this imperfect solution, another workaround to the absence of horizontal direct effect of directives lies with the obligation of consistent interpretation, also known as indirect effect,[1381] which may be defined as '*the duty of all national bodies to interpret, as far as possible, all national law in light of and in conformity with EU law*'.[1382] In broader conceptual terms: '*a norm of (EU) law is used as an aid to the interpretation of another rule; the latter is the one actually being applied by a court (or other authority) but is construed in the light of the former.*'[1383]

The Court started developing this solution in *Von Colson*, again a case on sex discrimination – and in fact, not a horizontal direct effect case but a rather classic question on the vertical direct effect of a directive. Two social workers were claiming damages from the Land Nordrhein-Westphalien, which had not hired them because they were women. In cases where employers had been found to practice discrimination in hiring, the German law implementing the Equal Treatment Directive only provided for limited damages, i.e. covering expenses incurred for submission of an application. The question arose whether other types of sanction should also be available, especially the possibility for victims of discrimination to claim damages. The Court looked at '*the actual purpose of the directive*' and the requirement laid down at Article 6, which '*by granting applicants for a post who have been discriminated against recourse to the courts, acknowledges that those candidates have rights of which they may avail themselves before the courts*'.[1384] The Court insisted that while the directive did not require a specific type of sanction against discrimination in hiring, the sanction had to '*guarantee*

1379 *Foster and others v British Gas*, C-188/89, para 20. See also Judgment of 20 March 2003, *Kutz-Bauer*, C-187/00, EU:C:2003:168, para 71; Order of 26 May 2005, *Sozialhilfeverband Rohrbach*, C-297/03, EU:C:2005:315, para 27.

1380 R. Gordon and R. Moffatt, *EU Law in Judicial Review* 162; Rosas and Armati, *EU Constitutional Law: An Introduction* 81.

1381 J.L. Da Cruz Vilaça, 'Le principe de l'effet utile du droit de l'Union dans la jurisprudence de la Cour' in A. Rosas, E. Levits and Y. Bot (eds), *The Court of Justice and the Construction of Europe: Analyses and Perspectives on Sixty Years of Case-law* (T.M.C. Asser 2013) 289.

1382 M. Bobek, 'The effects of EU law in the national legal systems' in C. Barnard and S. Peers (eds), *European Union Law* (Oxford University Press 2014) 153.

1383 G. Betlem, 'The Doctrine of Consistent Interpretation. Managing Legal Uncertainty' in J.M. Prinssen and A. Schrauwen (eds), *Direct Effect. Rethinking a Classic of EC Legal Doctrine* (Europa Law Publishing 2002) 79.

1384 *Von Colson and Kamann v Land Nordrhein-Westfalen*, C-14/83, para 22.

real and effective judicial protection' and '*have a real deterrent effect on the employer*'.[1385] Applying then the classic direct effect test, it admitted that there was no '*unconditional and sufficiently precise obligation*' in the directive regarding the type of sanction to be applied.[1386] So, the right not to be discriminated against on the basis of one's gender was clear; the issue was with the type of remedy available once such discrimination had taken place. In the absence of an unconditional and sufficiently precise obligation in the provision, the Court goes a step higher in the system within which this provision works: it relies on the obligation of the Member State to accomplish the objectives of the directive, and on the even broader obligation of sincere cooperation enshrined in the Treaty, which binds also the judicial authorities of the Member States – in order to conclude that '*it is for the national court to interpret and apply the legislation adopted for the implementation of the directive in conformity with the requirements of Community law, in so far as it is given discretion to do so under national law*', especially by looking at the '*wording and purpose*' of the directive.[1387]

The obligation of consistent interpretation was then applied to horizontal litigation, in *Marleasing* for the first time.[1388] It was systematised in the *Dominguez* ruling on the right to paid annual leave, where the Court prioritised the three possibilities for a national court to deal with effect of di-

1385 *Von Colson and Kamann v Land Nordrhein-Westfalen*, C-14/83, para 23. Swaine, 'Subsidiarity and Self-Interest: Federalism at the European Court of Justice' 23.

1386 *Von Colson and Kamann v Land Nordrhein-Westfalen*, C-14/83, para 27.

1387 *Von Colson and Kamann v Land Nordrhein-Westfalen*, C-14/83, paras 26-28. The same solution has been reiterated in *Pfeiffer and Others*, Joined cases C-397/01 to C-403/01, paras 110 and 113. Prechal S, 'EU Gender Equality Law: a source of inspiration for other EU legal fields?' (2008) European Gender Equality Law Review 10. Although it comes up most often in the interpretation of directives, the obligation of consistent interpretation applies also for other types of instruments, such as recommendations, as the Court held in *Grimaldi v Fonds des maladies professionnelles*, C-322/88, paras 18-19. According to Bobek there is also no obstacle to Treaty provisions or regulations producing such 'indirect effect': Bobek, 'The effects of EU law in the national legal systems' 154. In the *Pupino* case the Court extended the doctrine of indirect effect to Framework Decisions which existed under what was back then the third pillar of the EU: Judgment of 16 July 2005, *Pupino*, C-105/03, EU:C:2005:386; see Chalmers, Davies and Monti, *European Union Law: Cases and Materials* 300.

1388 Judgment of 13 November 1990, *Marleasing v Comercial Internacional de Alimentación*, C-106/89, EU:C:1990:395. This ruling has been said to have introduced the horizontal direct effect of directives '*through the back door*': Rasmussen, 'Towards a Normative Theory of Interpretation of Community Law' 145.

rectives. Consistent interpretation comes first, and applies to both vertical and horizontal situations, in so far as such interpretation is possible.[1389] Otherwise, comes the direct effect test, which allows for rights defined in the directive to be directly applicable in vertical litigation.[1390] As a last resort, the individual still has the possibility to claim damages.[1391] When it comes to applying directives in relations between individuals, the obligation of consistent interpretation therefore has become the default solution, having priority over the classic direct effect test.[1392] It works as a '*functional equivalent*' to the missing horizontal direct effect of directives.[1393]

What does this mean in practice for the identification and application of rights? Does it make a difference that consistent interpretation (or indirect effect) has priority over direct effect? As Bobek has pointed out, the line can be very thin between indirect and direct effect.[1394] The obligation of consistent interpretation does not challenge the relevance of the correlativity model, and it is consistent with the Court's general approach of maximising the useful effect of EU law. The main advantage of consistent interpretation is that it avoids asking the question in terms of 'horizontal' versus 'vertical' effect: instead the Court of Justice calls on the national courts to use their margin of appreciation in order to identify in their own law the same obligations and corresponding rights than those laid down in directives (and other EU law instruments).

1389 *Dominguez*, C-282/10, para 24 and case law cited.

1390 *Dominguez*, C-282/10, paras 36-41. In this case, while the provision contained a clear and precise obligation and therefore fulfilled the conditions for direct effect, it still could not have horizontal direct effect, like all directive provisions. The Court of Justice pointed out that the party opposite Mrs Dominguez in the proceedings was a social security body, and left it to the national court to determine whether this was a vertical or a horizontal situation and to draw the appropriate consequences.

1391 *Dominguez*, C-282/10, para 43.

1392 Mayeur-Carpentier, Clément-Wilz and Martucci, 'Chronique de droit administratif et droit de l'Union européenne, 1er janvier 2012 - 1er juillet 2012' 969; A. Gelblat 'Appréhender l'imprécision des droits : approche stratégique' La Revue des droits de l'homme (en ligne) 7 - 2015 <http://revdh.revues.org/1341> accessed 7 June 2016 para 22.

1393 Micklitz, 'The ECJ between the Individual Citizen and the Member States - A plea for a judge-made European law on remedies' 22.

1394 Bobek, 'The effects of EU law in the national legal systems' 155. Bobek categorizes indirect effect into weak, medium and strong, where weak is when EU law is used as simple confirmation of the meaning of a national provision and strong is when the words and meaning of the national provision have to be significantly twisted in order to achieve compliance with EU law.

The debate over the horizontal direct effect of directives nevertheless intensified with the *Mangold* and *Kücükdeveci* rulings on the application of the prohibition of age discrimination to an employer-employee (horizontal) relationship. In *Mangold*,[1395] the Court made clear that Directive 2000/78[1396] does not itself lay down the principle of equal treatment in the field of employment and occupation but has the sole purpose of laying down, in that field, a general framework for combating discrimination.[1397] In addition, it found that the principle of non-discrimination on grounds of age must be regarded as a general principle of Community law and that therefore '*observance of the general principle of equal treatment, in particular in respect of age, cannot as such be conditional upon the expiry of the period allowed the Member States for the transposition of a directive intended to lay down a general framework for combating discrimination on the grounds of age, [...] so far as [...] specific measures to implement such a directive are concerned.*'[1398] The Court therefore found the general principle to be applicable to the case in point, and found that the provision of German law that Mr Mangold was challenging was indeed contrary to EU law. In *Kücükdeveci*, the situation was different because the requirement of equal treatment in itself, a general principle now also codified at Article 21(1) of the Charter,[1399] was not precise enough to determine whether, in the case at hand, Ms. Kücükdeveci was indeed being discriminated against on grounds of her age because the period of employment she had completed before turning 25 was not taken into account in calculating her notice period of dismissal. But the Court explained that Directive 2000/78 '*gives specific expression*' to the principle of non-discrimination on grounds of age. The consequence was that the requirement of non-discrimination became sufficiently precise to have direct (horizontal) effect and thus provided the tools to identify both the rights of Ms. Kücükdeveci and the violation of those rights. The national court was thus under a duty to disapply the contrary provisions of national law.[1400]

1395 *Mangold*, C-144/04.

1396 Council Directive 2000/78/EC of 27 November 2000 establishing a general framework for equal treatment in employment and occupation (OJ L 303 p.16).

1397 *Mangold*, C-144/04, para 74. See also *Kücükdeveci*, C-555/07, para 20 and Judgment of 10 May 2011, *Römer*, C-147/08, EU:C:2011:286, para 59.

1398 *Mangold*, C-144/04, para 76.

1399 *Kücükdeveci*, C-555/07, paras 21-22.

1400 *Kücükdeveci*, C-555/07, para 51.

This solution has been harshly criticised, even characterised as '*hypocritical*' because the Court magically found that the general principle (and possibly the corresponding Charter right) had the same content as the directive.[1401] Yet, the ruling contains a clue that may help read sense into it. The Court expressly draws an analogy with *Defrenne II* when stating that the directive gives specific expression to the general principle of non-discrimination. The reader is however left alone to figure out how the analogy applies exactly. The paragraph from *Defrenne II* that is cited in *Kücükdeveci* indicated that the directive on the principle of equal pay for men and women provided '*further details regarding certain aspects of the material scope of Article 119*' and adopted '*various provisions whose essential purpose [was] to improve the legal protection of workers who may be wronged by failure to apply the principle of equal pay laid down by Article 119.*'[1402] It is almost as if the Court was minimising the substantive input of the directive. In *Kücükdeveci*, we have a general principle and Charter provision instead of a Treaty provision, but the idea is also that the main source of the right is in primary law and not in the directive which is not horizontally applicable. An additional clarification is provided in *Dansk Industri*, a more recent age discrimination case, in which the Court explained that Directive 2000/78 was adopted in order to '*facilitate the practical implementation of the principle of equal treatment and, in particular, to specify various possible exceptions to that principle, circumscribing those exceptions by the use of a clearer definition of their scope*'.[1403] So the directive functions as a 'facilitator' for the implementation of the general principle but it is not decisive with regard to the substance of the right arising from it.[1404]

It should be recalled that in *Defrenne II*, the Court insisted that while the transposition period for the directive had not yet expired, this did not mean that the Treaty provision which the directive was implementing could not apply.[1405] If the significance of Article 119 EEC was sufficiently clear to make it applicable to the case in point, there was no need to wait

1401 M. Blanquet and others, 'Chronique de jurisprudence - Droit général de l'Union européenne' (2012) Cahiers de droit européen 75 83.

1402 *Defrenne v SABENA*, C-43/75, para 54.

1403 *DI*, C-441/14, para 23.

1404 In a more recent judgment the Court expressly distinguished this case from one where a directive provision did *not* give concrete expression to a general principle of EU law and therefore could not be relied on in a dispute between individuals: Judgment of 7 August 2018, *Smith*, C-122/17, EU:C:2018:631, paras 46-48.

1405 *Defrenne v SABENA*, C-43/75, paras 66-68.

for implementing provisions of the directive applying that principle. In *Kücükdeveci*, the transposition period had expired but the transposition had not been correctly done. As soon as the expiration has brought the issue within the scope of EU law,[1406] the instrument of secondary law that gives expression to the right enshrined in the superior norm of primary law cannot have the effect of blocking the application of this right.[1407] The same solution was applied in *Römer*[1408] and then in *Egenberger*.[1409] In this sense these cases may be read as the logical (admittedly far-reaching) continuation of *Defrenne II*.

The principle according to which non-transposed directives do not have horizontal direct effect of directives, does not pose a major conceptual problem. Quite the contrary, it tends to confirm the basic correlation between rights and obligations. As the Court made clear in *Marshall*, the Treaty itself prevents directives from directly imposing obligations on private individuals.[1410] This limit to the scope of obligations translates into a corresponding limit to the possibility of identifying rights in directives. So far, the Court has developed two possibilities for extending the scope of obligations laid down in directives, resulting in a symmetrical extension of the scope of the correlative rights. One is the obligation of consistent interpretation; the other is the *Mangold/Kücükdeveci* solution which consists in combining the directive with the higher-ranking norm (Treaty provision, general principle, or Charter provision) to which it gives expression, and which has the ability to give rise to rights in horizontal situations.[1411] This of course raises issues with regard to legal certainty and the protection of legitimate expectations of individuals (such as employers) who are bound

---

1406 *Kücükdeveci*, C-555/07, paras 23-25.

1407 This suggested interpretation is in accordance with Pech's analysis of *Kücükdeveci* that '*Directive 2000/78 'disappeared' behind the general principle of equal treatment to which it gives expression and force.*' Pech, 'Between judicial minimalism and avoidance: the Court of Justice's sidestepping of fundamental constitutional issues in Römer and Dominguez' 29.

1408 Judgment of 10 May 2011, *Römer*, C-147/08, EU:C:2011:286, paras 60-61.

1409 Judgment of 17 April 2018, *Egenberger*, C-414/16, EU:C:2018:257.

1410 *Marshall v. Southampton and South-West Hampshire Area Health Authority*, C-152/84.

1411 Viewed in this light it appears that Charter provisions, much like Treaty provisions and general principles of EU law, can produce horizontal direct effects. Concerning the direct effect of general principles see J. Van Meerbeeck, 'Le mode opératoire des principes généraux : de la généralité in abstracto à l'effet direct in concreto' (Cahiers de droit européen - Les principes généraux du droit de l'Union européenne, Brussels, 10 September 2015).

by the identified obligations. Still, with the confirmation in *Dansk Industri* and *Egenberger* it appears that the Court does not foresee a different solution for the time being.[1412]

This review of the case law on discrimination also allows to address the criticism of a doctrinal branch which has been advocating an increased focus on rights in the Court's case law and condemning the lack of systematic reference to EU fundamental rights, especially in preliminary ruling references. The *Römer* and *Dominguez* cases have been criticized because in these cases the Court failed to refer to what would have been the relevant articles in the Charter (21(1) and 31(2)).[1413] Not addressing the role of these provisions has been characterised has a demonstration of '*judicial minimalism*'.[1414] In fact, the trend that emerges from the Court's case law on non-discrimination is one of expanding, not shrinking nor even stagnating, protection of individuals. These cases also show that reliance on the Charter is not indispensable for reaching a solution that is protective of individual rights. Relying on the general principle as a source of the right to non-discrimination is after all a way of insisting, like in *Dansk Industri*, that this rule comes from '*the constitutional traditions common to the Member States*'[1415] and therefore it reflects the consistency of the EU's system of protection of rights over time. Egenberger:

2.2.1.3.2. Protecting and balancing interests in anti-discrimination law

The case law on discrimination in the workplace also confirms the relevance of individual interests for conceptualising rights under EU law. In *Defrenne II* the Court stated that any individual having an interest in the fulfilment of an obligation imposed by the Treaty may claim it as a right.[1416] In the subsequent case law interest in non-discrimination is often implied and assumed. But some cases nevertheless expressly address this component of a right. We have already looked at the telling example of *Verholen*, at the intersection of EU social security law and EU law on dis-

1412 *DI*, C-441/14.

1413 *Römer*, C-147/08, and *Dominguez*, C-282/10. Lorenz, Groussot and Petursson, *The European Human Rights Culture - A Paradox of Human Rights Protection in Europe?* 173.

1414 Pech, 'Between judicial minimalism and avoidance: the Court of Justice's sidestepping of fundamental constitutional issues in Römer and Dominguez'.

1415 *DI*, C-441/14, para 22.

1416 *Defrenne v SABENA*, C-43/75, para 31.

crimination.[1417] The interest in getting the social security benefits lies not with the victim of the discrimination but with her husband. The prohibition of discrimination thus translates into a right for him.

This broadly understood notion of interest as a trigger for enforcing obligations was decisive in *Feryn*.[1418] The Belgian Centre for equal opportunities and combating racism, designated to promote equal treatment pursuant to Article 13 of Directive 2000/43,[1419] challenged the recruitment policy of the private company Feryn. One of the directors of this firm had publicly stated that they did not wish to recruit immigrants. The British and Irish governments had submitted in their observations that since there was no identified victim of discrimination, the provisions of the directive relating to direct discrimination did not apply to allege discrimination resulting from public statements made by an employer. The Court replied that the lack of an identifiable complainant was not sufficient to conclude that there was no direct discrimination and remarked that, since the employer's statement might suffice to discourage potential candidates from applying to positions with the company, the objective of the directive to foster '*socially inclusive labour market would be hard to achieve if the scope of Directive 2000/43 were to be limited to only those cases in which an unsuccessful candidate for a post, considering himself to be the victim of direct discrimination, brought legal proceedings against the employer*'.[1420] Therefore, in addition to the procedures which the directive requires to be available to victims of discrimination, Member States may also introduce or maintain '*provisions which are more favourable to the protection of the principle of equal treatment.*' Therefore, associations with a '*legitimate interest in ensuring compliance with the directive*' and especially the bodies designated under Article 13 of the directive may also challenge measures that are contrary to the prohibition of discrimination based on origin or ethnicity.[1421] More generally, this implies that individuals beyond those of the intended protective scope of a directive may also be in a position to challenge violations of this directive in court, as long as they have an interest in it.

1417 *Verholen and Others v Sociale Verzekeringsbank Amsterdam*, C-87/90 to C-89/90, p. 328.

1418 Judgment of 10 July 2008, *Feryn*, C-54/07, EU:C:2008:397.

1419 Council Directive 2000/43/EC of 29 June 2000 implementing the principle of equal treatment between persons irrespective of racial or ethnic origin (OJ L 180 p. 22).

1420 *Feryn*, C-54/07, para 24.

1421 *Feryn*, C-54/07, paras 26-27.

The *Kratzer* case illustrates *a contrario* what kind of interest may *not* function as a trigger for the right to equal treatment.[1422] Mr Kratzer had applied for a traineeship for the purpose of acquiring the formal status of applicant only in order to claim compensation for discrimination on the basis of Directive 2000/78 on equal treatment and Directive 2006/54.[1423] The Court held that such a person could not be regarded as a 'victim' or a 'person injured' within the meaning of the directive; in addition, the Court recalled that '*EU law cannot be relied on for abusive or fraudulent ends*'.[1424] It then applied its classic case law on identifying abuse of rights based on an objective and a subjective element.[1425] Although individual interest remains broadly understood for the purposes of activating obligations and correlated rights, the prohibition of abuse of rights sets a limit.

Finally, the right to non-discrimination is also, like any other right, not only activated by an interest but also balanced against other interests in concrete situations. Directive 2000/78 itself, and as the Court emphasised in *Dansk Industri*,[1426] lays down the possibilities for exceptions to the general principle of non-discrimination. Some practices constitute direct discrimination and are prohibited according to Article 4(1) unless they are justified by a '*genuine and determining occupational requirement, provided that the objective is legitimate and the requirement is proportionate*'. Other discriminatory measures may be allowed if they pursue a legitimate aim and are proportionate, otherwise they will be identified as indirect discrimination. So, all exceptions rely in one way or another on the principle of proportionality. The implications have been dissected in *G4S Secure Solutions* and *Bougnaoui*, two cases concerning discrimination on grounds of religion, which gained intensive media coverage – unsurprisingly given the '*social sensitivity inherent*' in the issues raised[1427]. Ms Achbita had been working as a receptionist under an employment contract of indefinite duration for the security company G4S. After three years on the job, she announced that she would wear her Islamic headscarf to work. This violated

1422 Judgment of 28 July 2016, *Kratzer*, C-423/15, EU:C:2016:604.

1423 Parliament and Council Directive 2006/54/EC of 5 July 2006 on the implementation of the principle of equal opportunities and equal treatment of men and women in matters of employment and occupation (OJ L 204 p. 23).

1424 *Kratzer*, C-423/15, paras 36-37.

1425 *Kratzer*, C-423/15, paras 38-42, citing especially Judgment of 13 March 2014, *SICES and Others*, C-155/13, EU:C:2014:145. On the prohibition of abuse of rights see p. 88 of this work.

1426 *DI*, C-441/14, para 23.

1427 Opinion of AG Kokott in *G4S Secure Solutions*, C-157/15, EU:C:2016:382, para 2.

G4S's internal ban on wearing any visible signs of political, philosophical or religious beliefs. She was dismissed on this basis and went to court to claim damages against her former employer. The case reached the Belgian Court of Cassation, which lodged a reference for preliminary ruling, asking whether the ban constituted direct discrimination in the meaning of Article 2 of Directive 2000/78. Ms Bougnaoui had been working as a design engineer for the company Micropole, in contact with clients who complained to her superiors about her wearing an Islamic veil. This led to her dismissal. This case, too, reached the Court of Cassation, which referred to the CJEU for a preliminary ruling, asking whether the wish of Micropole's customers not to have to deal with an employee wearing an Islamic headscarf could constitute a '*genuine and determining occupational requirement*' in the meaning of Article 4(1) of Directive 2000/78 and fall into the express derogation to the prohibition on direct discrimination.

Both Advocates General saw in these cases the need to deal not only with how to apply the system of exceptions and the distinction between direct and indirect discrimination within the meaning of Directive 2000/78, but also with how to assess the substance of the freedom of religion, which the ban in each case was potentially infringing. Ultimately, the problem was how to balance this right with the freedom to conduct a business (and the protection of the employer's economic interests). Concerning the qualification of the employer's freedom to conduct a business either as a 'genuine and determining occupational requirement' or a 'legitimate aim' to justify respectively direct or indirect discrimination, Advocate General Kokott relied on the freedom to conduct a business (as protected by Article 16 CFR) in order to conclude that the economic interest of an employer can constitute a genuine and determining occupational requirement and that, by extension, it also constitutes a legitimate aim that could justify indirect discrimination. Advocate General Sharpson took the view that it could not be characterised as a genuine and occupational requirement but might constitute a legitimate aim, the proportionality of the discriminatory measure with regard to this aim then needed to be assessed. So, the Advocates General did not grant the same relative importance to the freedom to conduct a business as a legitimate aim. The other point of divergence concerns the impact of a ban on external manifestations of religious identity. Advocate General Kokott submits that it would be an unnecessary '*sweeping assertion*' to assume that a headscarf ban would prevent Muslim women from integrating into society – Ms Achbita's precise case proves the point, since she requested to be allowed to wear her headscarf at work after having been worked without it for three years.[1428] By contrast, Advocate General Sharpston argues that '*to someone who is an observant member of a faith, religious identity is an integral part of that person's very being*', comparable to one's sex or skin colour.[1429] The divergence here is on whether the external manifestation of religion is essential to religious identity[1430] and on how much of a limitation on the freedom of religion the ban of such manifestation constitutes. If we reason in terms of effectiveness of rights, Sharpston's solution makes more sense: if we want rights to be effective (including the right to freedom of religion), the 'personal' choice to exercise them should be a real choice, not one which exposes their holders to dissuasive disadvantages.[1431] This approach preserves the uniform application of EU law and the effectiveness of the EU prohibition on discrimination, faithfully to the Court's original approach to discrimination ever since *Defrenne II*.

In its two rulings, interestingly, the Court points out that there is no definition of 'religion' in the Directive, so it relies on EU and ECHR instruments on freedom of conscience and religion, especially Article 10(1) of the Charter. It infers from these instruments that the concept of 'religion' in Article 1 of the directive '*should be interpreted as covering both the* forum internum, *that is the fact of having a belief, and the* forum externum, *that is the manifestation of religious faith in public*'.[1432] So the Court uses the definition of the 'right' to religious freedom in order to further define the right to equal treatment. Concerning a general ban on wearing religious signs, the Court admits that '*An employer's wish to project an image of neutrality towards customers relates to the freedom to conduct a business that is recognised in Article 16 of the Charter and is, in principle, legitimate, notably where the employer involves in its pursuit of that aim only those workers who are*

1428 Opinion of AG Kokott in *G4S Secure Solutions*, C-157/15, paras 123-124.

1429 Opinion of AG Sharpston in *Bougnaoui and ADDH*, C-188/15, EU:C:2016:553, para 118.

1430 As pointed out by AG Sharpston this issue has been discussed by AG Bot in another context: Opinion of Advocate General Bot in Joined Cases *Y and Z*, C-71/11 and C-99/11, EU:C:2012:224, concerning the notion of persecution on grounds of religion.

1431 A parallel may be drawn here with the Judgments of 17 December 2015 in *Seigneur v ECB*, F-95/14, EU:F:2015:155, para 59 and in *Bowles v ECB*, F-94/14, EU:F:2015:156, para 59 where the Civil Service Tribunal held that the choice to exercice representation mandates was part of the fundamental rights protected by Articles 27 and 28 CFR.

1432 *G4S Secure Solutions*, C-157/15, paras 26-28, *Bougnaoui and ADDH*, C-188/15, paras 28-30.

required to come into contact with the employer's customers'.[1433] It is therefore acceptable and will not constitute indirect discrimination in so far as the proportionality test allows to establish that the prohibition limited to strict necessity, which it is for the referring court to assess, taking '*into account the interests involved in the case*'.[1434] The individual measure in the *Bougnaoui* case, on the other hand, requires assessing whether it is justified by a genuine and determining occupational requirement. This can be determined on the basis of objective considerations relating to the nature of the activities, but not subjective considerations such as the willingness to take into account a client's wishes not to have services provided by a worker wearing an Islamic veil.[1435] The problem with these judgments is that, while they clarify what the prohibition on grounds of religion encompasses, it is not so clear what are the interests on the other side, i.e. the 'objective considerations' corresponding to the interests of society as a whole, and more importantly it is not clear who is in charge of identifying these interests: whether it is the private employer, the Member State, or the Union, is a question left open.

The case law on discrimination in the workplace nevertheless confirms the following basic elements about the relation between rights and interests. Interest is understood in a broad sense so that even individuals who are not themselves victims of discrimination may derive certain rights from EU anti-discrimination law. The limit to this generous approach is the prohibition on abuse of rights. Moreover, we see especially exemplified by the *G4S* and *Bougnaoui* cases on the right to equal treatment, that rights remain 'optimisation requirements' to be balanced with other rights and interests (including economic interests).[1436] In addition, these cases suggest that the right to non-discrimination may be grounded in another right, such as the freedom of religion, which seems to also ground the presumption that there is an interest in exercising this freedom.

1433 *G4S Secure Solutions*, C-157/15, para 38.
1434 *G4S Secure Solutions*, C-157/15, para 43.
1435 *Bougnaoui and ADDH*, C-188/15, para 40.
1436 See p. 85 of this work.

2.2.1.4. The 'new' Charter rights of workers to consultation and representation

The inclusion in the Charter of Article 27 on the right of workers to information, and consultation within the undertaking – which was absent from pre-Lisbon primary law[1437] – brings new pieces to our puzzle. In particular, the much-debated ruling *Association de Médiation Sociale* raises a number of issues. This association had refused the nomination of one of its workers, Mr Laboubi, as a trade union representative because the company did not have the minimum number of employees required by the French *Code du travail* for the nomination of such a representative. Indeed, based on the Code du travail, many employees of the AMS, with certain types of work contracts, were in fact not accounted for in the calculation of the number of employees. Yet, Article 27 of the Charter, titled '*Workers' right to information and consultation within the undertaking*', reads: '*Workers or their representatives must, at the appropriate levels, be guaranteed information and consultation in good time in the cases and under the conditions provided for by Union law and national laws and practices*'. Furthermore, Article 3(1) of EU Directive 2002/14 on the information and consultation of employees requires that '*all workers*' of an undertaking be taken into account for calculation of the number of employees.[1438] In the context of litigation between the AMS on the one hand, and Mr Laboubi and the local trade union section on the other hand, in order to determine whether the French legislation was compatible with EU law the French Cour de cassation referred the matter to the Court of Justice. The question was whether the right of workers to information and consultation, as laid down in Article 27 and specified in the directive, could have horizontal direct effect and whether the French provisions at issue were incompatible with it. Here the differences of approach between the Advocate General's Opinion and the Court's final ruling prove once more enlightening with regard to the concept of rights.[1439] In

1437 The Explanations cite the European Social Charter and the Community Charter on the rights of workers as sources of inspiration of this right, and add that: '*There is a considerable Union acquis in this field: Articles 154 and 155 of the Treaty on the Functioning of the European Union, and Directives 2002/14/EC (general framework for informing and consulting employees in the European Community), 98/59/EC (collective redundancies), 2001/23/EC (transfers of undertakings) and 94/45/EC (European works councils).*'.

1438 Parliament and Council Directive 2002/14/EC of 11 March 2002 establishing a general framework for informing and consulting employees in the European Community (OJ L 80 p. 29).

1439 As was the case in *Danske Slagterier*, C-445/06, as discussed p. 230 of this work.

fact, the ruling itself has given rise to a variety of interpretations which attest to its unfortunate lack of clarity; it is through comparison with the Opinion that interesting conclusions may be drawn with regard to the Charter's solidarity provisions and their ability to give rise to rights.

Advocate General Cruz Villalón saw in this case an opportunity to clarify the distinction between rights and principles laid down at Article 51(1) of the Charter and to put forward his interpretation of this provision. In his view, should the right to information and consultation fall into the category of 'principles,' there would be according to Article 52(5) CFR only '*limited possibilities*' of relying on it before a court. The main issue here was therefore '*to ascertain the possible status as a 'principle' of Article 27 of the Charter.*'[1440] He added that '*[t]he wording of the Charter shows that 'principles' contain obligations upon the public authorities, thus contrasting with 'rights', whose purpose is the protection of directly defined individual legal situations, though the specific expression of 'principles' at lower levels of the legal order is also possible.*' This means that a '*right requires an individual legal situation to be respected*', whereas 'principles' lay down '*much more general*' obligations: '*the public authorities, and in particular the legislature, are called upon to promote and transform the 'principle' into a judicially cognisable reality [...]*'.[1441] In a nutshell, according to the Advocate General, "*principles' are characterised by the concept of obligation.*'[1442] In his view, Article 27 should be categorised as one of these principles, for two main reasons, one systemic and one structural. The systemic reason is the fact that this provision is part of the Charter's 'Solidarity' title, which induces a presumption that it is a 'principle' and not a 'right'.[1443] The structural reason is the indeterminate content of the provision, reinforced by the phrase '*under the conditions provided for by Union law and national laws and practices*'.[1444] As already dis-

1440 Opinion of AG Cruz Villalón in *Association de médiation sociale*, C-176/12, para 42.

1441 Opinion of AG Cruz Villalón in *Association de médiation sociale*, C-176/12, para 50. In support of this interpretation he cites: M. Borowsky, 'Artikel 52', in J. Mayer, *Charta der Grundrechte der Europäischen Union*,(Nomos 2010, 3rd ed.); Burgorgue-Larsen, 'L'article II-112' 686; F. Mayer, 'Artikel 6 EUV', in E. Grabitz, M. Hilf and M. Nettesheim, *Das Recht der Europäischen Union – Kommentar* (Beck, 2010) paras 65 et seq.

1442 Opinion of AG Cruz Villalón in *Association de médiation sociale*, C-176/12, para 51.

1443 Opinion of AG Cruz Villalón in *Association de médiation sociale*, C-176/12, para 55.

1444 Opinion of AG Cruz Villalón in *Association de médiation sociale*, C-176/12, paras 53-54.

cussed in this study, the idea that conditionality should serve to a priori exclude the possibility for a provision to grant right is inconsistent with the Court's original method for identifying rights, since the unconditional character of a provision is part of the criteria to assess the practical applicability of a provision, not its abstract nature.[1445]

The Advocate General also suggested a method for practically applying the concept of 'principle' as it is enshrined in the Charter, and Article 27 in particular. According to him, the first sentence of Article 52(5)[1446] can be interpreted as meaning that secondary law must be controlled with regard to Charter principles only by confrontation with an intermediary layer of secondary legislation which would be explicitly intended to apply these principles (i.e. those that would '*give specific substantive and direct expression to the content of the 'principle*'[1447]). Article 3(1) of Directive 2002/14 precisely fulfils that function in relation to Article 27 of the Charter. Regarding the requirement that principles '*shall be judicially cognisable only in the interpretation of such acts and in the ruling on their legality*' (second sentence of Article 52(5)), the Advocate General states that this wording '*very implicitly but unequivocally excludes the possibility of directly relying on a 'principle' so as to exercise an individual right based upon that principle*'.[1448] He proposes to understand that the 'acts' referred to in the second sentence differ in scope from those referred to in the first sentence, in that the ones from the second sentence should be understood as all the acts that are *not* part of the intermediary layer.[1449] He then accepts the possibility for individuals to rely on directive combined with a 'principle' such as that which he has identified in Article 27 and he proposes an interpretation of Article 3(1) of the directive, which, he finds, precludes the application of the French legal provisions that were being challenged by Mr Laboubi and his union.[1450]

1445 See the Conclusion of Part 1 of this work, p. 224.

1446 As a reminder: '*The provisions of this Charter which contain* principles may be implemented by legislative and executive acts *taken by institutions, bodies, offices and agencies of the Union, and by acts of Member States when they are implementing Union law, in the exercise of their respective powers.*'

1447 Opinion of AG Cruz Villalón in *Association de médiation sociale*, C-176/12, para 63.

1448 Opinion of AG Cruz Villalón in *Association de médiation sociale*, C-176/12, para 68.

1449 Opinion of AG Cruz Villalón in *Association de médiation sociale*, C-176/12, para 70.

1450 Opinion of AG Cruz Villalón in *Association de médiation sociale*, C-176/12, paras 73-80.

All in all, the proposed solution holds water as long as its implicit premise – that rights and obligations are mutually exclusive – is not challenged.

The Court chose a different path. Unlike the Advocate General, it did not start from the rights/principles distinction laid down at Article 52(5) of the Charter and did not even mention it once in the ruling. Instead it took the problem from the other end and started by establishing the illegality of the French legal provisions with regard to Article 3(1) of the directive.[1451] Then, in accordance with established case law, it made clear that this provision could not produce horizontal direct effects and that, further, consistent interpretation was not possible here as it would lead to contra legem interpretation of national law.[1452] Finally the Court investigated whether Article 27 of the Charter could be applicable here in combination with Article 3(1) of the directive, and held that Article 27 could not be applied in *AMS* because it needed further specification. The following passage of the ruling is not to be overlooked: '*It is not possible to infer from the* wording *of Article 27 of the Charter or from the explanatory notes to that article that Article 3(1) of Directive 2002/14, as a directly applicable rule of law, lays down and addresses to the Member States a* prohibition *on excluding from the calculation of the staff numbers in an undertaking a specific category of employees initially included in the group of persons to be taken into account in that calculation*.'[1453] So the reason why no right could be identified in Article 27 in this case is that the Court was not able to identify a clear prohibition against the exclusion by the French legislator of certain categories of staff from the calculation. In other words, the content of the obligation upon the Member States was impossible to identify, and so was the content of any corresponding right, therefore there was no further need to assess the vertical or horizontal reach of the provision. By contrast, whether Article 27 was *intended* to be read as a right – either generally or specifically as opposed to a 'principle' in the meaning of Article 52(5) – was simply not an issue. *AMS* is thus a rather straightforward application of the classic concept of rights, which are correlates of clear and precise obligations (and cannot be identified if there are no such obligations). In no way does it validate the systematic opposition between rights and obligations proposed by the Advocate General.

Admittedly, the Court's judgment did not refute the Advocate General's suggestion either, which is probably *AMS* has been interpreted by many as

1451 *Association de médiation sociale*, C-176/12, paras 24-29.

1452 *Association de médiation sociale*, C-176/12, paras 33-40 and case law cited.

1453 *Association de médiation sociale*, C-176/12, para 46 (emphases added).

meaning that Article 27 should be categorised as a 'principle'. In the *Glatzel* ruling on the integration of disabled persons, the Court itself – but in a completely different formation[1454] – apparently assumed that such was the meaning of *AMS*, as it cited this case when it identified Article 26 of the Charter as a principle and explained that '*it must be given more specific expression in European Union or national law. Accordingly, that article cannot by itself confer on individuals a subjective right which they may invoke as such*'.[1455] However, this is much more in line with the Advocate General's Opinion in *AMS*, understanding rights and obligations as mutually exclusive concepts, than with the Court's actual solution in the same case, just highlighted above.

The Court's 'omission' of the distinction between rights and principles has the merit of avoiding a rigid and abstract categorisation of Charter provisions into 'rights' and 'principles', that would amount to considering the latter as obligations that have no correlative 'rights' unless further specified in secondary legislation. Instead, in *AMS* the Court pragmatically focuses on the precision and clarity of Article 27 and does not try to categorise it based on an intentionalist method of interpretation. In light of these elements, the *AMS* solution appears to be in line with the Court's original method for identifying rights. Interestingly, this provision was among those of the 'Solidarity' Title of the Charter which had originally been characterised in the literature as '*fully judicial rights*' because they were sufficiently clear and precise.[1456] If we follow the *van Gend en Loos/Defrenne* logic, the *AMS* judgment does not invalidate this view. Simply, in the factual circumstances of *AMS*, Article 27 could not provide a solution. This does not close the door to the possibility that it may be practically usable in other concrete circumstances, and thus directly confer rights on individuals.

1454 In *Glatzel* the formation was the Fifth Chamber (composed of T. von Danwitz, E. Juhász, A. Rosas, D. Šváby and C. Vajda), whereas for *AMS* it was the Grand Chamber (composed of V. Skouris, K. Lenaerts, R. Silva de Lapuerta, M. Ilešič and M. Safjan, J. Malenovský, E. Levits, J.-C. Bonichot, A. Arabadjiev, C. Toader, D. Šváby, M. Berger and A. Prechal).

1455 *Glatzel*, C-356/12, paras 77-78. Such is also the view of AG Jääskinen: in his Opinion in *Schönberger*, C-261/13 P, EU:C:2014:2107, para 58, he states that in *AMS* the Court classified the right to information and consultation as a 'principle'. It is also how Gordon and Moffatt understand the case: See Gordon and Moffatt, *EU Law in Judicial Review* 381.

1456 N.-L.A. Lorenz, X. Groussot and G.T. Petursson, *The European Human Rights Culture - A Paradox of Human Rights Protection in Europe?* (Martinus Nijhoff Publishers 2013) 196.

The later case law confirms as much: this possibility became reality in two EU civil service cases, *Seigneur* and *Bowles*.[1457] For determining whether employees deserved an additional salary advancement, an administrative circular required that they demonstrate excellent performance in their work over a certain period of time. This additional advancement was denied to two civil servants who could not demonstrate excellent performance in their work since they were fully dispensed of work in order to fulfill their representation mandates within the personnel committee and the pension oversight committee. Seigneur and Bowles claimed that the circular was violating Articles 27 and 28 of the Charter. The ECB pointed out that exercising representative functions resulted from a personal choice of the applicants ; the Civil Service Tribunal held that such a choice was in itself a fundamental right enshrined in Articles 27 and 28 CFR.[1458] The CST saw no problem in identifying the content of the rights applicable to this case. Concerned instead with the effectiveness of these rights, it held that their effective exercise would be hindered if the choice to exercice them led to dissuasive consequences. Ultimately, relying on Articles 27 and 28 and on the fundamental right to non-discrimination, the CST held that the contested provision in the circular was indeed illegal. This judgment sheds additional light on the *AMS* solution: Article 27 is not precise enough for the courts to be able to identify rights in certain concrete circumstances (such as in *AMS*, where the issue was indeed very complex), but its content is still perfectly useable as a right in other more straightforward situations (such as in *Seigneur* and *Bowles*).

The CST also did not need to rely on the distinction between rights and principles in order to reach a solution in *Michael Heath v. ECB*.[1459] Mr Heath, former employee of the European Central Bank, disagreed with the way his retirement pension had been calculated. Since the calculation had been made based on the applicable terms and conditions on employment, he challenged the legality of these terms and conditions, relying, among other provisions of EU and ECHR law, on Article 28 of the Charter. He argued that the trade unions should have been more directly involved in the elaboration of these terms and conditions. The CST agreed that Article 28 enshrines the right to freedom of association, especially the right for workers to organise unions to defend their interests, but it added that these

1457 *Seigneur v ECB*, F-95/14, and *Bowles v ECB*, F-94/14.

1458 *Seigneur v ECB*, F-95/14, EU:F:2015:155, para 59 and *Bowles v ECB*, F-94/14, para 59.

1459 Judgment of 29 September 2011, *Heath v ECB*, F-121/10, ECLI:EU:F:2011:174 and Judgment of 18 June 2013, *Heath v ECB*, T-645/11 P, ECLI:EU:T:2013:326.

rights do not translate into an obligation to establish procedures for collective bargaining, nor into an obligation to grant any codecision power to trade unions as regards the development of terms and conditions on employment.[1460] The General Court found that there was no need to rule on whether this was a correct interpretation of Article 28 to determine that the appeal was to be rejected.[1461] In any case, the CST's ruling can be read in the light of the classic approach based on the correlativity model again, in the sense that here the provision was not sufficiently precise to identify the right that Mr Heath was claiming.[1462]

By contrast with the Civil Service Tribunal, the General Court is perhaps more receptive to Advocate General Cruz Villalón's line of argument, even though the solutions it has reached so far are not necessarily incompatible with the correlativity model. In two orders of 11 November 2014 on the *Bergallou* and *Nguyen* cases it held that no individual procedural right for the members of the staff of the EU institutions could be found in Article 27 of the Charter. The applicants were arguing that each EU civil servant had a right, based on Article 27, to participate in the procedures establishing staff regulations. But the General Court answered that the participation of one person to the adoption of an EU act does not of itself individualise this person in relation to this act, unless applicable EU legislation grants specific procedural guarantees. The General Court added that the workers' rights to information and consultation and to negotiation and collective action enshrined in Articles 27 and 28 of the Charter could apply to the relations between the EU institutions and their staff, but that this application was limited to the cases and conditions laid down by Union law.[1463] The emphasis on the phrases '*under the conditions provided for by Union law and national laws and practices*' (Article 27) and '*in accordance with Union law and national laws and practices*' (Article 28), recalls the Ad-

1460 *Heath v ECB*, F-121/10, para 121.

1461 *Heath v ECB*, T-645/11 P, para 166.

1462 In the same way, in a case where the ex-spouse of a deceased civil servant relied on Article 25 (on the rights of the elderly) to claim pension rights from the Commission, the General Court held: '*l'article 25 de la Charte ne comporte pas de règle conférant aux particuliers un droit subjectif lié à un montant minimal de pension de survie au profit des personnes visées par l'article 27 de l'annexe VIII du statut.*' Judgment of 6 July 2016, *LM v Commission*, T-560/15 P, EU:T:2016:392, para 15.

1463 Order of 11 November 2014, *Bergallou v Parliament and Council*, T-22/14, EU:T:2014:954 paras 31-33 and exact same phrases in Order of 11 November 2014, *Nguyen v Parliament and Council*, T-20/14, EU:T:2014:955.

vocate General's Opinion in *AMS* and the Court's ruling in *Glatzel*.[1464] The GC followed the same approach in *Petsch*, where a contractual agent whose working hours had been increased claimed that his salary had been incorrectly adapted to the change. He argued that the wrongful adaptation of his salary amounted to a termination of his contract, which should not have been decided without prior consultation with the trade unions, claimed the violation of Articles 27 and 28 of the Charter. However the General Court highlighted as it had in the *Bergallou* and *Nguyen* cases, that the application of these provisions is to be framed by Union law.[1465] Mr Petsch was relying on a further provision of the Commission's general implementing provisions, but as the General Court held, while this provision indeed constitutes a rule giving further expression to Articles 27 and 28 of the Charter, it only governs the termination of contracts for groups of persons and is therefore not applicable to Mr Petsch's case.[1466] Arguably this does not invalidate the possibility for Articles 27 and 28 to give rise to rights; it only makes clear that the content of these provisions was not sufficient in itself to reach a solution in the concrete case.[1467] It remains to be seen whether the GC will always rely on the conditional phrasing of Articles 27 and 28 or whether it will be willing, in some cases, to acknowledge their immediate applicability.

Overall, the case law on Articles 27 and 28 to date does not challenge the relevance of the rights-obligations correlation for applying the Charter. The problem with these provisions is not specifically one of direct horizontal effect of Charter provisions, contrarily to what has been argued by some critics.[1468] In fact, while *AMS* confirms that there can be no horizontal direct effect for an untransposed directive, it contains no implication that a provision of the Charter could not be relied on in horizontal litigation. As Advocate General Cruz Villalón rightly pointed out, the heading of Article

1464 Opinion of AG Cruz Villalón in *Association de médiation sociale*, C-176/12 ; *Glatzel*, C-356/12.

1465 Judgment of 30 June 2015, *Petsch v Commission*, F-124/14, EU:F:2015:69, para 44.

1466 *Petsch v Commission*, F-124/14, paras 45-56.

1467 As pointed out by the GC, the claimant himself had explained very summarily why he thought his rights under the Charter were being violated by the contested measure. *Petsch v Commission*, F-124/14, paras 41-42.

1468 Guðmundsdóttir argues that *AMS* embodies the Court's refusal to extend the *Mangold/Kücükdeveci* approach to Article 27 in a horizontal situation. Guðmundsdóttir, 'A Renewed Emphasis on the Charter's Distinction Between Rights and Principles: Is a Doctrine of Judicial Restraint More Appropriate?' 693.

27 is "*Workers' right to information and consultation* within the undertaking', *the last detail meaning that it must be accepted that 'the undertaking' is in some way involved in the effectiveness of that right.*'[1469] The main issue lies with the substance of the Charter provisions, insufficiently detailed to be applicable of their own to a given situation. In such cases the relation between Charter provisions and secondary law becomes crucial. It is in this respect that *AMS* is puzzling. It looks at the possibility for a provision of primary law to have direct effect in isolation from its expression in secondary law (especially directives) and therefore is difficult to reconcile with the *Mangold-Kücükdeveci* approach.[1470]

2.2.1.5. Interim conclusions

The basic model of rights, obligations and interests applies very well to the variety of workers' rights analysed in this section. The different types of rights shed light on consistent and complementary aspects of the EU concept of rights, as correlatives of obligations activated by interests.

Concerning the correlativity between rights and obligations, firstly, social security cases exemplify the classic direct effect mechanism, giving full effectiveness to obligations of Member States under EU law via the medium of individual rights. This is complemented by reliance on the rights-obligations correlation also to claim damages from Member States where applicable. Secondly, the correlation also functions for administrative procedural rights, as illustrated by EU staff cases. Starting with *Alvis*, a long line of case law developed and refined the procedural guarantees which bind the EU administration towards its employees and translate into rights, also after Lisbon – and perhaps even more so, precisely because these guarantees now arise from a plurality of sources. Thirdly, specific issues concerning the rights of workers arise in horizontal relations (i.e. relations between employees and their employers from the private sector). Anti-discrimination law especially illustrates the problems for identifying rights in such relations. It is not that the Court is reluctant to acknowledge individual rights as such, but rather it is reluctant to impose obligations on individuals where the Treaty excludes this possibility, which is why the

---

1469 Opinion of AG Cruz Villalón in *Association de médiation sociale,* C-176/12, para 40.

1470 Vandamme, 'C'est arrivé près de chez vous! Het arrest Italmoda en het ontzeggen van rechten aan de particulier op grond van de EU-richtlijn' 157.

identification of rights in directives is such a sensitive issue. The absence of horizontal direct effect of these is actually a logical consequence of the right-obligation correlation: the impossibility to impose an obligation prevents the acknowledgement of a correlative right. The problem is that it limits the possibility to rely on a combination of sources, creating confusion as we see in the case law on the workers' right to participation and consultation enshrined in the Charter: this 'right' is rather easily applied in the vertical relations between the EU administration and its staff, but it has for now a limited impact in horizontal situations.[1471]

Regarding the notion of interest as the trigger for a right, the variety of interests which fulfil this function in the case law analysed in this section demonstrates that EU law takes workers into account not only as economic 'factors'. Instead, they are subjects with a broad array of interests which trigger the application of equally varied rights. In addition to the perhaps most obvious pecuniary interests such as claiming one's social security rights, other triggers for individual rights include interests relating to various aspects of one's career (advancement, participation); interests of individuals other than the intended beneficiary of a norm[1472]; and interests grounded in an expressly granted right (such as religious freedom[1473]).

2.2.2. Individual rights of Union citizens

The increasing focus on Union citizenship as a pillar of the European construction is '*emblematic not only of the special nature of Union law but also of the move away from a purely economic integration organisation towards and all-encompaasing 'union of peoples'*'.[1474] The formal notion of a 'citizenship of the Union' was instituted by the Maastricht Treaty.[1475] At first, it mostly encompassed a codification of existing rights for nationals of the Member

1471 As exemplified by the contrast between *Seigneur v ECB*, F-95/14 and *Bowles v ECB*, F-94/14, and *Association de médiation sociale*, C-176/12.

1472 Such as a husband's interest in relying on the prohibition on gender discrimination that is primarily intended to protect individuals in the situation of his wife: see *Verholen and Others v Sociale Verzekeringsbank Amsterdam*, C-87/90 to C-89/90, discussed p. 290 of this work.

1473 As in *G4S Secure Solutions*, C-157/15 and *Bougnaoui and ADDH*, C-188/15, discussed p. 307 of this work.

1474 Rosas and Armati, *EU Constitutional Law: An Introduction* 143.

1475 Article 17 EC. For an overview of the development of the notion see J. Shaw, 'E.U. Citizenship and Political Rights in an Evolving European Union' (2007) 75 Fordham Law Review 2549.

States, especially the right to free movement and the prohibition of discrimination on grounds of nationality. However, already in its original version the EU citizenship also contained a political element, i.e. Article 19 EC which granted the right to vote in elections for the European Parliament and in local elections. Since then it has evolved far beyond the notion of 'market citizenship'.[1476] This section looks at how the evolution of the rights of EU citizens to free movement and free residence enriches the basic model of rights, obligations and interests (2.2.2.1). It then tests the applicability of the classic concept of rights to the political rights of EU citizens (2.2.2.2).

2.2.2.1. The rights of Union citizens and their families to free movement and residence

The freedoms of movement and residence of Union citizens are proclaimed as 'rights' in the Treaties (Article 20(2)(a) TFEU and Article 21 TFEU). Since April 2004, replacing several previous directives on free movement, Directive 2004/38[1477] adds precisions and conditions for the implementation of the Treaty provisions citizenship. This directive codifies the consequences of the *Baumbast* judgment of 2002, which, as we shall see, may be considered as the seminal case on the free movement and residence of Union citizens.[1478] The case law on these rights is important for this study because of how the effectiveness rationale plays out in their application. The rights of free movement and residence are indeed triggered by a variety of interests that go far beyond the possibility to obtain finan-

1476 Shaw, 'E.U. Citizenship and Political Rights in an Evolving European Union' 2551. See also D. Kochenov, 'The Right to Have What Rights? EU Citizenship in Need of Clarification' (2013) 19 European Law Journal 502 504 and F. Wollenschläger, 'A New Fundamental Freedom beyond Market Integration', (2011) 17 *European Law Journal* 1. See also supporting the view that the market rationale is still relevant: N. Nic Shuibhne,'The Resilience of EU Market Citizenship', (2010) 47 *Common Market Law Review* 1597.

1477 Parliament and Council Directive 2004/38/EC of 29 April 2004 on the right of citizens of the Union and their family members to move and reside freely within the territory of the Member States amending Regulation (EEC) No 1612/68 and repealing Directives 64/221/EEC, 68/360/EEC, 72/194/EEC, 73/148/EEC, 75/34/EEC, 75/35/EEC, 90/364/EEC, 90/365/EEC and 93/96/EEC (OJ L 158 p. 77).

1478 Judgment of 17 September 2002, *Baumbast and R*, C-413/99, EU:C:2002:493.

cial benefits, and it is fascinating to see how far the personal scope of EU citizenship law stretches in order to protect these interests.

2.2.2.1.1. The rights of Union citizens to free movement and residence as an application of the classic relation between rights, obligations and interests

Regarding the free movement and residence of Union citizens, the correlation between individual rights and public obligations applies in a rather simple way. The Court held in *Baumbast* that the right to reside within the territory of the Member States under Article 18(1) EC (now 21(1) TFEU) '*is conferred directly on every citizen of the Union by a clear and precise provision of the EC Treaty*' and that Mr Baumbast, had the right to rely on this provision, '*purely as a national of a Member State, and consequently a citizen of the Union*'.[1479] However, the Court acknowledged that this right is not unconditional, since it '*is conferred subject to the limitations and conditions laid down by the Treaty and by the measures adopted to give it effect*'.[1480] The Court further specified that '*those limitations and conditions must be applied in compliance with the limits imposed by Community law and in accordance with the general principles of that law, in particular the principle of proportionality*'.[1481] In a nutshell: the provisions on EU citizenship give rise to rights in so far as they are clear and precise, and when the required conditions are satisfied.

These individual rights are mirrored by correlative obligations of Member States. By way of illustration, take the following case of action for a declaration of failure to fulfil obligations introduced by the Commission against Belgium.[1482] The Commission had received various complaints about Belgian legislation and administrative practice concerning both the conditions for granting residence permits and orders to leave Belgian territory issued to citizens of the Union. Concerning the first issue, the Court recalled the Baumbast judgment according to which '*The right to reside within the territory of the Member States under Article 18(1) EC is conferred directly on every citizen of the Union by a clear and precise provision of the EC Treaty subject to the limitations and conditions laid down by the EC Treaty and*

1479 *Baumbast and R*, C-413/99, para 84.

1480 *Baumbast and R*, C-413/99, para 85. See also *Trojani*, C-456/02, para 32 admitting that this right is '*not unconditional*'.

1481 *Baumbast and R*, C-413/99, para 91.

1482 Judgment of 23 March 2006, *Commission v Belgium*, C-408/03, EU:C:2006:192.

by the measures adopted to give it effect.'[1483] By excluding from the notion of sufficient personal resources, the income of a partner residing in the host Member State in the absence of an agreement concluded before a notary, Belgium has failed to fulfil its obligations under the Treaty. Concerning the second issue: '*The right of nationals of a Member State to enter the territory of another Member State and reside there for the purposes intended by the Treaty is a right conferred directly by the Treaty, or, as the case may be, by the provisions adopted for its implementation*', although since the right of residence under Article 18 EC is not unconditional, '*it is for the citizens of the Union to adduce the necessary evidence that they meet the conditions laid down in that regard by the relevant Community provisions*'.[1484] Automatic deportation however impairs '*the very substance of the right of residence directly conferred by Community law*'.[1485] The Court found that Belgium had failed to fulfil its obligations under Article 18 EC and the directive on the right of residence.[1486] So we have a clear and precise right – admittedly subject to some conditions, but Member States going beyond these conditions are in breach of their obligations and violate the correlative rights.

The basic right of free movement, often in conjunction with the prohibition of discrimination on the basis of nationality (and the correlative right to equal treatment), has allowed the Court to acknowledge and protect a variety of interests of Union citizens. Some of these, unsurprisingly, are financial entitlements. In *Martínez Sala*[1487] for instance, a Spanish national working in Germany was denied an allowance for her child because she did not have a valid residence permit for the period at which she applied. The starting point here was not her status as an EU citizen, but whether she was a worker and or employed person within the meaning of Article 48 EC on the freedom of movement of workers and Regulation No 1612/68 on the freedom of movement for workers[1488]. Either situation would give rise to a right to equal treatment based on what is now Article 18 TFEU (non-discrimination on the basis of nationality), meaning that

1483 *Commission v Belgium*, C-408/03, para 34. *Baumbast and R*, C-413/99, paras 84-85.

1484 *Baumbast and R*, C-413/99, paras 62-64.

1485 *Baumbast and R*, C-413/99, para 68.

1486 Council Directive 90/364/EEC of 28 June 1990 on the right of residence (OJ L 180 p. 26).

1487 Judgment of 12 May 1998, *Martínez Sala v Freistaat Bayern*, C-85/96, EU:C:1998:217.

1488 Council Regulation 1612/68 of 15 October 1968 on freedom of movement for workers within the Community (OJ L 257, 19/10/1968, p. 2).

she could not be requested to provide a document that nationals of the host member state were not required to produce. In this framework, EU citizenship came as a subsidiary protection to Ms Martínez Sala: since it is clear that she was residing lawfully in Germany, she came '*within the scope* ratione personae *of the provisions of the Treaty on European citizenship.*', which in turn gave her the right '*not to suffer discrimination on grounds of nationality within the scope of application* ratione materiae *of the Treaty*'.[1489] Intensifying the focus on the status of Union citizen, the *Grzelczyk* case famously led the Court to state that '*Union citizenship is destined to be the fundamental status of nationals of the Member States*'[1490] and that an EU citizen pursuing studies in a Member State other than his own can rely on the prohibition of all discrimination on grounds of nationality. *Trojani* provided an additional application of *Baumbast* by clarifying that, with regard to social assistance benefits, a citizen of the Union who is not economically active may rely on the same prohibition, if he has been lawfully resident in the host Member State for a certain time or possesses a residence permit.[1491] The notion of interests also manifests in the limits to this approach: one of the objectives of Directive 2004/38 is to '*prevent Union citizens who are nationals of other Member States from becoming an unreasonable burden on the social assistance system of the host Member State*', this notion of reasonableness justifies some restrictions to the grant of certain social benefits.[1492]

The right of EU citizens to free movement also entails the protection of the identity of Union citizens, again intersecting with the prohibition of discrimination on grounds of nationality. In *Garcia Avello*,[1493] two Spanish children born in Belgium were prevented from registering their last name as 'Garcia Weber', the combination of their father's and mother's name as is customary in Spain. The Court held that the children may rely on the prohibition of discrimination on grounds of nationality '*in regard to the rules governing their surname*'[1494] and recalled that '*the principle of non-discrimination requires that comparable situations must not be treated differently and that*

1489 *Martínez Sala v Freistaat Bayern*, C-85/96, paras 61-62.

1490 Judgment of 20 September 2001, *Grzelczyk*, C-184/99, EU:C:2001:458.

1491 Judgment of 7 September 2004, *Trojani*, C-456/02, EU:C:2004:488.

1492 Judgment of 11 November 2014, *Dano*, C-333/13, EU:C:2014:2358, para 74; Judgment of 15 September 2015, *Alimanovic*, C-67/14, EU:C:2015:597, para 50 and para 62; Judgment of 25 February 2016, *García-Nieto e.a.*, C-299/14, EU:C:2016:114, paras 22-23.

1493 Judgment of 2 October 2003, *Garcia Avello*, C-148/02, EU:C:2003:539.

1494 *Garcia Avello*, C-148/02, para 29.

different situations must not be treated in the same way';[1495] reaching the conclusion that in this case the Belgian authorities were in breach of EU law because the children in this specific situation might have difficulties proving their identity.[1496] In the same vein, the Court held in *Grunkin Paul* that the same serious inconvenience arose for a child holding the nationality of one Member State, but born and residing in another Member State, when the former State refuses the recognise the family name acquired by the child in the latter State. The resulting obligation for the EU citizen to use different names in the two Member States would infringe his right to free movement.[1497] Following this line of case law, for assessing whether there is an infringement of the right of EU citizens to free movement and residence, the notion of serious inconvenience is now taken into account at the administrative, professional and private levels.[1498]

The limits to the respect for the citizen's identity are identified by balancing interests, as exemplified in *Sayn-Wittgenstein*.[1499] Mrs Sayn-Wittgenstein was an Austrian national resident in Germany and had acquired a nobility title in Germany following her adoption by a German national. After she had used this title for several years, the Austrian authorities decided to suppress it, based on the constitutional abolition of all privileges, including titles of nobility. Before the CJEU, they argued that, unlike in *Grunkin Paul*, here the prohibition did not result in the obligation for the applicant to use different names in the two Member States and that in any case, the essential elements characterising the surname remained even if the nobility title was removed. The Court noted that '*a person's name is a constituent element of his identity and of his private life, the protection of which is enshrined*' in Article 7 CFR and Article 8 ECHR.[1500] It then identified a risk of doubts as to the person's identity, '*such as to hinder the exercise of the right which flows from Article 21 TFEU*' and therefore constituting a restriction on the

1495 *Garcia Avello*, C-148/02, para 31.

1496 *Garcia Avello*, C-148/02, para 36.

1497 Judgment of 14 October 2008, *Grunkin and Paul*, C-353/06, EU:C:2008:559, paras 21-24. Such an infringement may also arise where there is a discrepancy in the spelling of the name between two Member States following marriage and acquisition of joint surname, as was the case in Judgment of 12 May 2011, *Runevič-Vardyn and Wardyn*, C-391/09, EU:C:2011:291. Refusal of authorities to amend is possible if it does not give rise to serious inconvenience at administrative, professional and private levels.

1498 *Runevič-Vardyn and Wardyn*, C-391/09, para 76.

1499 Judgment of 22 December 2010, *Sayn-Wittgenstein*, C-208/09, EU:C:2010:806.

1500 *Sayn-Wittgenstein*, C-208/09, para 52.

freedoms conferred by this provision on all EU citizens.[1501] It was thus necessary to assess whether this restriction was justified by reasons of public policy – for which Member States have a certain degree of discretion but which may be relied on '*only if there is a genuine and sufficiently serious threat to a fundamental interest of society*'.[1502] The constitutional identity of Member States, protected by Article 4(2) TEU, may be taken into account as one of the public interests to be weighed in the balancing test.[1503] In *Sayn-Wittgenstein* the Court held that the Austrian ban on conferring nobility titles was an application of the principle of equal treatment, also recognised under EU law, and the measure did '*not appear disproportionate*'.[1504]

Illustrating the diversity of situations where EU citizenship rights apply, the *Petruhhin* judgment applied the freedom of movement in relation to extradition law. Mr Petruhhin, an Estonian national was arrested in Latvia and the Latvian authorities had responded favourably to the Russian authorities' request of extradition. Under Latvian law, had he been a Latvian national, he would have been protected from extradition. The Court held that this lower protection for non-Latvian EU citizens constituted a restriction to the freedom of movement of EU citizens, the proportionality of which must be controlled.[1505]

This overview reveals that the rights conferred by the status of EU citizens are no longer conditioned on economic considerations such as the requirement to be economically active in the host Member State. Symmetrically, they protect a variety of interests that go far beyond economic interests, such as the protection of the citizen's identity as it manifests in his or her patronym, and even a protection against extradition to a third country. This provides for a potentially ever-extensible range of concrete situations in which freedom of movement and residence applies under the 'umbrella' of Union citizenship. The dynamic rights-obligation correlation allows this right to translate into a variety of obligations on the Member States. The underlying effectiveness rationale is very powerful in this context: individuals rely on their fundamental status as EU citizens in order to protect their

1501 *Sayn-Wittgenstein*, C-208/09, paras 70-71. See also Judgment of 2 June 2016, *Bogendorff von Wolffersdorff*, C-438/14, EU:C:2016:401, para 40 and *Freitag*, C-541/15, para 38.

1502 *Sayn-Wittgenstein*, C-208/09, paras 86-87.

1503 *Sayn-Wittgenstein*, C-208/09, para 92. See also *Bogendorff von Wolffersdorff*, C-438/14, para 64.

1504 *Sayn-Wittgenstein*, C-208/09, paras 93-94.

1505 Judgment of 6 September 2016, *Petruhhin*, C-182/15, EU:C:2016:630, paras 32-34.

private and professional interests, and the Court acknowledges that the effective exercise of the right to free movement and residence attached to this status is only possible if these interests are taken into account. The same effectiveness logic is at work even more spectacularly in the development of the concept of derived rights.

2.2.2.1.2. A new manifestation of the effectiveness rationale: the concept of derived rights

The concept of an individual's right 'derived' from another individual's right developed essentially in relation with the freedom of movement and residence of EU citizens. This concept was originally used to emphasise the limits of the personal scope of the EU legislation on the free movement of workers.[1506] The Court then started accepting that to ensure the free movement of workers and economically active individuals it was necessary to also ensure that their family members could accompany them.[1507] The

1506 In the early case law on the social security of migrant workers, the Court held that a worker's family members could claim 'only' derived rights under Regulation No 1408/71, i.e. the rights acquired through their status as members of a worker's family. Judgment of 23 November 1976, *Kermaschek v Bundesanstalt für Arbeit*, C-40/76, EU:C:1976:157, para 7, Judgment of 17 December 1987, *Zaoui v CRAMIF*, C-147/87, EU:C:1987:576, para 11, Judgment of 16 July 1992, Hughes v Chief Adjudication Officer, C-78/91, EU:C:1992:331, para 25. Then in Judgment of 30 April 1996, *Bestuur van de Sociale Verzekeringsbank v Cabanis-Issarte,* C-308/93, EU:C:1996:169, para 31, the Court held that the distinction between 'rights in person and derived rights' could be dangerous because it '*may undermine the fun damental Community law requirement that its rules should be applied uniformly, by making their applicability to individuals depend on whether the national law relating to the benefits in question treats the rights concerned as rights in person or as derived rights, in the light of specific features of the domestic social security scheme*'. In consumer law, Member States also attempted to use the concept of derived rights in a restrictive way, but this was rejected by the Court: *Dillenkofer and Others v Bundesrepublik Deutschland*, Joined cases C-178/94, C-179/94, C-188 to C-190/94, para 40: '*the German and United Kingdom Governments' argument that the actual wording of Article 7 shows that this provision simply requires package travel organizers to provide sufficient evidence of security and that its lack of reference to any right of consumers to such security indicates that such a right is only an indirect and derived right must be rejected*'.

1507 See especially Judgment of 11 July 2002, *Carpenter*, C-60/00, EU:C:2002:434 where the Court held that the Member State of origin and establishment of an individual providing services to recipients in other Member States, could not deprive that provider's spouse, a third country national, from the right to re-

Baumbast case was the turning point where the concept of derived rights became central in the development of Union citizenship.[1508]

Mr Baumbast was a German national who had worked in the UK for several years and continued to reside there. The national court referred to the CJEU the question whether his children could continue their education in the UK under the provisions of Article 12 of Regulation No 1612/68. The Court held that '*to prevent a child of a citizen of the Union from continuing his education in the host Member State by refusing him permission to remain might dissuade that citizen from exercising the rights to freedom of movement laid down in Article 39 EC and would therefore create an obstacle to the effective exercise of the freedom thus guaranteed by the EC Treaty*'.[1509] The second problem was that the mother, the primary caretaker of the children, was not an EU national. The focus shifts onto the right of the children: if non-EU nationals in such a situation '*were refused the right to remain in the host Member State during the period of their children's education that might deprive those children of a right which is granted to them by the Community legislature*',[1510] i.e. the right conferred by Article 12 of Regulation 1612/68 to pursue '*under the best possible conditions, his education in the host Member State, (which) necessarily implies that that child has the right to be accompanied by the person who is his primary carer and, accordingly, that that person is able to reside with him in that Member State during his studies. To refuse to grant permission to remain to a parent who is the primary carer of the child exercising his right to pursue his studies in the host Member State infringes that right*'.[1511] So overall the Court has been receptive to the Baumbast family's argument that '*the provisions of Community law must be interpreted broadly so that the rights granted are effective*',[1512] relying on the basic idea that '*citizenship of the Union is destined to be the fundamental status of nationals of the Member States*'.[1513] The notion of dependency between Union citizens and their family members is since then essential in the determination of the derived

---

side in its territory. See also Judgment of 7 July 1992, *The Queen v Immigration Appeal Tribunal and Surinder Singh, ex parte Secretary of State for the Home Department*, C-370/90, EU:C:1992:296.

1508 *Baumbast and R*, C-413/99.

1509 *Baumbast and R*, C-413/99, para 52.

1510 *Baumbast and R*, C-413/99, para 71.

1511 *Baumbast and R*, C-413/99, para 73.

1512 *Baumbast and R*, C-413/99, para 65.

1513 *Baumbast and R*, C-413/99, para 82, *Garcia Avello*, C-148/02, para 22.

rights of the latter to accompany the former in the exercise of the freedom of movement and residence.[1514]

This notion and how it connects to derived rights and the effectiveness of the autonomous rights of Union citizens was further clarified in *Zhu and Chen*. A Chinese national was claiming the right to stay in the UK based on the right to free movement of her infant daughter, an Irish national. From the right of the child to stay in the UK, the Court derived the same right for the mother, without whom the child could not have effectively exercised her rights as an EU citizen.[1515] This case confirms the dynamism of the right-obligations correlation, since what seems like a single obligation on a Member State (to respect the freedom of movement and residence of an EU citizen) may translate into several jural correlatives, including here, a right for the baby and a derived right for the mother. As always, the correlation applies with various consequences in a potentially infinite number of real-life situations. Moreover, *Zhu and Chen* supports the notion that it is the interest of the individual, rather than his or her will or power (a baby being of course incapable of manifesting either will or power) that determines the existence of a right.[1516] Additionally, it highlights the importance of *actual* interests, as opposed to *pre-defined* protected interests, for triggering rights and corresponding obligations and therefore ensuring the effectiveness of EU law.

In addition, in *Zhu and Chen* the powerful effectiveness rationale overcomes the prohibition of abuse of rights. Indeed, the British government had suggested that Mrs Chen should not be allowed to stay in the UK because she had intentionally given birth in Northern Ireland so that the baby would benefit from the Irish *jus soli*, and then gone back to the UK to assert her Irish (i.e. European) daughter's right to stay. The abusive conduct, the argument went, should not be rewarded by acknowledging such

1514 Judgment of 10 May 2017, *Chavez-Vilchez and Others*, C-133/15, EU:C:2017:354 and Judgment of 30 June 2016, *NA*, C-115/15, EU:C:2016:487.

1515 *Zhu and Chen*, C-200/02, as analysed by K. Lenaerts, 'EU citizenship in the light of the case law of the CJEU' (Conference - EU Citizenship and Justice, Luxembourg, 14th and 15th September 2015). Advocate General Wathelet relies on the same reasoning in the *NA* case: Opinion of AG Wathelet in *NA*, C-115/15, EU:C:2016:259. See also Judgment of 10 October 2013, *Alokpa and Moudoulou*, C-86/12, EU:C:2013:645, para 28.

1516 See the overview of the debate between will theorists and interest theorists p. 43 of this work. The fact that the will theory excludes incapable individuals such as children is precisely one of the main arguments advanced *against* this theory by interest theorists.

a right.[1517] The Court however (again not so concerned about the abusive exercise of rights when it contributes to the effectiveness of EU law[1518]) held that such a conclusion would amount to allowing a Member State (the UK) to restrict the effects of another Member State (Ireland) granting nationality, and that this was prohibited by EU law.[1519]

It seems the UK found it difficult to draw all consequences from this case as in the 2014 *McCarthy* case it again defended measures restricting the free movement of family members of EU citizens in order to prevent abuse of rights.[1520] A British national and his Colombian wife resided in Spain and regularly travelled to the UK. The wife could not enter the UK without applying for a family permit, which was issued for a temporary period of six months after which the formalities had to be renewed. The UK legislation imposing these formalities was based on '*a general risk of abuse of rights or fraud.*'[1521] The Court held that the denial of entry for reasons of public policy, public security or public health had to be the result of an individual assessment of the situation of the family member[1522] and *that* '*pursuing an objective of general prevention in respect of widespread cases of abuse of rights or fraud would mean (…) that the mere fact of belonging to a particular group of persons would allow the Member States to refuse to recognise a right expressly conferred by Directive 2004/38 on family members of a Union citizen who are not nationals of a Member State, although they in fact fulfil the conditions laid down by that directive.*' The automaticity of such measures would '*disregard the very substance of the primary and individual right of Union citizens to move and reside freely within the territory of the Member States and of the derived rights*' of their family members who are third country nationals.[1523] Thus the concern for the protection of the 'substance' of EU citizenship rights has priority over the concern over the possible abusive use of these rights. The *Rendón Marín* and *CS* rulings have made clear that the fact that the non-EU parent and caretaker of a minor EU citizen should not be banned from the territory of a Member State for the sole reason that they have been criminally convicted, if that would result in also sending away the

---

1517 *Zhu and Chen*, C-200/02, para 34.

1518 As observed in Section 1.1.2.3.2. on the prohibition of abuse of rights: see p. 88 of this work.

1519 *Zhu and Chen*, C-200/02, paras 39-40.

1520 See also Judgment of 18 December 2014, *McCarthy*, C-202/13, EU:C:2014:2450, paras 57-58.

1521 *McCarthy*, C-202/13, para 43.

1522 *McCarthy*, C-202/13, para 46.

1523 *McCarthy*, C-202/13, paras 57-58.

child from the territory of the EU.[1524] It therefore seems that as a matter of principle the reprehensible conduct of the individual claiming either a derived right to stay in a Member State in order to ensure the effectiveness of the autonomous rights of an EU citizen matters little when balanced against the requirement of effectiveness of these autonomous rights.

The development of the concept of derived rights has enriched the reflection about the very substance of EU citizenship rights. *Ruiz Zambrano* was a case about the right to reside and work in Belgium of a Colombian couple with two Belgian children. Although the children had never used their free movement rights, the Court found that not issuing work and residence permits to the parents would amount to the deprivation of the children of the '*genuine enjoyment of the substance*' of their EU citizenship rights.[1525] From then on it seems that this 'substance' is no longer (exclusively) centred on the freedom of movement, and instead contains a more qualitative element consisting in '*the possibility of the whole family having a decent and secure life by European standards*'.[1526]

With regard to the sources of EU citizenship rights, it has been regretted that the Court privileges the provisions of the Treaty instead of drawing consequences from Charter provisions such as Article 7 on the respect for private and family life. The Court was accused of having adopted a minimalistic approach to fundamental rights in *Ruiz Zambrano*.[1527] But is it really 'minimalism' to give such a far-reaching effect to Article 20 TFEU? It would of course have been interesting to see how Article 7 could have applied. However, on the bright side, this case provides a telling example of how provisions of the Treaties (and the obligations and rights that they contain) can be as protective of individuals as provisions of a Charter expressly intended for that protection. In fact, *Ruiz Zambrano* shows that placing the Charter at the summit of a hypothetical hierarchy of sources

1524 Judgment of 13 September 2016, *Rendón Marín*, C-165/14, EU:C:2016:675; Judgment of 13 September 2016, *CS*, C-304/14, EU:C:2016:674.

1525 Judgment of 8 March 2011, *Ruiz Zambrano*, C-34/09, EU:C:2011:124, paras 42-43.

1526 Azoulai, 'The (Mis)Construction of the European Individual. Two Essays on Union Citizenship Law' 13.

1527 Lorenz, Groussot and Petursson, *The European Human Rights Culture - A Paradox of Human Rights Protection in Europe?* 173. The authors argue that in *Ruiz Zambrano*, the Court, '*in a cryptic reasoning focused merely on a citizenship provision (Article 20 TFEU) and failed to give guidelines on the right to family protection under Article 7 of the Charter. These cases reflect judicial minimalism in the context of EU fundamental rights.*' Kochenov, 'The Right to Have What Rights? EU Citizenship in Need of Clarification' 511.

rights is not necessary. It does not manifest judicial minimalism but rather constitutes a maximalist reading of Article 20 TFEU, fleshing out all its possible effects for individuals and Member States – which is why this case has been said to greatly increase the Court's *'rights pressure'*[1528] on the Member States.

The limits to this approach, drawn by the Court mainly in *McCarthy*, *Dereci* and *Iida*, help understand the rationale behind the concept of derived rights. In the 2011 *McCarthy* case, a Union citizen with dual Irish and British citizenship, who had always resided in the UK, had applied for a residence permit in the UK in order to obtain a right of residence for her husband, a third country national. The Court held that, since Mrs McCarthy had never exercised her right of free movement, the concept of 'beneficiary' for the purposes of Directive 2004/38 did not apply to her, nor to her spouse *'given that the rights conferred by that directive on the family members of a beneficiary of that directive are not autonomous rights of those family members, but derived rights, acquired through their status as members of the beneficiary's family'.*[1529] The Court likewise held that *'Article 21 TFEU is not applicable to a Union citizen who has never exercised his right of free movement, who has always resided in a Member State of which he is a national and who is also a national of another Member State, provided that the situation of that citizen does not include the application of measures by a Member State that would have the effect of depriving him of the genuine enjoyment of the substance of the rights conferred by virtue of his status as a Union citizen or of impeding the exercise of his right of free movement and residence within the territory of the Member States'.*[1530]

1528 Muir, 'The Court of Justice: a fundamental rights institution among others' 99-100 citing M. Shapiro, 'The European Court of Justice' in P. Craig and G. de Burca, *The Evolution of EU Law* (Oxford University Press 1999) 345.

1529 *McCarthy*, C-434/09, para 42. This statement will perhaps be qualified in a still pending case concerning an EU citizen who has become a national of her host Member State; the British authorities consider that neither she nor her family members may still be considered 'beneficiaries' under directive 2004/38. AG Bot argues that such an interpretation is incompatible with the effectiveness of rights conferred by Article 21(1) TFEU. Opinion of AG Bot in *Lounes*, C-165/16, EU:C:2017:407 (see especially para 86: '*To deprive her henceforward of the rights to which she has till now been entitled in respect of the residence of her family members because, by being naturalised, she has sought to become more deeply integrated in the host Member State, would annihilate the effectiveness of the rights which she derives from Article 21(1) TFEU*').

1530 *McCarthy*, C-434/09, para 56.

In *Dereci*, the applicants in the main proceedings were third-country nationals who wished to live with their family members, Austrian nationals residing in Austria and not having exercised the freedom of movement.[1531] Concerning the applicability of Treaty provisions on citizenship, the Court clarified *Ruiz Zambrano* by holding that '*the criterion relating to the denial of the genuine enjoyment of the substance of the rights conferred by virtue of European Union citizen status refers to situations in which the Union citizen has, in fact, to leave (...) the territory of the Union as a whole*'.[1532] In addition, '*the mere fact that it might appear desirable to a national of a Member State, for economic reasons or in order to keep his family together in the territory of the Union*' for those of his family members who are not Union citizens '*to reside with him in the territory of the Union, is not sufficient in itself to support the view that the Union citizen will be forced to leave Union territory if such a right is not granted*'.[1533]

Finally in *Iida* a Japanese national living in a Member State different from that where his spouse (a Union citizen) resided, was denied a right of residence, since he had not accompanied nor joined in the host Member State his spouse who had exercised her right of freedom of movement.[1534] Extending *McCarthy* and *Dereci*, the Court insisted that '*the Treaty provisions on citizenship of the Union do not confer any autonomous right on third-country nationals*' and that '*any rights conferred on third-country nationals by the Treaty provisions on Union citizenship are not autonomous rights of those nationals but rights derived from the exercise of freedom of movement by a Union citizen*'.[1535]

The effectiveness rationale is clearly at the heart of the reasoning in these three cases. The derived right loses its *raison d'être* when it would not help ensure the effective exercise of the autonomous right. As the Court explained in Iida, '*the purpose and justification of those derived rights are based on the fact that a refusal to allow them would be such as to interfere with the Union citizen's freedom of movement by discouraging him from exercising his rights of entry into and residence in the host Member State*'.[1536] *McCarthy* and *Dereci* have been interpreted as setting a limit to the possibility of taking into account the individual aspiration to family unity, and therefore as a re-

1531 Judgment of 15 November 2011, *Dereci and Others*, C-256/11, EU:C:2011:734.

1532 *Dereci and Others*, C-256/11, para 66.

1533 *Dereci and Others*, C-256/11, para 68.

1534 Judgment of 8 November 2012, *Iida*, C-40/11, EU:C:2012:691, para 65.

1535 *Iida*, C-40/11, paras 66-67. See also Judgment of 8 May 2013, *Ymeraga and Ymeraga-Tafarshiku*, C-87/12, EU:C:2013:291, para 34.

1536 *Iida*, C-40/11, para 68.

striction to Ruiz Zambrano.[1537] It makes sense in the light of *Iida:* this aspiration is accounted for only in so far as it impacts the effectiveness of the autonomous rights of Union citizens.

This rationale was again asserted in *Singh.* Several third country nationals were challenging the rejection by the Irish authorities of their applications to retain their right of residence following their divorce from EU citizens, who had left Ireland prior to the start of the divorce proceedings.[1538] They relied on Article 13(2) of the Directive, granting a right of residence to family members when divorce proceedings are initiated after three years of stay in the EU, including one in the host Member State. The Court started by pointing out that the rights conferred on family members of EU citizens by Directive 2004/38 are '*not autonomous rights (…) but rights derived from the exercise of freedom of movement by a Union citizen*' and that the '*purpose and justification of those derived rights are based on the fact that a refusal to allow such rights would be liable to interfere with the Union citizen's freedom of movement by discouraging him from exercising his rights of entry into and residence in the host Member State*'.[1539] Recalling then the solution in *Iida* that family members must be accompanying the Union citizen in the exercise of his freedom of movement in order to benefit from the Directive,[1540] the Court then looked at Article 13(2) of the Directive and considered that it corresponded '*to the purpose, stated in recital 15 in the preamble to the directive, of providing legal safeguards for family members in the event of the death of the Union citizen, divorce, (…), to ensure that in such circumstances family members already residing within the territory of the host Member State retain their right of residence exclusively on a personal basis*'.[1541] In other words, where the conditions are met, the derived right of residence becomes an autonomous right. However, if the Union citizen leaves the host Member States before the start of the divorce proceedings, the derived right disappears before it has had the possibility to give rise to an autonomous right: '*the later petition for divorce cannot have the effect of reviving that right, since*

1537 M. Dawson, 'How Does the European Court of Justice Reason? A Review Essay on the Legal Reasoning of the European Court of Justice' (2014) 20 European Law Journal 423 429.

1538 Judgment of 16 July 2015, *Singh and Others*, C-218/14, EU:C:2015:476. F. Strumia, 'Divorce immediately, or leave. Rights of third country nationals and family protection in the context of EU citizens' free movement: *Kuldip Singh and Others*' (2016) 53 Common Market Law Review 1373.

1539 *Singh and Others*, C-218/14, para 50.

1540 *Singh and Others*, C-218/14, para 52; *Iida*, C-40/11, para 61.

1541 *Singh and Others*, C-218/14, para 60.

Article 13 of Directive 2004/38 mentions only the 'retention' of an existing right of residence'.[1542]

The above overview shows that the case law on the rights of Union citizens covers an extremely broad array of particular situations. In this context, individual rights are components of a potentially infinite chain of rights and correlative obligations. Union citizenship becomes an increasingly inclusive umbrella of rights that apply, if that is in the legitimate interests of the citizens, beyond the holders of the status.

2.2.2.2. Political representation and participation rights

The basic principles concerning the democratic functioning of the EU are enshrined in Article 10 TEU, the first and third paragraph of which provide respectively that '*[t]he functioning of the Union shall be founded on representative democracy*' and that '*[e]very citizen shall have the right to participate in the democratic life of the Union*'. Article 11 TEU further organises the modalities of participatory democracy.[1543] These provisions are one step in a perhaps never-ending process of addressing and responding to the recurring criticism regarding the EU's 'democratic deficit' and 'legitimacy gap'.[1544] The public and academic debate on these issues had intensified

---

1542 *Singh and Others*, C-218/14, paras 62 and 67.

1543 On this evolution see J. Organ, 'Decommissioning Direct Democracy? A Critical Analysis of Commission Decision-Making on the Legal Admissibility of European Citizens Initiative Proposals' (2014) 10 European Constitutional Law Review 422 and A. Karatzia, 'The European Citizens' Initiative and the EU Institutional Balance: on Realism and the Possibilities of Affecting EU Lawmaking' (2017) 54 Common Market Law Review 177.

1544 P. Pescatore, 'Les exigences de la démocratie et la legitimité de la Communauté européenne' (1974) 10 Cahiers de Droit Européen 499; Rosas and Armati, *EU Constitutional Law: An Introduction* 126; F. Bignami, 'The Democratic Deficit in European Community Rulemaking: A Call for Notice and Comment in Comitology' (1999) 40 Harvard International Law Journal 451; R. Bellamy, 'Still in Deficit: Rights, Regulation, and Democracy in the EU' (2006) 12 European Law Journal 725; A. Føllesdal, 'Survey Article: The Legitimacy Deficits of the European Union' (2006) 14 The Journal of Political Philosophy 441; A.J. Menendez, 'The European Democratic Challenge: The Forging of a Supranational Volonté Générale' (2009) 15 European Law Journal 277; D. Curtin, 'Challenging Executive Dominance in European Democracy' (2014) 77 The Modern Law Review 1; Habermas, 'Democracy in Europe: Why the Development of the EU into a Transnational Democracy Is Necessary and How It Is Possible'.

with the first direct elections of the Members of the European Parliament[1545] and escalated during the ratification process of the Maastricht Treaty.[1546]

At this point the rights associated with democratic participation were given enhanced significance in the Union's constitutional system, mainly through two important changes. Firstly, the new treaty introduced the co-decision procedure to certain legislative areas, and extended the cooperation procedure to others, thus initating the European Parliament's evolution towards its status of co-legislator. It granted the Parliament the power to approve the composition of the Commission, and thus introduced a form of political control over EU executive power.[1547] The second key element of change was the introduction of the Union citizenship. We have just seen that this fundamental status confers a variety of 'spatial' rights to its holders and their family members. It also confers rights of representation and participation in the Union's democratic life. Following the Treaty of Lisbon, these rights are now codified in the Charter: Articles 39 and 40 enshrine the right to vote and to stand as a candidate at elections to the European Parliament and at municipal elections, Article 44 protects the right to petition the European Parliament. In an effort to strengthen direct democracy and citizen participation, the Treaty of Lisbon has also intro-

---

1545 Act concerning the election of the representatives of the European Parliament by direct universal suffrage annexed to Council Decision 76/787/ECSC, EEC, Euratom of 20 September 1976 (OJ L 278 p. 1), as amended by Council Decision 2002/772/EC, Euratom of 25 June 2002 and 23 September 2002 (OJ L 283 p. 1) ('the 1976 Act').

1546 Menendez, 'The European Democratic Challenge: The Forging of a Supranational Volonté Générale' 278; E. Lanza, 'Core of State Sovereignty and Boundaries of European Identity in the Lissabon-Urteil' (2010) 11 German Law Journal 399; R.A. Miller, 'Germany vs. Europe: The Principle of Democracy in German Constitutional Law and the Troubled Future of European Integration' (2014) 54 Virginia Journal of International Law 579. The debate has been particularly intense in the Germany at each important stage of the European integration process. This is due to the centrality of the principle of democracy, grounded in Article 20 GG, and complemented by Article 38 GG, which provides for the direct election of representatives to the Parliament. In each of its decisions concerning the transfer of sovereign State authority to the EU level, the Bundesverfassungsgericht has insisted on the principle of democracy most recently in the Lisbon Treaty case (BVerfG 123, 267) and the European Stability Mechanism case (BVerfG 132, 195).

1547 U. Bux, 'Le Parlement européen : contexte historique', *Fiches techniques sur l'Union européenne,* April 2017, <http://www.europarl.europa.eu/ftu/pdf/fr/FTU_1.3.1.pdf> accessed 17 July 2017.

duced the mechanism of the European Citizens' Initiative.[1548] The question here is: are the rights of individual citizens to political representation and participation 'rights' in the classic sense? In view of our (so far constant) observation that more discretion means a lower probability of identifying a right, if there are indeed individual rights to representation and participation, how do they relate to the discretion traditionally granted to institutional political actors?

2.2.2.2.1. The right to vote and to stand as a candidate at elections

In the pre-Lisbon case law on the right to vote in elections for the European Parliament, litigation arose from the lack of precision of this right with regard to its geographic and personal scope. The *Eman and Sevinger* case concerning Dutch nationals whose status as residents of Aruba deprived them of the right to vote is a prominent example.[1549] The Court held that neither the relevant Treaty provisions nor the 1976 Act contained rules defining '*expressly and precisely who are to be entitled to the right to vote and to stand as a candidate for the European Parliament*',[1550] and added that there is no '*unconditional right to vote*', meaning that criteria of residence were possible.[1551] However the principle of equal treatment, a general principle of EU law,[1552] prevents '*the criteria chosen from resulting in different treatment of nationals who are in comparable situations, unless that difference in treatment is objectively justified*'.[1553] In the case at hand, there seemed to be no sufficient objective justification to the rule according to which Netherlands nationals living in Aruba could not vote, while those living elsewhere abroad kept their right to vote. Should the national court find that the right to vote under EU law has indeed been infringed, the usual arsenal of remedies must be made available, in accordance with the princi-

---

1548 Article 11(4) TEU and Article 24, first sentence TFEU, complemented by the 'ECI Regulation': Parliament and Council Regulation No 211/2011 of 16 February 2011 on the citizens' initiative (OJ L 65 p.1). On the ECI see A. Karatzia, 'The European Citizens' Initiative: a laboratory for citizens' participation in EU law-making' (PhD thesis, University of Surrey 2016).

1549 Judgment of 12 September 2006, *Eman and Sevinger*, C-300/04, EU:C:2006:545.

1550 *Eman and Sevinger*, C-300/04, paras 40 and 43.

1551 *Eman and Sevinger*, C-300/04, para 52 and paras 54-55.

1552 *Eman and Sevinger*, C-300/04, para 57.

1553 *Eman and Sevinger*, C-300/04, para 61.

ples of equivalence and effectiveness and including the possibility to claim damages.[1554]

The case of voting rights of residents of Gibraltar led to an action for failure to fulfil obligations by the Kingdom of Spain against the United Kingdom, which constituted an interesting challenge *against* the granting of a right to vote.[1555] The Spanish government claimed that the UK had infringed the Treaty by conferring on Commonwealth citizens residing in Gibraltar the right to vote and to be elected in elections to the European Parliament.[1556] So, the issue was again how to define the geographic and personal scope of the right – but unlike in *Eman and Sevinger*, here the applicant was arguing that this scope was construed too broadly. The Court held that '*neither Article 190 EC nor the 1976 Act defines expressly and precisely who are to be entitled to the right to vote and to stand as a candidate in elections to the European Parliament. In themselves, those provisions do not exclude, therefore, a person who is not a citizen of the Union, such as a QCC resident in Gibraltar, from being entitled to the right to vote and stand for election*'. The Spanish government additionally submitted that the Treaties had established '*a clear link between citizenship of the Union and the right to vote and stand for election*', which meant that this right should be limited to EU citizens. Concerning this argument '*No clear conclusion can be drawn in that regard from Articles 189 EC and 190 EC, relating to the European Parliament, which state that it is to consist of representatives of the peoples of the Member States, since the term 'peoples', which is not defined, may have different meanings in the Member States and languages of the Union.*' Moreover, '*As regards the Treaty's articles relating to citizenship of the Union, no principle can be derived from them that citizens of the Union are the only persons entitled under all the other provisions of the Treaty, which would imply that Articles 189 EC and 190 EC apply to those citizens alone*'.[1557]

The common points to both cases is that the Court looked at whether the provisions on the right to vote contained sufficient precisions or express specifications to circumscribe a right. So in both cases, and just like for other types of rights, the identification of a right in a specific situation depends on the degree of discretion allowed in the implementation of the provision. The right to vote therefore exemplifies how a provision may or may not give rise to rights depending on the concrete circumstances. If we

1554 *Eman and Sevinger*, C-300/04, paras 65-72.

1555 Judgment of 12 September 2006, *Spain v United Kingdom*, C-145/04, EU:C:2006:543.

1556 In compliance with *Matthews v United Kingdom*, n°24833/94 (ECHR 1999).

1557 *Spain v United Kingdom*, C-145/04, paras 70-72.

look now at the (for now scarce) post-Lisbon case law on the right to vote, we see that it confirms this notion and thus illustrates the pitfall that consists in looking at Charter provisions through a strict 'rights'/'principles' filter. Indeed, Article 39 is one of the Charter's many contact points with the Treaties.[1558] Article 39(1) CFR is almost identical to Article 20(2)(b) TFEU and provides that '*[e]very citizen of the Union has the right to vote and to stand as a candidate at elections to the European Parliament in the Member State in which he or she resides, under the same conditions as nationals of that State.*' Article 39(2) CFR provides in the exact same terms as Article 14(3) TEU that '*[m]embers of the European Parliament shall be elected by direct universal suffrage in a free and secret ballot*'.

The *Delvigne* case on prisoner disenfranchisement raised the question of the practical significance of these provisions.[1559] A French prisoner had been permanently deprived of his right to vote as an automatic consequence of his condemnation for murder. This sanction, according to the French Criminal Code as it stood when the prisoner was condemned, was automatic for such crimes. Based on Article 39 CFR, Mr Delvigne challenged this sanction before the Tribunal d'instance of Bordeaux. The Tribunal d'instance asked the Court of Justice whether the general, automatic and indefinite ban that applied to Mr Delvigne was contrary to Article 39. The intervening Member States argued in favour of an interpretation which would restrict the applicability of Article 39 to situations where there is direct discrimination against EU nationals who have made use of their right to circulate within the EU. On the contrary, the European Parliament argued in this case that '*Article 39 of the Charter contains subjective rights laid down for the benefit of individuals*'; indeed, according to the EP, '*the right to vote recognised therein is not only guaranteed for citizens of the Union who vote in a Member State other than their Member State of nationality but also for nationals of the Member State in which they cast their vote*'. Moreover, the EP submitted that '*in order for practical effect to be given to Article 39(2) of the Charter, that provision must be construed as encompassing a subjective right which supplements Article 14(3) TEU. In that connection, universal*

1558 On the abundance of contact points between the Charter and other sources of fundamental rights, see p. 127 of this work.

1559 *Delvigne*, C-650/13. H. Van Eijken and J.W. Van Rossem, 'Prisoner disenfranchisement and the right to vote in elections to the European Parliament: Universal suffrage key to unlocking political citizenship?' (2016) 12 European Constitutional Law Review 114; A. Korzenov, 'The Right to Vote as an EU Fundamental Right and the Expanding Scope of Application of the EU Charter of Fundamental Rights' (2016) 75 The Cambridge Law Journal 24.

suffrage, which is the central notion for the purpose of defining the substance of that right, entails a ratio personae, in principle general, which affords unconditional protection not only for a citizen of the Union who votes in a Member State which is not his State of origin, but also for nationals of the Member State of the place where that citizen casts his vote.'[1560]

In its ruling the Court also refers to the connection (which the Explanations highlight) between Article 39(1) CFR and Article 20(2)(b) TFEU.[1561] As there is already case law on the meaning of Article 20(2)(b), the Court simply transposes that interpretation to Article 39(1) CFR and concludes that this provision does not apply to Mr Delvigne, because the latter is not a national of a Member State other than that in which he resides.[1562] Regarding Article 39(2), the Court finds that it '*constitutes the expression in the Charter of the right of Union citizens to vote in elections to the European Parliament*' based on Article 14(3) TEU, as suggested by the European Parliament and based on the Explanations which state that Article 39(2) '*takes over the basic principles of the electoral system in a democratic State.*'[1563] The Court then performs a proportionality test, based on Article 52(1) of the Charter, of the limitation of Mr Delvigne's right to vote. In light of the possibility provided by French law for cases such as Mr Delvigne's to be reviewed individually in order to assess the appropriateness of lifting the ban on voting, the Court finds that the limitation is not disproportionate.[1564]

This case calls for two observations. Firstly, once again, the Court steers clear of the rights/principles distinction.[1565] Even with the Parliament echoing the Explanations by referring to the notion of a 'subjective right', the Court avoids using that term and simply acknowledges that Article 39(2) contains a 'right'. Neither the characterisation of the provision as taking over 'principles' according to the Explanations, nor the fact that Article 14(3) TEU (of which Article 39(2) CFR is a duplicate) contains an 'obliga-

---

1560 Opinion of AG Cruz Villalón in *Delvigne*, C-650/13, EU:C:2015:363, paras 40-43.

1561 *Delvigne*, C-650/13, para 41.

1562 *Delvigne*, C-650/13, para 42: '*[...] that provision is confined to applying the principle of non-discrimination on grounds of nationality to the exercise of the right to vote in elections to the European Parliament, by providing that every citizen of the Union residing in a Member State of which he is not a national is to have the right to vote in those elections in the Member State in which he resides, under the same conditions as nationals of that State*' (citing *Spain* v *United Kingdom*, C-145/04, para 66).

1563 *Delvigne*, C-650/13, paras 41 and 44.

1564 *Delvigne*, C-650/13, para 57.

1565 Like in *Association de médiation sociale*, C-176/12, discussed in this work p. 351.

tion' on the Member States,[1566] constitute obstacles to finding that Article 39(2) grants a right.[1567] On the contrary, the analysis of the 'obligation' and 'right' aspects allows for the identification of the substance of the rule (whether this rule is primarily intended as a 'right' or 'principle,' or a 'right' or 'obligation,' is not an issue). This leads us to the second observation: Charter provisions are not taken as autonomous sources of rights; instead, in order to define the substance of each right, the Court relies both on Charter provisions and on the corresponding Treaty provisions, including the relevant case law where possible.

This rather classic approach is not unanimously accepted and a more restrictive approach to political participation rights may be observed in the case law of other courts. For instance, in *Chester and McGeoch*[1568] the UK Supreme Court had to rule on prisoner disenfranchisement. The applicants were claiming their 'right to vote' based on Article 20(2) TFEU, which the Explanations to the Charter equate to Article 39(1) CFR (Right to Vote and to Stand as a Candidate at Elections to the EP), and on ECtHR case law. The Supreme Court argued that nothing indicated that Article 39(1) CFR was meant to confer individual rights: '*had that been remotely intended, quite different explicit language would have been used*'[1569] – thus performing a purely intentionalist analysis. Unfortunately, it did not deem necessary to refer to the European Court of Justice for interpretation of that provision; therefore the case remained a domestic one. In light of the CJEU's stance on Article 20(2) in *Delvigne*, (i.e. that it applies only to EU citizens who reside in a Member State other than their own), the outcome would perhaps not have been different ultimately. Yet, it could have been a further occasion for the Court to reassert its correlativity-based method for identifying political representation rights. It is therefore regrettable that no reference for preliminary ruling was made, as it constitutes to say the least

1566 *Delvigne*, C-650/13, para 33.

1567 This is yet another echo of the Court's finding in *Defrenne II* that the label 'principle' on the prohibition on discrimination did not prevent it from giving rise to rights. Judgment of 8 April 1976, *Defrenne v. SABENA*, C-43/75, EU:C:1976:56, para. 28.

1568 R (on the application of Chester) v Secretary of State for Justice and McGeoch (AP) v The Lord President of the Council and another Scotland UKSC 63 (UK Supreme Court).

1569 R (on the application of Chester) v Secretary of State for Justice and McGeoch (AP) v The Lord President of the Council and another Scotland UKSC 63 (UK Supreme Court), para 59. See also L. Kadar and J. Shaw, 'Article 39' in S. Peers and others (eds), *The EU Charter of Fundamental Rights* (Hart Publishing 2014) 1054.

'a generous application of the acte clair *doctrine'*[1570] and also a questionable application of a sort of *Schutznorm* doctrine.

2.2.2.2.2. The right to petition

The right to petition the European Parliament was originally developed in the Rules of Procedure of the EP.[1571] It was then constitutionalised in the Maastricht Treaty, and is now enshrined in Article 227 TFEU and Article 44 CFR.[1572] This instrument has a very broad material scope of application since according to Rule 215(1) of the EP's Rules of Procedure the matter advanced by the petition must fall within the EU's field of activity.[1573] The second condition is that it must concern directly the author – Marty notes however that the legal service of the EP has maintained a broad interpretation of both conditions.[1574] In addition, it should be pointed out that the right of petition does not benefit only citizens of the Union, but also 'any natural or legal person residing or having its registered office in a Member State.'[1575]

The most prominent case to date concerning the right to petition is *Schönberger*, which went not only before the GC but then also on appeal before the Court of Justice. Mr Schönberger, a former civil servant at the European Parliament, had filed a petition against the decision of the latter

1570 A. Lansbergen, 'Prisoner Disenfranchisement in the United Kingdom and the Scope of EU Law: United Kingdom Supreme Court' (2014) 10 European Constitutional Law Review 126 137.

1571 Currently governed by Title IX on Petitions of the European Parliament's Rules of Procedure, 8th parliamentary term, 2014-2019.

1572 Articles 8D and 138D EC. N. Marty, 'Le droit de pétition devant la commission des pétitions du Parlement européen : un enjeu institutionnel' [2013] Revue des Affaires Européennes - Law & European Affairs 731 732. See also P. Magnette, 'La citoyenneté au-delà du vote. Droit de pétition et recours au médiateur', in P. Magnette, *De l'étranger au citoyen, Construire la citoyenneté européenne* (De Boeck Université 1997) 145-165.

1573 An example of a petition not accepted: Judgment 27 September 2012, *J v Parliament*, T-160/10, EU:T:2012:503. An Austrian citizen accused Austrian authorities of having confiscated some of his work and claimed that his right under Article 17 CFR had been infringed. He argued that the protection of fundamental rights was a field of activity of the EU, but the Court deemed the petition inadmissible based on Article 51 CFR.

1574 Marty, 'Le droit de pétition devant la commission des pétitions du Parlement européen : un enjeu institutionnel' 735-736.

1575 Article 44 CFR.

to grant him what he deemed an insufficient number of merit points.[1576] The Committee on Petitions of the Parliament examined the petition and closed the procedure by transferring it to the Directorate-General for Personnel. Mr Schönberger challenged this transfer decision before the Court. This case raised the question of how to construe the right of petition, set out in Article 20(2)(d) TFEU, Article 24, paragraph 2 TFEU, Article 227 TFEU and Article 44 CFR (so, again an illustration of the 'contact points' issue). It is also one of these cases where the contrast between the AG's Opinion and the final judgment is enlightening, especially with regard to the Court's response to the *Schutznorm*-pressure.

In his Opinion,[1577] Advocate General Jääskinen sets about to demonstrate why the right of petition should not be construed as a subjective right, but rather a political tool. As a first step, he mentions that the term 'right' in EU legislation does not automatically give rise to a subjective right. This view is supported by the existence of the rights/principles distinction laid down in Article 52(5) CFR. We know from the Explanations to the Charter that some 'rights' in the Charter are in fact not subjective individual rights. The Advocate General also refers to the *AMS* case in which, he believes, the Court categorised the right to information and consultation as a 'principle' (whereas in fact, it is not so clear whether the Court intended to do so). Indeed, he recalls, Article 27 CFR does not define an individual legal situation: it requires from the public bodies that they define an objective content (information and consultation of workers) and certain objectives (effectiveness of information, representativity based on the levels, in due time). Therefore, Jääskinen interprets Article 52(5) and the *AMS* judgment as meaning that a provision which lays down an obligation for public bodies by essence does *not* translate into a right.[1578] To back up his argument, he also recalls that EU law includes many instruments which are named 'rights' but do not open the way to judicial control.[1579] The AG argues that the right to petition falls into that category

1576 Judgment of 9 December 2014, *Schönberger*, C-261/13 P, ECLI:EU:C:2014:2423.

1577 Opinion of AG Jääskinen in *Schönberger*, C-261/13 P, ECLI:EU:C:2014:2107.

1578 Opinion of AG Jääskinen in *Schönberger*, C-261/13 P, paras 57-58.

1579 Such as the possibility to lodge a complaint based on the Code of good administrative behaviour, or the minimal norms established by the Commission for consultation of the public, which do not grant an individual right to a judicial remedy against the decisions which would be made in violation of these norms (Opinion of AG Jääskinen in *Schönberger*, C-261/13 P, ECLI:EU:C:2014:2107, para. 60). These happen to be non-binding tools, however, which of course is not the case of Charter and Treaty provisions – so the parallel drawn by the AG is of limited relevance.

and that it is fully respected as long as the applicant has been able to introduce its request, has been informed of the procedural steps within the European Parliament, and has received an answer – all the more since '*the substance of the right of petition lies in the possibility of formally making the Parliament aware of certain issues, without conferring on the applicant the directly to claim legal protection. It is not an individual right intended to produce legal effects with regard to the situation of a petitioner, but a political tool for participation in democratic life*'.[1580] The '*corollary to the right of petition*' is therefore limited to '*the Parliament's duty to establish the mechanisms to enable applicants to access the Parliament using efficient and transparent procedures.*'[1581] As a consequence, the control of the respect of the right to petition could not be initiated by an individual: '*a review by the EU Courts is required only if the Parliament's conduct reflects a serious and persistent infringement of the right of petition, calling into question the application of the petition instrument in itself.*'[1582]

The subsequent judgment reaches the same conclusion (i.e. dismissal of Mr Schönberger's action) but through a very different process, relying mainly on the correlation between rights and obligations. For deciding that a petition is inadmissible, there are clear and precise conditions to be respected (laid down in Article 227 TFEU and the rules adopted in application of it). The decision is subject to judicial review since such a decision '*is liable to affect the right of petition of the person concerned*',[1583] or as the GC had put in more dramatic terms, the decision to declare a petition inadmissible potentially affects the '*very essence*' of the fundamental right of citizens to submit a petition.[1584] The corollary, in light of the potential impacts on the effective exercise of the right, is the obligation for the petitions committee to provide a statement of reasons. This obligation is sup-

---

1580 Opinion of AG Jääskinen in *Schönberger*, C-261/13 P, para 78.

1581 Opinion of AG Jääskinen in *Schönberger*, C-261/13 P, para 80.

1582 Opinion of AG Jääskinen in *Schönberger*, C-261/13 P, para 81.

1583 *Schönberger*, C-261/13 P, para 22.

1584 Judgment of 7 March 2013, *Schönberger v Parliament*, T-186/11, EU:T:2013:111, para 16 ('*la décision de la commission des pétitions de déclarer irrecevable et, en conséquence, de classer sans suite une pétition est de nature à affecter l'essence même du droit fondamental des citoyens à présenter une pétition…*'), Judgment of 14 September 2011, *Tegebauer v Parliament*, T-308/07, EU:T:2011:466, para 21, Judgment of 10 September 2014, *Lomnici v Parliament*, T-650/13, EU:T:2014:796, para 32.

ported not only by the need to ensure adequate judicial review[1585] but also, as the GC explains, derives from '*the very nature*' of the right of petition, and contributes to legitimising the action of EU institutions.[1586] There is again this intertwining between systemic considerations on legitimacy and democratic functioning, and the insistance on the effectiveness of individual rights. '*By contrast, it is clear from the provisions of the TFEU and from the rules adopted by the Parliament for the organisation of the right of petition that, where the Parliament takes the view that a petition meets the conditions laid down in Article 227 TFEU, it has a broad discretion, of a political nature, as regards how that petition should be dealt with. It follows that a decision taken in that regard is not amenable to judicial review* (...)'.[1587] What we see here is the correlativity between rights and obligations at work. Where there are precise obligations to be observed, the individual has a corresponding right (to have his petition examined) and a corollary remedy (action for annulment). Conversely, where there is broad discretion, there is no corresponding right (to a certain answer on the substance of the petition[1588]) and no remedy. By contrast with the AG's restrictive approach to enforcement of the right to petition, the Court's judgment is consistent with its classic conception of the relation between rights and remedies, the latter being a logical and immediate consequence of the former. It is also in accordance with the idea that individuals when enforcing their rights play a simultaneous and equally important role for the activation of legality review and controlling the observance by institutions (here, the Parliament) of their obligations.

1585 *Schönberger*, C-261/13 P, para 23. In the same vein see *Tegebauer v Parliament*, T-308/07, paras 23-25, especially para 23, recalling that the obligation to give reasons for an individual decision aims to allow the concerned individual to assess whether there are motives to challenge it in court, and to allow the EU court to assess its legality. See also Order of 4 May 2016, *Pannonhalmi Főapátság v Parliament*, C-607/15 P, EU:C:2016:329, para 14. We have seen already how the obligation to state reasons connects with the right judicial review: see especially in this work p. 180, on *Kadi II*, Joined cases C-584/10 P, C-593/10 P and C-595/10 P.

1586 *Schönberger v Parliament*, T-186/11, para 17. See also *Tegebauer v Parliament*, T-308/07, para 29 and *Lomnici v Parliament*, T-650/13, para 33.

1587 *Schönberger*, C-261/13 P, para 24. See also *Tegebauer v Parliament*, T-308/07, EU:T:2011:466, para 21, *Schönberger v Parliament*, T-186/11, para 19; *Lomnici v Parliament*, T-650/13, para 34.

1588 *Schönberger v Parliament*, T-186/11, para 20 ; see also *Lomnici v Parliament*, T-650/13, para 36.

The notion of individual interest is also an important parameter in the judgment of the General Court (confirmed by the Court of Justice). The GC indeed started from the premise that only measures producing binding legal effects with the potential to affect the interests of the applicant could be challenged on the basis of Article 263 TFEU by significantly modifying his legal situation.[1589] Since there is no obligation to a certain substantive result of the petition procedure, the final outcome of such a procedure cannot affect the interests of the individual who submitted it, which is why it cannot be challenged on the basis of Article 263 TFEU.[1590] Keeping in mind that the right of petition is '*an instrument of citizen participation in the democratic life of the European Union*' and '*one of the means of ensuring direct dialogue between citizens of the European Union and their representatives*'[1591] it appears that the individual's interest is in the political participation process itself.

2.2.2.2.3. The right to submit a Citizens' Initiative

The possibility to submit a European Citizens' Initiative, provided by the ECI Regulation of 2011, is not as such characterised as a 'right' in the Treaties. It is instead the result of the implementation of Article 11(4) TEU ('*Not less than one million citizens who are nationals of a significant number of Member States may take the initiative of inviting the European Commission, within the framework of its powers, to submit any appropriate proposal on matters where citizens consider that a legal act of the Union is required for the purpose of implementing the Treaties*') and Article 24, first sentence TFEU, which requires the European Parliament and the Council to implement Article 11(4) TEU. Although the ECI procedure involves a (massive) group of individuals rather than one single individual, the similarities with the petition procedure cannot be ignored.[1592] In addition, the ECI Regulation does describe the ECI as a 'right': the first recital observes that according to the Treaties '*every citizen is to have the right to participate in the democratic life of the Union by way of a European citizens' initiative*' (which is in fact, a sort

1589 *Schönberger v Parliament*, T-186/11, para 15.

1590 *Schönberger v Parliament*, T-186/11, para 20; *Lomnici v Parliament*, T-650/13, para 39.

1591 *Schönberger*, C-261/13 P, para 17.

1592 Confirming this impression: the modalities of involvement of the Parliament in the process of examining an ECI are laid down in Rule 218 of the EP's Rules of Procedure, under Title IX, 'Petitions'.

of medley of Article 10, third paragraph and Article 11(4) TEU). Against this backdrop, the question arises as to whether we could characterise the possibility to submit an ECI as a 'right' in the sense that this study has been advancing so far, i.e., the correlative of an obligation, triggered by the existence of a particular interest.

The identification of a 'right' to submit an ECI is made possible by the conceptual correlation between obligations and rights, and the combination of several sources of rights. In *Anagnostakis*, the applicant was challenging the rejection of an ECI (submitted in the context of the Greek economic and financial crisis) seeking to have the EU legislature establish a principle of 'state of necessity' that would legitimate the refusal to repay public debt. The GC held that the refusal '*to register the proposed ECI is an action that may impinge upon the very effectiveness of the right of Union citizens to submit a citizens initiative that is enshrined in the first paragraph of Article 24 TFEU*'.[1593] This is remarkable since this provision is actually phrased as an obligation on the EP and the Council, which are tasked with adopting '*the provisions for the procedures and conditions required for a citizens' initiative*' – to be contrasted with the second paragraph of Article 24, which clearly mentions a 'right' to petition. Article 11(4) TEU could also have been identified as a primary law source for the right to submit an ECI since it provides that citizens 'may' submit an ECI. Nevertheless, the GC's solution exemplifies the fluidity between the provisions that provide for rights and those that impose obligations. It can also be suggested (although that is not explicit in the GC's reasoning) that the obligation of Article 24, first paragraph TFEU, has been given concrete expression as a right by the ECI regulation.

The idea that the right to submit an ECI encompasses certain procedural guarantees in the case of a decision of inadmissibility is another parallel to be drawn between the right to submit a petition and the right to submit an ECI.[1594] The GC has held in *Anagnostakis* that '*It is incumbent on the Commission, when it receives a proposal for a citizens' initiative, to appraise it and also to give reasons for any refusal to register it, given the effect of such a refusal on the effective exercise of the right enshrined in the Treaty. That follows from the very nature of this right which, as is pointed out in recital 1 of the*

1593 Judgment of 30 September 2015, *Anagnostakis v Commission*, T-450/12, EU:T:2015:739, (confirmed by Judgment of 12 September 2017, *Anagnostakis v Commission*, C-589/15 P, EU:C:2017:663), para 25.

1594 The analogy is noted in Order of 13 April 2016, *AJ - MV v Commission*, T-46/16, EU:T:2016:225, para 8. See also *Anagnostakis v Commission*, T-450/12, para 26 referring to case law on petition.

preamble to Regulation No 211/2011, is intended to reinforce citizenship of the Union and enhance the democratic functioning of the Union through the participation of citizens in the democratic life of the Union'.[1595] So the process of submitting the ECI is part of the 'very nature' of the right (if we use the GC's expression concerning the right of petition).

Concerning the substance of the right to the ECI and the Commission's correlative obligations, questions have been raised as to the exact degree of discretion which these allow on the Commission. Both parts of the admissibility criteria of Article 4(2)(b) of the ECI Regulation–that the ECI must not be 'manifestly outside the framework of the Commission's powers' and must pursue 'the purpose of implementing the Treaties'–allow for some discretion in the Commission's implementation.[1596] The way in which the Commission uses this discretion has been criticised in the literature, with Organ pointing out '*the formalistic, restrictive and sometimes selective approach taken, combined with the high number of proposals refused registration, [leaving] the Commission open to criticism in relation to its willingness to accept popular influence over the legislative agenda and a Union based on democracy*'.[1597]

Not surprisingly, the limits to the Commission's discretion are therefore being challenged also in court. An action for annulment was lodged against the Commission's decision rejecting the request for registration of the famous 'Stop TTIP' ECI asking the Commission to recommend that the Council cancel the negotiation mandate for the (in)famous Transatlantic Treaty on Investment and Trade (and the signature of its cousin CETA).[1598] The Commission responded that this was a request to take a preparatory act that could not in itself alter EU law and therefore the ECI

1595 *Anagnostakis v Commission*, T-450/12, para 26. See also Judgment of 19 April 2016, *Costantini and Others v Commission*, T-44/14, EU:T:2016:223, para 73; Judgment of 3 February 2017, *Minority SafePack - one million signatures for diversity in Europe v Commission*, T-646/13, EU:T:2017:59, para 17.

1596 J. Organ, 'Decommissioning Direct Democracy? A Critical Analysis of Commission Decision-Making on the Legal Admissibility of European Citizens Initiative Proposals' 10 European Constitutional Law Review 422 427.

1597 Organ, 'Decommissioning Direct Democracy? A Critical Analysis of Commission Decision-Making on the Legal Admissibility of European Citizens Initiative Proposals' 443.

1598 Council of the European Union, Directives for the negotiation of the Transatlantic Trade and Investment Partnership between the European Union and the United States of America, as adopted at the Foreign Affairs Council (Trade) on 14 June 2013, 11103/13, available at http://data.consilium.europa.eu/doc/document/ST-11103-2013-DCL-1/en/pdf.

fell outside the scope of the competences conferred on the Commission by the ECI Regulation. One of the first steps in the GC's reasoning was to highlight the relation between the '*principle of democracy*' enshrined in the preamble and Article 2 of the TEU and in the preamble to the Charter, and the '*general right*' of every citizen '*to participate in democratic life*'.[1599] The GC then insisted on the effectiveness of the ECI mechanism: '*The Commission's position (...) has the consequence of limiting considerably recourse to the ECI mechanism as an instrument of European Union citizen participation in the European Union's normative activity as carried out by means of the conclusion of international agreements*'. The Commission's reasoning, in so far as it '*definitively [prevents] European Union citizens from proposing any opening of negotiations relating to a new treaty to be negotiated by means of an ECI*', '*manifestly runs counter*' to the objectives pursued by the Treaties and the ECI Regulation.[1600] Expanding the teleological and systemic analysis, the GC added that '*The aim pursued by the ECI is to allow European Union citizens to participate more in the democratic life of the European Union, in particular, by (...) stimulating a democratic debate without having to await the adoption of the legal act whose modification or withdrawal is ultimately sought*'.[1601] In this sense, '*ECI proposals constitute an expression of the effective participation of citizens of the European Union in the democratic life thereof*'.[1602] The Commission's position that it has insufficient democratic legitimacy to adopt the act demanded by the ECI is therefore categorically rejected by the GC. The GC thus also rejects the Commission's view that the latter has no discretion and must reject the ECI because it manifestly falls outside the framework of its powers.

In addition, it must be pointed out that the limits to the Commission's discretion (and therefore, the intensity of its obligations with regard to how to treat an ECI) differ from the political discretion which the petition procedure allows the Parliament. This was clarified by the General Court in the *One fo Us* case.[1603] The 'One of Us' ECI asked that the EU should end the financing of activities '*which presuppose the destruction of human embryos, in particular in the areas of research, development aid and public health*'. Although the ECI met the formal conditions for being examined by the

---

1599 Judgment of 10 May 2017, *Efler and Others v Commission*, T-754/14, EU:T:2017:323, para 37.

1600 *Efler and Others v Commission*, T-754/14, para 38.

1601 *Efler and Others v Commission*, T-754/14, para 45.

1602 *Efler and Others v Commission*, T-754/14, para 47.

1603 Judgment of 23 April 2018, *One of Us and Others v Commission*, T-561/14, EU:T:2018:210.

Commission, the latter decided not to take the actions that were requested by the initiative. The core issue was thus whether Article 10 of the ECI regulation left discretion to the Commission for deciding on the follow-up to a successful ECI.[1604] Before the General Court, the Commission challenged the admissibility of the action for annulment against its decision by arguing that the *Schönberger* reasoning on petitions could be transposed to the case in point – i.e., that the ECI was subject to the institution's discretionary power regarding the action to be taken. However, the GC pointed out that the petition and the ECI were two different mechanisms and that the ECI was subject to more detailed and precise conditions. In particular, the ECI regulation requires that an acceptance or refusal by the Commission to take action should be supported by a '*clear, comprehensible and detailed*' statement of reasons. The GC concluded that a refusal to take action indeed amounted to an act with binding legal effects for the applicants, and that it could be challenged under Article 263 TFEU.[1605] This allowed for a detailed judicial review of the applicants' many substantive grounds for annulment.

One of these arguments was that, following a successful ECI and except in certain clearly defined cases, the Commission was obliged to submit a legislative proposal. The GC analysed the wording of relevant provisions and, taking into account also the intentions underlying these provisions, held that the right to the ECI was meant to foster democratic dialogue and involvement of citizens in the democratic process, but not to grant ECI applicants a power of legislative initiative.[1606] This is where the parallel with the right to petition becomes relevant again, since in both cases, then, there is no right to a certain substantive outcome (other than the petition or ECI being actually examined) and therefore no obligation to take action to reach that specific outcome.

1604 Karatzia, 'The European Citizens' Initiative and the EU Institutional Balance: on Realism and the Possibilities of Affecting EU Lawmaking' 199.

1605 *One of Us and Others v Commission*, T-561/14, paras 94-98. Importantly, the General Court also rejected the Commission's argument that the right to submit an ECI should not benefit from the same protection as the right to petition, since the former is not included as such in the Charter. On this point, the GC held: '*the fact remains that [the right to the ECI] is provided for under the primary law of the Union, namely in Article 11(4) TEU. It is therefore enshrined in an instrument that has the same legal value as that conferred on the Charter of Fundamental Rights.*' (see para 99).

1606 *One of Us and Others v Commission*, T-561/14, paras 103-118.

Concerning the relation between the right to submit an ECI and the interests involved, the 'One of Us' case had also led to an interesting order[1607] prior to the GC's judgment. Two NGOs, International Planned Parenthood Federation and Marie Stopes International, had asked to be allowed to intervene in the proceedings, arguing that they had an interest in its outcome. The GC recalled settled case law according to which '*the concept of an interest in the result of the case (…) must be defined in the light of the precise subject matter of the dispute and be understood as meaning a direct, existing interest in the ruling on the forms of order sought and not as an interest in relation to the pleas in law put forward. The expression 'result' is to be understood as meaning the operative part of the final judgment which the parties ask the Court to deliver. It is necessary, in particular, to ascertain whether the intervener is directly affected by the contested decision and whether its interest in the result of the case is established*'.[1608] The NGOs argued that three types of interests were indeed directly affected: first, their financial interests, given the risk of cuts in funding if the ECI succeeds; second, their reputation (since there is erroneous information about their activities in the ECI documents submitted before ECJ); third, '*questions of principle connected with the European Union's policy on reproductive freedom*' were at stake. Concerning the latter issue, they submitted that their intervention would '*facilitate the assessment of the case within its wider context*'.[1609]

The General Court was not convinced by any of these arguments. It replied that the financial interests of the NGOs were only very indirectly threatened since even if the Commission had to submit a legislative proposal it would then go through the whole legislative process. It also considered that the threat to the applicants' reputation does not concern the subject matter and the result of the case and, last, that '*the 'centre of gravity' of the present case does not concern questions connected with the EU's policy on reproductive freedom and that therefore the intervention of IPPF, (…) would not contribute to facilitating the Court's assessment of the context of the case*'.[1610] Thus, although the Order dismisses the application to intervene, it does not reveal a particularly restrictive conception of individual interests. It rather indicates that the 'centre of gravity' of the case is not the substance of the ECI and perhaps it is implicitly confirming that the right to submit an ECI is essentially a procedural right which does not open any claim as

1607 Order of 16 March 2016, *One of Us and Others v Commission*, T-561/14, EU:T:2016:173.

1608 *One of Us and Others v Commission*, T-561/14 (Order), para 19.

1609 *One of Us and Others v Commission*, T-561/14 (Order), paras 29-30.

1610 *One of Us and Others v Commission*, T-561/14 (Order), paras 38-42.

regards the substantial outcome of the procedure.[1611] On the longer run we will see whether even unsuccessful ECIs realise their expected potential of impacting the legislative process.[1612] The case law so far indicates that the Court, understandably, does not intend to become a forum for discussion of *substantive* issues that are meant to be debated in the legislative arena. This is precisely why the effectiveness of the *procedural* right to submit an ECI matters: it creates the conditions for this debate.

2.2.2.3. Interim conclusions

The European citizen holds a variety of rights. The Court does not limit itself to controlling only black-letter rights included in the notion of Union citizenship. It is also aware that the effectiveness of these rights is conditioned by the possibility for European citizens to preserve and develop their social and human relations and connections. Consequently, the implications of Union citizenship stretch beyond its holders, onto their family members who are third-country nationals. These non-citizens are attracted within the scope of EU citizenship law and become holders of 'derived' rights, the existence of which is conditioned by the link between these individuals and the EU citizens who hold autonomous rights. This concept of derived rights, as opposed to that of autonomous rights, is a significant contribution from the field of EU citizenship law to the more general concept of individual rights under EU law, which also works here as a correlative of Member State obligations activated by an ever broadening array of interests.

The representation and participation rights of EU citizens (and even other individuals, if we take the case of the right to petition) provide an additional confirmation that the strong relation between rights, obligations and interests works as a structuring force of the EU legal order, also in its political dimension. With regard to the right to vote, the Court avoids the binary opposition between rights and principles and instead acknowledges

1611 Karatzia's conclusion is also that: '*a formal and binding obligation on the Commission to submit a legislative initiative based on an ECI would be incompatible with the express wording of the Treaties, the ECI Regulation, and the existing institutional balance.*' Karatzia, 'The European Citizens' Initiative and the EU Institutional Balance: on Realism and the Possibilities of Affecting EU Lawmaking' 202.

1612 Karatzia, 'The European Citizens' Initiative and the EU Institutional Balance: on Realism and the Possibilities of Affecting EU Lawmaking' 206-208.

that the 'principle' of democratic participation and the obligation on the Member States to allow for direct universal suffrage for the EP elections, amounts to an individual right, the restriction of which is possible but subject to the observance of the proportionality principle. Likewise regarding the petition procedure, the Court looks at the obligations of the institution to which the petition has been submitted and deduces from these the corresponding rights. Finally, the ECI, absent from the Charter yet acknowledged as a 'fundamental right' in the case law, is an illustration that the identification of rights based on obligations laid down in the Treaties remains relevant even in the Lisbon constitutional framework.

The limits of these obligations are also the limits of the correlative rights. Institutions have broad political discretion in the answer they give on the substance of the petition or ECI: the substantial result of the procedure is where the obligation on the authorities ends, as well as the corresponding right for the individuals. As the case-law currently stands, political participation rights do not reach as far as a right to a certain outcome of the decision-making process, but they are very real *procedural* rights. It can be inferred that the interest of citizens here is to take part in the democratic process of participation, just like there is an inherent individual interest for a citizen to exercise his right to vote in the more classic system of democratic representation. These rights thus embody the recognised convergence of individual interests (of citizens) and common interests (of the EU polity).

2.2.3. Individual rights of asylum seekers in the EU

Asylum law is not the best area for bringing to light the beauty of the concept of rights under Union law. This might be due to the essence of the right to asylum, which is in great part conditioned on the (often difficult to prove) realisation of certain concrete circumstances outside the territory of the EU and the related infringement of other fundamental rights (2.2.3.1). Admittedly, the protection of applicants has been significantly increased by the Court, which has asserted and clarified the applicability of the rights to good administration in the procedures relating to international protection (2.2.3.2). However, an analysis of the 'Dublin system'[1613] re-

1613 Originally established by the Convention determining the State responsible for examining applications for asylum lodged in one of the Member States of the European Communities of 15 June 1990 – Dublin Convention OJ C 254 p.

veals that in this framework the implications of the concept of rights are reluctantly and restrictively acknowledged by the Member States and even by the Court (2.2.3.3).

2.2.3.1. A very conditional right to international protection

According to settled case law, the Geneva Convention[1614] constitutes '*the cornerstone of the international legal regime for the protection of refugees*'.[1615] The Union's asylum regime is organized within the Common European Asylum System.[1616] An important element of this system is the Qualification Directive (2004/83),[1617] which aims to '*guide the competent authorities of the Member States in the application of that convention on the basis of common*

1-12, replaced by Council Regulation (EC) No 343/2003 of 18 February 2003, establishing the criteria and mechanisms for determining the Member State responsible for examining an asylum application lodged in one of the Member States by a third-country national (OJ L 50/1 p. 1) ('Dublin II Regulation') replaced by Parliament and Council Regulation No 604/2013 of 26 June 2013 establishing the criteria and mechanisms for determining the Member State responsible for examining an application for international protection lodged in one of the Member States by a third-country national or a stateless person (recast) (OJ L 180/31 p. 31) ('Dublin III Regulation').

1614 UN General Assembly, *Convention Relating to the Status of Refugees*, 28 July 1951, United Nations, Treaty Series, vol. 189, p. 137, available at: http://www.refworld.org/docid/3be01b964.html [accessed 20 July 2017].

1615 See e.g. Judgment of 7 November 2013, *X and Others*, C-199/12 to C-201/12, EU:C:2013:720, para 39; Judgment of 17 June 2010, *Bolbol*, C-31/09, EU:C:2010:351, para 37; Judgment of 19 December 2012, *Abed El Karem El Kott and Others*, C-364/11, EU:C:2012:826, paras 42-43; Judgment of 2 December 2014, *A*, Joined cases C-148/13 to C-150/13, EU:C:2014:2406, para 45; Judgment of 26 February 2015, *Shepherd*, C-472/13, EU:C:2015:117, para 22.

1616 V. Chetail, 'The Common European Asylum System: *Bric-à-brac* or System?' in V. Chetail, P. de Bruycker and F. Maiani, (eds), *Reforming the Common European Asylum System. The New European Refugee Law* (Brill Nijhof 2016) 3-38.

1617 Council Directive 2004/83/EC of 29 April 2004 on minimum standards for the qualification and status of third country nationals or stateless persons as refugees or as persons who otherwise need international protection and the content of the protection granted (OJ L 304/12 p. 12) ('first Qualification Directive'), replaced in 2011 by Parliament and Council Directive 2011/95/EU of 13 December 2011 on standards for the qualification of third-country nationals or stateless persons as beneficiaries of international protection, for a uniform status for refugees or for persons eligible for subsidiary protection, and for the content of the protection granted (OJ L 337 p. 9) ('second Qualification Directive').

concepts and criteria'. The Qualification Directive (in both versions) must therefore be interpreted '*in a manner consistent with the Geneva Convention*' as well as with the Charter of Fundamental Rights.[1618] A 'well-founded fear of persecution' is the essential condition for granting the right to asylum. [1619] This translates into several more precise conditions and makes the right to asylum very dependent on the assessment of concrete circumstances[1620] and on the existence or threat of '*a severe violation of basic human rights, in particular the rights from which derogation cannot be made under Article 15(2) of the European Convention for the Protection of Human Rights and Fundamental Freedoms*'.[1621] At least, where these conditions are met, the Court has made clear that '*Member States are to grant refugee status to all third country nationals or stateless persons who qualify as a refugee*' in accordance with the Qualification Directive: '*Member States exercise no discretion in that respect*'[1622] – an other illustration of the correlation between rights and obligations and the opposite relation between discretion and rights.

The right to asylum is inherently circumstantial, which is exactly what we have seen so far concerning all types of rights since *Defrenne II.*[1623] But this characteristic is particularly important in the process of identifying the right to asylum precisely because the circumstances that are considered in this process are both external to the EU territory and very unstable. This is exemplified in *Abed El Karem El Kott:* three stateless persons of Palestinian origin had been subjected to violence in a United Nations refugee camp in Lebanon and subsequently fled to Hungary to ask for asylum.[1624] Their application was rejected by the Hungarian authorities on the ground that they had been under UN protection. However, although Article 12(1)(a) of Directive 2004/38 excluded granting the status of refugee to persons who were under protection of UN organs 'in application of Article 1D of the Geneva Convention), it also required that '*(w)hen such protection or assistance has ceased for any reason, without the position of such persons being definitely settled (…) those persons shall ipso facto be entitled to the benefits of this*

1618 See e.g. *X and Others*, C-199/12 to C-201/12, EU:C:2013:720, para 40; *Shepherd*, C-472/13, para 23; *A*, Joined cases C-148/13 to C-150/13, para 46.

1619 Second Qualification Directive: Recital 30, Article 2(d), Article 4(4), Article 5(2) and (3), Article 8(1)(a) and (2), Article 10(2), Article 11(2).

1620 Article 4 of the Second Qualification Directive provides for the criteria for the 'assessment of facts and circumstances'.

1621 Second Qualification Directive, Article 9(1)(a).

1622 Judgment of 24 June 2015, *T.*, C-373/13, EU:C:2015:413, para 63.

1623 *Defrenne v SABENA*, C-43/75.

1624 *Abed El Karem El Kott and Others*, C-364/11.

Directive'. The Court held that this provision did not '*entail an unconditional right to refugee status*' and that '*the authorities carrying out examination of the application for asylum must verify that the applicant actually sought assistance from the UN body, and that the assistance has ceased*', and that no other exceptions listed in Article 12 apply in the individual case.[1625] The assessment of factual circumstances is also crucial for granting subsidiary protection: beyond a certain degree of generalised violence in a country of origin, it is not even required that the applicant demonstrate that he is specifically and individually targeted by persecutions, in order to be granted the status.[1626] Conversely, '*the more the applicant is able to show that he is specifically affected by reason of factors particular to his personal circumstances, the lower the level of indiscriminate violence required for him to be eligible for subsidiary protection*'.[1627]

The variability of the factual and circumstantial conditions also makes the right unstable in time even after it has been granted. Article 11 of the Qualification Directive lays down the conditions for cessation of the international protection. Paragraphs 11(1), (e) and (f) and 11(2) of this provision provide that a change of circumstances in the country of origin, of a 'significant and non-temporary' nature, may suppress the well-founded fears of being exposed to acts of persecution amounting to severe violations of basic human rights. This is illustrated by the case of Iraqi nationals whose refugee status was revoked in application of Article 11, because the situation in their country was deemed no longer to ground such a fear of persecution.[1628] The Court held in this case that the abovementioned conditions of Article 11 are fulfilled '*when the factors which formed the basis of the refugee's fear of persecution may be regarded as having been permanently eradicated*'.[1629] It is however not clear how the character of 'permanence' would be demonstrated. In another case concerning a Turkish national who had been granted asylum in Germany and had engaged in activities with the Kurdish terrorist organization PKK, the Court accepted that the

1625 *Abed El Karem El Kott and Others*, C-364/11, paras 75-76.

1626 Judgment of 17 February 2009, *Elgafaji*, C-465/07, EU:C:2009:94.

1627 Judgment of 30 January 2014, *Diakite*, C-285/12, EU:C:2014:39, para 31 and *Elgafaji*, C-465/07, para 39.

1628 Judgment of 2 March 2010, *Salahadin Abdulla and Others*, Joined cases C-175/08, C-176/08, C-178/08 and C-179/08, EU:C:2010:105.

1629 *Salahadin Abdulla and Others*, Joined cases C-175/08, C-176/08, C-178/08 and C-179/08, para 73. See also *Abed El Karem El Kott and Others*, C-364/11, para 77.

status of refugee may be revoked for reasons of national security or public order, following an examination of the specific individual case.[1630]

In addition, the right to international protection is dependent on the well-founded fear of an infringement of a basic human right constituting an act of persecution.[1631] The persecution must in addition be exercised on the basis of the individual's belonging to a particular racial, national, social or religious group of his holding of a particular political opinion.[1632] This means that the analysis of a case will sometimes give rise to issues for defining and circumscribing not the right to asylum itself, but the other rights with which it is combined. In *Y and Z*, the applicants for international protection were Pakistani nationals and members of the Ahmadiyya religious community.[1633] In Pakistan this community was prohibited from manifesting this religion in public, even though for many of its members (including the applicants) the external manifestation is an essential aspect of it. The German authorities were arguing that there should be a distinction between the 'forum internum' and the 'forum externum' of religious freedom, meaning that an act of persecution justifying asylum could only concern the private aspects of that freedom and not its manifestation in public. The Court agreed that not any interference with the right to religious freedom guaranteed by Article 10(1) of the Charter could constitute an act of persecution that would justify granting refugee status. This is not particularly surprising: after all, even in the EU itself, interference with fundamental rights is admissible under certain conditions, following the idea that rights are not absolute rules but rather 'optimisation requirements'.[1634]

Therefore the question became how to determine which kind of violation of the right guaranteed by Article 10(1) CFR constitutes persecution within the meaning of Article 9(1) of the Qualification Directive.[1635] According to this provision, there must be a "*severe violation' of religious freedom having a significant effect on the person concerned in order for it to be possible for the acts in question to be regarded as acts of persecution*".[1636] For assessing the seriousness of the violation, the Court rejected the distinction between

1630 Judgment of 24 June 2015, *T.*, C-373/13, EU:C:2015:413.

1631 Second Qualification Directive, Article 9.

1632 Second Qualification Directive, Article 10.

1633 Judgment of 5 September 2012, *Y and Z*, Joined cases C-71/11 and C-99/11, EU:C:2012:518.

1634 Concerning the importance of the proportionality principle in the CJEU's case and what it says about the concept of rights, see p. 82 of this work.

1635 *Y and Z*, Joined cases C-71/11 and C-99/11, para 66.

1636 *Y and Z*, Joined cases C-71/11 and C-99/11, paras 58-59.

a 'core area' corresponding to the practice of faith in private circles, and an external dimension of the right to religious freedom: indeed, '*(s)uch a distinction is incompatible with the broad definition of 'religion' given by Article 10(1)(b) of the Directive, which encompasses all its constituent components, be they public or private, collective or individual*'.[1637] Therefore the assessment must focus on '*the nature of the repression inflicted on the individual and its consequences*', especially '*the severity of the measures and sanctions*'.[1638] In assessing the risk that the applicant will be subject to inhuman or degrading treatment, the competent authorities must take account of both '*objective and subjective*' factors, i.e. also subjective perception of the individual that the practice that he is prohibited from performing constitutes a necessary element in the exercise of his faith.[1639]

In the same way, for granting asylum following persecution on the basis of sexual orientation, the Court recalled the source of the protection: '*the fundamental rights specifically linked to the sexual orientation concerned in each of the cases in the main proceedings, such as the right to respect for private and family life, which is protected by Article 8 of the ECHR, to which Article 7 of the Charter corresponds, read together, where necessary, with Article 14 ECHR, on which Article 21(1) of the Charter is based*'[1640] and refused '*to distinguish acts that interfere with the core areas of the expression of sexual orientation, even assuming it were possible to identify them, from acts which do not affect those purported core areas*'.[1641] Here, too, the identification of the right to asylum depended on the identification of the allegedly infringed right. The Court again refused to exclusively associate the substance of this right with its internal and private characteristics, admitting that the substance of a right can also manifest in external and public expressions of it.[1642]

The identification of the right to asylum is therefore, like any other right, inherently dependent on concrete circumstances. In addition, it is conditioned on the infringement of other fundamental rights, the assessment of which is also highly complex. Where the conditions are fulfilled, however, Member States have no discretion and have an obligation to

1637 *Y and Z*, Joined cases C-71/11 and C-99/11, paras 62-63.

1638 *Y and Z*, Joined cases C-71/11 and C-99/11, paras 65-66.

1639 *Y and Z*, Joined cases C-71/11 and C-99/11, paras 70-71.

1640 Judgment of 7 November 2013, *X and Others*, Joined cases C-199/12 to C-201/12, EU:C:2013:720, para 54.

1641 *X and Others*, Joined cases C-199/12 to C-201/12, para 78.

1642 The Court stayed on the same line in *G4S Secure Solutions*, C-157/15 and *Bougnaoui and ADDH*, C-188/15. See p. 347 of this work.

grant asylum: the right to asylum thus also validates the correlation between obligations and rights.

2.2.3.2. The right to good administration in EU asylum law

In applying the guarantees of good administration to the procedures involving applicants for international protection, the Court's task, was complicated by the discrepancy between the scope of Article 41 CFR and the scope of the general principle on which it is based.[1643] The case law has however reached a point where the potential adverse effects on an individual's interests of the outcome of an asylum procedure are fully acknowledged, so that the Member States must observe the procedural obligations included in the principle of good administration when they conduct these procedures.

In the *M.* case, the Court was asked by an Irish court about the implications of Article 41, para 2 for the authorities of the Member States examining asylum applications. The Court avoided addressing the issue that the wording of Article 41 directed the obligations only at the EU institutions.[1644] It accepted that this provision was '*of general application*'[1645] but relied mostly on the case law on the rights of the defence, observance of which is '*a fundamental principle of EU* law'.[1646] Concerning the right to be heard, the Court reiterated the *Transocean* rationale: '*the Court has always affirmed the importance of the right to be heard and its very broad scope in the EU legal order, considering that that right must apply in all proceedings which are liable to culminate in a measure adversely affecting a person.*'[1647] More precisely, '*the right to be heard guarantees every person the opportunity to make known his views effectively during an administrative procedure and before the adoption of any decision liable to affect his interests adversely*'.[1648] Therefore, the right '*of the applicant for asylum to be heard must apply fully to the procedure in which*

1643 This problem was discussed in Section 1.2 of this work, p. 100.

1644 *M.*, C-277/11, para. 83-89. S. Platon, 'Chronique de jurisprudence de droit administratif européen (année 2014)' (2015) Droit administratif; R. Bousta, 'Droit des étrangers : mais à quoi sert le droit à une bonne administration?' La Revue des droits de l'homme [En ligne], 12 | 2017 <http://revdh.revues.org/3216> accessed 6 August 2017, point 39.

1645 *M.*, C-277/11, para 84.

1646 *M.*, C-277/11, para 81.

1647 *M.*, C-277/11, para 85.

1648 *M.*, C-277/11, para 87.

the competent national authority examines an application for international protection'.[1649] This means that in Member States where applications for asylum and for subsidiary protection are examined in two different procedures (like Ireland at the time of the *M.* case), the right to be heard must be guaranteed in each of these procedures.

By contrast, in *Y.S. and others,* applicants for residence in the Netherlands had been denied access to the legal analysis which provided internal advice on whether to grant them residence.[1650] They claimed their right of access to file based on Article 41(2)(b) CFR. Although the Court pointed out that '*the right to good administration, enshrined in that provision, reflects a general principle of EU law*',[1651] it declined to elaborate on how either the provision or the general principle could be interpreted in this case. The difference with the *M.* case could be explained by the fact that Mr M. had relied on the right to be heard as a general principle of EU law,[1652] whereas in *Y.S. and others* the focus was exclusively on Article 41 CFR. However, the unwillingness of the Court to reconnect this provision with the historical general principle is questionable in light of the EU's constitutional design, which, as discussed in Part 1, rather supports a pluralistic approach to sources of rights.[1653] From this perspective it makes no sense to have the right to good administration functioning through parallel but hermetically separate channels. Moreover, it is something of a paradox that before the Treaty of Lisbon, the Court redirected the focus from Article 41 of the – non-binding – Charter to the general principle of good administration;[1654] and that since the Charter has become binding, the individuals relying on it are disadvantaged because the Court will not perform that operation anymore.[1655] *Y.S. and Others* thus shows how relying exclusively on Charter-defined rights, instead of making use the continuity between the Charter and the general principles to construe those rights, can become disadvantageous to individuals and thus counterproductive – insofar, of course,

1649 *M.*, C-277/11, para 89.

1650 *Y.S and Others,* Joined cases C-141/12 and C-372/12.

1651 *Y.S and Others,* Joined cases C-141/12 and C-372/12, para 68.

1652 *M.*, C-277/11, para 49.

1653 See in particular the conclusions of Section 1.2 of this work, p. 162.

1654 *Sabou*, C-276/12, para 38, and *Kamino International Logistics and Datema Hellmann Worldwide Logistics*, Joined cases C-129/13 and C-130/13, paras 29 et seq.

1655 *Y.S and Others,* Joined cases C-141/12 and C-372/12, paras 67 to 69 and *Cicala,* C-482/10, para 28. Mihaescu Evans, 'The 'gaps' in protection stemming from the (problematic) coexistence of fundamental rights' sources in the EU legal order' 163.

as the aim of introducing the Charter was indeed to provide individuals with better protection.

Fortunately, the more recent case law signals a shift towards a reading of Article 41 in connection with the general principle of good administration on the basis of which it was drafted – perhaps also because the national courts have drawn lessons from *Y.S.* and frame their questions so that they will get their answers. In *N*, the national court asked for an interpretation of Directive 2004/38 '*in the light of the principle of good administration (…) and, in particular, as provided by Article 41 of the Charter*'.[1656] The Court held that, indeed, the right to good administration enshrined Article 41 indeed reflected a general principle of EU law and looked at the Irish procedural rules for examining applications for subsidiary protection in the light of this principle and the principle of effectiveness.[1657] It found that the Irish procedural rule according to which an application for subsidiary protection may be considered only after an application for refugee status has been refused was acceptable if both applications could be submitted at the same time and if the application of the rule did not result in an unreasonably long procedure for examining the application for subsidiary protection.[1658] In the *Mukarubega* case, a third-country national was requested to leave the French territory, and the Return Directive[1659] did not specify how the right to be heard fit into this procedure.[1660] The Court first considered Article 41(2) of the Charter (on the right to be heard before an unfavourable individual decision), and admitted that this provision was not addressed to the Member States but that the right to be heard was '*inherent in respect for the rights of the defence*', a general principle of EU law.[1661] The Court also relied on earlier case law, including *TUM*, to emphasise the obligation of the administration to give reasons for a decision, to hear the ad-

1656 Judgment of 8 May 2014, *N.*, C-604/12, EU:C:2014:302, para 24.

1657 *N.*, C-604/12, paras 49-50.

1658 *N.*, C-604/12, para 57. In *Danqua*, the Court added that the principle of effectiveness prohibited an Irish rule setting a two-week time limit to lodge an application for subsidiary protection after an application for asylum had been rejected, because such a rule did not practically put applicants '*in a position to avail themselves of the rights conferred on them by Directive 2004/38*'. Judgment of 20 October 2016, *Danqua*, C-429/15, EU:C:2016:789, paras 38-39 and paras 46-48.

1659 Parliament and Council Directive 2008/115/EC of 16 December 2008 on common standards and procedures in Member States for returning illegally staying third-country nationals (OJ L 348 p. 98) ('Return Directive').

1660 Judgment of 5 November 2014, *Mukarubega*, C-166/13, EU:C:2014:2336.

1661 *Mukarubega*, C-166/13, paras 44-45.

dressee's arguments and more generally the duty of care of the administration, all of which are, as recalled in *M.*, corollaries of the principle of the respect for the rights of the defence.[1662] The *Boudjlida* ruling follows a very similar reasoning and relies on *Mukarubega*, indicating that the Court's position on this issue is consolidating.[1663]

It is therefore by now established case law that the obligation to respect the rights of defence of the addressees of decisions which adversely affect their interests binds the national administrations when they take measures within the scope of the EU legislation on international protection, just like in other areas of EU law. Interestingly, in order to establish that the rights of defence have to be respected also by national administrations in spite of the phrasing of Article 41 CFR, the Court relies very much on general principles, which traditionally put more emphasis on the obligational aspect of good administration requirements. The case law on the procedural rights of applicants for international protection thus illustrates the protective power of a pluralistic approach to sources of rights, and sustains the conception of individual rights as correlatives of the obligations of Member State administrations.

2.2.3.3. The inconsistencies in the case law on the Dublin Regulation

Applicants for asylum arriving in the EU are not free to choose the Member State in which they will lodge their application. The Dublin Regulation lays down and prioritises the criteria for determining the Member State responsible for examining an application, and sets out the procedures for transferring those asylum seekers who apply in the 'wrong' Member State to the responsible Member State.[1664] These procedures are mostly framed in terms of the obligations of the Member States when requesting

1662 *Mukarubega*, C-166/13, para 48, citing *Technische Universität München v Hauptzollamt München-Mitte*, C-269/90, para 14 and *M.*, C-277/11, para 88.

1663 Judgment of 11 December 2014, *Boudjlida*, C-249/13, EU:C:2014:2431, paras 30-35. See also *Sacko,* C-348/16, paras 31-35.

1664 These transfers are hereafter referred to as 'Dublin transfers'. On the spirit and details of the Dublin system see C. Costello, *The Human Rights of Migrants and Refugees in European Law* (Oxford University Press 2016) 255-276. On the improvements (and remaining shortcomings) in the Dublin III Regulation (compared to Dublin II) see F. Maiani, 'The Dublin III Regulation: A New Legal Framework for a More Humane System?' in V. Chetail, P. De Bruycker and F. Maiani (eds), *Reforming the Common European Asylum System The New European Refugee Law* (Brill Nijhoff 2016) 101-142.

or accepting transfers. Yet they can have significant repercussions on the individuals who are transferred. Indeed, asylum seekers may have reasons for applying in one Member State rather than another, such as linguistic or cultural reasons, the presence of migrant communities, or social and economic motives. Therefore, as pointed out by Den Heijer, '*the outcome of a Dublin procedure may affect the personal interests of the asylum seekers in a rather fundamental way.*'[1665] Nevertheless, the Dublin system makes it very difficult for individuals to challenge such transfers. Compared to the Dublin II Regulation, Dublin III added some safeguards, which the Court has combined with the provisions of the Charter, thus increasing the procedural protection of 'dublinised' asylum seekers.[1666] This section however highlights the persisting issues and inconsistencies in the case law and argues that the restrictive conditions for challenging Dublin transfers result from a misapplication of the original concept of rights and of the classic relation between rights and remedies.[1667]

The first possibility to challenge a Dublin transfer was established in *N.S. and Others*, in the wake of an ECHR case, *M.S.S. v Belgium and Greece*, in which the ECtHR held that the Belgian authorities had infringed Article 3 ECHR on the prohibition of torture and inhuman or degrading treatment, by sending back an asylum seeker to Greece even though they could

---

1665 Den Heijer, 'Remedies in the Dublin Regulation: *Ghezelbash* and *Karim*' 869.

1666 'Dublinised' or 'dublinisé' is an expression used in civil society to designate asylum seekers who are the object of a transfer decision under the Dublin Regulation. See e.g. S. Wahnich, 'Sauver ceux qui pleurent', Chronique 'Historiques', Libération 8 February 2017 <http://www.liberation.fr/debats/2017/02/08/sauver-ceux-qui-pleurent_1547222> accessed 22 July 2017.

1667 Most of the litigation over the Dublin Regulation concerns challenges against transfer decisions. One exception is Judgment of 27 September 2012, *Cimade and GISTI*, C-179/11, EU:C:2012:594, the only asylum case so far to have reached the Court of Justice and which involved not individual asylum applicants but two NGOs challenging a French administrative circular which denied that the minimum conditions laid down in the Reception Conditions Directive applied to individuals on whom a transfer decision had been made. The Court held that this circular breached the Reception Conditions Directive and Article 1 CFR on the protection of human dignity, and that the requesting Member State's responsibility under this directive ended only once the transfer had been made (see especially para 56 and para 58). ('Reception Conditions Directive': Council Directive No 2003/9/EC of 27 January 2003 laying down minimum standards for the reception of asylum seekers (OJ L 031 p. 18), replaced by Parliament and Council Directive No 2013/33/EU of 26 June 2013 laying down standards for the reception of applicants for international protection (OJ L 180/96 p. 96)).

not have been unaware of the risks to which he would be exposed there in light of the deficiencies in that country's asylum procedure and reception conditions.[1668] In *N.S. and Others,* several asylum seekers were to be transferred from Ireland and the UK to Greece based on the Dublin Regulation. They challenged the transfer decisions, relying in the ECtHR's judgment and arguing that their transfer to Greece would constitute also a violation of their rights under the ECHR, the Geneva Convention and Article 4 CFR. The judgment in this case is the result of a perilous balancing exercise. The Court held that there was a general assumption that the treatment of asylum seekers in all Member States complied with these requirements, and then very cautiously added that it was '*not inconceivable*' that in a situation of '*major operational problems*' in the responsible Member State there could be 'a *substantial risk*' that an asylum seeker's fundamental rights would be violated following his transfer.[1669] Nevertheless, not '*any infringement of a fundamental right by the Member State responsible*' affects the obligations of the other Member States to comply with the Dublin Regulation, because, '*at issue here is the raison d'être of the European Union and the creation of an area of freedom, security and justice and, in particular, the Common European Asylum System, based on mutual confidence and a presumption of compliance, by other Member States, with (EU) law and, in particular, fundamental rights*'.[1670] In addition, regard must be had to the objective of the Dublin Regulation, which is to lay down '*a clear and effective method*' for quickly processing asylum applications.[1671] The Court therefore admits that the transfer would be incompatible with Article 4 CFR '*if there are substantial grounds for believing that there are systemic flaws in the asylum procedure and reception conditions for asylum applicants in the Member State responsible, resulting in inhuman or degrading treatment (…), of asylum seekers transferred to the territory of that Member State*'.[1672] In such a case, the transfer for the Member State responsible must not take place and the requesting Member State must apply the other criteria of the Dublin Regulation to determine the new Member State responsible for examining the application.[1673]

1668 *M.S.S. v Belgium and Greece,* n°30696/09 (ECHR 2011).

1669 Judgment of 21 December 2011, *N.S. and Others,* Joined cases C-411/10 and C-493/10, EU:C:2011:865, paras 80-81.

1670 *N.S. and Others,* Joined cases C-411/10 and C-493/10, para 83.

1671 *N.S. and Others,* Joined cases C-411/10 and C-493/10, paras 84-85.

1672 *N.S. and Others,* Joined cases C-411/10 and C-493/10, para 86.

1673 This was confirmed in Judgment of 14 November 2013, *Puid,* C-4/11, EU:C:2013:740.

This judgment is important because it makes clear that even though there is a presumption that EU Member States respect the fundamental rights of asylum seekers, this is not a conclusive presumption and it must allow for evidence to the contrary to be considered.[1674] It is also significant because it sheds light on the Dublin system as an instance of integrated – rather than segmented – administration, and the specific challenges that this growing integration causes in terms of protection of individuals. The Court does not allow the authorities of the requesting Member State to overlook systemic flaws in the requested Member State,[1675] since it could lead to violations of the individual's rights under Article 4 of the Charter.

The limits to this favourable solution for individuals were soon drawn in another case. *Abdullahi*[1676] indeed made clear that this situation of a systemic malfunctioning in the responsible Member State was the only situation where an applicant could challenge a Dublin transfer. In this case, a Somali national had entered the EU through Hungary and lodged an asylum application in Austria. The Austrian authorities found that in application of the Dublin allocation criteria, Hungary was the Member State responsible for examining Ms Abdullahi's application and had accepted to take her in charge; therefore, she was to be transferred back there. Ms Abdullahi challenged this decision, arguing that the allocation criteria had been erroneously applied by the Austrian authorities. The referring court therefore asked the Court of Justice whether an applicant for asylum had a right to request a review of the determination of the Member State responsible, on the ground that the criteria of Chapter III had been misapplied. In its answer, the Court insisted on the '*mutual confidence*' component of its N.S. judgment[1677] and again highlighted that the aim of the Dublin system was '*the establishment of a clear and workable method (…) not to compromise the objective of the rapid processing of asylum applications*'.[1678] Therefore, when the requested Member State has accepted to take charge of an applicant for asylum, '*the only way in which the applicant (…) can call into question the choice of (the) criterion is by pleading systemic deficiencies in the*

1674 *N.S. and Others*, Joined cases C-411/10 and C-493/10, paras 100-101.

1675 On the notion of systemic flaws and deficiencies in the Common European Asylum System see J. Vedsted-Hansen, 'Reception Conditions as Human Rights: Pan-European Standard or Systemic Deficiencies?' in V. Chetail, P. De Bruycker and F. Maiani (eds), *Reforming the Common European Asylum System The New European Refugee Law* (Brill Nijhoff 2016) 317-352.

1676 Judgment of 10 December 2013, *Abdullahi*, C-394/12, EU:C:2013:813.

1677 *Abdullahi*, C-394/12, paras 52-53.

1678 *Abdullahi*, C-394/12, para 59.

asylum procedure and in the conditions for the reception of applicants for asylum in that latter Member state, which provide substantial grounds for believing that the applicant for asylum would face a real risk of being subjected to inhuman or degrading treatment within the meaning of Article 4 of the Charter.'[1679]

As a result, it was impossible for individuals to rely on the provisions of the Dublin II Regulation setting out the obligations of the Member State administrations concerning the application of the allocation criteria and the implementation of the transfer procedures. This solution is highly problematic in the light of the classic concept of rights under Union law. Firstly, since under EU law the remedy is the immediate corollary of the right,[1680] *Abdullahi* in fact denies that the obligations of the Member States under EU law, even when they are clear, precise and are unconditional (or subject to conditions that are fulfilled), amount to rights for individuals. In other words, by denying the existence of the remedy, the Court in *Abdullahi* is denying the existence of rights correlative to the obligations enshrined in the Dublin Regulation. The resulting solution is even less protective of individuals than the one proposed by Advocate General Cruz Villalón. The AG distinguished between the provisions laying down obligations (concerning the cooperation between Member States), and those provisions specifically conferring rights on individuals.[1681] In his view, asylum seekers could only rely on the second category to challenge a transfer. The Court did not even consider this possibility in its judgment, remaining instead focused on the idea that the Dublin Regulation organises a system grounded on mutual trust between Member States, and where individuals have no active role to play.

Secondly, by relying exclusively on the objective of an efficient and quick procedure embodied by the Dublin Regulation, *Abdullahi* also plainly negates the importance of individual interests for triggering the control of the observance by Member States of their obligations under EU law. The inconsistency is even more blatant considering *MA and Others*, a case concerning the transfer of unaccompanied minors. The Court held in this case that a child's best interests, as protected by Article 24 CFR (which applies in the implementation of the Dublin Regulation as provided for by Article 51(1) CFR), must constitute '*a primary consideration*' in the application of

---

1679 *Abdullahi*, C-394/12, para 60.

1680 See the conclusions of Section 1.3. of this work, p. 222 concerning the relation between rights and remedies.

1681 Opinion of AG Cruz Villalón in *Abdullahi*, C-394/12, EU:C:2013:813, paras 44-47. This is consistent with his Opinion in *Association de médiation sociale*, C-176/12, ECLI:EU:C:2013:491. See p. 124 and p. 310 of this work.

the allocation criteria which concern minors.[1682] In particular, '*since unaccompanied minors form a category of particularly vulnerable persons, it is important not to prolong more than is strictly necessary the procedure for determining the Member State responsible, which means that, as a rule, unaccompanied minors should not be transferred to another Member State.*'[1683] As a consequence, the responsible Member State for processing the application of an unaccompanied minor is the State in which the minor is present after having lodged his application, even if he had previously applied for asylum in another Member State. The Dublin III Regulation takes this judgment into account and has a much more elaborate Article 6, paragraph (1) of which expressly provides that '*The best interests of the child shall be a primary consideration for Member States with respect to all procedures provided for in this Regulation*'. This is an unambiguous acknowledgement that the allocation criteria and the transfer procedures may have a significant impact on the individual interests of asylum seekers, and it further highlights the inconsistency in preventing them from challenging most decisions made on the basis of the Dublin Regulation.

This inconsistency was eventually mitigated by the entry into force of the Dublin III Regulation and its interpretation delivered in the *Ghezelbash* case.[1684] Mr Ghezelbash was an Iranian national who requested asylum in the Netherlands. The Dutch authorities found that France had already granted him a visa and lodged a take charge request, to which France agreed. Mr Ghezelbash challenged the decision, arguing that this decision resulted from a wrong application of Article 12 of the Dublin III Regulation.[1685] France and the Commission supported the view that a right of appeal exists only in respect of application of provisions that expressly confer rights on asylum seekers, reflecting fundamental rights protected under the Charter. Ghezelbash argued that Article 27(1), which guarantees access to a remedy '*in fact and in law, against a transfer decision*', conferred a right of appeal against application of all allocation criteria contained in Chapter III of the Dublin Regulation. The Court held that Article 27 must indeed be understood as being intended to ensure that Chapter III criteria are cor-

1682 Judgment of 6 June 2013, *MA and Others*, C-648/11, EU:C:2013:367, para 59.

1683 *MA and Others*, C-648/11, para 55.

1684 Judgment of 7 June 2016, *Ghezelbash*, C-63/15, EU:C:2016:409.

1685 This provision sets out the consequences, for the determination of the Member State responsible, of the applicant holding a residence document or a visa from one of the Member States of the EU.

rectly applied.[1686] By contrast with its findings in *Abdullahi*, the Court here held that this interpretation did not jeopardize the functions or aims of the regulation precisely because the judicial review would ensure the correct application of the provisions, without challenging the functioning of the whole system.[1687] *Ghezelbash* thus defeats '*the idea that the Dublin Regulation is purely an inter-State mechanism which should enable an individual asylum seeker to challenge his transfer to another Member State.*'[1688] The problem with *Ghezelbash* is that the Court has focused exclusively on the text and context of the Dublin III Regulation and how it differed from the previous version. It has not relied at all on the right to effective judicial protection as it is protected by Article 47 of the Charter. This is as unfortunate as it is peculiar, since Recital 19 of the Dublin Regulation requires that the regulation must be interpreted in accordance with Article 47 – which is exactly what Advocate General Sharpston had done in her Opinion.[1689] The same omission occurred in *CK and others*, where the Court held that the authorities must take into account evidence submitted by the applicant indicating a serious health condition before deciding whether a transfer decision is appropriate, and that the national courts operating in the context of the application of Article 27 of the Dublin Regulation must likewise take this evidence into account to control the legality of a transfer decision.[1690]

The case *Mengesteab*[1691] could have been an opportunity for the Court to further clarify the relation between the obligations of Member States, the rights of individuals and the remedies for enforcing these rights within the Dublin III framework. This case concerned the possibility for individuals to challenge a Dubin transfer in the case where Member State administrations have not respected the time limits set out in the regulation.[1692] An Eritrean national had arrived in Germany after entering the EU territory

---

1686 *Ghezelbash*, C-63/15, para 44. This solution was confirmed in Judgment of 7 June 2016, *Karim*, C-155/15, EU:C:2016:410, paras 22-27 (a failure to apply Article 19(2) must be challengeable in court).

1687 *Ghezelbash*, C-63/15, paras 53-59. Den Heijer, 'Remedies in the Dublin Regulation: *Ghezelbash* and *Karim*' 865.

1688 Den Heijer, 'Remedies in the Dublin Regulation: *Ghezelbash* and *Karim*' 866.

1689 Opinion of AG Sharpston in *Ghezelbash*, C-63/15, EU:C:2016:186, paras 82-91. Den Heijer, 'Remedies in the Dublin Regulation: *Ghezelbash* and *Karim*' 864-867.

1690 Judgment of 16 February 2017, *C.K. and Others*, C-578/16 PPU, EU:C:2017:127, para 75.

1691 Judgment of 26 July 2017, *Mengesteab*, C-670/16, EU:C:2017:587.

1692 The surface of this topic was scratched in the Order of 5 April 2017, *Ahmed*, C-36/17, EU:C:2017:273. The question was whether the provisions of the

through Italy and submitted an informal request for asylum. While the Dublin III Regulation sets a three-month time limit from the moment of the asylum application for lodging a take charge request, Germany lodged such a request to Italy more than three months after the informal application. The German administrative court asked the Court of Justice whether an individual may rely on the time limits for take charge requests as set out in the Dublin III Regulation to challenge a transfer decision. Advocate General Sharpston issued an interesting Opinion on this case. Importantly, she emphasised that *'[t]he rights to good administration and to an effective remedy (Articles 41 and 47 of the Charter) provide standards which are particularly relevant to the correct interpretation of Article 27(1) of the Dublin III Regulation.'*[1693] She argued that the time limits are central to the operation of the Dublin system, and provide certainty to both applicants and Member States. She rejected the argument that the time limits only govern inter-State relations, since the operation of those time limits has substantive implications for the applicants.[1694] Therefore, applicants should be able to challenge transfer decisions where Member States fail to meet the applicable time limits for take charge requests. Her proposed solution is therefore in line with the classic concept of individual rights as correlatives of obligations (of Member States, in the cases at hand); and it is consistent with the fundamental *ubi ius ibi remedium* principle that is enshrined in Article 47 CFR. However, in the judgment the Court kept to its previous approach from *Ghezelbash* looked only at the scope of judicial protection that was provided for in the Regulation itself.[1695] Only then, did it emphasise the clear wording of the relevant provisions and deduce that the concerned individuals should be allowed to rely on these provisions.[1696]

Dublin III Regulation governing the time limits for making a take-back request were applicable in a situation in which an individual had applied for international protection in Germany after being granted subsidiary protection by Italy. The Court gave a negative answer. There was no question of rights raised, the issue was put purely in terms of relation between the two Member States. But this did not solve the question of whether the relevant provisions could be relied on by an individual – it just clarified the circumstances in which they apply.

1693 Opinion of AG Sharpston in *Mengesteab*, C-670/16, EU:C:2017:480, para 104. See also Opinion of AG Sharpston in *Shiri*, C-201/16, EU:C:2017:579, para 37.

1694 Opinion of AG Sharpston in *Mengesteab*, C-670/16, see especially paras 89 and 95.

1695 *Mengesteab*, C-670/16, paras 53-58.

1696 *Mengesteab*, C-670/16, para 67.

Ghezelbash, C.K., and *Mengesteab* have thus established that 'dublinised' individuals may rely on provisions of the Dublin Regulation, beyond those that expressly confer rights. The approach of first looking at the remedy, and only then trying to identify the right, is however dangerously and unjustifiedly restrictive. A parallel with the *Berlioz* ruling supports this view. In that case, the Court held that, especially in the light of Article 47, even though the provisions of the directive at issue mainly organise exchanges between Member State administrations, individuals concerned must still have the possibility to request the judicial review of the application of these provisions.[1697] What holds true for a directive should be even more obvious for a regulation, especially since, '*by reason of their nature and their function in the system of the sources of Community law, regulations have direct effect and are as such, capable of creating individual rights which national courts must protect*'.[1698] Therefore it cannot be maintained that the provisions that concern cooperation between Member States within the framework of the Dublin Regulation should not be subjected to judicial control at the request of individuals, unless we ignore that the interests of asylum seekers are affected by the allocation of responsibility for processing, or unless we consider that these interests matter less than those of taxpayers affected by the exchange of tax information between Member States.

In *Shiri* the Court finally adopted a more openly consistent approach. An Iranian national who had applied for asylum in Bulgaria, then in Austria, was challenging the decision of the German authorities to transfer him back to Bulgaria. The CJEU had to interpret Article 29 of the Dublin III Regulation, which requires that from the moment when a Member State accepts to take charge or take back an asylum seeker, the Member State which had lodged the take charge or take back request must organise the transfer within a six months' timeframe.[1699] The Austrian court asked whether, once the six months have passed, the resquesting Member State becomes responsible for processing the asylum application. The Court drew a parallel with *Mengesteab* and answered positively.[1700] The Austrian court also asked whether Article 27 of the Dublin III Regulation, providing for the right to an effective remedy against a transfer decision, allowed an asylum applicant to challenge such a transfer also *after* the transfer decision had been made, if the six months' deadline imposed by Article 29 expired

1697 *Berlioz*, C-682/15. See the discussion of this case p. 202 of this work.

1698 *Politi v. Ministero delle finanze*, C-43/71, para. 9. See p. 209 of this work.

1699 The time limit is extended if the individual is being detained (one year) or has absconded (eighteen months).

1700 Judgment of 26 July 2017, *Shiri*, C-201/16, EU:C:2017:805, paras 30 and 31.

before the decision was executed. The Court again relied on an analogy with *Mengesteab* and answered that such was indeed the case. Interestingly, this time the Court followed Advocate General Sharpston's suggestion and expressly connected Article 27 of the Dublin III Regulation with the right to an effective remedy protected under Article 47 of the Charter.[1701] The Court thus recognised the relevance of Article 47 in litigation over the Dublin Regulation, and generalised the solutions of the earlier cases, so that no obligation imposed on Member States by the Dublin Regulation and potentially impacting individual interests can be left outside the scope of judicial review.[1702]

This clarification is even more welcome considering the Commission's proposal for a 'Dublin IV' Regulation.[1703] Article 28(1) of this proposal provides for an effective remedy against a transfer decision, but Article 28(4) provides that '*[t]he scope of the effective remedy provided in paragraph 1 shall be limited to an assessment of whether Articles 3(2) in relation to the existence of a risk of inhuman or degrading treatment or Articles 10 to 13 [laying down the criteria for determining the Member State responsible] and 18 [laying down provisions concerning dependent persons] are infringed upon.*' This restriction of the scope of the remedy, leaving out provisions that organise inter-State cooperation, clearly goes against the solution proposed above and disregards the basic idea that individuals have a right to the correct execution of the obligations of the Member State under EU law, and a corresponding remedy when this right is breached. As pointed out by Den Heijer, part of the problem came from the unwillingness of the Court to rely on Article 47 CFR in its case law concerning challenges against Dublin transfers: '*the Commission appears to follow up on the Court's implicit sugges-*

1701 The Court emphasised the objective laid down in recital 19 of the regulation, i.e. '*to guarantee effective protection of the rights of the persons concerned, legal safeguards and the right to an effective remedy in respect of decisions regarding transfers to the Member State responsible [...] in accordance, in particular, with Article 47 of the Charter of Fundamental Rights [...]*'. *Shiri*, C-201/16, para 44. See also Opinion of AG Sharpston in *Shiri*, C-201/16, para 37.

1702 This suggestion contradicts Den Heijer's argument that at least the application of the provisions of the Dublin Regulation which strictly '*govern the cooperation between Member States*' do not need to be subject to appeal. Den Heijer, 'Remedies in the Dublin Regulation: *Ghezelbash* and *Karim*' 867.

1703 Commission Proposal for a Regulation of the European Parliament and of the Council establishing the criteria and mechanisms for determining the Member State responsible for examining an application for international protection lodged in one of the Member States by a third-country national or a stateless person (recast), COM(2016) 270 final 2016:0133 (COD).

tion that it is within the discretion of the EU legislature to mould the scope of remedies.'[1704] With its ruling in *Shiri*, however, the Court finally started addressing the implications of Article 47 CFR in relation to the Dublin III Regulation. The even more flagrant contradiction between Article 47 and certain Dublin IV provisions might be all the more difficult to circumvent.

2.2.3.4. Interim conclusions

The right to international protection is dependent on many conditions, including the violation or threat of violation of another right, which make it difficult to assess. Perhaps even more complex issues lie with the way in which asylum seekers are treated as they await an answer to their application. The case law illustrates the continuing relevance, even after the entry into force of the Charter, of general principles of EU law as sources of rights and obligations. Indeed, the obligations included in the general principle of good administration are binding on the Member State, while the institutional scope of Article 41 CFR is limited to the EU institutions. It is by relying on the general principle that the Court has asserted and developed the procedural rights of applicants for international protection.[1705] In spite of these procedural safeguards, which undeniably enhance the protection of individuals facing Member State administration, it must be emphasised that EU law maintains '*a form of distance*', keeping asylum seekers '*in the position of objects of institutional cooperation*'.[1706] The possibility for asylum seekers to challenge transfer decisions remains limited because of the persisting idea that the provisions organising relations and exchanges between Member States do not give rise to rights and that therefore there is no need to provide individuals with a remedy to challenge their incorrect application. This form of *Schutznorm* pressure is even increasing, as the Dublin IV proposal seeks to limit the possibility to challenge Dublin transfers by identifying the provisions that are within the scope of judicial review – which means excluding the possibility of identifying rights and corresponding remedies in provisions that are not intended and identified as such. This is of course inconsistent with the classic concept of rights as correlatives of any clear, precise, unconditional obligation and with the *ubi ius*

1704 Den Heijer, 'Remedies in the Dublin Regulation: *Ghezelbash* and *Karim*' 866.

1705 This in line with the demonstration in Hofmann and Mihaescu, 'The Relation between the Charter's Fundamental Rights and the Unwritten General Principles of EU Law: Good Administration as the Test Case'.

1706 Editorial comments, 'EU law as a way of life' 368.

ibi remedium principle. The *Ghezelbash* case initiated a move to bring the Dublin III Regulation back in line with these essential features of the EU legal system. It remains to be seen whether the the same will happen with Dublin IV.

2.2.4. Conclusions

The case law reviewed in this section shows that the classic model of rights, obligations and interests applies to a variety of socio-economic, social and political rights. In fact, in view of the history of these rights and their basic characteristics, it is clear that we did not have to wait for the Charter to effectively have in EU law the '*indivisibility of rights*'.[1707] There is no major conceptual difference between these rights and the 'first generation' economic rights studied in Section 2.1: the general idea that an obligation imposed by EU law can translate into a correlative individual right if it coincides with an individual interest, applies to both generations of rights.[1708] The basic correlation between rights and obligations also explains the absence of horizontal direct effect of directives, and sustains the potential of general principles of Union law and Charter provisions to counterbalance the resulting lack of protection for individuals. Some new elements come to light and make the model more sophisticated, while some classic 'bugs' persist and generate new issues.

The first interesting development is the diversification of the interests that can trigger the application of obligations and corresponding rights. The case law on citizenship, political participation, and asylum exemplifies that the interest does not have to be an economically quantifiable interest. Union citizenship is particularly interesting in this respect, as the Court has recognised that the full enjoyment of free movement rights requires that the interests of citizens in leading a social and family life are taken into account. This in turn is causing the free movement rights to evolve into rights of integration into host Member States.[1709] Another important element is that the application of a right can be triggered by the infringement, or possible infringement of another right, which itself protects a

---

1707 Kenner, 'Economic and Social Rights in the EU Legal Order: The Mirage of Indivisibility' 15; La Torre, 'The Law beneath Right's Feet. Preliminary Investigation for a Study of the Charter of Fundamental Rights of the European Union' 534.

1708 See the conclusions of Section 2.1. p. 320.

1709 Editorial comments, 'EU law as a way of life' 360.

specific interest: for instance, both the right to equal treatment and the right to asylum can be construed in relation with the right to religious freedom.[1710]

Alongside these developments, and echoing the findings of Section 2.1., the *Schutznorm* pressure persists, for instance in the Opinions of Advocate Generals on the participation rights of workers in the undertaking, and of citizens in the Union's political life.[1711] This pressure even increases in the area of asylum law, where there is a tendency to restrict the possibility for asylum seekers to derive rights from Member States obligations under the Dublin system, and to access corresponding remedies. It also manifests itself in the debate over the construction of the distinction between 'rights' and 'principles' laid down at Articles 51(1) and 52(5) of the Charter. Indeed, a recurring suggestion is rely on a body of evidence that would signal the intention of the drafters to categorise each provision of the Charter into either justiciable 'rights' or 'principles' only laying down obligations on the authorities. Besides the fact that this intention is far from unequivocal, there is another more fundamental problem with this approach. It dismisses the Court's classic method of identifying individual rights, not based on abstract considerations but rather by checking the applicability of a given provision to a certain set of concrete circumstances. In the words of Prechal, the idea of a distinction between 'rights' and 'principles' '*has already been taken into account by the courts. However, any approach that decides a priori the degree of justiciability of the provisions concerned is highly unfortunate*'.[1712] The analysis of the (for now scarce) case law that (indirectly) addresses the rights/principles distinction confirms that the classic method is perfectly applicable to the Charter, as long as we understand the distinction fluidly and not rigidly. The continued relevance of the original concept of individual rights is arguably due precisely to this flexibility.

1710 See on the right to equal treatment in relation with the right to religious freedom see *G4S Secure Solutions*, C-157/15 and *Bougnaoui and ADDH*, C-188/15 (discussed p. 307 of this work). On the relation between the right to asylum and the right to religious freedom see *Y and Z*, Joined cases C-71/11 and C-99/11 (discussed p. 352 of this work).

1711 See respectively, Opinion of AG Cruz Villalón in *Association de Médiation Sociale*, C-176/12 and Opinion of AG Jääskinen in *Schönberger*, C-261/13 P.

1712 'Rights v principles, or how to remove fundamental rights from the jurisdiction of the courts' 183-184.

2.3. *Individual rights beyond individual interests*

In Section 2.1 we have looked at rights that come into existence due to economic individual interests, and in Section 2.2. at rights that come to life due to interests which, although not always economically quantifiable, can at least be individually isolated. What about interests that are neither strictly individualisable nor strictly economically assessable? 'Collective rights' are the object of an abundant legal literature, within and beyond the EU.[1713] Are individual rights within the Union's constitutional and legal framework inherently and exclusively connected with *individual* interests? Or can *collective* interests also function in such a way as to trigger the application of (individual) rights? Does the original concept of individual rights under EU law allow for collective interests to be properly taken into account? These questions are explored by examining how individual rights are identified and applied in three areas of Union law: consumer law (2.3.1), environmental law (2.3.2) and information law (2.3.3).

2.3.1. Individual rights in consumer law

Consumer law is highly symbolic of the protective power of Union law for individuals. There was no common policy on consumer protection at the inception of the EEC. It was the Single European Act that made a high level of consumer protection part of the objectives of the Community.[1714] This objective is now enshrined in the TFEU and detailed under Title XV.[1715] Consumers are now acknowledged by Union law not only as essen-

---

1713 E.g.: D. Feldman, 'Public Interest Litigation and Constitutional Theory in Comparative Perspective' (1992) 55 The Modern Law Review 44; R.F. Weber, 'Individual Rights and Group Rights in the European Community's Approach to Minority Languages' (2007) 17 Duke Journal of Comparative & International Law 361; P. Jones, 'Group Rights' The Stanford Encyclopedia of Philosophy (Spring 2014 Edition), ed E. Zalta, <http://plato.stanford.edu/archives/spr2014/entries/rights-group/> accessed 16 October 2015; K. Dowding and M. Van Hees, , 'The Construction of Rights' 97 American Political Science Review 281. L. Green, 'Two Views of Collective Rights' (1991) 4 Canadian Journal of Law and Jurisprudence 315.

1714 On the history of consumer protection in EU law see P. Nebbia and T. Askham, *EU Consumer Law* (Oxford University Press 2004), 5-59.

1715 Title XV entitled 'Consumer Protection' consists in Article 169 TFEU. Article 169(1) provides that: '*In order to promote the interests of consumers and to ensure a high level of consumer protection, the Union shall contribute to protecting the health,*

tial economic agents,[1716] but also as vulnerable individuals in need of specific protection against other private individuals, and who are able and encouraged to organise into groups and collectively defend their interests.[1717] The conceptual implications of these characteristics for individual rights may be considered from three successive angles. Firstly, the absence of horizontal direct effect of directives consistently limits the possibility to identify rights in these instruments, especially in the essentially horizontal relations governed by consumer law (2.1.3.1). Secondly, EU consumer law illustrates the power of the principle of effectiveness and the creativity with which the Court applies it, in order ensure that identified rights are effectively protected despite the inherently weak position of consumers towards sellers and suppliers (2.1.3.2). Thirdly, consumer law provides an interesting field of exploration for looking at how collective interests may develop into triggers for rights, much like individual interests. (2.1.3.3).

2.3.1.1. The challenge of identifying and protecting individual rights in horizontal relations

EU consumer law has been developed mainly by means of directives, yet it mostly regulates horizontal relations between economic actors (i.e. between consumers and sellers or suppliers). This brings us back to a familiar problem, that is, the limited possibility for directives to create rights on which individuals may rely before national courts.[1718] Consumer law does

---

safety and economic interests of consumers, as well as to promoting their right to information, education and to organize themselves to safeguard their interests'. Other relevant provisions include Article 4(2)(f), which provides that the Union and the Member States share the competence to legislate in the area of consumer protection and Article 12 TFEU, which requires that '*Consumer protection requirements shall be taken into account in defining and implementing other Union policies and activities*'.

1716 As highlighted by the European Commission, consumer expenditure accounts for 56% of EU GDP and is essential for reaching the objective of a '*smart, inclusive and sustainable growth*'. Commission Communication of 22.5.2012 'A European Consumer Agenda – Boosting confidence and growth' (COM(2012 225 final) 1.

1717 See L. Azoulai, 'Le droit de l'Union européenne comme mode de vie' (Université d'Aix-Marseille, Marseille, 27 May 2017), video available at https://blogdroiteuropeen.com/2017/06/12/le-droit-de-lunion-europeenne-comme-mode-de-vie-projet-de-recherche-du-prof-loic-azoulay/ accessed 3 August 2017.

1718 S. Weatherhill, *EU Consumer Law and Policy* (Edward Elgar 2005) 227.

not escape the absence of horizontal direct effect of directives, to which Member State liability is only an imperfect supplement.

Concerning the issue of horizontal direct effect, *Faccini Dori*[1719] laid down many elements which are still relevant for framing the relations between consumers and professionals under EU law. Ms Faccini Dori had signed a contract for an a contract English language course, from which she decided to retract within the minimum amount of time prescribed by Council Directive 85/577/EEC, which laid down rules to protect consumers in respect of contracts negotiated away from business premises.[1720] This directive had not been transposed into Italian law by the end of the transposition period. The referring court asked whether the provision which Ms Faccini Dori was invoking was sufficiently clear and precise and if so, whether it could be relied on by an individual against another individual. The Court held that the provision was indeed clear and precise since the minimum amount of time for a customer to change his mind after having entered a contract was clearly laid down.[1721] However, it confirmed its solution from *Marshall* according to which '*a directive cannot of itself impose obligations on an individual and cannot therefore be relied upon as such against an individual*'.[1722] Otherwise, a power would be recognised '*in the Community to enact obligations for individuals with immediate effect, whereas it has competence to do so only where it is empowered to adopt regulations*'.[1723] Exactly like in *Marshall*, the scope of the obligations laid down in the directive determines the scope of the correlative rights.[1724]

The introduction of Article 129a of the TEU, establishing the principle of a high degree of consumer protection,[1725] did not suppress the obstacle to the horizontal direct effect of directives on consumer protection. This was the question raised by the referring court in *El Corte Ingles*, and to

---

1719 Judgment of 14 July 1994, *Faccini Dori v Recreb*, C-91/92, EU:C:1994:292.

1720 Council Directive 85/577/EEC of 20 December 1985 to protect the consumer in respect of contracts negotiated away from business premises (OJ L 372 p. 31).

1721 *Faccini Dori v Recreb*, C-91/92, para 17.

1722 *Faccini Dori v Recreb*, C-91/92, para 20, referring to *Marshall v. Southampton and South-West Hampshire Area Health Authority*, C-152/84, para 48. See also, concerning consumer law: *Pfeiffer and Others*, Joined cases C-397/01 to C-403/01, para 108; Judgment of 25 October 2005, *Schulte*, C-350/03, EU:C:2005:637, para 70.

1723 *Faccini Dori v Recreb*, C-91/92, para 24.

1724 *Marshall v. Southampton and South-West Hampshire Area Health Authority*, C-152/84. See p. 298 of this work.

1725 Now Article 169(1) TFEU.

which the Court of Justice replied that the new provision merely assigned '*an objective to the Community (...) without also laying down any obligation on Member States or individuals*'; and therefore could not justify a change in the *Faccini Dori* solution.[1726] To avoid leaving consumers empty-handed, the Court has several times recalled that the classic supplements to the absence of horizontal direct effect apply also in consumer law. One is the obligation of consistent interpretation, that is, the obligation for the national court to interpret national law '*in the light of the wording and purpose of the directive so as to achieve the result pursued by the directive*'.[1727] Another supplement is the possibility to claim damages from Member States who have failed to transpose the relevant directives.[1728]

The Court applied its *Francovich* formula to the area of consumer law in *Dillenkofer*, a case which illustrates the Court's broad approach to the first liability condition of a rule entailing rights. The spotlight was on Article 7 of the Package Travel Directive, which established an obligation for the organiser and/or retailer party to the contract to provide sufficient evidence of security for the refund of money paid by the consumer and for his repatriation.[1729] Germany had not implemented that directive within the required time frame and several consumers (including Mr Dillenkofer) faced heavy expenses when the travel operators from whom they had purchased package travels went insolvent. After their claims against the companies had failed, they turned against the German government to seek compensation. One of the questions raised was whether Article 7 of the Directive '*entail[ed] the grant of rights to individuals*'.[1730] This corresponds to the *Francovich* rather than the *Brasserie* phrasing of the first liability condition – showing that the Court's terminology is not frozen in the '*intended to confer rights*' version. In order to answer this question, the Court relied on the wording, purpose and preamble of the Directive and it also stated that the

1726 Judgment of 7 March 1996, *El Corte Inglés v Blázquez Rivero*, C-192/94, para 20.

1727 *Faccini Dori v Recreb*, C-91/92, para 26; *Marleasing v Comercial Internacional de Alimentación*, C-106/89, para 8; Judgment of 16 December 1993, *Wagner Miret v Fondo de garantía salarial*, C-334/92, EU:C:1993:945, para 20, Judgment of 27 June 2000, *Océano Grupo Editorial and Salvat Editores*, Joined cases C-240/98 to C-244/98, EU:C:2000:346, para 30; *Pfeiffer and Others*, Joined cases C-397/01 to C-403/01, para 120.

1728 *El Corte Inglés v Blázquez Rivero*, C-192/94, para 22; *Faccini Dori v Recreb*, C-91/92, para 27.

1729 Council Directive 90/314/EEC of 13 June 1990 on package travel, package holidays and package tours (OJ L 158 p. 59) ('Package Travel Directive').

1730 *Dillenkofer and Others v Bundesrepublik Deutschland*, Joined cases C-178/94, C-179/94, C-188 to C-190/94, para 33.

fact that the Directive was intended to ensure the attainment of other objectives, i.e. ensuring the freedom to provide services (as the German and British government were arguing) did not preclude its provisions from also aiming to protect consumers.[1731] The Court also made clear that the absence of clear indication that Article 7 should confer rights did not prevent it from doing so, especially because any other solution would render the obligation laid down in that provision pointless.[1732] Thus, as Biondi and Farley point out, '*in true Court of Justice tradition*', the Court focused on the substance of the provision at issue, instead of performing a strictly literal-intentionalist interpretation, in order to verify whether it did entail the grant of rights to individuals.[1733] It did not examine the intention behind the isolated provision itself, but rather construed the obligation in the general system established by the directive and deduced from it the existence of a right.

Concerning the second condition of a sufficiently serious breach, the Court compared the situation at hand with that which had arisen in *Francovich*. While it was not clearly explained in *Francovich*, the Court here stated that there was a sufficiently serious breach whenever a Member State has taken no measures at all to transpose a directive. There was then only a yes-or-no question: has the obligation been breached or not? If the breach is established, then there is no need to evaluate the intensity of the breach and all that is necessary is to check the first liability condition (a rule intended to confer rights) and the third liability condition (causal link between the breach and the damage).[1734] In such a situation, thus, what will matter is the content of the right which the directive provides for. This approach was also applied to Article 7 of the Package Travel Directive in the subsequent *Rechberger* ruling, which made clear that there is also a 'sufficiently serious breach' when just one article of the directive has been incorrectly transposed, even if all other provisions of the directive have been

1731 *Dillenkofer and Others v Bundesrepublik Deutschland*, Joined cases C-178/94, C-179/94, C-188 to C-190/94, para 39.

1732 *Dillenkofer and Others v Bundesrepublik Deutschland*, Joined cases C-178/94, C-179/94, C-188 to C-190/94, para 40-41.

1733 Biondi and Farley, *The Right to Damages in European Law* 32.

1734 *Dillenkofer and Others v Bundesrepublik Deutschland*, Joined cases C-178/94, C-179/94, C-188 to C-190/94, para 20-28.

transposed.[1735] Indeed, the Member State '*enjoyed no margin of discretion as to the entry into force, in its own law, of the provisions of Article 7*'.[1736]

However, consumer law is not exempt from the influence of the *Schutznorm* doctrine that we have seen at work in many other contexts.[1737] The Court followed an intentionalist approach to the first liability condition in the heavily criticised *Peter Paul* case.[1738] In this case, a set of directives laid down a number of supervisory obligations for the national authorities vis-à-vis credit institutions.[1739] The preambles to these directives made clear that one of the objectives of harmonisation was the protection of depositors. Yet the Court found that the first liability condition was not met because the exact individual interests to be protected could not be determined.[1740] This does seem like a departure from the approach to rights that we have seen in direct effect cases, where any individual who has an interest in it may claim the execution of a clear, precise and unconditional obligation: there is no need, then, to identify the interests which the obligation *aims* to protect. Instead, in *Peter Paul*, there is a complete disconnection of obligations and rights: '*contrary to the claims of Paul and others, it*

1735 Judgment of 15 June 1999, *Rechberger and Others*, C-140/97, EU:C:1999:306. Biondi and Farley, *The Right to Damages in European Law* 33.

1736 *Rechberger and Others*, C-140/97, para 51.

1737 On the German *Schutznorm* doctrine, see p. 52 of this work; on how it puts pressure on the process of identifying rights conferred by EU law, see especially p. 161 and p. 190 of this work.

1738 Example of critical commentaries: M. Tison, 'Do Not Attack the Watchdog! Banking Supervisors Liability after Peter Paul' (2005) 42 Common Market Law Review 639; Reich, 'Horizontal Liability in EC Law: Hybridization of Remedies for Compensation in Case of Breaches of EC Rights' 718.

1739 Parliament and Council Directive 94/19/EC of 30 May 1994 on deposit-guarantee schemes, (OJ L 135 p. 5); First Council Directive 77/780/EEC of 12 December 1977 on the coordination of the laws, regulations and administrative provisions relating to the taking up and pursuit of the business of credit institutions (OJ L 322 p. 30); Council Directive 89/299/EEC of 17 April 1989 on the own funds of credit institutions (OJ L 124 p. 16); and Second Council Directive 89/646/EEC of 15 December 1989 on the coordination of laws, regulations and administrative provisions relating to the taking up and pursuit of the business of credit institutions and amending Directive 77/780 (OJ L 386 p. 1).

1740 Judgment of 12 October 2004, *Paul and Others*, C-222/02, EU:C:2004:606; S. Prechal, 'Protection of Rights: How Far?' in S. Prechal and B. Van Roermund (eds), *The Coherence of EU Law* (Oxford University Press 2008) 166; Biondi and Farley, *The Right to Damages in European Law* 36; Tison, 'Do Not Attack the Watchdog! Banking Supervisors Liability after Peter Paul'; L.A.D. Keus, 'Francovich in Nederland' (2005) Nederlands tijdschrift voor Europees recht 283 287.

does not necessarily follow either from the existence of [Member State obligations vis-à-vis credit institutions] or from the fact that the objectives pursued by those directives also include the protection of depositors that those directives seek to confer rights on depositors in the event that their deposits are unavailable as a result of defective supervision on the part of the competent national authorities.'[1741] In this perspective, the norm that is invoked must provide for the protection of certain persons in particular in order for the first liability condition to be fulfilled.

One could legitimately imagine that the Court's judgment in *Danske Slagterier*, an unambiguous rejection of the *Schutznorm* approach supported by the Advocate General in that case,[1742] would have buried *Peter Paul* once and for all. Yet, this approach resurfaced recently in the *Schmitt* case[1743] concerning the possibility to claim damages on the basis of Directive 93/42 on medical devices.[1744] This directive lays down essential requirements for medical devices marketed within the Union. Member States must designate 'notified bodies' which are in charge of monitoring the respect by manufacturers of these requirements. When the requirements are not or no longer met, the notified body must suspend or withdraw the certificate of conformity of the device. Mrs Schmitt had silicone breast implants (manufactured in France) fitted in Germany and had to have them removed after four years when it became know that these implants did not contain medical-grade silicone. She claimed damages from the notified body which, in her view, should have performed more thorough inspections on the manufacturer's premises, and would have then found out that the implants did not meet the standards. It was crucial for the German court to know whether the rules concerning the notified bodies in Directive 93/42 had a protective purpose for users of medical devices, in order to determine whether the notified body could incur liability under German civil liability law. The Court recalled its statement in *Peter Paul* that '*it does not necessarily follow from the fact that a directive imposes surveillance obligations on certain bodies [...]that the directive seeks to confer rights on [injured] parties in the event that those bodies fail to fulfil their obligations, and that is the case especially if the directive does not contain any express rule granting such rights.*'[1745] The Court added that the mere fact that the directive required

1741 *Paul and Others*, C-222/02, para 40.

1742 *Danske Slagterier*, C-445/06. See p. 230 of this work.

1743 Judgment of 16 February 2017, *Schmitt*, C-219/15, EU:C:2017:128.

1744 Council Directive 93/42/EEC of 14 June 1993 concerning medical devices (OJ L 169 p. 1).

1745 *Schmitt*, C-219/15, para 55, citing *Paul and Others*, C-222/02, paras 38 to 40.

notified bodies to take out civil liability insurance did not oblige Member States to set out a civil liability regime;[1746] however, the directive did not prevent it either, so that failure on the part of a notified body to fulfil its obligations '*may give rise to liability on its part vis-à-vis the end users of medical devices*'. The conditions for such liability were to be governed by national law, subject to the principles of equivalence and effectiveness.[1747]

It is not clear why the Court deemed it necessary to rely on *Peter Paul* and insisted that the surveillance obligations laid down in Directive 93/42 were not motivated by an intention to confer rights – especially since it did find in the end that the purpose of the notified body's involvement is to protect the end users of medical devices.[1748] As observed by Advocate General Sharpston, the notified body was not a public body;[1749] its relation with Mrs Schmitt was thus a horizontal relation and the issue was not one of State liability but of civil liability. This makes the reference to *Peter Paul* even less relevant, while the citation causes confusion as to the applicability of the *Schutznorm* doctrine in damages litigation.

The basic tools for identifying and protecting rights in EU law therefore do not give particularly thrilling results in terms of consumer protection. Since directives cannot directly impose obligations on individuals, there can be no correlative rights of consumers. Denial of horizontal direct effect means that the consumer was originally left with the costly and uncertain direct action against the State for damages;[1750] especially since damages litigation in consumer law is not immune to the influence of the *Schutznorm* doctrine. The gap was however filled rather spectacularly by the Union legislator, and the Court interpreting the legislation in the light of the principle of effectiveness.

2.3.1.2. The principle of effectiveness to the rescue

The EU legislator has taken several steps to increase consumer protection and make it more enforceable. The enactment of the Unfair Contract

1746 *Schmitt*, C-219/15, para 57.
1747 *Schmitt*, C-219/15, para 59.
1748 *Schmitt*, C-219/15, para 60.
1749 Opinion of AG Sharpston in Schmitt, C-219/15, EU:C:2016:694, para 27.
1750 S. Weatherhill, *EU Consumer Law and Policy* (Edward Elgar 2005) 227-244 (observing also that, next to private enforcement, Commission enforcement depends on limited means and variable political will).

Terms Directive[1751] in 1993, was one of the most important of these steps.[1752] In the words of the Court of Justice, the system of protection introduced by this directive '*is based on the idea that the consumer is in a weak position vis-à-vis the seller or supplier, as regards both his bargaining power and his level of knowledge*'.[1753] This leads to the consumer agreeing to terms drawn up in advance by the seller or supplier without being able to influence the content of those terms.[1754] To correct the imbalance, the directive introduces a notion of good faith and lists examples of terms that may be regarded as unfair. It requires that contract terms be drafted in intelligible language and provides that ambiguities are to be interpreted in favour of consumers. In addition, Article 6(1) states that unfair terms used in a contract concluded between a consumer and a seller or supplier '*shall… not be binding on the consumer*'. This, the Court has found in *Mostaza Claro*, is '*a mandatory provision which, taking into account the weaker position of one of the parties to the contract, aims to replace the formal balance which the latter establishes between the rights and obligations of the parties with an effective balance which re-establishes equality between them*'.[1755] The Court has thus built its case law in the light of this objective of an effective balance between the parties, so that the weaker parties, i.e. the consumers, can effectively exercise their rights. This amplified version of the principle of effectiveness has led to original developments concerning the relation between rights and remedies.

The most innovative and prominent evolution in this context is the development of the obligation for national courts to review of their own mo-

1751 Council Directive 93/13/EEC of 5 April 1993 on unfair terms in consumer contracts (OJ L 95 p. 29) ('Unfair Contract Terms Directive').

1752 Professor Elise Poillot calls this instrument the 'super-directive' of EU consumer law. E. Poillot, '*Gutiérrez Naranjo and Others*' (PhD Seminar Recent Developments in Theory and Practice of EU Law, University of Luxembourg, 27 June 2017).

1753 *Sánchez Morcillo and Abril García*, C-169/14, para 22; Judgment of 26 January 2017, *Banco Primus*, C-421/14, EU:C:2017:60, para 40.

1754 *Océano Grupo Editorial and Salvat Editores,* Joined cases C-240/98 to C-244/98, para 25; Judgment of 26 October 2006, *Mostaza Claro*, C-168/05, EU:C:2006:675, para 25; and Judgment of 6 October 2009, *Asturcom Telecomunicaciones*, C-40/08, EU:C:2009:615, para 29, Judgment of 14 June 2012, *Banco Español de Crédito*, C-618/10, EU:C:2012:349, para 39.

1755 Judgment of 26 October 2006, *Mostaza Claro*, C-168/05, EU:C:2006:675, para 36; *Asturcom Telecomunicaciones*, C-40/08, para 30; Judgment of 9 November 2010, *VB Pénzügyi Lízing,* C-137/08, EU:C:2010:659, para 47; Judgment of 21 December 2016, *Gutiérrez Naranjo*, Joined cases C-154/15 and C-307/15, EU:C:2016:980, para 55; *Banco Español de Crédito*, C-618/10, para 40.

tion the unfair nature of contract terms,[1756] which the Court justified especially in *Océano Grupo* and *Mostaza Claro*.[1757] The basic rationale underlying the obligation of *ex oficio* review is again the principle of effectiveness, combined with the teleological consideration that the aim of Article 6 of the Directive '*would not be achieved if the consumer were himself obliged to raise the unfair nature of [contract] terms*'.[1758] The Court highlighted that in disputes where amounts involved are often limited, lawyers' fees may suffice to dissuade the customer from challenging the application of an unfair term. Conversely, in Member States where consumers can defend themselves without lawyers, '*ignorance of the law*' may lead to the same result. In view of the real risk that the consumer '*is unaware of his rights or encounters difficulties in enforcing them*',[1759] the Court concluded in *Océano Grupo* that '*effective protection of the consumer may be attained only if the national court acknowledges that it has power to evaluate terms of this kind of its own motion*'.[1760] The Court reinforced this solution in *Mostaza Claro* by stating that it was justified by '*the nature and importance of the public interest underlying the protection which the Directive confers on consumers*'.[1761] The same logic of effectiveness applied in *Banco Español de Credito* in which the Court held that the Unfair Contract Terms Directive 93/13 precludes national legislation that does not permit the court hearing an application for an order for payment to determine of its own motion whether a term in a contract concluded between a seller or supplier and a consumer is unfair, in the case

---

1756 On ex oficio review in the context of consumer litigation see Östlund, 'Effectiveness of European Union Law versus Procedural Protection. Tracing the tension throughout the case-law of the Court of Justice on *ex officio* review by the national judge' especially 190-212; C. Lacchi, 'Preliminary References to the Court of Justice of the EU and Effective Judicial Protection: Towards a more protection-oriented approach of Article 267 TFEU' (PhD thesis, University of Luxembourg 2017) 62-68.

1757 *Océano Grupo Editorial and Salvat Editores*, Joined cases C-240/98 to C-244/98 and *Mostaza Claro*, C-168/05.

1758 *Océano Grupo Editorial and Salvat Editores*, Joined cases C-240/98 to C-244/98, para 26.

1759 *Mostaza Claro*, C-168/05, para 28.

1760 *Océano Grupo Editorial and Salvat Editores*, Joined cases C-240/98 to C-244/98, para 26. This requires the national court to favour a (consistent) interpretation '*that would allow it to decline of its own motion the jurisdiction conferred on it by virtue of an unfair term*': para 32.

1761 *Mostaza Claro*, C-168/05, para 38.

where that consumer has not lodged an objection.[1762] Again, this was justified by the '*significant risk that the consumers concerned will not lodge the objection required*'.[1763]

The development of consumer protection law also allows us to draw further conclusions regarding the relation of complementarity between the principle of effectiveness as an obligation of Member States, and the principle of effective judicial protection of individual rights. *Sanchez Morcillo* is particularly interesting in this respect.[1764] The Court was asked whether the Spanish system of mortgage enforcement proceedings concerning compensation in respect of the damage suffered by the consumer, was compatible with Article 7(1) of the Unfair Contract Terms Directive,[1765] read in combination with Article 47 of the Charter, in so far as this system restricted the possibility to appeal a first instance judgment. In the absence of harmonised rules at EU level, the matter was covered by the principle of national procedural autonomy, if the requirements of equivalence and effectiveness were satisfied. But the Court observed that the practical consequence of the procedural rule was that, since an appeal was possible only when an objection was upheld, while '*the seller or supplier may appeal against a decision which is contrary to its interests whilst, if the objection is dismissed, the consumer does not have that right*'.[1766] The ECJ admitted that '*the right to effective judicial protection under Article 47 […] does not entail a right of appeal against a first instance judgment*'.[1767] So the principle of effectiveness was decisive in the assessment: the Court pointed out that the obligation for the Member States to ensure the effectiveness of the rights that the parties derive from the directive '*implies a requirement of judicial protection, also guaranteed by Article 47 of the Charter*',[1768] and against this backdrop highlighted the potential catastrophic consequences for the consumer's interests of the application of the procedural rule, and the imbalance be-

1762 *Banco Español de Crédito*, C-618/10, paragraph 1 of the operative part. See also e.g. Judgment of 18 February 2016, *Finanmadrid EFC*, C-49/14, EU:C:2016:98, para 36.

1763 *Banco Español de Crédito*, C-618/10, para 54 and *Finanmadrid EFC*, C-49/14, para 52.

1764 *Sánchez Morcillo and Abril García*, C-169/14.

1765 '*Member States shall ensure that, in the interests of consumers and of competitors, adequate and effective means exist to prevent the continued use of unfair terms in contracts concluded with consumers by sellers or suppliers*'.

1766 *Sánchez Morcillo and Abril García*, C-169/14, para 30.

1767 *Sánchez Morcillo and Abril García*, C-169/14, para 36 (citing *Samba Diouf*, C-69/10, para 69). See also *Orizzonte Salute*, C-61/14, para 48.

1768 *Sánchez Morcillo and Abril García*, C-169/14, para 35.

tween the consumer and the seller with regard to the possibility to appeal.[1769] This led to the conclusion that the Spanish system was '*liable to jeopardise the effectiveness of consumer protection intended by Directive 93/13, read in conjunction with Article 47 of the Charter*'[1770] – which reveals a simultaneous concern for both the effectiveness of the overall system, and the effective protection of each individual's rights.

Interestingly, in the more recent case *Finanmadrid*, the Court did not rely on Article 47 to assess the compatibility with EU law of a Spanish rule of law that prevented national courts, ruling on the enforcement of an order for payment, from assessing *ex officio* whether a term in a consumer contract was unfair.[1771] The Court appears to have implicitly followed the Advocate General, who had observed that '*the level of judicial protection of the rights that consumers derive from Directive 93/13 is higher than that flowing from Article 47 of the Charter for the parties to a civil action involving EU law*'.[1772] The requirement for a court to conduct a review of its own motion does not derive from Article 47 CFR, but is '*a special feature of proceedings characterised by an imbalance between the parties. […] this requirement can only flow from the need to ensure that consumers are protected, as provided for in Article 6 of Directive 93/13*'.[1773] The ECJ held that the directive and the principle of effectiveness precluded the Spanish legislation at issue, while it did not see any incompatibility between the latter and Article 47.[1774]

The Court's dynamic application of the principle of effectiveness has thus multiplied the protective power of the Unfair Contract Terms Directive.[1775] In parallel to the jurisprudential development of the procedural protection of consumers, the Union legislator has introduced a battery of supplements in the system of consumer protection. These range from the

---

1769 *Sánchez Morcillo and Abril García*, C-169/14, paras 43-44.

1770 *Sánchez Morcillo and Abril García*, C-169/14, para 50.

1771 *Finanmadrid EFC*, C-49/14. See Lacchi, 'Preliminary References to the Court of Justice of the EU and Effective Judicial Protection: Towards a more protection-oriented approach of Article 267 TFEU' 66.

1772 Opinion of AG Szpunar in *Finanmadrid EFC*, C-49/14, EU:C:2015:746, para 90.

1773 Opinion of AG Szpunar in *Finanmadrid EFC*, C-49/14, para 92.

1774 *Finanmadrid EFC*, C-49/14, EU:C:2016:98, paras 54-57.

1775 The Court has also relied on the principle of effectiveness to identify an obligation for national courts to grant interim relief in relation to the Unfair Terms Directive: Judgment of 14 March 2013, *Aziz*, C-415/11, EU:C:2013:164. Likewise in *Naranjo* the principle of effectiveness led to the acknowledgement of a the right to repayment of amounts paid on the basis of contractual clauses that have been held by a court to be unfair. *Gutiérrez Naranjo*, Joined cases C-154/15 and C-307/15, paras 56-68.

reinforcement of certain substantive rights, especially obligations of (and correlative rights to) information,[1776] to a series of tailor-made liability regimes laid down in the Consumer Sales Directive, the Package Travel Directive, and the Product Liability Directive.[1777] In addition, the development of horizontal liability in competition law may also have an interesting impact for consumers, since it is not unrealistic to imagine that the logic of *Kone*[1778] will stretch further and that the effectiveness rationale will lead the Court to develop a more general principle of private liability that will benefit consumers.[1779]

2.3.1.3. From the protection of individual interests to the protection of collective interests: the future of functional subjectivation?

There is another angle from which the Union legislator seeks to ensure the effectiveness of EU consumer protection law; that is, by encouraging consumers to act collectively in defense of their interests. This positioning is

1776 On the obligation of information laid down by Article 4 of Directive 85/577, and how Member States must ensure that it translates into a right for individuals, see *Schulte*, C-350/03, para 100. On the transparency of clauses required by Directive 93/13, see Judgment of 21 March 2013, *RWE Vertrieb*, C-92/11, EU:C:2013:180. E. Poillot, 'Le contrôle de la transparence matérielle des clauses portant sur l'objet du contrat : une nouvelle arme en matière de lutte contre les clauses abusives' [2017] Recueil Dalloz n°19.

1777 Council Directive 85/374/EEC of 25 July 1985 on the approximation of the laws, regulations and administrative provisions of the Member States concerning liability for defective products (OJ L 210 p. 29). For a recent application of this Directive see Judgment of 21 June 2017, *W and Others*, C-621/15, EU:C:2017:484.

1778 *Kone and Others*, C-557/12, para 33.

1779 This possibility has been foreseen by the General Court in *Air Canada v Commission*, T-9/11, para 42; *Koninklijke Luchtvaart Maatschappij v Commission*, T-28/11, para 47; *Cathay Pacific Airways v Commission*, T-38/11, para 46; *Cargolux Airlines v Commission*, T-39/11, para 41; *Latam Airlines Group and Lan Cargo v Commission*, T-40/11, para 51; *British Airways v Commission*, T-48/11, para 43; *SAS Cargo Group and Others v Commission*, T-56/11, para 48; *Air France-KLM v Commission*, T-62/11, para 49; *Air France v Commission*, T-63/11, para 46; *Martinair Holland v Commission*, T-67/11, para 38; *Japan Airlines v Commission*, T-36/11, para 41; *Singapore Airlines and Singapore Airlines Cargo v Commission*, T-43/11, para 47. See p. 250 of this work.

clearly perceptible in the Consumer Injunctions Directive,[1780] Article 2(1)(a) of which states that judicial authorities must be empowered to order '*the cessation or prohibition of any infringement*' of a series of substantive consumer protection rules. Interestingly, these injunctions must be aimed at protecting the collective interests of consumers.[1781] The implications of this were analysed in *VKI v Amazon*, a judgment mostly known for having invalidated standard governing law clauses that gave consumers the impression that only the law of the Member State in which the company is located governs the contract, while the consumer also benefits from the legal protection that would apply under the Rome I Regulation[1782]. But *VKI v Amazon* is also important because of the approach to collective actions that it entails. The Court held the above conclusion was '*not affected by the collective nature of the action by means of which the validity of the terms is challenged. The fact that the action does not concern individual contracts actually concluded is inherent in the very nature of such a preventive collective action, in which an abstract review is carried out*'.[1783] The judgment made clear that the law applicable to an action for injunction is determined in accordance with Article 6(1) of the Rome I Regulation. The one applicable to the assessment of a particular contractual term must however always be determined pursuant to the Rome II Regulation[1784], whether that assessment is made in an individual or a collective action, so that the interpretation of this term does not vary depending on the kind of action brought, which would '*jeopardise the objective pursued by Directives 2006/22 and 93/13 of efficaciously putting an end to the use of unfair terms*'.[1785] Collective actions are

1780 Parliament and Council Directive 2009/22/EC of 23 April 2009 on injunctions for the protection of consumers' interests (OJ L 110 p. 30) ('Consumer Injunctions Directive'). Wilman, 'The end of the absence? The growing body of EU legislation on private enforcement and the main remedies it provides for' 910; M. Sullivan and R. Lahme, 'Class/collective actions in Europe: overview of applicable EU law principles', Thomson Reuters Practical Law, < https://uk.practicallaw.thomsonreuters.com/2-618-0602?transitionType=Default&contextData=(sc.Default)&firstPage=true&bhcp=1> accessed 3 August 2017.

1781 Article 1(1) and Recital 3 of the Consumer Injunctions Directive.

1782 Parliament and Council Regulation (EC) No 593/2008 of 17 June 2008 on the law applicable to contractual obligations (OJ L 177 p. 6) ('Rome I Regulation').

1783 Judgment of 28 July 2016, *Verein für Konsumenteninformation*, C-191/15, EU:C:2016:612, para 51.

1784 Parliament and Council Regulation (EC) No 864/2007 of 11 July 2007 on the law applicable to non-contractual obligations (OJ L 199 p. 40) ('Rome II Regulation').

1785 *Verein für Konsumenteninformation*, C-191/15, paras 57-60.

thus considered to contribute to the effectiveness of consumer protection law.

In addition, the European Commission launched an initiative on collective redress,[1786] which led to the issuance in June 2013 of the Recommendation on collective redress.[1787] This document puts forward a set of principles relating both to judicial and out-of-court collective redress (both injunctive and compensatory) that should be common across the Union.[1788] While it is not exclusively centred on consumer rights,[1789] the anchor point of this horizontal approach is consumer protection: the starting point of the initiative was the observation that '*[i]n the modern consumer oriented, globalised and digital economy accountability and confidence play a crucial role. Traders should be made accountable for their behaviour if that is detrimental for consumers*';[1790] and the Recommendation opens by emphasising the objective of '*a high level of consumer protection*'.[1791] Recital 6 reaffirms the faith in the classic mechanism of functional subjectivation as an efficient supplement to the Commission's action: '*[i]t is a core task of public enforcement to*

1786 European Commission, 'Judicial Redress – Collective Redress', June 2013, < http://ec.europa.eu/consumers/solving_consumer_disputes/judicial_redress/index_en.htm> accessed 3 August 2017.

1787 Commission Recommendation of 11 June 2013 on common principles for injunctive and compensatory collective redress mechanisms in the Member States concerning violations of rights granted under Union Law (OJ L 201 p. 60) ('Collective Redress Recommendation').

1788 Its Article 3(a) defines 'collective redress' means: (i) a legal mechanism that ensures a possibility to claim cessation of illegal behaviour collectively by two or more natural or legal persons or by an entity entitled to bring a representative action (injunctive collective redress); (ii) a legal mechanism that ensures a possibility to claim compensation collectively by two or more natural or legal persons claiming to have been harmed in a mass harm situation or by an entity entitled to bring a representative action (compensatory collective redress).

1789 Recital 7 of the Collective Redress Recommendation cites consumer protection, competition, environment protection, protection of personal data, financial services legislation, and investor protection, and adds that the principles set out '*should be applied horizontally and equally in those areas but also in any other areas where collective claims for injunctions or damages in respect of violations of the rights granted under Union law would be relevant*'. See also Parliament Resolution of 2 February 2012 'Towards a Coherent European Approach to Collective Redress'.

1790 European Commission, Consultation paper for discussion on the follow-up to the Green Paper on consumer collective redress, May-July 2009, <http://ec.europa.eu/consumers/archive/redress_cons/docs/consultation_paper2009.pdf > accessed 3 August 2017, p. 3.

1791 Collective Redress Recommendation, Recital 1.

prevent and punish the violations of rights granted under Union law. The possibility for private persons to pursue claims based on violations of such rights supplements public enforcement.' The Commission further observes that '*The possibility of joining claims and pursuing them collectively may constitute a better means of access to justice, in particular when the cost of individual actions would deter the harmed individuals from going to court*'.[1792]

The Court has however identified some limits to the development of collective litigation in consumer protection law. One important issue is how this developing trend connects with the traditional individual actions through which individuals defend their rights and pursue their particular interests. *Pohotovosť*,[1793] for instance, concerned the possibility for a consumer association to intervene in support of a consumer in a dispute over an individual contract. The Court observed that Article 7(2) of the Unfair Contract Terms Directive requires Member States to allow '*persons or organisations having a legitimate interest under national law in protecting consumers to take action*' in order to challenge in court unfair standard contract terms.[1794] However, the Court pointed out that there was nothing in the directive nor in the EU legislative framework on consumer protection that would expressly govern the role of consumer protection associations in individual disputes involving a consumer.[1795] Therefore, the possibility to grant and define such a role should be left up to the national legislator, within the limits set by the principles of equivalence and effectiveness.[1796] The Court also looked at whether the Charter could provide additional protection, but found that Article 38 requiring a high level of consumer protection could not by itself impose an interpretation of the directive that would encompass a right for consumer protection associations to intervene in individual disputes.[1797] Here it should be noted that the Court did not expressly refer to the distinction between 'rights' and 'principles' laid down in Article 52(5) CFR: like in many other contexts,[1798] it simply considered that the broad phrasing of the provision did not allow to solve the precise procedural question raised in the case in point. Neither could Article 47 CFR be helpful in this respect. The Court pointed out incidentally

1792 Collective Redress Recommendation, Recital 9.

1793 Judgment of 27 February 2014, *Pohotovosť*, C-470/12, EU:C:2014:101.

1794 *Pohotovosť*, C-470/12, para 43 and case law cited.

1795 *Pohotovosť*, C-470/12, para 45.

1796 *Pohotovosť*, C-470/12, para 46-48.

1797 *Pohotovosť*, C-470/12, para 52.

1798 See especially *Association de Médiation Sociale*, C-176/12, discussed p. 310 of this work.

that Slovakian law allowed individual consumers to mandate a consumer association to represent them in court, so that there was a place and function for associations in the Slovakian legal system. But this observation precisely illustrates that as long as the Commission's Recommendation remains a recommendation, there will be variable limits (depending on the domestic systems of Member States) to how much associations may be involved in the protection of the interests of consumers, and variable degrees of connection between collective and individual interests.

Another problem concerning the relationship between collective and individual actions, and how the protection of the various interests at stake functions in this relationship, arose in *Sales Sinués*,[1799] which focused on a provision of Spanish law requiring that an individual action brought by a consumer seeking a declaration that a contractual term was unfair must be suspended pending a final judgment on an ongoing collective action brought by a consumer association based on Article 7(2) of the Unfair Contract Terms Directive. The Court insisted on the need for a '*differentiated approach*' [1800] between the protection of consumers, who are in a weak position, and that of consumer associations, which although they must be able to play '*an essential role*' in order to achieve a high level of consumer protection in the EU, are not in an inferior position vis-à-vis a seller or supplier; there is no imbalance to correct, unlike in an individual action brought by a consumer;[1801] therefore, individual and collective actions have '*different purposes and legal effects*', which set limits on their procedural relationship.[1802] The consequence of the Spanish rule was that '*the consumer [could] no longer individually assert the rights recognized by Directive 93/13 by dissociating himself from (the) collective action*'.[1803] This led the consumer to forfeit '*the rights which he would be recognised as having in an individual action, namely to have the circumstance of his situation taken into account.*'[1804] This result was of course incompatible with the Unfair Contract Terms Directive. The lesson from this case is that the individual interests of consumers do not disappear behind collective interests defended by consumer associations, and consumers must be able to exercise their rights individually.

1799 Judgment of 14 April 2016, *Sales Sinués*, Joined cases C-381/14 and C-385/14, EU:C:2016:252.
1800 *Sales Sinués*, Joined cases C-381/14 and C-385/14, para 28.
1801 *Sales Sinués*, Joined cases C-381/14 and C-385/14, paras 26-27.
1802 *Sales Sinués*, Joined cases C-381/14 and C-385/14, para 30.
1803 *Sales Sinués*, Joined cases C-381/14 and C-385/14, para 35.
1804 *Sales Sinués*, Joined cases C-381/14 and C-385/14, para 40.

2.3.1.4. Interim conclusions

Consumer law challenges both essential components of the EU concept of individual rights. The correlation between obligations and rights necessarily means that directives that cannot directly impose obligations on individuals (sellers and suppliers) cannot either directly confer rights on individuals (consumers) in horizontal relations; State liability is an important but insufficient palliative to this gap. However, the correlation remains relevant for understanding consumer rights: in so far as the substantive obligations contained in the directives have been transposed by the Member States, the effectiveness of the correlative rights of consumers is ensured by an impressive set of procedural guarantees that go beyond the minimum requirements of Article 47 of Charter. The basic requirement that where there is a right, there is a remedy, remains, but what is more: where there is a consumer right, there is a super-remedy, allowing the national court to activate of itself a right whose holder may not even be aware that it exists. The other basic component, the notion of individual interest, is also enriched. Individual interests do not lose their function of activating rights; what is interesting is that, slowly but surely, an EU law on collective litigation is building up, in which collective interests may also be granted that function.

2.3.2. Individual rights in environmental law

The Treaty of Rome contained no express provision on the protection of the environment. The Community started developing its environmental policy through successive Environmental Action Programmes, the first of which relied on non-binding instruments, the following being more focused on environmental protection as instrumental to the integration process of the internal market.[1805] The EU's environmental policy has since

1805 First Environmental Action Programme (EAP): Declaration of the Council of the European Communities and of the representatives of the Governments of the Member States meeting in the Council of 22 November 1973 on the programme of action of the European Communities on the environment (OJ C 112, 20.12.1973); Second EAP: Resolution of the Council of the European Communities and of the Representatives of the Governments of the Member States meeting within the Council of 17 May 1977 on the continuation and implementation of a European Community policy and action programme on the environment (OJ C 139, 13.6.1977). Currently the 7th EAP is guiding the

then matured to a point where environmental protection is established as an aim in itself.[1806] This was first manifested in the introduction in Part III of the EEC Treaty, by the Single European Act in 1986, of a Title VII on environment,[1807]; the Maastricht Treaty then amended Articles 2 and 3 EC to include the objective of environmental protection. A turning point was the signing by the EU of the 1999 Aarhus Convention (AC),[1808] an international agreement which provides for access to environmental information, public participation in environmental decision-making, and access to justice in order to protect these two types of rights. Under the current setting Article 3 TEU requires the EU to '*work for the sustainable development of Europe based on (…) a high level of protection and improvement of the quality of the environment*'; Article 4 TFEU recognizes the environment as an area of shared competence; Article 11 TFEU refers to '*environmental protection requirements*'; and Articles 191 to 193 TFEU provide for express legislative environmental measures on the part of the Member States.[1809] In addition, Article 37 CFR provides that: '*A high level of environmental protection and the improvement of the quality of the environment must be integrated into the policies of the Union and ensured in accordance with the principle of sustainable development*'.

Admittedly, as pointed out by Prechal and Hancher, '*constitutionalising environmental interests does not necessarily imply the creation of automatically enforceable and justifiable rights.*'[1810] Of course, we know from Part I that for identifying individual rights the existence of clear and precise obligations matters just as much as the acknowledgement of interests. But precisely, there is an increasing number of such obligations in EU environmental law, so that the recent developments in this field may be characterised as a '*process of materialization of enforceable individual rights in the field of high en-*

EU environmental policy until 2020 (Decision No 1386/2013/EU of the European Parliament and of the Council of 20 November 2013 on a General Union Environment Action Programme to 2020 'Living well, within the limits of our planet' Text with EEA relevance (OJ L 354 p. 171).

1806 C. Hey, 'EU Environmental Policies: a short history of the policy strategies' European Environmental Bureau, 2005 <http://www.eeb.org/publication/chapter-3.pdf> accessed 2 March 2017.

1807 Single European Act (OJ L 169, 29.6.1987, p. 1).

1808 Convention on Access to Information, Public Participation in Decision-Making and Access to Justice in Environmental Matters (Aarhus Convention), 2161 UNTS 447; 38 ILM 517 (1999) ('Aarhus Convention'/'AC').

1809 Gordon and Moffatt, *EU Law in Judicial Review* 447.

1810 Prechal and Hancher, 'Individual Environmental Rights: Conceptual Pollution in EU Environmental Law?' 89.

vironmental protection.'[1811] The question therefore arises whether the EU concept of individual rights retains its original characteristics when applied in the area of environmental law. The two dimensions of this concept need to be examined: the correlativity between obligations and rights, and the activating function of interests. The latter dimension proves particularly problematic in the context of EU environmental law because of the difficulty of delineating and quantifying individual interests in environmental protection. This section first analyses how these issues arise and are addressed in the case law on sectoral environmental legislation (2.3.2.1) and in the case law on the early transversal environmental legislation, i.e. on impact assessments (2.3.2.2).[1812] In terms of transversal legislation, the EU has taken a significant leap by becoming a party to the Aarhus Convention. Individual rights in this setting are the object of Section 2.3.2.3 on the implementation of the AC before national courts, and Section 2.3.2.4 on the implementation of the AC before the EU courts.

2.3.2.1. The development of classic individual rights in sectoral environmental legislation

Early EU environmental case law provides an excellent example of the complementarity of actions by the Commission and by individuals as means of requesting from Member States the execution of their obligations under EU law, which the Court had already emphasised in *Van Gend en Loos*.[1813]

The first significant cases on the implementation of environmental directives were brought before the Court not by individuals, but by the Commission – however, individual rights were key in these rulings; they were

1811 A. Sikora, 'The Principle of High Environmental Protection as a Source of Enforceable Rights' (Cahiers de droit européen - Les principes généraux du droit de l'Union européenne, Brussels, 10 September 2015).

1812 The distinction for the purposes of analysing the whole body of EU environmental legislation is made e.g. in S. Scheuer, 'EU Environmental Policy Handbook. A Critical Analysis of EU Environmental Legislation' European Environmental Bureau, 2005 <http://www.eeb.org/?LinkServID=3E1E422E-AAB4-A68D-221A63343325A81B> accessed 6 March 2017.

1813 *Van Gend en Loos*, C-26/62, p. 13: '*The vigilance of individuals concerned to protect their rights amounts to an effective supervision in addition to the supervision entrusted […] to the diligence of the Commission and of the Member States.*' See also Section 1.1.2.1 of this work, p. 49, on the effectiveness rationale of individual rights.

the reason why the Commission launched infringement proceedings against Germany. All three cases from the *Commission v Germany* series from the early 1990s[1814] had in common that environmental directives[1815] had been transposed through instruments that were not clearly binding and did not have clear effects with regard to third parties.

In these judgments, the correlativity between obligations and rights plays its usual part, supported by the effectiveness rationale. In the first case, Germany claimed that 'administrative practice', based on a legal framework not explicitly nor specifically transposing the Groundwater Pollution Directive, nevertheless constituted adequate transposition of this directive. Ruling on the infringement procedure initiated by the Commission, the Court first analysed the directive as follows: '*the directive [...] seeks to protect the Community's groundwater in an effective manner by laying down specific and detailed provisions requiring the Member States to adopt a series of prohibitions, authorization schemes and monitoring procedures in order to prevent or limit discharges of certain substances. The purpose of those provisions of the directive is thus to create rights and obligations for individuals.*'[1816] Classically, the EU instrument lays down obligations which translate into further rights (and obligations) for individuals. In order for these rights to be practically applicable, however, they need to be unambiguous: hence the Member States' obligation to '*guarantee the full application of the directive in a sufficiently clear and precise manner so that, where the directive is intended to create rights for individuals, the persons concerned can ascertain the full extent of*

1814 Judgment of 28 February 1991, *Commission v Germany*, C-131/88, EU:C:1991:87, Judgment of 30 May 1991, *Commission v Germany*, C-59/89, EU:C:1991:225, Judgment of 17 October 1991, *Commission v Germany*, C-58/89, EU:C:1991:391.

1815 Respectively: Council Directive 80/68/EEC of 17 December 1979 on the protection of groundwater against pollution caused by certain dangerous substances (OJ L 20 p. 43) ('Groundwater Pollution Directive'); Council Directive 82/884/EEC of 3 December 1982 on a limit value for lead in the air, OJ 1982 L 378, p. 15 ('Lead Value Directive'); Council Directive 75/440/EEC of 16 June 1975 concerning the quality required of surface water intended for the abstraction of drinking water in the Member States (OJ L 194 p. 26) and Council Directive 79/869/EEC of 9 October 1979 concerning the methods of measurement and frequencies of sampling and analysis of surface water intended for the abstraction of drinking water in the Member States (OJ L 271 p. 44) ('Drinking Water Directives').

1816 *Commission v Germany*, C-131/88, para 7.

their rights and, where appropriate, rely on them before the national courts'.[1817] Upon close examination of the German legal framework compared to the provisions of the directive, the Court held that several provisions of the directive could not '*be regarded as having been implemented in German legislation with the precision and clarity necessary in order to satisfy fully the requirement of legal certainty*'.[1818] In the second *Germany v Commission* case in the series, the Commission was unsatisfied with the transposition of the Lead Value Directive by means of an administrative circular. Not only was it not clear from German law (even case law) whether a circular was binding on the administration; even worse, there was ambiguity as to whether a circular had effects on third parties. Therefore, it could not be claimed '*that individuals [were] in a position to know with certainty the full extent of their rights in order to rely on them where appropriate, before the national courts or that those whose activities [were] likely to give rise to nuisances [were] adequately informed of the extent of their obligations*'.[1819] Likewise, in the third case the implementation of the Drinking Water Directives through communications that do not have '*unquestionable binding force*'[1820] was found equally inappropriate. Germany was thus condemned in these second and third cases as well.[1821]

These three cases exemplify the dynamism of the correlativity model: obligations are laid down at the Union level, the Court deducts from these obligations an intention to confer rights, and derives thereof a further obligation to make these rights effective by laying them down in a clear and precise manner at the national level. The intention to confer rights is used not in a restrictive way but rather to strengthen the position of individuals

---

1817 *Commission v Germany*, C-131/88, para 6. The Court had hinted to this solution already in Judgment of 15 March 1990, *Commission v Netherlands*, C-339/87, EU:C:1990:119, regarding the transposition of a directive on the conservation of wild birds, ruling that an adequate legal framework needed to be established especially so that individuals could be aware of their rights and claim them in court if necessary.

1818 *Commission v Germany*, C-131/88, para 73.

1819 *Commission v Germany*, C-59/89, para 23.

1820 *Commission v Germany*, C-58/89, paras 17-18.

1821 Exactly like in the first case, the Court held that Germany had failed to fulfil its obligation to provide a legal framework that would '*guarantee the full application of the directive in a sufficiently clear and precise manner so that, where the directive is intended to create rights for individuals, the persons concerned can ascertain the full extent of their rights and, where appropriate, rely on them before the national courts*'. *Commission v Germany*, C-58/89, para 13; *Commission v Germany*, C-59/89, para 18; *Commission v Germany*, C-131/88.

relying on EU environmental law against national authorities. And it can be explained by the same effectiveness rationale materialising in the mechanism of functional subjectivation.[1822]

The correlativity between rights and obligations means that individuals may claim the execution of obligations contained in directives that have been wrongly transposed, or not transposed within the required timeframe, provided that these obligations are sufficiently clear, precise and unconditional.[1823] Case *Comitato di coordinamento per la difesa della Cava*[1824] provides such an example, and a good summary of how the correlativity model, through the case law on direct effect of directives, applies in EU environmental law. A group of citizens had mobilised against the decision of local authorities to develop a waste tip in their region. They relied on the directive on waste to challenge the decision in court.[1825] Specifically, they were invoking Article 4 of the directive which required that:

> '*Member States shall take the necessary measures to ensure that waste is disposed of without endangering human health and without harming the environment, and in particular:*
> - without risk to water, air, soil and plants and animals,
> - without causing a nuisance through noise or odours,
> - *without adversely affecting the countryside or places of special interest.*'

In order to assess whether this provision conferred rights on individuals,[1826] the Court first recalls the *Becker* and *Fratelli Costanzo* principle according to which '*wherever the provisions of a directive appear, as far as their subject-matter is concerned, to be unconditional and sufficiently precise, those provisions may be relied upon by an individual against the State where the State fails to implement the directive in national law by the end of the period pre-*

1822 The same supplementary use of the intention to confer rights has been observed in the case law on Member State liability: see p. 268 of this work.

1823 As established in *Van Duyn v. Home Office*, C-41/74. See p. 212 of this work.

1824 *Comitato di coordinamento per la difesa della Cava and Others v Regione Lombardia and* Others, C-236/92.

1825 Council Directive 75/442/EEC of 15 July 1975 on waste, OJ 1975 L 194, p. 39.

1826 It may be observed that the Italian court was seeking to ascertain whether the directive conferred '*subjective rights*' which could be implemented under the form of '*legitimate interests*' in Italian law. *Comitato di coordinamento per la difesa della Cava and Others v Regione Lombardia and Others*, C-236/92, para 5. Not for the first nor the last time, the Court ignores these terminological issues specific to the domestic system where the question originates and instead sticks to the term '*individual right*'. See e.g. *Olainfarm*, C-104/13, discussed p. 170 of this work.

scribed or where it fails to implement the directive correctly'.[1827] Then the Court recalls the definitions of 'unconditionality' – the character of a provision that is '*not subject, in its implementation or effects, to the taking of any measure either by the institutions of the Community or by the Member States*'[1828] – and sufficient precision – where the obligation imposed by the provision '*is set out in unequivocal terms*'.[1829] As for Article 4 of the directive, it '*indicates a programme*' and '*sets out the objectives*' that Member States must pursue, but it does not '*lay down any particular requirement restricting the freedom of the Member States regarding the way in which they organize the supervision of the activities*' referred to in the directive, nor does it require '*the adoption of specific measures or a particular method of waste disposal*'. It is therefore '*neither unconditional nor sufficiently precise and thus is not capable of conferring rights on which individuals may rely as against the State*'.[1830] As usual, the correlativity between rights and obligations also means *a contrario* that where obligations are not identifiable, there can also be no corresponding rights.[1831]

The obligations laid down by environmental directives often give rise to rights to scrutiny of (if not participation in) decision-making processes; but they do not necessarily grant rights to a substantive outcome. The line between these two types of rights is not always clear-cut, however, and one of the challenges arising from the development of environmental rights is to determine the exact substance, i.e. the material scope, of these rights. Such an issue arose in *Janecek*,[1832] concerning provisions of the Directive and the Regulation on ambient air quality assessment and management.[1833] Mr Janecek, whose health was being '*impaired*' because of the air quality, lived

1827 *Comitato di coordinamento per la difesa della Cava and Others v Regione Lombardia and* Others, C-236/92, para 8; citing Judgment of 19 January 1982, *Becker*, C-8/81, EU:C:1982:7 and *Fratelli Costanzo v. Comune di Milano*, C-103/88.

1828 *Comitato di coordinamento per la difesa della Cava and Others v Regione Lombardia and Others*, C-236/92, para 9 and case law cited.

1829 *Comitato di coordinamento per la difesa della Cava and Others v Regione Lombardia and Others*, C-236/92, para 10 and case law cited.

1830 *Comitato di coordinamento per la difesa della Cava and Others v Regione Lombardia and Others*, C-236/92, paras 12-14.

1831 The opposite relation between discretion and the existence of a right is also relevant here, even though it remains implicit. Indeed, in pointing out the '*freedom*' which the directive allows the Member States, the Court refers to an earlier ruling which had established that the same directive left a broad '*discretionary*' power to the Member States. *Traen*, C-372 to 374/85, para 22. Here, discretion seems to be equated with '*freedom*'.

1832 *Janecek*, C-237/07.

1833 Article 7(3) of Council Directive 96/62/EC of 27 September 1996 on ambient air quality assessment and management (OJ L 296 p. 55), as amended by Parlia-

near an air quality measuring station which indicated that the emissions of particulate matter PM_{10} were repeatedly exceeded. He applied before the administrative courts for an order requiring the Freistaat Bayern to draw up an air quality action plan in his district. The case went up the judicial ladder and the Federal Administrative Court referred to the Court of Justice in order to get an interpretation of EU law on two main issues, i.e. whether an individual could request from the authorities that they execute their obligation to draw an air quality plan, and whether such request could also have an impact on the content of the plan. Regarding the first issue, the Court observed that Article 7(3) of the Directive, on which Mr Janecek was relying, '*places the Member States under a clear obligation to draw up action plans both where there is a risk of the limit values being exceeded and where there is a risk of the alert thresholds being exceeded*'. This interpretation, the Court added, followed from "*a straightforward reading*" of the provision.[1834] The Court then recalled '*that individuals are entitled, as against public bodies, to rely on the provisions of a directive which are unconditional and sufficiently precise*'.[1835] The possibility for concerned persons to rely on obligations laid down in a directive matters in particular for this directive '*designed*' to '*protect public health*'.[1836] Consequently, '*the natural or legal persons directly concerned by a risk that the limit values or alert thresholds may be exceeded must be in a position to require the competent authorities to draw up an action plan where such a risk exists, if necessary by bringing an action before the competent courts*'.[1837]

According to Micklitz, *Janecek* thus exemplifies how the Court can be '*innovative in granting individuals standing where their actions produce collective effects*'[1838] – or in Dougan's words, it illustrates the Court's '*generous approach in harnessing the services of concerned individuals*' for implementation

ment and Council Regulation (EC) No 1882/2003 of 29 September 2003 (OJ L 284 p. 1).

1834 *Janecek*, C-237/07, para 35.

1835 *Janecek*, C-237/07, para 36, citing *Ratti*, C-148/78, para 20.

1836 *Janecek*, C-237/07, para 36.

1837 *Janecek*, C-237/07, para 38. The Court relies on the abovementioned *Commission v Germany* cases: '*the Court has held that, whenever the failure to observe the measures required by the directives which relate to air quality and drinking water, and which are designed to protect public health, could endanger human health, the persons concerned must be in a position to rely on the mandatory rules included in those directives*'.

1838 Micklitz, 'The ECJ between the Individual Citizen and the Member States - A plea for a judge-made European law on remedies' 24.

of Union environmental measures.[1839] In fact, in light of the classic *Van Gend en Loos/Defrenne* approach which allows any individual who has an interest in the fulfilment of an obligation to request it, the solution in *Janecek* is not particularly revolutionary. Of course, here the interest is not economic but it is purely a matter of health. But the general interest that consists in protecting human health is here individualised, literally embodied in one individual. The clear and precise obligation to draw up an action plan thus translates into a right for the individual who has the (non-economic) interest in doing so. The *ubi jus ibi remedium* logic then leads the Court to conclude that '*the natural or legal persons directly concerned by a risk that the limit values or alert thresholds may be exceeded must be in a position to require the competent authorities to draw up an action plan where such a risk exists, if necessary by bringing an action before the competent courts.*'[1840]

On the other hand, also in accordance with the correlativity model, where the directive allows discretion to the Member States, there is no clear and precise obligation that could translate into a right, so that, while Mr Janecek is indeed entitled to request the action plan to be drawn, he cannot request a specific action to be taken in order to respect the set limit values. Regarding the second issue, the Bundesverwaltungsgericht asks specifically whether the directive requires the authorities to take measures that would ensure that the limit value be respected. Here the Court first focuses on the wording of the relevant provision: '*According to Article 7(3) of Directive 96/62, action plans must include the measures "to be taken in the short term where there is a risk of the limit values and/or alert thresholds being exceeded, in order to reduce that risk and to limit the duration of such an occurrence". It follows from that very wording that the Member States are not obliged to take measures to ensure that those limit values and/or alert thresholds are never exceeded*'.[1841] Then it assesses the '*broad logic*' of the directive and finds that '*it is for the Member States to take measures capable of reducing to a minimum the risk of the limit values and/or alert thresholds being exceeded and the duration of such an occurrence, taking into account all the material circumstances and opposing interests*'.[1842] The ruling ends on the note that the directive does grant '*discretion*' to Member States as regards the nature of the measures, but that there are '*limits*' to this discretion and that the national

1839 Dougan, 'Who Exactly Benefits from the Treaties? The Murky Interaction Between Union and National Competence over the Capacity to Enforce EU Law' 94.
1840 *Janecek*, C-237/07, para 39.
1841 *Janecek*, C-237/07, para 44.
1842 *Janecek*, C-237/07, para 45.

court must control the '*adequacy*' of the measures with regard to the aim pursued by the directive as well as '*the balance which must be maintained between that objective and the various opposing public and private interests*'.[1843] This supports the view that the existence of discretion does not automatically mean that there is no obligation and no right, especially since assessing discretion is not a binary black-or-white question but rather a matter of where the cursor is set.[1844]

The logic of *Janecek* is also at work in the *ClientEarth* ruling from 2014, a case in which ClientEarth had initiated proceedings against the Secretary of State for the Environment and requested that the United Kingdom's air quality plans be revised, based on the new ambient air quality directive.[1845] With this new directive the legislator has moved the cursor: the discretion granted to the Member State has been restricted, compared to the earlier version of the ambient air quality directive on which Mr Janecek had relied. This time, the Court finds that the obligations imposed on the Member State consist not only in the elaboration of an action plan for ambient air quality, but also in the respect of certain limit values after expiration of the defined deadline. Like in *Janecek*, the question was raised as to the possibility for interested parties to seek a judicial order that would constrain the Member State into fulfilling its obligations. On this point, the Court follows closely its solution in *Janecek* and reaffirms the possibility for individuals to rely on unconditional and sufficiently precise provisions of directives, the obligation for the national court to perform consistent interpretation or disapply contrary national law, and the necessity to equip the corresponding right with a remedy. This means that the national courts should take '*any necessary measure, such as an order in the appropriate terms*'.[1846] Absent from the ruling is the question of interest, probably because it did not constitute a problem at the national level.[1847] *ClientEarth* is however perfectly consistent with the correlativity model and the *ubi jus ibi*

1843 *Janecek*, C-237/07, para 46.

1844 See the conclusions of Section 2.1 p. 320.

1845 Parliament and Council Directive 2008/50/EC of 21 May 2008 on ambient air quality and cleaner air for Europe, (OJ L 152 p. 1). *ClientEarth*, C-404/13. On this case see also, concerning the principle of effective judicial protection, p. 157 of this work.

1846 *ClientEarth*, C-404/13, paras 53-58.

1847 The English Divisional Court had laid down the criteria for standing in public interest challenges in the (in)famous Pergau Dam case (*R v Secretary of State for Foreign and Commonwealth Affairs, ex p World Development Movement Ltd* [1995] 1 WLR 386, confirmed by *R v Somerset County Council, ex p Dixon* [1998] Env LR 111).: especially, there must be a public interest at stake and the claimant

remedium principle. The degree of discretion is inversely proportional to the probability of identifying an obligation and a corresponding right; and the identification of a right combined with the requirement of effectiveness automatically translates into the obligation to provide a remedy.

The principle of effectiveness also impacts the temporal scope of the rights and obligations laid down in directives. It is probably not by chance that questions over the effects of directives before the end of the transposition period have arisen mostly in environmental law: environmental damage or evolution can be irreversible, making the objectives of the directives pointless. Environmental litigation has thus led the Court to stress that during the period prescribed for transposition of a directive, the Member States to which it is addressed '*must refrain from taking any measures liable seriously to compromise*' the attainment of the result prescribed by that directive.[1848] The Court elaborated on this finding and those from *Janecek* in Stichting Natuur en Milieu and held that the National Emission Ceilings Directive[1849] granted rights to individuals, who could claim before national courts, already during the transitional period, that Member States should adopt or envisage appropriate and coherent policies to pursue the objectives laid down in the directive.[1850]

By contrast, Article 37 of the Charter has not been used very successfully in litigation so far. It to date has been cited in merely ten judgments delivered by the ECJ.[1851] One of these cases was brought by an applicant to an EU civil service competition, who relied on Article 37 (among other EU law provisions) to challenge the prevalence of the paper version of the Official Journal over the electronic one. The CST dismissed the argument, em-

---

must demonstrate that, if standing were not granted, then a manifest illegality would not be challenged. Thus, on the whole, according to Gordon and Moffatt, '*at least where a challenge has significant public interest, an environmental pressure group will have standing to bring the challenge.*' In addition, other cases suggest that provided a claimant has sufficient interest to bring the challenge, no further standing restrictions will be imposed (*R (Kides) v South Cambridgeshire DC* [2002] 4 PLR 66; *R (Hammerton) v London Underground Ltd* [2002] EWHC 2307). Gordon and Moffatt, *EU Law in Judicial Review* 467. On the public interest challenge in English law see also Craig, 'Access to Mechanisms of Administrative Law' 772.

1848 *Inter-Environnement Wallonie*, C-129/96, para 45.

1849 Parliament and Council Directive 2001/81/EC of 23 October 2001 on national emission ceilings for certain atmospheric pollutants (OJ L 309 p. 22).

1850 Judgment of 26 May 2011, *Stichting Natuur en Milieu and Others*, C-165/09, EU:C:2011:348, see especially para 78 and paras 103-104.

1851 According to a search on www.curia.europa.eu on 8 October 2017.

phasising the general character of the provisions and their 'programmatic' character, and pointing out that it was unclear how they related to the applicant's claim.[1852] Interestingly, the CST did not rely on the rights/principles distinction to dismiss the relevance of Article 37 (which it could easily have done especially since it is one of the Charter's provisions which the Explanations explicitly describe a set of 'principles'). Instead, the CST emphasised that it was not able to use that provision in the concrete case at hand because it was too general to be applicable as such. This solution is in line with the well-established approach of assessing the practical applicability of a provision to a concrete case.

Less anecdotally, Article 37 has featured in a prominent series of cases concerning the EU's emissions trading system (ETS) within the legal framework on climate change mitigation.[1853] Several undertakings had been granted additional free allowances by German measures implementing the ETS. The Commission issued a decision rejecting these measures[1854] and the undertakings lodged an action for annulment against this

---

1852 Judgment of 12 March 2009, *Hambura v Parliament*, F-4/08, EU:F:2009:25, para 57.

1853 As organised by Parliament and Council Directive 2003/87/EC of 13 October 2003 establishing a scheme for greenhouse gas emission allowance trading within the Community and amending Council Directive 96/61/EC (OJ L 275 p. 32). The cases were the following: Judgment of 26 September 2014, *Arctic Paper Mochenwangen v Commission*, T-634/13, EU:T:2014:828 (appeal dismissed by Order of 13 September 2016, *Arctic Paper Mochenwangen v Commission*, C-551/14 P, EU:C:2016:684); Judgment of 26 September 2014, *Raffinerie Heide v Commission*, T-631/13, EU:T:2014:830 (appeal dismissed by Order of 13 September 2016, *Raffinerie Heide v Commission*, C-564/14 P, EU:C:2016:685); Judgment of 26 September 2014, *DK Recycling und Roheisen v Commission*, T-630/13, EU:T:2014:833 (appeal dismissed by Order of 22 June 2016, *DK Recycling und Roheisen v Commission*, C-540/14 P, EU:C:2016:469 (for a detailed analysis of this case see C. Mariotti, 'Theory and Practice of Emissions Trading in the European Union: Some Reflections on Allowance Allocation in Light of the DK Recycling Case' European Papers, Vol 1, 2016, No 3, European Forum, Insight of 22 December 2016, 1153-1170 <http://www.europeanpapers.eu/fr/europeanforum/theory-and-practice-emissions-trading-european-union-allowance-allocation#_ftn25> accessed 29 April 2017); Judgment of 26 September 2014, *Molda v Commission*, T-629/13, EU:T:2014:834; Judgment of 26 September 2014, *Romonta v Commission*, T-614/13, EU:T:2014:835 (appeal dismissed by Order of 13 September 2016, *Romonta v Commission*, C-565/14 P, EU:C:2016:698).

1854 Commission Decision of 5 September 2013 concerning national implementation measures for the transitional free allocation of greenhouse gas emission allowances in accordance with Article 11(3) of Directive 2003/87/EC of the European Parliament and of the Council (OJ L 240 p.27).

decision. They were claiming infringement of their freedom to pursue a trade and right to property. Importantly, Article 37 is not invoked by the applicants. It is instead part of the provisions which the Court mentions as setting the priorities that have to be taken into account and balanced with the fundamental rights of the operators of installations that are subject to the emission allowance trading scheme.[1855] This shows that even a Charter provision phrased in very broad terms still has its place in the adjudication process as it can serve as a guide for interpretation – but not necessarily to the advantage of individuals.

In conclusion, the case law on sectoral environmental legislation confirms that the basic characteristics of the EU concept of a right are valid also in this field. Individuals may rely on provisions of EU environmental law where these provisions are sufficiently clear and precise in defining obligations and where they have an interest in the performance of these obligations. The interest may be economic but it can also be non-economic, such as the protection of the individual's health. This broad conception of interest may be explained by the usual effectiveness rationale and it also raises the usual issues in some domestic procedural systems which condition access to court to a more restrictive conception of interest. The cases above thus also illustrate the common tension in the development of individual rights in the EU legal system. The *Schutznorm* issue and how it relates to the limits of the interest trigger very often resurfaces in environmental law, precisely because most provisions of EU environmental law aim to protect the general public rather than clearly identifiable individual interests.

2.3.2.2. The development of transversal environmental legislation: environmental impact assessment

The EU legal framework on environmental protection, which first developed based on sectoral legislation, has been supplemented with transversal legislation, mainly the Environmental Impact Assessment (EIA)

1855 *Arctic Paper Mochenwangen v Commission*, T-634/13, para 72; *Raffinerie Heide v Commission*, T-631/13; *DK Recycling und Roheisen v Commission*, T-630/13, para 73; *Molda v Commission*, T-629/13, para 74; *Romonta v Commission*, T-614/13, para 76.

directive.[1856] The introduction of this transversal legislation applying to all activities likely to affect the environment meant far-reaching obligations, potentially claimable by a broad range of interested individuals – and therefore, a reactivation of the debate on how the notion of interest relates to the EU concept of a right. Already the *Commission v Germany* cases described above had stirred confusion because they signalled that '(i)*n the interpretation of the CJEU, the concept of a norm granting individual rights (protective norm) includes also a provision that serves the protection of general public interest and protects the rights of individuals only indirectly*'.[1857]

Concerning the EIA directive, a typically controversial case was *Kraaijeveld*: an economic operator was challenging the legality of the decision of a Dutch local authority approving dyke reinforcement works, even though these would have had damaging effects on local businesses. As became clear during the proceedings, the local authority had failed to carry out the environmental assessment required by the EIA directive. The Court stated that '*it would be incompatible with the binding effect attributed to a directive (...) to exclude, in principle, the possibility that the obligation which it imposes may be invoked by those concerned. In particular, where the Community authorities have, by directive, imposed on Member States the obligation to pursue a particular course of conduct, the useful effect of such an act would be weakened if individuals were prevented from relying on it before their national courts (...)*.'[1858] The extent to which individuals may rely on the directive then depends on the discretion left to the Member States in pursuing the prescribed course of conduct.[1859] According to some commentators, this case is not about individual rights and not an example of direct effect for the benefit of individuals, but rather an instance of 'public interest effect' where individual parties are allowed to bring legal proceedings for the collective benefit – with the implication that *Kraaijeveld* would be opening

1856 Council Directive 85/337/EEC of 27 June 1985 on the assessment of the effects of certain public and private projects on the environment (OJ L 175, p. 40) ('the EIA Directive'), amended three times and codified in Parliament and Council Directive 2011/92/EU of 13 December 2011 on the assessment of the effects of certain public and private projects on the environment (OJ L 26 p. 1).

1857 Półtorak, 'Changes in the Level of the National Judicial Protection Under the EU Influence on the Example of the Polish Legal System' 234.

1858 Judgment of 24 October 1996, *Kraaijeveld and Others*, C-72/95, EU:C:1996:404, para 56.

1859 *Kraaijeveld and Others*, C-72/95, paras 56-61.

the door to the possibility of an *actio popularis.*[1860] Undeniably, this case exemplifies the power of the effectiveness rationale in the case law on rights, and the Court's continued reliance on individuals for ensuring the enforcement of the obligations which EU law imposes on Member States. *Kraaijeveld* should not be interpreted as a dismissal of the relevance of individual interests. On the contrary, it maintains that individual interests are pivotal as triggers for the application of rights. In this case, an individual's economic interest is at stake, as '*the removal of access to navigable waterways would be ruinous to Kraaijeveld's business, whose economic activity is related to waterways*'.[1861] Simultaneously, *Kraaijeveld* dismisses again the *Schutznorm* approach which requires the individual interest to have been *a priori* defined in the relevant provisions. What matters is the *actual* interest combined with a clearly identifiable obligation – which is why discretion remains relevant: here the limit to the Member State's discretion was in the obligation to perform an environmental impact assessment of the project.[1862]

The importance of individual interest for enforcement of the EIA directive by individuals is reaffirmed in *Wells.*[1863] A mining company was developing a quarry on the basis of authorisation that was issued in disrespect of the EIA directive and Mrs Wells, living nearby, started proceedings to get the administration to revoke or adapt the authorisation. The dispute was referred to the Court of Justice for a preliminary ruling. Having established the illegality of the authorisation in light of the directive, the Court then assessed the possibility for Mrs Wells, living nearby, to rely on the directive. The UK government was arguing that allowing this would amount to giving horizontal direct effect to the EIA directive, and violating the principle of legal certainty, since invalidating the authorisation would clearly have effects on the mining company. The Court confirmed its *Marshall* case law according to which directives '*can only create rights*', never obligations, for

1860 Dougan, *National Remedies Before the Court of Justice. Issues of Harmonisation and Differentiation* 41; see also Prechal and Hancher, 'Individual Environmental Rights: Conceptual Pollution in EU Environmental Law?' and J. Scott, *EC Environmental Law* (Longman 1998), ch 8; Hilson and Downes also identify a predominant 'public law effect' in *Kraaijeveld:* see Hilson and Downes, 'Making sense of rights: Community rights in E.C. law'.

1861 *Kraaijeveld and Others*, C-72/95, para 18.

1862 Prechal and Hancher, 'Individual Environmental Rights: Conceptual Pollution in EU Environmental Law?' 95. See also the same approach in Judgment of 19 September 2000, *Linster*, C-287/98, EU:C:2000:468, para 32; Judgment of 16 September 1999, *WWF and Others*, C-435/97, EU:C:1999:418, para 69.

1863 Judgment of 7 January 2004, *Wells*, C-201/02, EU:C:2004:12.

individuals.[1864] However, '*mere adverse repercussions*' on a private third party do not amount to obligations[1865] and merely constitute, in the words of Weatherhill, '*incidental adverse effect*' and is acceptable under EU law.[1866] This solution again highlights the instrumental rationale of individual rights, showing how the effectiveness of the rights granted by EU law trumps not only the contrary interests of Member States, but also those of other individuals – the only limit being that it should not create obligations for them.

The next question in *Wells* concerned the scope of the obligation to remedy the failure to carry out an EIA. The Court first stressed that under the principle of sincere cooperation '*the Member States are required to nullify the unlawful consequences of a breach of Community law*'.[1867] Nullification may occur by revocation or suspension of an authorisation already granted, or if the individual agrees, by financial compensation; the appropriate option being left for the national court to determine.[1868] Dougan has observed that with this solution, '*the Court of Justice did not seem to be suggesting that Directive 85/337/EEC was intended to confer rights on individual members of the public for the purposes of the Francovich case law, and that the claimant should thus benefit from a right to reparation conferred directly by Union law itself*' and that *Wells* thus shows particular deference to national procedural autonomy.[1869] But the case should not be read as excluding the possibility for violations of the EIA to give rise to State liability. Instead, the structure of the Court's reasoning should be read in the light of the convergence of effectiveness of EU law and individual interests. The starting point is the obligation to nullify the breach of EU law, and the best way to ensure the effective realisation of the objectives of the EIA directive is to 'go back' if possible to the point where an EIA should have been performed and to have it done. Unsurprisingly, damages only come second in the list of options because, as usual, liability functions as a supplement to direct ef-

---

1864 *Wells*, C-201/02, para 56, citing *Marshall v. Southampton and South-West Hampshire Area Health Authority*, C-152/84, para 48.

1865 *Wells*, C-201/02, para 57.

1866 S. Weatherhill, 'The Elusive Character of Private Autonomy in EU Law' in D. Leczykiewicz and S. Weatherhill (eds), *The Involvement of EU Law in Private Law Relationships* (Hart Publishing 2013) 16.

1867 *Wells*, C-201/02, para 64.

1868 *Wells*, C-201/02, paras 65-69.

1869 M. Dougan, 'Who Exactly Benefits from the Treaties? The Murky Interaction Between Union and National Competence over the Capacity to Enforce EU Law' 98.

fect.[1870] The concern for the individual interest that has been harmed by the violation of EU law is visible in the precision that awarding damages can be a solution 'if the individual so agrees'. *Wells* therefore gives one more illustration of the connection between direct effect and liability and of the double rationale of EU rights, serving both EU objectives and individual interests through the mechanism of functional subjectivation.

This reading is sustained by the more recent case *Leth*, where the owner of a property located near Vienna-Schechat airport was challenging the authorisation to develop the airport.[1871] The Court, relying on *Wells*, confirmed that the EIA directive '*confers on the individuals concerned a right to have the environmental effects of the project under examination assessed by the competent services and to be consulted in that respect*'.[1872] The Court also reasserted and clarified the solution from *Wells* that damages should be granted if consent cannot be revoked and if the individual agreed to it, and that in such a case the assessment of the Member State's liability should be conducted according to the *Brasserie* conditions.[1873] Here, the existence of a sufficiently serious breach of a rule of EU law intended to confer rights is easily established, precisely because the direct effect of this rule has been established.[1874] The Court leaves it to the Austrian court to determine whether there is a direct causality link between the omission of the EIA and the decrease in the value of Mrs Leth's property but it stresses that this link is not automatic and that it must be established that '*the harm disputed in the main proceedings results from a possible failure of the environmental impact assessment to perform a warning function*'.[1875] So, the right violated is the right to a certain conduct during the procedure, not the right to a substantive result, and the damages must result not from omission of the EIA alone but from the ensuing failure to meet the directive's objectives. Dougan has criticised this approach, arguing that '*the Court's conception of the material scope of the individual interests safeguarded under EU law is essentially monetarised: the Directive protects against (certain) pecuniary damage to property values, rather than the non-material interests of the individual, let alone the general interests of the natural environment*'.[1876] This is not very fair

1870 See e.g. p. 222 of this work.

1871 Judgment of 14 March 2013, *Leth*, C-420/11, EU:C:2013:166.

1872 *Leth*, C-420/11, para 32.

1873 *Leth*, C-420/11, para 41.

1874 *Leth*, C-420/11, para 44.

1875 *Leth*, C-420/11, paras 47-55.

1876 Dougan, 'Addressing Issues of Protective Scope within the Francovich Right to Reparation' 154.

to the Court, which was precisely being asked a very clear question, i.e. can the EIA also be considered to '*protect an individual against pecuniary damage as a result of a decrease in the value of his property?*'[1877] In other words, the question was in fact whether *not only* human health as such could be protected through the directive, but whether *also* financial interests could fall under the protective scope of the directive. And the Court's positive answer is simply yet another manifestation of its broad conception of individual interests as the trigger for rights (including the derived right to reparation where an obligation has been breached), ensuring the effectiveness of the objectives pursued by the directive.[1878]

Comparably to what happens concerning sectoral environmental legislation, when it comes to transversal legislation the new guarantee of Article 37 CFR does not seem to add much to the preexisting system of protection of environmental rights. This is illustrated in a case[1879] in which an Italian environmental NGO was challenging the validity of a provision of the Strategic Environmental Assessment Directive (SEA) Directive,[1880] considering that it left too much discretion to the Member States and therefore did not ensure that the objective of a high level of environmental protection set out Article 191 TFEU and Article 37 CFR would be fulfilled. The Court first assessed the validity of the directive provision in the light of Article 191 and found that the EU legislature had committed no manifest error of assessment that could affect the validity of the provision. The Court then pointed out the correspondence between Article 191 TFEU and Article 37 CFR, relying on the Explanations. Based on Article 52(2) CFR, which pro-

---

1877 Judgment of 14 March 2013, *Leth*, C-420/11, EU:C:2013:166, para 18.

1878 See a converging analysis of the case in Thorson, *Individual Rights in EU Law* 239, and at 252 pointing out AG Kokott's Opinion that the possibility to claim damages reinforces the effectiveness of the directive: Opinion of AG Kokott in *Leth*, C-420/11, EU:C:2012:701, paras 51-53. AG Kokott stresses again the 'warning function' of the EIA in her Opinion in *Comune di Corridonia and Aldo Alessandrini Provincia di Macerata and Others*, Joined cases C-196/16 and C-197/16, EU:C:2017:249, para 56.

1879 Judgment of 21 December 2016, *Associazione Italia Nostra Onlus*, C-444/15, EU:C:2016:978.

1880 Parliament and Council Directive 2001/42/EC of 27 June 2001 on the assessment of the effects of certain plans and programmes on the environment (OJ L 197 p. 30) ('the SEA Directive'). An analysis of the spirit and content of the SEA Directive and an assessment of how it overlaps with the EIA Directive is available in: SHEATE W and others, *The Relationship between the EIA and SEA Directives* (Imperial College London Consultants, Final Report to the European Commission, 2005) <http://ec.europa.eu/environment/archives/eia/pdf/final_report_0508.pdf> accessed 29 April 2017.

vides that rights recognised by the Charter for which provision is made in the Treaties '*are to be exercised under the conditions and within the limits defined by those Treaties*', the Court did not deem necessary to conduct a separate assessment of validity in the light of Article 37 CFR and found that this provision had not been infringed either.[1881] This once more highlights the redundancy of the rights/principles distinction, as the connection between the Treaties and the Charter was sufficient to establish the impossibility to apply the Charter provision in the concrete case.

The case law on environmental impact assessment confirms the correlativity model and illustrates the two functions of individual rights in EU law: protecting individual interests and ensuring the effectiveness of EU (environmental) legislation. Relying on the latter rationale, the Court maintains its broad understanding of the notion of individual interest in the face of *Schutznorm* pressures in domestic legal systems.

2.3.2.3. The Aarhus Convention and EU Environmental procedural rights: broadening the notion of individual interest in domestic proceedings

The Aarhus Convention entails three 'pillars': access to environmental information, participation in the decision-making process, and access to effective judicial mechanisms.[1882] It was approved on behalf of the Community by Decision 2005/370.[1883] A set of directives – the so-called 'Aarhus Package' – was adopted in order to adapt existing directives to the AC.[1884] Directive 2003/4 provides for specific remedies for when the right of access to environmental information has been violated.[1885] Directive 2003/35 lays down the right of participation in decision-making processes, including in

---

1881 *Associazione Italia Nostra Onlus*, C-444/15, paras 62-63.

1882 C. Poncelet, 'Access to Justice in Environmental Matters - Does the European Union Comply with its Obligations?' (2012) 24 Journal of Environmental Law 287 288.

1883 Council Decision 2005/370/EC of 17 February 2005 on the conclusion, on behalf of the European Community, of the Convention on access to information, public participation in decision-making and access to justice in environmental matters (OJ L 124 p. 1).

1884 C. Poncelet, 'Access to Justice in Environmental Matters - Does the European Union Comply with its Obligations?' 289.

1885 Parliament and Council Directive 2003/4/EC of 28 January 2003 on public access to environmental information and repealing Council Directive 90/313/EEC (OJ L 041 p. 26).

those provided for by the EIA Directive.[1886] The Environmental Liability (EL) directive[1887] provides that citizens may submit requests to national authorities concerning possible environmental damage and by doing so contribute to preventing it (which constitutes a form of participation too). The transposition effort appears to have neglected the 'third pillar' concerning effective legal remedies.[1888] Therefore the question arises whether the AC itself may give rise to rights (especially rights of access to court) which individuals can rely on directly.

The first relevant case on this issue is the so-called 'Slovakian brown bears' case.[1889] Some economic operators had submitted applications for derogations or authorisations to get hunting licenses, access to protected areas or use of chemicals in these protected areas. The NGO Lesoochranáske zoskupenie VLK ('zoskupenie') applied to be a party to the administrative proceedings concerning these derogations and authorisations. The application was rejected and the zoskupenie lodged an appeal relying on Article 9(3) AC, which provides that '*each Party shall ensure that, where they meet the criteria, if any, laid down in its national law, members of the public have access to administrative or judicial procedures to challenge acts and omissions by private persons and public authorities which contravene provisions of its national law relating to the environment*'. In dispute was the possibility for individuals such as the zoskupenie to rely on this provision before national authorities. The Court started by stressing that the AC now forms '*an integral part of the legal order of the European Union*'.[1890] Since the AC covers an area where the EU and the Member States have mixed competence, the Court then had to check whether the EU had exercised its powers or not; in the latter case this would mean that the obligations deriving from 9(3) AC would still be covered by national law. The Court observed that environmental protection is an EU external competence under the Treaties and that the Habitats Directive[1891] is being relied on, which

1886 Parliament and Council Directive 2003/35/EC of 26 May 2003 (OJ L 156 p. 17).

1887 Parliament and Council Directive 2004/35/EC of 21 April 2004 on environmental liability with regard to the prevention and remedying of environmental damage (OJ L 43 p. 56) ('Environmental Liability Directive').

1888 Poncelet, 'Access to Justice in Environmental Matters - Does the European Union Comply with its Obligations?' 290.

1889 Judgment of 9 March 2011, *Lesoochranárske zoskupenie VLK v Ministerstvo životného prostredia Slovenskej republiky*, C-240/09, EU:C:2011:125.

1890 *Lesoochranárske zoskupenie VLK*, C-240/09, para 30.

1891 Council Directive 92/43/EEC of 21 May 1992 on the conservation of natural habitats and of wild fauna and flora (OJ L 206 p. 7) ('Habitats Directive').

means that the dispute falls within the scope of EU law.[1892] However, for the time being EU law only explicitly regulates, through the Aarhus Regulation,[1893] the application of Article 9(3) AC before EU institutions. Nevertheless, '*Where a provision can apply both to situations falling within the scope of national law and to situations falling within the scope of EU law, it is clearly in the interest of the latter that, in order to forestall future differences of interpretation, that provision should be interpreted uniformly, whatever the circumstances in which it is to apply*'.[1894] The Court therefore finds it relevant to assess the direct effect of Article 9(3) and recalls the classic criteria for assessing direct effect, applicable to international agreements of the EU: regard must be had to '*the purpose and nature of the agreement*' and the '*wording*' of the provision, which must contain '*a clear and precise obligation which is not subject, in its implementation or effects, to the adoption of any subsequent measure*'.[1895] The problem lies with the second part of the test, i.e. the wording of Article 9(3), which does not contain '*any clear and precise obligation capable of directly regulating the legal position of individuals. Since only members of the public who meet the criteria, if any, laid down by national law are entitled to exercise the rights provided for in Article 9(3), that provision is subject, in its implementation or effects, to the adoption of a subsequent measure.*'[1896] So, in itself, Article 9(3) AC has no direct effect.

There is however a way to mitigate the absence of direct effect of Article 9(3). The Court highlights that Member States have the responsibility of ensuring that the rights conferred on individuals by EU environmental law – in this case, the Habitats Directive – are effectively protected, especially with regard to the principles of equivalence and effectiveness.[1897] Therefore '*it is inconceivable that Article 9(3) of the Aarhus Convention be interpreted in such a way as to make it in practice impossible or excessively difficult to exercise*

1892 *Lesoochranárske zoskupenie VLK*, C-240/09, paras 32-38.

1893 Parliament and Council Regulation 1367/2006 of 6 September 2006 on the application of the provisions of the Aarhus Convention on Access to Information, Public Participation in Decision-making and Access to Justice in Environmental Matters to Community institutions and bodies (OJ L 264 p.13) ('Aarhus Regulation').

1894 *Lesoochranárske zoskupenie VLK*, C-240/09, para 42.

1895 *Lesoochranárske zoskupenie VLK*, C-240/09, para 44. Concerning the direct effect of international agreements see p. 251 of this work.

1896 *Lesoochranárske zoskupenie VLK*, C-240/09, para 45. See also Judgment of 15 March 2018, *North East Pylon Pressure Campaign and Sheehy*, C-470/16, EU:C:2018:185, para 52.

1897 *Lesoochranárske zoskupenie VLK*, C-240/09, para 47-48.

rights conferred by EU law'.[1898] This means that the national court should interpret its national law '*in a way which, to the fullest extent possible, is consistent with the objectives laid down in Article 9(3) of the Aarhus Convention*' and '*the objective of effective judicial protection of the rights conferred by EU law*' and in particular '*so as to enable an environmental protection organisation, such as the zoskupenie, to challenge before a court a decision taken following administrative proceedings liable to be contrary to EU environmental law*'.[1899] This case makes even clearer that the triggering of rights and accordingly of an effective remedy is not conditioned by the existence of a protective intention of individuals. The Habitats Directive aims to protect a variety of species, yet it grant rights to individuals (and especially NGOs). The Aarhus Convention thus reinforces the broad conception of interest as a trigger for application of rights. As such, it strengthens the effectiveness of the EU sectoral environmental legislation that developed in the previous decades by facilitating the claiming of the rights that arise from it.

These developments have renewed the debate and the judicial dialogue regarding the extent to which Member States might need to adapt their procedural systems in order to ensure the effective application of the rights (especially environmental rights) conferred by EU law. This question is intrinsically connected with that of how to reconcile diverging conceptions of a right. In *Bund für Umwelt und Naturschutz*, a case involving a German local branch of the Friends of the Earth NGO,[1900] the EU concept of a right again collided with the German conception of a subjective public right. A private company intended to construct a coal-fired power station and was delivered a partial permit for the project by the administration, based on the requirements on the EIA directive. Friends of the Earth initiated proceedings against this decision, based on substantive provisions from the Habitats Directive. Unsure how to assess the admissibility of the action, the administrative court lodged a reference for preliminary ruling on the interpretation of the EIA directive. The problem arose from the condition that, under German law, an action challenging an administrative measure is admissible only if that measure affects the claimant's individual public rights or interests, as clearly defined and delimited by the provision which is being relied on.[1901] So, as Advocate General Sharpston puts it

---

1898 *Lesoochranárske zoskupenie VLK*, C-240/09, para 49.

1899 *Lesoochranárske zoskupenie VLK*, C-240/09, para 50-51.

1900 Judgment of 12 May 2011, *Bund für Umwelt und Naturschutz Deutschland, Landesverband Nordrhein Westfalen*, C-115/09, EU:C:2011:289.

1901 *Bund für Umwelt und Naturschutz Deutschland, Landesverband Nordrhein Westfalen*, C-115/09, para 31.

(and as the German government admits), the right to a remedy depends upon the existence of individual substantive rights.[1902] Yet the relevant provisions of German environmental law are primarily aimed at the protection of the general public, not of individual rights. As a consequence, non-governmental organisations promoting environmental protection were in fact excluded from the possibility to rely before the courts on these provisions.[1903]

However, Article 10a of the directive, based on Article 9(2) AC, provides that the conditions for the admissibility of such actions may consist, at the national level, in one of the two following: either the existence of '*a sufficient interest in bringing the action*' or on the applicant alleging '*the impairment of a right*'. The EIA directive explicitly requires that environmental protection organisations must be regarded as fulfilling one of these conditions (depending on the condition adopted in the Member State). Therefore, the Court holds that these organisations must be entitled to access to court to challenge the legality of decisions which fall within the field of application of the directive. Therefore, Member States cannot deprive environmental protection organisations which fulfil the criteria of '*the opportunity of playing the role granted to them*' by the EIA directive interpreted in the light of the AC (the former being an implementation of the latter). Therefore, '*the concept of 'impairment of a right' cannot depend on conditions which only other physical or legal persons can fulfil*' and more generally '*the 'rights capable of being impaired' which the environmental protection organisations are supposed to enjoy must necessarily include the rules of national law implementing EU environment law and the rules of EU environment law having direct effect.*'[1904] In other words, with regard at least to environmental NGOs the Member State must allow for all rules of EU law giving rise to rights to also translate into rights for the purposes of applying the EAI directive in the national system. Although the Court insists that Member States have discretion in defining what constitutes a 'sufficient interest' or the 'impairment of a right' and may therefore maintain a system function-

1902 Opinion of AG Sharpston in *Bund für Umwelt und Naturschutz Deutschland, Landesverband Nordrhein Westfalen*, C-115/09, EU:C:2010:773, para 75.

1903 Only in some carefully limited cases, especially as regards associations for environmental protection, has a participation right been acknowledged as such. Voßkuhle and Kaiser, 'Grundwissen – Öffentliches Recht: Das subjektiv-öffentliche Recht' 18.

1904 *Bund für Umwelt und Naturschutz Deutschland, Landesverband Nordrhein Westfalen*, C-115/09, paras 42-48.

ing with a notion of 'subjective public rights',[1905] they must avoid a restrictive interpretation of this notion that would threaten the objective of ensuring wide access to justice.[1906] Having made this clear the Court assesses the direct effect of the applicable provisions of the Habitats Directive, and finds that since they are indeed '*unconditional and sufficiently precise*'[1907] individuals such as NGOs may rely on them '*even where, on the ground that the rules relied on protect only the interests of the general public and not the interests of individuals, national procedural law does not permit this.*'[1908]

This solution entailing a broad conception of individual interest has been extended recently in *Gruber.*[1909] The Court had to deal with the issue that under Austrian law, neighbours of an area affected by a project (here, the construction of a retail park) could not challenge an official decision that the project does not require an environmental impact assessment, nor object to the permission given for the project on the basis that it ought to have been subject to such an assessment. The Court was asked whether this was compatible with the EIA Directive. AG Kokott noted that the notion of 'concerned' persons, who can rely on the duty to conduct and EIA is often '*misunderstood*' as being so broad that it creates '*a potentially very wide category of possible right-holders*' and therefore might permit an *actio popularis.*[1910] This fear, expressed by the Austrian government at the oral hearing, is unfounded since the EIA directive does limit the notion of 'public concerned': Article 1(2)(e) defines this as the public '*affected or likely to be affected by, or having an interest in, the environmental decision-making*', and Article 1(2)(d) provides that the 'public' encompasses '*natural and legal persons*'. This means that the NGOs currently excluded by Austrian law from preliminary screening procedures concerning the necessity of an EIA must be allowed to participate in these procedures, but it does not mean that *anyone* may participate.[1911] The Court follows the AG's approach and relies copiously on *Bund für Umwelt und Naturschutz*: the EIA Directive must be

1905 *Bund für Umwelt und Naturschutz Deutschland, Landesverband Nordrhein Westfalen*, C-115/09, para 50.

1906 *Bund für Umwelt und Naturschutz Deutschland, Landesverband Nordrhein Westfalen*, C-115/09, paras 36 and 45.

1907 *Bund für Umwelt und Naturschutz Deutschland, Landesverband Nordrhein Westfalen*, C-115/09, para 54.

1908 *Bund für Umwelt und Naturschutz Deutschland, Landesverband Nordrhein Westfalen*, C-115/09, para 59.

1909 Judgment of 16 April 2015, *Gruber*, C-570/13, EU:C:2015:231.

1910 Opinion of AG Kokott in *Gruber*, C-570/13, EU:C:2014:2374, para 35. Thorson, *Individual Rights in EU Law* 305.

1911 Opinion of AG Kokott in *Gruber*, C-570/13, paras 35-42.

read in the light of the AC and although Member States have discretion as to how they define a 'sufficient interest' and the 'impairment of a right', this discretion is limited by '*the need to respect the objective of ensuring wide access to justice for the public concerned*' and therefore the exercise by Member States of their procedural autonomy cannot result in the exclusion of neighbours from the process of assessing the necessity of an EIA.[1912] *Gruber* thus maintains the same line as in *Bund für Umwelt und Naturschutz*, which required Member States to adopt a broad understanding of interest so that environmental NGOs would not be excluded from the decision-making process; here the same applies for individual neighbours of a property where a project is being developed.

A second case involving the Slovakian NGO Lesoochranáske zoskupenie VLK[1913] further explores the limits of Member State discretion on the determination of interest for the purposes of participation in decision-making on environmental issues. An undertaking had applied for an authorisation to build an enclosure in a special protection area for peregrine falcons. LZ applied to be party to the administrative authorisation procedure (this being the only way to contest a decision contrary to the Habitats Directive). It was denied that possibility and only granted the status of 'interested person' which allowed for much more limited participation. The authorisation was granted. While the zoskupenie could still appeal the authorisation, the question was whether EU law allowed for domestic rules of procedure which did not to provide the possibility to appeal the rejection of the status of party to procedure before the procedure was actually over. The Court dealt with this question by recalling the meta-principle of effectiveness of EU law which requires that directives (such as the Habitats Directive) may be relied on by individuals in legal proceedings and that '*the national courts be able to take that directive into consideration as an element of EU law in order, inter alia, to review whether a national authority which has granted an authorisation relating to a plan or project has complied with its obligations*' under the directive, '*and has thus kept within the limits of the discretion granted to the competent national authorities by that provision*'.[1914] In addition, Article 6(3) of the Habitats Directive '*provides that the competent national authorities, before agreeing to a plan or project as referred to in that provision, must, if appropriate, obtain the opinion of the general public. That provision must be read in conjunction with Article 6(1)(b) of the [AC], an instrument*

1912 *Gruber*, C-570/13, paras 34-44.
1913 *Lesoochranárske zoskupenie VLK*, C-243/15.
1914 *Lesoochranárske zoskupenie VLK*, C-243/15, para 44.

which forms an integral part of the EU legal order.' The latter provision confers on the public '*in particular, the right to participate 'effectively during the environmental decision-making' by submitting, 'in writing or, as appropriate, at a public hearing or inquiry with the applicant, any comments, information, analyses or opinions that it considers relevant to the proposed activity'.* There must be '*early public participation, when all options are open and effective public participation can take place*'.[1915] Since the zoskupenie falls within the concept of 'public concerned' in the sense of the AC, it '*derives*' a '*right to participate*' from Article 6 AC.[1916] Then the Court reads Article 9(2) AC in the light of Article 19(1) TEU and Article 47 CFR and finds that this provision '*limits the discretion available to the Member States when determining the detailed rules for the legal actions which it envisages*'.[1917] Therefore NGOs '*must be able to rely*' on rules of national law implementing EU environmental law and on rules of EU environmental law having direct effect.[1918] Finally, having conceded that '*in the absence of EU rules governing the matter, it is for the domestic legal system of each Member State to lay down the detailed procedural rules governing actions for safeguarding rights which individuals derive from EU law, the Member States being responsible for ensuring that those rights are effectively protected in each case*',[1919] the Court actually assesses whether the Slovakian mechanism of interested party is sufficient, and finds it is not. This case is therefore yet another instance of how the requirement of effectiveness of EU environmental law, materialising in substantial and procedural rights, requires adjustments to the principle of the procedural autonomy of Member States.[1920]

As part of the 'Aarhus Package', the Environmental Liability Directive is an important element in the transversal legislation on environmental protection that ensures compliance with the sectoral legislation. This directive explicitly codifies the right of individuals and NGOs to request action by the competent authorities and to ask for judicial review of inaction.[1921] So far there are very few cases (less than 20) on the EL directive. Several of

1915 *Lesoochranárske zoskupenie VLK*, C-243/15, paras 45-46.

1916 *Lesoochranárske zoskupenie VLK*, C-243/15, paras 46-47.

1917 *Lesoochranárske zoskupenie VLK*, C-243/15, para 58.

1918 *Lesoochranárske zoskupenie VLK*, C-243/15, paras 59-60.

1919 *Lesoochranárske zoskupenie VLK*, C-243/15, para 65.

1920 S. Xefteri, 'Note d'actualité droit de l'environnement de l'UE 1/2017', Blogdroiteuropeen, février 2017, <http://wp.me/p6OBGR-1Cl> accessed 30 April 2017.

1921 B. Van den Broek and L. Enneking, 'Public Interest Litigation in the Netherlands. A Multidimensional Take on the Promotion of Environmental Interests by Private Parties through the Courts' (2014) 10 Utrecht Law Review 77 80. See also R.K.L. Tham, 'The Impact of the Environmental Liability Directive

these result from Commission actions for failure to correctly transpose the directive[1922] and most cases do not deal with rights. One case, that of Mr *Folk*, deserves closer attention here.

Mr *Folk*[1923] has fishing rights in the river Mürz downstream from a hydroelectric powerplant. The activity of the powerplant causes decrease of the fish population, which damages Mr Folk's business. One of the questions from the referring court is whether Articles 12 and 13 of the EL Directive preclude a national provision which does not allow persons holding fishing rights to initiate a review procedure ('the Article 13 review procedure') in relation to environmental damage as defined in Article 2(1)(b) of that directive. Indeed, the applicable Austrian law provisions do not mention fishing rights and therefore exclude the possibility for holders of such rights from lodging an environmental complaint in respect of damage relating to their fishing rights. Article 12(1) of the EL directive, entitled 'Request for action', lists three categories of persons entitled to submit observations on environmental damage and request the authorities to take action: persons '*affected or likely to be affected*' by such damage, persons '*having a sufficient interest in environmental decision-making*' relating to the damage, or persons '*alleging the impairment of a right*', where domestic administrative procedural law requires it as a precondition. The provision allows the Member States discretion to determine what constitutes a '*sufficient interest*' and the '*impairment of a right*'. This naturally poses a problem, for it could be interpreted as meaning that Member States are free to restrict standing according to a *Schutznorm* approach (which is exactly the interpretation put forward by the Austrian government). However, the Court finds that the Member States do not have discretion as regards the right to a review procedure for all three categories of persons listed in Article 12(1), and observes that persons holding fishing rights are able to come within all three categories and must therefore be granted standing.[1924] This solu-

---

2004/35 on English Law' Exeter Papers in European Law No 14 <http://law.exeter.ac.uk/cels/eupapers.shtml> accessed 19 May 2016.

1922 Judgment of 22 December 2008, *Commission v Finland*, C-328/08, EU:C:2008:775; Judgment of 11 December 2008, *Commission v France*, C-330/08, EU:C:2008:720; Judgment of 24 March 2009, *Commission v Luxembourg*, C-331/08, EU:C:2009:185; Judgment of 19 May 2009, *Commission v Greece*, C-368/08, EU:C:2009:326; Judgment of 12 March 2009, *Commission v Slovenia*, C-402/08, EU:C:2009:157; Judgment of 18 June 2009, *Commission v United Kingdom*, C-417/08, EU:C:2009:384; Judgment of 11 September 2014, *Commission v Germany*, C-525/12, EU:C:2014:2202.

1923 Judgment of 1 June 2017, *Folk*, C-529/15, EU:C:2017:419.

1924 *Folk*, C-529/15, paras 54-56.

tion is perfectly consistent with the Court's classic approach of allowing individuals (including NGOs) interested in the fulfilment of obligations laid down in EU environmental obligations to contribute to the enforcement of these obligations.

The question is then whether there is indeed procedural autonomy left in the implementation of environmental rights. In fact, it is doubtful whether the CJEU's approach leaves any 'discretion' to the Member States in this area. Where they choose to use the 'impairment of a right' criterion in order to determine access to court based on Article 9(2) AC they are required to admit that NGOs may be holders of rights even though the domestic conception of a right might preclude it – the assumption being that environmental NGOs have an interest in the fulfilment of obligations laid down in EU environmental legislation. The broad understanding of interest, as component of the EU concept of right, thus trumps the restrictive conception of a protected interest that determines access to court in systems such as the German or Austrian – not only when it comes to assessing the standing of environmental NGOs,[1925] but also that of private individuals (e.g. neighbours to a site where a project will be developed). This is after all, in line with the 1991 *Commission v Germany* cases,[1926] and the more recent *Commission v Germany* case from 2015 shows the difficulty in implementing this approach in the German system.[1927] The persisting resistance is commensurate with the far-reaching implications of a solution which entails, at least to a certain extent, substituting the EU concept of a right for the domestic one, if this is necessary for domestic remedies to ensure the respect of EU rights (which it is, precisely, in systems where the existence of a remedy is determined by the existence of a 'protected interest').

The post-Aarhus case law on environmental rights thus follows the Court's previously established logic of relying on a broad array of individual interests in order to translate into effective rights the obligations laid

1925 Case *Djurgården-Lilla Värtans Miljöskyddsförening* had allowed for the criteria for identifying such NGOs to be laid down by national law (for instance, the requirement that the association would have as its object the protection of the environment), but made clear that these criteria must be limited to what is necessary for the purposes of verification and cannot nullify the protective EU provisions. Judgment of 15 October 2009, *Djurgården-Lilla Värtans Miljöskyddsförening*, C-263/08, EU:C:2009:631, para 45. See also M. Dougan, 'Who Exactly Benefits from the Treaties? The Murky Interaction Between Union and National Competence over the Capacity to Enforce EU Law' 103.

1926 *Commission v Germany*, C-131/88, *Commission v Germany*, C-59/89, and *Commission v Germany*, C-58/89. See p. 434 of this work.

1927 *Commission v Germany*, C-137/14.

down in EU environmental law. When these rights are claimed before national courts, the Court of Justice stretches this logic so far that it could almost be thought to be favourable to an *actio popularis* – at the very least, the possibility of it does not seem to curb its support for the increasingly prominent role of individuals in the enforcement of EU environmental law within the legal systems of the Member States. This approach must now be contrasted with what happens when individuals attempt to play the same part on the EU level, through direct challenge of EU acts.

2.3.2.4. The Aarhus Regulation and the persisting rights deficit on the EU level

When it comes to claiming environmental rights against the acts or actions of EU institutions, unfortunately there is not really a before and an after Aarhus. The landmark case on standing before EU Courts in environmental matters remains *Greenpeace*, which is simply an application of the *Plaumann* restrictive interpretation of the criterion of individual concern.[1928] The so-called Aarhus Regulation (AR) from 2006 was supposed to implement the AC's requirement concerning effective remedies, especially by providing NGOs with the possibility to activate the internal review mechanism set out at Article 10(1) AR.[1929] However, the substantive scope of this procedure is limited to '*an administrative act adopted under environmental law, or an alleged administrative omission (to adopt such an act)*'. Article 2(1)(g) AR defines administrative acts '*any measure of individual scope under environmental law, taken by a Community institution or body, and having a legally binding and external effect*'. This also has the effect of restricting the scope of the internal review mechanism, since the term '*individual*' ex-

1928 Judgment of 2 April 1998, *Greenpeace and Others v Commission*, C-321/95 P, EU:C:1998:153. A comparable problem was ruled on by the General Court in Order of 22 December 1995, *Danielsson and Others v Commission*, T-219/95, EU:T:1995:219, where the applicants were challenging a Commission decision that consented to French nuclear tests in the Pacific Ocean, and the Court found that they were not individually concerned by the decision (see in particular paras 68 and 76).

1929 M. Schaap and R. Imbers, 'Access to environmental justice for NGOs: interplay between the Aarhus Convention, the EU Lisbon Treaty and the European Convention on Human Rights' in A. Jakubowski, K. Wierczy Ska and K. Wierczyńska (eds), *Fragmentation vs the Constitutionalisation of International Law: A Practical Inquiry* (Routledge 2016) 248.

cludes from the mechanism most environmental decisions.[1930] As we shall now see, the Court has done nothing to advance an interpretation of either Article 263(4) TFEU or Article 10(1) AR that would allow for environmental rights to be as effectively protected against the acts of the EU as they are against the acts of the Member States.

Shortly after the entry into force of the EL Directive, two NGOs tried to challenge two Commission decisions which led to the extension of the use of certain plant protection chemicals in some Member States. They advanced a series of arguments in favour of the admissibility of their action for annulment. First, they argued that as environmental NGOs they should automatically have standing in actions for annulment of acts entailing a potential setback in terms of environmental protection. This argument, of course, had little chance of being accepted by the Court, especially starting from the UPA position that it would be necessary to assess whether '*the applicants are concerned by the (...) decisions by reason of certain attributes peculiar to them or there is a factual situation which differentiates them from all other persons in relation to those decisions*'.[1931] And indeed the Court did not depart from its *UPA* line and rejected this first argument.[1932] Secondly, the applicants relied on the EL Directive and argued that as NGOs promoting environmental protection and meeting the requirements under national law they should be '*entitled to submit observations to the competent authority and to request that authority to take action under that directive*', and therefore also have standing to bring an action for annulment in the case at hand. However, the Court held that 'competent authorities' in the EL Directive were exclusively national authorities and the procedural rights provided for by the EL Directive could not be relied upon against EU institutions.[1933] The applicants also argued that their special consultative status should translate into a given procedural guarantee, but the Court denied that there was anything in the legal framework supporting this claim and added that '*Community law, as it now stands, does not provide for a right to*

1930 Schoukens, 'Access to Justice in Environmental Cases after the Rulings of the Court of Justice of 13 January 2015: Kafka Revisited?' 50-51; Poncelet, 'Access to Justice in Environmental Matters - Does the European Union Comply with its Obligations?' 303-306.

1931 Order of 28 November 2005, *EEB and Stichting Natuur en Milieu v Commission*, T-236/04 and T-241/04, EU:T:2005:426, paras 52-53.

1932 *EEB and Stichting Natuur en Milieu v Commission*, T-236/04 and T-241/04, para 56.

1933 *EEB and Stichting Natuur en Milieu v Commission*, T-236/04 and T-241/04, para 59.

bring a class action before the Community courts'.[1934] Finally the applicants had claimed that they should be granted standing based on the principle of effective judicial protection and here again the Court maintained its *UPA* line.[1935] The action was dismissed because applicants could not manage to prove individual concern – or to convince the Court to redefine this criterion.[1936] This case is therefore an explicit rejection of the possibility of an environmental actio popularis and an illustration that the necessary individualisation of interests as a condition of access to court causes serious issues in an area such as environmental law where many interests are inherently *not* individualisable.

The criterion of direct concern is also a problem for environmental NGOs trying to access the EU courts, as exemplified by the General Court's order in a case where several NGOs were challenging a Commission implementing regulation approving the substance sulfoxaflor as an ingredient of plant protection products.[1937] The GC held that the implementing regulation had '*neither the purpose nor the consequence of granting rights or imposing obligations on subjects other than the Member States and the potential applicants for authorisations to place products on the market*'.[1938] In addition, the GC assessed whether there could be direct concern of each separate applicant, given that they were putting forward different arguments. One of the applicants was an association of beekeepers who argued that by threatening bee populations the regulation was infringing the right to property and freedom to conduct a business of its members. The GC held that these rights were not directly at stake and that they might be infringed at the stage where Member States would issue authorisation for products containing sulfoxaflor; therefore, the members of the beekeeping association were not directly concerned by the regulation.[1939] The other two applicants were environmental protection organisations who argued

1934 *EEB and Stichting Natuur en Milieu v Commission*, T-236/04 and T-241/04, paras 62-63.

1935 *EEB and Stichting Natuur en Milieu v Commission*, T-236/04 and T-241/04, paras 65-68.

1936 See also Order of 2 June 2008, *WWF-UK v Council*, T-91/07, 2008 II-00081*, para 88, confirmed by Order of 5 May 2009, *WWF-UK v Council*, C-355/08 P, EU:C:2009:286.

1937 Commission Implementing Regulation (EU) No 540/2011 of 25 May 2011 implementing Regulation (EC) No 1107/2009 of the European Parliament and of the Council as regards the list of approved active substances (OJ L 153 p. 1).

1938 Order of 28 September 2016, *PAN Europe and Others v Commission*, T-600/15, EU:T:2016:601, para 27.

1939 *PAN Europe and Others v Commission*, T-600/15, paras 31-36.

that the regulation was impacting the objectives of their Europe-wide campaign on the protection of bees against insecticides. The GC recalled settled case law according to which environmental NGOs '*are entitled to effective judicial protection of the rights they derive from the EU legal order, but the right to such protection cannot call into question the conditions laid down for all natural or legal persons in the fourth paragraph of Article 263 TFEU*'[1940] and noted that, although they have a right to conduct their campaigns, they '*have no right, in the legal order of the European Union, that protects the objectives of their campaigns from being influenced by acts of the European Union*'. The impact of the regulation on their campaign could therefore only be 'factual', not 'legal'.[1941] Therefore they were not directly concerned by the regulation either. The reasoning of the GC here is strangely reminiscent of the *Schutznorm* approach that the Court so relentlessly dismisses when domestic courts seek to apply it: it seems like only a legally protected interest (as opposed to a 'factual' one) could allow for a right to be identified.

Once the absence of direct concern is established, the GC goes through the other arguments brought forward by the applicants. Article 37 CFR '*contains a principle providing for a general obligation on the European Union in respect of the objectives to be pursued in the framework of its policies, and not a right to bring actions in environmental matters before the Courts of the European Union*' and as a 'principle' in the meaning of Article 52(5) it does not give rise to direct claims.[1942] Article 47 CFR '*is not intended to change the system of judicial review laid down by the Treaties*'. Finally, the AC, as an international agreement, prevails over EU secondary legislation but not over primary legislation, including Article 263 TFEU.[1943] The lockdown is complete with the GC pointing out that '*the applicants have failed to demonstrate that the fourth paragraph of Article 263 TFEU, as interpreted by the Courts of the European Union, was incompatible with Article 9(3) of the Aarhus Convention. It is, in fact, the Aarhus Convention itself, when it refers to members of the public who 'meet the criteria, if any, laid down [in] national law', which makes the rights that Article 9(3) is supposed to give to members of the public conditional upon meeting the eligibility criteria arising under the fourth paragraph of Ar-*

1940 *PAN Europe and Others v Commission*, T-600/15, para 39. See also Order of 24 September 2009, *Município de Gondomar* v *Commission*, C-501/08 P, EU:C:2009:580, para 38 and Order of 13 March 2015, *European Coalition to End Animal Experiments* v *ECHA*, T-673/13, EU:T:2015:167, para 63.

1941 *PAN Europe and Others v Commission*, T-600/15, para 40.

1942 *PAN Europe and Others v Commission*, T-600/15, para 47-48.

1943 *PAN Europe and Others v Commission*, T-600/15, paras 53-56.

ticle 263 TFEU'.[1944] The GC thus grants the EU much more discretion to define these criteria, than Member States are allowed according to the case law analysed in the previous section.

The internal review mechanism of Article 10(1) AR has not been the object of much litigation so far[1945] but for now it does not appear to mitigate the shortcomings of Article 263 TFEU, although the General Court initially attempted to read it in such a way. In the *Vereniging Milieudefensie* case, the Commission had accepted that the Netherlands postpone the deadline for attaining limit values for nitrogen dioxide in certain areas. The Vereniging Milieudefensie submitted a request for internal review (under Article 10(1) AR) of the acceptance decision. The 'individual scope' criterion was however not fulfilled and the request was therefore rejected. The NGO challenged the rejection before the General Court, which held that, since Article 10(1) AR was an implementation of Article 9(3) AC, the former could be reviewed in light of the latter.[1946] This was based on the *Nakajima* exception according to which, where a regulation is intended to implement an obligation imposed on the EU institutions under an international treaty, the CJEU must be able to review the legality of that regulation in the light of the international treaty without having to assess first the direct effect of the provision.[1947] The GC found that the restriction of the applicability of the review mechanism to acts of individual scope violated Article 9(3) AC. In another case, two other NGOs, Stichting Natuur en Milieu and Pesticide Action Network, requested an internal review of a regulation setting certain maximum residue levels in certain products.[1948] The Commission again rejected the request, also because the regulation was not an 'administrative act', i.e. a 'measure of individual scope' within the meaning of the AR. The GC likewise held that on that point the AR incorrectly imple-

1944 *PAN Europe and Others v Commission*, T-600/15, para 60.

1945 As of May 2017, only a dozen cases of the Court of Justice and General Court refer to Article 10 AR.

1946 Judgment of 14 June 2012, *Vereniging Milieudefensie and Stichting Stop Luchtverontreiniging Utrecht v Commision*, T-396/09, EU:T:2012:301, para 58.

1947 *Vereniging Milieudefensie and Stichting Stop Luchtverontreiniging Utrecht v Commision*, T-396/09, para 54; *Nakajima All Precision v Council*, C-69/89. See on the direct effect of international agreements, p. 251 of this work.

1948 Commission Regulation (EC) No 149/2008 of 29 January 2008 amending Regulation (EC) No 396/2005 of the European Parliament and of the Council by establishing Annexes II, III and IV setting maximum residue levels for products covered by Annex I thereto (OJ L 58 p. 1).

mented Article 9(3) AC, because it excluded the Commission's regulatory activities from the scope of the review mechanism.[1949]

On appeal against the GC's ruling in *Vereniging Milieudefensie*, the Court dismissed the General Court's application of the *Nakajima* rationale and held that '*the effects, within the EU legal order, of provisions of an agreement concluded by the European Union with non-member States may not be determined without taking account of the international origin of the provisions in question*'; therefore the assessment must be made on the basis '*of the agreement's spirit, general scheme or terms*'.[1950] The Court recalled its established case law according to which an international agreement could be relied on by individuals '*only where, first, the nature and the broad logic of that agreement do not preclude it and, secondly, those provisions appear, as regards their content, to be unconditional and sufficiently precise*'.[1951] Consistently with its findings from the Slovakian brown bears case,[1952] the Court held that Article 9(3) AC did not contain an unconditional and sufficiently precise obligation '*capable of directly regulating the legal position of individuals*', especially given that only members of the public who met the criteria laid down in national law were entitled to exercise the rights provided for in Article 9(3).[1953] The Court finally quashed the GC's judgment and dismissed the action. The same went for the action against the GC's judgment in *Sticht-*

1949 Judgment of 14 June 2012, *Stichting Natuur en Milieu and Pesticide Action Network Europe v Commission*, T-338/08, EU:T:2012:300, para 70.

1950 *Council and Others v Vereniging Milieudefensie and Stichting Stop Luchtverontreiniging Utrecht*, Joined cases C-401/12 P to C-403/12 P, para 53.

1951 *Council and Others v Vereniging Milieudefensie and Stichting Stop Luchtverontreiniging Utrecht*, Joined cases C-401/12 P to C-403/12 P, para 54 and case law quoted, especially: *Intertanko and Others*, C-308/06, para 45; *FIAMM and Others v Council and Commission*, C-120/06 P and C-121/06 P, paras 110 and 120; *Air Transport Association of America and Others*, C-366/10, para 54.

1952 *Lesoochranárske zoskupenie VLK*, C-240/09, para 44.

1953 *Council and Others v Vereniging Milieudefensie and Stichting Stop Luchtverontreiniging Utrecht*, C-401/12 P to C-403/12 P, para 55. In a later case the GC acknowledged this solution and dismissed an action for annulment challenging the rejection of a request for review of a decision that did not constitute a measure of general application: Judgment of 29 June 2015, *Frank Bold Society v Commission*, T-19/13, EU:T:2015:520, para 36. See also Order of 17 July 2015, *European Environmental Bureau*, T-565/14, EU:T:2015:559, para 33, confirming that 'administrative acts' in the meaning of the AR cannot be understood as encompassing measures of general application.

ing Natuur en Milieu and PAN Europe.[1954] As observed by Schoukens, the result is particularly disturbing because there is no doubt that the AR intended to implement the EU's obligations under the AC – even judging just from the title of the Regulation: '*on the application of the provisions of*' the AC.[1955] The problem is that in this situation, unlike in the Slovakian brown bears case, there is no such thing as an obligation of consistent interpretation to make up for the absence of direct effect.

The Court maintains a consistent line between its case law on the internal review mechanism and its case law on the action for annulment, as the *ClientEarth v Commission* ruling issued a few months later illustrates.[1956] ClientEarth had challenged a decision refusing access to certain documents on the conformity of the legislation of various Member States with EU environmental law. At stake was the conformity of Article 4(2) of Regulation 1049/2001[1957] with the AC. It was even less difficult here for the Court to find that the challenged EU law provision was not an implementation of the AC and that therefore the *Nakajima* exception was not applicable.[1958] Again the Court relied on the criteria of unconditionality and precision and ruled out the possibility for the appellant (ClientEarth) to rely on Article 4(4)(c) AC.[1959] This judgment is also relevant for information rights outside the scope of environmental law and will therefore be further analysed in Section 2.3.3, but it does confirm the *Vereniging Milieudefensie* ruling and it likewise illustrates the restriction that arises from assimilating the direct effect of a provision of international (environmental) law with its ability to serve as a basis for legality review.[1960]

1954 Judgment of 13 January 2015, *Council and Commission v Stichting Natuur en Milieu and Pesticide Action Network Europe*, EU:C:2015:5, Joined cases C-404/12 P and C-405/12 P, EU:C:2015:5.

1955 Schoukens, 'Access to Justice in Environmental Cases after the Rulings of the Court of Justice of 13 January 2015: Kafka Revisited?' 58.

1956 Judgment of 16 July 2015, *ClientEarth v. Commission*, C-612/13 P, EU:C:2015:486.

1957 Parliament and Council Regulation of 30 May 2001 regarding public access to European Parliament, Council and Commission documents (OJ L 145, 31/05/2001 p. 43-48).

1958 *ClientEarth v. Commission*, C-612/13 P, paras 36-37.

1959 *ClientEarth v. Commission*, C-612/13 P, para 42. See also Opinion of AG Cruz Villalón in *ClientEarth v Commission*, C-612/13 P, EU:C:2015:218, paras 67-69.

1960 B. Pirker, 'Cases C-401 to 403/12 and C-404 to 405/12: no review of legality in light of the Aarhus Convention' 29 January 2015, available at http://europeanlawblog.eu/2015/01/29/cases-c-401-to-40312-and-c-404-to-40512-no-review-of-legality-in-light-of-the-aarhus-convention/ (accessed 26 April 2017).

The limited impact of the existence of the internal review mechanism in terms of effective protection of rights is not only due to the restrictive criteria that give access to the procedure, but also to the restrictive nature of the procedure itself. This was illustrated in a case concerning a Commission decision authorising the marketing of GMOs for animal feed. Three NGOs had asked for internal review of this decision but the request was rejected. They subsequently lodged an action for annulment against that rejection, relying on Regulation 1829/2003 on genetically modified food and feed.[1961] The GC first noted that the AR did not give a right to challenge the legality of the authorisation decision but only to challenge the refusal to perform an internal review of that decision.[1962] Concerning the grounds that applicants must indicate in a request for review, given that the access of NGOs '*to relevant information is usually restricted to information that is publicly available*' requiring them to prove the illegality of the decision would be placing too heavy a burden on them; instead it is sufficient that they bring forward '*a set of material raising serious doubts as to the lawfulness of the authorisation decision*'.[1963] However, the substantial review is then limited because of the Commission's broad discretion, which is why on the part of the substantial pleas that were admissible, the GC controlled only whether there had been manifest errors of assessment and eventually dismissed the action.[1964] This is of course one of the limits of procedural environmental rights – that even when they apply they do not guarantee a certain outcome on the substance. When their application is severely restricted, the chances of obtaining a result on the substance are all the more limited.

Unsurprisingly given all these restrictions, the Aarhus Convention Compliance Committee (the body monitoring the implementation of the AC) has found that neither the mechanism of action for annulment under Article 263 TFEU nor the mechanism of internal review provided for by the AR, under their current interpretation and application by the CJEU, constitute appropriate implementation of the AC's third pillar.[1965] Environmental protection NGOs are thus caught between a rock and a hard place:

1961 Parliament and Council Regulation 1829/2003 of 22 September 2003 on genetically modified food and feed (OJ L 268 p. 1).

1962 Judgment of 15 December 2016, *TestBioTech and Others v Commission*, T-177/13, EU:T:2016:736, paras 66-70.

1963 *TestBioTech and Others v Commission*, T-177/13, para 88.

1964 Xefteri, 'Note d'actualité droit de l'environnement de l'UE 1/2017' 10-12.

1965 ACCC Findings and Recommendations with regard to Communication ACCC/C/2008/32 (Part II) Concerning Compliance by the European Union, as

on the one hand, they face the challenge of having to prove at least direct concern, if not individual *and* direct concern, before being admitted to claim environmental rights; on the other hand, the review mechanism that relieves them of this burden only allows for review of a limited range of acts, i.e. only acts of individual scope. The Court's refusal to depart from its restrictive interpretation of Article 263(4) TFEU is not specific to environmental law; it is consistent with a position already assessed and criticised in this study.[1966] The restrictive interpretation of the criteria laid down in Article 10 AR, however, could have been avoided without requiring adjustments of the Court's stance on Article 263(4).

Besides the General Court's suggestion discussed above in *Vereniging Milieudefensie* and *Stichting Natuur en Milieu*, a solution was also proposed by Advocate General Jääskinen, who in his Opinion in *Vereniging Milieudefensie* has suggested that the assessment of the direct effect of an international agreement and the ability of its provisions to be used for legality review should be decoupled. This would allow to accept that while Article 9(3) does not create individual rights (as made clear in the Slovakian brown bears case),[1967] it still creates a clear obligation on the EU authorities, in the light of which Article 10 AR could be reviewed.[1968] The AG indeed noted that '*the obligation to guarantee access to justice*' enshrined in Article 9(3) '*is sufficiently clear to preclude a rule which would have the object or the effect of removing certain categories of non-legislative decisions taken by public*

adopted on 17 March 2017 (advance unedited version). See also the commentary by B. Pirker, 'Implementation of the Aarhus Convention by the EU - an Inconvenient Truth from the Compliance Committee' 24 April 2017 <http://europeanlawblog.eu/2017/04/24/implementation-of-the-aarhus-convention-by-the-eu-an-inconvenient-truth-from-the-compliance-committee/> accessed 30 April 2017. The ACCC had previously suggested that the new wording of Article 263(4) TFEU could provide '*a possible means for ensuring compliance*' with Article 9 AC: ACCC Findings and Recommendations with regard to Communication ACCC/C/2008/32 (Part I), ECE/MP.PP/C.1/2011/4/Add.1, 24 August 2011, para 91.

1966 See p. 212 of this work.

1967 *Lesoochranárske zoskupenie VLK*, C-240/09, para 45.

1968 Opinion of AG Jääskinen in Council and Others v Vereniging Milieudefensie and Stichting Stop Luchtverontreiniging Utrecht, C-401/12 P to C-403/12 P, EU:C:2014:310. See a commentary of this Opinion by Schoukens, 'Access to Justice in Environmental Cases after the Rulings of the Court of Justice of 13 January 2015: Kafka Revisited?' 61.

authorities from the scope of the review to be conducted by the national courts.'[1969] In fact, this conclusion may be reached without decoupling rights from obligations.[1970] Direct effect is always a matter of assessing the applicability of a norm in a concrete case: it may contain a sufficiently precise obligation and therefore a correlative right for the purposes of one specific case but not for another. We have seen this in a number of cases such as *Defrenne II*,[1971] and more recently in the case law on Article 27 CFR, the ability of which to give rise to rights is contingent on the specifics of each concrete case.[1972] There is no reason why the provisions of the AC, forming '*an integral part of the EU legal system*',[1973] should not function in the same way and thus, where practically applicable, be used to review provisions of EU secondary law such as those of the AR.[1974] This solution relying on the classic correlativity model (instead of departing from it as AG Jääskinen suggests) would allow to identify at least some aspects of the internal review mechanism that may be contrary to the obligations and correlative rights laid down in the AC – mainly, as Jääskinen rightly points out, the exclusion of some non-legislative acts from the scope of review.

For the time being, it appears that the signing of the Aarhus Convention has not led the Court to relax the standing conditions for action for annulment in environmental matters. The repeatedly denounced flaws of the system of remedies before the EU courts are exacerbated in the field of environmental law, where proving an individual interest is often very difficult. And the restrictive conditions for access to the internal review mechanism laid down in the Aarhus Regulations certainly do not supplement the gaps in protection left by Article 263 TFEU. Against this backdrop, there remains a risk that, in the enforcement of EU environmental law, not all interests would be taken into account, i.e. environmental interest groups would not have the means of contributing to the enforcement of EU envi-

1969 Opinion of AG Jääskinen in Council and Others v Vereniging Milieudefensie and Stichting Stop Luchtverontreiniging Utrecht, C-401/12 P to C-403/12 P, EU:C:2014:310, paras 90-95.

1970 See Opinion of AG Kokott in *East Sussex City Council*, C-71/14, EU:C:2015:234, para. 41 where she emphasises this symmetry: The Aarhus Convention '*establishes a set of environmental obligations (and corresponding rights for the public)*'.

1971 *Defrenne v SABENA*, C-43/75.

1972 See p. 351 of this work.

1973 *Lesoochranárske zoskupenie VLK*, C-240/09, para 30.

1974 As the GC held in *European Environmental Bureau*, T-565/14, para 31: The AC '*has primacy over secondary Community legislation*' and the AR '*must be interpreted in conformity with that convention*'.

ronmental law because there is no strictly speaking 'individual' interest in doing so.[1975]

2.3.2.5. Interim conclusions

The case law concerning environmental rights claimed by individuals in their national courts is very encouraging in the sense that the Court of Justice has defended in this context a broad conception of interest, making it easier for individuals (especially, but not only, environmental NGOs) to claim the rights that they derive from EU environmental legislation. These developments, however, also highlight the discrepancy between the protection of environmental rights on the domestic and EU levels.[1976] The ACCC has rightly pointed out that it is insufficient to rely on the enforcement of individual environmental rights within the legal systems of Member States while such effective enforcement is not made possible where acts of the EU itself are at stake.[1977]

Because the push for more environmental protection came from outside the EU with the signature of an international agreement, the observed per-

---

1975 The risk was already pointed out in 2001 by Prechal and Hancher, 'Individual Environmental Rights: Conceptual Pollution in EU Environmental Law?' 105.

1976 H. Schoukens, 'Access to Justice in Environmental Cases after the Rulings of the Court of Justice of 13 January 2015: Kafka Revisited?' 62; Pirker, 'Cases C-401 to 403/12 and C-404 to 405/12: no review of legality in light of the Aarhus Convention'; A.J.C. Roger, 'A lost opportunity for improving access to justice in environmental matters: the CJEU on the invocability of the Aarhus Convention', 15 February 2015, available at http://eulawanalysis.blogspot.lu/2015/02/a-lost-opportunity-for-improving-access.html (accessed 26 April 2017); Poncelet, 'Access to Justice in Environmental Matters - Does the European Union Comply with its Obligations?'.

1977 '*While the system of judicial review in the national courts of the EU Member States and the request for preliminary ruling is a significant element for ensuring consistent application and proper implementation of EU law in the Member States, it cannot be a basis for generally denying members of the public access to the EU Courts to challenge decisions, acts and omissions by EU institutions and bodies. Nor does the system of preliminary review amount to appellate system with regard to decisions, acts and omissions by the EU institutions and bodies. Thus, with respect to decisions, acts and omissions of EU institutions and bodies, the system of preliminary ruling does neither in itself meet the requirements of access to justice in article 9 of the Convention nor compensate for the strict jurisprudence of the EU Courts*'. European Union ACCC/C/2008/32 (Part I), ECE/MP.PP/C.1/2011/4/Add.1, May 2011, para. 90.

sisting discrepancy in the protection of rights between the national and EU levels also sheds additional light on the weaknesses of the EU concept of a right, especially at the interface between EU and international law. The CJEU has welcomed the Aarhus Convention in so far as it has contributed to reinforcing the grip of EU law on the legal systems of Member States, and especially by constraining Member States into departing from the *Schutznorm* approach to rights and adopting an ever broader conception of individual interest. This allows the classic model to flourish according to the mechanism of functional subjectivation: EU environmental obligations can be claimed as rights by individuals who have an interest in the fulfilment of these obligations. By contrast, the CJEU has not been very receptive to the AC as an exogenous source of rights to be claimed against the EU institutions. It seems that the Court fails to see the 'effectiveness' rationale of rights in this context, seeing them only as a threat to the action of the EU institutions, which would explain why it prefers to minimise the array of interests that may give rise to rights. Yet it should be pointed out that the procedural rights arising from the AC are meant to be used to ensure the effective enforcement by individuals of EU environmental legislation. As the Court itself in the Slovakian brown bears case put it: '*it is inconceivable that Article 9(3) of the Aarhus Convention be interpreted in such a way as to make it in practice impossible or excessively difficult to exercise rights conferred by EU law*'.[1978]

2.3.3. Information rights

'*Applicants who defend the interest of all of us can never stand out*'.[1979]

Transparency became a prominent stake in the EU in the early 1990s with the Danish rejection of the Maastricht Treaty, followed by a narrow acceptance of it in France. In response to these votes which were interpreted as expressing distrust of the EU and its institutions, measures were taken to enhance the transparency of the EU institutions, especially through the de-

1978 The irony was also pointed out by Roger, 'A lost opportunity for improving access to justice in environmental matters: the CJEU on the invocability of the Aarhus Convention'.

1979 Van Wolferen, 'The Limits to the CJEU's Interpretation of Locus Standi, a Theoretical Framework' 919.

velopment of the right of access to documents.[1980] Following the Interinstitutional declaration on democracy, transparency, and subsidiarity issued in 1993,[1981] the Council and Commission each adopted decisions granting individuals a general right of access to their documents.[1982] This was then formalised in the Treaty of Amsterdam, which included a 'right of access to European Parliament, Council, and Commission documents' (Article 255 TEC), and then in the Charter of Fundamental Rights guaranteeing a 'right of access to documents' (Article 42 CFR). Finally, '*after a long, bitter set of negotiations*'[1983] the Regulation on public access to documents of all three institutions was adopted.[1984] In addition, since the entry into force of the Lisbon Treaty, Article 15(3) TFEU has become the legal basis for public access to documents, applying to all Union institutions, bodies, offices and agencies.

The right of access to documents has occasionally been described by the EU Courts as a general principle of EU law,[1985] and as a '*fundamental right*'[1986]. Yet a general principle does not give rise to rights in all circum-

---

1980 Bignami, 'Three Generations of Participation Rights in European Administrative Proceedings' 11.

1981 Interinstitutional declaration on democracy, transparency, and subsidiarity. Bulletin of the European Communities, No. 10/93, pp. 118-120.

1982 Council Decision 93/731/EC of 20 December 1993 on public access to Council documents (OJ L 340 p. 43) (Decision 93/731) - Article 1(1): '*The public shall have access to Council documents under the conditions laid down in this Decision*'. Commission Decision 94/90/ECSC, EC, Euratom of 8 February 1994 on public access to Commission documents (OJ L 46 p. 58) ('Decision 94/90'), adopting a Code of conduct (annexed to the decision) which opens with the following so-called 'general principle': '*The public will have the widest possible access to documents held by the Commission and the Council*'.

1983 Bignami, 'Three Generations of Participation Rights in European Administrative Proceedings' 11.

1984 Regulation (EC) 1049/2001 of the European Parliament and of the Council of 30 May 2001 regarding public access to European Parliament, Council and Commission documents (OJ L 145/43) ('Transparency Regulation').

1985 More precisely, 'general principle of transparency' in Judgment of 13 September 2007, *Commission v Italy*, C-260/04, EU:C:2007:508, para 25, and 'general principle of access to documents' in Judgment of 19 July 1999, *Rothmans v Commission*, T-188/97, EU:T:1999:156, paras 53-54.

1986 Judgment of 27 November 2007, *Pitsiorlas v Council and ECB*, Joined cases T-3/00 and T-337/04, EU:T:2007:357, paras 221 and 231. In addition, according to Lenaerts with the incorporation of the right of access to documents in the Charter this right has been 'unequivocally "upgraded" to a fundamental right': K. Lenaerts, "In the Union we trust": Trust-enhancing principles of Community law' (2004) 41 Common Market Law Review 317 322.

stances; and a 'fundamental right' included in the Charter does not necessarily constitute a 'right' in every context either. In addition, the right of access to document is often described as a 'public right', which is a very unusual term in EU law[1987] and which might suggest that this 'right' is not connected with an individualisable interest. Does this correspond to a new concept to be distinguished from the classic EU concept of a right? In order to tackle this questions we need to isolate the components of this classic concept in situations where individuals request access to documents of the institutions, and assess how these components function together. The case law on the right of access to documents as it originally developed based on the decisions by the Commission and the Council concerning public access to their documents reflects a straightforward application of the classic EU concept of a right, i.e. the combination of a clear, precise and unconditional obligation with an individual interest understood in a broad way (3.3.2.1). Regulation 1049/2001 appears to have worked as a game changer (or at least it has been interpreted as such by the Court) not only because it has reinforced the conditional character of the right of access to documents and weakened the interest trigger (3.3.2.2) but also because it has led to a shift in the overall approach to individual and public interests (3.3.2.3).

2.3.3.1. Early developments of the right of access to documents

How does the right of access to documents in its early form fit with our classic understanding of a right as the correlative of an obligation, the application of which is triggered by an individual interest? The case law on the Commission and Council decisions on access to documents shows that the Court applied these classic elements in order to circumscribe and protect the right of access to documents.

Let us first look at how the correlativity model applies. The first important case, *Carvel and Guardian*,[1988] concerned Decision 93/731 on public access to Council documents. Mr. Carvel, a journalist at the Guardian, was denied access to a number of documents, including the Coreper preparatory reports, the minutes, the attendance and voting records and the deci-

1987 A search on the curia website for the term 'public right' gives 47 documents, of which 41 concern the public right of access to documents (search date: 11 May 2017).

1988 Judgment of 19 October 1995, *Carvel and Guardian Newspapers v Council*, T-194/94, EU:T:1995:183.

sions of both the Council of Ministers for Social Affairs and the Council of Ministers for Justice, as well as the minutes of the Council of Ministers for Agriculture.[1989] Decision 93/731 provided for two types of exceptions to its general rule laid down in Article 1(1) that '*the public shall have access to Council documents*': compulsory exceptions laid down at Article 4(1) describing situations where access '*shall not be granted*',[1990] and the exception laid down in Article 4(2) – on which the Council was relying in *Carvel* – providing that: '*Access to a Council document may be refused in order to protect the confidentiality of the Council's proceedings*'. It all hangs on the 'may' as opposed to 'shall': as the Court of First Instance explained, '*The Council is therefore obliged under Article 4(1) to refuse access to documents where certain circumstances exist. Under Article 4(2), however, the Council enjoys a discretion as to whether or not to refuse a request for access to documents relating to its proceedings*'. In exercising this discretion the Council must '*genuinely balance the interest of citizens in gaining access to its documents against any interest of its own in maintaining the confidentiality of its deliberations*'.[1991] Consequently, '*whenever access to documents is requested, the Council must balance the interests defined above and reach a decision in accordance with the applicable procedure*'.[1992] The CFI looks at the extent of the discretion in order to 'define' the 'scope' of Article 4(2).[1993] Then the Court reviews the Council's decision in the light of this obligation and finds that no balancing of interests

1989 In fact he did obtain the documents from the Social Affairs Council '*because of an administrative error*', '*owing to the novelty of the procedure for allowing public access to documents of the Council and its practical implementation*', in the Council's own words (*Carvel and Guardian Newspapers v Council*, T-194/94, para 34), showing that the Institution itself was unprepared to deal with that kind of request at the time and was also adjusting to the new requirements laid down by Decision 93/731.

1990 Decision 93/731, Article 4(1) provided that '*access to a Council document shall not be granted*' where its disclosure could undermine: '*the protection of the public interest (public security, international relations, monetary stability, court proceedings, inspections and investigations)*', '*the protection of the individual and of privacy*', '*the protection of commercial and industrial secrecy*', '*the protection of the Community's financial interests*', '*the protection of confidentiality as requested by the natural or legal person who supplied any of the information contained in the document or as required by the legislation of the Member State which supplied any of that information*'.

1991 *Carvel and Guardian Newspapers v Council*, T-194/94, paras 64-65. See also Judgment of 17 June 1998, *Svenska Journalistförbundet v Council*, T-174/95, EU:T:1998:127, para 113.

1992 *Carvel and Guardian Newspapers v Council*, T-194/94, para 67.

1993 *Carvel and Guardian Newspapers v Council*, T-194/94, para 69.

took place, the Council having considered that it had no discretion and had to deny access.[1994] What comes out of this is that, even though we are looking at a Decision governing 'citizens' rights of access to documents',[1995] in fact the reasoning is about obligations and discretion. Exactly like we have seen in many other areas, the assessment of discretion serves to identify the extent of the institution's obligation and the individual's corresponding right. In the subsequent evaluation of whether the Council correctly exercised its discretion, the Court insists that the institution must '*genuinely balance the interest of citizens in gaining access to its documents against any interest of its own in maintaining the confidentiality of its deliberations*'.[1996] In this case it found that this 'genuine balance' had not been struck and therefore annulled the Council' decision.

Shortly afterwards the CFI followed the same approach in order to interpret Decision 94/90 on public access to Commission documents. The World Wildlife Fund had requested access to documents concerning the use of EC structural funds to finance the building of an interpretative centre in Ireland. The request was denied based on '*the protection of the public interest (in particular, inspections and investigations) and the protection of the Commission's interest in the confidentiality of its own proceedings*'.[1997] In order to assess whether the refusal was legal in the light of Decision 94/90 the CFI first laid down its method, which consisted firstly in examining 'the legal force' of Decision 94/90 adopting a Code of Conduct, and secondly in determining 'the scope of the exceptions'.[1998] As for the first step, i.e. assessing the legal force, the Court held that '*Decision 94/90 constitutes the Commission's response to the calls made by the European Council to reflect at Community level the right of citizens to have access to documents held by public authorities, a right which is recognized in the domestic legislation of most of the Member States*'. In other words, the Court was faithful to its preferred method of interpretation: considering the instrument in relation to the system as a whole, taking into account the dynamism of the system, and seeking confirmation in the domestic legal system of the Member States. Then the CFI looked at the logic of the document: '*By adopting Decision 94/90, the Commission has indicated to citizens who wish to gain access to documents which it holds that their requests will be dealt with according to the procedures,*

1994 *Carvel and Guardian Newspapers v Council*, T-194/94, para 71-78.
1995 *Carvel and Guardian Newspapers v Council*, T-194/94, para 62.
1996 *Carvel and Guardian Newspapers v Council*, T-194/94, para 65.
1997 Judgment of 5 March 1997, *WWF UK v Commission*, T-105/95, EU:T:1997:26, para 15.
1998 *WWF UK v Commission*, T-105/95, para 53.

conditions and exceptions laid down for the purpose. Although Decision 94/90 is, in effect, a series of obligations which the Commission has voluntarily assumed for itself as a measure of internal organization, it is nevertheless capable of conferring on third parties legal rights which the Commission is obliged to respect.'[1999] This was consistent with the case law on the ability of decisions of the institutions to give rise to rights – which had been established since the 1970s in the context of direct effect.[2000] In fact the Court's reasoning here is very similar to that which characterised the founding cases on direct effect: nothing prevents the obligations from also being interpreted as rights, and this is sufficient, in light of the broad logic of the EU legal system, to identify these rights.[2001] This ruling, like *Carvel and Guardian*, therefore illustrates the relevance of the correlativity model for conceptualising the right of access to documents (at least in its early years) and it confirms that decisions give rise to rights not only to individuals facing Member State administrations, but also EU institutions.

In its second step of determining the scope of the exceptions, this judgment also touches upon the notion of interest. The CFI first makes clear that '... *where a general principle is established and exceptions to that principle are then laid down, the exceptions should be construed and applied strictly, in a manner which does not defeat the application of the general rule. In particular, the grounds for refusing a request for access to Commission documents, set out in the Code of Conduct as exceptions, should be construed in a manner which will not render it impossible to attain the objective of transparency expressed in the response of the Commission to the calls of the European Council*'.[2002] In the light of the general rule the Court then insists on the distinction between the mandatory exceptions provided for by Decision 94/90 and the other cate-

---

1999 *WWF UK v Commission*, T-105/95, paras 54-55. See also Case T-83/96 *van der Wal* v*Commission* [1998] ECR II-545, paragraph 41, and Case T-124/96 *Interporc* v*Commission* [1998] ECR II-231, paragraph 46.

2000 *Grad v Finanzamt Traunstein*, 9/70, para 9. Regarding decisions the same method was applied later in: *Hansa Fleisch v. Landrat des Kreises Schleswig-Flensburg*, C-156/91, paras 12-13; Judgment of 12 December 1990, *Kaefer and Procacci v French State*, C-100/89, EU:C:1990:456, para 24; Judgment of 28 September 1999, *Fruchthandelsgesellschaft Chemnitz v Commission*, T-254/97, EU:T:1999:178, para 29 and case law cited. See p. 241 of this work.

2001 *Van Gend en Loos*, C-26/62.

2002 *WWF UK v Commission*, T-105/95, para 56. See also Judgment of 19 July 1999, *Hautala v Council*, T-14/98, EU:T:1999:157, para 84.

gory of exceptions '*drafted in discretionary terms*',[2003] and holds that the exercise of discretion precisely entails the obligation to strike '*a genuine balance between, on the one hand, the interest of the citizen in obtaining access to those documents and, on the other, its own interest in protecting the confidentiality of its deliberations*'.[2004] The CFI eventually annuls the denial of access because the Commission has not even attempted to strike this balance.[2005]

Carvel and *WWF* thus have in common a willingness to narrowly interpret the exceptions to the general rule, and confirm that the existence of discretion does not automatically amount to the absence of an obligation and correlative right. On the contrary, it is a matter of degree and of whether the identifiable obligation is practically applicable to a concrete case. The CFI confirmed its approach in subsequent case law, occasionally giving reason to the administration[2006] but also requiring, where possible (and when it would not constitute an unreasonable burden on the administration) to select those passages that could be disclosed from each document instead of imposing blanket exclusions of entire documents.[2007]

The relevance of the right-obligation correlativity being clear, we still need to examine how the other classic component of a right, i.e. the interest in enforcement of the correlative obligation, applies in the case law on access to documents. What is peculiar in the *Carvel* and *WWF* line of case law is that the obligation to balance individual interests on the one hand, with those of third parties, the general public and the institutions on the

---

2003 The Court explains the distinction by distinguishing between different types of interests: *WWF UK v Commission*, T-105/95, para 60: '*The Court considers that the distinction between these two categories of exception in the Code of Conduct is explained by the nature of the interest which the categories seek respectively to protect. The first category, comprising the 'mandatory exceptions', effectively protects the interest of third parties or of the general public in cases where disclosure of particular documents by the institution concerned would risk causing harm to persons who could legitimately refuse access to the documents if held in their own possession. On the other hand, in the second category, relating to the internal deliberations of the institution, the interest of the institution alone is at stake.*'.

2004 *WWF UK v Commission*, T-105/95, paras 58-59, citing *Carvel and Guardian Newspapers v Council*, T-194/94, paras 64-65.

2005 *WWF UK v Commission*, T-105/95, para 70.

2006 In Judgment of 14 October 1999, *Bavarian Lager*, T-309/97, EU:T:1999:257, the CFI relied on *WWF* but this time dismissed the action for annulment against the denial of access, because the protection of the confidentiality of infringement proceedings justified the refusal.

2007 *Hautala v Council*, T-14/98 and Judgment of 6 February 1998, *Interporc Im- und Export v Commission*, T-124/96, EU:T:1998:25. Bignami, 'Three Generations of Participation Rights in European Administrative Proceedings' 11.

other hand, appears to be inherent in the right of access to documents. This would imply in turn that the individual interest in requesting access to document is *presumed* to exist. This suggestion is confirmed by the Court's broad interpretation of an applicant's interest in seeking annulment of a decision denying access to documents. In *Svenska Journalistförbundet v Council,* the Swedish Journalists' Union had lodged requests both with the Council (relying on Decision 93/731) and with the Swedish authorities in order to access Council documents relating to the setting up of the European Police Office. As they readily admitted, their intention was to test the Council's compliance with transparency principles. The result of the experiment was unequivocal: they obtained 18 out of 20 requested documents from the Swedish authorities, whereas the ratio was exactly opposite in the Council's response, denying access to to 18 of the 20 requested documents. The Council justified its refusal by explaining that the release of these documents could be harmful to the public interest (public security) and that they related to the Council's proceedings, including the positions taken by the members of the Council, and were therefore covered by the duty of confidentiality. In the subsequent action introduced by the journalists' union against the denial of access, the Council disputed the applicant's interest in seeking annulment, arguing that in spite of being addressee of the contested decision '*the applicant (could not) derive any benefit from obtaining access to documents which (were) already in its possession*'.[2008] The Council was thus trying to play the card of the extra 'interest' filter in a situation where direct and individual concern did not have to be demonstrated given that the challenged act was an individual decision.[2009]

However, the Court highlighted that '*The objective of Decision 93/731 is to give effect to the principle of the largest possible access for citizens to information with a view to strengthening the democratic character of the institutions and the trust of the public in the administration. Decision 93/731, like Decision 94/90, does not require that members of the public must put forward reasons for seeking access to requested documents*'. The combination of these teleological and systemic considerations led the Court to conclude that '*a person who is refused access to a document or to part of a document has, by virtue of that very fact, established an interest in the annulment of the decision.*'.[2010] We have here a very clear confirmation that *any* individual interest may function as a trig-

2008 *Svenska Journalistförbundet v Council,* T-174/95, para 55.

2009 Concerning the notion of interest in bringing proceedings see note 874 of this work.

2010 *Svenska Journalistförbundet v Council,* T-174/95, paras 66-67 relying in particular on *Interporc Im- und Export v Commission,* T-124/96, para 48.

ger for a right; even more so when the instrument laying down the correlative obligation, also creates a presumption that a corresponding interest exists.

All in all, the right of access to documents was born a very classic individual right. Decisions 93/731 and 94/90 laid down obligations to which correlative rights could be identified, and individual interest in enforcing them was so broadly understood that it could be *presumed* to exist. This broad understanding of the ability of institutional arrangements to grant rights, and the reliance on a '*teleological reasoning that placed the initial code of conduct adopted by two decision-making institutions in the context of its broader democratic purpose*', allowed the EU Courts to develop '*a constitutional perspective on access to document provisions* avant la lettre'.[2011] The Transparency Regulation to a certain extent builds on the early case law but it also shifts the balance between the different components of its 'ancestors'.

2.3.3.2. The 'right' of access to documents in Regulation 1049/2011: a very conditional obligation

According to recital 4 of the Transparency Regulation, its purpose is '*to give the fullest possible effect to the right of public access to documents and to lay down the general principles and limits on such access in accordance with Article 255(2) of the EC Treaty*'. The 'right' itself is laid down at Article 2(1): '*Any citizen of the Union, and any natural or legal person residing or having its registered office in a Member State, has a right of access to documents of the institutions, subject to the principles, conditions and limits defined in this Regulation*'.[2012] This affirmation of a 'right' is in itself a departure from the approach of Decisions 93/731 and 94/90, which did not phrase the general rule in terms of a 'right'. The 'institutions', as indicated by the title of the Regulation, are the Parliament, the Council and the Commission. Article

2011 D. Curtin, H.C.H. Hofmann and J. Mendes, 'Constitutionalising EU Executive Rule-Making Procedures: A Research Agenda' (2013) 19 European Law Journal 1 7.

2012 Article 2(2) adds that natural or legal persons not residing or not having a registered office in a Member State may be granted that right. The Commission's proposal for reviewing the Transparency Regulation entails the suppression of this distinction and the broadening of the personal scope of the Regulation to 'any natural or legal person', regardless of nationality or place of residence. Proposal for a Regulation of the European Parliament and of the Council regarding public access to European Parliament, Council and Commission documents, /* COM/2008/0229 final - COD 2008/0090 */, Article 2.

2(3) clarifies the material scope of the right: '*This Regulation shall apply to all documents held by an institution, that is to say, documents drawn up or received by it and in its possession, in all areas of activity of the European Union*' – which, as further clarified by the Court, means that the right of access concerns existing 'documents'[2013] specifically and not 'information' in general.[2014] In addition, Article 4(6) integrates previously mentioned case law by providing that '*If only parts of the requested document are covered by any of the exceptions, the remaining parts of the document shall be released*'. Looking closely at Regulation 1049/2001 and the relevant case law it appears that we have a 'right' that is 'subject' to so many 'principles, conditions and

---

2013 See e.g. judgment of 2 October 2014, *Strack v Commission*, C-127/13 P, EU:C:2014:2250, para 38: '*the right of access to documents held by the institutions (...) applies only to existing documents in the possession of the institution concerned*'. However the CFI held in Judgment of 25 June 2002, *British American Tobacco (Investments) v Commission*, T-311/00, EU:T:2002:167, paras 31-32, as well as in *Pitsiorlas v Council and ECB*, Joined cases T-3/00 and T-337/04, para 109, that: '*in order to ensure the effective judicial protection of persons who, on requesting access, are confronted with answers from administrative bodies stating that they are not in possession of the documents requested or that those documents do not exist, the Court considers that those answers amount to refusals to grant access which affect the interests of the applicants for access and are therefore actionable.*' As pointed out by the Court of Justice in *Strack* '*Any other outcome would make impossible review by the European Union judicature of the merits of decisions refusing access to documents held by the institutions, since it would suffice for the institution concerned to state that a document does not exist to avoid judicial review altogether*' (para 40).

2014 Judgment of 25 April 2007, *WWF European Policy Programme v Council*, T-264/04, EU:T:2007:114, paras 76-77: '*the concept of a document must be distinguished from that of information. The public's right of access to the documents of the institutions covers only documents and not information in the wider meaning of the word and does not imply a duty on the part of the institutions to reply to any request for information from an individual*'. In this case, the World Wildlife Fund had requested access to information concerning an item on the agenda of a Council meeting; the Court held that '*since there (were) no minutes or other documents relating to the first item on the agenda of the meeting of the Committee of 19 December 2003, the Council was not obliged to provide the applicant with information on the content of that item at the meeting*' (para 77). Concerning another requested document, the CFI further held that the minutes that the applicants had asked for had never been held by the Council since they had been drafted by participants of Member States in the Committee (para 86). This formalist interpretation potentially opens a regrettable possibility for institutions to circumvent their obligations under the Transparency Regulation and may paradoxically encourage informal discussions: no notes taken (or at least, no notes taken by the institutions) at a meeting, no document, no right of access....

limits' that although it might be clear and precise, it is definitely not unconditional.

The possibility to rely on Article 2(1) is conditional in the sense that it will be determined by whether or not the situation is covered by exceptions listed at Article 4. These exceptions are divided in two. The mandatory exceptions listed at Article 4(1) include (a) public security, defence, foreign relations and financial, currency and economic policy and (b) the protection of privacy, in particular data protection. The second category of exceptions is much more innovative in the sense that it departs significantly from what could have been called the discretionary exception under Decisions 93/731 and 94/90. Article 4(2) indeed requires that '*the institutions shall refuse access*' where disclosure would undermine the protection of commercial interests of a natural or legal person; court proceedings and legal advice; or the purpose of inspections, investigations and audits. By comparison to the Decisions, the exception has become stronger ('shall' has replaced 'may') and a condition has been added: '*unless there is an overriding public interest in disclosure*'. With a similar structure, Article 4(3), also under the condition that there be no overriding public interest in disclosure, provides that access to documents drawn up by an institution for internal use or received by an institution and relating to a matter where a decision has not been taken by the institutions, as well as documents containing opinions for internal use in deliberations and preliminary consultations, shall be refused if disclosure '*would seriously undermine the institution's decision-making process*'.

Another type of exception may be read in Article 4(5) which provides that '*(a) Member State may request the institution not to disclose a document originating from that Member State without its prior agreement*'. In an early case following the adoption of the Transparency Regulation, this provision had been interpreted as mandatory by the General Court.[2015] Then the Court of Justice made clear that Article 4(5) entailed no right of veto for the Member States, and only allowed for their participation in assessing the applicability of Article 4(1) to (3).[2016] Otherwise '*without any objective reason*', '*the effectiveness*' of the right of public access '*would be substantially*

2015 Judgment of 17 March 2005, *Scippacercola v Commission*, T-187/03, EU:T:2005:108.

2016 Judgment of 18 December 2007, *Sweden v Commission*, C-64/05, EU:C:2007:802, para 75 and further para 76: '*the prior agreement of the Member State referred to in Article 4(5) resembles not a discretionary right of veto but a form of assent confirming that none of the grounds of exception under Article 4(1) to (3) is present*'. See also Judgment of 14 February 2012, *Germany v Commission*,

reduced'.[2017] Not for the first nor probably the last time, the Court appears to be more protective of individuals and the effectiveness of their rights against Member States, than against EU institutions. It remains up to the EU institutions (under the control of the CJEU if need be) to assess the applicability of the system of exceptions laid down at Article 4.

According to the Court, this system of exceptions '*is based on a balancing of the opposing interests in a given situation, that is to say, first, the interests which would be favoured by the disclosure of the documents in question and, secondly, those which would be jeopardised by such disclosure. The decision taken on a request for access to documents depends on which interest must prevail in the particular case*'.[2018] The application of the exceptions is therefore inherently a balancing exercise between different interests, that ground a variety of limits and conditions on the right of access to documents. Discretion, just like for other rights, is a key indicator for interpreting these limits and conditions and thus for circumscribing this right.

The mandatory exceptions listed at Article 4(1) function as rather straightforward conditions: if one of them is fulfilled, then there is no right of access. The Court established its reading grid for this provision in *Sison*.[2019] The Court held that '*the particularly sensitive and essential nature of the interests*' protected by this provision combined with its imperative char-

---

T-59/09, EU:T:2012:75, para 35; Judgment of 13 January 2011, *IFAW Internationaler Tierschutz-Fonds v Commission*, T-362/08, EU:T:2011:6, paras 73-74 confirmed on this point by Judgment of 21 June 2012, *IFAW Internationaler Tierschutz-Fonds v Commission*, C-135/11 P, EU:C:2012:376, para 33 (sent back to the GC, case T-362/08 RENV pending).

2017 *Sweden v Commission*, C-64/05, EU:C:2007:802, para 64.

2018 Judgment of 27 February 2014, *Commission v EnBW*, C-365/12 P, EU:C:2014:112, para 63, citing Judgment of 14 November 2013, *LPN and Finland* v *Commission*, C-514/11 P, EU:C:2013:738, para 42. This is consistent with Recital 11 of the Transparency Regulation: '*In principle, all documents of the institutions should be accessible to the public. However, certain public and private interests should be protected by way of exceptions. The institutions should be entitled to protect their internal consultations and deliberations where necessary to safeguard their ability to carry out their tasks. In assessing the exceptions, the institutions should take account of the principles in Community legislation concerning the protection of personal data, in all areas of Union activities*'.

2019 Judgment of 1 February 2007, *Sison v Council*, C-266/05 P, EU:C:2007:75 confirming Judgment of 26 April 2005, *Sison v Council*, Joined cases T-110/03, T-150/03 and T-405/03, EU:T:2005:143.

acter[2020] '*confers on the decision which must thus be adopted by the institution a complex and delicate nature which calls for the exercise of particular care. Such a decision requires, therefore, a margin of appreciation*'.[2021] In addition, the criteria set out at Article 4(1)(a) '*are very general, since access must be refused, as is clear from the wording of that provision, if disclosure of the document concerned would 'undermine' the protection of the 'public interest' as regards, inter alia, 'public security' and 'international relations*'.[2022] It is of course not new that the more general and the less precise a provision, the broader the discretion it leaves to the duty-holder and the lower the probability of identifying a right that individuals could claim.

What is less usual is the Court's next observation that '*it is clear from examination of the preparatory documents which preceded the adoption of that regulation that various proposals intended to define more precisely the scope of the public-interest exceptions to which Article 4(1) of that regulation refers, which would undoubtedly have enabled the opportunities for judicial review in regard to the institution's assessment to be correspondingly increased, were not accepted*'.[2023] This is peculiar because, as already pointed out, the Court traditionally did not often rely on preparatory works for interpreting provisions of EU law and rather avoided the intentionalist method of interpretation, especially when it came to identifying rights.[2024] The reference to preparatory works here serves to reinforce a reading of Article 4(1) already unfavourable to individuals, who are faced with the broad discretion of the institutions in the assessment of the criteria and see their chances of being granted a right of access to documents correspondingly restricted.

Nevertheless, there are limits to this discretion, as several judgments made clear. For instance, the third indent of Article 4(1)(a) concerning the protection of the public interest as regards international relations has been often relied on, sometimes abusively by the EU institutions and the Mem-

---

2020 The Court added at para 46 that '*as regards the exceptions to the right of access provided for by that provision, refusal of access by the institution is mandatory where disclosure of a document to the public would undermine the interests which that provision protects, without the need, in such a case and in contrast to the provisions, in particular, of Article 4(2), to balance the requirements connected to the protection of those interests against those which stem from other interests.*'.

2021 *Sison v Council*, C-266/05 P, para 35. See also Judgment of 27 November 2012, *Steinberg v Commission*, T-17/10, EU:T:2012:625, para 63; Judgment of 12 September 2013, *Besselink v Council*, T-331/11, EU:T:2013:419, para 32.

2022 *Sison v Council*, C-266/05 P, para 36.

2023 *Sison v Council*, C-266/05 P, para 37.

2024 S. Miettinen and M. Kettunen, 'Travaux to the Treaties: Treasures or trivia?' (European Studies Association conference, Boston 5 March 2015).

ber States.[2025] In one case the Council had refused to disclose the opinion of its legal service concerning the legal basis for negotiating an international agreement with the USA (to make available to the US Treasury Department financial messaging data to prevent and combat terrorism and terrorist financing).[2026] In the subsequent action for annulment the Council argued in favour of a presumption of the existence of a threat to the credibility of the EU in the negotiations of international agreements, which would prohibit the disclosure of documents discussing the legal basis for such agreements. The Court of Justice, siding with the General Court, did not accept this presumption and held that the risk involved in disclosing positions taken within the institutions with regard to the choice of a legal basis for an international agreement, '*does not in itself establish the existence of a threat to the European Union's interest in the field of international relations*' and that '*the mere fear of disclosure of the existence of divergent opinions within the institutions regarding the appropriate legal basis on which to adopt a decision authorising the opening of negotiations on behalf of the EU is not a sufficient basis for concluding that the public interest in the field of international relations may be undermined*'.[2027] Therefore, and more generally as regards Article 4(1), there has to be a genuine assessment in each case, of whether the public interest may be undermined.

However, because of the discretion granted to the institutions by Article 4(1), the review of legality of this assessment is limited: the Court controls the respect of procedural rules, of the duty to state reasons, as well as the manifest error of assessment of the facts or the misuse of powers.[2028] The limited possibility for review has of course led to the validation by the

---

2025 The Court has clarified the notion of 'international relations' in case opposing Germany and the Commission concerning the disclosure of documents relating to an infringement procedure: the Court held that the relations between the EU institutions and the Member States are not 'international relations', especially because another interpretation '*would make it possible for a significant proportion of the documents relating to EU activities to be removed from the scope of the public right of access to documents of the institutions*' and would therefore '*undermine the objective of transparency pursued by Regulation No 1049/2001*'. *Germany v Commission*, T-59/09, para 65.

2026 Judgment of 4 May 2012, *In 't Veld v Council*, T-529/09, EU:T:2012:215 confirmed by Judgment of 3 July 2014, *Council v in 't Veld*, C-350/12 P, EU:C:2014:2039.

2027 *Council v in 't Veld*, C-350/12 P, para 44.

2028 *Sison v Council*, C-266/05 P, para 34 and paras 64-68; *Council v in 't Veld*, C-350/12 P, para 63; *Besselink v Council*, T-331/11, para 34; *Steinberg v Commission*, T-17/10, para 64; *WWF European Policy Programme v Council*, T-264/04, para 40.

Court of several denials of access to documents based on Article 4(1)(a) concerning the protection of the public interest[2029] as well as Article 4(1)(b) concerning the protection of privacy and the integrity of the individual.[2030]

In addition to the mandatory exceptions laid down in Article 4(1) of the Transparency Regulation, the right of access to documents is also subject to the exceptions of Article 4, paragraphs (2) and (3). These paragraphs have a similar structure, ending with an '*exception to the exception*' where an overriding public interest may be identified.[2031] The exceptions in these provisions should therefore be applied differently from those listed at Article 4(1).[2032] The state of affairs on Article 4, paragraphs (2) and (3) is provided in *ClientEarth.* The NGO had challenged the refusal of access to Commis-

---

2029 Based on the first and second indent (public security, defence and military matters): reports drawn up during a European Community Monitoring Mission in Croatia carried out during the conflicts in former Yugoslavia (Judgment of 3 October 2012, *Jurašinović v Council*, T-465/09, EU:T:2012:515, confirmed by Judgment of 28 November 2013, *Jurašinović v Council*, C-576/12 P, EU:C:2013:777); documents relating to funding decisions for grants to Israeli and Palestinian NGOs under the Partnership for Peace programme (*Steinberg v Commission*, T-17/10). Based on the third indent (international relations): documents relating to the negotiations between the EU and Turkey concerning the return to Turkey of asylum applicants (Judgment of 7 February 2018, *Access Info Europe v Commission*, T-851/16, EU:T:2018:69), documents relating to trade negotiations between the EU and India (Judgment of 7 June 2013, *Stichting Corporate Europe Observatory v Commission*, T-93/11, EU:T:2013:308, confirmed by Judgment of 4 June 2015, *Stichting Corporate Europe Observatory v Commission*, C-399/13 P, EU:C:2015:360), document on the draft Anti-Counterfeiting Trade Agreement (Judgment of 19 March 2013, *In 't Veld v Commission*, T-301/10, EU:T:2013:135, denial partially sanctioned because of a manifest error of assessment). Based on the third and fourth indents (international relations and financial, monetary or economic policy): documents concerning the meeting of the so-called 'Article 133 Committee' of the Council that advises and makes proposals to the EC on the negotiation of international trade agreements (*WWF European Policy Programme v Council*, T-264/04).

2030 *Umbach v Commission*, T-474/08, confirmed by Order of 14 April 2011, *Umbach v Commission*, C-609/10 P, EU:C:2011:263 (documents relating to a tender procedure).

2031 H.C.H. Hofmann, 'Individual Rights and Information in EU Public Law', in A.S. Lind, I. Österdal and J. Reichel (eds), *Transparency in the future – Swedish openness 250 years* (Ragulka 2017) p. 72.

2032 *WWF European Policy Programme v Council*, T-264/04, para 44: '*The exceptions set out in Article 4(1) of Regulation No 1049/2001 are framed in mandatory terms and it follows that the institutions are obliged to refuse access to documents falling under any one of those mandatory exceptions once the relevant circumstances are shown to*

sion studies on Member State compliance with certain EU environmental directives (i.e., documents from the pre-litigation stage of infringement proceedings). The Commission had argued that the information sought was protected since it is part of an ongoing investigation into Member States' compliance with EU law. The Court confirmed that '*such studies are among the instruments available to the Commission*' in order to assess the respect by Member States of their obligation to transpose EU directives '*in order to decide, when necessary, to initiate infringement proceedings against those Member States which it considers to be in breach of EU law. The studies fall, consequently, within the scope of the concept of 'investigations*'.[2033]

The General Court had considered that a presumption of confidentiality could apply to these documents. The Court of Justice accepted that it is in principle '*open to the EU institution concerned to base its decisions in that regard on general presumptions which apply to certain categories of documents, as considerations of a generally similar kind are likely to apply to requests for disclosure relating to documents of the same nature*',[2034] and then summed up its earlier case law, identifying five types of documents '*which enjoy a general presumption of confidentiality*'[2035]: the documents in an administrative file relating to a procedure for reviewing State aid[2036]; the pleadings lodged by an institution in court proceedings[2037]; the documents exchanged between the Commission and notifying parties or third parties in the course of merger control proceedings[2038]; the documents concerning an infringe-

---

exist (...). Those exceptions are therefore different from the exceptions relating to the interest of the institutions in maintaining the confidentiality of their deliberations laid down in Article 4(3) of Regulation No 1049/2001, in the application of which the institutions enjoy a discretion which allows them to balance, on the one hand, their interest in maintaining the confidentiality of their deliberations against, on the other hand, the interest of the citizen in gaining access to documents (...)' (citing by analogy, *WWF UK v Commission*, T-105/95 para 58 and *Carvel and Guardian Newspapers v Council*, T-194/94, paras 64-65).

2033 *ClientEarth v. Commission*, C-612/13 P, para 62.

2034 *ClientEarth v Commission*, C-612/13 P, para 69; *Commission* v *EnBW*, C-365/12 P, para 65 and case law cited; Judgment of 1 July 2008, *Sweden and Turco v Council*, Joined cases C-39/05 P and C-52/05 P, EU:C:2008:374, para 50.

2035 *ClientEarth v Commission*, C-612/13 P, para 77.

2036 Judgment of 29 June 2010, *Commission* v *Technische Glaswerke Ilmenau*, C-139/07 P, EU:C:2010:376, paras 58-61; see also Judgment of 14 July 2016, *Sea Handling v Commission*, C-271/15 P, EU:C:2016:557, para 36.

2037 Judgment of 21 September 2010, *Sweden and Others* v *API and Commission*, Joined cases C-514/07 P, C-528/07 P and C-532/07 P, EU:C:2010:541, para 94.

2038 Judgment of 28 June 2012, *Commission* v *Éditions Odile Jacob*, C-404/10 P, EU:C:2012:393, para 123.

ment procedure during its pre-litigation stage[2039]; and the documents relating to proceedings under Article 101 TFEU.[2040] The Court then pointed out that all these cases concerned ongoing administrative or judicial proceedings.[2041] In such situations the general presumption of confidentiality supposedly helps preserve a '*climate of mutual trust*' and the possibility to reach an amicable solution.[2042] The presumption has the effect of not obliging the institution to examine whether the disclosure would undermine protected interests in a given case.[2043] Even though it should be interpreted strictly,[2044] this '*judge-made general presumption of confidentiality of documents*'[2045] is very problematic. Not only is it inconsistent with the telos of Regulation 1049/2001. It also strongly alters the system of Article 4 which the Court itself described as one based on the balancing of interests.[2046]

When it is either presumed or established that disclosure would undermine a protected interest, the 'overriding public interest' test must apply for the individual to access the documents.[2047] The notion of 'overriding

2039 *LPN and Finland* v *Commission*, Joined cases C-514/11 P and C-605/11 P, para 65.

2040 *Commission* v *EnBW*, C-365/12 P, para 93.

2041 *ClientEarth v. Commission*, C-612/13 P, para 78.

2042 *ClientEarth v. Commission*, C-612/13 P, paras 75-76.

2043 *LPN and Finland* v *Commission*, C-514/11 P, para 68; *Sea Handling v Commission*, C-271/15 P, paras 67-69.

2044 Concerning documents which are not part of a pre-litigation file and which have not given rise to a formal procedure, disclosure is not impeded by a general presumption of confidentiality and it should be accepted or denied on a case by case basis: see *ClientEarth v. Commission*, C-612/13 P, paras 78-83. Likewise, in a famous case concerning access to 'trilogue' tables, documenting informal discussions between the Commission, the Parliament and the Council, the GC held that such discussions were essential parts of the legislative process and that transparency, in this context, was of particular importance. No general presumption of non-disclosure could be justified and the institutions also could not demonstrate that the public interest protected by Article 4(A) would be specifically and actually undermined by disclosure. The GC therefore annulled the refusal to disclose the documents. Judgment of 22 March 2018, *De Capitani v Parliament*, T-540/15, EU:T:2018:167.

2045 Hofmann, 'Individual Rights and Information in EU Public Law' p. 75.

2046 See *Commission v EnBW*, C-365/12 P, para 63 and Recital 11 of Regulation 1049/2001, cited at note 2018 in this work.

2047 The Court has held that the existence of a presumption of confidentiality does not rule out the possibility of demonstrating that there is an overriding public interest which justifies the disclosure of the documents: *Commission* v *Éditions*

public interest' was famously clarified in *Sweden and Turco.*[2048] The applicant argued that the principles of democracy and citizen participation in the legislative process in themselves constitute an overriding public interest, whereas the Council was claiming a 'space to think' to maintain internal advice confidential. '*The possibility for citizens to find out the considerations underpinning legislative action is a precondition for the effective exercise of their democratic rights*',[2049] thus clearly laying down '*the main principle of public access and its linkage with the principle of democracy*'.[2050] The conclusion from *Sweden and Turco* is that the Transparency Regulation imposes in principle '*an obligation to disclose the opinions of the Council's legal service relating to a legislative process*', because this serves '*the transparency and openness of the legislative process and strengthens the democratic right of European citizens to scrutinize the information which has formed the basis of a legislative act*' as required by the preamble of the Transparency Regulation.[2051]

Although *Sweden and Turco* had established that '*the overriding public interest capable of justifying the disclosure of a document must not necessarily be distinct from the principles which underlie Regulation No 1049/2001*',[2052] the subsequent case law shows a tendency to be more restrictive as regards the type of circumstances that can constitute an overriding public interest. The Court has indeed held that '*general considerations cannot provide an appropriate basis for establishing that, in the present case, the principle of transparency was in some sense especially pressing and capable, therefore, of prevailing over the reasons justifying the refusal to disclose the documents in question*', so that the applicant must rely on precise circumstances to demonstrate the existence of an overriding public interest.[2053] The problem with this approach is of course that if there is no access to documents it might be difficult to give precise indications.

Odile Jacob, para 126 and Judgment of 25 September 2014, *Spirlea v Commission,* T-306/12, EU:T:2014:816, para 90.

2048 *Sweden and Turco v Council*, Joined cases C-39/05 P and C-52/05 P.

2049 *Sweden and Turco v Council*, Joined cases C-39/05 P and C-52/05 P, para 46.

2050 D. Curtin and P. Leino-Sandberg, *Openness, Transparency and the Right of Access to Documents in the EU. In-depth analysis for the PETI committee* (European Parliament DG for Internal Policies, Policy Department C: Citizens' Rights and Constitutional Affairs, 2016).

2051 *Sweden and Turco v Council*, Joined cases C-39/05 P and C-52/05 P, paras 67-68.

2052 *Sweden and Turco v Council*, Joined cases C-39/05 P and C-52/05 P, paras 74-75 and *LPN and Finland* v *Commission*, C-514/11 P, para 92.

2053 *LPN and Finland* v *Commission*, C-514/11 P, paras 93-94; *ClientEarth and International Chemical Secretariat v ECHA*, T-245/11, para 193; *Deza v ECHA*, T-189/14, para 124; *Spirlea v Commission*, T-306/12, paras 91-92.

The Court's restrictive conception of the notion of an overriding public interest is also manifested in cases where the relation between the Transparency Regulation and the Aarhus Regulation is being questioned. In *LPN*, the environmental NGO had requested access in order to be in a position to supplement the information held by the Commission concerning a dam construction project which was the subject of an infringement procedure, and therefore take active part in the procedure. It was relying both on the Transparency Regulation and on the Aarhus Regulation. Supported by the Finnish observations, it argued that the GC instead of only checking conditions under Article 9 AR should also have checked whether an overriding public interest in the meaning of Article 4(2) AR could have justified disclosure. The Court held that although the preamble of the AR '*stresses the importance of providing adequate environmental information and effective opportunities for public participation in environmental decision-making, the fact remains that such participation cannot be relied upon in order to justify access to the documents relating to an infringement procedure. In accordance with Article 9 of that regulation, Community institutions and bodies are to provide opportunities for the public to participate only where they prepare, modify or review plans or programmes relating to the environment. However, infringement procedures are not referred to in that article*.'[2054] Such a compartmentalised reading of EU information and participation law, by contrast with a systemic one, contributes to restricting the information and participation rights of NGOs in environmental matters on the EU level.

The same problem arose in a recent case where the overlap between the Aarhus Regulation and the Transparency Regulation was also at stake. The Dutch branch of Greenpeace and Pesticide Action Network Europe (PAN Europe) made a request, on the basis of the Transparency Regulation and the AR, for access to several documents relating to the initial authorisation for the placing of a rather infamous substance, glyphosate, on the market.[2055] The request was denied based on the first indent of Article 4(2) of the Transparency Regulation (protection of commercial interests of a natural or legal person). The applicants argued that there was an overriding public interest in disclosure of the information requested since it related to emissions into the environment within the meaning of the first sentence of Article 6(1) AR. The GC upheld this plea, accepting a broad understanding of information related to emissions into the environment as any informa-

2054 *LPN and Finland* v *Commission*, C-514/11 P, para 96.

2055 Judgment of 23 November 2016, *Commission v Stichting Greenpeace Nederland and PAN Europe*, C-673/13 P, EU:C:2016:889.

tion that relates, '*in a sufficiently direct manner*', to emissions into the environment.[2056]

However, on appeal the Court of Justice went for a much more restrictive understanding of the concept of information, arguing that a broader approach '*would to a large extent deprive the concept of 'environmental information' as defined in Article 2(1)(d) [AR] of any meaning. Such an interpretation would deprive of any practical effect the possibility, laid down in the first indent of Article 4(2) of Regulation No 1049/2001, for the institutions to refuse to disclose environmental information on the ground, inter alia, that such disclosure would have an adverse effect on the protection of the commercial interests of a particular natural or legal person and would jeopardise the balance which the EU legislature intended to maintain between the objective of transparency and the protection of those interests. It would also constitute a disproportionate interference with the protection of business secrecy ensured by Article 339 TFEU*'.[2057] The Court therefore quashed the GC's judgment. In painting such a dramatic picture of the consequences of a broad understanding of the concept of environmental information, the Court opposes an 'objective' of transparency with the private interests in non-disclosure, perhaps forgetting that this objective of transparency also corresponds to concrete interests and that access to documents is supposed to be a 'right'. The Court makes this right conditional on the absence of competing interests and does not fully take into account the interests in transparency. Thus the EU citizens are left with merely a residual right of access to documents.

2.3.3.3. Presumption or suppression of the interest trigger?

The system of Article 4 being inherently one of balancing interests, it is worth asking where and how the individual interest in having access to documents (which, if the classic EU concept of a right applies here, should have a certain weight in activating the right of access to documents) fits in this system.

According to Article 6(1) of Regulation 1049/2001, an applicant for access to documents '*is not obliged to state reasons for the application*'. As a consequence, he also does not have to demonstrate any interest in having ac-

---

2056 Judgment of 8 October 2013, Stichting Greenpeace Nederland and PAN Europe v Commission, T-545/11, EU:T:2013:523, para 53.

2057 *Commission v Stichting Greenpeace Nederland and PAN Europe*, C-673/13 P, para 81.

cess to the documents requested.[2058] '*That is a concrete expression of the principles of openness and transparency which must drive the action taken by the institutions of the European Union, and of the democratic nature of those institutions*'.[2059] This means that an institution cannot base a denial of access on the absence of arguments which might justify disclosure[2060] and that there is no abuse in basing a request of access to documents on strictly private interests.[2061]

The same logic applies for assessing the admissibility of an action for annulment of a denial of access. The challenge being directed at an individual decision, there is of course no need to prove direct and/or individual concern.[2062] However, the legal interest in bringing proceedings must also be tested. For instance, in the *Pitsiorlas* case the applicant had asked for a series of documents on the Basle/Nyborg agreement and had been provided only with two documents which 'well represented' the agreement in its entirety according to the ECB. The ECB argued that the action was 'devoid of purpose' and abusive in so far as the applicant's request had essentially been satisfied. The Court found this paradoxical since it was also stated that the agreement was confidential.[2063] So it held that it could not be considered that the request had been satisfied and that '*a person who is refused access to a document or to part of a document has, by virtue of that very fact, established an interest in the annulment of the decision refusing access*'.[2064] The action was consequently deemed admissible. So the individual interest fil-

---

2058 *Sison v Council*, C-266/05 P, paras 62-64 and 80-83. See also Judgment of 8 November 2007, *Bavarian Lager v Commission*, T-194/04, EU:T:2007:334, para 92. The Court has stressed in Judgment of 26 January 2010, *Internationaler Hilfsfonds v Commission*, C-362/08 P, EU:C:2010:40, para 56 and Judgment of 21 October 2010, *Agapiou Joséphidès v Commission and EACEA*, T-439/08, EU:T:2010:442, para 74 that '*Regulation No 1049/2001 confers a very extensive right of access to the documents of the institutions concerned, there being, in accordance with Article 6(1) of the regulation, no requirement to state reasons for the application in order to enjoy that right*'.

2059 Judgment of 15 July 2015, *Dennekamp v Parliament*, T-115/13, EU:T:2015:497, para 52.

2060 Judgment of 7 June 2011, *Toland v Parliament*, T-471/08, EU:T:2011:252, para 84.

2061 Judgment of 9 June 2010, *Éditions Jacob v Commission*, T-237/05, EU:T:2010:224, para 188.

2062 Article 263(4) TFEU provides that any natural or legal person may '*institute proceedings against an act addressed to that person*'.

2063 *Pitsiorlas v Council and ECB*, Joined cases T-3/00 and T-337/04, para 86.

2064 *Pitsiorlas v Council and ECB*, Joined cases T-3/00 and T-337/04, para 89, citing *Svenska Journalistförbundet v Council*, T-174/95, para 67.

ter (direct and/or individual concern *and* interest in bringing proceedings) that usually has such restrictive effects for individual applicants in an action before the EU Courts, is relatively loose when it comes to claiming a right of access to documents.[2065]

The downside to this approach is that the particular interest that may be asserted by a requesting party in obtaining access to a document concerning it individually *cannot* be taken into account even when the applicant itself relies on it. In *Sison* the applicant had found himself on a list of persons targeted by a Council decision establishing restrictive measures with a view to combating terrorism.[2066] He requested access to documents which had served as the basis for elaborating this list. The Council denied the access, based on the exception of public security and international relations provided for at Article 4(1)(a) of the Transparency Regulation. In the ensuing action for annulment one of the arguments advanced by the applicant was that he had a legitimate interest in obtaining access to those documents, since they concerned him personally and had led to his inclusion on the list at issue. The Court however observed (relying on Articles 2(1), 6(1), 12(1) of Regulation 1049/2001, its title and recitals 4 and 11) that the purpose of the Transparency Regulation '*is to give the general public a right of access to documents of the institutions and not to lay down rules designed to protect the particular interest which a specific individual may have in gaining access to one of them*'.[2067] Looking at how a provision functions in relation to the broader system in which it exists in order to assess its ability to give rise to a right is not particularly revolutionary.[2068] More original is the thorough '*analysis of the preparatory documents which led to the adoption of Regulation No 1049/2001*' in the next paragraph, revealing that '*consideration was paid to the possibility of extending the subject-matter of that regulation by providing for account to be taken of certain specific interests of which persons could avail themselves in order to obtain access to a particular document*' but that this possibility was eventually not incorporated in the Transparency Regu-

2065 Some actions have nevertheless been dismissed for lack of interest in bringing proceedings: see e.g. Judgment of 7 March 2013, *Henkel and Henkel France v Commission*, T-64/12, EU:T:2013:116 and Judgment of 23 September 2015, *Schroeder v Council and Commission*, T-205/14, EU:T:2015:673.

2066 *Sison v Council*, C-266/05 P, confirming Judgment of 26 April 2005, *Sison v Council*, Joined cases T-110/03, T-150/03 and T-405/03, EU:T:2005:143.

2067 *Sison v Council*, C-266/05 P, paras 43-44.

2068 This was already the Court's approach in *Van Gend en Loos*, C-26/62, as discussed in this work p. 22.

lation.[2069] It follows that '*the particular interest of an applicant in obtaining access to documents cannot be taken into account by the institution called upon to rule on the question whether the disclosure to the public of those documents would undermine the interests protected by Article 4*'. This applies to interests protected by Article 4(1) because '*as regards the exceptions to the right of access provided for by that provision, refusal of access by the institution is mandatory where disclosure of a document to the public would undermine the interests which that provision protects, without the need, in such a case and in contrast to the provisions [...] of Article 4(2), to balance the requirements connected to the protection of those interests against those which stem from other interests*'.[2070]

This approach of contrasting Article 4(1) and Article 4(2) could have led to imagine that, *a contrario*, individual interests may have been taken into account in the balancing exercise required by Article 4(2). Yet the General Court did not take this view and instead ruled in another case that '*if the rules on exceptions provided for in Article 4(2) of Regulation No 1049/2001 are based on the weighing-up of conflicting interests in a given situation, namely, on the one hand, the interests that would be threatened by disclosure of the documents concerned and, on the other, the interests that would be favoured by such disclosure, as regards the latter set of interests, only an overriding public interest can be taken into account*'.[2071] Therefore, the interest of the applicant is irrelevant also in assessing overriding public interest for purposes of applying 4(2).[2072] Individual interest is in fact, quite simply, taken out of the Article 4 equation.

This is further exemplified by the complicated relation between the right of access to documents and procedural rights in administrative proceedings.[2073] In *Franchet and Byk*, the applicants were the object of an investigation and they were seeking access to documents relating this investigation. They submitted that the right to a fair hearing constituted an overriding public interest because '*even if the right to a fair hearing primarily protects*

2069 *Sison v Council*, C-266/05 P, para 45. See the same reasoning in Judgment of 12 May 2015, *Unión de Almacenistas de Hierros de España v Commission*, T-623/13, EU:T:2015:268, paras 85-88.

2070 *Sison v Council*, C-266/05 P, para 46.

2071 *Unión de Almacenistas de Hierros de España v Commission*, T-623/13, para 89.

2072 *Unión de Almacenistas de Hierros de España v Commission*, T-623/13, para 90; Judgment of 21 October 2010, *Umbach v Commission*, T-474/08, EU:T:2010:443, paras 59 and 62.

2073 For an analysis of this relation in the light of the principle of good administration see Mihaescu Evans, 'The right to good administration at the crossroads of the various sources of fundamental rights in the EU integrated administrative system' 211-225.

a private interest, this is also an overriding right which constitutes the basis of the rule of law and democracy in a State. In particular, access to the courts and to effective judicial protection is at issue.'[2074] This after all was not inconsistent in the light of the double rationale of administrative procedural rights that the Court has so often emphasised.[2075] The GC however took the view that under Article 2(1) of the Transparency Regulation, '*the beneficiaries of the right of access to documents of the institutions are '[a]ny citizen of the Union, and any natural or legal person residing or having its registered office in a Member State'. That provision makes it clear that the purpose of the regulation is to guarantee access for everyone to public documents and not merely access for the requesting party to documents concerning him*'.[2076] The consequences of this very intentionalist reading is that '*the particular interest which may be asserted by a requesting party in obtaining access to a document concerning him personally cannot be taken into account*'.[2077] The GC further justified its interpretation by explaining that '*[t]he general interest which the applicants claim is the right to a fair hearing. It is certainly true that the right to a fair hearing is in itself a general interest. However, the fact that this right is manifested in the present case by the applicants' individual interest in defending themselves implies that the interest which the applicants invoke is not a general, but rather a private, interest.*'[2078] The GC finally held that '*the right to a fair hearing invoked by the applicants as an overriding interest is not an overriding public interest justifying disclosure of the requested documents*'.[2079]

The systematic dismissal of the relevance of individual interests for identifying an overriding public interest looks like a new, reverse *Schutznorm* approach. The *Schutznorm* approach requires that rights arise only of individual interests that were intended to be protected, and not of norms pursuing only a general interest. Here, the individual interest is dismissed because only an inherently 'public' interest may be 'overriding'. The underlying logic is in fact the same in both cases: we have a complete disconnection between individual and general interests, instead of a search for convergence, which was the very rationale of the original EU concept of individual rights.

The absence of an obligation to state reasons and to demonstrate interest also backfires in a (so far) more marginal but still disturbing way. In three

---

2074 *Franchet and Byk v Commission*, T-48/05, para 65.
2075 See p. 308 of this work.
2076 *Franchet and Byk v Commission*, T-48/05, para 136.
2077 *Franchet and Byk v Commission*, T-48/05, para 137.
2078 *Franchet and Byk v Commission*, T-48/05, para 138.
2079 *Franchet and Byk v Commission*, T-48/05, para 139.

cases, pharmaceutical companies had applied for interim suspension and annulment of decisions by EU agencies (the European Medicines Agency in *PTC* and *MSD*, the European Chemicals Agency in *Deza*) based on the Transparency Regulation granting to third parties access to certain documents containing information submitted in applications for marketing authorisation of some medicinal and chemical products. In all three cases the General Court granted interim relief because disclosure of the report to the third party '*would place the applicant in a vulnerable situation*' especially because the third party '*would immediately take cognisance of that report and could use it straightaway for any purpose it deemed useful, since Article 6(1) of Regulation No 1049/2001 does not require the party requesting access to give reasons explaining that request. The applicant would thus have to expect that the disclosure of that report would be liable to weaken its competitive position.*'[2080] The same reasoning has applied in another case when France opposed the disclosure of a draft law which fell within the scope of an EU directive and the conformity of which with EU law was being assessed by the Commission. The GC again emphasised that the issue was amplified because '*under Article 6(1) of Regulation No 1049/2001, an applicant is not obliged to state reasons for his application.*'[2081] The absence of an obligation to state reasons and to demonstrate interest becomes an additional argument *against* granting access to documents. While for now limited to the specific context of interim relief proceedings,[2082] this approach of transforming the absence of an obligation to state reasons into a source of suspicion as to the motives

---

2080 Order of 20 July 2016, *PTC Therapeutics International v EMA*, T-718/15 R, EU:T:2016:425, para 113 (on appeal the Court of Justice did not explicitly address this argument but upheld the GC's finding that '*disclosure of the report at issue would, with a sufficient degree of probability, place PTC at risk of serious and irreparable harm*' - Order of 1 March 2017, *EMA v PTC Therapeutics International*, C-513/16 P, EU:C:2017:148, para 126). See also Order of 25 July 2014, *Deza v ECHA*, T-189/14 R, EU:T:2014:686, para 89; Order of 20 July 2016, *MSD Animal Health Innovation and Intervet international v EMA*, T-729/15 R, EU:T:2016:435, para 104 (Confirmed by Order of 1 March 2017, *EMA v MSD Animal Health Innovation and Intervet international*, C-512/16 P(R), EU:C:2017:149).

2081 Order of 1 September 2015, *France v Commission*, T-344/15 R, EU:T:2015:583, para 40.

2082 Eventually, when judging these cases, the General Court did not refer to Article 6 of the Transparency Regulation in its reasoning. It dismissed the actions for annulment against decisions of respectively the European Chemicals Agency, the Commission, and the European Medicines Agency to disclose certain information which the applicant deemed confidential (Judgment of 13 January 2017, *Deza v ECHA*, T-189/14, EU:T:2017:4, Judgment of 5 April 2017,

underlying a request to access documents is nevertheless questionable. Firstly, because it does not seem necessary to go down that path in order to assess whether disclosure would harm the party opposing it; secondly, because this approach is completely inconsistent with the Court's so far unyielding position that the interest of the applicant in submitting a request should not be taken into account.

2.3.3.4. Interim conclusions

As things now stand the right of access to documents constitutes a rather atypical right. It is not new that a right arises from an unconditional obligation, or at least a conditional one in a situation where the required condition (i.e. the absence of an exception provided for by Article 4 of the Transparency Regulation) is fulfilled – in which case the obligation becomes applicable, giving the applicant the right of access to the requested documents. What is more disturbing is the Court's interpretation of the conditions, which is so generous towards stakeholders opposed to disclosure that it significantly limits the possibility for Article 2(1) to give rise to a right. It does not look like Article 42 of the Charter will help reinforce this right. This provision has been relied on in only 17 cases so far and never in a decisive way.[2083] In line with the Explanations on Article 42, the Court has pointed out that the right of access to documents in the Charter corresponds to Article 15 TFEU(3), which (unlike Article 42) provides in its second subparagraph that the '*general principles and limits on grounds of public or private interest governing this right*' shall be determined through the ordinary legislative procedure. In accordance with Article 52(2) of the Charter, this right is therefore governed by Regulation 1049/2001, which was adopted on the basis of Article 255 EC (the predecessor of Article 15 TFEU).[2084] The upgrading of the right of access to documents to the status

France v Commission, T-344/15, EU:T:2017:250, Judgment of 5 February 2018, *PTC Therapeutics International v EMA*, T-718/15, EU:T:2018:66, Judgment of 5 February 2018, *MSF Animal Health Innovation and Intervet International v EMA*, T-729/15, EU:T:2018:67.

2083 According to a search on the curia website on 15 May 2017.

2084 Order of 2 September 2014, *Verein Natura Havel and Vierhaus v Commission*, T-538/13, EU:T:2014:738, paras 68-70; Judgment of 25 March 2015, *Sea Handling SpA v Commission*, T-456/13, EU:T:2015:185, para 50; Judgment of 26 May 2016, *International Management Group v Commission*, T-110/15, EU:T:2016:322, para 23.

of fundamental right therefore does not alter the limits and conditions to which it is subjected.

Also problematic is the Court's approach to individual interest. Individual interest is presumed when it comes to claiming the right, which at least has the advantage of facilitating access to judicial review of a non-disclosure decision. However, this seemingly favourable approach turns out to be illusory as individual interest is then completely dismissed from the balancing process that allows identifying the obligation and correlative right. This process in itself is also rather atypical, since so far it seemed like there were two distinct successive phases of first identifying a right and then balancing it against other norms.[2085] What is also atypical in the case law on access to documents is the reliance on preparatory works in order to apply an intentionalist method of interpretation. It is not clear why this method would make any sense now that 27 or 28 Member States are negotiating legislative instruments, considering that it was not favoured when there were 6 Member States. The negotiations on the Transparency Regulation were particularly tense and difficult:[2086] should this be an argument for or against reliance on preparatory works? What is clear is that the intentionalist approach is favouring the development of a sort of reverse *Schutznorm* approach, which strictly dissociates individual interest from the notion of public interest and dismisses the former as a parameter for assessing the existence of the latter. The interest in requesting access to documents thus runs the risk of being drowned out by the variety of opposing interests that are protected by the Transparency Regulation. Of course, these interests, including those of the institutions and of private parties, deserve protection. The problem is that NGOs and citizens advocating transparency are statistically more likely to be on the side of the applicant being denied access, than on that of the individual opposing disclosure. And it is not always easy to determine whether the EU institution denying access is genuinely doing so in the name of a relatively abstract EU general interest. In this asymmetrical setting, the dismissal of an 'individual interest' component in the public right of access to documents is rather unfortunate in an area where functional subjectivation would make perfect sense, given the overarching objective of improving transparency and the sense of citizenship in the EU.

2085 See this work's section on the proportionality principle p. 82.

2086 Bignami, 'Three Generations of Participation Rights in European Administrative Proceedings' 11.

2.3.4. Conclusions

Based on the jurisprudential developments from the past two decades analysed in this section, it is safe to say that on an overall level, non-individualisable interests are increasingly taken into account in the EU legal order. This is seen most notably in the way that consumer protection associations, as well as environment protection associations, are enabled to actively take part in the enforcement of EU law. These developments suggest that an individual right is not only granted to any individual who has a personal interest in the execution of an obligation laid down by EU law, but also to any individual representing a collective interest in the execution of such an obligation.

This section also highlights two types of circumstances where this does not work. One is environmental litigation before the EU courts. The other is litigation over access to documents of the EU institutions, also before the EU courts. Thus we can at least partically agree with Dougan's point that '*EU law has yet to develop a coherent framework for addressing the interaction between individual rights and collective interests.*'[2087] Based on the findings from this section, it should be added that the necessary framework is already in place in the decentralised enforcement system before nationals courts. What is sorely lacking is coherence between this system, and the centralised one of litigation before the EU courts.

2.4. Conclusion of Part 2

Part 1 of this work identified the basic characteristics of individual rights under EU law, that is, their defining relation with obligations and interests. Part 2 tested the resilience and relevance of this original connection as it developed along three generations of individual rights. Undeniably, and as confirmed by Section 2.1, individual rights first took shape as means of enforcing obligations laid down by provisions of economic law, and their development was fuelled by the purpose of advancing economic interests. The mechanism of functional subjectivation ensured that economic agents such as traders and sellers, pursuing their particular interests, would simultaneously advance the Community/Union's *telos* of a deepening economic

2087 Dougan, 'Addressing Issues of Protective Scope within the Francovich Right to Reparation' 154.

integration. Perhaps individuals in this setting were indeed merely means to an end (at least, this can be neither proven nor refuted).

Nonetheless, the case law reviewed in this Part 2 amply illustrates the resilience and flexibility of the original concept of individual rights. Section 2.2 demonstrated that the relation between rights, obligations and interests remains an essential structuring force of the evolving constitutional and legal order of the EU. The concept of individual rights proves ever more dynamic and adaptable in view of the need to protect an increasing variety of individual interests beyond the economic sphere. Not only economic agents in the strict sense have individual rights: so do employees, Union citizens, and asylum seekers. These characters all pursue interests which function as triggers for activating rights and correlative obligations. The model works in 'vertical' relations such as those between an EU citizen having exercised his right to free movement, and the administration of the host Member State. It also applies in 'horizontal' relations in the economic and socio-economic realm (i.e., in relations between competitors, or relations between employers and employees). In addition, the dynamism of the rights-obligations correlation combined with the powerful effectiveness rationale notably gave rise to the concept of derived rights, a key element of Union citizenship law. Another point that highlights the flexibility of the original concept of individual rights is that improvements in the protection of individuals are transposable across different areas of EU law. For instance, administrative procedural rights originally protected economic actors in their relations with the Commission as an enforcer of competition law, and EU civil servants in their relations with their employer. The Court built on this case law to assert the procedural protection of asylum seekers interacting with the immigration authorities of the Member States implementing EU asylum law. Additionnally, Section 2.3 explored the perspectives for collective interests to be likewise accepted as triggers for individual rights. There seems to be no major conceptual obstacle for such a development, at least if we look at the development of collective litigation in the national courts of the Member States. This evolution, especially in consumer law and environmental law, attests that collective interests can functions as triggers for the individual rights of associations, including the right of access to court.

This second part of the study also confirms and elaborates on major issues that Part 1 had identified. Firstly, the influence of the *Schutznorm* approach, focusing on the existence of a protective intention in order to identify a right, is perceptible in many disputes. The Court's resistance to this doctrine is uneven depending on the area of EU law in which it manifests itself. In the case law on Member State liability for violations of EU (mostly economic) law, the protective intention is clearly pushed into the background. Instead, the classic conception of rights as correlatives of obligations serves as the reference point for identifying individual rights, like in *Danske Slagterier.*[2088] There is no such clear-cut reaction to the *Schutznorm* pressure in the case law on Union liability so far. Likewise, when it comes to applying social provisions of the Charter, the Court for now circumvents the problem arising from the protective intention approach. In *AMS*, it did not validate an intentionalist approach to the rights/principles distinction, nor did it take the chance to clearly reassert that the process of identifying a right should be based on an assessment of the practical applicability of a provision in concrete circumstances, not on an abstract (and uncertain) labelling of this provision as either a 'right' or a 'principle'.[2089] Finally, as regards the Dublin system of allocation of responsibility for processing asylum applications, the Union legislator as well as the Member States submitting observations in specific cases, try to restrict the access to a remedy to only provisions that clearly define certain rights. The Court so far has not clearly responded that any obligation of the Member State administrations under the Dublin regulation has the potential to give rise to a correlative right and therefore also to the right to a remedy.

Secondly, another aspect in dire need of improvement and enhanced coherence concerns the difficulty for individuals to assert their rights as correlatives of the institutions of the Union, as opposed to national administrations or other individuals. In the first place, the outlook remains grim in terms of the collective interests that the Court accepts as triggers for rights to be claimed against the EU institutions. This is especially illustrated by the difficulties of environmental protection associations to assert their participation rights on the EU level, and the laborious enforcement of the right of access to documents of the EU institutions. More generally, in an action for annulment, the interest is filtered so strictly when checking the admissibility, that once assessing whether there actually is a right, the interest criterion is of course already fulfilled. Only the content of the obligation and correlative right is left to be assessed, while so many interests are potentially left unprotected. Strict standing conditions are supposed to avoid the development of an *actio popularis* and the overloading of the EU Courts.[2090] Still, in terms of avoiding a work overload, the Court is very

2088 *Danske Slagterier*, C-445/06. See p. 230 of this work.

2089 *Association de Médiation Sociale*, C-176/12. See p. 351 of this work.

2090 Waelbroeck and Bombois, 'Des requérants 'privilégiés' et des autres... A propos de l'arrêt Inuit et de l'exigence de protection juridictionnelle effective des particuliers en droit européen' 68-69.

self-protective, and much less concerned with the risk that its domestic counterparts could be overloaded with legal actions based on EU law. The result is that while individual rights that are correlatives of obligations imposed by Union law on Member States and individuals blossom in litigation before national courts, the same cannot be said of those rights that should arise as correlatives of the obligations of the Union's own institutions.

Conclusion

> *'As long as the Court goes on handing down judgments that enable ordinary men and women to savor the fruits of integration, it will continue to demonstrate its usefulness.'*[2091]

This study has put forward a definition of individual rights that allows to think and reason about rights in a coherent yet flexible manner. It has shed light on the relation between rights, obligations and interests and how this relation shapes and reflects the nature and function of individual rights in the legal order of the European Union. The study also addressed the challenges generated by the evolution of the Union's constitutional framework, and the potential impact thereof on the definition and relevance of the concept of individual rights under Union law.

The original definition of individual rights as correlatives of obligations, triggered into existence by interests in the fulfilment of these obligations, resists the test of time and the successive reconfigurations of the Union's legal order. The basic concept of individual rights could already be inferred from the CJEU's original method for identifying these rights developed in *Van Gend en Loos* and *Defrenne II*. We have observed through the analytical lens of the rights/obligations/interests relation, how individual rights evolved into a self-standing concept, emancipated from the specific frame of the direct effect doctrine, yet retaining their original characteristics. The original definition of individual rights also reflects their significance and function within the EU legal order. In a virtuous circle of functional subjectivation, individuals, by pursuing their own interests, also fulfil a crucial function of activating the process of legality review, thereby ensuring the effective enforcement of EU law. Additionally, the development concept of individual rights parallels the ever-increasing inclusiveness of the EU legal order, as more and more categories of right-holders may be identified: providers of goods and services, workers, agricultors, tenderers, taxpayers, civil servants, citizens, voters, asylum seekers, consumers, and the list gets longer.

The study has emphasised that the correlation between rights and obligations functions in a pragmatic and dynamic way. It is not a tool for ab-

2091 Mancini and Keeling, 'Language, Culture and Politics in the Life of the European Court of Justice' 413.

stractly determining whether a given provision gives rise to rights; instead, it means that the degree of discretion allowed by the provision (assessed by looking at clues such as clarity, unconditionality, and precision) is inversely proportional to the probability of identifying a right. Indeed, individual rights come to life in concrete circumstances. No matter whether is it phrased as a right or obligation, a provision of EU law can give rise to no right at all, or a broad array of different rights. This dynamism has allowed the concept of individual rights to remain relevant all along the process of constitutional integration. For instance, in order to ensure the effectiveness of individual rights conferred by the status of Union citizen, the Court of Justice developed the additional concept of derived rights. A prime example of this was case *Zhu and Chen*, in which what could seem at first sight like a single obligation of a Member State towards an EU citizen translated into two correlative rights (a right for the infant EU citizen, and a derived right for her mother, to remain in the host Member State).[2092] Another example is the jurisprudential response to the transformations in the Union's administrative structure. We have come a long way from *Van Gend en Loos* to *Berlioz*.[2093] In *Van Gend en Loos*, a right was recognised to a transport company as a correlative of the Dutch administration's obligation to refrain from imposing a custom duty. In *Berlioz*, a taxpayer's right correlative to an obligation of the French tax authorities translated into a further obligation for the Luxembourgish administration to control the decision of its French counterpart; this in turn, in accordance with the right to an effective remedy, required the Luxembourgish courts to control the observance of these obligations.

The resilience and problem-solving potential of the original concept of individual rights in view of the challenges of the deepening European integration is also due to its ability to accommodate to a broad variety of interests. The interests that historically triggered individual rights were predominantly the interests of economic actors such as traders and agricultors. This study has highlighted the gradual and smooth expansion of the range of interests able to trigger individual rights. Notably, subjectively defined interests are increasingly taken into account – especially the interests of EU citizens to have a family life, and to retain their identity as they move across Member State borders. Importantly, the relevant interests are not only interests in substantive results. Indeed, the interest of the European individual in being included in diverse processes is also increasingly recog-

2092 *Zhu and Chen*, C-200/02.

2093 *Van Gend en Loos*, C-26/62; *Berlioz*, C-682/15.

nised. There are individual rights to be actively involved in the political and administrative life of the Union: the right to vote and stand as candidate to the elections of the European Parliament, the right to play a role in the initiation of legislative processes, the right to participate in administrative decision-making. What is more, the evolution is not only qualitative: besides individual interests, collective interests are now, with the support of the Union's legislature, recognised as possible triggers for rights. This is demonstrated by the growing weight of collective litigation, especially in consumer law and environmental law. Against this backdrop, the principle of proportionality remains an essential tool for ensuring that the interests protected by rights are optimally balanced with other relevant interests.

It must also be stressed that not only expressly protected interests can function as triggers for rights. It is in the Union's best interest that as many individuals as possible engage in the mechanism of functional subjectivation and contribute to the enforcement of the rights and obligations laid down by Union law. The effectiveness rationale thus underpins the generosity with which the Court admitted an increasingly broad array of interests as triggers for individual rights, no matter whether the provisions that are claimed by individuals are expressly intended to protect them. Admittedly, there is one way in which the protective intention underlying a provision can add a layer of protection. In the face of a public liability claim, the judge may rely on the intention which underpins a given provision in order to check whether that provision is intended to confer rights. Still, although this intentionalist method of interpretation may be decisive in some cases, it works merely as a supplement to the direct effect test, which comes in where the latter test fails – it is not a substitute for that test in the first place. In other words, the most important impact that the detection of an intention to grant a right can have is to occasionally expand the scope of a right. Even this should not be systematically assumed, since not everything labelled 'right' easily gives rise to individual rights, as the case law on the 'right' of access to documents unfortunately illustrates. Conversely, the absence of a clearly expressed protective intention does not restrict the scope of the right. This is regularly confirmed by the Court, in cases such as *Danske Slagterier*, *Olainfarm*, and *Berlioz*.[2094] For this reason, when it comes to identifying rights, it is important to dissociate the protective intention underlying a provision, and the protective scope of this provision. The protective scope is not fully pre-determined. Rather, the personal, ma-

2094 *Danske Slagterier*, C-445/06; *Olainfarm*, C-104/13; *Berlioz*, C-682/15.

terial, temporal, institutional scopes of a right are all optional, modular filters for delineating this right in a concrete situation.

However, this study has also identified a tension, both in the case law and the literature, between the above-described generous approach to interests as triggers for rights, and a more restrictive conception of rights and interests. The latter approach can be traced back to the German *Schutznorm* doctrine according to which the identification of a subjective right in a given provision is conditioned to the existence of an express legislative intention to protect a specific interest. The tension in the method for identifying individual rights signals a conceptual misunderstanding over both the nature and the function of individual rights under Union law. Firstly, conditioning the identification of a right to the existence of a protective intention, amounts to denying that rights can be reflections of obligations – when in fact, that is exactly what they are. Secondly, the *Schutznorm* approach undermines the mechanism of functional subjectivation, since it negates the function of individuals as agents of enforcement of EU law. The paradox of this approach is that while focusing on the notion of 'protective' intention, it is in fact much less protective of individuals than the original method for identifying rights designed in *Van Gend en Loos* and *Defrenne II*. This is illustrated in certain branches of the case law where the Court proves more receptive to the *Schutznorm* doctrine – such as in litigation over Union liability, or State aid law.

By contrast, the proposed definition of individual rights allows for a harmonious, consistent and protective approach to all sources of rights. As this study has emphasised, the logical correlativity between rights and obligations does not establish any hierarchy between the two concepts. Therefore, it applies irrespective of how strong a norm or body of norms emphasises either the 'right' or 'obligation' dimension. Thinking of rights and obligations as correlatives is thus the best way to make sense of the plurality of sources of rights that characterises the Union's legal order. A telling example is the right to an effective remedy, which the Court keeps developing by connecting a general principle originally based on the obligations of the Member States, a right enshrined at Article 47 CFR, and a further complementary obligation laid down by Article 19(1) TEU. The suggested approach also goes against a strict and abstract categorisation of Charter provisions into 'rights' on which individuals could rely and 'principles' that would oblige the EU and Member State authorities to act in a certain way, but have no immediate effects for individuals. Instead, the ability of a Charter provision (like of other provisions of Union law) to give rise to rights should always be assessed in concrete circumstances.

Finally, this book sheds light on the diversity of relations within which individual rights come to life. While the conferral of individual rights in so-called 'horizontal' relations is still an intensely debated and still open issue, it has been argued in this work that when it comes to identifying and protecting individual rights, the fracture line is not (or no longer) between vertical and horizontal relations. The Court's creative use of the principle of effectiveness ensures that it is increasingly possible for individuals to claims rights conferred by EU law not only in their relations with Member State administrations but also in horizontal relations, as the recent developments in competition law and consumer law illustrate. Rather, it is the relation between individuals and the EU institutions that stands apart. Most of the cases in which the Court was relatively responsive to the *Schutznorm* doctrine (or variants of it) were cases where individuals were challenging acts of the Union's institutions. In these situations, a restrictive conception of the relevant interests often blocks the materialisation of institutional obligations into correlative individual rights. The resulting asymmetry is increasingly blatant as the European integration process deepens and the Union's institutions gain more and more competences, and it is unsustainable in a Union based on the rule of law. It is up to the Union's judicature, possibly encouraged by the legislature, to correct this incoherence and to ensure that in the constitutional process of integration all relevant interests are – consistently – taken seriously.

Table of cases

Judgments and Orders of the Court of Justice

Judgment of 29 November 1956, *Fédération charbonnière de Belgique v High Authority*, C-8/55, EU:C:1956:11

Judgment of 12 July 1957, *Algera and Others v Assemblée commune*, Joined cases C-7/56 and C-3 to C-7/57, EU:C:1957:7

Judgment of 4 February 1959, *Stork & Co. v High Authority of the European Coal and Steel Community*, C-1/58, EU:C:1959:4

Judgment of 23 February 1961, *De gezamenlijke Steenkolenmijnen in Limburg v High Authority*, C-30/59, EU:C:1961:2

Judgment of 22 March 1961, *S.N.U.P.A.T. v High Authority*, Joined cases C-42/59 and C-42/59, EU:C:1961:5

Judgment of 14 July 1961, *Vloeberghs v High Authority*, C-9/60, EU:C:1961:18

Judgment of 6 April 1962, *De Geus en Uitdenbogerd v Bosch and others*, C-13/61, EU:C:1962:11

Judgment of 12 July 1962, *Koninklijke Nederlandsche Hoogovens en Staalfabrieken v High Authority*, C-14/61, EU:C:1962:28

Judgment of 14 December 1962, *Wöhrmann v Commission of the EEC*, C-31/62, EU:C:1962:49

Judgment of 5 February 1963, *Van Gend en Loos*, C-26/62, EU:C:1963:1

Judgment of 4 July 1963, *Alvis v Council of the EEC*, 32/62, EU:C:1963:15

Judgment of 15 July 1963, *Plaumann v Commission of the EEC*, C-25/62, EU:C:1963:17

Judgment of 19 March 1964, *Unger v Bedrijfsvereniging voor Detailhandel en Ambachten*, C-75/63, EU:C:1964:19

Judgment of 15 July 1964, *Costa v E.N.E.L.*, C-6/64, EU:C:1964:66

Judgment of 1 July 1965, *Toepfer v Commission of the EEC*, Joined cases C-106 and 107/63, EU:C:1965:65

Judgment of 13 July 1965, *Lemmerz Werke* v High Authority, C-111/63, C:1965:76

Judgment of 16 June 1966, *Lütticke v Hauptzollamt Saarlouis*, C-57/65, EU:C:1966:34

Judgment of 5 July 1967, *De Moor v Caisse de pension des employés privés*, C-2/67, EU:C:1967:28

Judgment of 14 July 1967, *Kampffmeyer and Others v Commission of the EEC*, Joined cases C-5/66, C-13/66, C-16/66, C-21/66, EU:C:1967:31

Judgment of 3 April 1968, *Molkerei Zentrale Westfalen-Lippe v Hauptzollamt Paderborn*, C-28/67, EU:C:1968:17

Judgment of 19 December 1968, *Salgoil v Ministerio del commercio con l'estero*, C-13/68, EU:C:1968:54

Judgment of 13 February 1969, *Walt Wilhelm and Others v Bundeskartellamt*, C-14/68, EU:C:1969:4

Judgment of 12 November 1969, *Caisse de maladie des CFL and Others v Compagnie d'assurance sur la vie et contre les accidents*, C-27/69, EU:C:1969:56

Judgment of 12 November 1969, *Stauder*, C-26/69, EU:C:1969:57

Judgment of 6 October 1970, *Grad v Finanzamt Traunstein*, 9/70, EU:C:1970:78

Judgment of 17 December 1970, *Internationale Handelsgesellschaft*, 11/70, EU:C:1970:114

Judgment of 17 December 1970, *Spa Sace v Ministero delle finanze*, C-33/70, EU:C:1970:118

Judgment of 28 April 1071, *Lütticke v Commission*, C-4/69, EU:C:1971:40

Judgment of 13 May 1971, *International Fruit Company and Others v Commission*, C-41 to C-44/70, EU:C:1971:53

Judgment of 25 May 1971, *Defrenne v. Belgian State*, C-80/70, EU:C:1971:55

Judgment of 2 December 1971, *Zuckerfabrik Schöppenstedt v Council*, 5/71, EU:C:1971:116

Judgment of 14 December 1971, *Politi v. Ministero delle finanze*, C-43/71, EU:C:1971:122

Judgment of 5 June 1973, *Commission v Council*, C-81/72, EU:C:1973:60

Judgment of 19 June 1973, *Capolongo v Azienda Agricola Maya*, C-77/72, EU:C:1973:65

Judgment of 10 October 1973, *Fratelli Variola Spa v Amministrazione delle finanze dello Stato*, C-34/73, EU:C:1973:101

Judgment of 11 December 1973, *Lorenz GmbH v Bundesrepublik Deutschland and Others*, C-120/73, EU:C:1973:152

Judgment of 11 December 1973, *Lohrey v Bundesrepublik Deutschland and Others*, C-141/73, EU:C:1973:155

Judgment of 21 January 1974, *BRT v Sabam*, C-127/73, EU:C:1974:25

Judgment of 14 May 1974, *Nold v Commission*, 4/73, EU:C:1974:51

Judgment of 23 October 1974, *Transocean Marine Paint Association v Commission*, C-17/74, EU:C:1974:106

Judgment of 3 December 1974, *Van Binsbergen* v *Bedrijfsvereniging Metaalnijverheid*, C-33/74, EU:C:1974:131

Judgment of 4 December 1974, *Van Duyn v. Home Office*, C-41/74, EU:C:1974:133

Judgment of 28 October 1975, *Rutili*, C-36/75, EU:C:1975:137

Judgment of 17 February 1976, *Rewe-Zentrale v Hauptzollamt Landau-Pfalz*, C-45/75, EU:C:1976:22

Judgment of 8 April 1976, *Defrenne v. SABENA*, C-43/75, EU:C:1976:56

Judgment of 15 June 1976, *CNTA v Commission*, C-74/74, EU:C:1976:84

Judgment of 23 November 1976, *Kermaschek v Bundesanstalt für Arbeit*, C-40/76, EU:C:1976:157

Judgment of 16 December 1976, *Rewe v Landwirtschaftskammer für das Saarland*, 33/76, EU:C:1976:188

Judgment of 16 December 1976, *Comet BV v Produktschap voor Siergewassen*, 45/76, EU:C:1976:191

Judgment of 1 February 1977, *Verbond nederlandse ondernemingen v Inspecteur der invoerrechten en accijnzen*, C-51/76, EU:C:1977:12

Judgment of 22 March 1977, *Ianelli v Meroni*, C-74/76, EU:C:1977:51

Judgment of 22 March 1977, *Steinike and Weinlig*, C-78/76, EU:C:1977:52

Judgment of 5 July 1977, *Bela Mühle v Grows Farm*, C-114/76, EU:C:1977:116

Judgment of 9 March 1978, *Simmenthal*, C-106/77, EU:C:1978:49

Judgment of 3 May 1978, *Töpfer v Commission*, C-112/77, EU:C:1978:94

Judgment of 29 November 1978, *Redmond*, C-83/78, EU:C:1978:214

Judgment of 13 April 1978, *Mollet v Commission*, C-75/77, EU:C:1978:84

Judgment of 25 May 1978, *HNL v Council and Commission*, Joined cases C-83 and C-94/76, 4, 15 and 40/77, EU:C:1978:113

Judgment of 7 February 1979, *Knoors v Staatssecretaris van Economische Zaken*, C-115/78, EU:C:1979:31

Judgment of 13 February 1979, *Hoffmann-La Roche v Commission*, C-85/76, EU:C:1979:36

Judgment of 5 April 1979, *Ratti*, C-148/78, EU:C:1979:110

Judgment of 26 June 1979, *Pigs and Bacon Commission*, C-177/78, EU:C:1979:164

Judgment of 4 October 1979, *Dumortier v Council*, C-64/76, EU:C:1979:223

Judgment of 4 October 1979, *Ireks-Arkady GmbH contre Conseil et Commission des Communautés européennes*, C-238/78, EU:C:1979:226

Judgment of 4 October 1979, *DGV v Council and Commission*, Joined cases C-241, C-242 and C-246 to C-249/78, EU:C:1979:227

Judgment of 13 December 1979, *Hauer*, C-44/79, EU:C:1979:290

Judgment of 22 May 1980, *Regina v Secretary of State for Home Affairs, ex parte Santillo*, C-131/79, EU:C:1980:131

Judgment of 17 September 1980, *Philip Morris v Commission*, C-730/79, EU:C:1980:209

Judgment of 5 May 1981, *Dürbeck v Hauptzollamt Frankfurt a. M.*, C-112/80, EU:C:1981:94

Judgment of 27 May 1981, *Amministrazione delle Finanze dello Stato* v. *Essevi SpA and Carlo Salengo*, C-142 and C-143/80, EU:C:1981:121

Judgment of 17 December 1981, *Ludwigshafener Walzmühle v Council and Commission*, Joined cases C-197 to C-200, C-243, C-245 and C-247/80, EU:C:1981:311

Judgment of 19 January 1982, *Becker*, C-8/81, EU:C:1982:7

Judgment of 3 March 1982, *Alpha Steel v Commission*, C-14/81, EU:C:1982:76

Judgment of 14 December 1982, *Procureur de la République v Waterkeyn*, C-314/81, EU:C:1982:430

Judgment of 22 September 1983, *Auer v Ministère Public*, 271/82, EU:C:1983:243

Judgment of 9 November 1983, *Ammistrazione delle finanze dello Stato v San Giorgio*, C-199/82, EU:C:1983:318

Judgment of 15 December 1983, *Rienks*, C-5/83, EU:C:1983:382

Judgment of 15 March 1984, *Tradax v Commission*, 64/82, EU:1984:106

Judgment of 10 April 1984, *Von Colson and Kamann v Land Nordrhein-Westfalen*, C-14/83, EU:C:1984:153

Judgment of 9 October 1984, *Heineken*, Joined cases 91/83 and 127/83, EU:C:1984:307

Judgment of 14 November 1984, *Intermills v Commission*, C-323/82, EU:C:1984:345

Judgment of 10 January 1985, *Leclerc and Others v 'Au Blé Vert and Others*, C-229/83, EU:C:1985:1

Judgment of 11 July 1985, *Salerno and Others v Commission and Council*, C-87/77, C-130/77, C-22/83, C-9 and C-10/84, EU:C:1985:318

Judgment of 7 November 1985, *Adams v Commission*, C-154/83, EU:C:1985:448

Judgement of 15 January 1986, *Hurd v Jones*, 44/84, EU:C:1986:2

Judgment of 26 February 1986, *Marshall v. Southampton and South-West Hampshire Area Health Authority*, C-152/84, EU:C:1986:84

Judgment of 23 April 1986, *Les Verts*, C-294/83, EU:C:1986:166

Judgment of 15 May 1986, *Johnston v Chief Constable of the Royal Ulster Constabulary*, 222/84, EU:C:1986:206

Judgment of 10 July 1986, *DEFI v Commission*, C-282/85, EU:C:1986:316

Judgment of 8 October 1986, *Leussink-Brummelhuis v Commission*, C-169/83 and C-136/84, EU:C:1986:371

Judgment of 14 January 1987, *Zuckerfabrik Bedburg v Council and Commission*, C-281/84, EU:C:1987:3

Judgment of 12 May 1987, *Traen*, joined cases C-372 to 374/85, EU:C:1987:222,

Judgment of 30 September 1987, *Demirel v. Stadt Schwäbisch Gmünd*, C-12/86, EU:C:1987:400

Judgment of 8 October 1987, *Kolpinghuis Nijmegen*, C-80/86, EU:C:1987:431

Judgment of 15 October 1987, *Unectef v Heylens*, 222/86, EU:C:1987:442

Judgment of 22 October 1987, *Foto-Frost v Hauptzollamt Lübeck-Ost*, C-314/85, EU:C:1987:452

Judgment of 17 December 1987, *Zaoui v CRAMIF*, C-147/87, EU:C:1987:576

Judgment of 25 February 1988, *Bianco and Girard v Directeur général des douanes and droits indirects*, C-331/85, C-376/85 and C-378/85, EU:C:1988:97

Judgment of 8 March 1988, *Exécutif régional wallon v Commission*, Joined cases C-62/87 and C-72/87, EU:C:1988:132

Judgment of 28 April 1988, *Mulder v Minister van Landbouw and Visserij*, C-120/86, EU:C:1988:213

Judgment of 20 September 1988, *Beentjes v State of the Netherlands*, C-31/87, EU:C:1988:422

Judgment of 22 September 1988, *Land de Sarre v Ministre de l'Industrie*, C-187/87, EU:C:1988:439

Judgment of 22 June 1989, *Fratelli Costanzo v. Comune di Milano*, C-103/88, EU:C:1989:256

Judgment of 27 June 1989, *Kühne*, C-50/88, EU:C:1989:262

Judgment of 29 June 1989, *Vreugdenhil* 22/88, EU:C:1989:277

Judgment of 17 January 1989, *Vainker v Parliament*, C-293/87, EU:C:1989:8

Judgment of 23 May 1989, *Top Hit Holzvertrieb v Commission*, C-378/87, EU:C:1989:209

Judgment of 11 July 1989, *Schräder v Hauptzollamt Gronau*, C-265/87, EU:C:1989:303

Judgment of 12 July 1989, *Binder v Hauptzollamt Bad Reichenhall*, C-161/88, EU:C:1989:312

Judgment of 13 July 1989, *Wachauf v Bundesamt für Ernährung und Forstwirtschaft*, C-5/88, EU:C:1989:321

Judgment of 21 September 1989, *Hoechst AG v Commission*, C-46/87, EU:C:1989:337

Judgment of 21 November 1989, *UCDV v Commision*, C-244/88, EU:C:1989:588

Judgment of 13 December 1989, *Grimaldi v Fonds des maladies professionnelles*, C-322/88, EU:C:1989:646

Judgment of 15 March 1990, *Commission v Netherlands*, C-339/87, EU:C:1990:119

Judgment of 27 March 1990, *Cargill v Commission*, C-229/88, EU:C:1990:138

Judgment of 8 May 1990, *Biehl v Administration des contributions*, C-175/88, EU:C:1990:186

Judgment of 19 June 1990, *The Queen v Secretary of State for Transport, ex parte Factortame*, C-213/89, EU:C:1990:257

Judgment of 26 June 1990, *Sofrimport SARL v Commission*, C-152/88, EU:C:1990:259

Judgment of 6 June 1990, *AERPO and Others v Commission*, C-119/88, EU:C:1990:231

Judgment of 12 July 1990, *Foster e.a. v British Gas*, C-188/89, EU:C:1990:313

Judgment of 3 October 1990, *Bouchoucha*, C-61/89, EU:C:1990:343

Judgment of 13 November 1990, *Marleasing v Comercial Internacional de Alimentación*, C-106/89, EU:C:1990:395

Judgment of 12 December 1990, *Kaefer and Procacci v French State*, C-100/89, EU:C:1990:456

Judgment of 31 January 1991, *Office national de l'emploi v Kziber*, C-18/90, EU:C:1991:36

Judgment of 21 February 1991, *Zuckerfabrik Süderdithmarschen and Zuckerfabrik Soest v Hauptzollamt Itzehoe and Hauptzollamt Paderborn*, Joined Cases C-143/88 and C-92/89, EU:C:1991:65

Judgment of 28 February 1991, *Commission v Germany*, C-131/88, EU:C:1991:87

Judgment of 28 February 1991, *Delimitis v Henninger Bräu*, C-234/89, EU:C:1991:91

Judgment of 7 May 1991, *Nakajima All Precision v Council*, C-69/89, EU:C:1991:186

Judgment of 30 May 1991, *Commission v Germany*, C-59/89, EU:C:1991:225

Judgment of 18 June 1991, *ERT v DEP*, C-260/89, EU:C:1991:254

Judgment of 27 June 1991, *Al-Jubail Fertilizer Company and Others v Council*, C-49/88, EU:C:1991:276

Judgment of 27 June 1991, *Mecanarte-Metalurgica da Lagoa v Alfandega do Porto*, C-348/89, EU:C:1991:278

Judgment of 11 July 1991, *Verholen and Others v Sociale Verzekeringsbank Amsterdam*, C-87/90 to C-89/90, EU:C:1991:314

Judgment of 17 October 1991, *Commission v Germany*, C-58/89, EU:C:1991:391

Judgment of 19 November 1991, *Francovich and Bonifaci v. Italy*, Joined Cases C-6/90 and C-9/90, EU:C:1991:428

Judgment of 21 November 1991, *Technische Universität München v Hauptzollamt München-Mitte*, C-269/90, EU:C:1991:438

Judgment of 21 November 1991, *Fédération nationale du commerce extérieur des produits alimentaires and Others v France*, C-354/90, EU:C:1991:440

Judgment of 28 November 1991, *BEUC v Commission*, C-170/89, EU:C:1991:450

Judgment of 10 January 1992, *Kühn v Landwirtschaftskammer Weser-Ems*, C-177/90, EU:C:1992:2

Judgment of 30 January 1992, *Schönherr v Economic and Social Committee*, T-25/90, ECR, EU:T:1992:8

Judgment of 12 February 1992, *Netherlands and PTT Netherlands v Commission*, C-48/90 and C-66/90, EU:C:1992:63

Judgment of 13 March 1992, *Vreugdenhil v Commission*, C-282/90, EU:C:1992:124

Judgment of 8 April 1992, *Commission v Germany*, C-62/90, EU:C:1992:169

Judgment of 7 July 1992, *The Queen v Immigration Appeal Tribunal and Surinder Singh, ex parte Secretary of State for the Home Department*, C-370/90, EU:C:1992:296

Judgment of 19 May 1992, *Mulder and Others v Council and Commission*, C-104/89 and C-37/90, EU:C:1992:217

Judgment of 16 July 1992, Hughes v Chief Adjudication Officer, C-78/91, EU:C:1992:331

Judgment of 10 November 1992, *Hansa Fleisch v. Landrat des Kreises Schleswig-Flensburg*, C-156/91, EU:C:1992:423

Judgment of 3 December 1992, *Oleificio Borelli v Commission*, C-97/91, EU:C:1992:491

Judgment of 16 December 1992, *Lornoy and Others v Belgian State,* C-17/91, EU:C:1992:514

Judgment of 16 December 1992, *Demoor and Others v Belgian State,* Joined Cases C-144/91 and C-145/91, EU:C:1992:518

Judgment of 3 March 1993, *General Milk Products* v *Hauptzollamt Hamburg-Jonas,* C-8/92, EU:C:1993:82

Judgment of 17 mars 1993, *Sloman Neptun v Bodo Ziesemer*, C-72/91 and C-73/91, EU:C:1993:97

Judgment of 18 mars 1993, *Parliament v Frederiksen*, C-35/92 EU:C:1993:104

Judgment of 2 August 1993, *Larsy v INASTI*, C-31/92, EU:C:1993:166

Judgment of 16 December 1993, *Wagner Miret v Fondo de garantía salarial*, C-334/92, EU:C:1993:945

Judgment of 23 February 1994, *Comitato di coordinamento per la difesa della Cava and Others v Regione Lomardia and* Others, C-236/92, EU:C:1994:60

Judgment of 9 March 1994, *TWD v Bundesrepublik Deutschland,* C-188/92, EU:C:1994:90

Judgment of 20 April 1994, *Yousfi v Belgian State*, C-58/93, EU:C:1994:160

Judgment of 18 May 1994, *Codorniu v Council,* C-309/89, EU:C:1994:197

Judgment of 29 June 1994, *Fiskano v Commission*, C-135/92, EU:C:1994:267

Judgment of 14 July 1994, *Faccini Dori v Recreb*, C-91/92, EU:C:1994:292

Judgment of 5 October 1994, *X v Commission,* C-404/92 P, EU:C:1994:361

Judgment of 5 October 1994, *TV10 v Commissariaat voor de Media,* C-23/93, EU:C:1994:362

Judgment of 5 October 1994, *Germany v Council,* C-280/93, EU:C:1994:367

Judgment of 13 December 1994, *SMW Winzersekt v Land Rheinland-Pfalz*, C-306/93, EU:C:1994:407

Judgment of 14 February 1995, Finanzamt Köln-Altstadt v Schumacker, C-279/93, EU:C:1995:31

Judgment of 5 April 1995, *Krid v Caisse nationale d'assurance vieillesse des travailleurs salariés*, C-103/94, EU:C:1995:97

Judgment of 17 October 1995, *The Queen v Minister of Agriculture, Fisheries and Food, ex parte Fishermen's Organisations and Others*, C-44/94, EU:C:1995:325

Judgment of 14 December 1995, *Peterbroeck, Van Campenhout & Cie v Belgian State,* C-312/93, EU:C:1995:437

Judgment of 14 December 1995, *Van Schijndel v Stichting Pensioenfonds voor Fysiotherapeuten*, C-430/93 and C-431/93, EU:C:1995:441

Judgment of 15 December 1995, *Union royale belge des sociétés de football association and Others v Bosman and Others*, C-415/93, EU:C:1995:463

Judgment of 15 February 1996, *Duff and Others*, C-63/93, EU:C:1996:51

Judgment of 5 March 1996, *Brasserie du pêcheur v Bundesrepublik Deutschland and The Queen v Secretary of State for Transport, ex parte Factortame*, C-46/93 and C-48/93, EU:C:1996:79

Judgment of 7 March 1996, *El Corte Inglés v Blázquez Rivero*, C-192/94, EU:C:1996:88

Judgment of 12 March 1996, *Pafitis and Others,* C-441/93, EU:C:1996:92

Judgment of 26 March 1996, *The Queen v H.M. Treasury, ex parte British Telecommunications*, C-392/93, EU:C:1996:131

Judgment of 30 April 1996, *Bestuur van de Sociale Verzekeringsbank v Cabanis-Issarte,* C-308/93, EU:C:1996:169

Judgment of 2 May 1996, *Brennet* v *Paletta*, C-206/94, EU:C:1996:182

Judgment of 14 May 1996, *Faroe Seafood and Føroya Fiskasøla*, C-153/94, EU:C:1996:198

Judgment of 23 May 1996, *The Queen v Ministry of Agriculture, Fisheries and Food, ex parte Hedley Lomas (Ireland)*, C-5/94, EU:C:1996:205

Judgment of 11 July 1996, *SFEI and Others*, C-39/94, EU:C:1996:285

Judgment of 10 September 1996, *Taflan-Met and Others*, C-277/94, EU:C:1996:315

Judgment of 26 September 1996, *Arcaro*, C-168/95, EU:C:1996:363

Judgment of 3 October 1996, *Hallouzi-Choho v Bestuur van de Sociale Verzekeringsbank*, C-126/95, EU:C:1996:368

Judgment of 8 October 1996, *Dillenkofer and Others v Bundesrepublik Deutschland*, Joined Cases C-178/94, C-179/94, C-188 to C-190/94, EU:C:1996:375

Judgment of 17 October 1996, *Denkavit Internationaal and Others v Bundesamt für Finanzen*, C-283/94, EU:C:1996:387

Judgment of 24 October 1996, *Commission* v *Lisrestal and Others*, C-32/95 P, EU:C:1996:402

Judgment of 24 October 1996, *Kraaijeveld and Others*, C-72/95, EU:C:1996:404

Judgment of 12 December 1996, *Ministero delle Finanze v Foods Import*, C-38/95, EU:C:1996:488

Judgment of 12 December 1996, *Olasagasti and Others v Amministrazione delle Finanze dello Stato*, Joined Cases 47 to 50/95, C-60/95, C-81/95, C-92/95 and C-148/95, EU:C:1996:489

Judgment of 14 January 1997, *Comateb and Others v Directeur général des douanes and droits indirects*, C-192/95 to C-218/95, EU:C:1997:12

Judgment of 20 March 1997, *Land Rheinland-Pfalz v Alcan Deutschland*, C-24/95, EU:C:1997:163

Judgment of 15 April 1997, *Irish Farmers Association and Others v Minister for Agriculture, Food and Forestry, Ireland and Attorney General*, C-22/94, EU:C:1997:187

Judgment of 15 January 1998, *Babahenini v Belgian State*, C-113/97, EU:C:1998:13

Judgment of 2 April 1998, *Norbrook Laboratories v Ministry of Agriculture, Fisheries and Food*, C-127/95, EU:C:1998:151

Judgment of 2 April 1998, *Greenpeace and Others v Commission*, C-321/95 P, EU:C:1998:153

Judgment of 2 April 1998, *Commission v Sytraval and Brink's France*, C-367/95 P, EU:C:1998:154

Judgment of 28 April 1998, *Metronome Musik v Music Point Hokamp*, C-200/96, EU:C:1998:172

Judgment of 12 May 1998, *Martínez Sala v Freistaat Bayern*, C-85/96, EU:C:1998:217

Judgment of 14 May 1998, *Windpark Groothusen v Commission*, C-48/96 P, EU:C:1998:223

Judgment of 12 May 1998, *Kefalas and others v Elliniko Dimosio and Organismos Oikonomikis Anasygkrotisis Epicheiriseon*, C-367/96, EU:C:1998:222

Judgment of 16 June 1998, *Lemmens*, C-227/97, EU:C:1998:296

Judgment of 22 September 1998, *Coote v Granada Hospitality*, C-185/97, EU:C:1998:424

Judgment of 10 December 1998, *Schröder and Thamann v Commission*, C-221/97 P, EU:C:1998:597

Judgment of 17 December 1998, *IP*, C-2/97, EU:C:1998:613

Judgment of 9 February 1999, *Dilexport Srl* v. *Amministrazione delle Finanze dello Stato*, C-343/96, EU:C:1999:59

Judgment of 25 February 1999, *Carbonari*, C-131/97, EU:C:1999:98

Judgment of 9 March 1999, *Centros*, C-212/97, EU:C:1999:126

Judgment of 15 June 1999, *Rechberger and Others*, C-140/97, EU:C:1999:306

Judgment of 16 September 1999, *WWF and Others*, C-435/97, EU:C:1999:418

Judgment of 23 November 1999, *Portugal v Council*, C-149/96, EU:C:1999:574

Judgment of 23 March 2000, *Diamantis*, C-373/97, EU:C:2000:150

Judgment of 6 June 2000, *Angonese*, C-281/98, EU:C:2000:296

Judgment of 27 June 2000, *Océano Grupo Editorial and Salvat Editores*, Joined cases C-240/98 to C-244/98, EU:C:2000:346

Judgment of 4 July 2000, *Bergaderm and Goupil v Commission*, C-352/98 P, EU:C:2000:361

Judgment of 13 July 2000, *Centrosteel*, C-456/98, EU:C:2000:402

Judgment of 19 September 2000, *Linster*, C-287/98, EU:C:2000:468

Judgment of 21 September 2000, *Michailidis*, C-441/98 and C-442/98, EU:C:2000:479

Judgment of 14 December 2000, *Emsland-Stärke*, C-110/99, EU:C:2000:695

Judgment of 18 January 2001, *Stockholm Lindöpark*, C-150/99, EU:C:2001:34

Judgment of 22 February 2001, *Gomes Valente*, C-393/98, EU:C:2001:109

Judgment of 8 March 2001, *Metallgesellschaft and Others*, C-397/98 and C-410/98, EU:C:2001:134

Judgment of 26 June 2001, *BECTU*, C-173/99, EU:C:2001:356

Judgment of 28 June 2001, *Larsy*, C-118/00, EU:C:2001:368

Judgment of 20 September 2001, *Grzelczyk*, C-184/99, EU:C:2001:458

Judgment of 20 September 2001, *Courage and Crehan*, C-453/99, EU:C:2001:465

Judgment of 11 July 2002, *Carpenter*, C-60/00, EU:C:2002:434

Judgment of 23 April 2002, *Nygård*, C-234/99, EU:C:2002:244

Judgment of 25 July 2002, *Unión de Pequeños Agricultores*, C-50/00 P, EU:C:2002:462

Judgment of 17 September 2002, *Baumbast and R*, C-413/99, EU:C:2002:493

Judgment of 17 September 2002, *Muñoz and Superior Fruiticola*, C-253/00, EU:C:2002:497

Judgment of 5 November 2002, Überseering, C-208/00, EU:C:2002:632

Judgment of 10 December 2002, *Commission v Camar and Tico*, C-312/00 P, EU:C:2002:736

Judgment of 20 March 2003, *Kutz-Bauer*, C-187/00, EU:C:2003:168

Judgment of 8 May 2003, *ATRAL*, C-14/02, EU:C:2003:265

Judgment of 12 June 2003, *Schmidberger*, C-112/00, EU:C:2003:333

Judgment of 24 July 2003, *Altmark Trans and Regierungspräsidium Magdeburg*, C-280/00, EU:C:2003:415

Judgment of 11 September 2003, *Safalero*, C-13/01, EU:C:2003:447

Judgment of 30 September 2003, *Inspire Art*, C-167/01, EU:C:2003:512

Judgment of 30 September 2003, *Köbler*, C-224/01, EU:C:2003:513

Judgment of 2 October 2003, *Weber's Wine World and Others*, C-147/01, EU:C:2003:533

Judgment of 2 October 2003, *Garcia Avello*, C-148/02, EU:C:2003:539

Judgment of 21 October 2003, *van Calster and Cleeren*, Joined cases C-261/01 and C-262/01, EU:C:2003:571

Judgment of 27 November 2003, *Enirisorse*, Joined cases C-34/01 to C-38/01, EU:C:2003:640

Judgment of 9 December 2003, Case C-129/00, *Commission* v. *Italy*, EU:C:2003:656

Judgment of 11 December 2003, *Barbier*, C-364/01, EU:C:2003:665

Judgment of 7 January 2004, *Wells*, C-201/02, EU:C:2004:12

Judgment of 30 March 2004, *Rothley and Others v Parliament*, C-167/02 P, EU:C:2004:193

Judgment of 1 April 2004, *Commission v Jégo-Quéré*, C-263/02 P, EU:C:2004:210

Judgment of 15 July 2004, *Spain* v *Commission*, C-501/00, EU:C:2004:438

Judgment of 7 September 2004, *Trojani*, C-456/02, EU:C:2004:488

Judgment of 5 October 2004, *Pfeiffer and Others*, C-397/01 to C-403/01, EU:C:2004:584

Judgment of 12 October 2004, *Paul and Others*, C-222/02, EU:C:2004:606

Judgment of 19 October 2004, *Zhu and Chen*, C-200/02, EU:C:2004:639

Judgment of 11 November 2004, C-216/02, *Zuchtverband für Ponys*, EU:C:2004:703

Judgment of 17 February 2005, *Linneweber and Akritidis*, Joined cases C-453/02 and C-462/02, EU:C:2005:92

Judgment of 22 February 2005, *Commission v max.mobil*, C-141/02 P, EU:C:2005:98

Judgment of 12 April 2005, *Commission v United Kingdom*, C-61/03, EU:C:2005:210

Order of 26 May 2005, *Sozialhilfeverband Rohrbach*, C-297/03, EU:C:2005:315

Judgment of 16 July 2005, *Pupino*, C-105/03, EU:C:2005:386

Judgment of 12 July 2005, *Commission v CEVA and Pfizer*, C-198/03 P, EU:C:2005:445

Judgment of 12 July 2005, *Alliance for Natural Health*, C-154/04, EU:C:2005:449

Judgment of 15 September 2005, *Ireland v Commission*, C-199/03, EU:C:2005:548

Judgment of 6 October 2005, *Scott v Commission*, C-276/03 P, EU:C:2005:590

Judgment of 25 October 2005, *Schulte*, C-350/03, EU:C:2005:637

Judgment of 22 November 2005, *Mangold*, C-144/04, EU:C:2005:709

Judgment of 6 December 2005, *Gaston Schul* C-461/03, EU:C:2005:742

Judgment of 13 December 2005, *Commission v Aktionsgemeinschaft Recht und Eigentum*, C-78/03 P, EU:C:2005:761

Judgment of 21 February 2006, *Halifax and Others*, C-255/02, EU:C:2006:121

Judgment of 16 March 2006, *Emsland-Stärke*, C-94/05, EU:C:2006:185

Judgment of 23 March 2006, *Commission v Belgium*, C-408/03, EU:C:2006:192

Judgment of 15 June 2006, *Dokter and Others*, C-28/05, EU:C:2006:408

Judgment of 27 June 2006, *Parliament v Council*, C-540/03, EU:C:2006:429

Judgment of 13 July 2006, *Manfredi*, Joined cases C-295/04 to C-298/04, EU:C:2006:461

Judgment of 9 March 2006, *Spain v Council*, C-310/04, EU:C:2006:521

Judgment of 12 September 2006, *Spain v United Kingdom*, C-145/04, EU:C:2006:543

Judgment of 12 September 2006, *Cadbury Schweppes and Cadbury Schweppes Overseas*, C-196/04, EU:C:2006:544

Judgment of 12 September 2006, *Eman and Sevinger*, C-300/04, EU:C:2006:545

Judgment of 5 October 2005, *Transalpine Ölleitung in Österreich*, C-368/04, EU:C:2006:644

Judgment of 26 October 2006, *Mostaza Claro*, C-168/05, EU:C:2006:675

Judgment of 9 November 2006, *Commission v De Bry*, C-344/05 P, EU:C:2006:710

Judgment of 1 February 2007, *Sison v Council*, C-266/05 P, EU:C:2007:75

Judgment of 13 March 2007, *Unibet*, C-432/05, EU:C:2007:163

Judgment of 19 April 2007, *Holcim (Deutschland) v Commission*, C-282/05 P, EU:C:2007:226

Judgment of 22 June 2006, *Belgium and Forum 187 v Commission*, Joined cases C-182/03 and C-217/03, EU:C:2006:416

Judgment of 28 June 2007, *JP Morgan Fleming Claverhouse Investment Trust and The Association of Investment Trust Companies*, C-363/05, EU:C:2007:391

Judgment of 5 July 2007, *Kofoed*, C-321/05, EU:C:2007:408

Judgment of 13 September 2007, *Commission v Italy*, C-260/04, EU:C:2007:508

Judgment of 11 December 2007, *The International Transport Workers' Federation and The Finnish Seamen's Union*, C-438/05, EU:C:2007:772

Judgment of 18 December 2007, *Sweden v Commission*, C-64/05, EU:C:2007:802

Judgment of 18 December 2007, *Laval un Partneri*, C-341/05, EU:C:2007:809

Judgment of 21 February 2008, *Tele2 Telecommunication*, C-426/05, EU:C:2008:103

Judgment of 15 April 2008, *Impact*, C-268/06, EU:C:2008:223

Judgment of 3 June 2008, *Intertanko and Others*, C-308/06, EU:C:2008:312

Judgment of 1 July 2008, Sweden and Turco v Council, Joined cases C-39/05 P and C-52/05 P, EU:C:2008:374

Judgment of 10 July 2008, *Feryn*, C-54/07, EU:C:2008:397

Judgment of 25 July 2008, *Janecek*, C-237/07, EU:C:2008:447

Judgment of 3 September 2008, *Kadi and Al Barakaat International Foundation v Council and Commission*, C-402/05 P and C-415/05 P, EU:C:2008:461

Judgment of 17 July 2008, *Raccanelli*, C-94/07, EU:C:2008:425

Judgment of 9 September 2008, *FIAMM and Others v Council and Commission*, C-120/06 P and C-121/06 P, EU:C:2008:476

Judgment of 14 October 2008, *Grunkin and Paul*, C-353/06, EU:C:2008:559

Judgment of 18 December 2008, *Sopropé*, C-349/07, EU:C:2008:746

Judgment of 22 December 2008, *British Aggregates v Commission*, C-487/06 P, EU:C:2008:757

Judgment of 22 December 2008, *Commission v Finland*, C-328/08, EU:C:2008:775

Judgment of 11 december 2008, *Commission v France*, C-330/08, EU:C:2008:720

Judgment of 20 January 2009, *Schultz-Hoff and Others*, Joined cases C-350/06 and C-520/06, EU:C:2009:18

Judgment of 17 February 2009, *Elgafaji*, C-465/07, EU:C:2009:94

Judgment of 12 March 2009, *Commission v Slovenia*, C-402/08, EU:C:2009:157

Judgment of 24 March 2009, *Danske Slagterier*, C-445/06, ECLI:EU:C:2009:178

Judgment of 24 March 2009, *Commission v Luxembourg*, C-331/08, EU:C:2009:185

Order of 5 May 2009, *WWF-UK v Council*, C-355/08 P, EU:C:2009:286

Judgment of 19 May 2009, *Commission v Greece*, C-368/08, EU:C:2009:326

Judgment of 18 June 2009, *Commission v United Kingdom*, C-417/08, EU:C:2009:384

Judgment of 9 July 2009, *3F v Commission*, C-319/07 P, EU:C:2009:435

Judgment of 16 July 2009, *Mono Car Styling*, C-12/08, EU:C:2009:466

Order of 24 September 2009, *Município de Gondomar* v *Commission*, C-501/08 P, EU:C:2009:580

Judgment of 6 October 2009, *Asturcom Telecomunicaciones*, C-40/08, EU:C:2009:615

Judgment of 15 October 2009, *Djurgården-Lilla Värtans Miljöskyddsförening*, C-263/08, EU:C:2009:631

Judgment of 29 October 2009, *SKF*, C-29/08, EU:C:2009:665

Judgment of 17 December 2009, *Réexamen M v EMEA*, C-197/09 RX-II, EU:C:2009:804

Judgment of 19 January 2010, *Kücükdeveci*, C-555/07, EU:C:2010:21

Judgment of 26 January 2010, *Internationaler Hilfsfonds v Commission*, C-362/08 P, EU:C:2010:40

Judgment of 28 January 2010, *Uniplex (UK)*, C-406/08, EU:C:2010:45

Judgment of 2 March 2010, *Salahadin Abdulla and Others*, Joined cases C-175/08, C-176/08, C-178/08 and C-179/08, EU:C:2010:105

Judgment of 18 March 2010, *Alassini and Others*, C-317 to C-320/08, EU:C:2010:146

Judgment of 22 March 2010, *SPM v Council and Commission*, C-39/09 P, EU:C:2010:157

Judgment of 17 June 2010, *Bolbol*, C-31/09, EU:C:2010:351

Judgment of 29 June 2010, *Commission* v *Technische Glaswerke Ilmenau*, C-139/07 P, EU:C:2010:376

Judgment of 8 July 2010, *Afton Chemical*, C-343/09, EU:C:2010:419

Judgment of 15 July 2010, *Commission v Germany*, C-271/08, EU:C:2010:426

Judgment of 21 September 2010, *Sweden and Others* v *API and Commission*, Joined cases C-514/07 P, C-528/07 P and C-532/07 P, EU:C:2010:541

Judgment of 21 October 2010, *Accardo and Others*, C-227/09, EU:C:2010:624,

Judgment of 9 November 2010, *VB Pénzügyi Lízing*, C-137/08, EU:C:2010:659

Judgment of 9 November 2010, *Volker und Markus Schecke and Eifert*, Joined cases C-92/09 and C-93/09, EU:C:2010:662

Judgment of 18 November 2010, *NDSHT v Commission*, C-322/09 P, EU:C:2010:701

Judgment of 25 November 2010, *Fuß*, C-429/09, ECLI:EU:C:2010:717

Judgment of 16 December 2010, *Kahla Thüringen Porzellan v Commission*, C-537/08 P, EU:C:2010:769

Judgment of 16 December 2010, *Skoma-Lux*, C-339/09, EU:C:2010:781

Judgment of 22 December 2010, *Sayn-Wittgenstein*, C-208/09, EU:C:2010:806

Judgment of 22 December 2010, *DEB*, C-279/09, EU:C:2010:811

Opinion of 8 March 2011, 1/09, EU:C:2011:123

Judgment of 8 March 2011, *Ruiz Zambrano*, C-34/09, EU:C:2011:124

Judgment of 9 March 2011, *Lesoochranárske zoskupenie VLK v Ministerstvo životného prostredia Slovenskej republiky*, C-240/09, EU:C:2011:125

Judgment of 17 March 2011, *AJD Tuna*, C-221/09, EU:C:2011:153

Judgment of 5 May 2011, *McCarthy*, C-434/09, EU:C:2011:277

Judgment of 10 May 2011, *Römer*, C-147/08, EU:C:2011:286

Judgment of 12 May 2011, *Bund für Umwelt und Naturschutz Deutschland, Landesverband Nordrhein Westfalen*, C-115/09, EU:C:2011:289

Judgment of 24 May 2011, *Commission v Kronoply and Kronotex*, C-83/09 P, EU:C:2011:341

Judgment of 14 June 2011, *Pfleiderer*, C-360/09, EU:C:2011:389

Judgment of 28 July 2011, *Samba Diouf*, C-69/10, EU:C:2011:524

Judgment of 6 September 2011, *Lady & Kid and Others*, C-398/09, EU:C:2011:540

Judgment of 13 October 2011, *Deutsche Post and Germany v Commission*, C-463/10 P, EU:C:2011:656

Judgment of 22 September 2011, *Belgium v Deutsche Post and DHL International*, C-148/09 P, EU:C:2011:603

Judgment of 27 October 2011, *Austria v Scheucher-Fleisch and Others*, C-47/10 P, EU:C:2011:698

Judgment of 15 November 2011, *Dereci and Others*, C-256/11, EU:C:2011:734

Judgment of 21 December 2011, *France v People's Mojahedin Organization of Iran*, C-27/09 P, EU:C:2011:853

Judgment of 21 December 2011 *Air Transport Association of America and Others*, C-366/10, EU:C:2011:864

Judgment of 21 December 2011, *N.S. and Others*, C-411/10 and C-493/10, EU:C:2011:865

Judgment of 21 December 2011, *Cicala*, C-482/10, EU:C:2011:868

Judgment of 24 January 2012, *Dominguez*, C-282/10, EU:C:2012:33

Judgment of 14 June 2012, *Banco Español de Crédito*, C-618/10, EU:C:2012:349

Judgment of 5 September 2012, *Y and Z*, Joined cases C-71/11 and C-99/11, EU:C:2012:518

Judgment of 21 June 2012, *IFAW Internationaler Tierschutz-Fonds v Commission*, C-135/11 P, EU:C:2012:376

Judgment of 28 June 2012, *Commission* v *Éditions Odile Jacob*, C-404/10 P, EU:C:2012:393

Judgment of 19 July 2012, *Littlewoods Retail and Others*, C-591/10, EU:C:2012:478

Judgment of 27 September 2012, *Cimade and GISTI*, C-179/11, EU:C:2012:594

Judgment of 6 November 2012, *Otis and Others*, C-199/11, EU:C:2012:684

Judgment of 8 November 2012, *Iida*, C-40/11, EU:C:2012:691

Judgment of 22 November 2012, *M.*, C-277/11, EU:C:2012:744

Judgment of 27 November 2012, *Pringle*, C-370/12, EU:C:2012:756

Judgment of 19 December 2012, *Abed El Karem El Kott and Others*, C-364/11, EU:C:2012:826

Judgment of 22 January 2013, *Sky Österreich*, C-283/11, EU:C:2013:28

Judgment of 31 January 2013, *D. and A.*, C-175/11, EU:C:2013:45

Judgment of 26 February 2013, *Åkerberg Fransson*, C-617/10, EU:C:2013:105

Judgment of 14 March 2013, *Aziz*, C-415/11, EU:C:2013:164

Judgment of 14 March 2013, *Leth*, C-420/11, EU:C:2013:166

Judgment of 21 March 2013, *RWE Vertrieb*, C-92/11, EU:C:2013:180

Judgment of 11 April 2013, *Edwards and Pallikaropoulos*, C-260/11, EU:C:2013:221

Judgment of 8 May 2013, *Ymeraga and Ymeraga-Tafarshiku*, C-87/12, EU:C:2013:291

Judgment of 30 May 2013, *Halaf*, C-528/11, EU:C:2013:342

Judgment of 13 June 2013, *Ryanair v Commission*, C-287/12 P, EU:C:2013:395

Judgment of 27 June 2013, *Agrokonsulting-04*, C-93/12, EU:C:2013:432

Judgment of 18 July 2013, *Commission and Others v Kadi*, Joined cases C-584/10 P, C-593/10 P and C-595/10 P, EU:C:2013:518

Judgment of 10 September 2013, *G. and R*, C-383/13 PPU, EU:C:2013:533

Judgment of 3 September 2013, *Idromacchine and Others v Commission*, C-34/12 P, EU:C:2013:552

Judgment of 26 September 2013, *Texdata Software GmbH*, C-418/11, EU:C:2013:588

Judgment of 3 October 2013, *Inuit Tapiriit Kanatami and Others v Parliament and Council*, C-583/11 P, EU:C:2013:625

Judgment of 10 October 2013, *Alokpa and Moudoulou*, C-86/12, EU:C:2013:645

Judgment of 17 October 2013, *Schaible*, C-101/12, EU:C:2013:661

Judgment of 17 October 2013, *Schwarz*, C-291/12, EU:C:2013:670

Judgment of 22 October 2013, *Sabou*, C-276/12, EU:C:2013:678

Judgment of 7 November 2013, *X and Others*, Joined cases C-199/12 to C-201/12, EU:C:2013:720

Judgment of 14 November 2013, *LPN and Finland* v *Commission*, C-514/11 P, EU:C:2013:738

Judgment of 14 November 2013, *Puid*, C-4/11, EU:C:2013:740

Judgment of 28 November 2013, *Council v. Manufacturing Support & Procurement Kala Naft*, C-348/12 P, EU:C:2013:776

Judgment of 7 November 2013, *X and Others*, C-199/12 to C-201/12, EU:C:2013:720

Judgment of 28 November 2013, *Jurašinović v Council*, C-576/12 P, EU:C:2013:777

Judgment of 19 December 2013, *Telefonica v Commission*, C-274/12 P, EU:C:2013:852

Judgment of 15 January 2014, *Association de médiation sociale*, C-176/12, EU:C:2014:2

Judgment of 30 January 2014, *Diakite*, C-285/12, EU:C:2014:39

Judgment of 27 February 2014, *Stichting Woonpunt and Others v Commission*, C-132/12 P, EU:C:2014:100

Judgment of 27 February 2014, *Pohotovosť*, C-470/12, EU:C:2014:101

Judgment of 27 February 2014, *Commission v EnBW*, C-365/12 P, EU:C:2014:112

Judgment of 6 March 2014, *Siragusa*, C-206/13, EU:C:2014:126

Judgment of 13 March 2014, *SICES and Others*, C-155/13, EU:C:2014:145

Judgment of 8 April 2014, *Digital Rights Ireland and Seitlinger and Others*, C-293/12, EU:C:2014:238

Judgment of 8 May 2014, *N.*, C-604/12, EU:C:2014:302

Judgment of 15 May 2014, *Almos Agrárkülkereskedelmi*, C-337/13, EU:C:2014:328

Judgment of 22 May 2014, *Glatzel*, C-356/12, EU:C:2014:350

Judgment of 27 May 2014, *Spasic*, C-129/14 PPU, EU:C:2014:586

Judgment of 5 June 2014, *Kone and Others*, C-557/12, EU:C:2014:1317

Judgment of 3 July 2014, *Council v in 't Veld*, C-350/12 P, EU:C:2014:2039

Judgment of 3 July 2014, *Kamino International Logistics and Datema Hellmann Worldwide Logistics*, Joined cases C-129/13 and C-130/13, EU:C:2014:2041

Judgment of 17 July 2014, *Y.S. and Others*, Joined cases C-141/12 and C-372/12, EU:C:2014:2081

Judgment of 17 July 2014, *Sánchez Morcillo and Abril García*, C-169/14, EU:C:2014:2099

Judgment of 3 September 2014, *GMAC UK*, C-589/12, EU:C:2014:2131

Judgment of 11 September 2014, *Commission v Germany*, C-525/12, EU:C:2014:2202

Judgment of 17 September 2014, *Liivimaa Lihaveis*, C-562/12, EU:C:2014:2229

Judgment of 23 October 2014, *Olainfarm*, C-104/13, EU:C:2014:2316

Judgment of 9 October 2014, *Traum*, C-492/13, EU:C:2014:2267

Judgment of 5 November 2014, *Mukarubega*, C-166/13, EU:C:2014:2336

Judgment of 11 November 2014, *Dano*, C-333/13, EU:C:2014:2358

Judgment of 19 November 2014, *ClientEarth*, C-404/13, EU:C:2014:2382

Judgment of 2 December 2014, *A*, Joined cases C-148/13 to C-150/13, EU:C:2014:2406

Judgment of 9 December 2014, *Schönberger*, C-261/13 P, ECLI:EU:C:2014:2423

Judgment of 11 December 2014, *Boudjlida*, C-249/13, EU:C:2014:2431

Judgment of 18 December 2014, *McCarthy*, C-202/13, EU:C:2014:2450

Judgment of 18 December 2014, *M'Bodj*, C-542/13, EU:C:2014:2452

Judgment of 18 December 2014, *Schoenimport 'Italmoda' Mariano Previti and Others*, C-131/13, C-163/13 and C-164/13, EU:C:2014:2455

Judgment of 13 January 2015, *Council and Others v Vereniging Milieudefensie and Stichting Stop Luchtverontreiniging Utrecht*, C-401/12 P to C-403/12 P, EU:C:2015:4

Judgment of 13 January 2015, *Council and Commission v Stichting Natuur en Milieu and Pesticide Action Network Europe*, EU:C:2015:5, C-404/12 P and C-405/12 P, EU:C:2015:5

Judgment of 4 February 2015, *Melchior*, C-647/13, EU:C:2015:54

Judgment of 26 February 2015, *Shepherd*, C-472/13, EU:C:2015:117

Judgment of 17 March 2015, *AKT*, C-533/13, EU:C:2015:173

Judgment of 4 June 2015, *Stichting Corporate Europe Observatory v Commission*, C-399/13 P, EU:C:2015:360

Judgment of 24 June 2015, *T.*, C-373/13, EU:C:2015:413

Judgment of 25 June 2015, *Indėlių ir investicijų draudimas et Nemaniūnas*, C-671/13, EU:C:2015:418

Judgment of 16 July 2015, *ClientEarth v. Commission*, C-612/13 P, EU:C:2015:486

Judgment of 16 July 2015, *Larentia + Minerva*, C-108/14, EU:C:2015:496

Judgment of 16 July 2015, *Singh and Others*, C-218/14, EU:C:2015:476

Judgment of 10 September 2015, *Wojciechowski*, C-408/14, EU:C:2015:591

Judgment of 15 September 2015, *Alimanovic*, C-67/14, EU:C:2015:597

Judgment of 6 October 2015, *Delvigne*, C-650/13, EU:C:2015:648

Judgment of 6 October 2015, *East Sussex County Council*, C-71/14, EU:C:2015:656

Judgment of 6 October 2015, *T-Mobile Czech Republic et Vodafone Czech Republic*, C-508/14, EU:C:2015:657

Judgment of 15 October 2015, *Commission v Germany*, C-137/14, EU:C:2015:683

Judgment of 6 October 2015, *Schrems*, C-362/14, EU:C:2015:650

Judgment of 6 October 2015, *Orizzonte Salute*, C-61/14, EU:C:2015:655

Judgment of 17 December 2015, *WebMindLicenses*, C-419/14, EU:C:2015:832

Judgment of 25 February 2016, *García-Nieto e.a.*, C-299/14, EU:C:2016:114.

Judgment of 7 April 2016, *ONEm and M.*, C-284/15, EU:C:2016:220

Judgment of 16 April 2015, *Gruber,* C-570/13, EU:C:2015:231

Judgment of 18 February 2016, *Finanmadrid EFC,* C-49/14, EU:C:2016:98

Judgment of 14 April 2016, *Sales Sinués,* Joined cases C-381/14 and C-385/14, EU:C:2016:252

Judgment of 19 April 2016, *DI*, C-441/14, EU:C:2016:278

Order of 4 May 2016, *Pannonhalmi Főapátság v Parliament,* C-607/15 P, EU:C:2016:329

Judgment of 2 June 2016, *Bogendorff von Wolffersdorff,* C-438/14, EU:C:2016:401

Judgment of 14 June 2016, *Marchiani v Parliament,* C-566/14 P, EU:C:2016:437

Order of 22 June 2016, *DK Recycling und Roheisen v Commission,* C-540/14 P, EU:C:2016:469

Judgment of 7 June 2016, *Karim,* C-155/15, EU:C:2016:410

Judgment of 30 June 2016, *NA*, C-115/15, EU:C:2016:487

Judgment of 14 July 2016, *Sea Handling v Commission,* C-271/15 P, EU:C:2016:557

Judgment of 19 July 2016, *Kotnik and others,* C-526/14, EU:C:2016:570

Judgment of 28 July 2016, *Verein für Konsumenteninformation,* C-191/15, EU:C:2016:612

Judgment of 6 September 2016, *Petruhhin,* C-182/15, EU:C:2016:630

Judgment of 13 September 2016, *CS*, C-304/14, EU:C:2016:674

Judgment of 13 September 2016, *Rendón Marín*, C-165/14, EU:C:2016:675

Order of 13 September 2016, *Arctic Paper Mochenwangen v Commission*, C-551/14 P, EU:C:2016:684

Judgment of 13 October 2016 *Polkomtel,* C-231/15, EU:C:2016:769

Order of 13 September 2016, *Raffinerie Heide v Commission,* C-564/14 P, EU:C:2016:685

Judgment of 20 October 2016, *Danqua,* C-429/15, EU:C:2016:789

Opinion of AG Sharpston in Schmitt, C-219/15, EU:C:2016:694

Order of 13 September 2016, *Romonta v Commission,* C-565/14 P, EU:C:2016:698

Judgment of 20 September 2016, *Ledra Advertising v Commission and ECB,* C-8/15 P, EU:C:2016:701

Judgment of 8 November 2016, *Lesoochranárske zoskupenie VLK*, C-243/15, EU:C:2016:838

Judgment of 23 November 2016, *Commission v Stichting Greenpeace Nederland and PAN Europe,* C-673/13 P, EU:C:2016:889

Judgment of 21 December 2016, *AGET Iraklis,* C-201/15, EU:C:2016:972

Judgment of 21 December 2016, *Associazione Italia Nostra Onlus*, C-444/15, EU:C:2016:978

Judgment of 21 December 2016, *Gutiérrez Naranjo*, Joined cases C-154/15 and C-307/15, EU:C:2016:980

Judgment of 26 January 2017, *Banco Primus*, C-421/14, EU:C:2017:60

Judgment of 15 February 2017, *British Film Institute,* C-592/15, EU:C:2017:117

Judgment of 16 February 2017, *C.K. and Others,* C-578/16 PPU, EU:C:2017:127

Judgment of 16 February 2017, *Schmitt,* C-219/15, EU:C:2017:128

Order of 1 March 2017, *EMA v PTC Therapeutics International,* C-513/16 P, EU:C:2017:148

Order of 1 March 2017, *EMA v MSD Animal Health Innovation and Intervet international*, C-512/16 P(R), EU:C:2017:149

Judgment of 7 March 2017, *X and X*, C-638/16 PPU, EU:C:2017:173

Judgment of 8 March 2017, *Viasat Broadcasting UK v Commission*, C-660/15 P, EU:C:2017:178

Judgment of 9 March 2017, *Poland v Commission*, C-105/16 P, EU:C:2017:191

Judgment of 14 March 2017, *G4S Secure Solutions*, C-157/15, EU:C:2017:203

Judgment of 14 March 2017, *Bougnaoui and ADDH*, C-188/15, EU:C:2017:204

Judgment of 4 April 2017, *European Ombudsman v Staelen*, C-337/15 P, EU:C:2017:256

Judgment of 5 April 2017, *Orsi*, Joined cases C-217/15 and C-350/15, EU:C:2017:264

Order of 5 April 2017, *Ahmed*, C-36/17, EU:C:2017:273

Judgment of 10 May 2017, *Chavez-Vilchez and Others*, C-133/15, EU:C:2017:354

Judgment of 16 May 2017, *Berlioz Investment Fund*, C-682/15, EU:C:2017:373

Judgment of 18 May 2017, *Fondul Proprietatea*, C-150/16, EU:C:2017:388

Judgment of 1 June 2017, *Folk*, C-529/15, EU:C:2017:419

Judgment of 8 June 2017, *Freitag*, C-541/15, EU:C:2017:432

Judgment of 14 June 2017, *Online Games and Others*, C-685/15, EU:C:2017:452

Judgment of 14 June 2017, *Compass Contract Services*, C-38/16, EU:C:2017:454

Judgment of 19 July 2017, *Abercrombie & Fitch Italia*, C-143/16, EU:C:2017:566

Judgment of 21 June 2017, *W and Others*, C-621/15, EU:C:2017:484

Judgment of 6 June 2013, *MA and Others*, C-648/11, EU:C:2013:367

Judgment of 18 May 2017, *Litdana*, C-624/15, EU:C:2017:389

Judgment of 26 July 2017, *Mengesteab*, C-670/16, EU:C:2017:587

Judgment of 12 September 2017, *Anagnostakis v Commission*, C-589/15 P, EU:C:2017:663

Judgment of 20 December 2017, *Spain v Council*, C-521/15, EU:C:2017:982

Judgment of 20 December 2017, *Caterpillar Financial Services*, C-500/16, EU:C:2017:996

Judgment of 20 December 2017, *Erzeugerorganisation Tiefkühlgemüse*, C-516/16, EU:C:2017:1011

Judgment of 21 February 2018, *Kreuzmayr*, C-628/16, EU:C:2018:84

Judgment of 14 March 2018, *Astellas Pharma*, C-557/16, EU:C:2018:181

Judgment of 15 March 2018, *North East Pylon Pressure Campaign and Sheehy*, C-470/16, EU:C:2018:185

Judgment of 17 April 2018, *Egenberger*, C-414/16, EU:C:2018:257

Judgment of 7 August 2018, *Smith*, C-122/17, EU:C:2018:631

Opinions of Advocates General

Opinion of AG Lagrange in *Conf. des prod. de fruits v Conseil CEE*, C-16/62, EU:C:1962:40

Opinion of AG Reischl in *Cucchi v Avez*, C-77/76, EU:C:1977:68

Opinion of AG Reischl in *Just*, C-68/79, EU:C:1979:272

Opinion of AG Reischl in *Amministrazione delle finanze dello Stato v Denkavit italiana*, C-61/79, EU:C:1980:2

Opinion of AG Mancini in *Luxembourg v Parliament,* C-230/81, EU:C:1982:417

Opinion of AG Slynn, *Tradax v Commission*, 64/82, EU:1983:300

Opinion of AG Lenz in *Finsider v Commission,* Joined cases 63 and 147/84, EU:C:1985:253

Opinion of AG Darmon in *Verholen and Others v Sociale Verzekeringsbank Amsterdam*, C-87/90 to C-89/90, EU:C:1991:223

Opinion of AG Jacobs in *Technische Universität München v Hauptzollamt München-Mitte*, C-269/90, EU:C:1991:317

Opinion of AG Darmon in *Vreugdenhil*, C-282/90, EU:C:1992:12

Opinion of AG Van Gerven in *Banks v British Coal,* C-128/92, EU:C:1993:860

Opinion of AG Tesauro in *Pafitis and Others,* C-441/93, EU:C:1995:368

Opinion of AG Tesauro in *Brasserie du pêcheur v Bundesrepublik Deutschland and The Queen v Secretary of State for Transport, ex parte Factortame*, Joined cases C-46/93 and C-48/93, EU:C:1995:407

Opinion of AG Fennelly in *Lemmens*, C-227/97, EU:C:1998:61

Opinion of AG Léger, *Linster,* C-287/98, EU:C:2000:3

Opinion of AG Alber in *Emsland-Stärke,* C-110/99, EU:C:2000:252

Opinion in *Muñoz and Superior Fruiticola*, C-253/00, EU:C:2001:697

Opinion of AG Jacobs in *Unión de Pequeños Agricultores v Council*, C-50/00 P, EU:C:2002:197

Opinion of AG Ruiz-Jarabo Colomer in *Zuchtverband für Ponys,* C-216/02, ECLI:EU:C:2004:25

Opinion of AG Maduro in *Commission v max-mobil*, C-141/02 P, EU:C:2004:646

Opinion of AG Geelhoed in *Franz Egenberger*, C-313/04, EU:C:2005:733

Opinion of AG Mazak in *Palacios de la Villa,* C-411/05, EU:C:2007:106

Opinion of AG Maduro in *Sweden v Commission*, C-64/05 P, EU:C:2007:433

Opinion of AG Sharpston in *Bartsch*, C-427/06, EU:C:2008:297

Opinion of AG Trstenjak in *Danske Slagterier*, C-445/06, EU:C:2008:464

Opinion of AG Mengozzi in *DEB,* C-279/09, EU:C:2010:489

Opinion of AG Sharpston in *Bund für Umwelt und Naturschutz Deutschland, Landesverband Nordrhein Westfalen*, C-115/09, EU:C:2010:773

Opinion of AG Bot in *Scattolon*, C-108/10, EU:C:2011:211

Opinion of AG Cruz Villalón in *Scarlet Extended,* C-70/10, EU:C:2011:255

Opinion of AG Cruz Villalón in *Prigge e.a.*, C-447/09, EU:C:2011:321

Opinion of AG Trstenjak in *Dominguez,* C-282/10, EU:C:2011:559

Opinion of AG Bot in *Sky Österreich*, C-283/11, EU:C:2012:341

Opinion of AG Kokott in *Leth,* C-420/11, EU:C:2012:701

Opinion of AG Mengozzi in *Texdata Software,* C-418/11, EU:C:2013:50

Opinion of AG Cruz Villalón in *Association de médiation sociale,* C-176/12, ECLI:EU:C:2013:491

Opinion of AG Cruz Villalón in *Abdullahi,* C-394/12, EU:C:2013:813

Opinion of AG Jääskinen in *Council and Others v Vereniging Milieudefensie and Stichting Stop Luchtverontreiniging Utrecht*, C-401/12 P to C-403/12 P, EU:C:2014:310

View of AG Jääskinen in *Spasic*, C-129/14 PPU, EU:C:2014:739

Opinion of AG Cruz Villalón in *Digital Rights Ireland*, C-293/12, EU:C:2014:845

Opinion of AG Jääskinen in *Schönberger*, C-261/13 P, EU:C:2014:2107

Opinion of AG Mengozzi in *Melchior*, C-647/13, EU:C:2014:2301

Opinion of AG Kokott in *Gruber*, C-570/13, EU:C:2014:2374

Opinion of AG Szpunar in *AKT*, C-533/13, EU:2014:2392

Opinion of AG Cruz Villalón in *ClientEarth v Commission*, C-612/13 P, EU:C:2015:218

Opinion of AG Kokott in *East Sussex City Council*, C-71/14, EU:C:2015:234

Opinion of AG Cruz Villalón in *Delvigne*, C-650/13, EU:C:2015:363

Opinion of AG Mengozzi in *Wojciechowski*, C-408/14, EU:C:2015:393

Opinion of AG Mengozzi in *Arjona Camacho*, C-407/14, EU:C:2015:534

Opinion of AG Wathelet in *WebMindLicenses*, C-419/14, EU:C:2015:606

Opinion of AG Sharpston in *Ghezelbash*, C-63/15, EU:C:2016:186

Opinion of AG Wathelet in *NA*, C-115/15, EU:C:2016:259

Opinion of AG Bot in *Daouidi*, C-395/15, EU:C:2016:371

Opinion of AG Kokott in *G4S Secure Solutions*, C-157/15, EU:C:2016:382

Opinion of AG Sharpston in *Bougnaoui and ADDH*, C-188/15, EU:C:2016:553

Opinion of AG Bobek in *Folk*, C-529/15, EU:C:2017:1

Opinion of AG Wathelet in *Berlioz Investment Fund*, C-682/15, EU:C:2017:2

Opinion of AG Mengozzi in *X and X*, C-638/16 PPU, EU:C:2017:93

Opinion of AG Sánchez-Bordona in *Compass Contract Services*, C-38/16, EU:C:2017:163

Opinion of AG Bobek in *Abercrombie & Fitch Italia*, C-143/16, EU:C:2017:235

Opinion of AG Kokoktt in *Puškár*, C-73/16, EU:C:2017:253

Opinion of AG Szpunar in *Unibet International*, C-49/16, EU:C:2017:270

Opinion of AG Bobek in *Bionorica SE and Diapharm GmbH & Co. KG v European Commission*, Joined cases C-596/15 P and C-597/15 P, EU:C:2017:297

Opinion of AG Kokott in *Comune di Corridonia and Aldo Alessandrini Provincia di Macerata and Others*, Joined cases C-196/16 and C-197/16, EU:C:2017:249

Opinion of AG Saugmandsgaard Øe in *Associação Sindical dos Juízes Portugueses*, C-64/16, EU:C:2017:395

Opinion of AG Bot in *Lounes*, C-165/16, EU:C:2017:407

Opinion of AG Sharpston in *Mengesteab*, C-670/16, EU:C:2017:480

Opinion of AG Sharpston in *Shiri*, C-201/16, EU:C:2017:579

Judgments and Orders by the Court of First Instance/General Court

Judgment of 7 February 1991 in *Tagaras v Court of Justice*, T-18/89, EU:T:1991:8

Judgment of 27 June 1991, *Stahlwerke Peine-Selzgitter v Commission*, T-120/89, EU:T:1991:32

Judgment of 21 October 1992, *Maurissen v European Court of Auditors*, T-23/91, ECR, EU:T:1992:106

Judgment of 6 December 1994 in *Lisrestal*, T-450/93, ECR, EU:T:1994:290

Judgment of 13 July 1995, *O'Dwyer and Others v Council*, Joined cases T-466/93, T-469/93, T-473/93, T-474/93 and T-477/93, EU:T:1995:136

Judgment of 14 September 1995, *Antillean Rice Mills e.a. v Commission*, T-480/93 and T-483/93, EU:T:1995:162

Judgment of 14 September 1995, *Lefebvre and Others v Commission*,T-571/93, ECR, EU:T:1995:163

Judgment of 19 October 1995, *Carvel and Guardian Newspapers v Council*, T-194/94, EU:T:1995:183

Order of 22 December 1995, *Danielsson and Others v Commission*, T-219/95, EU:T:1995:219

Judgment of 16 January 1996, *Candiotte v Council*, T-108/94, EU:T:1996:5

Judgment of 18 September 1996, *Climax Paper Converters v Council*, T-155/94, EU:T:1996:118

Judgment of 24 September 1996, *Dreyfus v Commission*, T-485/93, EU:T:1996:126

Judgment of 22 January 1997, *Opel Austria v Council*, T-115-94, ECR, EU:T:1997:3

Judgment of 5 March 1997, *WWF UK v Commission*, T-105/95, EU:T:1997:26

Judgment of 19 March 1997, *Oliveira v Commission*, T-73/95, EU:T:1997:39

Judgment of 19 June 1997, *Air Inter v Commission*, T-260/94, EU:T:1997:89

Judgment of 14 July 1997, *Interhotel v Commission*, T-81/95, EU:T:1997:117

Judgment of 17 December 1997, *EFMA v Council*, T-121/95, EU:T:1997:198

Judgment of 18 December 1997, *Ajinomoto and The NutraSweet Company v Council*, T-159/94, EU:T:1997:209

Judgment of 18 December 1997, *Inter-Environnement Wallonie*, C-129/96, EU:C:1997:628

Judgment of 6 February 1998, *Interporc Im- und Export v Commission*, T-124/96, EU:T:1998:25

Judgment of 17 June 1998, *Svenska Journalistförbundet v Council*, T-174/95, EU:T:1998:127

Judgment of 19 November 1998, *Champion Stationery Mfg and others v Council*, T-147/97, EU:T:1998:266

Judgment of 9 July 1999, *New Europe Consulting and Brown v Commission*, T-231/97, EU:T:1999:146

Judgment of 19 July 1999, *Rothmans v Commission*, T-188/97, EU:T:1999:156

Judgment of 19 July 1999, *Hautala v Council*, T-14/98, EU:T:1999:157

Judgment of 28 September 1999, *Fruchthandelsgesellschaft Chemnitz v* Commission, T-254/97, EU:T:1999:178

Judgment of 14 October 1999, *Bavarian Lager*, T-309/97, EU:T:1999:257

Judgment of 7 December 1999, *Interporc v Commission*, T-92/98, EU:T:1999:308

Judgment of 22 March 2000, *Coca-Cola v Commission*, T-125/97 and 127/97, EU:T:2000:84

Judgment of 27 June 2000, *Meyer v Commission*, T-72/99, EU:T:2000:170

Judgment of 24 October 2000, *Fresh Marine v Commission*, T-178/98, EU:T:2000:240

Judgment of 26 October 2000, *Carlo Ripa di Meana and Others v Parliament*, T-83/99, EU:T:2000:244

Judgment of 20 March 2001 in *Cordis v Commission*, T-18/99, EU:T:2001:95

Judgment of 11 January 2002 in *Biret International v Council*, T-174/00, EU:T:2002:2

Judgment of 30 January 2002, *max.mobil v Commission*, T-54/99, EU:T:2002:20

Judgment of 6 June 2002, *Airtours v Commission*, T-342/99, EU:T:2002:146

Judgment of 25 October 2002, *Tetra Laval v Commission*, T-5/02, EU:T:2002:264

Judgment of 21 November 2002, *Kundan and Tata v Council*, T-88/98, EU:T:2002:280

Judgment of 9 July 2003, *Vlaams Fonds voor Sociale Integratie van Personen met een Handicap v Commission*, T-102/00, EU:T:2003:192

Judgment of 29 April 2004 in *Tokai Carbon e.a. v Commission* T-236/01, T-239/01, T-244/01 to T-246/01, T-251/01 and T-252/01, EU:T:2004:118

Judgment of 3 February 2005, *Chiquita Brands and Others v Commission*, T-19/01, EU:T:2005:31

Judgment of 17 March 2005, *Scippacercola v Commission*, T-187/03, EU:T:2005:108

Judgment of 14 April 2005, *Sniace SA v Commission*, T-141/03, EU:T:2005:129

Judgment of 26 April 2005, *Sison v Council*, Joined cases T-110/03, T-150/03 and T-405/03, EU:T:2005:143

Judgment of 21 September 2005, *Kadi v Council and Commission*, T-315/01, EU:T:2005:332

Judgment of 19 October 2005, *Cofradía de pescadores "San Pedro" de Bermeo and Others v Council*, T-415/03, ECR, EU:T:2005:365

Judgment of 24 November 2015, *Marcuccio* v *Commission*, T-236/02, EU:T:2005:417

Order of 28 November 2005, *EEB and Stichting Natuur en Milieu v Commission*, T-236/04 and T-241/04, EU:T:2005:426

Judgment of 14 December 2005 in *FIAMM and FIAMM Technologies v Council and Commision*, T-69/00, EU:T:2005:449

Order of 14 December 2005, *Arizona Chemical and Others v Commission*, EU:T:2005:458

Judgment of 30 March 2006, *Yedaş Tarim ve Otomotiv Sanayi ve Ticaret v Council and Commission*, T-367/03, EU:T:2006:96

Judgment of 25 April 2007, *WWF European Policy Programme v Council*, T-264/04, EU:T:2007:114

Judgment of 8 May 2007, *Citymo v Commission*, T-271/04, ECR, EU:T:2007:128

Judgment of 11 July 2007, *Asklepios Kliniken*, T-167/04, EU:T:2007:215

Judgment of 12 September 2007, *Nikolaou v Commission*, T-259/03, ECR, EU:T:2007:254

Judgment of 8 November 2007, *Bavarian Lager v Commission*, T-194/04, EU:T:2007:334

Judgment of 8 July 2008, *Franchet and Byk v Commission*, T-48/05, ECR, EU:T:2008:257

Judgment of 9 September 2008, *MyTravel v Commission*, T-212/03, EU:T:2008:315

Judgment of 27 November 2007, *Pitsiorlas v Council and ECB*, Joined cases T-3/00 and T-337/04, EU:T:2007:357

Judgment of 13 November 2008, *SPM v Council and Commission*, T-128/05, EU:T:2008:494

Judgment of 9 July 2009, *Ristic and others v Parliament*, T-238/07, EU:T:2009:263

Judgment of 7 September 2009, *Liga para Protecção da Natureza v Commission*, T-186/08, EU:T:2009:309

Order of 30 September 2009, *Ivanov v Commission*, T-166/08, EU:T:2009:375

Judgment of 3 March 2010, *Artegodan v Commission*, T-429/05, EU:T:2010:60

Judgment of 19 March 2010, *Gollnisch v Parliament*, T-42/06, EU:T:2010:102

Judgment of 12 May 2010, *Bui Van v Commission*, T-491/08 P, EU:T:2010:191

Judgment of 28 April 2010, *BST v Commission*, T-452/05, EU:T:2010:167

Judgment of 9 June 2010, *Éditions Jacob v Commission*, T-237/05, EU:T:2010:224

Judgment of 21 October 2010, *Agapiou Joséphidès v Commission and EACEA*, T-439/08, EU:T:2010:442

Judgment of 21 October 2010, *Umbach v Commission*, T-474/08, EU:T:2010:443

Judgment of 13 January 2011, *IFAW Internationaler Tierschutz-Fonds v Commission*, T-362/08, EU:T:2011:6

Judgment of 7 June 2011, *Toland v Parliament*, T-471/08, EU:T:2011:252

Order of 14 April 2011, *Umbach v Commission*, C-609/10 P, EU:C:2011:263

Judgment of 14 September 2011, *Tegebauer v Parliament*, T-308/07, EU:T:2011:466

Judgment of 8 November 2011, *Idromacchine and Others v Commission*, T-88/09, EU:T:2011:641
Judgment of 20 October 2011, *Danfoss and Sauer-Danfoss*, C-94/10, EU:C:2011:674

Judgment of 23 November 2011, *Sison v Council*, T-341/07, ECR, EU:T:2011:687

Judgment of 14 February 2012, *Germany v Commission*, T-59/09, EU:T:2012:75

Judgment of 22 May 2012, *Aitic Penteo v OHIM - Atos Worldline*, T-585/10, ECR, EU:T:2012:251

Judgment of 14 June 2012, *Stichting Natuur en Milieu and PAN Europe v Commission*, T-338/08, EU:T:2012:300

Judgment of 14 June 2012, *Vereniging Milieudefensie and Stichting Stop Luchtverontreiniging Utrecht v Commision*, T-396/09, EU:T:2012:301

Judgment of 19 June 2012, *Jaramillo v EIB*, T-234/11 P, EU:T:2012:311

Judgment of 4 May 2012, *In 't Veld v Council*, T-529/09, EU:T:2012:215

Judgment 27 September 2012, *J v Parliament*, T-160/10, EU:T:2012:503

Judgment of 3 October 2012, *Jurašinović v Council*, T-465/09, EU:T:2012:515

Judgment of 27 November 2012, *Steinberg v Commission*, T-17/10, EU:T:2012:625

Judgment of 6 December 2012, *Evropaïki Dynamiki v Commission*, T-167/10, EU:T:2012:651

Judgment of 7 March 2013, *Schönberger v Parliament*, T-186/11, EU:T:2013:111

Judgment of 7 March 2013, *Henkel and Henkel France v Commissio*n, T-64/12, EU:T:2013:116

Judgment of 19 March 2013, In 't Veld v Commission, T-301/10, EU:T:2013:135

Judgment of 16 May 2013, *Gap granen & producten v Commission*, T-437/10, EU:T:2013:248

Judgment of 7 June 2013, *Stichting Corporate Europe Observatory v Commission*, T-93/11, EU:T:2013:308

Judgment of 18 June 2013, *Heath v ECB*, T-645/11 P, ECLI:EU:T:2013:326

Judgment of 12 September 2013, *Besselink v Council*, T-331/11, EU:T:2013:419

Judgment of 8 October 2013, Stichting Greenpeace Nederland and PAN Europe v Commission, T-545/11, EU:T:2013:523

Judgment of 14 November 2013, *LPN and Finland* v *Commission*, Joined cases C-514/11 P and C-605/11 P, EU:C:2013:738

Judgment of 16 July 2014, *Hassan v Council*, T-572/11, ECR, EU:T:2014:682

Order of 25 July 2014, *Deza v ECHA*, T-189/14 R, EU:T:2014:686

Order of 2 September 2014, *Verein Natura Havel and Vierhaus v Commission*, T-538/13, EU:T:2014:738

Judgment of 10 September 2014, *Lomnici v Parliament*, T-650/13, EU:T:2014:796

Judgment of 25 September 2014, *Spirlea v Commission*, T-306/12, EU:T:2014:816

Judgment of 26 September 2014, *Arctic Paper Mochenwangen v Commission*, T-634/13, EU:T:2014:828

Judgment of 26 September 2014, *Raffinerie Heide v Commission*, T-631/13, EU:T:2014:830

Judgment of 26 September 2014, *DK Recycling und Roheisen v Commission*, T-630/13, EU:T:2014:833

Judgment of 26 September 2014, *Molda v Commission*, T-629/13, EU:T:2014:834

Judgment of 26 September 2014, *Romonta v Commission*, T-614/13, EU:T:2014:835

Judgment of 5 November 2014, *Vtesse Network v Commission*, T-362/10, EU:T:2014:928

Order of 11 November 2014, *Bergallou v Parliament and Council*, T-22/14, EU:T:2014:954

Order of 11 November 2014, *Nguyen v Parliament and Council*, T-20/14, EU:T:2014:955

Judgment of 19 November 2014, *Ntouvas v ECDC*, T-223/12, ECR, EU:T:2014:975

Judgment of 19 November 2014, *European Dynamics Luxembourg and Evropaïki Dinamiki*, T-40/12 and T-183/12, ECR, EU:T:2014:972

Judgment of 29 June 2015, *Frank Bold Society v Commission*, T-19/13, EU:T:2015:520

Order of 13 March 2015, *European Coalition to End Animal Experiments* v *ECHA*, T-673/13, EU:T:2015:167

Judgment of 25 March 2015, *Sea Handling SpA v Commission*, T-456/13, EU:T:2015:185

Judgment of 14 April 2015, *Ayadi v Commission*, T-527/09 RENV, EU:T:2015:205

Judgment of 22 April 2015, T-320/09, *Planet v Commission*, EU:T:2015:223

Judgment of 29 April 2015 in *Staelen v Ombudsman*, T-217/11, ECR, EU:T:2015:238

Judgment of 12 May 2015, *Unión de Almacenistas de Hierros de España v Commission*, T-623/13, EU:T:2015:268

Judgment of 15 July 2015, *Dennekamp v Parliament*, T-115/13, EU:T:2015:497

Judgment of 13 May 2015, *Niki Luftfahrt v Commission*, T-511/09, EU:T:284

Order of 1 September 2015, *France v Commission*, T-344/15 R, EU:T:2015:583

Order of 17 July 2015, *European Environmental Bureau*, T-565/14, EU:T:2015:559

Judgment of 23 September 2015, *Schroeder v Council and Commission*, T-205/14, EU:T:2015:673

Judgment of 23 September 2015 in *ClientEarth and International Chemical Secretariat v ECHA*, T-245/11, EU:T:2015:675

Judgment of 30 September 2015, *Anagnostakis v Commission*, T-450/12, EU:T:2015:739

Judgment of 28 October 2015, *Al-Faqih and Others v Commission*, T-134/11, EU:T:2015:812

Judgment of 3 December 2015 in *CN v Parliament*, T-343/13, EU:T:2015:926

Judgment of 16 December 2015, *Martinair Holland v Commission*, T-67/11, EU:T:2015:984

Judgment of 16 December 2015, *Cathay Pacific Airways v Commission*, T-38/11, EU:T:2015:985

Judgment of 16 December 2015, *Latam Airlines Group and Lan Cargo v Commission*, T-40/11, EU:T:2015:986

Judgment of 16 December 2015, *British Airways v Commission*, T-48/11, EU:T:2015:988

Judgment of 16 December 2015, *Singapore Airlines and Singapore Airlines Cargo v Commission*, T-43/11, EU:T:2015:989

Judgment of 16 December 2015, *SAS Cargo Group and Others v Commission*, T-56/11, EU:T:2015:990

Judgment of 16 December 2015, *Cargolux Airlines v Commission*, T-39/11, EU:T:2015:991

Judgment of 16 December 2015, *Japan Airlines v Commission*, T-36/11, EU:T:2015:992

Judgment of 16 December 2015, *Air France v Commission*, T-63/11, EU:T:2015:993

Judgment of 16 December 2015, *Air Canada v Commission*, T-9/11, EU:T:2015:994

Judgment of 16 December 2015, *Koninklijke Luchtvaart Maatschappij v Commission*, T-28/11, EU:T:2015:995

Judgment of 16 December 2015, *Air France-KLM v Commission*, T-62/11, EU:T:2015:996

Order of 16 March 2016, *One of Us and Others v Commission*, T-561/14, EU:T:2016:173

Judgment of 19 April 2016, *Costantini and Others v Commission*, T-44/14, EU:T:2016:223

Judgment of 10 May 2016, *Mikhalchanka v Council*, T-693/13, EU:T:2016:283

Judgment of 26 May 2016, *International Management Group v Commission*, T-110/15, EU:T:2016:322

Judgment of 6 July 2016, *LM v Commission*, T-560/15 P, EU:T:2016:392

Order of 20 July 2016, *PTC Therapeutics International v EMA*, T-718/15 R, EU:T:2016:425

Order of 20 July 2016, *MSD Animal Health Innovation and Intervet international v EMA*, T-729/15 R, EU:T:2016:435

Order of 28 September 2016, *PAN Europe and Others v Commission*, T-600/15, EU:T:2016:601

Judgment of 29 November 2016, *T & L Sugars and Sidul Açúcares v Commission*, T-279/11, EU:T:2016:683

Judgment of 15 December 2016, *TestBioTech and Others v Commission*, T-177/13, EU:T:2016:736

Judgment of 13 January 2017, *Deza v ECHA*, T-189/14, EU:T:2017:4

Judgment of 3 February 2017, *Minority SafePack - one million signatures for diversity in EUrope v Commission*, T-646/13, EU:T:2017:59

Judgment of 5 April 2017, *France v Commission*, T-344/15, EU:T:2017:250

Judgment of 24 April 2017, *HF v Parliament*, T-584/16, EU:T:2017:282

Judgment of 10 May 2017, *Efler and Others v Commission*, T-754/14, EU:T:2017:323

Judgment of 16 May 2017, *Agria Polska and Others v Commission*, T-480/15, EU:T:2017:339

Judgment of 26 July 2017, *Sacko*, C-348/16, EU:C:2017:591

Judgment of 25 October 2017, *Shiri*, C-201/16, EU:C:2017:805

Judgment of 5 February 2018, *PTC Therapeutics International v EMA*, T-718/15, EU:T:2018:66

Judgment of 5 February 2018, *MSF Animal Health Innovation and Intervet International v EMA*, T-729/15, EU:T:2018:67

Judgment of 7 February 2018, *Access Info Europe v Commission*, T-851/16, EU:T:2018:69

Judgment of 22 March 2018, *De Capitani v Parliament*, T-540/15, EU:T:2018:167

Judgment of 23 April 2018, *One of Us and Others v Commission*, T-561/14, EU:T:2018:210

Judgments of the Civil Service Tribunal

Judgment in *Nijs v Court of Auditors*, F-5/07, EU:F:2008:84

Judgment of 11 September 2008, *Bui Van v Commission*, F-51/07, EU:F:2008:112

Judgment of 12 March 2009, *Hambura v Parliament*, F-4/08, EU:F:2009:25

Order of 23 September 2010, *Bui Van v Commission*, F-51/07 RENV, EU:F:2010:108

Judgment of 1st December 2010, *Nolin v Commission*, F-82/09, EU:F:2010:154

Judgment of 29 September 2011, *Heath v ECB*, F-121/10, ECLI:EU:F:2011:174

Judgment of 5 December 2012, *Z v Court of Justice*, F-88/09 and F-48/10, EU:F:2012:171

Judgment of 14 May 2014, *Delacroix v EEAS*, F-11/13, EU:F:2014:91

Judgment of 19 June 2014 *BN v Parliament*, F-157/12, EU:F:2014:164

Judgment of 17 September 2014, *Wahlström v Frontex*, F-117/13, EU:F:2014:215

Judgment of 17 March 2015, *AX v ECB*, F-73/13, EU:F:2015:9

Judgment of 15 April 2015, *Pipiliagkas v Commission*, F-96/13, EU:F:2015:29

Judgment of 30 June 2015, *Petsch v Commission*, F-124/14, EU:F:2015:69

Judgment of 15 December 2015, *Guittet v Commission*, F-141/14, EU:F:2015:149

Judgment of 17 December 2015, *Seigneur v ECB*, F-95/14, EU:F:2015:155

Judgment of 17 December 2015, *Bowles v ECB*, F-94/14, EU:F:2015:156

Judgment of 5 February 2016, *GV v EEAS*, F-137/14, EU:F:2016:14

Judgments of the European Court of Human Rights

Matthews v United Kingdom, n°24833/94 (ECHR 1999)

Goodwin v United Kingdom, n°28957/95 (ECHR 2002)

Bosphorus Hava Yolları Turizm ve Ticaret Anonim Şirketi v Ireland, n°45036/98 (ECHR 2005)

M.S.S. v Belgium and Greece, n°30696/09 (ECHR 2011)

Tchokontio Happi v France, n°65829/12 (ECHR 2015)

Judgments of the International Court of Justice

ICJ Judgment of 25 May 1926, *German interests in Polish Upper Silesia*, CPJI, Series A, No7

Judgments of national courts

Denmark

Supreme Court (Højesteret), 6 December 2016, Case 15/2014 (First Chamber), *DI v Estate of A*

France

Syndicat des propriétaires et contribuables du quartier Croix-de-Seguey-Tivoli, CE, 21 décembre 1906, Rec. p. 962

Arrighi, CE, section, 6 nov 1936, Rec. p 966

Ministre de l'intérieur c/ Cohn-Bendit, CE, ass, 22 déc 1978, Rec. Lebon p. 524

Cons. const., 25 juillet 1979, n° 79-105 DC, *Droit de grève à la radio et à la télévision*

Nicolo, CE, ass., 20 oct 1989, n°108243

Fédération nationale des syndicats d'exploitants agricoles et autres du 11 juillet 2001, n°s 219494, 221021, 221274, 221275, 221421, Rec.

Mme Perreux, CE, ass., 30 oct 2009, n°298348

Germany

BVerfGE 27, 297/307

BVerfGE 37, 271

BVerfGE 46, 160

BVerfGE 49, 89

BVerfGE 53, 30

BVerfG 123, 267

BVerfG 132, 195

BVerwG, 3.12.1959, MDR 1960 338

Italy

Council of State, Opinion of 26 February 1965

Constitutional Court, Judgment of 27 December 1973, Case 183/73, *Frontini and associates*, Giurisprudenza Costituzionale, 1973, 2406

Poland

Order of the Sąd Najwyższy of 20 February 2008, III SK 23/07

United Kingdom

R v Secretary of State for Foreign and Commonwealth Affairs, ex p World Development Movement Ltd [1995] 1 WLR 386.

R. v Lord Chancellor, ex p. Witham [1998] Q.B. 575.

R (Kides) v South Cambridgeshire DC [2002] 4 PLR 66

R (Hammerton) v London Underground Ltd [2002] EWHC 2307.

R (on the application of Chester) v Secretary of State for Justice and McGeoch (AP) v The Lord President of the Council and another Scotland UKSC 63 (UK Supreme Court)

R v Somerset County Council, ex p Dixon [1998] Env LR 111.

ACCC Findings and Recommendations

ACCC Findings and Recommendations with regard to Communication ACCC/C/2008/32 (Part II) Concerning Compliance by the European Union, as adopted on 17 March 2017 (advance unedited version)

ACCC Findings and Recommendations with regard to Communication ACCC/C/2008/32 (Part I), ECE/MP.PP/C.1/2011/4/Add.1, 24 August 2011

Table of legal acts

Legal acts of the European Union

Treaties

Treaty establishing the European Coal and Steel Community (ECSC Treaty/Treaty of Paris), 18 April 1951, 261 UNTS 140, Expired by its terms 23 July 2002

Treaty instituting the European Economic Community (EEC Treaty/Treaty of Rome), 1957 294 UNTS 17

Single European Act (OJ L 169, 29.6.1987, p. 1–28).

Treaty on the European Union (Maastricht Treaty), OJ 1992 191/1

Treaty amending the Treaty on the European Union, the Treaties establishing the European Communities and certain related acts (Treaty of Amsterdam), OJ 1997 C 340/1

Treaty amending the Treaty on European Union, the Treaties establishing the European Communities and certain related acts (OJ 2001 C 80) (Treaty of Nice)

Treaty establishing a Constitution for Europe, OJ 2004 C 310/1

Charter of Fundamental Rights of the European Union, OJ 2007 C 303/1

Treaty of Lisbon Amending the Treaty on European Union and the Treaty Establishing the European Community, OJ 2007 C 306/1

Consolidated Version of the Treaty on European Union, OJ 2010 C 83/01

Consolidated Version of the Treaty on the Functioning of the European Union (TFEU), OJ 2008 C 115/47

Regulations

Council Regulation No 3 of 25 September 1958 on social security for migrant workers, OJ, English Special Edition 1952-1958(I), p. 63

Council Regulation (EEC) No 20 of 4 April 1962 on the gradual establishment of the common organization of the market in pigmeat (OJ 1962 p. 945)

Council Regulation 19/62/EEC of 4 April 1962 on the Progressive Establishment of a Common Organisation of the Market in Cereals' (OJ 1962 30/933)

Council Regulation (EEC) No 121/67/EEC of 13 June 1967 on the common organization of the market in pigmeat (OJ 1967 p. 2283)

Council Regulation 120/67/EEC of 13 June 1967 on the common organization of the market in cereals (OJ 1967 2269/67)

Council Regulation (EEC) No 1612/68 of 15 October 1968 on freedom of movement for workers within the Community (OJ, English Special Edition 1968 (II), p. 475)

Council Regulation (EEC) No 1035/72 of 18 May 1972 on the common organization of the market in fruit and vegetables (OJ, English Special Edition, 1972 (II) p. 437)

Council Regulation (EEC) No 1408/71 of 14 June 1971 on the application of social security schemes to employed persons, to self-employed persons and to members of their families moving within the Community, as amended and updated by Council Regulation (EEC) No 2001/83 of 2 June 1983 (OJ L 230, p.6), as amended by Council Regulation (EEC) No 1248/92 of 30 April 1992 (OJ L 136, p. 7)

Council Regulation (EEC) No 2707/72 of 19 December 1972 laying down the conditions for applying protective measures for fruit and vegetables (OJ, English Special Edition 1972, p. 3)

Council Regulation (EEC) No 754/76 of 25 March 1976 on the customs treatment applicable to goods returned to the customs territory of the Community (OJ L 89 p. 1)

Council Regulation (EEC) No 563/76 of 15 March 1976 on the compulsory purchase of skimmed-milk powder held by intervention agencies for use in feeding-stuffs (OJ L 67 p.18)

Commission Regulation No 1687/76 of 30 June 1976 laying down common detailed rules for verifying the use and/or destination of products from intervention (OJ L 190 p. 1)

Council Regulation (EEC) No 1697/79 of 24 July 1979 on the post-clearance recovery of import duties or export duties which have not been required of the person liable for payment on goods entered for a customs procedure involving the obligation to pay such duties (OJ L 197 p. 1)

Council Regulation (EEC) No 1785/81 of 30 June 1981 on the common organisation of the markets in the sugar sector (OJ L 177 p. 4), as amended by Council Regulation (EC) No 3290/94 of 22 December 1994 on the adjustments and transitional arrangements required in the agriculture sector in order to implement the agreements concluded during the Uruguay Round of multilateral trade negotiations (OJ L 349 p. 105)

Council Regulation (EEC) No 857/84 of 31 March 1984 adopting general rules for the application of the levy referred to in Article 5c of Regulation (EEC) No 804/68 in the milk and milk products sector (OJ L 90 p. 13), as supplemented by Commission Regulation No 1371/84 of 16 May 1984 laying down detailed rules for the application of the additional levy referred to in Article 5c of Regulation (EEC) No 804/68 (OJ L 132 p. 11)

Council Regulation (EEC) No 1914/87 of 2 July 1987 introducing a special elimination levy in the sugar sector for the 1986/87 marketing year (OJ L 183 p.5)

Council Regulation 816/92 of 31 March 1992 amending Regulation 804/68 on the common organization of the market in milk and milk products (OJ L 86 p. 83)

Council Regulation 748/93 of 17 March 1993 amending Regulation 3950/92 establishing an additional levy in the milk and milk products sector (OJ L 77 p. 16)

Council Regulation (EC) No 3697/93 of 20 December 1993 withdrawing tariff concessions in accordance with Article 23(2) and Article 27(3)(a) of the Free Trade Agreement between the Community and Austria (General Motors Austria) (OJ L 343 p. 1)

Commission Regulation (EC) No 1423/95 of 23 June 1995 laying down detailed implementing rules for the import of products in the sugar sector other than molasses (OJ L 141 p. 16)

Commission Regulation (EC) No 1249/96 of 28 June 1996 on rules of application (cereal sector import duties) for Council Regulation (EEC) No 1766/92 (OJ L 161 p. 125)

Council Regulation (EC) No 2200/96 of 28 October 1996 on the common organization of the market in fruit and vegetables (OJ L 297 p. 1)

Parliament and Council Regulation (EC) No 45/2001 of 18 December 2000 on the protection of individuals with regard to the processing of personal data by the Community institutions and bodies and on the free movement of such data (OJ L 8 p. 1)

Parliament and Council Regulation of 30 May 2001 regarding public access to European Parliament, Council and Commission documents (OJ L 145 p. 43-48)

Council Regulation (EC) No 881/2002 of 27 May 2002, imposing certain specific restrictive measures directed against certain persons and entities associated with Usama bin Laden, the Al-Qaida network and the Taliban, and repealing Council Regulation (EC) No 467/2001 prohibiting the export of certain goods and services to Afghanistan, strengthening the flight ban and extending the freeze of funds and other financial resources in respect of the Taliban of Afghanistan (OJ L 139 p. 9–22)

Council Regulation (EC) No 343/2003 of 18 February 2003, establishing the criteria and mechanisms for determining the Member State responsible for examining an asylum application lodged in one of the Member States by a third-country national (OJ L 50/1 p. 1-10)

Parliament and Council Regulation 1829/2003 of 22 September 2003 on genetically modified food and feed (OJ L 268 p. 1-23)

Parliament and Council Regulation No 1367/2006 of 6 September 2006 on the application of the provisions of the Aarhus Convention on Access to Information, Public Participation in Decision-making and Access to Justice in Environmental Matters to Community institutions and bodies (OJ L 264 p.13-19)

Parliament and Council Regulation (EC) No 864/2007 of 11 July 2007 on the law applicable to non-contractual obligations (Rome II) (OJ L 199 p. 40-49)

Commission Regulation (EC) No 149/2008 of 29 January 2008 amending Regulation (EC) No 396/2005 of the European Parliament and of the Council by establishing Annexes II, III and IV setting maximum residue levels for products covered by Annex I thereto (OJ L 58 p. 1-398)

Parliament and Council Regulation (EC) No 593/2008 of 17 June 2008 on the law applicable to contractual obligations (Rome I) (OJ L 177 p. 6-16)

Parliament and Council Regulation No 211/2011 of 16 February 2011 on the citizens' initiative (OJ L 65 p.1)

Parliament and Council Regulation No 604/2013 of 26 June 2013 establishing the criteria and mechanisms for determining the Member State responsible for examining an application for international protection lodged in one of the Member States by a third-country national or a stateless person (recast) (OJ L 180/31 p. 31)

Council Regulation 2015/1589 of 13 July 2015 laying down detailed rules for the application of Article 108 of the TFEU (OJ L 248 p.9)

Directives

Council Directive 64/221/EEC of 25 February 1964 on the co-ordination of special measures concerning the movement and residence of foreign nationals which are justified on grounds of public policy, public security or public health (OJ 056 p.850)

Council Directive 64/433/EEC of 26 June 1964 on health conditions for the production and marketing of fresh meat (OJ, English Special Edition 1963-64, p. 185), as amended by Council Directive 91/497/EEC of 29 July 1991 (OJ L 268, p. 69)

Council Directive 67/228/EEC of 11 April 1967 on the harmonisation of legislation of Member States concerning turnover taxes (OJ 71/1303 p. 14)

Council Directive 74/577/EEC of 18 November 1974 on stunning of animals before slaughter (OJ L 316 p. 10)

Council Directive 75/440/EEC of 16 June 1975 concerning the quality required of surface water intended for the abstraction of drinking water in the Member States (OJ L 194 p. 26)

Council Directive 75/442/EEC of 15 July 1975 on waste (OJ L 194 p. 39)

Council Directive 76/207/EEC of 9 February 1976 on the implementation of the principle of equal treatment for men and women as regards access to employment, vocational training and promotion, and working conditions (OJ L 39 p. 40)

Second Council Directive 77/91/EEC of 13 December 1976 on coordination of safeguards which, for the protection of the interests of members and others, are required by Member States of companies within the meaning of the second paragraph of Article 58 of the Treaty, in respect of the formation of public limited liability companies and the maintenance and alteration of their capital, with a view to making such safeguards equivalent (OJ L 26 p. 1)

Council Directive 77/388/EEC of 17 May 1977 on the harmonisation of the laws of the Member States relating to turnover taxes - Common system of value added tax: uniform basis of assessment (OJ L 145 p. 1)

First Council Directive 77/780/EEC of 12 December 1977 on the coordination of the laws, regulations and administrative provisions relating to the taking up and pursuit of the business of credit institutions (OJ L 322 p. 30)

Council Directive 79/7/EEC of 19 December 1978 on the progressive implementation of the principle of equal treatment for men and women in matters of social security (OJ L 6 p. 24)

Council Directive 79/869/EEC of 9 October 1979 concerning the methods of measurement and frequencies of sampling and analysis of surface water intended for the abstraction of drinking water in the Member States (OJ L 271 p. 44)

Council Directive 80/68/EEC of 17 December 1979 on the protection of groundwater against pollution caused by certain dangerous substances (OJ L 20 p. 43)

Council Directive 80/987/EEC of 20 October 1980 on the approximation of the laws of the Member States relating to the protection of employees in the event of the insolvency of the employer (OJ L 283 p. 23)

Council Directive 81/851/EEC of 28 September 1981 on the approximation of the laws of the Member States relating to veterinary medicinal products (OJ L 317 p. 1)

Council Directive 81/852/EEC of 28 September 1981 on the approximation of the laws of the Member States relating to analytical, pharmaco-toxicological and clinical standards and protocols in respect of the testing of veterinary medicinal products (OJ L 317 p. 16)

Council Directive 82/884/EEC of 3 December 1982 on a limit value for lead in the air (OJ L 378, p. 15)

Council Directive 85/337/EEC of 27 June 1985 on the assessment of the effects of certain public and private projects on the environment (OJ L 175 p. 40)

Council Directive 85/577/EEC of 20 December 1985 to protect the consumer in respect of contracts negotiated away from business premises (OJ L 372 p. 31).

Council Directive 89/299/EEC of 17 April 1989 on the own funds of credit institutions (OJ L 124 p. 16)

Second Council Directive 89/646/EEC of 15 December 1989 on the coordination of laws, regulations and administrative provisions relating to the taking up and pursuit of the business of credit institutions and amending Directive 77/780 (OJ L 386 p. 1)

Council Directive 89/662/EEC of 11 December 1989 concerning veterinary checks in intra-Community trade with a view to the completion of the internal market (OJ L 395 p. 13)

Council Directive 89/665/EEC of 21 December 1989 on the coordination of the laws, regulations and administrative provisions relating to the application of review procedures to the award of public supply and public works contracts (OJ L 395 p. 33)

Council Directive 90/314/EEC of 13 June 1990 on package travel, package holidays and package tours (OJ L 158/59 p. 59)

Council Directive 90/427/EEC of 26 June 1990 on the zootechnical and genealogical conditions governing intra-Community trade in equidæ (OJ L 224 p. 55)

Council Directive 90/364/EEC of 28 June 1990 on the right of residence (OJ L 180 p. 26)

Council Directive 90/435/EEC of 23 July 1990 on the common system of taxation applicable in the case of parent companies and subsidiaries of different Member States (OJ L 225 p. 6)

Council Directive 92/13/EEC of 25 February 1992 coordinating the laws, regulations and administrative provisions relating to the application of Community rules on the procurement procedures of entities operating in the water, energy, transport and telecommunications sectors (OJ L 76 p. 14)

Council Directive 92/43/EEC of 21 May 1992 on the conservation of natural habitats and of wild fauna and flora (OJ L 206 p. 7)

Council Directive 92/85/EEC of 19 October 1992 on the introduction of measures to encourage improvements in the safety and health at work of pregnant workers and workers who have recently given birth or are breastfeeding (tenth individual Directive within the meaning of Article 16 (1) of Directive 89/391/EEC) (OJ L 348 p. 1)

Council Directive 93/13/EEC of 5 April 1993 on unfair terms in consumer contracts (OJ 1993 L 95 p. 29)

Council Directive 93/42/EEC of 14 June 1993 concerning medical devices (OJ L 169 p. 1)

Council Directive 93/104/EC of 23 November 1993 concerning certain aspects of the organisation of working time (OJ L 307 p. 18)

Parliament and Council Directive 94/19/EC of 30 May 1994 on deposit-guarantee schemes (OJ L 135 p. 5)

Council Directive 94/45/EC of 22 September 1994 on the establishment of a European Works Council or a procedure in Community-scale undertakings and Community-scale groups of undertakings for the purposes of informing and consulting employees (OJ L 254 p. 64)

Parliament and Council Directive 95/46/EC of 24 October 1995 on the protection of individuals with regard to the processing of personal data and on the free movement of such data (OJ L 281 p. 31)

Council Directive 96/34/EC of 3 June 1996 on the framework agreement on parental leave concluded by UNICE, CEEP and the ETUC (OJ L 145 p. 4)

Council Directive 85/337/EEC of 27 June 1985 on the assessment of the effects of certain public and private projects on the environment (OJ L 175 p. 40), as amended by Directive 2003/35/EC of the European Parliament and of the Council of 26 May 2003 (OJ L 156 p. 17).

Council Directive 96/62/EC of 27 September 1996 on ambient air quality assessment and management (OJ L 296 p. 55), as amended by Regulation (EC) No 1882/2003 of the European Parliament and of the Council of 29 September 2003 (OJ L 284 p. 1)

Council Directive 98/59/EC of 20 July 1998 on the approximation of the laws of the Member States relating to collective redundancies (OJ L 225 p. 16)

Council Directive 2000/43/EC of 29 June 2000 implementing the principle of equal treatment between persons irrespective of racial or ethnic origin (OJ L 180 p. 22)

Council Directive 2000/78/EC of 27 November 2000 establishing a general framework for equal treatment in employment and occupation (OJ L 303 p.16)

Council Directive 2001/23/EC of 12 March 2001 on the approximation of the laws of the Member States relating to the safeguarding of employees' rights in the event of transfers of undertakings, businesses or parts of undertakings or businesses (OJ L 82 p. 16)

Parliament and Council Directive 2001/42/EC of 27 June 2001 on the assessment of the effects of certain plans and programmes on the environment (OJ L 197 p. 30)

Parliament and Council Directive 2001/81/EC of 23 October 2001 on national emission ceilings for certain atmospheric pollutants (OJ L 309 p. 22)

Parliament and Council Directive 2001/83/EC of 6 November 2001 on the Community code relating to medicinal products for human use (OJ L 311 p. 67), as amended by Parliament and Council Regulation (EC) No 1394/2007 of 13 November 2007 (OJ L 324 p. 121, and corrigendum OJ 2009 L 87 p. 174)

Parliament and Council Directive 2002/21/EC of 7 March 2002 on a common regulatory framework for electronic communications networks and services (OJ L 108 p. 33)

Parliament and Council Directive 2002/14/EC of 11 March 2002 establishing a general framework for informing and consulting employees in the European Community (OJ L 80 p. 29)

Council Directive No 2003/9/EC of 27 January 2003 laying down minimum standards for the reception of asylum seekers (OJ L 031 p. 18)

Parliament and Council Directive 2003/4/EC of 28 January 2003 on public access to environmental information and repealing Council Directive 90/313/EEC (OJ L 041 p. 26)

Parliament and Council Directive 2003/35/EC of 26 May 2003 (OJ L 156, p. 17)

Parliament and Council Directive 2003/87/EC of 13 October 2003 establishing a scheme for greenhouse gas emission allowance trading within the Community and amending Council Directive 96/61/EC (OJ L 275 p. 32)

Parliament and Council Directive 2003/88/EC of 4 November 2003 concerning certain aspects of the organisation of working time (OJ L 299 p. 9)

Council Directive 2004/83/EC of 29 April 2004 on minimum standards for the qualification and status of third country nationals or stateless persons as refugees or as persons who otherwise need international protection and the content of the protection granted (OJ L 304/12 p. 12)

Parliament and Council Directive 2006/24/EC of 15 March 2006 on the retention of data generated or processed in connection with the provision of publicly available electronic communications services or of public communications networks and amending Directive 2002/58/EC (OJ L 105/54 p. 54)

Parliament and Council Directive 2004/35/EC of 21 April 2004 on environmental liability with regard to the prevention and remedying of environmental damage (OJ L 43 p. 56)

Parliament and Council Directive 2006/54/EC of 5 July 2006 on the implementation of the principle of equal opportunities and equal treatment of men and women in matters of employment and occupation (OJ L 204 p. 23).

Parliament and Council Directive 2008/50/EC of 21 May 2008 on ambient air quality and cleaner air for Europe (OJ L 152 p. 1)

Parliament and Council Directive 2008/115/EC of 16 December 2008 on common standards and procedures in Member States for returning illegally staying third-country nationals (OJ L 348 p. 98)

Parliament and Council Directive 2009/22/EC of 23 April 2009 on injunctions for the protection of consumers' interests (OJ L 110 p. 30)

Parliament and Council Directive No 2009/30/EC as regards the specification of petrol, diesel and gas-oil and introducing a mechanism to monitor and reduce greenhouse gas emissions and amending Council Directive 1999/32/EC as regards the specification of fuel used by inland waterway vessels and repealing Directive 93/12/EEC (OJ L 140 p. 88)

Council Directive 2011/16/EU of 15 February 2011 on administrative cooperation in the field of taxation and repealing Directive 77/799/EEC (OJ L 64 p. 1)

Parliament and Council Directive 2011/92/EU of 13 December 2011 on the assessment of the effects of certain public and private projects on the environment (OJ L 26 p. 1)

Parliament and Council Directive 2011/95/EU of 13 December 2011 on standards for the qualification of third-country nationals or stateless persons as beneficiaries of international protection, for a uniform status for refugees or for persons eligible for subsidiary protection, and for the content of the protection granted (OJ L 337 p. 9)

Parliament and Council Directive No 2013/33/EU of 26 June 2013 laying down standards for the reception of applicants for international protection (OJ L 180/96 p. 96)

Directive 2014/104/EU of the European Parliament and of the Council of 26 November 2014 on certain rules governing actions for damages under national law for infringements of the competition law provisions of the Member States and of the European Union (OJ L 349 p. 1)

Parliament and Council Directive 98/30/EC of 22 June 1998 concerning common rules for the internal market in natural gas (OJ L 204 p. 1) and Parliament and Council Directive 2003/55/EC of 26 June 2003 concerning common rules for the internal market in natural gas and repealing Directive 98/30/EC (OJ L 176 p. 57)

Parliament and Council Directive 2002/22/EC of 7 March 2002 on Universal Service and users' rights relating to electronic communications networks and services (Universal Service Directive) (OJ L 108 p. 51)

Decisions

Council Decision of 13 May 1965 on the harmonization of certain provisions affecting competition in transport by rail, road and inland waterway (OJ special edition 1965 p. 67)

Act concerning the election of the representatives of the European Parliament by direct universal suffrage annexed to Council Decision 76/787/ECSC, EEC, Euratom of 20 September 1976 (OJ L 278 p. 1), as amended by Council Decision 2002/772/EC, Euratom of 25 June 2002 and 23 September 2002 (OJ L 283 p. 1)

Council Decision 85/73/EEC of 15 June 1988 on the levels of the fees to be charged for health inspections and controls of fresh meat pursuant to Directive 85/73/EEC (OJ L 194/24)

Commission Decision 92/353/EEC of 11 June 1992 laying down the criteria for the approval or recognition of organizations and associations which maintain or establish stud-books for registered equidae (OJ L 192 p. 63)

Council Decision 93/731/EC of 20 December 1993 on public access to Council documents (OJ L 340 p. 43)

Commission Decision 94/90/ECSC, EC, Euratom of 8 February 1994 on public access to Commission documents (OJ L 46 p. 58).

Council Framework Decision of 19 July 2002 on combating trafficking in human beings (OJ L 203 p. 1)

Council Decision 2005/370/EC of 17 February 2005 on the conclusion, on behalf of the European Community, of the Convention on access to information, public participation in decision-making and access to justice in environmental matters (OJ L 124 p. 1)

Commission Decision of 5 September 2013 concerning national implementation measures for the transitional free allocation of greenhouse gas emission allowances in accordance with Article 11(3) of Directive 2003/87/EC of the European Parliament and of the Council (OJ L 240 p.27)

Decision No 1386/2013/EU of the European Parliament and of the Council of 20 November 2013 on a General Union Environment Action Programme to 2020 'Living well, within the limits of our planet' Text with EEA relevance (OJ L 354 p. 171)

Recommendations

Commission Recommendation to the Member States of 23 July 1962 concerning the adoption of a European schedule of occupational diseases (OJ 1962, 80, p. 2188)

Commission Recommendation 66/462 of 20 July 1966 on the conditions for granting compensation to persons suffering from occupational diseases (OJ 1966, 147, p. 26)

Commission Recommendation of 11 June 2013 on common principles for injunctive and compensatory collective redress mechanisms in the Member States concerning violations of rights granted under Union Law (OJ L 201 p. 60)

Protocols, Resolutions, Declarations, Communications, Proposals

First Environmental Action Programme (EAP): Declaration of the Council of the European Communities and of the representatives of the Governments of the Member States meeting in the Council of 22 November 1973 on the programme of action of the European Communities on the environment (OJ C 112, 20.12.1973)

Resolution of the Council of the European Communities and of the Representatives of the Governments of the Member States meeting within the Council of 17 May 1977 on the continuation and implementation of a European Community policy and action programme on the environment (OJ C 139, 13.6.1977)

Commission Memorandum on Accession of the Communities to the European Convention on Human Rights (COM (79) final, Bulletin of the European Communities, Supplement 2/79)

Community Charter of the Fundamental Social Rights of Workers, adopted at the meeting of the European Council held in Strasbourg on 9 December 1989

Interinstitutional declaration on democracy, transparency, and subsidiarity. Bulletin of the European Communities, No. 10/93, pp. 118-120

Commission Communication on the Charter of Fundamental Rights of the European Union, 13.9.2000 (COM(2000) 559 final)

Communication from the Commission on the legal nature of the Charter of Fundamental Rights of the European Union, 28.10.2000 (COM (2000) 664 final)

European Parliament resolution of 15 March 2007 on compliance with the Charter of Fundamental Rights in the Commission's legislative proposals: methodology for systematic and rigorous monitoring, 15.3.2007 (2005/2169(INI))

Explanations relating to the Charter of Fundamental Rights (2007 OJ C 303/17)

Protocol on the application of the Charter of Fundamental Rights of the European Union to Poland and to the United Kingdom (2007 OJ C 306/156)

Proposal for a Regulation of the European Parliament and of the Council regarding public access to European Parliament, Council and Commission documents, /* COM/2008/0229 final - COD 2008/0090 */

Commission Communication of 22.5.2012 'A European Consumer Agenda – Boosting confidence and growth' (COM(2012 225 final)

Council Directives for the negotiation of the Transatlantic Trade and Investment Partnership between the European Union and the United States of America, as adopted at the Foreign Affairs Council (Trade) on 14 June 2013, 11103/13, available at http://data.consilium.europa.eu/doc/document/ST-11103-2013-DCL-1/en/pdf

Commission Proposal for a Regulation of the European Parliament and of the Council establishing the criteria and mechanisms for determining the Member State responsible for examining an application for international protection lodged in one of the Member States by a third-country national or a stateless person (recast), COM(2016) 270 final 2016:0133 (COD)

European Parliament resolution of 19 January 2017 on a European Pillar of Social Rights (2016/2095(INI))

Protocol (No 7) on the Privileges and Immunities of the European Union (OJ C 326, 26/10/2012 p. 266)

Codes of Conduct, Rules and Guidelines

European Parliament's Rules of Procedure, 8th parliamentary term, 2014-2019, January 2017 version, available at: http://www.europarl.europa.eu/sides/getDoc.do?pubRef=-//EP//NONSGML+RULES-EP+20170116+0+DOC+PDF+V0//EN&language=EN [accessed 8 August 2017]

International agreements, conventions and treaties

General Agreement on Tariffs and Trade (GATT), October 30, 1947, 61 Stat. A-11, 55 U.N.T.S. 194

UN General Assembly, *Universal Declaration of Human Rights*, 10 December 1948, 217 A (III), available at: http://www.refworld.org/docid/3ae6b3712c.html [accessed 19 April 2017]

Council of Europe, *European Convention for the Protection of Human Rights and Fundamental Freedoms, as amended by Protocols Nos. 11 and 14*, 4 November 1950, ETS 5, available at: http://www.refworld.org/docid/3ae6b3b04.html [accessed 8 August 2017]

UN General Assembly, *Convention Relating to the Status of Refugees*, 28 July 1951, United Nations, Treaty Series, vol. 189, p. 137, available at: http://www.refworld.org/docid/3be01b964.html [accessed 19 April 2017]

Agreement creating an association between the European Economic Community and Turkey, OJ of 29.12.1964, L217, p. 3687

UN General Assembly, *International Covenant on Civil and Political Rights*, 16 December 1966, United Nations, Treaty Series, vol. 999, p. 171, available at: http://www.refworld.org/docid/3ae6b3aa0.html [accessed 11 December 2015].

UN General Assembly, *International Covenant on Economic, Social and Cultural Rights*, 16 December 1966, United Nations, Treaty Series, vol. 993, p. 3, available at: http://www.refworld.org/docid/3ae6b36c0.html [accessed 11 December 2015].

United Nations, *Vienna Convention on the Law of Treaties*, 23 May 1969, United Nations, Treaty Series, vol. 1155, p. 331, available at: http://www.refworld.org/docid/3ae6b3a10.html [accessed 15 December 2016]

Cooperation agreement between the European Economic Community and Morocco, OJ 1978 L274/2

Council of Europe, *Convention for the Protection of Individuals with Regard to the Automatic Processing of Individual Data*, 28 January 1981, ETS 108, available at: http://www.refworld.org/docid/3dde1005a.html [accessed 19 April 2017]

Convention implementing the Schengen Agreement of 14 June 1985 between the Governments of the States of the Benelux Economic Union, the Federal Republic of Germany and the French Republic on the gradual abolition of checks at their common borders (OJ L 239, 22/09/2000, p. 19)

UN General Assembly, *Convention on the Rights of the Child*, 20 November 1989, United Nations, Treaty Series, vol. 1577, p. 3, available at: http://www.refworld.org/docid/3ae6b38f0.html [accessed 19 April 2017]

Convention determining the State responsible for examining applications for asylum lodged in one of the Member States of the European Communities of 15 June 1990 – Dublin Convention OJ C 254 p. 1-12

Agreement on the European Economic Area (EEA Agreement), 1994 OJ L1 572

Convention drawn up on the basis of Article K.3 of the Treaty on European Union, on the protection of the European Communities' financial interests (OJ C 316, 27/11/1995 p. 49)

Council of Europe, *European Social Charter (Revised)*, 3 May 1996, ETS 163, available at: http://www.refworld.org/docid/3ae6b3678.html [accessed 19 April 2017]

Council of Europe, *Convention on Human Rights and Biomedicine*, 4 April 1997, ETS 164

Convention drawn up on the basis of Article K.3 (2) (c) of the Treaty on European Union on the fight against corruption involving officials of the European Communities or officials of Member States of the European Union (OJ C 195, 25/06/1997 p. 2-11)

Convention on Access to Information, Public Participation in Decision-Making and Access to Justice in Environmental Matters (Aarhus Convention), 2161 UNTS 447; 38 ILM 517 (1999)

Constitutional and legal acts of Member States

Belgium

Belgian Constitution, 1831, as coordinated in 1994, last modified in 2014.

Bulgaria

Bulgarian Administrative Procedure Code, in force from 12.7.2006, amend. sg. 27/25 March 2014 (English translation available at http://www.cadastre.bg/node/7941, accessed 19 March 2017)

France

French Constitution of 4 October 1958, last modified on 23 July 2008.

Preamble to the French Constitution of 27 October 1946.

Germany

Basic Law for the Federal Republic of Germany, 23 May 1949 (English version available at: http://www.refworld.org/docid/4e64d9a02.html, accessed 21 March 2017)

Verwaltungsgerichtsordnung, 21.1.1960, BGBI. I 1960 p. 17

Ireland

Constitution of Ireland, 1937, last amended on 29 August 2015.

Italy

Constitution of Italy, 22 December 1947, (English version available at: http://www.refworld.org/docid/3ae6b59cc.html, accessed 20 March 2017)

Spain

Spanish Constitution, 1978 (Agencia Estatal Boletín Oficial del Estado)

United Kingdom

Human Rights Act 1998 [United Kingdom of Great Britain and Northern Ireland], 9 November 1998.

Bibliography

Monographs

AALTO P, *Public liability in EU law: Brasserie, Bergaderm and beyond* (Bloomsbury Publishing 2011)

ALEXY R, *Theorie der Grundrechte* (Suhrkamp 1985)

ALEXY R, *A Theory of Constitutional Rights* (Oxford University Press 2002)

AUBERT JL, SAVAUX E, *Introduction au droit et thèmes fondamentaux du droit civil* (Sirey 2016)

AUNE A-C, *Le phénomène de multiplication des droits subjectifs en droit des personnes et de la famille* (Presses Universitaires d'Aix-Marseille 2007)

AVILA H, *Theory of Legal Principles* (Springer 2007)

BALLOT E, *Les insuffisances de la notion de droits fondamentaux* (mare & martin 2014)

BASSET A, *Pour en finir avec l'interprétation. Usage des techniques d'interprétation dans les jurisprudences constitutionnelles française et allemande* (Institut universitaire Varenne 2015)

Bagińska E, *Damages for Violations of Human Rights* (Springer 2015)

BATAILLER F, *Le Conseil d'Etat, Juge constitutionnel* (L.G.D.J. 1966)

BEBR G, *Development of Judicial Control of the European Communities* (Springer 2013)

BECK G, *The Legal Reasoning of the CJEU* (Hart 2012)

BELJIN S, *Staatshaftung im Europarecht* (Beck 2000)

BERROD F, *La systématique des voies de droit communautaires* (Dalloz, coll. Nouvelle bibliothèque de thèses 2003)

BERRY E and HARGREAVES S, *European Union Law* (Oxford University Press 2007)

BIONDI A and FARLEY M, *The Right to Damages in European Law* (Kluwer Law International 2009)

BIOY X, *Droits fondamentaux et libertés publiques* (Monchrestien, Lextenso éditions 2011)

BOBEK M, *Central European Judges Under the European Influence. The Transformative Power of the EU Revisited* (Hart Publishing 2015)

BORCHARDT K-D, *Der Grundsatz des Vertrauensschutzes im Europäischen Gemeinschaftsrecht* (N.P. Engel Verlag 1988)

BOUVERESSE A, *Le pouvoir discrétionnaire dans l'ordre juridique communautaire* (Bruylant 2010)

BRAIBANT G, *La Charte des droits fondamentaux de l'Union européenne* (Seuil 2001)

CAPITANT D, *Les effets juridiques des droits fondamentaux en Allemagne* (L.G.D.J. 2001)

CARBONNIER J, *Droit et passion du droit* (Flammarion 1996)

CARBONNIER J, *Droit civil : Introduction, Les personnes* (Presses universitaires de France 1984)

CARRERA S, *In Search of the Perfect Citizen? The Intersection Between Integration, Immigration, and Nationality in the EU* (BRILL 2009)

CHALMERS D, DAVIES G and MONTI G, *European Union Law: Cases and Materials* (2nd edn, Cambridge University Press 2010)

CLAES M, *National Courts' Mandate in the European Constitution* (Hart Publishing 2006)

CONWAY G, *The Limits of Legal Reasoning and the European Court of Justice* (Cambridge University Press 2012)

CORNU G, *Droit civil. Introduction. Les personnes. Les biens* (8th edn, Montchrestien 1997)

COSTELLO C, *The Human Rights of Migrants and Refugees in European Law* (Oxford University Press 2016)

CREPEAU P-A, *L'intensité de l'obligation juridique ou Des obligations de diligence, de résultat et de garantie* (Yvon Blais 1989)

DABIN J, *Le droit subjectif* (Dalloz 2008)

DAVID R, *International Encyclopedia of Comparative Law. Volume II - The Legal Systems of the World, Their Comparison and Unification. Chapter 3 - Sources of Law* (Mohr Siebeck 1984)

DELEUZE N and BERTRAND-MIKOVIC A, *Introduction générale au droit : le droit objectif, les droits subjectifs, l'action en justice* (Studyrama 2005)

DERO-BUGNY D, *Les rapports entre la Cour de justice de l'Union européenne et la Cour européenne des droits de l'homme* (Bruylant 2015)

DI MAJO A, *La tutela civile dei diritti*, vol 3 (4th edn, Giuffrè editore 2003)

DOUGAN M, *National Remedies Before the Court of Justice. Issues of Harmonisation and Differentiation* (Hart Publishing 2004)

DOUGLAS-SCOTT S, *Constitutional Law of the European Union* (Pearson Education 2002)

DUGUIT L, *Traité de droit constitutionnel* (2nd edn, Fontemoing 1921)

DUGUIT L, *Manuel de droit constitutionnel* (4th edn, E. DE BOCCARD 1923)

DWORKIN R, *Taking Rights Seriously* (Harvard University Press 1977)

ECK L, *L'abus de droit en droit constitutionnel* (L'Harmattan 2010)

ELEUTHERIADES PZ, *Legal Rights* (Oxford University Press 2008)

ELLIS E and WATSON P, *EU anti-discrimination law* (Oxford University Press 2012)

FEYEREISEN M, GUILLOT J and SALVADOR S, *Procédure administrative contentieuse* (Promoculture Larcier 2013)

FOULQUIER N, *Les droits publics subjectifs des administrés. Emergence d'un concept en droit administratif français du XIXè au XXè siècle* (Dalloz 2003)

FREDMAN S, *Human Rights Transformed. Positive Rights and Positive Duties* (Oxford University Press 2008)

FROMONT M, *Droit administratif des Etats européens* (Presses universitaires de France 2006)

GAILLARD E, *Le pouvoir en droit privé* (BEBYAI 1985)

GAILLET A, *L'individu contre l'Etat. Essai sur l'évolution des recours de droit public dans l'Allemagne du XIXè siècle* (Dalloz 2012)

GICQUEL J and GICQUEL JE, *Droit constitutionnel et institutions politiques* (Montchrestien, Lextenso éditions 2008)

GORDON R and MOFFATT R, *EU Law in Judicial Review* (2nd edn, Oxford University Press 2014)

GRZESZICK B, *Rechte und Ansprüche. Eine Rekonstruktion des Staatshaftungsrechts aus den subjektiven öffentlichen Rechten* (Mohr Siebeck 2002)

HABERMAS J, *Between Facts and Norms: Contributions to a Discourse Theory of Law and Democracy* (REHG W trans, The MIT Press 1993)

HABERMAS J, *Droit et démocratie. Entre faits et normes*, (BOUCHINDHOMME C and ROCHLITZ R trans, Gallimard 1997)

HARTLEY TC, *The Foundations of European Community Law* (5th edn, Oxford University Press 2003)

HARTLEY TC, *The Foundations of European Union Law* (Oxford University Press 2010)

HEUSCHLING L, *Etat de droit, Rechtsstaat, Rule of law* (Nouvelle bibliothèque de thèses, Dalloz 2002)

HOFMANN HCH, ROWE GC and TÜRK AH, *Administrative Law and Policy of the European Union* (Oxford University Press 2011)

IGNATIEFF M, *The Rights Revolution* (Anansi 2000)

IONESCU O, *La notion de droit subjectif dans le droit privé* (Sirey 1931)

JELLINEK G, *System der subjektiven öffentlichen Rechte* (1905)

JHERING (VON) R, *Der Geist des römischen Rechts auf den verschiedenen Stufen seiner Entwicklung* (Benno Schwabe 1954 8th ed)

JERHING (VON) R, *La lutte pour le droit* (O. JOUANJAN ed., O. DE MEULENAERE trans, Dalloz 2006, first published 1890)

JOSSERAND L, *De l'esprit des droits et de leur relativité. Théorie dite de l'abus des droits* (Dalloz 1939)

KACZMAREK L, *La Responsabilité pour fait normal : Etude critique sur son originalité en matière civile extracontractuelle* (Editions Publibook 2012)

KACZOROWSKA A, *European Union Law* (Routledge 2008)

KELSEN H, *General Theory of Norms* (Oxford University Press 1991)

KOLB R, *La bonne foi en droit international public. Contribution à l'étude des principes généraux de droit* (The Graduate Institute 2000)

KOMINOS AP, *EC Private Antitrust Enforcement: Decentralised Application of EC Competition Law by National Courts* (Hart 2008)

KÜNNECKE M, *Tradition and Change in Administrative Law: an Anglo-German comparison* (Springer 2007)

LANGLET D and MAHMOUDI S, *EU Environmental Law and Policy* (Oxford University Press 2016)

LASSER M, *Judicial Deliberations. A Comparative Analysis of Judicial Transparency and Legitimacy* (Oxford University Press 2004)

LASSER M, *Judicial Transformations: The Rights Revolution in the Courts of Europe* (Oxford University Press 2009)

LE SUEUR A, SUNKIN M and MURKENS JEK, *Public Law. Text, Cases, and Materials* (2nd edn, Oxford University Press 2010)

LECOURT R, *L'Europe des juges* (Bruylant 1976)

LECUYER Y, *Mémento de la jurisprudence de la CEDH* (Hachette Education 2012)

LENAERTS K, MASELIS I and GUTMAN K, *EU Procedural Law* (Oxford University Press 2014)

LEPETIT-COLLIN H, *Recherches sur le plein contentieux objectif* (L.G.D.J., collection Thèses 2011)

LEVINET M, *Théorie générale des droits et libertés* (4th edn, L.G.D.J. , Anthemis/ Nemesis 2012)

LEWIS E and others, *Non-Contractual Liability of the EU for Damage Sustained by Women Who Received PIP Breast Implants* (Amsterdam International Law Clinic, 2013)

LORENZ N-LA, GROUSSOT X and PETURSSON GT, *The European Human Rights Culture - A Paradox of Human Rights Protection in Europe?* (Martinus Nijhoff Publishers 2013)

LOUGHLIN M, *The Idea of Public Law* (Oxford University Press 2003)

LOUGHLIN M, *Foundations of Public Law* (Oxford University Press 2010)

LYONS T, *EC Customs Law* (Oxford University Press 2001)

MACCORMICK N, *Institutions of Law* (Oxford University Press 2007)

MASING J, *Die Mobilisierung des Bürgers für die Durchsetzung des Rechts: europäische Impulse für eine Revision der Lehre vom subjektiv-öffentlichen Recht* (Duncker & Humblot 1997)

MAURER H, *Allgemeines Verwaltungsrecht* (11 edn, Beck 1997)

MAURER H, *Allgemeines Verwaltungsrecht* (17 edn, Beck 2009)

MEDINA ALCOZ L, *Libertad y autoridad en el derecho administrativo. Derecho subjetivo e interés legítimo: una revisión* (Marcial Pons 2016)

MENDES J, *Participation in EU Rule-Making. A Rights-Based Approach* (Oxford University Press 2011)

MICKLITZ H-W and WEATHERHILL S, *European Economic Law* (Asghate Dartmouth 1997)

MILUTINOVIC V, *The 'Right to Damages' under EU Competition Law: from Courage v Crehan to the White Paper and Beyond* (Kluwer Law International 2010)

NEBBIA P and ASKHAM T, *EU Consumer Law* (Oxford University Press 2004)

NETTESHEIM M, *Die mitgliedstaatliche Durchführung von EG-Richtlinien* (Duncker & Humblot 1999)

OST F, *Droit et intérêt, vol. 2 : Entre droit et non-droit, l'intérêt : essai sur les fonctions qu'exerce la notion d'intérêt en droit privé* (Publications des Facultés universitaires Saint-Louis 1990)

PALMER E, *Judicial Review, Socio-Economic Rights and the Human Rights Act* (Hart Publishing 2007)

POIARES MADURO M, *We the Court* (Hart 1998)

Półtorak N, *European Union Rights in National Courts* (Wolters Kluwer 2015)

POULET-GIBOT LECLERC N, *Droit administratif: sources, moyens, contrôles* (Bréal 2007)

PRECHAL S, *Directives in EC Law* (Oxford University Press 2006)

RICCI J-C, *Droit civil - Les biens* (Hachette Education 2013)

ROSAS A and ARMATI L, *EU Constitutional Law : An Introduction* (Hart 2012)

ROUBIER P, *Droits subjectifs et situations juridiques* (2nd edn, Dalloz 2005)

ROUSSET M and ROUSSET O, *Droit administratif - Tome 2. Le contentieux administratif* (2nd edn, Presses universitaires de Grenoble 2004)

SAJÓ A, *Abuse: The Dark Side of Fundamental Rights* (Eleven International Publishing 2006)

SAÜBERLICH U, *Die außervertragliche Haftung im Gemeinschaftsrecht. Eine Untersuchung der Mehrpersonenverhältnisse* (Springer 2005)

STAEBE E, *Rechtsschutz bei gemeinschaftswidrigen Beihilfen vor europäischen und deutschen Gerichten* (Duncker & Humblot 2001)

SAURUGGER S, *Théories et concepts de l'intégration européenne* (Presses de la Fondation nationale des sciences politiques 2009)

SCHERMERS H, *Judicial Protection in the European Communities* (Springer 2013)

SCHLACKE S, *Überindividueller Rechtsschutz: Phänomenologie und Systematik überindividueller Klagebefugnisse im Verwaltungs- und Gemeinschaftsrecht, insbesondere am Beispiel des Umweltrechts* (Mohr Siebeck 2008)

SCHWARZE J, *European Administrative Law* (Sweet & Maxwell 2006)

SCOTT J, *EC Environmental Law* (Longman 1998)

SIMON D (ed), MARIATTE F and RITLENG D, *Contentieux de l'Union européenne : 1/ Annulation, exception d'illégalité* (Lamy 2010)

SIMON D, MARIATTE F and MUNOZ R, *Contentieux de l'Union européenne : 2/ Carence, Responsabilité* (Lamy 2011)

SOMMERMANN, K-P, *Staatsziele und Staatszielbestimmungen* (Mohr Siebeck 1997)

SUMNER LW, *The Moral Foundation of Rights* (Clarendon Press 1987)

SUPIOT A, *Homo juridicus. Essai sur la fonction anthropologique du Droit* (Seuil 2005)

THORSON B, *Individual Rights in EU Law* (Springer 2016)

TRIDIMAS T, *The General Principles of EU Law* (2nd edn, Oxford University Press 2006)

TÜRK AH, *The Concept of Legislation in European Community Law - A Comparative Perspective* (Kluwer 2006)

TÜRK AH, *Judicial review in EU law* (Edward Elgar Publishing 2010)

VAN RAEPENBUSCH S, *Droit institutionnel de l'Union et des Communautés européennes* (De Boeck 2000)

VILLEY M, *Le droit et les droits de l'Homme* (3rd edn, Presses universitaires de France 1998)

VILLEY M, *La formation de la pensée juridique moderne* (2nd edn, Presses universitaires de France 2013)

VIRALLY M, *La pensée juridique* (3rd edn, Editions Panthéon-Assas, LGDJ 2010)

WAKEFIELD J, *Judicial Protection through the Use of Article 288(2) EC* (Kluwer Law International 2002)

WALDRON J, *The Right to Private Property* (Clarendon Press 1988)

WALDRON J, *Law and Disagreement* (Oxford University Press 1999)

WALINE M, *L'individualisme et le droit* (Dalloz 2007)

WEATHERHILL S, *EU Consumer Law and Policy* (Edward Elgar 2005)

WHITE AR, *Rights* (Clarendon Press 1984)

WIDDERSHOVEN R and MEIJ AWH, *Europees recht en het Nederlands bestuursrecht: preadviezen* (Samson H.D. Tjeenk Willink 1996)

WINDSCHEID B, *Lehrbuch des Pandektenrechts* (KIPP T ed, 9th edn, Buddeus 1906)

WITZ C, *Droit privé allemand, 1, Actes juridiques, droits subjectifs (BGB, Partie générale, Loi sur les conditions générales d'affaires)* (Litec 1992)

Edited books and book chapters

ABELSHAUSER W, "Integration à la Carte' The Primacy of Politics and the Economic Integration of Western Europe in the 1950s' in MARTIN S (ed), *The Construction of Europe Essays in Honour of Emile Noël* (Kluwer Academic Publishers 1994)

ALEXY R, 'Rights and Liberties as Concepts' in ROSENFELD M and SAJO A (eds), *Oxford Handbook of Comparative Constitutional Law* (Oxford University Press 2012)

ANCEL P, 'Abus de droit (Interdiction de l'—)' in ANDRIANTSIMBAZOVINA J et al (eds) *Dictionnaire des Droits de l'Homme* (Presses universitaires de France 2008)

ARNULL A, 'The action for annulment: A case of double standards?' in O'KEEFE D and BAVASSO A (eds), *Judicial Review in European Union Law* (Kluwer Law International 2000)

AUGSBERG I, 'Methoden des europäischen Verwaltungsrechts' in TERHECHTE JP (ed) *Verwaltungsrecht der Europäischen Union* (1st edn, Nomos)

AZOULAI L, 'Le principe de bonne administration' in AUBY J-B and DUTHEIL DE LA ROCHERE J (eds), *Droit administratif européen* (Bruylant 2007)

AZOULAI L, BARBOU DES PLACES S and PATAUT E, 'Being a Person in the European Union' in AZOULAI L and others (eds), *Constructing the Person in EU Law: Rights, Roles, Identities* (Bloomsbury Publishing 2016)

BAILEY SH, 'Grounds for Judicial Review: Due Process, Natural Justice, and Fairness' in FELDMAN D (ed) *English Public Law* (2nd edn, Oxford University Press 2009)

BAILLEUX A, 'Les droits de la défense et les (autres) droits fondamentaux devant les juridictions de l'Union européenne' in MAHIEU S (ed) *Contentieux de l'Union européenne Questions choisies* (Larcier 2014)

BARDIN M, 'Depuis l'arrêt Algera, retour sur une utilisation "discrète" du droit comparé par la Cour de justice de l'Union européenne' in DI MANNO T (ed) *Le recours au droit comparé par le juge* (Bruylant 2014)

BARNARD C, 'The 'Opt-Out' for the UK and Poland from the Charter of Fundamental Rights: Triumph or Rhetoric over Reality?', GRILLER S and ZILLER J (eds), *The Lisbon Treaty*, vol 11 (Springer 2008)

BAST J, 'Legal Instruments' in VON BOGDANDY A and BAST J (eds), *Principles of European Constitutional Law* (Hart Publishing 2006)

BELJIN S, 'Rights in EU Law' in PRECHAL S and VAN ROERMUND B (eds), *The Coherence of EU Law The Search for Unity in Divergent Concepts* (Oxford University Press 2008)

BENGOETXEA J and JÄÄSKINEN N, 'Rights and Diverse Effects in EU Law: A Hohfeldian Approach to the Doctrine of Direct Effect of Directives' in BANAKAR R (ed) *Rights in Context - Law and Justice in Late Modern Society* (Ashgate 2010)

BERNARD N, 'A 'New Governance' Approach to Economic, Social and Cultural Rights in the EU' in HERVEY T and KENNER J (eds), *Economic and Social Rights under the EU Charter of Fundamental Rights A Legal Perspective* (Hart 2003)

BETLEM G, 'The Doctrine of Consistent Interpretation. Managing Legal Uncertainty' in PRINSSEN JM and SCHRAUWEN A (eds), *Direct Effect Rethinking a Classic of EC Legal Doctrine* (Europa Law Publishing 2002)

BIGNAMI F, 'Regulation and the courts: judicial review in comparative perspective' in BIGNAMI F and ZARING D, *Comparative Law and Regulation. Understanding the Global Regulatory Process* (Elgar 2016)

BOBEK M, 'The effects of EU law in the national legal systems' in BARNARD C and PEERS S (eds), *European Union Law* (Oxford University Press 2014)

BOBEK M, 'Why There is no Principle of "Procedural Autonomy" of the Member States', in DE WITTE B and MICKLITZ H (eds), *The European Court of Justice and the Autonomy of the Member States* (Intersentia 2012)

BOK AJ, 'Judicial Review of Administrative Decisions by the Dutch Administrative Courts: recours objectif or recours subjectif? A Survey including French and German law' in STROINK FAM (ed), *Judicial Lawmaking and Administrative Law* (Intersentia nv 2005)

BOROWSKI M, 'The Charter of Fundamental Rights in the Treaty on European Union' in TRYBUS M and RUBINI L (eds), *The Treaty of Lisbon and the Future of European Law and Policy* (Edward Elgar 2012)

BOROWSKY M, 'Artikel 52,' in MAYER J, *Charta der Grundrechte der Europäischen Union*,(Nomos 2010, 3rd ed.)

BRENNINKMEIJER AFM, 'The Influence of Court of Justice Case Law on the Procedural Law of the Member States' in VERVAELE JAE (ed) *Administrative Law Application and Enforcement of Community Law in the Netherlands* (Kluwer 1994)

BURGORGUE-LARSEN L, 'L'article II-112' in BURGORGUE-LARSEN L and others (eds), *Traité établissant une Constitution pour l'Europe : commentaire article par article Tome 2, Partie II La Charte des droits fondamentaux de l'Union* (Bruylant 2005)

CARTABIA M, 'The Italian Constitutional Court and the Relationship Between the Italian legal system and the European Union' in SLAUGHTER AM, STONE SWEET A and WEILER JHH (eds), *The European Court and National Courts – Doctrine and Jurisprudence. Legal Change in Its Social Context* (Hart 1998)

CHETAIL V, 'The Common European Asylum System: *Bric-à-brac* or System?' in CHETAIL V, DE BRUYCKER P and MAIANI F (eds), *Reforming the Common European Asylum System The New European Refugee Law* (Brill Nijhof 2016)

CLAES M, 'The European Union, its Member States and their Citizens' in LECZYKIEWICZ D and WEATHERHILL S (eds), *The Involvement of EU Law in Private Law Relationships* (Hart Publishing 2013)

CRAIG P, 'Access to Mechanisms of Administrative Law' in FELDMAN D (ed) *English Public Law* (2nd edn, Oxford University Press 2009)

CRAIG P, 'Rights, Legality, and Legitimacy' in CRAIG P (ed) *The Lisbon Treaty: Law, Politics, and Treaty Reform* (Oxford University Press 2010)

CURTIN D and MORTELMANS K, 'Application and Enforcement of Community Law by the Member States: Actors in Search of a Third Generation Script,' in D. CURTIN and T. HEUKELS (eds), *Institutional Dynamics of European Integration, Essays in Honour of H.G. Schermers*, vol. II, (Martinus Nijhoff Publishers 1994)

DA CRUZ VILACA JL, 'Le principe de l'effet utile du droit de l'Union dans la jurisprudence de la Cour' in ROSAS A and others (eds), *The Court of Justice and the Construction of Europe: Analyses and Perspectives on Sixty Years of Case-law* (T.M.C. Asser 2013)

DE BURCA G, 'The Language of Rights and European Integration' in SHAW J and MORE G (eds), *New Legal Dynamics of European Union* (Clarendon Press 1995)

DEDERICHS M and CHRISTENSEN R, 'Inhaltsanalyse als methodisches Instrument zur Untersuchung von Gerichtsentscheidungen, vorgeführt am Beispiel der Rechtssprechung des EuGH' in F. MÜLLER and I. BURR (eds), *Rechtssprache Europas. Reflexion der Praxis von Sprache und Mehrsprachigkeit im supranationalen Recht* (Duncker & Humblot 2004)

DE GROOT GR, 'Law, Legal Language and the Legal system: Reflections on the Problems of Translating Legal Texts,' in GESSNER V, HOELAND A and VARGA C, *European Legal Cultures* (Dartmouth 1996)

DE SCHUTTER O, 'Les droits et principes sociaux dans la Charte des droits fondamentaux de l'Union européenne' in CARLIER JY and DE SCHUTTER O (eds), *La Charte des droits fondamentaux de l'Union européenne* (Bruylant 2002)

DE WITTE B, 'Direct Effect, Primacy and the Nature of the Legal Order' in DE BURCA G and CRAIG P (eds), *The Evolution of EU Law* (2nd edn, Oxford University Press 2011)

DEDERICHS M and CHRISTENSEN R, 'Inhaltsanalyse als methodisches Instrument zur Untersuchung von Gerichtsentscheidungen, vorgeführt am Beispiel der Rechtsprechung des EuGH' in MÜLLER F and BURR I (eds), *Rechtssprache Europas Reflexion der Praxis von Sprache und Mehrsprachigkeit im supranationalen Recht* (Duncker & Humblot 2004)

DOUGAN M, 'The Impact of the General Principles of Union Law upon Private Relationships' in LECZYKIEWICZ D and WEATHERHILL S (eds), *The Involvement of EU Law in Private Law Relationships* (Hart Publishing 2013)

DOUGAN M, 'Who Exactly Benefits from the Treaties? The Murky Interaction Between Union and National Competence over the Capacity to Enforce EU Law', *The Cambridge Yearbook of European Legal Studies, Volume 12* (Hart 2010)

DREXL J, 'Competition Law as Part of the European Constitution' in VON BOGDANDY A and BAST J (eds), *Principles of European Constitutional Law* (Hart Publishing 2006)

DWORKIN R, 'Rights as Trumps' in WALDRON J (ed) *Theories of Rights* (Oxford University Press 1984)

EBNER M and GAMBARO E, 'The Notion of State Aid' in SANTA MARIA A (ed), *Competition and State Aid. An Analysis of the EC Practice* (Kluwer Law International 2007)

EDWARD D 'National Courts—the Powerhouse of Community Law' in J. Bell and others (eds), *Cambridge Yearbook of European Legal Studies, Volume 5* (Bloomsbury 2004)

EDWARD DOA, 'Direct Effect: Myth, Mess or Mystery?' in PRINSSEN JM and SCHRAUWEN A (eds), *Direct Effect Rethinking a Classic of EC Legal Doctrine* (Europa Law Publishing 2002)

EIJSBOUTS T, 'Direct Effect, the Test and the Terms. In Praise of a Capital Doctrine of EU Law' in PRINSSEN JM and SCHRAUWEN A (eds), *Direct Effect Rethinking a Classic of EC Legal Doctrine* (Europa Law Publishing 2002)

EVERLING U, 'The European Union Between Community and National Policies and Legal Orders' in VON BOGDANDY A and BAST J (eds), *Principles of European Constitutional Law* (Hart Publishing 2006)

FELDMAN D, 'Remedies for Violations of Convention Rights' in FELDMAN D (ed) *English Public Law* (2nd edn, Oxford University Press 2009)

FREDMAN S and WESSON M, 'Social, Economic, and Cultural Rights' in FELDMAN D (ed) *English Public Law* (2nd edn, Oxford University Press 2009)

GARDBAUM S, 'The structure and scope of constitutional rights' in T. GINSBURG, R. DIXON (eds.) *Comparative Constitutional Law* (Elgar Publishing 2011)

GARRETT G, 'The Politics of Legal Integration in the European Union' (1995) 49 International Organization 171. W. MATTLI W and A.-M. SLAUGHTER, 'Law and Politics in the European Union: A Reply to Garrett' (1995) 49 International Organization 183

GERKRATH J, 'Direct Effect in Germany and France' in PRINSSEN JM and SCHRAUWEN A (eds), *Direct Effect Rethinking a Classic of EC Legal Doctrine* (Europa Law Publishing 2002)

GRABITZ E, 'Liability for Legislative Acts' in SCHERMERS HG, HEUKELS T and MEAD P (eds), *Non-contractual liability of the European Communities* (Martinus Nijhoff Publishers 1988)

GRAZIADEI M, 'Rights in the European Landscape: A Historical and Comparative Profile' in PRECHAL S and VAN ROERMUND B (eds), *The Coherence of EU Law The Search for Unity in Divergent Concepts* (Oxford University Press 2008)

GRIFFITHS RT, 'Europe's First Constitution: The European Political Community, 1952-1954' in MARTIN S (ed), *The Construction of Europe Essays in Honour of Emile Noël* (Kluwer Academic Publishers 1994)

GUASTINI R, 'L'interprétation de la constitution' in TROPER M and CHAGNOL-LAUD D (eds), *Traité international de droit constitutionnel* (Dalloz 2012)

HART HLA, 'Bentham on Legal Rights' in HART HLA (ed) *Essays on Bentham: Jurisprudence and Political Theory* (Clarendon Press 1982)

HILSON C, 'Legality Review of Member States Discretion under Directives' in TRIDIMAS T and NEBBIA P (eds), *European Union Law for the Twenty-First Century: Volume 1: Rethinking the New Legal Order* (Bloomsbury Publishing 2004)

HOFMANN HCH, 'Individual Rights and Information in EU Public Law', in LIND AS, ÖSTERDAL I and REICHEL J (eds), *Transparency in the future – Swedish openness 250 years* (Ragulka 2017)

HOFMANN HCH, 'The Legal Framework to Subsidies and State Aid Review' in HOFMANN HCH and MICHEAU C (eds), *State Aid Law of the European Union* (Oxford University Press 2016)

HOFMANN HCH, 'Effective Judicial Remedies Before the National Courts' in WARD A and others (eds), *The EU Charter of Fundamental Rights* (Hart 2014)

HOFMANN HCH and TÜRK AH, 'The challenges of Europe's integrated administration' in ERIKSEN EO and JOERGES C (eds), *Law, Democracy and Solidarity in Europe's Post-National Constellation* (ARENA 2006)

HOLLAND S, 'Economic and Social Cohesion in the 1990's' in MARTIN S (ed), *The Construction of Europe Essays in Honour of Emile Noël* (Kluwer Academic Publishers 1994)

HOURQUEBIE F, 'Les droits publics subjectifs: échec de l'importation d'une théorie allemande en droit administratif français?' in MELLERAY F (ed) *L'argument de droit comparé en droit administratif français* (Bruylant 2007)

HUNT J, 'Fair and Just Working Conditions' in HERVEY T and KENNER J (eds), *Economic and Social Rights under the EU Charter of Fundamental Rights A Legal Perspective* (Hart 2003)

JACQUE JP, 'The Role of Law in European Integration', in GESSNER V, HOELAND A and VARGA C, *European Legal Cultures* (Darthmouth 1996)

JAEGER M, 'Les voies de recours sont-elles des vases communicants?' in RODRÍGUEZ IGLESIAS GC (ed), *Mélanges en hommage à Fernand Schockweiler* (Nomos 1999)

JANS JH and PRINSSEN JM, 'Direct Effect: Convergence or Divergence? A Comparative Perspective' in PRINSSEN JM and SCHRAUWEN A (eds), *Direct Effect Rethinking a Classic of EC Legal Doctrine* (Europa Law Publishing 2002)

JONES A, 'Private Enforcement of EU Competition Law: A Comparison with, and Lessons from, the US (January 14, 2016)' in BERGSTRÖM M, IACOVIDES M and STRAND M (eds), *Harmonising EU Competition Litigation: The New Directive and Beyond* (Hart Publishing 2016) - TLI Think! Paper 10/2016 Available at SSRN: https://ssrn.com/abstract=2715796

KADAR L and SHAW J, 'Article 39' in PEERS S and others (eds), *The EU Charter of Fundamental Rights* (Hart Publishing 2014)

KADELBACH S, 'Union Citizenship' in VON BOGDANDY A and BAST J (eds), *Principles of European Constitutional Law* (Hart Publishing 2006)

KENNEDY D, 'The International Human Rights Regime: Stil Part of the Problem?' in DICKINSON R and others (eds), *Examining Critical Perspectives on Human Rights* (Cambridge University Press 2012)

KENNER J, 'Economic and Social Rights in the EU Legal Order: The Mirage of Indivisibility' in HERVEY T and KENNER J (eds), *Economic and Social Rights under the EU Charter of Fundamental Rights A Legal Perspective* (Hart 2003)

KORNEZOV A, 'When David Teaches EU Law to Goliath: A Generational Upheaval in the Making' in BOBEK M (ed), *Central European Judges Under the European Influence* (Hart Publishing 2015)

KRAMER MH, SIMMONDS NE and STEINER H, *A Debate Over Rights* (Oxford University Press 1998)

KRAMER MH, 'Rights Without Trimmings' in KRAMER MH, SIMMONDS NE and STEINER H, *A Debate Over Rights* (Oxford University Press 1998)

LECZYKIEWICZ D, 'The Constitutional Dimension of Private Law Liability Rules in the EU' in LECZYKIEWICZ D and WEATHERHILL S (eds), *The Involvement of EU Law in Private Law Relationships* (Hart Publishing 2013)

LENAERTS K and GUTIERREZ-FONS JA, 'The Place of the Charter in the EU Constitutional Edifice' in PEERS S and others (eds), *The EU Charter of Fundamental Rights A Commentary* (Hart Publishing 2014)

MACCORMICK N, 'Rights in Legislation' in HACKER PMS and RAZ J (eds), *Law, Morality and Society: Essays in Honour of HLA Hart* (Clarendon Press 1977)

MAGNETTE P, 'La citoyenneté au-delà du vote. Droit de pétition et recours au médiateur', in MAGNETTE P, *De l'étranger au citoyen, Construire la citoyenneté européenne* (De Boeck Université 1997)

MAIANI F, 'The Dublin III Regulation: A New Legal Framework for a More Humane System?' in CHETAIL V, DE BRUYCKER P and MAIANI F (eds), *Reforming the Common European Asylum System The New European Refugee Law* (Brill Nijhoff 2016)

MAYER F, 'Artikel 6 EUV', in Grabitz E, Hilf M and Nettesheim M, *Das Recht der Europäischen Union – Kommentar* (Beck, 2010)

MELOT R, 'La conception wébérienne des droits subjectifs : un parcours de l'histoire économique au débat sur la légitimité politique' in COUTU M and ROCHER G (eds), *La légitimité de l'Etat et du droit autour de Max Weber* (Presses Université Laval 2005)

MENDES J, 'Participation and participation rights in EU law and governance' in HOFMANN HCH and TÜRK AH (eds), *Legal Challenges in EU Administrative Law Towards an Integrated Administration* (Edward Elgar 2009)

MICKLITZ H-W, 'The Interest in Public Interest Litigation' in MICKLITZ H-W and REICH N (eds), *Public Interest Litigation before European Courts* (Nomos 1997)

MILUTINOVIC V, 'The 'Right to Damages' in a 'System of Parallel Competences': A Fresh Look at BRT v. SABAM and its Subsequent Interpretation (July 1, 2013)'. Forthcoming in: LOWE P and MARQUIS M (eds), *European Competition Law Annual 2011: Integrating Public and Private Enforcement Implications for Courts and Agencies* (Hart Publishing, 2014) < https://ssrn.com/abstract=2293649≥ accessed 30 May 2017

MUIR E, 'The Court of Justice: a fundamental rights institution among others' in DAWSON M, DE WITTE B and MUIR E eds, *Judicial Activism at the European Court of Justice* (Edward Elgar 2013)

NEFRAMI E, 'Quelques réflexions sur l'article 19, paragraphe 1, alinéa 2, TUE et l'obligation de l'Etat membre d'assurer la protection juridictionnelle effective dans les domaines couverts par le droit de l'Union' in BOUTAYEB C (ed) *La Constitution, l'Europe et le droit Mélanges en l'honneur de Jean-Claude Masclet* (Publications de la Sorbonne 2013)

NEVILLE BROWN L, 'Is there a general principle of abuse of rights in European Community law?' in CURTIN D and HEUKELS T (eds), *Institutional Dynamics of European Integration Essays in Honour of Henry G Schermers*, vol II (Martinus Nijhoff 1994)

NOLLKAEMPER A, 'The Direct Effect of Public International Law' in PRINSSEN JM and SCHRAUWEN A (eds), *Direct Effect Rethinking a Classic of EC Legal Doctrine* (Europa Law Publishing 2002)

PEERS S, 'The Rebirth of the EU's Charter of Fundamental Rights' in BARNARD C and ODUDU O (eds), *The Cambridge Yearbook of European Legal Studies, Volume 13* (Hart 2011)

PEERS S, 'Taking Rights Away? Limitations and Derogations', in S. Peers, A. Ward (eds), *The European Union Charter of Fundamental Rights* (Hart Publishing 2004) 141

PESCATORE P, 'Van Gend en Loos, 3 February 1963: A view from within' in POIARES MADURO M and AZOULAI L (eds), *The Past and Future of EU Law: The Classics of EU Law Revisited on the 50th Anniversary of the Rome Treaty* (Hart 2010)

PITTIE M and JUSSIAUX A, 'Les recours en responsabilité non contractuelle devant le juge de l'Union européenne' in MAHIEU S (ed) *Contentieux de l'Union européenne Questions choisies* (Larcier 2014)

POIARES MADURO M, 'The Double Constitutional Life of the Charter of Fundamental Rights of the European Union' in HERVEY T and KENNER J (eds), *Economic and Social Rights under the EU Charter of Fundamental Rights A Legal Perspective* (Hart 2003)

Półtorak N, 'Changes in the Level of the National Judicial Protection Under the EU Influence on the Example of the Polish Legal System' in BOBEK M (ed), *Central European Judges Under the European Influence* (Hart Publishing 2015)

PRECHAL S, 'Direct Effect Reconsidered, Redefined and Rejected' in PRINSSEN JM and SCHRAUWEN A (eds), *Direct Effect Rethinking a Classic of EC Legal Doctrine* (Europa Law Publishing 2002)

PRECHAL S, 'Rights v principles, or how to remove fundamental rights from the jurisdiction of the courts' in DE ZWAAN J and others (eds), *The European Union: An Ongoing Process of Integration - Liber Amicorum Alfred E Kellermann* (T.M.C. Asser Press 2004)

PRECHAL S, 'Protection of Rights: How Far?' in PRECHAL S and VAN ROERMUND B (eds), *The Coherence of EU Law* (Oxford University Press 2008)

PRECHAL S and VAN ROERMUND B, 'Binding Unity in EU Legal Order: An Introduction' in PRECHAL S and VAN ROERMUND B (eds), *The Coherence of EU Law: The Search for Unity in Divergent Concepts* (Oxford University Press 2008)

RANGEON F, 'Droits-libertés et droits-créances : les contradictions du préambule de la Constitution de 1946' in KOUBI G (ed) *Le Préambule de la constitution de 1946 : antinomies juridiques et contradictions politiques* (Presses universitaires de France 1996)

RAULUS H, 'The Charter of Fundamental Rights as a set of constitutional principles' in TRYBUS M and RUBINI L (eds), *The Treaty of Lisbon and the Future of European Law and Policy* (Edward Elgar 2012)

RAVO LM, 'The role of the Principle of Effective Judicial Protection and its Impact on National Jurisdictions' *Sources of Law and Legal Protection (Triestine Lecture 1)* (EUT Edizioni Università di Trieste 2012)

REICH N, 'The Impact of the Non-Discrimination Principle on Private Autonomy' in LECZYKIEWICZ D and WEATHERHILL S (eds), *The Involvement of EU Law in Private Law Relationships* (Hart Publishing 2013)

REICH N, "System der subjectiven öffentlichen Rechte' in the Union: A European Constitution for Citizens of Bits and Pieces' in Academy of European Law (ed) *Collected Courses of the Academy of European Law*, vol VI - 1 (Martinus Nijhoff Publishers 1998)

ROTT P, 'The Court of Justice's Principle of Effectiveness and its Unforeseeable Impact on Private Law Relationships' in LECZYKIEWICZ D and WEATHERHILL S (eds), *The Involvement of EU Law in Private Law Relationships* (Hart Publishing 2013)

RUIZ-JARABO COLOMER D, 'Once Upon a Time–Francovich: From Fairy Tale to Cruel Reality?' in POIARES MADURO M and AZOULAI L (eds), *The Past and Future of EU Law: the Classics of EU Law Revisited on the 50th Anniversary of the Rome Treaty* (Hart Publishing 2010)

RYAN B, 'The Charter and Collective Labour Law' in HERVEY T and KENNER J (eds), *Economic and Social Rights under the EU Charter of Fundamental Rights A Legal Perspective* (Hart 2003)

SACK, PG 'Law and Custom: Reflections on the Relation between English Law and the English Language' in GESSNER V, HOELAND A and VARGA C, *European Legal Cultures* (Dartmouth 1996)

SAUTER W, 'Proportionality in EU Law: A Balancing Act?' in Barnard C, Albors-Llorens A, Gehring MW (eds), *Cambridge Yearbook of European Legal Studies, Vol 15* 439

SCHAAP M and IMBERS R, 'Access to environmental justice for NGOs: interplay between the Aarhus Convention, the EU Lisbon Treaty and the European Convention on Human Rights' in JAKUBOWSKI A, WIERCZY SKA K and Wierczyńska K (eds), *Fragmentation vs the Constitutionalisation of International Law: A Practical Inquiry* (Routledge 2016)

SHAPIRO M, 'The European Court of Justice' in CRAIG P and DE BURCA G, *The Evolution of EU Law* (Oxford University Press 1999)

SHAW J, 'Citizens' Rights and Access to Law' in MICKLITZ H-W and REICH N (eds), *Public Interest Litigation before European Courts* (Nomos 1997)

SHAW J, 'Citizenship of the Union: Towards Post-National Membership?' in Academy of European Law (ed) *Collected Courses of the Academy of European Law*, vol VI - 1 (Martinus Nijhoff Publishers 1998)

SIMMONDS NE, 'Rights at the Cutting Edge' in KRAMER MH and others (eds), *A Debate Over Rights* (Oxford University Press 1998)

SIMON D, 'SABENA is dead, Gabrielle Defrenne's case is still alive: the old lady's testament...' in POIARES MADURO M and AZOULAI L (eds), *The Past and Future of EU law: the Classics of EU Law Revisited on the 50th Anniversary of the Rome Treaty* (Hart 2010)

SUNKIN M, 'Grounds for Judicial Review: Illegality in the Strict Sense' in FELDMAN D (ed) *English Public Law* (2nd edn, Oxford University Press 2009)

SUNKIN M, 'Remedies Available in Judicial Review Proceedings' in FELDMAN D (ed) *English Public Law* (2nd edn, Oxford University Press 2009)

TENORE M, 'The Scope for 'Consistent Interpretation' in the Area of Dividend Taxation' in PISTONE P (ed), *Legal Remedies in European Tax Law* (IBFD 2009)

THOMA R, 'Das System der subjektiven öffentlichen Rechte und Pflichten' in DREIER H (ed) *Rechtsstaat - Demokratie - Grundrechte* (Mohr Siebeck 1932)

VAN GERVEN W, 'Bridging the Unbridgeable - Community and National Tort Laws After Francovich and Brasserie' in MICKLITZ H-W and REICH N (eds), *Public Interest Litigation before European Courts* (Nomos 1997)

VAN LEUVEN N, 'Droits et principes de la Charte des droits fondamentaux de l'Union européenne : pas d'opposition simple entre hard law et soft law' in HACHEZ I and others (eds), *Les sources du droit revisitées Volume 1 - Normes internationales et constitutionnelles* (Anthemis 2012)

VAN MEERBEECK J, 'Les principes généraux du droit de l'Union européenne' in HACHEZ I and others (eds), *Les sources du droit revisitées Volume 1 - Normes internationales et constitutionnelles* (Anthemis 2012)

VAN ROSSEM JW, 'The Autonomy of EU Law: More is Less?' in WESSEL RA and BLOCKMANS S (eds), *Between Autonomy and Dependence* (T.M.C. Asser Press 2013)

VEDSTED-HANSEN J, 'Reception Conditions as Human Rights: Pan-European Standard or Systemic Deficiencies?' in CHETAIL V, DE BRUYCKER P and MAIANI F (eds), *Reforming the Common European Asylum System The New European Refugee Law* (Brill Nijhoff 2016)

VOIGTS H-M, *Die Subjektivierung von Gemeinwohlinteressen als Demokratisierung der Verwaltung* (LIT Verlag 2016)

VON DANWITZ T, *Verwaltungsrechtliches System und europäische Integration* (Mohr Siebeck 1996)

VOS E, 'EU Risk Regulation reviewed by the European Courts' in VAN ASSELT MBA and others (eds), *Trade, Health and the Environment - The European Union put to the test* (Routledge 2014)

WALLACE C and SHAW J, 'Education, Multiculturalism and the Charter of Fundamental Rights of the European Union' in HERVEY T and KENNER J (eds), *Economic and Social Rights under the EU Charter of Fundamental Rights A Legal Perspective* (Hart 2003)

WALUCHOW W, 'Constitutions as Living Trees: an Idiot Defends' in DYZENHAUS D and others (eds), *Law and Morality: Readings in Legal Philosophy* (University of Toronto Press 2007)

WARD A, 'More than an 'Infant Disease'. Individual Rights, EC Directives, and the Case for Uniform Remedies' in PRINSSEN JM and SCHRAUWEN A (eds), *Direct Effect Rethinking a Classic of EC Legal Doctrine* (Europa Law Publishing 2002)

WATHELET M, 'Du concept de l'effet direct à celui de l'invocabilité au regard de la jurisprudence récente de la Cour de justice' in HOSKINS M and ROBINSON W (eds), *A True European Essays for Judge David Edward* (Hart Publishing 2003)

WATHELET M and WILDERMEERSCH J, *Contentieux européen* (2 edn, Larcier 2014)

WEATHERHILL S, 'The Elusive Character of Private Autonomy in EU Law' in LECZYKIEWICZ D and WEATHERHILL S (eds), *The Involvement of EU Law in Private Law Relationships* (Hart Publishing 2013)

WEBER D, 'Some Remarks on the Application of Community Law, Its Legal Effects and the Relationship between These Concepts' in PISTONE P (ed), *Legal Remedies in European Tax Law* (IBFD 2009)

WIDDERSHOVEN R, 'Naar een bestuurs(proces)rechtelijk Ius Commune in Europa' in STEYGER E and others (eds), *Europees recht en het Nederlands bestuursrecht* (VAR-reeks 1996)

WOEHRLING J-M, 'La France peut-elle se passer du principe de confiance légitime ?' in *Gouverner, administrer, juger Liber amicorum Jean Waline, Mélanges en l'honneur de Jean Waline* (Dalloz 2002)

WOUTERS J and VAN EECKHOUTTE D, 'Giving Effect to Customary International Law Through European Community Law' in PRINSSEN JM and SCHRAUWEN A (eds), *Direct Effect Rethinking a Classic of EC Legal Doctrine* (Europa Law Publishing 2002)

Peer-reviewed journal articles

Editorial comments, 'EU law as a way of life' (2017) 54 Common Market Law Review 357

ABBOT C and LEE M, 'Economic Actors in EU Environmental Law' (2015) 34 Yearbook of European Law 26

ACAR T, 'Appréhender l'imprécision des droits : approche linguistique' La Revue des droits de l'homme (en ligne) 7 - 2015 <http://revdh.revues.org/1191> accessed 7 June 2016

ADAM S, DEVISSCHER P and VAN ELSUWEGE P, 'Chronique de jurisprudence communautaire : les relations extérieures (1er janvier 2006-31 décembre 2008)' (2009) Cahiers de droit européen 465

AGUDO GONZALEZ J, 'Evolucion y negacion del derecho subjetivo' (2011) Revista Digital de Derecho Administrativo 9

ALEXY R, 'On Balancing and Subsumption' (2003) Ratio Juris 433-449

AMAR AR, 'The Bill of Rights as a Constitution' (1992) 100 Yale Law Journal 1131

APPEL I and SINGER J, 'Verfahrensvorschriften als subjektive Rechte' (2007) Juristische Schulung 913

ARNULL A, 'Case C-432/05, Unibet (London) Ltd and Unibet (International) Ltd v Justitiekanslern, judgment of the Grand Chamber of 13 March 2007' (2007) 44 Common Market Law Review 1763

ATRIA F, 'Social Rights: A Reply' (2015) 24 Social & Legal Studies 628

AUGENSTEIN D, 'Engaging the Fundamentals: On the Autonomous Substance of EU Fundamental Rights Law' (2013) 14 German Law Journal 1917

AZOULAI L, ''Integration through law' and us' (2016) 14 International Journal of Constitutional Law 449

BABAC B, 'La nouvelle procédure administrative et le nouveau contentieux administratif en Croatie - Sur quelques implications des différences dans le traitement de l'objet du litige administratif au regard du contrôle de la légalité de l'action administrative' (2012) 49 Zbornik radova Pravnog fakulteta u Splitu 325

BAQUERO CRUZ J, 'What's Left of the Charter? Reflections on Law and Political Mythology' (2008) 15 Maastricht Journal of European and Comparative Law 65

BARAV A, 'Enforcement of Community Rights in the National Courts: the Case for Jurisdiction to Grant an Interim Relief' (1989) 26 Common Market Law Review 369

BARENTS R, 'Een grondwet voor Europa (VI): de grondrechten' (2005) Nederlands tijdschrift voor Europees recht 39

BARENTS R, 'EU Procedural Law and Effective Legal Protection' (2014) 51 Common Market Law Review 1437

BASILIEN-GAINCHE M-L, 'Cour de Justice de l'Union européenne : Notion de permis de séjour formellement limité' (2012) Lettre 'Actualités Droits-Libertés' du CREDOF

BECKER F and CAMPBELL A, 'The Direct Effect of European Directives: Towards the Final Act?' (2007) 13 Columbia Journal of European Law 401

BELLAMY R, 'Still in Deficit: Rights, Regulation, and Democracy in the EU' (2006) 12 European Law Journal 725

BENLOLO-CARABOT M, 'Chapitre 2. Les droits sociaux dans l'ordre juridique de l'Union Européenne' La Revue des droits de l'homme (en ligne), 1 - 2012, 84 <http:// revdh.revues.org/120> accessed 23 January 2014

BENNET M, 'Le droit et l'analyse philosophique des droits selon W.N. Hohfeld' (2011) 21 Klesis Revue philosophique 133

BIGNAMI F, 'Creating European Rights: National Values and Supranational Interests' (2005) 11 Columbia Journal of European Law 241

BIGNAMI F, 'The Democratic Deficit in European Community Rulemaking: A Call for Notice and Comment in Comitology' (1999) 40 Harvard International Law Journal 451

BIRKS P, 'Rights, Wrongs, and Remedies' (2000) 20 Oxford Journal of Legal Studies 1

BLANQUET M and others, 'Chronique de jurisprudence - Droit général de l'Union européenne' (2012) Cahiers de droit européen 75

BOGDANDY V, 'National legal scholarship in the European legal area-A manifesto' (2012) 10 International Journal of Constitutional Law 614

BOLGAR V, 'L'intérêt général dans la théorie et dans la pratique' (1965) 17 Revue internationale de droit comparé 329

BONNARD R, 'Léon Duguit. Ses oeuvres. Sa doctrine' (1929) Extrait de la Revue du Droit public et de la Science politique en France et à l'Etranger 5

BOUCOBZA I and ROBITAILLE D, 'Standards jurisprudentiels et contrôle de l'obligation étatique. Des contrôles à géométrie variable' La Revue des droits de l'homme (en ligne), 298 <http://revdh.revues.org/142> accessed 5 September 2016

BOUSTA R, 'Droit des étrangers : mais à quoi sert le droit à une bonne administration?' La Revue des droits de l'homme [En ligne], 12 | 2017 ≤http://revdh.revues.org/3216> accessed 6 August 2017

BOUSTA R, 'Who Said There is a 'Right to Good Administration'? A Critical Analysis of Article 41 of the Charter of Fundamental Rights of the European Union' (2013) 19 European Public Law 481

BREDA V, 'A European Constitution in a Multinational Europe or a Multinational Constitution for Europe?' (2006) 12 European Law Journal 330

BRITO VIEIRA M and CARREIRA DA SILVA F, 'Getting rights right: Explaining social rights constitutionalization in revolutionary Portugal' (2013) 11 International Journal of Constitutional Law 898

BROHM WINFRIED V, 'Soziale Grundrechte und Staatszielbestimmungen in der Verfassung', JuristenZeitung, 1994, p. 213

BRUNESSEN B, 'Retour sur un classique. Quelques remarques sur la catégorie des principes généraux du droit de l'Union européenne' (2013) Revue française de droit administratif 1217

BUIJZE AWGJ, 'Het Hof van Justitie in Kamino-Datema: horen in bezwaar onder voorwaarden gesanctioneerd' (2014) Nederlands tijdschrift voor Europees recht 299

BURGORGUE-LARSEN L, 'Ombres et Lumières de la constitutionnalisation de la Charte des droits fondamentaux de l'Union européenne' (2004) Cahiers de droit européen 683

BURLEY A and MATTLI W, 'Europe Before the Court: A Political Theory of Legal Integration' (1993) 47 International Organization 41

CALLIES C, 'Kohärenz und Konvergenz beim europäischen Individualrechtsschutz - Der Zugang zum Gericht im Lichte des Grundrechts auf effektiven Rechtsschutz' (2002) 49 Neue Juristische Wochenschrift 3577

CARANTA R, 'Governmental Liability after Francovich' (1993) 52 Cambridge Law Journal 272

CERNAT A, 'The Term of Subjective Right in the Romanian Public Law Doctrine' [2005] Manager – Juridical

CHALMERS D and BARROSO L, 'What Van Gend en Loos stands for' (2014) 12 International Journal of Constitutional Law 105

COLLIOT-THELENE C, 'Pour une politique des droits subjectifs : la lutte pour les droits comme lutte politique' (2009) 59 L'Année sociologique 231

COLLIOT-THELENE C, 'Après la souveraineté : que reste-t-il des droits subjectifs?' Eurostudia, vol 2, n°2, 2006, 3 <http://id.erudit.org/iderudit/014585ar> accessed 30 July 2016.

CONTIADES X and FOTIADOU A, 'Social rights in the age of proportionality: Global economic crisis and constitutional litigation' (2012) 10 International Journal of Constitutional Law 660

COPPEL J and O'NEILL A, 'The European Court of Justice: Taking Rights Seriously?' (1992) 29 Common Market Law Review 669

COSTA J-P, 'Concepts juridiques dans la jurisprudence de la Cour européenne des droits de l'Homme : de l'influence de différentes traditions nationales' (2004) Revue trimestrielle des droits de l'homme 101

CURTIN D, HOFMANN HCH and MENDES J, 'Constitutionalising EU Executive Rule-Making Procedures: A Research Agenda' (2013) 19 European Law Journal 1

CURTIN D, 'Challenging Executive Dominance in European Democracy' (2014) 77 The Modern Law Review 1

DASHWOOD A, 'The Principle of Direct Effect in European Community Law' (1982) 16 Journal of Common Market Studies 229

Daukšienė I and BUDNIKAS A, 'Has the action for failure to act in the European Union lost its purpose?' (2014) 7 Baltic Journal of Law & Politics 209

DAWSON M, 'How Does the European Court of Justice Reason? A Review Essay on the Legal Reasoning of the European Court of Justice' (2014) 20 European Law Journal 423

DE BAERE G and ROES T, 'EU Loyalty as Good Faith' (2015) 64 International & Comparative Law Quarterly 829

DE BURCA G, 'After the EU Charter of Fundamental Rights: The Court of Justice as a Human Rights Adjudicator?' (2013) 20 Maastricht Journal of European and Comparative Law 168

DE MOL M et al., 'Inroepbaarheid in rechte van het Handvest van de Grondrechten van de Europese Unie: Toepassingsgebied en het onderscheid tussen "rechten" en "beginselen', 60 SEW (2012) 222

DE MUNNIK NJM, 'Geen ambsthalve toepassing van Europees recht. Vragen van het CBb inzake Van der Weerd e.a. beantwoord' (2007) Nederlands tijdschrift voor Europees recht 246

DEN HEIJER M, 'Remedies in the Dublin Regulation: *Ghezelbash* and *Karim*' (2017) 54 Common Market Law Review 859

DENVIR J, 'Towards a Political Theory of Public Interest Litigation' (1976) 54 North Carolina Law Review 1133

DEROSIER J-P, 'Enquête sur la limite constitutionnelle : du concept à la notion' (2008) 76 Revue française de droit constitutionnel 785

DE ROY C, 'Visie op de verhoudingen tussen burger en bestuur enerzijds, en tussen bestuur en rechter anderzijds, en de gevolgen hiervan op de organisatie van het administratief contentieux' jura falconis, jg 39, 2002-2003, nr 3, 429 <https://www.law.kuleuven.be/jura/art/39n3/deroy.htm> accessed 24 January 2016

DICKSON B, 'The EU Charter of Fundamental Rights in the case law of the European Court of Human Rights' European Human Rights Law Review 2015(1) 27

DONIER, 'Le droit au service public, reflet des obligations pesant sur les personnes publiques' La Revue des droits de l'homme (en ligne), 393 <http://revdh.revues.org/151> accessed 5 September 2016

DONIER V and others, 'Les débiteurs des droits sociaux' La Revue des droits de l'homme (en ligne), 388 <http://revdh.revues.org/161> accessed 1 September 2016

DOUGAN M, 'Addressing Issues of Protective Scope within the Francovich Right to Reparation' (2017) 13 European Constitutional Law Review 124

DOUGAN M, 'The Treaty of Lisbon 2007: Winning Minds, Not Hearts' (2008) 45 Common Market Law Review 617

DOWDING K and VAN HEES M, 'The Construction of Rights' (2003) 97 American Political Science Review 281

DUGUIT L, 'Souveraineté et liberté - Neuvième leçon, La souveraineté nationale à l'intérieur. La liberté de l'individu.' Revue générale du droit online, 2014, numéro 18567 <www.revuegeneraledudroit.eu/?p=18567> accessed 31 July 2016

DUGUIT L, 'Les doctrines juridiques objectivistes' Extraits de la Revue du Droit public et de la Science politique en France et à l'Etranger (Octobre-Novembre-Décembre 1927), Revue générale du droit online, 2014, numéro 17072 >www.revuegeneraledudroit.eu/?p=17072> accessed 31 July 2016

EILMANSBERGER T, 'The Relationship between Rights and Remedies in EC Law: in Search of the Missing Link' (2004) 41 Common Market Law Review 1199

ELEFTHERIADIS P, 'The Direct Effect of Community Law: Conceptual Issues' (1996) 16 Yearbook of European Law 205

ELLIOTT M, 'Constitutional Legislation, European Union Law and the Nature of the United Kingdom's Contemporary Constitution' (2014) 10 Columbia Journal of European Law 379

EMINESCU Y, 'Les juristes roumains et l'essor du droit comparé à l'Ecole de droit de Paris' (1989) 41 Revue internationale de droit comparé 737

ENGLE E, 'Taking the Right Seriously: Hohfeldian Semiotics and Rights Discourse' (2010) 3 The Crit 84

FAUVARQUE-COSSON B, 'La confiance légitime et l'estoppel' (2007) 11 Electronic Journal of Comparative Law 1

FELDMAN D, 'Public Interest Litigation and Constitutional Theory in Comparative Perspective' (1992) 55 The Modern Law Review 44

FENNELLY N, 'Legal Interpretation at the European Court of Justice' (1996) 20 Fordham International Law Journal 656

FERCOT C, 'Précision et droits de l'Homme dans les ordres juridiques allemand et suisse' La Revue des droits de l'homme (en ligne) 7 - 2015 <http://revdh.revues.org/1330> accessed 7 June 2016

FERNANDEZ MARTIN JM, 'El principio de tutela judicial efectiva de los derechos subjetivos derivados del Derecho comunitario: evolución y alcance' (1994) Revista de Instituciones europeas 845

FINNIS JM, 'Some Professorial Fallacies About Rights' (1972) Scholarly Works

FØLLESDAL A, 'Survey Article: The Legitimacy Deficits of the European Union' (2006) 14 The Journal of Political Philosophy 441

FOSSUM JE, 'The European Union in Search of an Identity' (2003) 2 European Journal of Political Theory 319

FRANKEN AA and VAN KAMPEN PTC, 'Toetsing van plaatsing op een sanctielijst na Kadi II' (2014) Nederlands tijdschrift voor Europees recht 116

FRIEDBACHER TJ, 'Motive Unmasked: The European Court of Justice, the Free Movement of Goods and the Search for Legitimacy' (1996) 2 European Law Journal 226

FROMONT M, 'L'influence du droit français et du droit allemand sur les conditions de recevabilité du recours en annulation devant la Cour de Justice des Communautés européennes' [1966] Revue trimestrielle de droit européen 47

GAILLET A, 'Chronique de droit administratif allemand (2012), 1. Le droit au recours des associations : l'orientation subjective du procès administratif allemand à l'épreuve du droit européen et conventionnel de l'environnement' (2013) Droit administratif

GALMOT Y, 'Réflexions sur le recours au droit comparé par la Cour de justice des Communautés européennes' (1990) Revue française de droit administratif 255

GARLAND D, 'On the Concept of 'Social Rights' (2015) 24 Social & Legal Studies 622

GÁSPÁR-SZILÁGYI S, 'The Primacy and Direct Effect of EU International Agreements' (2015) 21 European Public Law 343

GAY L, 'Droit de grève et liberté syndicale dans la jurisprudence constitutionnelle : des libertés "particulières"?' Nouveaux Cahiers du Conseil constitutionnel n°45 (Le Conseil constitutionnel et le droit social) - October 2014

GELBLAT A, 'Appréhender l'imprécision des droits : approche stratégique' La Revue des droits de l'homme (en ligne) 7 - 2015 <http://revdh.revues.org/1341> accessed 7 June 2016

GERKRATH J, 'Les principes généraux du droit ont-ils encore un avenir en tant qu'instrument de protection des droits fondamentaux dans l'Union européenne?' (2006) Revue des Affaires Européennes - Law & European Affairs 31

GEURSEN WW, 'Handhaving van het objectieve gemeenschapsrecht via het effectiviteitsbeginsel vs. subjectieve rechtsbescherming via het nationaalrechtelijke verbod op reformatio in peius' (2009) Nederlands tijdschrift voor Europees recht 131

GEWIRTH A, 'Why Rights are Indispensable' (1986) 95 Mind 329

GEWIRTH A, 'Rights and Duties' (1988) 97 Mind 441

GOLDONI M, 'Constitutional Pluralism and the Question of the European Common Good' (2012) 18 European Law Journal 385

GOLDSMITH L, 'The Charter of Rights-A Brake Not an Accelerator' (2004) European Human Rights Law Review 473

GOODIN RE and GIBSON D, 'Rights, Young and Old' (1997) 17 Oxford Journal of Legal Studies 185

GREEN L, 'Two Views of Collective Rights' (1991) 4 Canadian Journal of Law and Jurisprudence 315

GREER SL and SOKOL T, 'Rules for Rights: European Law, Health Care and Social Citizenship' (2014) 20 European Law Journal 66

GRIMMEL A, "This is not Life as it is Lived Here': The Court of Justice of the EU and the Myth of Judicial Activism in the Foundational Period of Integration through Law' (2014) 7 European Journal of Legal Studies 61

GROULIER C, 'Norme permissive et droit public' (Université de Limoges 2006)

GRÜNDLER T, 'La doctrine des libertés fondamentales à la recherche des droits sociaux' La Revue des droits de l'homme (en ligne), 103 <http://revdh.revues.org/1 22> accessed 5 September 2016

GRZESZICK B, 'Das Grundrecht auf eine gute Verwaltung - Strukturen und Perspektiven des Charta-Grundrechts auf eine gute Verwaltung' (2006) Europarecht 161

GUÐMUNDSDÓTTIR D, 'A Renewed Emphasis on the Charter's Distinction Between Rights and Principles: Is a Doctrine of Judicial Restraint More Appropriate?' (2015) 52 Common Market Law Review 685

GUTMAN HW, 'Academic Determinism: The Division of the Bill of Rights' (1981) 54 California Law Review 295

GUTTERIDGE HC, 'Abuse of Rights' (1933) 5 Cambridge Law Journal 22

HABERMAS J, 'Democracy in Europe: Why the Development of the EU into a Transnational Democracy Is Necessary and How It Is Possible' (2015) 21 European Law Journal 546

HACHEZ I 'Précision et droits de l'homme dans l'ordre juridique belge : focus sur la notion polysémique d'effet direct' La Revue des droits de l'homme (en ligne) 7 - 2015 <http://revdh.revues.org/1261> accessed 7 June 2016

HALPIN A, 'Rights, Duties, Liabilities, and Hohfeld' (2007) 13 Legal Theory 23

HARBO T.-I., 'The Function of the Proportionality Principle in EU Law' (2010) 16 European Law Journal 158

HAURIOU M, 'Recours pour excès de pouvoir et tierce opposition, Note sous Conseil d'Etat, 8 décembre 1899 (Ville d'Avignon), 15 décembre 1899 (Adda) S. 1900.3.73' Revue générale du droit on line, 2015, numéro 15407 <www.revuegeneraledudroit.eu/?p=15407> accessed 22 January 2016.

HERINGA AW and VERHEY L, 'The EU Charter: Text and Structure' (2001) 8 Maastricht Journal of European and Comparative Law 11

HILSON C, 'Rights and Principles in EU Law: A Distinction Without Foundation?' (2008) 15 Maastricht Journal of European and Comparative Law 93

HILSON C and DOWNES T, 'Making sense of rights: Community rights in E.C. law' (1999) European Law Review 121

HINTON EF, 'Strengthening the Effectiveness of Community Law: Direct Effect, Article 5 EC, and the European Court of Justice' (1998) 31 NYU Journal of International Law and Politics 307

HOFMANN HCH and MIHAESCU B, 'The Relation between the Charter's Fundamental Rights and the Unwritten General Principles of EU Law: Good Administration as the Test Case' (2013) 9 European Constitutional Law Review 73

HOFMANN HCH, 'Mapping the European administrative space' (2008) 31 West European Politics 662

HOHFELD WN, 'Some Fundamental Legal Conceptions as Applied in Judicial Reasoning' (1913) 23 Yale Law Journal

HOHFELD WN, 'Fundamental Legal Conceptions as Applied in Judicial Reasoning' (1917) Yale Law Journal, Faculty Scholarship Series Paper 4378 <http://digitalcommons.law.yale.edu/fss_papers/4378>

HOLMES OW, 'Codes, and the Arrangement of the Law' (1870) 5 American Law Review

HOLMWOOD J, 'Social Rights and Complex Freedom: A Comment on Fernando Atria' (2015) Social & Legal Studies 614

JACOBS FG, 'The Evolution of the European Legal Order' (2004) 41 Common Market Law Review 303

JANS JH and DE GRAAF KJ, 'Bevoegdheid = verplichting? Enkele opmerkingen over de uitspraak van het Hof van Justitie in de zaak Kühne & Heinz (2004) Nederlands tijdschrift voor Europees recht 98

JIMENEZ LOBEIRA PC, 'EU Citizenship and Political Identity: The Demos and Telos Problems' (2012) 18 European Law Journal 504

KAPSALI V, 'L'opposabilité du droit au logement précisée par le Conseil d'Etat' (2013) Droit administratif

KARATZIA A, 'The European Citizens' Initiative and the EU Institutional Balance: on Realism and the Possibilities of Affecting EU Lawmaking' (2017) 54 Common Market Law Review 177

KATROUGALOS GS, 'The Implementation of Social Rights in Europe' (1996) 2 Columbia Journal of European Law 277

KEAT R, 'Individual Rights as Social Rights' (2015) 24 Social & Legal Studies

KEUS LAD, 'Francovich in Nederland' (2005) Nederlands tijdschrift voor Europees recht 283

KHOSLA M, 'Making social rights conditional: Lessons from India' (2010) 8 International Journal of Constitutional Law 739

KLATT M, 'Positive rights: Who decides? Judicial review in balance' (2015) 13 International Journal of Constitutional Law 354

KOCHENOV D, 'The Right to Have What Rights? EU Citizenship in Need of Clarification' (2013) 19 European Law Journal 502

KORNEZOV A, 'The Right to Vote as an EU Fundamental Right and the Expanding Scope of Application of the EU Charter of Fundamental Rights' (2016) 75 The Cambridge Law Journal 24

Kostova-Bourgeix A, 'Cour de justice, 1er mars 2005, *A. Owusu c/ N.B. Jackson*, aff. C-281/02' Revue des affaires européennes 307

KROMMENDIJK J, 'Principled Silence or Mere Silence on Principles? The Role of the EU Charter's Principles in the Case Law of the Court of Justice' (2015) 11 European Constitutional Law Review 321

LANSBERGEN A, 'Prisoner Disenfranchisement in the United Kingdom and the Scope of EU Law: United Kingdom Supreme Court' (2014) 10 European Constitutional Law Review 126

LANZA E, 'Core of State Sovereignty and Boundaries of European Identity in the Lissabon-Urteil' (2010) 11 German Law Journal 399

LAURENT E, 'L'intérêt général dans l'Union européenne. Du fédéralisme doctrinal aux biens publics européens?' (2007) Regards croisés sur l'économie 27

LA TORRE M, 'The Law beneath Right's Feet. Preliminary Investigation for a Study of the Charter of Fundamental Rights of the European Union' (2002) 8 European Law Journal 515

LENAERTS A, 'The General Principle of the Prohibition of Abuse of Rights: A Critical Position on Its Role in a Codified European Contract Law' (2010) 6 European Review of Private Law 1121

LENAERTS K, 'Exploring the Limits of the EU Charter of Fundamental Rights' (2012) 8 European Constitutional Law Review 375

LENAERTS K, "In the Union we trust': Trust-enhancing principles of Community law' (2004) 41 Common Market Law Review 317

LENAERTS K, 'Fundamental Rights to be included in a Community Catalogue' (1991) 16 European Law Review 367

LENAERTS K and GUTIERREZ-FONS JA, 'To Say What the Law of the EU Is: Methods of Interpretation and the ECJ' (2014) 20 Columbia Journal of European Law 3

LEVINSON DJ, 'Empire-Building Government in Constitutional Law' (2004) 118 Harvard Law Review 915

MANCINI GF and KEELING DT, 'Language, Culture and Politics in the Life of the European Court of Justice' (1995) 1 Columbia Journal of European Law 397

MARTINES F, 'Direct Effects of International Agreements of the European Union' (2014) 25 The European Journal of International Law 129

MARTY N, 'Le droit de pétition devant la commission des pétitions du Parlement européen : un enjeu institutionnel' [2013] Revue des Affaires Européennes - Law & European Affairs 731

MATTLI W and SLAUGHTER A.-M., 'Law and Politics in the European Union: A Reply to Garrett' (1995) 49 International Organization 183

MAUGÜé C, 'Le Conseil constitutionnel et le droit supranational' (2003) Pouvoirs 53

MAYEUR-CARPENTIER C, CLEMENT-WILZ L and MARTUCCI F, 'Chronique de droit administratif et droit de l'Union européenne, 1er janvier 2012 - 1er juillet 2012' (2012) Revue française de droit administratif 961

MEEHAN E, 'Citizenship and the European Community' (1993) 64 The Political Quarterly 172

MELLERAY F, 'La revanche d'Emmanuel Lévy? L'introduction du principe de protection de la confiance légitime en droit public français' (2004) 56-57 Droit et société 143

MENDES J, 'Discretion, Care and Public Interests in the EU Administration: Probing the Limits of Law' (2016) 53 Common Market Law Review 2

MENENDEZ AJ, 'The European Democratic Challenge: The Forging of a Supranational Volonté Générale' (2009) 15 European Law Journal 277

MICHALEIDES-NOUAROS G, 'L'évolution récente de la notion de droit subjectif' (1966) Revue trimestrielle de droit civil

MIHAESCU EVANS B, 'The 'gaps' in protection stemming from the (problematic) coexistence of fundamental rights' sources in the EU legal order' (2016) Cahiers de droit européen

MILLARD E, 'Précision et effectivité des droits de l'homme' La Revue des droits de l'homme (en ligne) 7 - 2015 <http://revdh.revues.org/1215> accessed 7 June 2016

MILLARD E, 'La justiciabilité des droits sociaux : une question théorique et politique' La Revue des droits de l'homme (en ligne), 452 <http://revdh.revues.org/1 59> accessed 10 January 2017

MILLER RA, 'Germany vs. Europe: The Principle of Democracy in German Constitutional Law and the Troubled Future of European Integration' (2014) 54 Virginia Journal of International Law 579

MILLER GP, 'Liberty and Constitutional Architecture: The Rights-Structure Paradigm' (1993) 16 Harvard Journal of Law & Public Policy 87

MITRANY D, 'The Prospect of Integration: Federal or Functional' (1965) 4 Journal of Common Market Studies 119

MOYSE PE, 'L'abus de droit : l'anténorme - partie II' (2012) 58 McGill Law Journal 1

NEACSU D, 'The Draft of the EU Charter of Fundamental Rights: A Step in the Process of Legitimizing EU as a Political Entity and Economic-Social Rights as Fundamental Human Rights' (2001) 7 Columbia Journal of European Law 141

O'CALLAGHAN P, 'Reversing Ubi Remedium Ibi Jus in the Common Law: The Right of Privacy' (2007) 15 European Review of Private Law 659

ORGAN J, 'Decommissioning Direct Democracy? A Critical Analysis of Commission Decision-Making on the Legal Admissibility of European Citizens Initiative Proposals' (2014) 10 European Constitutional Law Review 422

PARRET LYM, 'Effectieve rechtsbescherming: eindeloos potentieel, ongeleid projectiel?' (2012) Nederlands tijdschrift voor Europees recht 157

PAUNIO E and LINDROOS-HOVINHEIMO S, 'Taking Language Seriously: An Analysis of Linguistic Reasoning and Its Implications in EU Law' (2010) 16 European Law Journal 395

PECH L, 'Between judicial minimalism and avoidance: the Court of Justice's sidestepping of fundamental constitutional issues in Römer and Dominguez' (2012) 49 Common Market Law Review 1841

PEIFFERT O, 'Un possible malentendu en droit de l'Union européenne : le « droit subjectif » comme condition de l'effet direct' (2017) RTDeur 655

PESCATORE P, 'Les exigences de la démocratie et la legitimité de la Communauté européenne' (1974) 10 Cahiers de Droit Européen 499

PETERSEN E, 'L'influence possible du droit anglais sur le recours en annulation auprès de la Cour de justice des communautés européennes' [1966] Revue trimestrielle de droit européen 256

PIC E, 'Faire de la terminologie en droit?' (2007) Cahiers du CIEL 57

PLATON S, 'Chronique de jurisprudence de droit administratif européen (année 2014)' (2015) Droit administratif

POIARES MADURO M, 'Interpreting European Law: Judicial Adjudication in a Context of Constitutional Pluralism' (2007) 1 European Journal of Legal Studies 1

POILLOT E, 'Le contrôle de la transparence matérielle des clauses portant sur l'objet du contrat : une nouvelle arme en matière de lutte contre les clauses abusives' [2017] Recueil Dalloz n°19

POLLICINO O, 'Legal Reasoning of the Court of Justice in the Context of the Principle of Equality Between Judicial Activism and Self-restraint' (2004) 5 German Law Journal 283

PONCELET C, 'Access to Justice in Environmental Matters - Does the European Union Comply with its Obligations?' (2012) 24 Journal of Environmental Law 287

PRECHAL S, 'Community Law in National Courts: The Lessons from *Van Schijndel*' (1998) 35 Common Market Law Review 681

PRECHAL S, 'Does Direct Effect Still Matter?' (2000) 37 Common Market Law Review 1047

PRECHAL S, 'Member State Liability and Direct Effect: What's the Difference After All?' (2006) 17 European Business Law Review 299

PRECHAL S, 'EU Gender Equality Law: a source of inspiration for other EU legal fields?' (2008) European Gender Equality Law Review

PRECHAL S and HANCHER L, 'Individual Environmental Rights: Conceptual Pollution in EU Environmental Law?' (2001) 2 Yearbook of European Environmental Law 89

PRECHAL S and WIDDERSHOVEN R, 'Redefining the Relationship between 'Rewe-effectiveness' and Effective Judicial Protection' (2011) 4 Review of European Administrative Law 31

TOUBES MUNIZ J, 'Legal Principles and Legal Theory' (1997) 10 Ratio Juris 267

RASMUSSEN H, 'Towards a Normative Theory of Interpretation of Community Law' [1992] The University of Chicago Legal Forum 135

RASMUSSEN M, 'Revolutionizing European Law: A history of the Van Gend en Loos judgment' (2014) 12 International Journal of Constitutional Law 136

RAZ J, 'On the Nature of Rights' (1984) 93 Mind 194

RAZ J, 'Rights and Individual Well-Being' (1992) 5 Ratio Juris 127

REICH N, 'Union Citizenship - Metaphor or Source of Rights?' (2001) 7 European Law Journal 4

REICH N, 'Horizontal Liability in EC Law: Hybridization of Remedies for Compensation in Case of Breaches of EC Rights' (2007) 44 Common Market Law Review 705

RIDEAU J, 'Ordre juridique de l'Union européenne - Sources non écrites' JurisClasseur Europe Traité, Cote 04

RIJKEN CRJJ, 'Het Hof als hoeder van de fundamentale rechten in de zaak Kadi en Al Barakaat' (2009) Nederlands tijdschrift voor Europees recht 140

ROBIN-OLIVIER S, 'The evolution of direct effect in the EU: Stocktaking, problems, projections' (2014) 12 International Journal of Constitutional Law 165

ROMAN D, 'La justiciabilité des droits sociaux ou les enjeux de l'édification d'un Etat de droit social' La Revue des droits de l'homme (en ligne), 2 <http://revdh.revues.org/635> accessed 1 September 2016

ROMAN D, 'Les droits civils au renfort des droits sociaux. L'interchangeabilité des droits fondamentaux dans le discours judiciaire.' La Revue des droits de l'homme (en ligne), 320 <http://revdh.revues.org/144> accessed 1 September 2016

ROSAS A and KAILA H, 'L'application de la Charte des droits fondamentaux de l'Union européenne par la Cour de justice : un premier bilan' [2011] Il Diritto dell'Unione Europea 1

ROULHAC C, 'Introduction' La Revue des droits de l'homme (en ligne) 7 - 2015 <http://revdh.revues.org/1312> accessed 7 June 2016

RUFFERT M, 'Rights and Remedies in European Community Law: a Comparative View' (1997) 34 Common Market Law Review 319

RUIZ FABRI H, 'Is There a Case - Legally and Politically - for Direct Effect of WTO Obligations?' (2014) 25 European Journal of International Law 151

RUIZ FABRI H, 'Principes généraux du droit communautaire et droit comparé' (2007) 45 Droits 127

SALES P, 'Rights and Fundamental Rights in English Law' (2016) 75 The Cambridge Law Journal 86

SCHILLING T, 'Beyond Multilingualism: On Different Approaches to the Handling of Diverging Language Versions of a Community Law' (2010) 16 European Law Journal 47

SCHLAG P, 'How to Do Things With Hohfeld' (2014) 78 Law and Contemporary Problems

SCHOUKENS H, 'Access to Justice in Environmental Cases after the Rulings of the Court of Justice of 13 January 2015: Kafka Revisited?' (2015) 31 Utrecht Journal of International and European Law 46

SCHWARZE J, 'Judicial Review of European Administrative Procedure' (2004) 68 Law and Contemporary Problems 85

SEMMELMANN C, 'General Principles in EU Law between a Compensatory Role and an Intrinsic Value' (2013) 19 European Law Journal 457

SHARPSTON E, 'European Community Law and the Doctrine of Legitimate Expectations: How Legitimate, and for Whom' (1990) 11 Northwestern Journal of International Law & Business 87

SHAW J, 'E.U. Citizenship and Political Rights in an Evolving European Union' (2007) 75 Fordham Law Review 2549

SIMON D, 'Y a-t-il des principes généraux de droit communautaire?' (1991) 14 Droits 73

SIMON D, 'Protection juridictionnelle effective' (2011) Europe comm. 38

SIMON D and RIGAUX A, 'La responsabilité des Etats membres en cas de violation du droit communautaire revisitée, ou comment le problème technique de l'odeur sexuelle des porcs non castrés conduit à trancher des questions fondamentales' (2009) 19 Europe

SIMONATI A, 'The Principles of Administrative Procedure and the EU Courts: an Evolution in Progress?' (2011) 4 Review of European Administrative Law 45

SIRINELLI J, 'La subjectivisation du recours pour excès de pouvoir' (2016) Revue française de droit administratif 529

SMISMANS S, 'European Civil Society: Shaped by Discourses and Institutional Interests' (2003) 9 European Law Journal 473

SMITH M, 'Four German Jurists. II' (1896) 11 Political Science Quarterly 278

SNELL J, 'Fundamental Rights Review of National Measures: Nothing New under the Charter?' (2015) 21 European Public Law 285

NIC SHUIBHNE N,'The Resilience of EU Market Citizenship', (2010) 47 Common Market Law Review 1597

STRUMIA F, 'Divorce immediately, or leave. Rights of third country nationals and family protection in the context of EU citizens' free movement: *Kuldip Singh and Others*' (2016) 53 Common Market Law Review 1373

SUEUR J.-J. 'Imprécision des droits de l'Homme : quelle imprécision?' La Revue des droits de l'homme (en ligne) 7 - 2015 <http://revdh.revues.org/1313> accessed 7 June 2016

SWAINE ET, 'Subsidiarity and Self-Interest: Federalism at the European Court of Justice' (2000) 41 Harvard International Law Journal 1

Šadl U, 'The Role of Effet Utile in Preserving the Continuity and Authority of European Union Law: Evidence from the Citation Web of the Pre-accession Case Law of the Court of Justice of the EU' European Journal of Legal Studies, Summer 2015 - Volume 8 - Issue 1 <http://www.ejls.eu/18/209UK.htm> accessed 8 January 2017

TISON M, 'Do Not Attack the Watchdog! Banking Supervisors Liability after Peter Paul' (2005) 42 Common Market Law Review 639

VAN DEN BROEK B and ENNEKING L, 'Public Interest Litigation in the Netherlands. A Multidimensional Take on the Promotion of Environmental Interests by Private Parties through the Courts' (2014) 10 Utrecht Law Review 77

VAN DROOGHENBROECK S, 'L'article 17 de la CEDH est-il indispensable ?' [2001] Revue trimestrielle des droits de l'homme (no spécial : Le droit face à la montée du racisme et de la xénophobie) 543

VAN EIJKEN H and VAN ROSSEM JW, 'Prisoner disenfranchisement and the right to vote in elections to the European Parliament: Universal suffrage key to unlocking political citizenship?' (2016) 12 European Constitutional Law Review 114

VAN EIJKEN H and VERHOEVEN MJM, "Lost in translation: Een bespreking van het arrest Skoma-Lux: de doorwerking van niet officieel gepubliceerde verordeningen' (2008) Nederlands tijdschrift voor Europees recht 165

VAN GERVEN W, 'Of Rights, Remedies and Procedures' (2000) 37 Common Market Law Review 501

VAN GERVEN W, 'Remedies for Infringements of Fundamental Rights' (2004) 10 European Public Law 261

VAN GERVEN W, 'Articles 30, 48, 52 and 59 after *Keck & Mithouard*, and Protection of Rights Arising from Directives after *Faccini Dori*' (1996) Columbia Journal of European Law 217

VAN GERVEN W, 'Principe de proportionnalité, abus de droit et droits fondamentaux' [1992] Journal des tribunaux 305

VAN GESTEL R and MICKLITZ H-W, 'Why Methods Matter in European Legal Scholarship' (2014) 20 European Law Journal 292

VAN HOEK AAH and RIJKEN CRJJ, 'Rechtsbescherming en het recht van verdediging bij plaatsing op de Europese terrorismelijst - de zaak-Mujahedin-e Kalq v De Raad' (2007) Nederlands tijdschrift voor Europees recht 284

VAN ROOSMALEN HJTM and PAHLADSINGH A, 'Het Handvest van de grondrechten van de Europese Unie: beweging in de rechtspraak' (2013) Nederlands tijdschrift voor Europees recht 83

VAN WAEYENBERGE A and PECHO P, 'L'arrêt Unibet et le traité de Lisbonne - un pari sur l'avenir de la protection juridictionnelle effective' (2008) 44 Cahiers de droit européen 126

VAN WOLFEREN M, 'The Limits to the CJEU's Interpretation of Locus Standi, a Theoretical Framework' (2016) 12 Journal of Contemporary European Research 914

VANDAMME J, 'C'est arrivé près de chez vous! Het arrest Italmoda en het ontzeggen van rechten aan de particulier op grond van de EU-richtlijn' (2015) Nederlands tijdschrift voor Europees recht 154

VARUHAS JNE, 'Judicial Review: Standing and Remedies' (2013) 72 The Cambridge Law Journal 243

VON ARNAUD A, 'Theorie und Methode des Grundrechtsschutzes in Europa - am Beispiel des Grundsatzes der Verhältnismässigkeit' (2008) Europarecht 41

VON BOGDANDY A, 'Founding Principles of EU Law: A Theoretical and Doctrinal Sketch' (2010) 16 European Law Journal 95

VON BOGDANDY A, 'Deutsche Rechtswissenschaft im europäischen Rechtsraum' (2011) 66 Juristen Zeitung 1

VON DANWITZ T and PARASCHAS K, 'A Fresh Start for the Charter: Fundamental Questions on the Application of the European Charter of Fundamental Rights' (2012) 35 Fordham International Law Journal 1396

VOßKUHLE A and KAISER A-B, 'Grundwissen – Öffentliches Recht: Das subjektiv-öffentliche Recht' (2009) Juristische Schulung 16

WAELBROECK D and BOMBOIS T, 'Des requérants "privilégiés" et des autres... A propos de l'arrêt Inuit et de l'exigence de protection juridictionnelle effective des particuliers en droit européen"' [2014] Cahiers de droit européen 21

WALDRON J, 'Critical Notice' (1985) 94 Mind 281

WALDRON J, 'A Rights-Based Critique of Constitutional Rights' (1993) 13 Oxford Journal of Legal Studies 18

WALKER N, 'Legal Theory and the European Union' EUI Working Paper Law 2005/16

WALLACE W, 'Europe as a Confederation: the Community and the Nation-State' (1982) 21 Journal of Common Market Studies 57

WEILER J, 'Does Europe Need a Constitution? Demos, Telos and the German Maastricht Decision' (1995) 1 European Law Journal 219

WEILER JHH, 'A Constitution for Europe? Some Hard Choices' (2002) 40 Journal of Common Market Studies 563

WEILER JHH, 'Community, Member States and European Integration: Is the Law Relevant?' (1982) 21 Journal of Common Market Studies 39

WEILER JHH, 'Van Gend en Loos: The individual as subject and object and the dilemma of European legitimacy' (2014) 12 International Journal of Constitutional Law 94

WEILER JHH and LOCKHART NJS, ''Taking Rights Seriously' Seriously: The European Court and its Fundamental Rights Jurisprudence - Part I' (1995) 32 Common Market Law Review 51

WEILER JHH and LOCKHART NJS, ''Taking Rights Seriously' Seriously: the European Court and its Fundamental Rights Jurisprudence - Part II' (1995) 32 Common Market Law Review 579

WEISSE-MARCHAL C, 'Quelle réparation pour les dommages causés aux particuliers par la violation d'une directive communautaire dépourvue d'effet direct ?' (2000) Revue française de droit administratif 402

WERNICKE S, 'Au nom de qui? The European Court of Justice between Member States, Civil Society and Union Citizens' (2007) 13 European Law Journal 380

WILKINSON MA, 'Civil Society and the Re-imagination of European Constitutionalism' (2003) 9 European Law Journal 451

WILLIAMS G, 'The Concept of Legal Liberty' (1956) 56 Columbia Law Review 1129

WILMAN FG, 'The end of the absence? The growing body of EU legislation on private enforcement and the main remedies it provides for' (2016) 53 Common Market Law Review 887

WOLLENSCHLÄGER F, 'A New Fundamental Freedom beyond Market Integration', (2011) 17 European Law Journal 1

WYATT D, 'Horizontal effect of fundamental freedoms and the right to equality after *Viking* and *Mangold*, and the implications for Community competence' (2008) 4 Croatian Yearbook of European Law and Policy 1

YOUNG KG, 'Rights and Queues: On Distributive Contests in the Modern State' (2016) 55 Columbia Journal of Transnational Law 65

Zalasiński A, 'Proportionality of Anti-Avoidance and Anti-Abuse Measures in the ECJ's Direct Tax Case Law' (2007) 35 Intertax 310

ZATJAY I, 'La permanence des concepts du droit romain dans les systèmes juridiques continentaux' (1966) 18 Revue internationale de droit comparé 353

ZUMBANSEN P, 'Semantics of European Law' (1999) 5 European Law Journal 114

Theses

BIGIAOUI-DUHAMEL L, 'L'abus de droit en droit du travail' (Thèse de doctorat en droit privé, Université Paris 1 2002)

BOBIC A, 'Prohibition of Abuse of Rights in EU Law' (Master's thesis, University of Zagreb, Faculty of Law, Jean Monnet Chair of European Public Law 2011)

DE VOS N, 'Europeanisering van het vertrouwensbeginsel. Betekenis van het Europese vertrouwensbeginsel voor de equivalente beginselen in Nederland, Frankrijk en België in het kader van een groeiend ius commune' (Universiteit Utrecht 2011)

KARATZIA A, 'The European Citizens' Initiative: a laboratory for citizens' participation in EU law-making' (PhD thesis, University of Surrey 2016)

IONESCU RN, 'L'abus de droit en droit communautaire' (Thèse pour le doctorat en droit, Universitat Autònoma de Barcelona and Université Toulouse I - Sciences sociales 2009)

LACCHI C, 'Preliminary References to the Court of Justice of the EU and Effective Judicial Protection: Towards a more protection-oriented approach of Article 267 TFEU' (PhD thesis, University of Luxembourg 2017)

MARTY N, 'La Notion de Bonne Administration: À la Confluence des Droits Européens et du Droit Administratif Français' (PhD thesis, University of Montpellier 2007)

MIHAESCU EVANS B, 'The right to good administration at the crossroads of the various sources of fundamental rights in the EU integrated administrative system' (PhD thesis, University of Luxembourg 2014)

NIVERT N, 'Intérêt général et droits fondamentaux' (Thèse pour l'obtention du grade de Docteur en droit public, Université de la Réunion 2012)

ÖSTLUND A, 'Effectiveness of European Union Law versus Procedural Protection. Tracing the tension throughout the case-law of the Court of Justice on *ex officio* review by the national judge' (PhD thesis, University of Luxembourg 2017)

RAMADAN AM, 'L'abus du droit de brevet : étude comparée de droit français et égyptien' (Thèse de doctorat en droit privé et sciences criminelles, Université de Montpellier et Université d'Alexandrie 2012)

Working papers, electronic articles and blog posts

ARCURI A and POLI S, 'What Price for the Community Enforcement of WTO Law?' EUI Working Paper 2010/01

ARESTIS G, 'Fundamental rights in the EU: three years after Lisbon, the Luxembourg perspective' College of Europe Research Papers in Law 2/2013

AZOULAI L, 'L'autonomie de l'individu européen et la question du statut' EUI Department of Law Research paper 2013/14

AZOULAI L, 'The (Mis)Construction of the European Individual. Two Essays on Union Citizenship Law' EUI Working Paper Law 2014/14

BILCHITZ D, 'Article Review: David Bilchitz on Matthias Klatt's 'Positive Rights: Who Decides? Judicial Review in Balance' ' International Journal of Constitutional Law Blog, August 26, 2015, 359 <http://www.iconnectblog.com/2015/08/article-review-david-bilchitz-on-matthias-klatts-positive-rights-who-decides-judicial-review-in-balance> accessed 27 August 2015

BIGNAMI F, 'Three Generations of Participation Rights in European Administrative Proceedings' Jean Monnet Working Paper 11/03

CAMPBELL K, 'Legal Rights' The Stanford Encyclopedia of Philosophy (Fall 2013 Edition), ed ZALTA, E <http://plato.stanford.edu/archives/fall2013/entries/legal-rights/> accessed 10 November 2014

DANI M, 'The subjectification of the citizen in European public law' EUI Working Paper, Law 2015/02

HAGNER F, Les particuliers et l'ordre juridique communautaire : l'égalité de traitement entre les hommes et les femmes (euryopa - Institut européen de l'Université de Genève 2003)

HOFMANN HCH, 'The Right to an 'Effective Judicial Remedy' and the Changing Conditions of Implementing EU Law' Law Working Paper 2013-02

JOERGES C, 'The Law in the Process of Constitutionalizing Europe' EUI Working Papers, Law 2002/4

MICKLITZ H-W, 'The ECJ between the Individual Citizen and the Member States - A plea for a judge-made European law on remedies' EUI Working Paper Law 2011/15

MARIOTTI C, 'Theory and Practice of Emissions Trading in the European Union: Some Reflections on Allowance Allocation in Light of the DK Recycling Case' European Papers, Vol 1, 2016, No 3, European Forum, Insight of 22 December 2016, 1153-1170 ≤http://www.europeanpapers.eu/fr/europeanforum/theory-and-practice-emissions-trading-european-union-allowance-allocation#_ftn25≥ accessed 29 April 2017

Millénaire 3, 'L'antidiscrimination, une volonté de l'Union européenne' Discriminations "raciales" et politiques antidiscriminatoires - Fiche n°1 <http://www.millenaire3.com/uploads/tx_ressm3/syntheses_discrim_fiche1.pdf> accessed 14 April 2015

REICH N, 'Rights without Duties? Reflections on the State of Liability Law in the Multilevel Governance System of the Community: Is There a Need for a More Coherent Approach in European Private Law?' (2009) EUI Working Papers, Law 2009/10

MILLER V, The Treaty Establishing a Constitution for Europe: Part II (The Charter of Fundamental Rights) (House of Commons Library, Research Paper 04/85, 2004)

OEHLER U, 'Environmental Liability and GMOs in the EU and in Germany' Exeter Papers in European Law No 15 <http://law.exeter.ac.uk/cels/eupapers.shtml> accessed 19 May 2016

PAQUES M and DONNAY L, 'Juridiction ordinaire et juridiction administrative en droit belge' <https://orbi.ulg.ac.be/bitstream/2268/9929/1/Juridiction%20ordinaire%20et%20juridiction%20administrative%20n%20droit%20belge.pdf> accessed 24 January 2016

PIRKER B, 'Cases C-401 to 403/12 and C-404 to 405/12: no review of legality in light of the Aarhus Convention' 29 January 2015 <http://europeanlawblog.eu/2015/01/29/cases-c-401-to-40312-and-c-404-to-40512-no-review-of-legality-in-light-of-the-aarhus-convention/> accessed 26 April 2017

PIRKER B, 'Implementation of the Aarhus Convention by the EU - an Inconvenient Truth from the Compliance Committee' 24 April 2017 <http://europeanlawblog.eu/2017/04/24/implementation-of-the-aarhus-convention-by-the-eu-an-inconvenient-truth-from-the-compliance-committee/> accessed 30 April 2017

PORAT B, 'Rights-Based Law v. Duty-Based Law: Old Dilemma, New Perspective' Hebrew University of Jerusalem Legal Research Paper No 16-04 <http://papers.ssrn.com/sol3/papers.cfm?abstract_id=2696463> accessed 12 January 2016

SADURSKI W, 'Rights and Moral Reasoning: An Unstated Assumption' EUI Working Paper, Law 2007/38

SADURSKI W, 'Constitutional Courts in the Process of Articulating Constitutional Rights in the Post-Communist States of Central and Eastern Europe, Part I: Social and Economic Rights' EUI Working Paper Law 2002/14

SCHNEBEL V, 'Le juge administratif, un nouveau juge de la constitutionnalité des lois? 14 November 2011 <http://chevalierdesgrandsarrets.com/2011/11/14/le-juge-administratif-un-nouveau-juge-de-la-constitutionnalité-des-lois/> accessed 20 April 2015

ROGER AJC, 'A lost opportunity for improving access to justice in environmental matters: the CJEU on the invocability of the Aarhus Convention,' 15 February 2015, available at http://eulawanalysis.blogspot.lu/2015/02/a-lost-opportunity-for-improving-access.html (accessed 26 April 2017)

SULLIVAN M and LAHME R, 'Class/collective actions in Europe: overview of applicable EU law principles', Thomson Reuters Practical Law, < https://uk.practicallaw.thomsonreuters.com/2-618-0602?transitionType=Default&contextData=(sc.Default)&firstPage=true&bhcp=1> accessed 3 August 2017

THAM RKL, 'The Impact of the Environmental Liability Directive 2004/35 on English Law' Exeter Papers in European Law No 14 <http://law.exeter.ac.uk/cels/eupapers.shtml> accessed 19 May 2016.

VAN DUFFEL S, 'From Objective Right to Subjective Rights: The Franciscans and the Interest and Will Conceptions of Rights' National University of Singapore, 2 <http://ssrn.com/abstract=1467455>

WENAR L, 'Rights' The Stanford Encyclopedia of Philosophy (Fall 2011 Edition), ed ZALTA, E <http://plato.stanford.edu/archives/fall2011/entries/rights/> accessed 10 November 2014

XEFTERI S, 'Note d'actualité droit de l'environnement de l'UE 1/2017', Blogdroiteuropeen, février 2017, <http://wp.me/p6OBGR-1Cl> accessed 30 April 2017

ZACCARONI G, 'Ultra vires review e applicazione orizzontale del principio di non discriminazione sulla base dell'età : una riflessione (a freddo) su Dansk Industri', SIDIBlog, May 2017, < http://www.sidiblog.org/2017/05/04/ultra-vires-review-e-applicazione-orizzontale-del-principio-di-non-discriminazione-sulla-base-delleta-una-riflessione-a-freddo-su-dansk-industri/> accessed 13 August 2017

Reports and official publications

'Le Tiers et le droit public - Le rapport roumain' Association Henri Capitant, Journées panaméennes, 18 au 22 mai 2015, Les tiers <http://www.henricapitant.org/storage/app/media/pdfs/evenements/tiers_droits_public_2015/Roumanie_7.pdf>

'Le juge administratif et le droit de l'Union européenne', Conseil d'Etat, 23 September 2015, <http://www.conseil-etat.fr/Decisions-Avis-Publications/Etudes-Publications/Dossiers-thematiques/Le-juge-administratif-et-le-droit-de-l-Union-europeenne> accessed 22 June 2017

AUBY J-M, Les recours juridictionnels contre les actes administratifs spécialement économiques dans le droit des Etats membres de la CEE (Commission européenne, Etudes, Série concurrence - rapprochement des législations, 1971)

BUTT ME, KÜBERT J and SCHULTZ CA, *Droits sociaux fondamentaux en Europe* (Document de travail, Parlement Européen, Direction générale des études, Séries affaires sociales, SOCI 104 FR, 2000)

BUX U, 'Le Parlement européen : contexte historique', *Fiches techniques sur l'Union européenne,* April 2017, <http://www.europarl.europa.eu/ftu/pdf/fr/FTU_1.3.1.pdf> accessed 17 July 2017

CURTIN D and LEINO-SANDBERG P, *Openness, Transparency and the Right of Access to Documents in the EU. In-depth analysis for the PETI committee* (European Parliament DG for Internal Policies, Policy Department C: Citizens' Rights and Constitutional Affairs, 2016)

EDWARD DOA, Oral Evidence Taken before the European Scrutiny Committee on Wednesday 17 November 2004, uncorrected transcript available at https://www.publications.parliament.uk/pa/cm200304/cmselect/cmeuleg/uc1064-ii/uc106402.htm (accessed 18 April 2017)

EU Network of Independent Experts on Fundamental Rights, 'Commentary of the Charter" <http://ec.europa.eu/justice/fundamental-rights/files/networkcommentaryfinal_en.pdf> accessed 9 October 2015

European Commission, 'Judicial Redress – Collective Redress', June 2013, < http://ec.europa.eu/consumers/solving_consumer_disputes/judicial_redress/index_en.htm> accessed 3 August 2017

European Commission, Consultation paper for discussion on the follow-up to the Green Paper on consumer collective redress, May-July 2009, <http://ec.europa.eu/consumers/archive/redress_cons/docs/consultation_paper2009.pdf > accessed 3 August 2017

HEY C, 'EU Environmental Policies: a short history of the policy strategies' European Environmental Bureau, 2005 ≤http://www.eeb.org/publication/chapter-3.pdf≥ accessed 2 March 2017

LADENBURGER C, 'European Institutional Report' in LAFFRANQUE J (ed) *The Protection of Fundamental Rights Post-Lisbon: The Interaction between the Charter of Fundamental Rights of the European Union, the European Convention on Human Rights and National Constitutions* (Reports of the XXC FIDE Congress, Tallinn, 2012)

PINAULT M, *Rapport de la délégation française* (8ème colloque de l'Association des Conseils d'Etat et des Juridictions administratives suprêmes de l'Union européenne, du 12 au 15 mai 1982, Copenhague - "La notion de l'intérêt en contentieux administratif (intérêt personnel, intérêt collectif, l'action populaire) notamment en matière d'environnement", 1982)

SCHEUER S, 'EU Environmental Policy Handbook. A Critical Analysis of EU Environmental Legislation' European Environmental Bureau, 2005 ≤http://www.eeb.org/?LinkServID=3E1E422E-AAB4-A68D-221A63343325A81B≥ accessed 6 March 2017

SHEATE W and others, *The Relationship between the EIA and SEA Directives* (Imperial College London Consultants, Final Report to the European Commission, 2005) <http://ec.europa.eu/environment/archives/eia/pdf/final_report_0508.pdf> accessed 29 April 2017

UIBO L, 'Defending Estonia's interests in the Court of Justice of the European Union' Estonian Ministry of Foreign Affairs Yearbook 2010 ≤http://www.vm.ee/en/yearbook-2010≥ accessed 14 February 2017

Conference and seminar interventions, conference papers and interviews

AZOULAI L, 'Le droit de l'Union européenne comme mode de vie' (Université d'Aix-Marseille, Marseille, 27 May 2017), video available at https://blogdroiteuropeen.com/2017/06/12/le-droit-de-lunion-europeenne-comme-mode-de-vie-projet-de-recherche-du-prof-loic-azoulay/ accessed 3 August 2017

BLANCHET T, 'Evolution of EU citizenship and the rights attached to it' (Conference - EU Citizenship and Justice, Luxembourg, 14th and 15th September 2015)

CESPEDES R, 'Hohfeld's Taxonomy Revisited: an Update from the Theory of Rights and Modern Public Law, Family Law and Human Rights Law' 'Tis Forty Years Since: Britain & Ireland in Europe, Europe in Britain & Ireland' The changing landscape of theory and practice, The University of Edinburgh, Edinburgh Law School, 2-3 September 2013

COLE M, HOFMANN HCH and SCHILTZ J-L, 'The Future of Data Transfers outside of the European Union' (Seminar at the University of Luxembourg, 20 April 2016)

DELAPORTE F, 'Droit luxembourgeois et droits européens', Interview by WARIN C, (*blogdroiteuropéen*, 2016) <https://blogdroiteuropeen.com/2016/11/10/droit-luxembourgeois-et-droits-europeens-interview-de-francis-delaporte-partie-2/> accessed 20 March 2017

KOMBILA-IBOUANGA H, 'La proportionnalité en tant que principe du droit de l'Union' (VIIIe Congrès mondial de droit constitutionnel, Mexico, 6-10 December 2010)

LAPOINTE U, 'Boyle, Martin. 2001. "Chapitre I: Legal legitimacy and the Principles of Private and Public Autonomy", *Towards Justice and Validity: An Investigation into Habermas' Theory of Legitimacy*, Mémoire de maîtrise, Carleton University, pp. 6-45', in FLEURY G, LAPOINTE U, ROCH L, DEMERS V, 'Légitimité et gouvernance dans les oeuvres de Jürgen Habermas (Raison et légitimité et Droit et démocratie)' Chaire de responsabilité sociale et de développement durable ESG-UQAM, Recueil de textes CEH/RT-34-2005, Deuxième séminaire de la série annuelle 2004-2005 sur la gouvernance, 6 octobre 2005

LAW S, 'The Rationales, Reasoning and Methodology Underpinning the Judicial Recognition of Principles of Union Law' (Cahiers de Droit européen - Les principes généraux du droit de l'Union européenne, Bruxelles, 10 September 2015)

LENAERTS K, 'EU citizenship in the light of the case law of the CJEU' (Conference - EU Citizenship and Justice, Luxembourg, 14th and 15th September 2015)

LENAERTS K, 'Les défis actuels de la Cour de justice', Interview by TAMBOU O, (*blogdroiteuropéen*, 2016) <https://blogdroiteuropeen.com/2016/04/01/interview-du-president-koen-lenaerts-partie-2-les-defis-actuels-de-la-cjue/> accessed 6 July 2016

MIETTINEN S and KETTUNEN M, 'Travaux to the Treaties: Treasures or trivia?' (European Studies Association conference, Boston 5 March 2015)

ORTINO M, 'A Reading of the EU Constitutional Legal System Through the Principle of Effectiveness' (Cahiers de droit européen - Les principes généraux du droit de l'Union européenne, Brussels, 10 September 2015)

E. Poillot, '*Gutiérrez Naranjo and Others*' (PhD Seminar Recent Developments in Theory and Practice of EU Law, University of Luxembourg, 27 June 2017)

POTVIN-SOLIS, 'Principe général de non-discrimination et situation purement interne' (Cahiers de droit européen - Les principes généraux du droit de l'Union européenne, Brussels, 10 September 2015)

PRECHAL S, 'The relation between the rights arising from the Charter and general principles of law' (The protection of fundamental rights in the EU: future challenges, Luxembourg, 22 October 2012)

RAPOPORT C, 'L'opposabilité des 'droits-créances' constitutionnels en droit public français' (Communication présentée aux journées de l'association française de droit constitutionnel, www.droitconstitutionnel.org/congresParis/comC8/RapoportTXTpdf, accessed 20 March 2017)

RODRÍGUEZ PM, 'The principle of legal certainty and the limits to the application of EU law' (Cahiers de droit européen - Les principes généraux du droit de l'Union européenne, Brussels, 10 September 2015)

ROTOLO A and SARTOR G, 'Deontic Logic. Introductory materials', Summer School on Law and Logic, European University Institute and Harvard Law School 2015 <http://lawandlogic.org/coursebasic/session-5-2-2/> accessed 25 August 2015

SAFJAN M, 'A Union of Effective Judicial Protection. Addressing a multi-level challenge through the lens of Article 47 CFREU' (King's College London, February 2014)

SEVER S, 'General Principles of Law and the Charter of Fundamental Rights' (Cahiers de droit européen - Les principes généraux du droit de l'Union européenne, Brussels, 10 September 2015)

SIKORA A, 'The Principle of High Environmental Protection as a Source of Enforceable Rights' (Cahiers de droit européen - Les principes généraux du droit de l'Union européenne, Brussels, 10 September 2015)

TURGIS S, 'Notions autonomes et concurrence des juges' (La concurrence des juges en Europe Le dialogue en question(s), Faculté de Droit de Tours, 25-26-27 November 2015)

VAN MEERBEECK J, 'Le mode opératoire des principes généraux : de la généralité in abstracto à l'effet direct in concreto' (Cahiers de droit européen - Les principes généraux du droit de l'Union européenne, Brussels, 10 September 2015)

VITORINO, Speaking points European Convention, 29 October 2002, Brussels, SPEECH/02/531

ZETTERQUIST O, 'Fundamental Rights and the Fundamentals of the European Constitution' (Seminar at the University of Luxembourg, 26 June 2014)

Journalistic and literary works

RIVAIS R, 'Strasbourg garantit le droit au logement opposable' SOS Conso, Le Monde <http://sosconso.blog.lemonde.fr/2015/04/17/strasbourg-garantit-le-droit-au-logement-opposable/> accessed 17 April 2015

VOLTAIRE, 'Onzième lettre écrite par le proposant à M. Covelle', *Œuvres complètes de Voltaire, Tome 46* (1784 La Société littéraire-typographique) 447.

WAHNICH S, 'Sauver ceux qui pleurent,' Chronique 'Historiques,' Libération 8 February 2017 <http://www.liberation.fr/debats/2017/02/08/sauver-ceux-qui-pleurent_1547222> accessed 22 July 2017

WITTGENSTEIN L, *Recherches philosophiques* (Gallimard 2014)

Index